# Motif Reference Manual

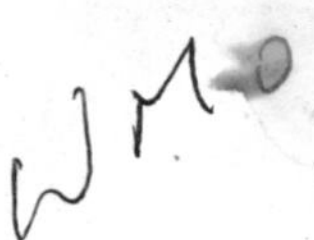

# Volume Six B

---

# Motif Reference Manual

---

by Paula M. Ferguson

UIL Material by David Brennan

*O'Reilly & Associates, Inc.*

**Motif Reference Manual**
by Paula M. Ferguson
UIL Material by David Brennan


Printed in the United States of America.

**Editor:** Tim O'Reilly

**Production Editors:** Eileen Kramer
Clairemarie Fisher O'Leary

**Printing History:**

June 1993: First edition.

This book is printed on acid-free paper with 50% recycled content, 10-15% post-consumer waste. O'Reilly & Associates is committed to using paper with the highest recycled content available consistent with high quality.

ISBN 1-56592-038-4

# Table of Contents

# Figures

# Preface

## About the Motif Toolkit

The Motif toolkit, from the Open Software Foundation (OSF), is based on the X Toolkit Intrinsics (Xt), which is the standard mechanism on which many of the toolkits written for the X Window System are based. Xt provides a library of user-interface objects called widgets and gadgets, which provide a convenient interface for creating and manipulating X windows, colormaps, events, and other cosmetic attributes of the display. In short, widgets can be thought of as building blocks that the programmer uses to construct a complete application.

However, the widgets that Xt provides are generic in nature and impose no user-interface policy whatsoever. Providing the look and feel of an interface is the job of a user-interface toolkit such as Motif. Motif provides a complete set of widgets that are designed to implement the application look and feel specified in the *Motif Style Guide* and the *Motif Application Environment Specification*. The Motif toolkit also includes a library of functions for creating and manipulating the widgets and other aspects of the user interface.

The Motif toolkit has other components in addition to the widget set and related functions. Motif provides a User Interface Language (UIL) for describing the initial state of a user interface. UIL is designed to permit rapid prototyping of the user interface for an application. The Motif Resource Manager (Mrm) functions provide the interface between C language application code and UIL. Motif also provides the Motif Window Manager (*mwm*). The appearance and behavior of this window manager is designed to be compatible with the appearance and behavior of the Motif widget set.

## About This Manual

This manual contains reference material on the Motif toolkit. The first edition of Volume Six, which was based on Motif 1.1, included the Motif reference material in appendices. This second edition is based on Motif 1.2, which is the latest major release of the Motif toolkit. Motif 1.2 is based on Release 5 of the Xlib and Xt specifications (X11R5). This release of Motif provides many new features, including new widget classes and several new functions. In order to cover all of the material, it became necessary to split Volume Six into two separate manuals, a programming manual and a reference manual. Volume Six A is the *Motif Programming Manual* and Volume Six B is the *Motif Reference Manual*.

This manual is part of the sixth volume in the O'Reilly & Associates X Window System Series. It includes reference pages for each of the Motif functions and macros, for the Motif and Xt Intrinsics widget classes, for the Mrm functions, for the Motif clients, and for the UIL file format, data types, and functions. A permuted index and numerous quick reference appendices are also provided.

Volume Six B includes reference pages for all of the new functions and widgets in Motif 1.2. When the functionality of an existing routine or widget has changed in Motif 1.2, the reference page explains the differences between the two versions. Volume Six B also provides a complete set of reference material for UIL and Mrm, which was not covered in the previous edition.

Volumes Six A and B are designed to be used together. Volume Six A provides a complete programmer's guide to the Motif toolkit. Each chapter of the book covers a particular component of the Motif toolkit. Each chapter includes basic tutorial material about creating and manipulating the component, intermediate-level information about the configurable aspects of the component, and any advanced programming topics that are relevant. The chapters also provide numerous programming examples.

To get the most out of the examples in Volume Six A, you will need the exact calling sequences of each function from Volume Six B. To understand fully how to use each of the routines described in Volume Six B, all but the most experienced Motif programmers will need the explanations and examples in Volume Six A.

While the Motif toolkit is based on Xt, the focus of this manual is on Motif itself, not on the X Toolkit Intrinsics. Reference pages for the Xt widget classes are included here to provide a complete picture of the widget class hierarchy. Many reference pages mention related Xt routines, but the functionality of these routines is not described. Detailed information about Xt is provided by Volume Four, *X Toolkit Intrinsics Programming Manual, Motif Edition*, and Volume Five, *X Toolkit Intrinsics Reference Manual*.

## How This Manual is Organized

Volume Six B is designed to make it easy and fast to look up virtually any fact about the Motif toolkit. It contains reference pages and numerous helpful appendices.

The book is organized as follows:

| | |
|---|---|
| Preface | Describes the organization of the book and the conventions it follows. |
| Permuted Index | Provides a standard UNIX permuted index for all reference pages, regardless of section. |
| Section 1 | *Motif Functions and Macros*, contains reference pages for all of Motif functions and macros. |
| Section 2 | *Motif and Xt Widget Classes*, contains reference pages for the widget classes defined by the Motif toolkit and the X Toolkit Intrinsics. |
| Section 3 | *Mrm Functions*, contains reference pages for the Motif Resource Manager functions that are used in conjuctions with the User Interface Language. |

Section 4 — *Motif Clients*, contains reference pages for the Motif clients: *mwm*, *uil*, and *xmbind*.

Section 5 — *UIL File Format*, contains reference pages that describe the file format of a User Interface Language module.

Section 6 — *UIL Data Types*, contains reference pages for the data types supported by the User Interface Language.

Section 7 — *UIL Functions*, contains reference pages for the User Interface Language functions.

Appendix A — *Function Summaries*, provides quick reference tables that list each Motif function alphabetically and also by functional groups.

Appendix B — *Data Types*, lists and explains in alphabetical order the structures, enumerated types, and other typedefs used for arguments to Motif and Mrm functions.

Appendix C — *Table of Motif Resources*, lists all of the resources provided by Motif and Xt widget classes, along with their types and the classes that define them.

Appendix D — *Table of UIL Objects*, lists all of the objects supported by the User Interface Language, along with their corresponding Motif widget classes.

Appendix E — *New Features in Motif 1.2*, lists the new functions, widget classes, and widget resources in Motif 1.2.

Index — Should help you to find what you need to know.

## Assumptions

This book assumes that the reader is familiar with the C programming language and the concepts and architecture of the X Toolkit, which are presented in Volume Four, *X Toolkit Intrinsics Programming Manual, Motif Edition*, and Volume Five, *X Toolkit Intrinsics Reference Manual*. A basic understanding of the X Window System is also useful. For some advanced topics, the reader may need to consult Volume One, *Xlib Programming Manual*, and Volume Two, *Xlib Reference Manual*.

## Related Documents

The following books on the X Window System are available from O'Reilly & Associates, Inc.:

| | |
|---|---|
| Volume Zero | *X Protocol Reference Manual* |
| Volume One | *Xlib Programming Manual* |
| Volume Two | *Xlib Reference Manual* |
| Volume Three | *X Window System User's Guide, Motif Edition* |
| Volume Four | *X Toolkit Intrinsics Programming Manual, Motif Edition* |
| Volume Five | *X Toolkit Intrinsics Reference Manual* |
| Volume Six A | *Motif Programming Manual* |
| Volume Seven | *XView Programming Manual* with accompanying reference volume. |
| Volume Eight | *X Window System Administrator's Guide* |

*PHIGS Programming Manual*

*PHIGS Reference Manual*

*PEXlib Programming Manual*

*PEXlib Reference Manual*

Quick Reference *The X Window System in a Nutshell*

## Conventions Used in This Book

*Italic* is used for:

- UNIX pathnames, filenames, program names, user command names, options for user commands, and variable expressions in syntax sections.
- New terms where they are defined.

`Typewriter Font` is used for:

- Anything that would be typed verbatim into code, such as examples of source code and text on the screen.
- Variables, data structures (and fields), symbols (defined constants and bit flags), functions, macros, and a general assortment of anything relating to the C programming language.
- All functions relating to Motif, Xt, and Xlib.
- Names of subroutines in example programs.

`Italic Typewriter Font` is used for:

- Arguments to functions, since they could be typed in code as shown but are arbitrary names that could be changed.

*Helvetica Italic* is used for:

- Titles of examples, figures, and tables.

**Boldface** is used for:

- Chapter headings, section headings, and the names of buttons and menus.

## Request for Comments

To help us provide you with the best documentation possible, please write to tell us about any problems you find in this manual or how you think it could be improved.

Our U.S. mail address, e-mail address, and phone numbers are as follows:

O'Reilly & Associates, Inc.
103 Morris Street, Suite A
Sebastopol, CA 95472
800-998-9938
international +1 707-829-0515
UUCP: uunet!ora!motif    Internet: motif@ora.com

## Obtaining Motif

If your hardware vendor is an OSF member, they may be able to provide Motif binaries for your machine. Various independent vendors also provide binaries for some machines. Source licenses must be obtained directly from OSF:

OSF Direct Channels
Open Software Foundation
11 Cambridge Center
Cambridge, MA 02142
USA
+1 617 621-7300
Internet: direct@osf.org

# Acknowledgements

This book developed out of the realization that it would be impossible to update the first edition of Volume Six to cover Motif 1.2 without dividing the original book into two books. Dan Heller, David Flanagan, Adrian Nye, and Tim O'Reilly all provided valuable suggestions on how best to expand the original reference appendices into a full-fledged reference manual.

The Motif reference pages in this book are based on the reference appendices from the first edition, which were developed by Daniel Gilly. His work meant that I didn't have to start from scratch, and thus saved many hours of toil. The OSF/Motif reference material also provided a helpful foundation from which to explore the complexities of the Motif toolkit. Many of the Motif examples in the book were borrowed from the first edition of Volume Six. These example were written by Dan Heller, although they have been updated for Motif 1.2

Dave Brennan, of HaL Computer Systems, took on the unenviable task of learning everything there is to know about UIL and Mrm, so that he could write the UIL reference material. He did a great job.

Adrian Nye deserves special recognition for freeing me to work on this project, when I'm sure that he had other projects he would have liked to send my way. I don't think either one of us had any idea how involved this update project would become. The other inhabitants of the "writer's block" at O'Reilly & Associates, Valerie Quercia, Linda Mui, and Ellie Cutler, provided support that kept me sane while I was working on the book. Extra gratitude goes to Linda Mui for her work on the cross references and the reference tables; her knowledge of various tools prevented me from doing things the hard way. Tim O'Reilly also provided editorial support that improved the quality of the reference material.

Special thanks go to the people who worked on the production of this book. The final form of this book is the work of the staff at O'Reilly & Associates. The authors would like to thank Chris Reilly for the figures, Ellie Cutler for indexing, Lenny Muellner for tools support, Eileen Kramer for copyediting and production of the final copy, and Clairemarie Fisher O'Leary for final proofing and printing. Thanks also to Donna Woonteiler for her patience in answering my questions and helping me to understand the production process.

Despite the efforts of all of these people, the authors alone are responsible for any errors or omissions that remain.

*Paula M. Ferguson*

# Permuted Index

*The permuted index takes the brief descriptive string from the title of each reference page and rotates (permutes) the string so that each keyword will at one point start the* second, *or center, column of the line. The beginning and end of the original string are indicated by a slash when they are in other than their original position; if the string is too long, it is truncated.*

*To find the command you want, simply scan down the middle of the page, looking for a keyword of interest. Once you find the keyword you want, you can read (with contortions) the brief description of the command that makes up the entry. If things still look promising, you can look all the way over to the right for the name of the relevant reference page.*

# Permuted Index



## How to Use the Permuted Index

The permuted index takes the brief descriptive string from the title of each reference page and rotates (permutes) the string so that each keyword will at one point start the *second*, or center, column of the line. The beginning and end of the original string are indicated by a slash when they are in other than their original position; if the string is too long, it is truncated.

To find the command you want, simply scan down the middle of the page, looking for a keyword of interest. Once you find the keyword you want, you can read (with contortions) the brief description of the command that makes up the entry. If things still look promising, you can look all the way over to the right for the name of the relevant reference page.

## The Permuted Index

Permuted Index

Permuted Index

Permuted Index

# Section 1

## Motif Functions and Macros

*This section describes the functions and macros available in the Motif toolkit. Functions are presented alphabetically.*

*The first reference page,* Introduction, *explains the format and contents of each of the following pages.*

## In This Section:



☞

XmFontListInitFontContext
XmFontListNextEntry
XmFontListRemoveEntry
XmGetAtomName
XmGetColorCalculation
XmGetColors
XmGetDestination
XmGetDragContext
XmGetFocusWidget
XmGetMenuCursor
XmGetPixmap
XmGetPixmapByDepth
XmGetPostedFromWidget
XmGetSecondaryResData
XmGetTabGroup
XmGetTearOffControl
XmGetVisibility
XmGetXmDisplay
XmGetXmScreen
XmInstallImage
XmInternAtom
XmIsMotifWMRunning
XmIs***Object***
XmIsTraversable
XmListAddItem
XmListAddItemUnselected
XmListDeleteAllItems
XmListDeleteItem
XmListDeleteItemsPos
XmListDeletePos
XmListDeletePositions
XmListDeselectAllItems
XmListDeselectItem
XmListDeselectPos
XmListGetKbdItemPos
XmListGetMatchPos
XmListGetSelectedPos
XmListItemExists
XmListItemPos
XmListPosSelected
XmListPosToBounds
XmListReplaceItems
XmListReplaceItemsPos
XmListReplItemsPosUnsel
XmListReplItemsUnselected
XmListReplacePositions
XmListSelectItem
XmListSelectPos
XmListSetAddMode
XmListSetBottomItem
XmListSetBottomPos
XmListSetHorizPos
XmListSetItem
XmListSetKbdItemPos
XmListSetPos
XmListUpdateSelectedList
XmListYToPos
XmMainWindowSep
XmMainWindowSetAreas
XmMapSegmentEncoding
XmMenuPosition
XmMessageBoxGetChild
XmOptionButtonGadget
XmOptionLabelGadget
XmProcessTraversal
XmRegisterSegmentEncoding
XmRemoveProtocolCallback
XmRemoveProtocols
XmRemoveTabGroup
XmRemWMProtocolCallback
XmRemoveWMProtocols
XmRepTypeAddReverse
XmRepTypeGetId
XmRepTypeGetNameList
XmRepTypeGetRecord
XmRepTypeGetRegistered
XmRepTypeInTearOffModConv
XmRepTypeRegister
XmRepTypeValidValue
XmResolveAllPartOffsets
XmResolvePartOffsets
XmScaleGetValue
XmScaleSetValue
XmScrollBarGetValues
XmScrollBarSetValues
XmScrollVisible
XmScrolledWindowSetAreas
XmSelectionBoxGetChild
XmSetColorCalculation
XmSetFontUnit
XmSetFontUnits
XmSetMenuCursor
XmSetProtocolHooks
XmSetWMProtocolHooks
XmStringBaseline
XmStringByteCompare
XmStringCompare
XmStringConcat
XmStringCopy
XmStringCreate
XmStringCreateLocalized
XmStringCreateLtoR
XmStringCreateSimple
XmStringDirectionCreate
XmStringDraw
XmStringDrawImage
XmStringDrawUnderline
XmStringEmpty
XmStringExtent
XmStringFree
XmStringFreeContext
XmStringGetLtoR
XmStringGetNextComponent
XmStringGetNextSegment
XmStringHasSubstring
XmStringHeight
XmStringInitContext
XmStringLength
XmStringLineCount
XmStringNConcat
XmStringNCopy
XmStringPeekNextComponent
XmStringSegmentCreate
XmStringSeparatorCreate
XmStringWidth
XmTargetsAreCompatible

XmTextClearSelection
XmTextCopy
XmTextCut
XmTextDisableRedisplay
XmTextEnableRedisplay
XmTextFindString
XmTextFindStringWcs
XmTextGetBaseline
XmTextGetCursorPosition
XmTextGetEditable
XmTextGetInsertionPosition
XmTextGetLastPosition
XmTextGetMaxLength
XmTextGetSelection
XmTextGetSelectionPosition
XmTextGetSelectionWcs
XmTextGetSource
XmTextGetString
XmTextGetStringWcs
XmTextGetSubstring
XmTextGetSubstringWcs
XmTextGetTopCharacter
XmTextInsert
XmTextInsertWcs
XmTextPaste
XmTextPosToXY
XmTextRemove
XmTextReplace
XmTextReplaceWcs
XmTextScroll
XmTextSetAddMode
XmTextSetCursorPosition
XmTextSetEditable
XmTextSetHighlight
XmTextSetInsertionPosition
XmTextSetMaxLength
XmTextSetSelection
XmTextSetSource
XmTextSetString
XmTextSetStringWcs
XmTextSetTopCharacter
XmTextShowPosition
XmTextXYToPos
XmToggleButtonGetState
XmToggleButtonSetState
XmTrackingEvent
XmTrackingLocate
XmTranslateKey
XmUninstallImage
XmUpdateDisplay
XmVaCreateSimpleCheckBox
XmVaCreateSimpleMenuBar
XmVaCreateSimpleOptMenu
XmVaCreateSimplePopupMenu
XmVaCreSimpPulldownMenu
XmVaCreateSimpleRadioBox
XmWidgetGetBaselines
XmWidgetGetDisplayRect

# Introduction

This page describes the format and contents of each reference page in Section 1, which covers the Motif functions and macros.

## Name

Function – a brief description of the function.

## Synopsis

This section shows the signature of the function: the names and types of the arguments, and the type of the return value. If header file other than *<Xm/Xm.h>* is needed to declare the function, it is shown in this section as well.

### Inputs

This subsection describes each of the function arguments that pass information to the function.

### Outputs

This subsection describes any of the function arguments that are used to return information from the function. These arguments are always of some pointer type, so you should use the C address-of operator (**&**) to pass the address of the variable in which the function will store the return value. The names of these arguments are sometimes suffixed with `_return` to indicate that values are returned in them. Some arguments both supply and return a value; they will be listed in this section and in the "Inputs" section above. Finally, note that because the list of function arguments is broken into "Input" and "Output" sections, they do not always appear in the same order that they are passed to the function. See the function signature for the actual calling order.

### Returns

This subsection explains the return value of the function, if any.

## Availability

This section appears for functions that were added in Motif 1.2, and also for functions that are now superseded by other, preferred, functions.

## Description

This section explains what the function does and describes its arguments and return value. If you've used the function before and are just looking for a refresher, this section and the synopsis above should be all you need.

## Usage

This section appears for most functions and provides less formal information about the function: when and how you might want to use it, things to watch out for, and related functions that you might want to consider.

## Example

This section appears for some of the most commonly used Motif functions, and provides an example of their use.

### Structures

This section shows the definition of any structures, enumerated types, typedefs, or symbolic constants used by the function.

### Procedures

This section shows the syntax of any prototype procedures used by the function.

### See Also

This section refers you to related functions, widget classes, and clients. The numbers in parentheses following each reference refer to the sections of this book in which they are found.

# XmActivateProtocol

## Name

XmActivateProtocol – activate a protocol.

## Synopsis

```
#include <Xm/Protocols.h>
void XmActivateProtocol (shell, property, protocol)
    Widget shell;
    Atom property;
    Atom protocol;
```

### Inputs

| | |
|---|---|
| *shell* | Specifies the widget associated with the protocol property. |
| *property* | Specifies the property that holds the protocol data. |
| *protocol* | Specifies the protocol atom. |

## Description

`XmActivateProtocol()` activates the specified *protocol*. If the *shell* is realized, `XmActivateProtocol()` updates its protocol handlers and the specified *property*. If the *protocol* is active, the protocol atom is stored in *property*; if the *protocol* is inactive, the protocol atom is not stored in *property*.

## Usage

A protocol is a communication channel between applications. Protocols are simply atoms, stored in a property on the top-level shell window for the application. `XmActivateProtocol()` makes the shell able to respond to `ClientMessage` events that contain the specified *protocol*. Before you can activate a protocol, the protocol must be added to the *shell* with `XmAddProtocols()`. Protocols are automatically activated when they are added. The inverse routine is `XmDeactivateProtocol()`.

## See Also

*XmActivateWMProtocol*(1), *XmAddProtocols*(1), *XmDeactivateProtocol*(1), *XmInternAtom*(1), *VendorShell*(2).

# XmActivateWMProtocol



## Name

XmActivateWMProtocol – activate the XA_WM_PROTOCOLS protocol.

## Synopsis

```
#include <Xm/Protocols.h>
void XmActivateWMProtocol (shell, protocol)
    Widget shell;
    Atom protocol;
```

### Inputs

| | |
|---|---|
| *shell* | Specifies the widget associated with the protocol property. |
| *protocol* | Specifies the protocol atom. |

## Description

`XmActivateWMProtocol()` is a convenience routine that calls `XmActivate-Protocol()` with *property* set to `XA_WM_PROTOCOL`, the window manager protocol property.

## Usage

The property `XA_WM_PROTOCOLS` is a set of predefined protocols for communication between clients and window managers. Before you can activate the protocols, they must be added to the *shell* with `XmAddProtocols()` or `XmAddWMProtocols()`. Protocols are automatically activated when they are added. The inverse routine is `XmDeactivate-WMProtocol()`.

## See Also

*XmActivateProtocol*(1), *XmAddProtocols*(1), *XmAddWMProtocols*(1), *XmDeactivateWMProtocol*(1), *XmInternAtom*(1), *VendorShell*(2).

# XmAddProtocolCallback

## Name

XmAddProtocolCallback – add client callbacks to a protocol.

## Synopsis

```
#include <Xm/Protocols.h>
void XmAddProtocolCallback (shell, property, protocol, callback, closure)
    Widget shell;
    Atom property;
    Atom protocol;
    XtCallbackProc callback;
    XtPointer closure;
```

### Inputs

| | |
|---|---|
| *shell* | Specifies the widget associated with the protocol property. |
| *property* | Specifies the property that holds the protocol data. |
| *protocol* | Specifies the protocol atom. |
| *callback* | Specifies the procedure to invoke when the protocol message is received. |
| *closure* | Specifies any client data that is passed to the *callback*. |

## Description

XmAddProtocolCallback() adds client callbacks to a protocol. The routine verifies that the protocol is registered, and if it is not, it calls XmAddProtocols(). XmAddProtocolCallback() adds the callback to the internal list of callbacks, so that it is called when the corresponding client message is received.

## Usage

A protocol is a communication channel between applications. Protocols are simply atoms, stored in a property on the top-level shell window for the application. To communicate using a protocol, a client sends a ClientMessage event containing a property and protocol, and the receiving client responds by calling the associated protocol callback routine. XmAddProtocolCallback() allows you to register these callback routines.

## See Also

*XmAddProtocols*(1), *XmAddWMProtocolCallback*(1), *XmInternAtom*(1), *VendorShell*(2).

# XmAddProtocols

## Name

XmAddProtocols – add protocols to the protocol manager.

## Synopsis

```
#include <Xm/Protocols.h>
void XmAddProtocols (shell, property, protocols, num_protocols)
    Widget shell;
    Atom property;
    Atom *protocols;
    Cardinal num_protocols;
```

### Inputs

*shell* Specifies the widget associated with the protocol property.

*property* Specifies the property that holds the protocol data.

*protocols* Specifies a list of protocol atoms.

*num_protocols*
Specifies the number of atoms in *protocols*.

## Description

`XmAddProtocols()` registers a list of protocols to be stored in the specified *property* of the specified *shell* widget. The routine adds the protocols to the protocol manager and allocates the internal tables that are needed for the protocol.

## Usage

A protocol is a communication channel between applications. Protocols are simply atoms, stored in a property on the top-level shell window for the application. `XmAddProtocols()` allows you to add protocols that can be understood by your application. The inverse routine is `XmRemoveProtocols()`. To communicate using a protocol, a client sends a `ClientMessage` event containing a property and protocol, and the receiving client responds by calling the associated protocol callback routine. Use `XmAddProtocolCallback()` to add a callback function to be executed when a client message event containing the specified protocol atom is received.

## See Also

*XmAddProtocolCallback*(1), *XmAddWMProtocols*(1), *XmInternAtom*(1), *XmRemoveProtocols*(1), *VendorShell*(2).

# XmAddTabGroup

## Name

XmAddTabGroup – add a widget to a list of tab groups.

## Synopsis

```
void XmAddTabGroup (tab_group)
    Widget tab_group;
```

### Inputs

*tab_group* Specifies the widget to be added.

## Availability

In Motif 1.1, `XmAddTabGroup()` is obsolete. It has been superceded by setting `XmNnavigationType` to `XmEXCLUSIVE_TAB_GROUP`.

## Description

`XmAddTabGroup()` makes the specified widget a separate tab group. This routine is retained for compatibility with Motif 1.0 and should not be used in newer applications. If traversal behavior needs to be changed, this should be done directly by setting the `XmNnavigationType` resource, which is defined by Manager and Primitive.

## Usage

A tab group is a group of widgets that can be traversed using the keyboard rather than the mouse. Users move from widget to widget within a single tab group by pressing the arrow keys. Users move between different tab groups by pressing the Tab or Shift-Tab keys. If the *tab_group* widget is a manager, its children are all members of the tab group (unless they are made into separate tab groups). If the widget is a primitive, it is its own tab group. Certain widgets must not be included with other widgets within a tab group. For example, each List, Scrollbar, OptionMenu, or multi-line Text widget must be placed in a tab group by itself, since these widgets define special behavior for the arrow or Tab keys, which prevents the use of these keys for widget traversal. The inverse routine is `XmRemoveTabGroup()`.

## See Also

*XmGetTabGroup*(1), *XmRemoveTabGroup*(1),
*XmManager*(2), *XmPrimitive*(2).

# XmAddWMProtocolCallback

## Name

XmAddWMProtocolCallback – add client callbacks to an XA_WM_PROTOCOLS protocol.

## Synopsis

```
#include <Xm/Protocols.h>
void XmAddWMProtocolCallback (shell, protocol, callback, closure)
    Widget shell;
    Atom protocol;
    XtCallbackProc callback;
    XtPointer closure;
```

### Inputs

| | |
|---|---|
| *shell* | Specifies the widget associated with the protocol property. |
| *protocol* | Specifies the protocol atom. |
| *callback* | Specifies the procedure to invoke when the protocol message is received. |
| *closure* | Specifies any client data that is passed to the *callback*. |

## Description

`XmAddWMProtocolCallback()` is a convenience routine that calls `XmAddProtocol-Callback()` with *property* set to `XA_WM_PROTOCOL`, the window manager protocol property.

## Usage

The property `XA_WM_PROTOCOLS` is a set of predefined protocols for communication between clients and window managers. To communicate using a protocol, a client sends a `ClientMessage` event containing a property and protocol, and the receiving client responds by calling the associated protocol callback routine. `XmAddWMProtocolCallback()` allows you to register these callback routines with the window manager protocol property. The inverse routine is `XmRemoveWMProtocolCallback()`.

## Example

The following code fragment shows the use of `XmAddWMProtocolCallback()` to save the state of an application using the `WM_SAVE_YOURSELF` protocol:

```
Atom wm_save_yourself;

wm_save_yourself =
    XmInternAtom (XtDisplay (toplevel), "WM_SAVE_YOURSELF", False);
XmAddWMProtocols (toplevel, &wm_save_yourself, 1);
XmAddWMProtocolCallback (toplevel, wm_save_yourself, save_state, toplevel);
```

`save_state` is a callback routine that saves the state of the application.

## See Also

*XmAddProtocolCallback*(1), *XmInternAtom*(1), *XmRemoveWMProtocolCallback*(1), *VendorShell*(2).

# XmAddWMProtocols



## Name

XmAddWMProtocols – add the XA_WM_PROTOCOLS protocols to the protocol manager.

## Synopsis

```
#include <Xm/Protocols.h>
void XmAddWMProtocols (shell, protocols, num_protocols)
     Widget shell;
     Atom *protocols;
     Cardinal num_protocols;
```

### Inputs

*shell* Specifies the widget associated with the protocol property.

*protocols* Specifies a list of protocol atoms.

*num_protocols*
Specifies the number of atoms in *protocols*.

## Description

XmAddWMProtocols() is a convenience routine that calls XmAddProtocols() with *property* set to XA_WM_PROTOCOL, the window manager protocol property.

## Usage

The property XA_WM_PROTOCOLS is a set of predefined protocols for communication between clients and window managers. XmAddWMProtocols() allows you to add this protocol so that it can be understood by your application. The inverse routine is XmRemoveWMProtocols(). To communicate using a protocol, a client sends a ClientMessage event containing a property and protocol, and the receiving client responds by calling the associated protocol callback routine. Use XmAddWMProtocolCallback() to add a callback function to be executed when a client message event containing the specified protocol atom is received.

## Example

The following code fragment shows the use of XmAddWMProtocols() to add the window manager protocols, so that the state of an application can be saved using the WM_SAVE_YOURSELF protocol:

```
Atom wm_save_yourself;

wm_save_yourself =
    XmInternAtom (XtDisplay (toplevel), "WM_SAVE_YOURSELF", False);
XmAddWMProtocols (toplevel, &wm_save_yourself, 1);
XmAddWMProtocolCallback (toplevel, wm_save_yourself, save_state, toplevel);
```

save_state is a callback routine that saves the state of the application.

## See Also

*XmAddProtocols*(1), *XmAddWMProtocolCallback*(1), *XmInternAtom*(1), *XmRemoveWMProtocols*(1), *VendorShell*(2).

# XmCascadeButtonHighlight



## Name

XmCascadeButtonHighlight, XmCascadeButtonGadgetHighlight – set the highlight state of a CascadeButton.

## Synopsis

```
#include <Xm/CascadeB.h>
void XmCascadeButtonHighlight (cascadeButton, highlight)

#include <Xm/CascadeBG.h>
void XmCascadeButtonGadgetHighlight (cascadeButton, highlight)

    Widget cascadeButton;
    Boolean highlight;
```

### Inputs

*cascadeButton*
Specifies the CascadeButton or CascadeButtonGadget.

*highlight* Specifies the highlight state.

## Description

`XmCascadeButtonHighlight()` sets the state of the shadow highlight around the specified *cascadeButton*, which can be a CascadeButton or a CascadeButtonGadget. `XmCascadeButtonGadgetHighlight()` sets the highlight state of the specified *cascadeButton*, which must be a CascadeButtonGadget. Both routines draw the shadow if *highlight* is `True` and erase the shadow if *highlight* is `False`.

## Usage

CascadeButtons do not normally display a shadow like other buttons, so the highlight shadow is often used to show that the button is armed. `XmCascadeButtonHighlight()` and `XmCascadeButtonGadgetHighlight()` provide a way for you to cause the shadow to be displayed.

## See Also

*XmCascadeButton*(2), *XmCascadeButtonGadget*(2).

# XmChangeColor

## Name

XmChangeColor – update the colors for a widget.

## Synopsis

```
void XmChangeColor (widget, background)
    Widget widget;
    Pixel background;
```

### Inputs

| | |
|---|---|
| *widget* | Specifies the widget whose colors are to be changed. |
| *background* | Specifies the background color. |

## Availability

Motif 1.2 and later.

## Description

`XmChangeColor()` changes all of the colors for the specified *widget* based on the new *background* color. The routine recalculates the foreground color, the select color, and the top and bottom shadow colors and updates the corresponding resources for the widget. `XmChangeColor()` uses the default color calculation procedure unless a customized color calculation procedure has been set with `XmSetColorCalculation()`.

## Usage

`XmChangeColor()` is a convenience routine for changing all of the colors for a widget, based on the *background* color. Without the routine, an application would have to call `XmGetColors()` to get the new colors and then set the `XmNforeground`, `XmNtopShadowColor`, `XmNbottomShadowColor`, `XmNselectColor` resources for the widget with `XtSetValues()`.

## See Also

*XmGetColorCalculation*(1), *XmGetColors*(1), *XmSetColorCalculation*(1).

# XmClipboardBeginCopy

## Name

XmClipboardBeginCopy – set up storage for a clipboard copy operation.

## Synopsis

```
#include <Xm/CutPaste.h>
int XmClipboardBeginCopy (display, window, clip_label, widget, callback,
        item_id)
    Display *display;
    Window window;
    XmString clip_label;
    Widget widget;
    XmCutPasteProc callback;
    long *item_id;
```

### Inputs

| | |
|---|---|
| *display* | Specifies a connection to an X server; returned from XOpenDisplay() or XtDisplay(). |
| *window* | Specifies a window ID that identifies the client to the clipboard. |
| *clip_label* | Specifies a label that is associated with the data item. |
| *widget* | Specifies the widget that receives messages requesting data that has been passed by name. |
| *callback* | Specifies the callback function that is called when the clipboard needs data that has been passed by name. |

### Outputs

| | |
|---|---|
| *item_id* | Returns the ID assigned to the data item. |

### Returns

ClipboardSuccess on success or ClipboardLocked if the clipboard is locked by another application.

## Description

XmClipboardBeginCopy() is a convenience routine that calls XmClipboardStart-Copy() with identical arguments and with a *timestamp* of CurrentTime.

## Usage

XmClipboardBeginCopy() can be used to start a normal copy operation or a copy-by-name operation. In order to pass data by name, the *widget* and *callback* arguments to XmClipboardBeginCopy() must be specified.

## Procedures

The XmCutPasteProc has the following format:

```
typedef void (*XmCutPasteProc) (Widget, * int, * int, * int)
    Widget widget;
```

```
int *data_id;
int *private_id;
int *reason;
```

An XmCutPasteProc takes four arguments. The first argument, *widget*, is the widget passed to the callback routine, which is the same widget as passed to XmClipboardBeginCopy(). The *data_id* argument is the ID of the data item that is returned by XmClipboardCopy() and *private_id* is the private data passed to XmClipboardCopy(). The *reason* argument takes the value XmCR_CLIPBOARD_DATA_REQUEST, which indicates that the data must be copied to the clipboard, or XmCR_CLIPBOARD_DATA_DELETE, which indicates that the client can delete the data from the clipboard. Although the last three parameters are pointers to integers, the values are read-only and changing them has no effect.

## See Also

*XmClipboardCancelCopy*(1), *XmClipboardCopy*(1), *XmClipboardCopyByName*(1), *XmClipboardEndCopy*(1), *XmClipboardStartCopy*(1).

# XmClipboardCancelCopy



## Name

XmClipboardCancelCopy – cancel a copy operation to the clipboard.

## Synopsis

```
#include <Xm/CutPaste.h>
int XmClipboardCancelCopy (display, window, item_id)
    Display *display;
    Window window;
    long item_id;
```

### Inputs

*display* Specifies a connection to an X server; returned from `XOpenDisplay()` or `XtDisplay()`.

*window* Specifies a window ID that identifies the client to the clipboard.

*item_id* Specifies the ID of the data item.

### Returns

`ClipboardSuccess` on success, `ClipboardLocked` if the clipboard is locked by another application, or `ClipboardFail` on failure.

## Description

`XmClipboardCancelCopy()` cancels the copy operation that is in progress and frees temporary storage that has been allocated for the operation. The function returns `ClipboardFail` if `XmClipboardStartCopy()` has not been called or if the data item has too many formats.

## Usage

A call to `XmClipboardCancelCopy()` is valid only between calls to `XmClipboardStartCopy()` and `XmClipboardEndCopy()`. `XmClipboardCancelCopy()` can be called instead of `XmClipboardEndCopy()` when you need to terminate a copying operation before it completes. If you have previously locked the clipboard, `XmClipboardCancelCopy()` unlocks it, so you should not call `XmClipboardUnlock()`.

## See Also

*XmClipboardBeginCopy*(1), *XmClipboardCopy*(1), *XmClipboardEndCopy*(1), *XmClipboardStartCopy*(1).

# XmClipboardCopy

## Name

XmClipboardCopy – copy a data item to temporary storage for later copying to the clipboard.

## Synopsis

```
#include <Xm/CutPaste.h>
int XmClipboardCopy (display, window, item_id, format_name, buffer, length,
        private_id, data_id)
    Display *display;
    Window window;
    long item_id;
    char *format_name;
    char *buffer;
    unsigned long length;
    int private_id;
    int *data_id;
```

### Inputs

| | |
|---|---|
| *display* | Specifies a connection to an X server; returned from XOpenDisplay() or XtDisplay(). |
| *window* | Specifies a window ID that identifies the client to the clipboard. |
| *item_id* | Specifies the ID of the data item. |
| *format_name* | Specifies the name of the format of the data item. |
| *buffer* | Specifies the buffer from which data is copied to the clipboard. |
| *length* | Specifies the length of the data being copied to the clipboard. |
| *private_id* | Specifies the private data that is stored with the data item. |

### Outputs

| | |
|---|---|
| *data_id* | Returns an ID for a data item that is passed by name. |

### Returns

ClipboardSuccess on success, ClipboardLocked if the clipboard is locked by another application, or ClipboardFail on failure.

## Description

XmClipboardCopy() copies the data item specified by *buffer* to temporary storage. The data item is moved to the clipboard data structure when XmClipboardEndCopy() is called. The *item_id* is the ID of the data item returned by XmClipboardStartCopy() and *format_name* is a string that describes the type of the data.

Since the data item is not actually stored in the clipboard until XmClipboardEndCopy() is called, multiple calls to XmClipboardCopy() add data item formats to the same data item or will append data to an existing format. The function returns ClipboardFail if Xm-ClipboardStartCopy() has not been called or if the data item has too many formats.



Motif Functions and Macros

## Usage

`XmClipboardCopy()` is called between calls to `XmClipboardStartCopy()` and `XmClipboardEndCopy()`. If you need to make multiple calls to `XmClipboardCopy()` to copy a large amount of data, you should call `XmClipboardLock()` to lock the clipboard for the duration of the copy operation.

When there is a large amount of clipboard data and the data is unlikely to be retrieved, it can be copied to the clipboard by name. Since the data itself is not copied to the clipboard until it is requested with a retrieval operation, copying by name can improve performance. To pass data by name, call `XmClipboardCopy()` with *buffer* specified as NULL. A unique number is returned in *data_id* that identifies the data item for later use. When another application requests data that has been passed by name, a callback requesting the actual data will be sent to the application that owns the data and the owner must then call `XmClipboardCopyByName()` to transfer the data to the clipboard. Once data that is passed by name has been deleted from the clipboard, a callback notifies the owner that the data is no longer needed.

## Example

The following callback shows the sequence of calls needed to copy data to the clipboard:

```
static void to_clipbd(widget, client_data, call_data)
Widget widget;
XtPointer client_data;
XtPointer call_data;
{
    unsigned long item_id = 0;
    int           status;
    XmString      clip_label;
    char          buffer[32];
    Display      *dpy = XtDisplayOfObject(widget);
    Window        window = XtWindowOfObject(widget);
    char         *data = (char *) client_data;

    sprintf(buffer, "%s", data);
    clip_label = XmStringCreateLocalized("Data");

    /* start a copy; retry until unlocked */
    do
        status = XmClipboardStartCopy(dpy, window,
            clip_label, CurrentTime, NULL, NULL, &item_id);
    while (status == ClipboardLocked);

    XmStringFree(clip_label);

    /* copy the data; retry until unlocked */
    do
        status = XmClipboardCopy(dpy, window, item_id, "STRING",
            buffer, (long)strlen(buffer)+1, 0, NULL);
    while (status == ClipboardLocked);

    /* end the copy; retry until unlocked */
```

```
        do
            status = XmClipboardEndCopy(dpy, window, item_id);
        while (status == ClipboardLocked);
    }
```

## See Also

*XmClipboardBeginCopy*(1), *XmClipboardCancelCopy*(1), *XmClipboardCopyByName*(1), *XmClipboardEndCopy*(1), *XmClipboardStartCopy*(1).

# XmClipboardCopyByName

## Name

XmClipboardCopyByName – copy a data item passed by name.

## Synopsis

```
#include <Xm/CutPaste.h>
int XmClipboardCopyByName (display, window, data_id, buffer, length,
        private_id)
    Display *display;
    Window window;
    int data_id;
    char *buffer;
    unsigned long length;
    int private_id;
```

### Inputs

*display* — Specifies a connection to an X server; returned from XOpenDisplay() or XtDisplay().

*window* — Specifies a window ID that identifies the client to the clipboard.

*data_id* — Specifies the ID number assigned to the data item by XmClipboard-Copy().

*buffer* — Specifies the buffer from which data is copied to the clipboard.

*length* — Specifies the length of the data being copied to the clipboard.

*private_id* — Specifies the private data that is stored with the data item.

### Returns

ClipboardSuccess on success or ClipboardLocked if the clipboard is locked by another application.

## Description

XmClipboardCopyByName() copies the actual data to the clipboard for a data item that has been previously passed by name. The data that is copied is specified by *buffer*. The *data_id* is the ID assigned to the data item by XmClipboardCopy().

## Usage

XmClipboardCopyByName() is typically used for incremental copying; new data is appended to existing data with each call to XmClipboardCopyByName(). If you need to make multiple calls to XmClipboardCopyByName() to copy a large amount of data, you should call XmClipboardLock() to lock the clipboard for the duration of the copy operation.

Copying by name improves performance when there is a large amount of clipboard data and when this data is likely never to be retrieved, since the data itself is not copied to the clipboard until it is requested with a retrieval operation. Data is passed by name when XmClipboard-Copy() is called with a *buffer* value of NULL. When a client requests the data passed by name, the *callback* registered by XmClipboardStartCopy() is invoked. See XmClipboardStartCopy() for more information about the format of the callback. This callback calls XmClipboardCopyByName() to copy the actual data to the clipboard.

## Example

The following XmCutPasteProc callback shows the use of XmClipboardCopyByName() to copy data passed by name:

```
static void copy_by_name(widget, data_id, private_id, reason)
Widget widget;
int *data_id, *private_id, *reason;
{
    Display     *dpy = XtDisplay(toplevel);
    Window       window = XtWindow(toplevel);
    int          status;
    char         buffer[32];

    if (*reason == XmCR_CLIPBOARD_DATA_REQUEST) {
        sprintf(buffer, "stuff");

        do
            status = XmClipboardCopyByName(dpy, window, *data_id, buffer,
                strlen(buffer)+1, *private_id);
        while (status != ClipboardSuccess);
    }
```

## See Also

*XmClipboardBeginCopy*(1), *XmClipboardCopy*(1), *XmClipboardEndCopy*(1), *XmClipboardStartCopy*(1).

# XmClipboardEndCopy

## Name

XmClipboardEndCopy – end a copy operation to the clipboard.

## Synopsis

```
#include <Xm/CutPaste.h>
int XmClipboardEndCopy (display, window, item_id)
    Display *display;
    Window window;
    long item_id;
```

### Inputs

| | |
|---|---|
| *display* | Specifies a connection to an X server; returned from `XOpenDisplay()` or `XtDisplay()`. |
| *window* | Specifies a window ID that identifies the client to the clipboard. |
| *item_id* | Specifies the ID of the data item. |

### Returns

`ClipboardSuccess` on success, `ClipboardLocked` if the clipboard is locked by another application, or `ClipboardFail` on failure.

## Description

`XmClipboardEndCopy()` locks the clipboard, places data that has been accumulated by calling `XmClipboardCopy()` into the clipboard data structure, and then unlocks the clipboard. The *item_id* is the ID of the data item returned by `XmClipboardStartCopy()`. The function returns `ClipboardFail` if `XmClipboardStartCopy()` has not been called previously.

## Usage

`XmClipboardEndCopy()` frees temporary storage that was allocated by `XmClipboardStartCopy()`. `XmClipboardStartCopy()` must be called before `XmClipboardEndCopy()`, which does not need to be called if `XmClipboardCancelCopy()` has already been called.

## Example

The following callback shows the sequence of calls needed to copy data to the clipboard:

```
static void to_clipbd(widget, client_data, call_data)
Widget widget;
XtPointer client_data;
XtPointer call_data;
{
    unsigned long item_id = 0;
    int           status;
    XmString      clip_label;
    char          buffer[32];
    Display      *dpy = XtDisplayOfObject(widget);
```

```
    Window          window = XtWindowOfObject(widget);
    char           *data = (char *) client_data;

    sprintf(buffer, "%s", data);
    clip_label = XmStringCreateLocalized("Data");

    /* start a copy; retry until unlocked */
    do
        status = XmClipboardStartCopy(dpy, window,
            clip_label, CurrentTime, NULL, NULL, &item_id);
    while (status == ClipboardLocked);

    XmStringFree(clip_label);

    /* copy the data; retry until unlocked */
    do
        status = XmClipboardCopy(dpy, window, item_id, "STRING",
            buffer, (long)strlen(buffer)+1, 0, NULL);
    while (status == ClipboardLocked);

    /* end the copy; retry until unlocked */
    do
        status = XmClipboardEndCopy(dpy, window, item_id);
    while (status == ClipboardLocked);
}
```

## See Also

*XmClipboardBeginCopy*(1), *XmClipboardCancelCopy*(1), *XmClipboardCopy*(1), *XmClipboardCopyByName*(1), *XmClipboardStartCopy*(1).

# XmClipboardEndRetrieve



## Name

XmClipboardEndRetrieve – end a copy operation from the clipboard.

## Synopsis

```
#include <Xm/CutPaste.h>
int XmClipboardEndRetrieve (display, window)
    Display *display;
    Window window;
```

### Inputs

*display* Specifies a connection to an X server; returned from `XOpenDisplay()` or `XtDisplay()`.

*window* Specifies a window ID that identifies the client to the clipboard.

### Returns

`ClipboardSuccess` on success or `ClipboardLocked` if the clipboard is locked by another application.

## Description

`XmClipboardEndRetrieve()` ends the incremental copying of data from the clipboard.

## Usage

A call to `XmClipboardEndRetrieve()` is preceded by a call to `XmClipboardStartRetrieve()`, which begins the incremental copy, and calls to `XmClipboardRetrieve()`, which incrementally retrieve the data items from clipboard storage. `XmClipboardStartRetrieve()` locks the clipboard and it remains locked until `XmClipboardEndRetrieve()` is called.

## Example

The following code fragment shows the sequence of calls needed to perform an incremental retrieve. Note that this code does not store the data as it is retrieved:

```
int           status;
unsigned long received;
char          buffer[32];
Display      *dpy = XtDisplayOfObject(widget);
Window        window = XtWindowOfObject(widget);

do
    status = XmClipboardStartRetrieve(dpy, window, CurrentTime);
while (status == ClipboardLocked);

do {
    /* retrieve data from clipboard */
    status = XmClipboardRetrieve(dpy, window, "STRING",
        buffer, sizeof(buffer), &received, NULL)
```

```
} while (status == ClipboardTruncate);

status = XmClipboardEndRetrieve(dpy, window);
```

## See Also

*XmClipboardRetrieve*(1), *XmClipboardStartRetrieve*(1).

# XmClipboardInquireCount

## Name

XmClipboardInquireCount – get the number of data item formats available on the clipboard.

## Synopsis

```
#include <Xm/CutPaste.h>
int XmClipboardInquireCount (display, window, count, max_format_-
        name_length)
    Display *display;
    Window window;
    int *count;
    int *max_format_name_length;
```

### Inputs

*display* Specifies a connection to an X server; returned from `XOpenDisplay()` or `XtDisplay()`.

*window* Specifies a window ID that identifies the client to the clipboard.

### Outputs

*count* Returns the number of data item formats available for the data on the clipboard.

*max_format_name_length*
Returns the maximum length of data item format names.

### Returns

`ClipboardSuccess` on success, `ClipboardLocked` if the clipboard is locked by another application, or `ClipboardNoData` if there is no data on the clipboard.

## Description

`XmClipboardInquireCount()` returns the number of data formats available for the current clipboard data item and the length of its longest format name. The *count* includes the formats that were passed by name. If there are no formats available, *count* is 0 (zero).

## Usage

To inquire about the formats of the data on the clipboard, you use `XmClipboardInquireCount()` and `XmClipboardInquireFormat()` in conjunction. `XmClipboardInquireCount()` returns the number of formats for the data item and `XmClipboardInquireFormat()` allows you to iterate through all of the formats.

## See Also

*XmClipboardInquireFormat*(1).

# XmClipboardInquireFormat

## Name

XmClipboardInquireFormat – get the specified clipboard data format name.

## Synopsis

```
#include <Xm/CutPaste.h>
int XmClipboardInquireFormat (display, window, index, format_name_buf,
        buffer_len, copied_len)
    Display *display;
    Window window;
    int index;
    XtPointer format_name_buf;
    unsigned long buffer_len;
    unsigned long *copied_len;
```

### Inputs

*display* Specifies a connection to an X server; returned from `XOpenDisplay()` or `XtDisplay()`.

*window* Specifies a window ID that identifies the client to the clipboard.

*index* Specifies the index of the format name to retrieve.

*buffer_len* Specifies the length of *format_name_buf* in bytes.

### Outputs

*format_name_buf*
Returns the format name.

*copied_len* Returns the length (in bytes) of the string copied to *format_name_buf*.

### Returns

`ClipboardSuccess` on success, `ClipboardLocked` if the clipboard is locked by another application, `ClipboardTruncate` if *format_name_buf* is not long enough to hold the returned data, or `ClipboardNoData` if there is no data on the clipboard.

## Description

`XmClipboardInquireFormat()` returns a format name for the current data item in the clipboard. The format name returned is specified by *index*, where 1 refers to the first format. If *index* exceeds the number of formats for the data item, then `XmClipboardInquireFormat()` returns a value of 0 (zero) in the *copied_len* argument. `XmClipboardInquireFormat()` returns the format name in the *format_name_buf* argument. This argument is a buffer of a fixed length that is allocated by the programmer. If the buffer is not large enough to hold the format name, the routine copies as much of the format name as will fit in the buffer and returns `ClipboardTruncate`.

## Usage

To inquire about the formats of the data on the clipboard, you use `XmClipboardInquireCount()` and `XmClipboardInquireFormat()` in conjunction. `XmClipboardInquireCount()` returns the number of formats for the data item and `XmClipboardInquireFormat()` allows you to iterate through all of the formats.

## See Also

*XmClipboardInquireCount*(1).

# XmClipboardInquireLength

## Name

XmClipboardInquireLength – get the length of the data item on the clipboard.

## Synopsis

```
#include <Xm/CutPaste.h>
int XmClipboardInquireLength (display, window, format_name, length)
    Display *display;
    Window window;
    char *format_name;
    unsigned long *length;
```

### Inputs

*display* Specifies a connection to an X server; returned from `XOpenDisplay()` or `XtDisplay()`.

*window* Specifies a window ID that identifies the client to the clipboard.

*format_name* Specifies the format name for the data.

### Outputs

*length* Returns the length of the data item for the specified *format*.

### Returns

`ClipboardSuccess` on success, `ClipboardLocked` if the clipboard is locked by another application, or `ClipboardNoData` if there is no data on the clipboard for the requested format.

## Description

`XmClipboardInquireLength()` returns the length of the data stored under the specified *format_name* for the current clipboard data item. If no data is found corresponding to *format_name* or if there is no item on the clipboard, `XmClipboardInquireLength()` returns a *length* of 0 (zero). When a data item is passed by name, the length of the data is assumed to be passed in a call to `XmClipboardCopy()`, even though the data has not yet been transferred to the clipboard.

## Usage

`XmClipboardInquireLength()` provides a way for an application to find out how much data is on the clipboard, so that it can allocate a buffer that is large enough to retrieve the data with one call to `XmClipboardRetrieve()`.

## Example

The following code fragment demonstrates how to use `XmClipboardInquireLength()` to retrieve all of the data on the clipboard:

```
int          status, recvd, length;
char        *data;
Display     *dpy = XtDisplayOfObject(widget);
Window       window = XtWindowOfObject(widget);
```

```
do
    status = XmClipboardInquireLength(dpy, window, "STRING", &length);
while (status == ClipboardLocked);

if (length != 0) {
    data = XtMalloc(length+1);

    do
        status = XmClipboardRetrieve(dpy, window,
            "STRING", data, length+1, &recvd, NULL);
    while (status == ClipboardLocked);

    if (status != ClipboardSuccess || recvd != length) {
        XtWarning("Failed to receive all clipboard data");
    }
}
```

## See Also

*XmClipboardRetrieve*(1).

## Name

XmClipboardInquirePendingItems – get a list of pending data ID/private ID pairs.

## Synopsis

```
#include <Xm/CutPaste.h>
int XmClipboardInquirePendingItems (display, window, format_name,
        item_list, count)
    Display *display;
    Window window;
    char *format_name;
    XmClipboardPendingList *item_list;
    unsigned long *count;
```

### Inputs

*display* Specifies a connection to an X server; returned from `XOpenDisplay()` or `XtDisplay()`.

*window* Specifies a window ID that identifies the client to the clipboard.

*format_name* Specifies the format name for the data.

### Outputs

*item_list* Returns an array of *data_id*/*private_id* pairs for the specified *format*.

*count* Returns the number of items in the *item_list* array.

### Returns

`ClipboardSuccess` on success or `ClipboardLocked` if the clipboard is locked by another application.

## Description

`XmClipboardInquirePendingItems()` returns a list of pending *data_id*/*private_id* pairs for the specified *format_name*. The *data_id* and *private_id* arguments are specified in the clipboard functions for copying and retrieving. A data item is considered pending under these conditions: the application that owns the data item originally passed it by name, the application has not yet copied the data, and the data item has not been deleted from the clipboard. If there are no pending data items for the specified *format_name*, the routine returns a *count* of 0 (zero). The application is responsible for freeing the memory that is allocated by `XmClipboardInquirePendingItems()` to store the list. Use `XtFree()` to free the memory.

## Usage

An application should call `XmClipboardInquirePendingItems()` before exiting, to determine whether data that has been passed by name should be copied to the clipboard.

## Structures

The `XmClipboardPendingList` is defined as follows:

```
typedef struct {
    long DataId;
    long PrivateId;
} XmClipboardPendingRec, *XmClipboardPendingList;
```

## See Also

*XmClipboardStartCopy*(1).

# XmClipboardLock

## Name

XmClipboardLock – lock the clipboard.

## Synopsis

```
#include <Xm/CutPaste.h>
int XmClipboardLock (display, window)
    Display *display;
    Window window;
```

### Inputs

*display* Specifies a connection to an X server; returned from `XOpenDisplay()` or `XtDisplay()`.

*window* Specifies a window ID that identifies the client to the clipboard.

### Returns

`ClipboardSuccess` on success or `ClipboardLocked` if the clipboard is locked by another application.

## Description

`XmClipboardLock()` locks the clipboard on behalf of an application, which prevents access to the clipboard by other applications. If the clipboard has already been locked by another application, the routine returns `ClipboardLocked`. If the same application has already locked the clipboard, the lock level is increased.

## Usage

An application uses `XmClipboardLock()` to ensure that clipboard data is not changed by calls to clipboard functions by other applications. An application does not need to lock the clipboard between calls to `XmClipboardStartRetrieve()` and `XmClipboardEndRetrieve()`, because the clipboard is locked automatically between these calls. `XmClipboardUnlock()` allows other applications to access the clipboard again.

## See Also

*XmClipboardEndCopy*(1), *XmClipboardEndRetrieve*(1), *XmClipboardStartCopy*(1), *XmClipboardStartRetrieve*(1), *XmClipboardUnlock*(1).

# XmClipboardRegisterFormat



## Name

XmClipboardRegisterFormat – register a new format for clipboard data items.

## Synopsis

```
#include <Xm/CutPaste.h>
int XmClipboardRegisterFormat (display, format_name, format_length)
    Display *display;
    char *format_name;
    unsigned long format_length;
```

### Inputs

*display* Specifies a connection to an X server; returned from `XOpenDisplay()` or `XtDisplay()`.

*format_name* Specifies the string name for the format.

*format_length*
Specifies the length of the format in bits (8, 16, or 32).

### Returns

`ClipboardSuccess` on success, `ClipboardBadFormat` if the format is not properly specified, `ClipboardLocked` if the clipboard is locked by another application, or `ClipboardFail` on failure.

## Description

`XmClipboardRegisterFormat()` registers a new format having the specified *format_name* and *format_length*. `XmClipboardRegisterFormat()` returns `ClipboardFail` if the format is already registered with the specified length or `ClipboardBadFormat` if *format_name* is NULL or *format_length* is not 8, 16, or 32 bits.

## Usage

`XmClipboardRegisterFormat()` is used by applications that support cutting and pasting of arbitrary data types. Every format that is stored on the clipboard needs to have a length associated with it, so that clipboard operations between applications that run on platforms with different byte-swapping orders function properly. This routine is not needed for format types that are defined by the ICCCM because those formats are preregistered. If you are registering your own data structure as a format, you should choose an appropriate name and use 32 as the format size.

## See Also

*XmClipboardStartCopy*(1).

# XmClipboardRetrieve

## Name

XmClipboardRetrieve – retrieve a data item from the clipboard.

## Synopsis

```
#include <Xm/CutPaste.h>
int XmClipboardRetrieve (display, window, format_name, buffer, length,
        num_bytes, private_id)
    Display *display;
    Window window;
    char *format_name;
    char *buffer;
    unsigned long length;
    unsigned long *num_bytes;
    int *private_id;
```

### Inputs

| | |
|---|---|
| *display* | Specifies a connection to an X server; returned from `XOpenDisplay()` or `XtDisplay()`. |
| *window* | Specifies a window ID that identifies the client to the clipboard. |
| *format_name* | Specifies the format name for the data. |
| *buffer* | Specifies the buffer to which the clipboard data is copied. |
| *length* | Specifies the length of *buffer*. |

### Outputs

| | |
|---|---|
| *num_bytes* | Returns the number of bytes of data copied into *buffer*. |
| *private_id* | Returns the private data that was stored with the data item. |

### Returns

`ClipboardSuccess` on success, `ClipboardLocked` if the clipboard is locked by another application, `ClipboardTruncate` if *buffer* is not long enough to hold the returned data, or `ClipboardNoData` if there is no data on the clipboard for the requested format.

## Description

`XmClipboardRetrieve()` fetches the current data item from the clipboard and copies it to the specified *buffer*. The *format_name* specifies the type of data being retrieved. The *num_bytes* parameter returns the amount of data that is copied into *buffer*. The routine returns `ClipboardTruncate` when all of the data does not fit in the *buffer*, to indicate that more data remains to be copied.

## Usage

`XmClipboardRetrieve()` can be used to retrieve data in one large piece or in multiple smaller pieces. To retrieve data in one chunk, call `XmClipboardInquireLength()` to determine the size of the data on the clipboard. Multiple calls to `XmClipboard-Retrieve()` with the same *format_name*, between calls to

`XmClipboardStartRetrieve()` and `XmClipboardEndRetrieve()`, copy data incrementally. Since the clipboard is locked by a call to `XmClipboardStart-Retrieve()`, it is suggested that your application call any clipboard inquiry routines between this call and the first call to `ClipboardRetrieve()`.

## Example

The following code fragment shows the sequence of calls needed to perform an incremental retrieve. Note that this code does not store the data as it is retrieved:

```
int           status;
unsigned long received;
char          buffer[32];
Display      *dpy = XtDisplayOfObject(widget);
Window        window = XtWindowOfObject(widget);

do
    status = XmClipboardStartRetrieve(dpy, window, CurrentTime);
while (status == ClipboardLocked);

do {
    /* retrieve data from clipboard */
    status = XmClipboardRetrieve(dpy, window, "STRING",
        buffer, sizeof(buffer), &received, NULL)
} while (status == ClipboardTruncate);

status = XmClipboardEndRetrieve(dpy, window);
```

## See Also

*XmClipboardEndRetrieve*(1), *XmClipboardInquireLength*(1), *XmClipboardLock*(1), *XmClipboardStartRetrieve*(1), *XmClipboardUnlock*(1).

# XmClipboardStartCopy

## Name

XmClipboardStartCopy – set up storage for a clipboard copy operation.

## Synopsis

```
#include <Xm/CutPaste.h>
int XmClipboardStartCopy (display, window, clip_label, timestamp, widget,
        callback, item_id)
    Display *display;
    Window window;
    XmString clip_label;
    Time timestamp;
    Widget widget;
    XmCutPasteProc callback;
    long *item_id;
```

### Inputs

| | |
|---|---|
| *display* | Specifies a connection to an X server; returned from XOpenDisplay() or XtDisplay(). |
| *window* | Specifies a window ID that identifies the client to the clipboard. |
| *clip_label* | Specifies a label that is associated with the data item. |
| *timestamp* | Specifies the time of the event that triggered the copy operation. |
| *widget* | Specifies the widget that receives messages requesting data that has been passed by name. |
| *callback* | Specifies the callback function that is called when the clipboard needs data that has been passed by name. |

### Outputs

| | |
|---|---|
| *item_id* | Returns the ID assigned to the data item. |

### Returns

ClipboardSuccess on success or ClipboardLocked if the clipboard is locked by another application.

## Description

XmClipboardStartCopy() creates the storage and data structures that receive clipboard data. During a cut or copy operation, an application calls this function to initiate the operation. The data that is copied to the structures becomes the next clipboard data item.

Several arguments to XmClipboardStartCopy() provide identifying information. The *window* argument specifies the window that identifies the application to the clipboard; an application should pass the same window ID to each clipboard routine that it calls. *clip_label* assigns a text string to the data item that could be used as the label for a clipboard viewing window. The *timestamp* passed to the routine must be a valid timestamp. The *item_id* argument returns a number that identifies the data item. An application uses this number to specify the data item in other clipboard calls.

## Usage

Since copying a large piece of data to the clipboard can take a long time and it is possible that the data will never be requested by another application, the clipboard copy routines provide a mechanism to copy data by name. When a clipboard data item is passed by name, the application does not need to copy the data to the clipboard until it has been requested by another application. In order to pass data by name, the *widget* and *callback* arguments to `XmClipboardStartCopy()` must be specified. *widget* specifies the ID of the widget that receives messages requesting that data be passed by name. All of the message handling is done by the clipboard operations, so any valid widget ID can be used. *callback* specifies the procedure that is invoked when the clipboard needs the data that was passed by name and when the data item is removed from the clipboard. The callback function copies the actual data to the clipboard using `XmClipboardCopyByName()`.

## Example

The following routines show the sequence of calls needed to copy data by name. The `to_clipbd` callback shows the copying of data and `copy_by_name` shows the callback that actually copies the data:

```
static void to_clipbd(widget, client_data, call_data)
Widget widget;
XtPointer client_data;
XtPointer call_data;
{
    unsigned long item_id = 0;
    int           status;
    XmString      clip_label;
    Display      *dpy = XtDisplayOfObject(widget);
    Window        window = XtWindowOfObject(widget);
    void          copy_by_name();
    unsigned long size = DATA_SIZE;
    char         *data = (char *) client_data;

    clip_label = XmStringCreateLocalized("Data");

    /* start a copy; retry until unlocked */
    do
        status = XmClipboardStartCopy(dpy, window,
            clip_label, CurrentTime, widget, copy_by_name, &item_id);
    while (status == ClipboardLocked);

    XmStringFree(clip_label);

    /* copy the data; retry until unlocked */
    do
        status = XmClipboardCopy(dpy, window, item_id, "STRING",
            NULL, size, 0, NULL);
    while (status == ClipboardLocked);

    /* end the copy; retry until unlocked */
```

```
    do
        status = XmClipboardEndCopy(dpy, window, item_id);
    while (status == ClipboardLocked);
}

static void copy_by_name(widget, data_id, private_id, reason)
Widget widget;
int *data_id, *private_id, *reason;
{
    Display     *dpy = XtDisplay(toplevel);
    Window       window = XtWindow(toplevel);
    int          status;
    char         buffer[32];

    if (*reason == XmCR_CLIPBOARD_DATA_REQUEST) {
        sprintf(buffer, "stuff");

        do
            status = XmClipboardCopyByName(dpy, window, *data_id, buffer,
                strlen(buffer)+1, *private_id);
        while (status != ClipboardSuccess);
    }
```



## Procedures

The `XmCutPasteProc` has the following format:

```
typedef void (*XmCutPasteProc) (Widget, * int, * int, * int)
    Widget widget;
    int *data_id;
    int *private_id;
    int *reason;
```

An `XmCutPasteProc` takes four arguments. The first argument, *widget*, is the widget passed to the callback routine, which is the same widget as passed to `XmClipboardBeginCopy()`. The *data_id* argument is the ID of the data item that is returned by `XmClipboardCopy()` and *private_id* is the private data passed to `XmClipboardCopy()`. The *reason* argument takes the value `XmCR_CLIPBOARD_DATA_REQUEST`, which indicates that the data must be copied to the clipboard, or `XmCR_CLIPBOARD_DATA_DELETE`, which indicates that the client can delete the data from the clipboard. Although the last three parameters are pointers to integers, the values are read-only and changing them has no effect.

## See Also

*XmClipboardBeginCopy*(1), *XmClipboardCancelCopy*(1), *XmClipboardCopy*(1), *XmClipboardCopyByName*(1), *XmClipboardEndCopy*(1), *XmClipboardLock*(1), *XmClipboardRegisterFormat*(1), *XmClipboardUndoCopy*(1), *XmClipboardUnlock*(1), *XmClipboardWithdrawFormat*(1).

# XmClipboardStartRetrieve



## Name

XmClipboardStartRetrieve – start a clipboard retrieval operation.

## Synopsis

```
#include <Xm/CutPaste.h>
int XmClipboardStartRetrieve (display, window, timestamp)
    Display *display;
    Window window;
    Time timestamp;
```

### Inputs

| | |
|---|---|
| *display* | Specifies a connection to an X server; returned from `XOpenDisplay()` or `XtDisplay()`. |
| *window* | Specifies a window ID that identifies the client to the clipboard. |
| *timestamp* | Specifies the time of the event that triggered the retrieval operation. |

### Returns

`ClipboardSuccess` on success or `ClipboardLocked` if the clipboard is locked by another application.

## Description

`XmClipboardStartRetrieve()` starts a clipboard retrieval operation by telling the clipboard that an application is ready to start copying data from the clipboard. `XmClipboardStartRetrieve()` locks the clipboard until `XmClipboardEndRetrieve()` is called. The *window* argument specifies the window that identifies the application to the clipboard; an application should pass the same window ID to each clipboard routine that it calls. The *timestamp* passed to the routine must be a valid timestamp.

## Usage

Multiple calls to `XmClipboardRetrieve()` with the same *format_name*, between calls to `XmClipboardStartRetrieve()` and `XmClipboardEndRetrieve()`, copy data incrementally.

## Example

The following code fragment shows the sequence of calls needed to perform an incremental retrieve. Note that this code does not store the data as it is retrieved:

```
int           status;
unsigned long received;
char          buffer[32];
Display      *dpy = XtDisplayOfObject(widget);
Window        window = XtWindowOfObject(widget);

do
    status = XmClipboardStartRetrieve(dpy, window, CurrentTime);
while (status == ClipboardLocked);
```

```
do {
    /* retrieve data from clipboard */
    status = XmClipboardRetrieve(dpy, window, "STRING",
        buffer, sizeof(buffer), &received, NULL)
} while (status == ClipboardTruncate);

status = XmClipboardEndRetrieve(dpy, window);
```

### See Also

*XmClipboardEndRetrieve*(1), *XmClipboardInquireCount*(1), *XmClipboardInquireFormat*(1), *XmClipboardInquireLength*(1), *XmClipboardInquirePendingItems*(1), *XmClipboardLock*(1), *XmClipboardRetrieve*(1), *XmClipboardUnlock*(1).

# XmClipboardUndoCopy

## Name

XmClipboardUndoCopy – remove the last item copied to the clipboard.

## Synopsis

```
#include <Xm/CutPaste.h>
int XmClipboardUndoCopy (display, window)
    Display *display;
    Window window;
```

### Inputs

*display* Specifies a connection to an X server; returned from `XOpenDisplay()` or `XtDisplay()`.

*window* Specifies a window ID that identifies the client to the clipboard.

### Returns

`ClipboardSuccess` on success or `ClipboardLocked` if the clipboard is locked by another application.

## Description

`XmClipboardUndoCopy()` deletes the item most recently placed on the clipboard, provided that the application that originally placed the item has matching values for *display* and *window*. If the values do not match, no action is taken. The routine also restores any data item that was deleted from the clipboard by the call to `XmClipboardCopy()`.

## Usage

Motif maintains a two-deep stack of items that have been placed on the clipboard. Once an item has been copied to the clipboard, the copy can be undone by calling `XmClipboard-UndoCopy()`. Calling this routine twice undoes the last undo operation.

## See Also

*XmClipboardBeginCopy*(1), *XmClipboardCopy*(1), *XmClipboardCopyByName*(1), *XmClipboardEndCopy*(1), *XmClipboardStartCopy*(1).

## Name

XmClipboardUnlock – unlock the clipboard.

## Synopsis

```
#include <Xm/CutPaste.h>
int XmClipboardUnlock (display, window, remove_all_locks)
    Display *display;
    Window window;
    Boolean remove_all_locks;
```

### Inputs

*display* — Specifies a connection to an X server; returned from `XOpenDisplay()` or `XtDisplay()`.

*window* — Specifies a window ID that identifies the client to the clipboard.

*remove_all_locks* — Specifies whether nested locks should be removed.

### Returns

`ClipboardSuccess` on success or `ClipboardFail` if the clipboard is not locked or if it is locked by another application.

## Description

`XmClipboardUnlock()` unlocks the clipboard, which allows other applications to access it. If *remove_all_locks* is `True`, all nested locks are removed. If it is `False`, only one level of lock is removed.

## Usage

Multiple calls to `XmClipboardLock()` can increase the lock level, and normally, each `XmClipboardLock()` call requires a corresponding call to `XmClipboardUnlock()`. However, by setting *remove_all_locks* to `True`, nested locks can be removed with a single call.

## See Also

*XmClipboardBeginCopy*(1), *XmClipboardCancelCopy*(1), *XmClipboardEndCopy*(1), *XmClipboardEndRetrieve*(1), *XmClipboardLock*(1), *XmClipboardStartCopy*(1), *XmClipboardStartRetrieve*(1).

# XmClipboardWithdrawFormat



## Name

XmClipboardWithdrawFormat – indicate that an application does not want to supply a data item any longer.

## Synopsis

```
#include <Xm/CutPaste.h>
int XmClipboardWithdrawFormat (display, window, data_id)
    Display *display;
    Window window;
    int data_id;
```

### Inputs

| | |
|---|---|
| *display* | Specifies a connection to an X server; returned from `XOpenDisplay()` or `XtDisplay()`. |
| *window* | Specifies a window ID that identifies the client to the clipboard. |
| *data_id* | Specifies the ID for the passed-by-name data item. |

### Returns

`ClipboardSuccess` on success or `ClipboardLocked` if the clipboard is locked by another application.

## Description

`XmClipboardWithdrawFormat()` withdraws a data item that has been passed by name from the clipboard. The *data_id* is the ID that was assigned to the item when it was passed by `XmClipboardCopy()`.

## Usage

Despite its name, `XmClipboardWithdrawFormat()` does not remove a format specification from the clipboard. The routine provides an application with a way to withdraw data of a particular format from the clipboard.

## See Also

*XmClipboardBeginCopy*(1), *XmClipboardCopy*(1), *XmClipboardCopyByName*(1), *XmClipboardStartCopy*(1).

# XmCommandAppendValue

## Name

XmCommandAppendValue – append a compound string to the command.

## Synopsis

```
#include <Xm/Command.h>
void XmCommandAppendValue (widget, command)
    Widget widget;
    XmString command;
```

### Inputs

| | |
|---|---|
| *widget* | Specifies the Command widget. |
| *command* | Specifies the string that is appended. |

## Description

`XmCommandAppendValue()` appends the specified *command* to the end of the string that is displayed on the command line of the specified Command *widget*.

## Usage

`XmCommandAppendValue()` is a convenience routine that changes the value of the `XmN-command` resource of the Command widget.

## See Also

*XmCommandSetValue*(1),
*XmCommand*(2).

# XmCommandError



## Name

XmCommandError – display an error message in a Command widget.

## Synopsis

```
#include <Xm/Command.h>
void XmCommandError (widget, error)
    Widget widget;
    XmString error;
```

### Inputs

*widget* Specifies the Command widget.

*error* Specifies the error message to be displayed.

## Description

XmCommandError() displays an error message in the history region of the specified Command *widget*. The error string remains displayed until the next command takes effect.

## Usage

XmCommandError() displays the error message as one of the items in the XmNhistoryItems list. When the next command is entered, the error message is deleted from the list.

## See Also

*XmCommand*(2).

# XmCommandGetChild

## Name

XmCommandGetChild – get the specified child of a Command widget.

## Synopsis

```
#include <Xm/Command.h>
Widget XmCommandGetChild (widget, child)
    Widget widget;
    unsigned char child;
```

### Inputs

| | |
|---|---|
| *widget* | Specifies the Command widget. |
| *child* | Specifies the child of the Command widget. Pass one of the following possible values: XmDIALOG_COMMAND_TEXT, XmDIALOG_PROMPT_LABEL, XmDIALOG_HISTORY_LIST, or XmDIALOG_WORK_AREA. |

### Returns

The widget ID of the specified child of the Command *widget*.

## Description

XmCommandGetChild() returns the widget ID of the specified *child* of the Command *widget*.

## Usage

XmDIALOG_COMMAND_TEXT specifies the command text entry area, XmDIALOG_PROMPT_LABEL specifies the prompt string for the command line, XmDIALOG_HISTORY_LIST specifies the command history list, and XmDIALOG_WORK_AREA specifies any work area child that has been added to the Command widget. For more information on the different children of the Command widget, see the manual page in Section 2, *Motif and Xt Widget Classes*.

## Structures

The possible values for *child* are:

```
XmDIALOG_COMMAND_TEXT          XmDIALOG_HISTORY_LIST
XmDIALOG_PROMPT_LABEL          XmDIALOG_WORK_AREA
```

## See Also

*XmCommand*(2).

# XmCommandSetValue

## Name

XmCommandSetValue – replace the command string.

## Synopsis

```
#include <Xm/Command.h>
void XmCommandSetValue (widget, command)
    Widget widget;
    XmString command;
```

### Inputs

| | |
|---|---|
| *widget* | Specifies the Command widget. |
| *command* | Specifies the string that is displayed. |

## Description

`XmCommandSetValue()` replaces the currently displayed command-line text of the specified Command *widget* with the string specified by *command*. Specifying a zero-length string clears the command line.

## Usage

`XmCommandSetValue()` is a convenience routine that changes the value of the `XmNcommand` resource of the Command widget.

## See Also

*XmCommandAppendValue*(1),
*XmCommand*(2).

# XmConvertUnits

## Name

XmConvertUnits – convert a value to a specified unit type.

## Synopsis

```
int XmConvertUnits (widget, orientation, from_unit_type, from_value,
      to_unit_type)
    Widget widget;
    int orientation;
    int from_unit_type;
    int from_value;
    int to_unit_type;
```

### Inputs

*widget* Specifies the widget for which to convert the data.

*orientation* Specifies the screen orientation that is used in the conversion. Pass either XmHORIZONTAL or XmVERTICAL.

*from_unit_type*
Specifies the unit type of the value that is being converted.

*from_value* Specifies the value that is being converted.

*to_unit_type*
Specifies the new unit type of the value.

### Returns

The converted value or 0 (zero) if the input parameters are not specified correctly.

## Description

XmConvertUnits() converts the value specified in *from_value* into the equivalent value in a different unit of measurement. This function returns the resulting value if successful; it returns 0 (zero) if *widget* is NULL or if incorrect values are supplied for orientation or conversion unit arguments. *orientation* matters only when conversion values are font units, which are measured differently in the horizontal and vertical dimensions.

## Usage

XmConvertUnits() allows an application to manipulate resolution-independent values. XmPIXELS specifies a normal pixel value, Xm100TH_MILLIMETERS specifies a value in terms of 1/100 of a millimeter, Xm1000TH_INCHES specifies a value in terms of 1/1000 of an inch, Xm100TH_POINTS specifies a value in terms of 1/100 of a point (1/72 of an inch), and Xm100TH_FONT_UNITS specifies a value in terms of 1/100 of a font unit. A font unit has horizontal and vertical components which are specified by the Screen resources XmNhorizontalFontUnit and XmNverticalFontUnit.

## Structures

The possible values for *from_unit_type* and *to_unit_type* are:

```
XmPIXELS                     Xm100TH_POINTS
Xm100TH_MILLIMETERS          Xm100TH_FONT_UNITS
Xm1000TH_INCHES
```

## See Also

*XmSetFontUnits*(1),
*XmScreen*(2).

## Name

XmCreate*Object* – create an instance of a particular widget class or compound object.

## Synopsis

### Simple Widgets

```
#include <Xm/ArrowB.h>
Widget XmCreateArrowButton (parent, name, arglist, argcount)

#include <Xm/ArrowBG.h>
Widget XmCreateArrowButtonGadget (parent, name, arglist, argcount)

#include <Xm/BulletinB.h>
Widget XmCreateBulletinBoard (parent, name, arglist, argcount)

#include <Xm/CascadeB.h>
Widget XmCreateCascadeButton (parent, name, arglist, argcount)

#include <Xm/CascadeBG.h>
Widget XmCreateCascadeButtonGadget (parent, name, arglist, argcount)

#include <Xm/Command.h>
Widget XmCreateCommand (parent, name, arglist, argcount)

#include <Xm/DialogS.h>
Widget XmCreateDialogShell (parent, name, arglist, argcount)

#include <Xm/DragIcon.h>
Widget XmCreateDragIcon (parent, name, arglist, argcount)

#include <Xm/DrawingA.h>
Widget XmCreateDrawingArea (parent, name, arglist, argcount)

#include <Xm/DrawnB.h>
Widget XmCreateDrawnButton (parent, name, arglist, argcount)

#include <Xm/FileSB.h>
Widget XmCreateFileSelectionBox (parent, name, arglist, argcount)

#include <Xm/Form.h>
Widget XmCreateForm (parent, name, arglist, argcount)

#include <Xm/Frame.h>
Widget XmCreateFrame (parent, name, arglist, argcount)

#include <Xm/Label.h>
Widget XmCreateLabel (parent, name, arglist, argcount)
```

```
#include <Xm/LabelG.h>
Widget XmCreateLabelGadget (parent, name, arglist, argcount)

#include <Xm/List.h>
Widget XmCreateList (parent, name, arglist, argcount)

#include <Xm/MainW.h>
Widget XmCreateMainWindow (parent, name, arglist, argcount)

#include <Xm/MenuShell.h>
Widget XmCreateMenuShell (parent, name, arglist, argcount)

#include <Xm/MessageB.h>
Widget XmCreateMessageBox (parent, name, arglist, argcount)

#include <Xm/PanedW.h>
Widget XmCreatePanedWindow (parent, name, arglist, argcount)

#include <Xm/PushB.h>
Widget XmCreatePushButton (parent, name, arglist, argcount)

#include <Xm/PushBG.h>
Widget XmCreatePushButtonGadget (parent, name, arglist, argcount)

#include <Xm/RowColumn.h>
Widget XmCreateRowColumn (parent, name, arglist, argcount)
Widget XmCreateRadioBox (parent, name, arglist, argcount)
Widget XmCreateWorkArea (parent, name, arglist, argcount)

#include <Xm/Scale.h>
Widget XmCreateScale (parent, name, arglist, argcount)

#include <Xm/ScrollBar.h>
Widget XmCreateScrollBar (parent, name, arglist, argcount)

#include <Xm/ScrolledW.h>
Widget XmCreateScrolledWindow (parent, name, arglist, argcount)

#include <Xm/SelectioB.h>
Widget XmCreateSelectionBox (parent, name, arglist, argcount)

#include <Xm/Separator.h>
Widget XmCreateSeparator (parent, name, arglist, argcount)

#include <Xm/SeparatoG.h>
Widget XmCreateSeparatorGadget (parent, name, arglist, argcount)
```

```
#include <Xm/Text.h>
Widget XmCreateText (parent, name, arglist, argcount)

#include <Xm/TextF.h>
Widget XmCreateTextField (parent, name, arglist, argcount)

#include <Xm/ToggleB.h>
Widget XmCreateToggleButton (parent, name, arglist, argcount)

#include <Xm/ToggleBG.h>
Widget XmCreateToggleButtonGadget (parent, name, arglist, argcount)
```

**Dialog Objects**

```
#include <Xm/BulletinB.h>
Widget XmCreateBulletinBoardDialog (parent, name, arglist, argcount)

#include <Xm/FileSB.h>
Widget XmCreateFileSelectionDialog (parent, name, arglist, argcount)

#include <Xm/Form.h>
Widget XmCreateFormDialog (parent, name, arglist, argcount)

#include <Xm/MessageB.h>
Widget XmCreateErrorDialog (parent, name, arglist, argcount)
Widget XmCreateInformationDialog (parent, name, arglist, argcount)
Widget XmCreateMessageDialog (parent, name, arglist, argcount)
Widget XmCreateQuestionDialog (parent, name, arglist, argcount)
Widget XmCreateTemplateDialog (parent, name, arglist, argcount)
Widget XmCreateWarningDialog (parent, name, arglist, argcount)
Widget XmCreateWorkingDialog (parent, name, arglist, argcount)

#include <Xm/SelectioB.h>
Widget XmCreatePromptDialog (parent, name, arglist, argcount)
Widget XmCreateSelectionDialog (parent, name, arglist, argcount)
```

**Menu Objects**

```
#include <Xm/RowColumn.h>
Widget XmCreateMenuBar (parent, name, arglist, argcount)
Widget XmCreateOptionMenu (parent, name, arglist, argcount)
Widget XmCreatePopupMenu (parent, name, arglist, argcount)
Widget XmCreatePulldownMenu (parent, name, arglist, argcount)
```

**Simple Menu Objects**

```
#include <Xm/RowColumn.h>
Widget XmCreateSimpleCheckBox (parent, name, arglist, argcount)
Widget XmCreateSimpleMenuBar (parent, name, arglist, argcount)
Widget XmCreateSimpleOptionMenu (parent, name, arglist, argcount)
Widget XmCreateSimplePopupMenu (parent, name, arglist, argcount)
```

```
Widget XmCreateSimplePulldownMenu (parent, name, arglist, argcount)
Widget XmCreateSimpleRadioBox (parent, name, arglist, argcount)
```

#### Scrolled Objects

```
#include <Xm/List.h>
Widget XmCreateScrolledList (parent, name, arglist, argcount)

#include <Xm/Text.h>
Widget XmCreateScrolledText (parent, name, arglist, argcount)

    Widget parent;
    String name;
    ArgList arglist;
    Cardinal argcount;
```

#### Inputs

| | |
|---|---|
| *parent* | Specifies the widget ID of the parent of the new widget. |
| *name* | Specifies the string name of the new widget for resource lookup. |
| *arglist* | Specifies the resource name/value pairs used in creating the widget. |
| *argcount* | Specifies the number of name/value pairs in *arglist*. |

#### Returns

The widget ID of the widget that is created.

### Availability

`XmCreateDragIcon()` and `XmCreateTemplateDialog()` are only available in Motif 1.2 and later.

### Description

The `XmCreate*()` routines are convenience routines for creating an instance of a particular widget class or a particular compound object. Each creation routine takes the same four arguments: the parent's widget ID, the name of the new widget, a list of resource name/value pairs, and the number of name/value pairs.

The simple creation routines create a single widget with the default resource settings for the widget class, except for `XmCreateRadioBox()` and `XmCreateWorkArea()`, which create specially configured RowColumn widgets.

The dialog creation routines are convenience routines for creating a particular unmanaged widget as a child of a DialogShell. The *parent* argument specifies the parent of the DialogShell and *name* specifies the string name of the particular widget that is created. The name of the DialogShell is the string that results from appending "_popup" to the name of the widget. The routines return the widget ID of the widget that is created as the child of the DialogShell.

The menu creation routines are convenience routines for creating particular types of menu objects. Each routine creates a RowColumn widget with specific resource settings that configure the widget to operate as the particular type of menu. `XmCreatePopupMenu()` and `XmCreatePulldownMenu()` create the RowColumn widget as the child of a MenuShell.

The simple menu creation routines are convenience routines for creating particular configurations of RowColumn widgets and their children. For example, `XmCreateSimpleCheckBox()` creates a CheckBox with ToggleButtonGadgets as its children.

`XmCreateScrolledList()` and `XmCreateScrolledText()` are convenience routines that create a List or Text widget as the child of a ScrolledWindow. The *parent* argument specifies the parent ofthe ScrolledWindow and *name* specifies the string name of the List or Text widget. The name of the ScrolledWindow is the string that results from appending "`SW`" to the name of the widget. The routines return the widget ID of the List or Text widget.

## Usage

Each widget or compound object that can be created with an `XmCreate*()` routine can also be created using `XtCreateWidget()`. The simple Motif creation routines are simply veneers to `XtCreateWidget()`. The rest of the Motif creation routines create multiple widgets and/or set specific widget resources. In order to use `XtCreateWidget()` to create these objects, you need to have a complete understanding of the compound object that you are trying to create. For more information on each widget and compound object that can be created, see the appropriate manual page in cmtr02 ].

## See Also

*XmArrowButtonGadget*(2), *XmArrowButton*(2), *XmBulletinBoardDialog*(2), *XmBulletinBoard*(2), *XmCascadeButtonGadget*(2), *XmCascadeButton*(2), *XmCheckBox*(2), *XmCommand*(2), *XmDialogShell*(2), *XmDragIcon*(2), *XmDrawingArea*(2), *XmDrawnButton*(2), *XmErrorDialog*(2), *XmFileSelectionBox*(2), *XmFileSelectionDialog*(2), *XmFormDialog*(2), *XmForm*(2), *XmFrame*(2), *XmInformationDialog*(2), *XmLabelGadget*(2), *XmLabel*(2), *XmList*(2), *XmMainWindow*(2), *XmMenuBar*(2), *XmMenuShell*(2), *XmMessageBox*(2), *XmMessageDialog*(2), *XmOptionMenu*(2), *XmPanedWindow*(2), *XmPopupMenu*(2), *XmPromptDialog*(2), *XmPulldownMenu*(2), *XmPushButtonGadget*(2), *XmPushButton*(2), *XmQuestionDialog*(2), *XmRadioBox*(2), *XmRowColumn*(2), *XmScale*(2), *XmScrollBar*(2), *XmScrolledList*(2), *XmScrolledText*(2), *XmScrolledWindow*(2), *XmSelectionBox*(2), *XmSelectionDialog*(2), *XmSeparatorGadget*(2), *XmSeparator*(2), *XmTemplateDialog*(2), *XmTextField*(2), *XmText*(2), *XmToggleButtonGadget*(2), *XmToggleButton*(2), *XmWarningDialog*(2), *XmWorkingDialog*(2).

# XmCvtCTToXmString

## Name

XmCvtCTToXmString – convert compound text to a compound string.

## Synopsis

```
XmString XmCvtCTToXmString (text)
    char *text;
```

### Inputs

*text* Specifies the compound text that is to be converted.

### Returns

The converted compound string.

## Description

`XmCvtCTToXmString()` converts the specified *text* string from compound text format, which is an X Consortium Standard defined in *Compound Text Encoding*, to a Motif compound string. The routine assumes that the compound text is NULL-terminated and NULLs within the compound text are handled correctly. If *text* contains horizontal tabulation (HT) control characters, the result is undefined. `XmCvtCTToXmString()` allocates storage for the converted compound string. The application is responsible for freeing this storage using `XmStringFree()`.

## Usage

Compound text is an encoding that is designed to represent text from any locale. Compound text strings identify their encoding using embedded escape sequences. The compound text representation was standardized for X11R4 for use as a text interchange format for interclient communication. An application must call `XtAppInitialize()` before calling `XmCvtCTToXmString()`. The conversion of compound text to compound strings is implementation dependent. `XmCvtCTToXmString()` is the complement of `XmCvtXmStringToCT()`.

## See Also

*XmCvtXmStringToCT*(1).

# XmCvtStringToUnitType

## Name

XmCvtStringToUnitType – convert a string to a unit-type value.

## Synopsis

```
void XmCvtStringToUnitType (args, num_args, from_val, to_val)
    XrmValuePtr args;
    Cardinal *num_args;
    XrmValue *from_val;
    XrmValue *to_val;
```

### Inputs

*args* Specifies additional XrmValue arguments that are need to perform the conversion.

*num_args* Specifies the number of items in *args*.

*from_val* Specifies value to convert.

### Outputs

*to_val* Returns the converted value.

## Availability

In Motif 1.2, XmCvtStringToUnitType() is obsolete. It has been superceded by a new resource converter that uses the RepType facility.

## Description

XmCvtStringToUnitType() converts the string specified in *from_val* to one of the unit-type values: XmPIXELS, Xm100TH_MILLIMETERS, Xm1000TH_INCHES, Xm100TH_POINTS, or Xm100TH_FONT_UNITS. This value is returned in *to_val*.

## Usage

XmCvtStringToUnitType() should not be called directly; it should be installed as a resource converter using the R3 routine XtAddConverter(). The routine only needs to be installed if the XmNunitType resource for a widget is being set in a resource file. In this case, XmCvtStringToUnitType() must be installed with XtAddConverter() before the widget is created. Use the following call to XtAddConverter() to install the converter:

```
XtAddConverter (XmRString, XmRUnitType, XmCvtStringToUnitType, NULL, 0);
```

In Motif 1.2, the use of XmCvtStringToUnitType() as a resource converter is obsolete. A new resource converter that uses the RepType facility has replaced the routine.

## See Also

*XmGadget*(2), *XmManager*(2), *XmPrimitive*(2).

# XmCvtXmStringToCT



## Name

XmCvtXmStringToCT – convert a compound string to compound text.

## Synopsis

```
char * XmCvtXmStringToCT (string)
    XmString string;
```

### Inputs

*string* Specifies the compound string that is to be converted.

### Returns

The converted compound text string.

## Description

`XmCvtXmStringToCT()` converts the specified Motif compound *string* to a string in X11 compound text format, which is described in the X Consortium Standard *Compound Text Encoding*.

## Usage

Compound text is an encoding that is designed to represent text from any locale. Compound text strings identify their encoding using embedded escape sequences. The compound text representation was standardized for X11R4 for use as a text interchange format for interclient communication. `XmCvtXmStringToCT()` is the complement of `XmCvtCTToXmString()`.

In Motif 1.2, an application must not call `XmCvtXmStringToCT()` until after `XtAppInitialize()` is called, so that the locale is established correctly. The routine uses the font list tag of each compound string segment to select a compound text format for the segment. A mapping between font list tags and compound text encoding formats is stored in a registry.

If the compound string segment tag is associated with `XmFONTLIST_DEFAULT_TAG` in the registry, the converter calls `XmbTextListToTextProperty()` with the `XCompoundTextStyle` encoding style and uses the resulting compound text for the segment. If the compound string segment tag is mapped to a registered MIT charset, the routine creates the compound text using the charset as defined in the X Consortium Standard *Compound Text Encoding*. If the compound string segment tag is associated with a charset that is not `XmFONTLIST_DEFAULT_TAG` or a registered charset, the converter creates the compound text using the charset and the text as an "extended segment" with a variable number of octets per character. If the compound string segment tag is not mapped in the registry, the result depends upon the implementation.

## See Also

*XmCvtCTToXmString*(1), *XmMapSegmentEncoding*(1), *XmRegisterSegmentEncoding*(1).

# XmDeactivateProtocol

## Name

XmDeactivateProtocol – deactivate a protocol.

## Synopsis

```
#include <Xm/Protocols.h>
void XmDeactivateProtocol (shell, property, protocol)
    Widget shell;
    Atom property;
    Atom protocol;
```

### Inputs

| | |
|---|---|
| *shell* | Specifies the widget associated with the protocol property. |
| *property* | Specifies the property that holds the protocol data. |
| *protocol* | Specifies the protocol atom. |

## Description

`XmDeactivateProtocol()` deactivates the specified *protocol* without removing it. If the *shell* is realized, `XmDeactivateProtocol()` updates its protocol handlers and the specified *property*. A protocol may be active or inactive. If *protocol* is active, the protocol atom is stored in *property*; if *protocol* is inactive, the protocol atom is not stored in *property*.

## Usage

A protocol is a communication channel between applications. Protocols are simply atoms, stored in a property on the top-level shell window for the application. `XmDeactivate-Protocol()` allows a client to temporarily stop participating in the communication. The inverse routine is `XmActivateProtocol()`.

## See Also

*XmActivateProtocol*(1), *XmDeactivateWMProtocol*(1), *XmInternAtom*(1), *VendorShell*(2).



 

# XmDeactivateWMProtocol



## Name

XmDeactivateWMProtocol – deactivate the XA_WM_PROTOCOLS protocol.

## Synopsis

```
#include <Xm/Protocols.h>
void XmDeactivateWMProtocol (shell, protocol)
    Widget shell;
    Atom protocol;
```

### Inputs

*shell* Specifies the widget associated with the protocol property.

*protocol* Specifies the protocol atom.

## Description

`XmDeactivateWMProtocol()` is a convenience routine that calls `XmDeactivateProtocol()` with *property* set to `XA_WM_PROTOCOL`, the window manager protocol property.

## Usage

The property `XA_WM_PROTOCOLS` is a set of predefined protocols for communication between clients and window managers. `XmDeactivateWMProtocol()` allows a client to temporarily stop participating in the communication with the window manager. The inverse routine is `XmActivateWMProtocol()`.

## See Also

*XmActivateWMProtocol*(1), *XmDeactivateProtocol*(1), *XmInternAtom*(1), *VendorShell*(2).

# XmDestroyPixmap

## Name

XmDestroyPixmap – remove a pixmap from the pixmap cache.

## Synopsis

```
Boolean XmDestroyPixmap (screen, pixmap)
    Screen *screen;
    Pixmap pixmap;
```

### Inputs

| | |
|---|---|
| *screen* | Specifies the screen on which the pixmap is located. |
| *pixmap* | Specifies the pixmap. |

### Returns

`True` on success or `False` if there is no matching pixmap and screen in the cache.

## Description

`XmDestroyPixmap()` removes the specified *pixmap* from the pixmap cache when it is no longer needed. A pixmap is not completely freed until there are no further reference to it.

## Usage

The pixmap cache maintains a per-client list of the pixmaps that are in use. Whenever a pixmap is requested using `XmGetPixmap()`, an internal reference counter for the pixmap is incremented. `XmDestroyPixmap()` decrements this counter, so that when it reaches 0 (zero), the pixmap is removed from the cache.

## See Also

*XmGetPixmap*(1), *XmInstallImage*(1), *XmUninstallImage*(1).

# XmDragCancel



## Name

XmDragCancel – cancel a drag operation.

## Synopsis

```
#include <Xm/DragDrop.h>
void XmDragCancel (dragcontext)
    Widget dragcontext;
```

### Inputs

*dragcontext* Specifies the ID of the DragContext object for the drag operation that is being cancelled.

## Availability

Motif 1.2 and later.

## Description

`XmDragCancel()` cancels the drag operation that is in progress for the specified *dragcontext*. If the DragContext has any actions pending, they are terminated. The routine can only be called by the client that initiated the drag operation. `XmDragCancel()` frees the DragContext object associated with the drag operation.

## Usage

`XmDragCancel()` allows an initiating client to cancel a drag operation if it decides that that the operation should not continue for whatever reason. Calling `XmDragCancel()` is equivalent to the user pressing `KCancel` during the drag. The `XmNdropStartCallback` informs the initiating client of the cancellation by setting the `dropAction` field to `XmDROP_CANCEL`. So that it can undo any drag-under effects under the dynamic protocol, the receiving client gets an `XmCR_DROP_SITE_LEAVE_MESSAGE` when the drag is cancelled.

## See Also

*XmDragStart*(1),
*XmDragContext*(2).

## Name

XmDragStart – start a drag operation.

## Synopsis

```
#include <Xm/DragDrop.h>
Widget XmDragStart (widget, event, arglist, argcount)
    Widget widget;
    XEvent *event;
    ArgList arglist;
    Cardinal argcount;
```

### Inputs

| | |
|---|---|
| *widget* | Specifies the widget or gadget that contains the data that is being dragged. |
| *event* | Specifies the event that caused the drag operation. |
| *arglist* | Specifies the resource name/value pairs used in creating the DragContext. |
| *argcount* | Specifies the number of name/value pairs in *arglist*. |

### Returns

The ID of the DragContext object that is created.

## Availability

Motif 1.2 and later.

## Description

`XmDragStart()` starts a drag operation by creating and returning a DragContext object. The DragContext stores information that the toolkit needs to process a drag transaction. The DragContext object is widget-like, in that it uses resources to specify its attributes. The toolkit frees the DragContext upon completion of the drag and drop operation.

The *widget* argument to `XmDragStart()` should be the smallest widget that contains the source data for the drag operation. The *event* that starts the drag operation must be a `ButtonPress` event. The *arglist* and *argcount* parameters work as for any creation routine; any DragContext resources that are not set by the arguments are retrieved from the resource database or set to their default values.

## Usage

Motif 1.2 supports the drag and drop model of selection actions. In a widget that acts as a drag source, a user can make a selection and then drag the selection, using `BTransfer`, to other widgets that are registered as drop sites. These drop sites can be in the same application or another application.

In Motif 1.2, the Text and TextField widgets, the List widget, and Label and its subclasses are set up to act as drag sources by the toolkit. In order for another widget to act as a drag source, it must have a translation for `BTransfer`. The action routine for the translation calls `XmDragStart()` to initiate the drag and drop operation.

The only DragContext resource that must be specified when `XmDragStart()` is called is the `XmNconvertProc` procedure. This resource specifies a procedure of type `XtConvertSelectionIncrProc` that converts the source data to the format(s) requested by the receiving client. The specification of the other resources, such as those for operations and drag-over visuals, is optional. For more information about the DragContext object, see the manual page in Section 2, *Motif and Xt Widget Classes.*

## Example

The following routines show the use of `XmDragStart()` in setting up a ScrollBar to function as a drag source. When the ScrollBar is created, the translations are overridden to invoke `StartDrag` when `BTransfer` is pressed:

```
/* global variable */
Atom                    COMPOUND_TEXT;

/* start the drag operation */
static void StartDrag(widget, event, params, num_params)
Widget   widget;
XEvent   *event;
String   *params;
Cardinal *num_params;
{
   Argargs[10];
   int  n;
   Atom exportList[1];

   exportList[0] = COMPOUND_TEXT;

   n = 0;
   XtSetArg (args[n], XmNexportTargets, exportList); n++;
   XtSetArg (args[n], XmNnumExportTargets, XtNumber(exportList)); n++;
   XtSetArg (args[n], XmNdragOperations, XmDROP_COPY); n++;
   XtSetArg (args[n], XmNconvertProc, ConvertProc); n++;
   XtSetArg (args[n], XmNclientData, widget); n++;
   XmDragStart (widget, event, args, n);
}

/* define translations and actions */
static char dragTranslations[] =
     "#override <Btn2Down>: StartDrag()";

static XtActionsRec dragActions[] =
     { {"StartDrag", (XtActionProc)StartDrag} };

void main (argc, argv)
unsigned int argc;
char **argv;
{

   Arg              args[10];
```

```
    int             n;
    Widget          top, bboard, scrollbar;
    XtAppContext    app;
    XtTranslations  parsed_trans;

    XtSetLanguageProc (NULL, (XtLanguageProc)NULL, NULL);

    top = XtAppInitialize (&app, "Drag", NULL, 0, &argc, argv, NULL, NULL, 0);

    COMPOUND_TEXT = XmInternAtom (XtDisplay (top), "COMPOUND_TEXT", False);

    n = 0;
    bboard = XmCreateBulletinBoard (top, "bboard", args, n);
    XtManageChild (bboard);

    /* override button two press to start a drag */
    parsed_trans = XtParseTranslationTable (dragTranslations);
    XtAppAddActions (app, dragActions, XtNumber (dragActions));

    n = 0;
    XtSetArg (args[n], XmNtranslations, parsed_trans); n++;
    XtSetArg (args[n], XmNorientation, XmHORIZONTAL); n++;
    XtSetArg (args[n], XmNwidth, 100); n++;
    scrollbar = XmCreateScrollBar (bboard, "scrollbar", args, n);
    XtManageChild (scrollbar);

    XtRealizeWidget (top);
    XtAppMainLoop (app);
}
```



## See Also

*XmDragCancel*(1),
*XmDragContext*(2).

# XmDropSiteConfigureStackingOrder

## Name

XmDropSiteConfigureStackingOrder – change the stacking order of a drop site.

## Synopsis

```
#include <Xm/DragDrop.h>
void XmDropSiteConfigureStackingOrder (widget, sibling, stack_mode)
    Widget widget;
    Widget sibling;
    Cardinal stack_mode;
```

### Inputs

| | |
|---|---|
| *widget* | Specifies the widget ID associated with the drop site. |
| *sibling* | Specifies an optional widget ID of a sibling drop site. |
| *stack_mode* | Specifies the stacking position. Pass either `XmABOVE` or `XmBELOW`. |

## Availability

Motif 1.2 and later.

## Description

`XmDropSiteConfigureStackingOrder()` changes the stacking order of a drop site relative to its siblings. The routine changes the stacking order of the drop site associated with the specified *widget*. The stacking order is changed only if the drop sites associated with *widget* and *sibling* are siblings in both the widget hierarchy and the drop site hierarchy. The parent of both of the widgets must be registered as a composite drop site.

If *sibling* is specified, the stacking order of the drop site is changed relative to the stack position of the drop site associated with *sibling*, based on the value of *stack_mode*. If *stack_mode* is `XmABOVE`, the drop site is positioned just above the sibling; if *stack_mode* is `XmBELOW`, the drop site is positioned just below the sibling. If *sibling* is not specified, a *stack_mode* of `XmABOVE` causes the drop site to be placed at the top of the stack, while a *stack_mode* of `BELOW` causes it to be placed at the bottom of the stack.

## Usage

A drop site for drag and drop operations can be a composite drop site, which means that it has children which are also drop sites. The stacking order of the drop sites controls clipping of drag-under effects during a drag and drop operation. When drop sites overlap, the drag-under effects of the drop sites lower in the stacking order are clipped by the drop sites above them, regardless of whether or not the drop sites are active. You can use `XmDropSite-ConfigureStackingOrder()` to modify the stacking order. Use `XmDropSiteQuery-StackingOrder()` to get the current stacking order.

## See Also

*XmDropSiteQueryStackingOrder*(1), *XmDropSiteRegister*(1),
*XmDropSite*(2).

# XmDropSiteEndUpdate



## Name

XmDropSiteEndUpdate – end an update of multiple drop sites.

## Synopsis

```
#include <Xm/DragDrop.h>
void XmDropSiteEndUpdate (widget)
f
    Widget widget;
```

### Inputs

*widget* Specifies any widget in the hierarchy associated with the drop sites that are to be updated.

## Availability

Motif 1.2 and later.

## Description

`XmDropSiteEndUpdate()` finishes an update of multiple drop sites. The *widget* parameter specifies a widget in the widget hierarchy that contains all of the widgets associated with the drop sites being updated. The routine uses *widget* to identify the shell that contains all of the drop sites.

## Usage

`XmDropSiteEndUpdate()` is used with `XmDropSiteStartUpdate()` and `XmDropSiteUpdate()` to update information about multiple drop sites in the DropSite registry. `XmDropSiteStartUpdate()` starts the update processing, `XmDropSiteUpdate()` is called multiple times to update information about diferent drop sites, and `XmDropSiteEndUpdate()` completes the processing. These routines optimize the updating of drop site information. Calls to `XmDropSiteStartUpdate()` and `XmDropSiteEndUpdate()` can be nested recursively.

## See Also

*XmDropSiteStartUpdate*(1), *XmDropSiteUpdate*(1),
*XmDropSite*(2).

## Name

XmDropSiteQueryStackingOrder – get the stacking order of a drop site.

## Synopsis

```
#include <Xm/DragDrop.h>
Status XmDropSiteQueryStackingOrder (widget, parent_return, child_returns,
        num_child_returns)
    Widget widget;
    Widget *parent_return;
    Widget **child_returns;
    Cardinal *num_child_returns;
```

### Inputs

*widget* Specifies the widget ID associated with a composite drop site.

### Outputs

*parent_return*
: Returns the widget ID of the parent of the specified *widget*.

*child_returns*
: Returns a list of the children of *widget* that are registered as drop sites.

*num_child_returns*
: Returns the number of children in *child_returns*.

### Returns

A non-zero value on success or 0 (zero) on failure.

## Availability

Motif 1.2 and later.

## Description

`XmDropSiteQueryStackingOrder()` retrieves information about the stacking order of drop sites. For the specified *widget*, the routine returns its parent and a list of its children that are registered as drop sites. The children are returned in *child_returns*, which lists the children in the current stacking order, with the lowest child in the stacking order at the beginning of the list and the top child at the end of the list. `XmDropSiteQueryStackingOrder()` allocates storage for the list of returned children. The application is responsible for managing this storage, which can be freed using `XtFree()`. The routine returns a non-zero value on success or 0 (zero) on failure.

## Usage

A drop site for drag and drop operations can be a composite drop site, which means that it has children which are also drop sites. The stacking order of the drop sites controls clipping of drag-under effects during a drag and drop operation. When drop sites overlap, the drag-under effects of the drop sites lower in the stacking order are clipped by the drop sites above them, regardless of whether or not the drop sites are active. Use `XmDropSiteQueryStacking-Order()` to get the current stacking order for a composite drop site. You can use `XmDrop-SiteConfigureStackingOrder()` to modify the stacking order.

Text and TextField widgets are automatically registered as drop sites by the Motif toolkit. In early versions of Motif 1.2, these drop sites do not appear in the list of drop site children returned by `XmDropSiteQueryStackingOrder()`.

## See Also

*XmDropSiteConfigureStackingOrder*(1), *XmDropSiteRegister*(1),
*XmDropSite*(2).

## Name

XmDropSiteRegister – register a drop site.

## Synopsis

```
#include <Xm/DragDrop.h>
void XmDropSiteRegister (widget, arglist, argcount)
    Widget widget;
    ArgList arglist;
    Cardinal argcount;
```

### Inputs

| | |
|---|---|
| *widget* | Specifies the widget ID that is to be associated with the drop site. |
| *arglist* | Specifies the resource name/value pairs used in registering the drop site. |
| *argcount* | Specifies the number of name/value pairs in *arglist*. |

## Availability

Motif 1.2 and later.

## Description

XmDropSiteRegister() registers the specified *widget* as a drop site, which means the widget has a drop site associated with it in the DropSite registry. Drop sites are widget-like, in that they use resources to specify their attributes. The *arglist* and *argcount* parameters work as for any creation routine; any drop site resources that are not set by the arguments are retrieved from the resource database or set to their default values. If the drop site is registered with XmNdropSiteActivity set to XmDROP_SITE_ACTIVE and XmNdropProc set to NULL, the routine generates a warning message.

## Usage

Motif 1.2 supports the drag and drop model of selection actions. In a widget that acts as a drag source, a user can make a selection and then drag the selection, using BTransfer, to other widgets that are registered as drop sites. The DropSite registry stores information about all of the drop sites for a display. Text and TextField widgets are automatically registered as drop sites when they are created. An application can register other widgets as drop sites using XmDropSiteRegister(). Once a widget is registered as a drop site, it can participate in drag and drop operations. A drop site can be removed from the registry using XmDropSiteUnregister(). When a drop site is removed, the widget no longer participates in drag and drop operations.

A drop site for drag and drop operations can be a composite drop site, which means that it has children which are also drop sites. If the drop site being registered is a descendant of a widget that has already been registered as a drop site, the XmNdropSiteType resource of the ancestor must be set to XmDROP_SITE_COMPOSITE. A composite drop site must be registered as a drop site before its descendants are registered. The stacking order of the drop sites controls clipping of drag-under effects during a drag and drop operation. When drop sites overlap, the drag-under effects of the drop sites lower in the stacking order are clipped by the drop sites above them, regardless of whether or not the drop sites are active. When a descendant drop site is registered, it is stacked above all of its sibling drop sites that have already been registered.

## Example

The following routine shows the use of `XmDropSiteRegister()` to register a Label widget as a drop site. When a drop operation occurs in the Label, the `HandleDrop` routine, which is not shown here, handles the drop:

```
/* global variable */
Atom      COMPOUND_TEXT;

void main (argc, argv)
unsigned int argc;
char **argv;
{
   Arg          args[10];
   int          n;
   Widget       top, bb, label;
   XtAppContext app;
   Atom         importList[1];

   XtSetLanguageProc (NULL, (XtLanguageProc)NULL, NULL);

   top = XtAppInitialize (&app, "Drop", NULL, 0, &argc, argv, NULL, NULL, 0);

   n = 0;
   bb = XmCreateBulletinBoard (top, "bb", args, n);
   XtManageChild (bb);

   COMPOUND_TEXT = XmInternAtom (XtDisplay(top), "COMPOUND_TEXT", False);

   n = 0;
   label = XmCreateLabel (bb, "Drop Here", args, n);
   XtManageChild (label);

   /* register the label as a drop site */
   importList[0] = COMPOUND_TEXT;
   n = 0;
   XtSetArg (args[n], XmNimportTargets, importList); n++;
   XtSetArg (args[n], XmNnumImportTargets, 1); n++;
   XtSetArg (args[n], XmNdropSiteOperations, XmDROP_COPY);
   XtSetArg (args[n], XmNdropProc, HandleDrop); n++;
   XmDropSiteRegister (label, args, n);

   XtRealizeWidget (top);
   XtAppMainLoop (app);
}
```

## See Also

*XmDropSiteConfigureStackingOrder*(1), *XmDropSiteEndUpdate*(1), *XmDropSiteQueryStackingOrder*(1), *XmDropSiteRetrieve*(1), *XmDropSiteStartUpdate*(1), *XmDropSiteUpdate*(1), *XmDropSiteUnregister*(1), *XmDisplay*(2), *XmDropSite*(2), *XmScreen*(2).

# XmDropSiteRetrieve

## Name

XmDropSiteRetrieve – get the resource values for a drop site.

## Synopsis

```
#include <Xm/DragDrop.h>
void XmDropSiteRetrieve (widget, arglist, argcount)
    Widget widget;
    ArgList arglist;
    Cardinal argcount;
```

### Inputs

| | |
|---|---|
| *widget* | Specifies the widget ID associated with the drop site. |
| *arglist* | Specifies the resource name/address pairs that contain the resource names and addresses into which the resource values are stored. |
| *argcount* | Specifies the number of name/value pairs in *arglist*. |

## Availability

Motif 1.2 and later.

## Description

`XmDropSiteRetrieve()` gets the specified resources for the drop site associated with the specified *widget*. Drop sites are widget-like, in that they use resources to specify their attributes. The *arglist* and *argcount* parameters work as for `XtGetValues()`.

## Usage

`XmDropSiteRetrieve()` can be used to get the current attributes of a drop site from the DropSite registry. The DropSite registry stores information about all of the drop sites for a display. An initiating client can also use `XmDropSiteRetrieve()` to retrieve information about the current drop site by passing the DragContext for the operation to the routine. The initiator can access all of the drop site resources except `XmNdragProc` and `XmdropProc` using this technique.

## See Also

*XmDropSiteRegister*(1), *XmDropSiteUpdate*(1),
*XmDropSite*(2).

# XmDropSiteStartUpdate

## Name

XmDropSiteStartUpdate – start an update of multiple drop sites.

## Synopsis

```
#include <Xm/DragDrop.h>
void XmDropSiteStartUpdate (widget)
    Widget widget;
```

### Inputs

*widget* Specifies any widget in the hierarchy associated with the drop sites that are to be updated.

## Availability

Motif 1.2 and later.

## Description

`XmDropSiteStartUpdate()` begins an update of multiple drop sites. The *widget* parameter specifies a widget in the widget hierarchy that contains all of the widgets associated with the drop sites being updated. The routine uses *widget* to identify the shell that contains all of the drop sites.

## Usage

`XmDropSiteStartUpdate()` is used with `XmDropSiteUpdate()` and `XmDropSiteEndUpdate()` to update information about multiple drop sites in the DropSite registry. `XmDropSiteStartUpdate()` starts the update processing, `XmDropSiteUpdate()` is called multiple times to update information about diferent drop sites, and `XmDropSiteEndUpdate()` completes the processing. These routines optimize the updating of drop site information. Calls to `XmDropSiteStartUpdate()` and `XmDropSiteEndUpdate()` can be nested recursively.

## See Also

*XmDropSiteEndUpdate*(1), *XmDropSiteUpdate*(1),
*XmDropSite*(2).

# XmDropSiteUnregister



## Name

XmDropSiteUnregister – remove a drop site.

## Synopsis

```
#include <Xm/DragDrop.h>
void XmDropSiteUnregister (widget)
    Widget widget;
```

### Inputs

*widget* Specifies the widget ID associated with the drop site.

## Availability

Motif 1.2 and later.

## Description

`XmDropSiteUnregister()` removes the drop site associated with the specified *widget* from the DropSite registry. After the routine is called, the widget cannot be the receiver in a drag and drop operation. The routine frees all of the information associated with the drop site.

## Usage

Motif 1.2 supports the drag and drop model of selection actions. In a widget that acts as a drag source, a user can make a selection and then drag the selection, using `BTransfer`, to other widgets that are registered as drop sites. Once a widget is registered as a drop site with `XmDropSiteRegister()`, it can participate in drag and drop operations. Text and TextField widgets are automatically registered as drop sites when they are created. `XmDropSiteUnregister()` provides a way to remove a drop site from the registry, so that the widget no longer participates in drag and drop operations.

## See Also

*XmDropSiteRegister*(1),
*XmDropSite*(2).

# XmDropSiteUpdate

## Name

XmDropSiteUpdate – change the resource values for a drop site.

## Synopsis

```
#include <Xm/DragDrop.h>
void XmDropSiteUpdate (widget, arglist, argcount)
    Widget widget;
    ArgList arglist;
    Cardinal argcount;
```

### Inputs

| | |
|---|---|
| *widget* | Specifies the widget ID associated with the drop site. |
| *arglist* | Specifies the resource name/value pairs used in updating the drop site. |
| *argcount* | Specifies the number of name/value pairs in *arglist*. |

## Availability

Motif 1.2 and later.

## Description

`XmDropSiteUpdate()` changes the resources for the drop site associated with the specified *widget*. Drop sites are widget-like, in that they use resources to specify their attributes. The *arglist* and *argcount* parameters work as for `XtSetValues()`.

## Usage

`XmDropSiteUpdate()` can be used by itself to update the attributes of a drop site. The routine can also be used with `XmDropSiteStartUpdate()` and `XmDropSiteEndUpdate()` to update information about multiple drop sites in the DropSite registry. `XmDropSiteStartUpdate()` starts the update processing, `XmDropSiteUpdate()` is called multiple times to update information about diferent drop sites, and `XmDropSiteEndUpdate()` completes the processing. The DropSite registry stores information about all of the drop sites for a display. These routines optimize the updating of drop site information by sending all of the updates at once, rather than processing each one individually.

## See Also

*XmDropSiteEndUpdate*(1), *XmDropSiteRegister*(1), *XmDropSiteStartUpdate*(1),
*XmDropSiteUnregister*(1),
*XmDropSite*(2).

# XmDropTransferAdd

## Name

XmDropTransferAdd – add drop transfer entries to a drop operation.

## Synopsis

```
#include <Xm/DragDrop.h>
void XmDropTransferAdd (drop_transfer, transfers, num_transfers)
    Widget drop_transfer;
    XmDropTransferEntryRec *transfers;
    Cardinal num_transfers;
```

### Inputs

*drop_transfer*
: Specifies the ID of the DropTransfer object to which the entries are being added.

*transfers*
: Specifies the additional drop transfer entries.

*num_transfer*
: Specifies the number of drop transfer entries in *transfers*.

## Availability

Motif 1.2 and later.

## Description

`XmDropTransferAdd()` specifies a list of additional drop transfer entries that are to be processed during a drop operation. The *widget* argument specifies the DropTransfer object associated with the drop operation. *transfers* is an array of `XmDropTransferEntryRec` structures that specifies the targets of the additional drop transfer operations. `XmDropTransferAdd()` can be used to modify the DropTransfer object until the last call to the `XmNtransferProc` is made. After the last call, the result of modifying the DropTransfer object is undefined.

## Usage

The toolkit uses the DropTransfer object to manage the transfer of data from the drag source to the drop site during a drag and drop operation. `XmDropTransferAdd()` provides a way for a drop site to specify additional target formats after a drop operation has started. The routine adds the entries to the `XmNdropTransfers` resource. The attributes of a DropTransfer object can also be manipulated with `XtSetValues()` and `XtGetValues()`.

## Structures

`XmDropTransferEntryRec` is defined as follows:

```
typedef struct {
    XtPointer client_data;  /* data passed to the transfer proc */
    Atom      target;       /* target format of the transfer */
} XmDropTransferEntryRec, *XmDropTransferEntry;
```

## See Also

*XmDropTransferStart*(1),
*XmDragContext*(2), *XmDropTransfer*(2).

# XmDropTransferStart

## Name

XmDropTransferStart – start a drop operation.

## Synopsis

```
#include <Xm/DragDrop.h>
Widget XmDropTransferStart (widget, arglist, argcount)
    Widget widget;
    ArgList arglist;
    Cardinal argcount;
```

### Inputs

| | |
|---|---|
| *widget* | Specifies the ID of the DragContext object associated with the operation. |
| *arglist* | Specifies the resource name/value pairs used in creating the DropTransfer. |
| *argcount* | Specifies the number of name/value pairs in *arglist*. |

### Returns

The ID of the DropTransfer object that is created.

## Availability

Motif 1.2 and later.

## Description

`XmDropTransferStart()` starts a drop operation by creating and returning a DropTransfer object. The DropTransfer stores information that the toolkit needs to process a drop transaction. The DropTransfer is widget-like, in that it uses resources to specify its attributes. The toolkit frees the DropTransfer upon completion of the drag and drop operation.

The *widget* argument to `XmDropTransferStart()` is the DragContext object associated with the drag operation. The *arglist* and *argcount* parameters work as for any creation routine; any DropTransfer resources that are not set by the arguments are retrieved from the resource database or set to their default values.

## Usage

Motif 1.2 supports the drag and drop model of selection actions. In a widget that acts as a drag source, a user can make a selection and then drag the selection, using `BTransfer`, to other widgets that are registered as drop sites. These drop sites can be in the same application or another application. The toolkit uses the DropTransfer object to manage the transfer of data from the drag source to the drop site. `XmDropTransferStart()` is typically called from within the `XmNdropProc` procedure of the drop site.

The attributes of a DropTransfer object can be manipulated with `XtSetValues()` and `XtGetValues()` until the last call to the `XmNtransferProc` procedure is made. You can also use `XmDropTransferAdd()` to add drop transfer entries to be processed. After the last call to `XmNtransferProc`, the result of using the DropTransfer object is undefined. For more information about the DropTransfer object, see the manual page in Section 2, *Motif and Xt Widget Classes*.

## Example

The following routine shows the use of `XmDropTransferStart()` in the `HandleDrop` routine, which is the `XmNdropProc` procedure for a Label widget that is being used as a drop site:

```
/* global variable */
Atom     COMPOUND_TEXT;

static void HandleDrop(widget, client_data, call_data)
Widget          widget;
XtPointer       client_data;
XtPointer       call_data;
{
   XmDropProcCallback       DropData;
   XmDropTransferEntryRec   transferEntries[1];
   XmDropTransferEntry      transferList;
   Arg                      args[10];
   int                      n;

   DropData = (XmDropProcCallback) call_data;

   n = 0;

   if ((DropData->dropAction != XmDROP) ||
       (DropData->operation != XmDROP_COPY)) {
     XtSetArg (args[n], XmNtransferStatus, XmTRANSFER_FAILURE); n++;
   }
   else {
     transferEntries[0].target = COMPOUND_TEXT;
     transferEntries[0].client_data = (XtPointer) widget;
     transferList = transferEntries;
     XtSetArg (args[n], XmNdropTransfers, transferEntries); n++;
     XtSetArg (args[n], XmNnumDropTransfers, XtNumber (transferEntries)); n++;
     XtSetArg (args[n], XmNtransferProc, TransferProc); n++;
   }

   XmDropTransferStart (DropData->dragContext, args, n);
}
```

## See Also

*XmDropTransferAdd*(1),
*XmDragContext*(2), *XmDropTransfer*(2).

# XmFileSelectionBoxGetChild



## Name

XmFileSelectionBoxGetChild – get the specified child of a FileSelectionBox widget.

## Synopsis

```
#include <Xm/FileSB.h>
Widget XmFileSelectionBoxGetChild (widget, child)
    Widget widget;
    unsigned char child;
```

### Inputs

*widget* Specifies the FileSelectionBox widget.

*child* Specifies the child of the FileSelectionBox widget. Pass one of the values from the list below.

### Returns

The widget ID of the specified child of the FileSelectionBox.

## Description

XmFileSelectionBoxGetChild() returns the widget ID of the specified *child* of the FileSelectionBox widget.

## Usage

XmDIALOG_APPLY_BUTTON, XmDIALOG_CANCEL_BUTTON, XmDIALOG_HELP_-BUTTON, and XmDIALOG_OK_BUTTON specify the action buttons in the widget. Xm-DIALOG_DEFAULT_BUTTON specifies the current default button. XmDIALOG_DIR_LIST and XmDIALOG_DIR_LIST_LABEL specify the directory list and its label, while Xm-DIALOG_LIST and XmDIALOG_LIST_LABEL specify the file list and its label. Xm-DIALOG_FILTER_LABEL and XmDIALOG_FILTER_TEXT specify the filter text entry area and its label, while XmDIALOG_TEXT and XmDIALOG_SELECTION_LABEL specify the file text entry area and its label. XmDIALOG_SEPARATOR specifies the separator and Xm-DIALOG_WORK_AREA specifies any work area child that has been added to the FileSelection-Box. For more information on the different children of the FileSelectionBox, see the manual page in Section 2, *Motif and Xt Widget Classes*.

## Structures

The possible values for *child* are:

XmDIALOG_APPLY_BUTTON
XmDIALOG_CANCEL_BUTTON
XmDIALOG_DEFAULT_BUTTON
XmDIALOG_DIR_LIST
XmDIALOG_DIR_LIST_LABEL
XmDIALOG_FILTER_LABEL
XmDIALOG_FILTER_TEXT
XmDIALOG_HELP_BUTTON
XmDIALOG_LIST
XmDIALOG_LIST_LABEL
XmDIALOG_OK_BUTTON
XmDIALOG_SELECTION_LABEL
XmDIALOG_SEPARATOR
XmDIALOG_TEXT
XmDIALOG_WORK_AREA

## See Also

*XmFileSelectionBox*(2).

# XmFileSelectionDoSearch

## Name

XmFileSelectionDoSearch – start a directory search.

## Synopsis

```
#include <Xm/FileSB.h>
void XmFileSelectionDoSearch (widget, dirmask)
    Widget widget;
    XmString dirmask;
```

### Inputs

*widget* Specifies the FileSelectionBox widget.

*dirmask* Specifies the directory mask that is used in the directory search.

## Description

`XmFileSelectionDoSearch()` starts a directory and file search for the specified FileSelectionBox *widget*. *dirmask* is a text pattern that can include wildcard characters. `XmFileSelectionDoSearch()` updates the lists of directories and files that are displayed by the FileSelectionBox. If *dirmask* is non-`NULL`, the routine restricts the search to directories that match the *dirmask*.

## Usage

`XmFileSelectionBoxDoSearch()` allows you to force a FileSelectionBox to reinitialize itself, which is useful if you want to set the directory mask directly.

## See Also

*XmFileSelectionBox*(2).

# XmFontListAdd

## Name

XmFontListAdd – create a new font list.

## Synopsis

```
XmFontList XmFontListAdd (oldlist, font, charset)
    XmFontList oldlist;
    XFontStruct *font;
    XmStringCharSet charset;
```

### Inputs

| | |
|---|---|
| *oldlist* | Specifies the font list to which *font* is added. |
| *font* | Specifies the font structure. |
| *charset* | Specifies a tag that identifies the character set for the font. |

### Returns

The new font list, *oldlist* if *font* or *charset* is NULL, or NULL if *oldlist* is NULL.

## Availability

In Motif 1.2, `XmFontListAdd()` is obsolete. It has been superceded by `XmFontListAppendEntry()`.

## Description

`XmFontListAdd()` makes a new font list by adding the font structure specified by *font* to the old font list. The routine returns the new font list and deallocates *oldlist*. *charset* specifies the character set that is associated with the font. It can be `XmSTRING_DEFAULT_CHARSET`, which takes the character set from the current language environment, but this value may be removed from future versions of Motif.

`XmFontListAdd()` searches the font list cache for a font list that matches the new font list. If the routine finds a matching font list, it returns that font list and increments its reference count. Otherwise, the routine allocates space for the new font list and caches it. In either case, the application is responsible for managing the memory associated with the font list. When the application is done using the font list, it should be freed using `XmFontListFree()`.

## Usage

A font list contains entries that describe the fonts that are in use. In Motif 1.1, each entry associates a font and a character set. In Motif 1.2, each entry consists of a font or a font set and an associated tag. `XmFontListAdd()` is retained for compatibility with Motif 1.1 and should not be used in newer applications.

## See Also

*XmFontListAppendEntry*(1), *XmFontListFree*(1).

# XmFontListAppendEntry



## Name

XmFontListAppendEntry – append a font entry to a font list.

## Synopsis

```
XmFontList XmFontListAppendEntry (oldlist, entry)
    XmFontList oldlist;
    XmFontListEntry entry;
```

### Inputs

| | |
|---|---|
| *oldlist* | Specifies the font list to which *entry* is appended. |
| *entry* | Specifies the font list entry. |

### Returns

The new font list or `oldlist` if *entry* is NULL.

## Availability

Motif 1.2 and later.

## Description

`XmFontListAppendEntry()` makes a new font list by appending the specified *entry* to the old font list. If *oldlist* is NULL, the routine creates a new font list that contains the single *entry*. `XmFontListAppendEntry()` returns the new font list and deallocates *oldlist*. The application is responsible for freeing the font list entry using `XmFontListEntryFree()`.

As of Motif 1.2.1, there is a bug in `XmFontListEntryFree()` that causes it to free the font or font set, rather than the font list entry. As a workaround, you can use `XtFree()` to free the font list entry.

`XmFontListAppendEntry()` searches the font list cache for a font list that matches the new font list. If the routine finds a matching font list, it returns that font list and increments its reference count. Otherwise, the routine allocates space for the new font list and caches it. In either case, the application is responsible for managing the memory associated with the font list. When the application is done using the font list, it should be freed using `XmFontListFree()`.

## Usage

In Motif 1.2, a font list contains font list entries, where each entry consists of a font or font set and an associated tag. Before a font list entry can be added to a font list, it has to be created with `XmFontListEntryCreate()` or `XmFontListEntryLoad()`.

## Example

The following code fragment shows how you can use `XmFontListAppendEntry()` to create a font list:

```
    Widget              toplevel;
    XmFontListEntry     entry1, entry2, entry3;
    XmFontList          fontlist;

    entry1 = XmFontListEntryLoad(XtDisplay(toplevel),
        "-*-courier-*-r-*--12-*", XmFONT_IS_FONT, "tag1");
    entry2 = XmFontListEntryLoad(XtDisplay(toplevel),
        "-*-courier-bold-o-*--14-*", XmFONT_IS_FONT, "tag2");
    entry3 = XmFontListEntryLoad(XtDisplay(toplevel),
        "-*-courier-medium-r-*--18-*", XmFONT_IS_FONT, "tag3");
    fontlist = XmFontListAppendEntry(NULL, entry1);
    fontlist = XmFontListAppendEntry(fontlist, entry2);
    fontlist = XmFontListAppendEntry(fontlist, entry3);
#ifdef BUG_FIXED
    XmFontListEntryFree(entry1);
    XmFontListEntryFree(entry2);
    XmFontListEntryFree(entry3);
#else
    XtFree(entry1);
    XtFree(entry2);
    XtFree(entry3);
#endif
    .
    .
    .
    XtVaCreateManagedWidget("widget_name", xmLabelWidgetClass, toplevel,
        XmNfontList,        fontlist,
        NULL);

    XmFontListFree(fontlist);
    .
    .
    .
```

## See Also

*XmFontListEntryCreate*(1), *XmFontListEntryFree*(1), *XmFontListEntryLoad*(1), *XmFontListFree*(1), *XmFontListRemoveEntry*(1).

Motif Functions and Macros

# XmFontListCopy

## Name

XmFontListCopy – copy a font list.

## Synopsis

```
XmFontList XmFontListCopy (fontlist)
    XmFontList fontlist;
```

### Inputs

*fontlist*    Specifies the font list to be copied.

### Returns

The new font list or NULL if *fontlist* is NULL.

## Description

XmFontListCopy() makes and returns a copy of *fontlist*. The routine searches the font list cache for the font list, returns the font list, and increments its reference count. The application is responsible for managing the memory associated with the font list. When the application is done using the font list, it should be freed using XmFontListFree().

## Usage

A font list contains entries that describe the fonts that are in use. In Motif 1.1, each entry associates a font and a character set. In Motif 1.2, each entry consists of a font or a font set and an associated tag. XmFontListCopy() makes a correct copy of the font list regardless of the type of entries in the list.

When a font list is assigned to a widget, the widget makes a copy of the font list, so it is safe to free the font list. When you retrieve a font list from a widget using XtGetValues(), you should not alter the font list directly. If you need to make changes to the font list, use XmFontListCopy() to make a copy of the font list and then change the copy.

## See Also

*XmFontListFree*(1).

# XmFontListCreate

## Name

XmFontListCreate – create a font list.

## Synopsis

```
XmFontList XmFontListCreate (font, charset)
    XFontStruct *font;
    XmStringCharSet charset;
```

### Inputs

*font* Specifies the font structure.

*charset* Specifies a tag that identifies the character set for the font.

### Returns

The new font list or NULL if *font* or *charset* is NULL.

## Availability

In Motif 1.2, `XmFontListCreate()` is obsolete. It has been superceded by `XmFontListAppendEntry()`.

## Description

`XmFontListCreate()` creates a new font list that contains a single entry with the specified *font* and *charset*. *charset* specifies the character set that is associated with the font. It can be XmSTRING_DEFAULT_CHARSET, which takes the character set from the current language environment, but this value may be removed from future versions of Motif.

`XmFontListCreate()` searches the font list cache for a font list that matches the new font list. If the routine finds a matching font list, it returns that font list and increments its reference count. Otherwise, the routine allocates space for the new font list and caches it. In either case, the application is responsible for managing the memory associated with the font list. When the application is done using the font list, it should be freed using `XmFontListFree()`.

## Usage

A font list contains entries that describe the fonts that are in use. In Motif 1.1, each entry associates a font and a character set. In Motif 1.2, each entry consists of a font or a font set and an associated tag. `XmFontListCreate()` is retained for compatibility with Motif 1.1 and should not be used in newer applications.

## See Also

*XmFontListAppendEntry*(1).

# XmFontListEntryCreate

## Name

XmFontListEntryCreate – create a font list entry.

## Synopsis

```
XmFontListEntry XmFontListEntryCreate (tag, type, font)
     char *tag
     XmFontType type;
     XtPointer font;
```

### Inputs

| | |
|---|---|
| *tag* | Specifies the tag for the font list entry. |
| *type* | Specifies the type of the *font* argument. Pass either XmFONT_IS_FONT or XmFONT_IS_FONTSET. |
| *font* | Specifies the font or font set. |

### Returns

A font list entry.

## Availability

Motif 1.2 and later.

## Description

XmFontListEntryCreate() makes a font list entry that contains the specified *font*, which is identified by *tag*. *type* indicates whether *font* specifies an XFontSet or a pointer to an XFontStruct. *tag* is a NULL-terminated string that identifies the font list entry. It can have the value XmFONTLIST_DEFAULT_TAG, which identifies the default font list entry in a font list.

XmFontListEntryCreate() allocates space for the new font list entry. The application is responsible for managing the memory associated with the font list entry. When the application is done using the font list entry, it should be freed using XmFontListEntryFree().

As of Motif 1.2.1, there is a bug in XmFontListEntryFree() that causes it to free the font or font set, rather than the font list entry. As a workaround, you can use XtFree() to free the font list entry.

## Usage

In Motif 1.2, a font list contains font list entries, where each entry consists of a font or font set and an associated tag. XmFontListEntryCreate() creates a font list entry using an XFontStruct returned by XLoadQueryFont() or an XFontSet returned by XCreateFontSet(). The routine does not copy the font structure, so the XFontStruct or XFontSet must not be freed until all references to it have been freed. The font list entry can be added to a font list using XmFontListAppendEntry().

## Example

The following code fragment shows how to create font list entries using `XmFontList-EntryCreate()`:

```
    Widget              toplevel;
    XFontStruct         *font1, *font2;  /* Previously loaded fonts */
    XFontSet            fontset3;        /* Previously created font sets */
    XmFontListEntry     entry1, entry2, entry3;
    XmFontList          fontlist;

    entry1 = XmFontListEntryCreate("tag1", XmFONT_IS_FONT, font1);
    entry2 = XmFontListEntryCreate("tag2", XmFONT_IS_FONT, font2);
    entry3 = XmFontListEntryCreate("tag3", XmFONT_IS_FONTSET, fontset3);
    fontlist = XmFontListAppendEntry(NULL, entry1);
    fontlist = XmFontListAppendEntry(fontlist, entry2);
    fontlist = XmFontListAppendEntry(fontlist, entry3);
#ifdef BUG_FIXED
    XmFontListEntryFree(entry1);
    XmFontListEntryFree(entry2);
    XmFontListEntryFree(entry3);
#else
    XtFree(entry1);
    XtFree(entry2);
    XtFree(entry3);
#endif
    .
    .
    .
    XtVaCreateManagedWidget("widget_name", xmLabelWidgetClass, toplevel,
        XmNfontList,        fontlist,
        NULL);

    XmFontListFree(fontlist);
    .
    .
    .
```

## See Also

*XmFontListAppendEntry*(1), *XmFontListEntryFree*(1), *XmFontListEntryGetFont*(1), *XmFontListEntryGetTag*(1), *XmFontListEntryLoad*(1), *XmFontListRemoveEntry*(1).

# XmFontListEntryFree



## Name

XmFontListEntryFree – free the memory used by a font list entry.

## Synopsis

```
void XmFontListEntryFree (entry)
    XmFontListEntry *entry;
```

### Inputs

*entry* Specifies the font list entry that is to be freed.

## Availability

Motif 1.2 and later.

## Description

`XmFontListEntryFree()` deallocates storage used by the specified font list *entry*. The routine does not free the `XFontSet` or `XFontStruct` data structure associated with the font list entry.

## Usage

In Motif 1.2, a font list contains font list entries, where each entry consists of a font or font set and an associated tag. A font list entry can be created using `XmFontListEntryCreate()` or `XmFontListEntryLoad()` and then appended to a font list with `XmFontList-AppendEntry()`. Once the entry has been appended to the necessary font lists, it should be freed using `XmFontListEntryFree()`.

As of Motif 1.2.1, there is a bug in `XmFontListEntryFree()` that causes it to free the font or font set, rather than the font list entry. As a workaround, you can use `XtFree()` to free the font list entry.

## Example

The following code fragment shows the use of `XmFontListEntryFree()`:

```
    Widget              toplevel;
    XmFontListEntry     entry1, entry2, entry3;
    XmFontList          fontlist;

    entry1 = XmFontListEntryLoad(XtDisplay(toplevel),
        "-*-courier-*-r-*--12-*", XmFONT_IS_FONT, "tag1");
    entry2 = XmFontListEntryLoad(XtDisplay(toplevel),
        "-*-courier-bold-o-*--14-*", XmFONT_IS_FONT, "tag2");
    entry3 = XmFontListEntryLoad(XtDisplay(toplevel),
        "-*-courier-medium-r-*--18-*", XmFONT_IS_FONT, "tag3");
    fontlist = XmFontListAppendEntry(NULL, entry1);
    fontlist = XmFontListAppendEntry(fontlist, entry2);
    fontlist = XmFontListAppendEntry(fontlist, entry3);
#ifdef BUG_FIXED
    XmFontListEntryFree(entry1);
```

```
        XmFontListEntryFree(entry2);
        XmFontListEntryFree(entry3);
    #else
        XtFree(entry1);
        XtFree(entry2);
        XtFree(entry3);
    #endif
        .
        .
        .
        XtVaCreateManagedWidget("widget_name", xmLabelWidgetClass, toplevel,
            XmNfontList,        fontlist,
            NULL);

        XmFontListFree(fontlist);
        .
        .
        .
```

## See Also

*XmFontListAppendEntry*(1), *XmFontListEntryCreate*(1), *XmFontListEntryLoad*(1), *XmFontListNextEntry*(1), *XmFontListRemoveEntry*(1).

Motif Functions and Macros

# XmFontListEntryGetFont



## Name

XmFontListEntryGetFont – get the font information from a font list entry.

## Synopsis

```
XtPointer XmFontListEntryGetFont (entry, type_return)
    XmFontListEntry entry;
    XmFontType *type_return;
```

### Inputs

| | |
|---|---|
| *entry* | Specifies the font list entry. |

### Outputs

| | |
|---|---|
| *type_return* | Returns the type of the font information that is returned. Valid types are `XmFONT_IS_FONT` or `XmFONT_IS_FONTSET`. |

### Returns

An `XFontSet` or a pointer to an `XFontStruct`.

## Availability

Motif 1.2 and later.

## Description

`XmFontListEntryGetFont()` retrieves the font information for the specified font list *entry*. When the font list entry contains a font, *type_return* is `XmFONT_IS_FONT` and the routine returns a pointer to an `XFontStruct`. When the font list entry contains a font set, *type_return* is `XmFONT_IS_FONTSET` and the routne returns the `XFontSet`. The `XFontSet` or `XFontStruct` that is returned is not a copy of the data structure, so it must not be freed by an application.

## Usage

The `XmFontList` and `XmFontListEntry` types are opaque, so if an application needs to perform any processing on a font list, it has to use special functions to cycle through the font list entries and retrieve information about them. These routines use a `XmFontContext` to maintain an arbitrary position in a font list. `XmFontListEntryGetFont()` can be used to get the font structure for a font list entry once it has been retrieved from the font list using `XmFontListNextEntry()`.

## See Also

*XmFontListEntryCreate*(1), *XmFontListEntryGetTag*(1), *XmFontListEntryLoad*(1), *XmFontListNextEntry*(1).

# XmFontListEntryGetTag

## Name

XmFontListEntryGetTag – get the tag of a font list entry.

## Synopsis

```
char* XmFontListEntryGetTag (entry)
    XmFontListEntry entry;
```

### Inputs

*entry* Specifies the font list entry.

### Returns

The tag for the font list entry.

## Availability

Motif 1.2 and later.

## Description

`XmFontListEntryGetTag()` retrieves the tag of the specified font list *entry*. The routine allocates storage for the tag string; the application is responsible for freeing the memory using `XtFree()`.

## Usage

The `XmFontList` and `XmFontListEntry` types are opaque, so if an application needs to perform any processing on a font list, it has to use special functions to cycle through the font list entries and retrieve information about them. These routines use a `XmFontContext` to maintain an arbitrary position in a font list. `XmFontListEntryGetTag()` can be used to get the tag of a font list entry once it has been retrieved from the font list using `XmFontListNextEntry()`.

## See Also

*XmFontListEntryCreate*(1), *XmFontListEntryGetFont*(1), *XmFontListEntryLoad*(1), *XmFontListNextEntry*(1).

# XmFontListEntryLoad

## Name

XmFontListEntryLoad – load a font or create a font set and then create a font list entry.

## Synopsis

```
XmFontListEntry XmFontListEntryLoad (display, font_name, type, tag)
    Display *display;
    char *font_name;
    XmFontType type;
    char *tag;
```

### Inputs

| | |
|---|---|
| *display* | Specifies a connection to an X server; returned from `XOpenDisplay()` or `XtDisplay()`. |
| *font_name* | Specifies an X Logical Font Description (XLFD) string. |
| *type* | Specifies the type of *font_name*. Pass either `XmFONT_IS_FONT` or `XmFONT_IS_FONTSET`. |
| *tag* | Specifies the tag for the font list entry. |

### Returns

A font list entry or `NULL` if the font cannot be found or the font set cannot be created.

## Availability

Motif 1.2 and later.

## Description

`XmFontListEntryLoad()` either loads a font or creates a font set depending on the value of *type* and then creates a font list entry that contains the font data and the specified *tag*. *font_name* is an XLFD string which is parsed as either a font name or a base font name list. *tag* is a `NULL`-terminated string that identifies the font list entry. It can have the value `XmFONTLIST_DEFAULT_TAG`, which identifies the default font list entry in a font list.

If *type* is set to `XmFONT_IS_FONT`, the routine uses the `XtCvtStringToFontStruct()` converter to load the font struct specified by *font_name*. If the value of *type* is `XmFONT_IS_FONTSET`, `XmFontListEntryLoad` uses the `XtCvtStringToFontSet` converter to create a font set in the current locale.

`XmFontListEntryLoad()` allocates space for the new font list entry. The application is responsible for managing the memory associated with the font list entry. When the application is done using the font list entry, it should be freed using `XmFontListEntryFree()`.

As of Motif 1.2.1, there is a bug in `XmFontListEntryFree()` that causes it to free the font or font set, rather than the font list entry. As a workaround, you can use `XtFree()` to free the font list entry.

## Usage

In Motif 1.2, a font list contains font list entries, where each entry consists of a font or font set and an associated tag. `XmFontListEntryLoad()` sets up the font data and creates a font list entry. The font list entry can be added to a font list using `XmFontListAppendEntry()`.

## Example

The following code fragment shows how to create font list entries using `XmFontListEntryLoad()`:

```
    Widget              toplevel;
    XmFontListEntry     entry1, entry2, entry3;
    XmFontList          fontlist;

    entry1 = XmFontListEntryLoad(XtDisplay(toplevel),
        "-*-courier-*-r-*--12-*", XmFONT_IS_FONT, "tag1");
    entry2 = XmFontListEntryLoad(XtDisplay(toplevel),
        "-*-courier-bold-o-*--14-*", XmFONT_IS_FONT, "tag2");
    entry3 = XmFontListEntryLoad(XtDisplay(toplevel),
        "-*-courier-medium-r-*--18-*", XmFONT_IS_FONT, "tag3");
    fontlist = XmFontListAppendEntry(NULL, entry1);
    fontlist = XmFontListAppendEntry(fontlist, entry2);
    fontlist = XmFontListAppendEntry(fontlist, entry3);
#ifdef BUG_FIXED
    XmFontListEntryFree(entry1);
    XmFontListEntryFree(entry2);
    XmFontListEntryFree(entry3);
#else
    XtFree(entry1);
    XtFree(entry2);
    XtFree(entry3);
#endif
    .
    .
    .
    XtVaCreateManagedWidget("widget_name", xmLabelWidgetClass, toplevel,
        XmNfontList,        fontlist,
        NULL);

    XmFontListFree(fontlist);
    .
    .
    .
```

## See Also

*XmFontListAppendEntry*(1), *XmFontListEntryCreate*(1), *XmFontListEntryFree*(1), *XmFontListEntryGetFont*(1), *XmFontListEntryGetTag*(1), *XmFontListRemoveEntry*(1).

# XmFontListFree



## Name

XmFontListFree – free the memory used by a font list.

## Synopsis

```
void XmFontListFree (fontlist)
    XmFontList fontlist;
```

### Inputs

*fontlist*    Specifies the font list that is to be freed.

## Description

`XmFontListFree()` deallocates storage used by the specified *fontlist*. The routine does not free the `XFontSet` or `XFontStruct` data structures associated with the font list.

## Usage

A font list contains entries that describe the fonts that are in use. In Motif 1.1, each entry associates a font and a character set. In Motif 1.2, each entry consists of a font or a font set and an associated tag. `XmFontListFree()` frees the storage used by the font list but does not free the associated font data structures.

It is important to call `XmFontListFree()` rather than `XtFree()` because Motif caches font lists. A call to `XmFontListFree()` decrements the reference count for the font list; the font list is not actually freed until the reference count reaches 0 (zero).

## Example

The following code fragment shows the use of `XmFontListFree()`:

```
    Widget              toplevel;
    XmFontListEntry     entry1, entry2, entry3;
    XmFontList          fontlist;

    entry1 = XmFontListEntryLoad(XtDisplay(toplevel),
        "-*-courier-*-r-*--12-*", XmFONT_IS_FONT, "tag1");
    entry2 = XmFontListEntryLoad(XtDisplay(toplevel),
        "-*-courier-bold-o-*--14-*", XmFONT_IS_FONT, "tag2");
    entry3 = XmFontListEntryLoad(XtDisplay(toplevel),
        "-*-courier-medium-r-*--18-*", XmFONT_IS_FONT, "tag3");
    fontlist = XmFontListAppendEntry(NULL, entry1);
    fontlist = XmFontListAppendEntry(fontlist, entry2);
    fontlist = XmFontListAppendEntry(fontlist, entry3);
#ifdef BUG_FIXED
    XmFontListEntryFree(entry1);
    XmFontListEntryFree(entry2);
    XmFontListEntryFree(entry3);
#else
    XtFree(entry1);
    XtFree(entry2);
    XtFree(entry3);
```

```
#endif
    .
    .
    .
    XtVaCreateManagedWidget("widget_name", xmLabelWidgetClass, toplevel,
        XmNfontList,        fontlist,
        NULL);

    XmFontListFree(fontlist);
    .
    .
    .
```

## See Also

*XmFontListAppendEntry*(1), *XmFontListCopy*(1), *XmFontListRemoveEntry*(1).

# XmFontListFreeFontContext



## Name

XmFontListFreeFontContext – free a font context.

## Synopsis

```
void XmFontListFreeFontContext (context)
    XmFontContext context;
```

### Inputs

*context* Specifies the font list context that is to be freed.

## Description

`XmFontListFreeFontContext()` deallocates storage used by the specified font list *context*.

## Usage

The `XmFontList` type is opaque, so if an application needs to perform any processing on a font list, it has to use special functions to cycle through the font list. These routines use a `XmFontContext` to maintain an arbitrary position in a font list. `XmFontListFreeFontContext()` is the last of the three font context routines that an application should call when processing a font list, as it frees the font context data structure. An application begins by calling `XmFontListInitFontContext()` to create a font context and then makes repeated calls to `XmFontListNextEntry()` or `XmFontListGetNextFont()` to cycle through the font list.

## See Also

*XmFontListGetNextFont*(1), *XmFontListInitFontContext*(1), *XmFontListNextEntry*(1).

# XmFontListGetNextFont

## Name

XmFontListGetNextFont – retrieve information about the next font list element.

## Synopsis

```
Boolean XmFontListGetNextFont (context, charset, font)
     XmFontContext context;
     XmStringCharSet *charset;
     XFontStruct **font;
```

### Inputs

*context* Specifies the font context for the font list.

### Outputs

*charset* Returns the tag that identifies the character set for the font.

*font* Returns the font structure for the current font list element.

### Returns

`True` if the values being returned are valid or `False` otherwise.

## Availability

In Motif 1.2, `XmFontListGetNextFont()` is obsolete. It has been superceded by `XmFontListNextEntry()`.

## Description

`XmFontListGetNextFont()` returns the character set and font for the next element of the font list. *context* is the font context created by `XmFontListInitFontContext()`. The first call to `XmFontListGetNextFont()` returns the first font list element. Repeated calls to `XmFontListGetNextFont()` using the same context access successive font list elements. The routine returns `False` when it has reached the end of the font list.

## Usage

A font list contains entries that describe the fonts that are in use. In Motif 1.1, each entry associates a font and a character set. In Motif 1.2, each entry consists of a font or a font set and an associated tag. `XmFontListGetNextFont()` is retained for compatibility with Motif 1.1 and should not be used in newer applications. If the routine is called with a font context that contains a font set, it returns the first font of the font set.

The `XmFontList` type is opaque, so if an application needs to perform any processing on a font list, it has to use special functions to cycle through the font list. These routines use a `XmFontContext` to maintain an arbitrary position in a font list. `XmFontListGetNextFont()` cycles through the fonts in a font list. `XmFontListInitFontContext()` is called first to create the font context. When an application is done processing the font list, it should call `XmFontListFreeFontContext()` with the same *context* to free the allocated data.

## See Also

*XmFontListFreeFontContext*(1), *XmFontListInitFontContext*(1), *XmFontListNextEntry*(1).

# XmFontListInitFontContext

## Name

XmFontListInitFontContext – create a font context.

## Synopsis

```
Boolean XmFontListInitFontContext (context, fontlist)
     XmFontContext *context;
     XmFontList fontlist;
```

### Inputs

*fontlist* Specifies the font list.

### Outputs

*context* Returns the allocated font context structure.

### Returns

`True` if the font context is allocated or `False` otherwise.

## Description

`XmFontListInitFontContext()` creates a font context for the specified *fontlist*. This font *context* allows an application to access the information that is stored in the font list. `XmFontListInitFontContext()` allocates space for the font context. The application is responsible for managing the memory associated with the font context. When the application is done using the font context, it should be freed using `XmFontListFreeFontContext()`.

## Usage

The `XmFontList` type is opaque, so if an application needs to perform any processing on a font list, it has to use special functions to cycle through the font list. These routines use a `XmFontContext` to maintain an arbitrary position in a font list. `XmFontListInitFontContext()` is the first of the three font context routines that an application should call when processing a font list, as it creates the font context data structure. The *context* is passed to `XmFontListNextEntry()` or `XmFontListGetNextFont()` to cycle through the font list. When an application is done processing the font list, it should call `XmFontListFreeFontContext()` with the same *context* to free the allocated data.

## See Also

*XmFontListFreeFontContext*(1), *XmFontListGetNextFont*(1), *XmFontListInitFontContext*(1), *XmFontListNextEntry*(1).

Motif Functions and Macros

# XmFontListNextEntry



## Name

XmFontListNextEntry – retrieve the next font list entry in a font list.

## Synopsis

```
XmFontListEntry XmFontListNextEntry (context)
    XmFontContext context;
```

### Inputs

*context* Specifies the font context for the font list.

### Returns

A font list entry or NULL if the context refers to an invalid entry or if it is at the end of the font list.

## Availability

Motif 1.2 and later.

## Description

XmFontListNextEntry() returns the next font list entry in a font list. *context* is the font context created by XmFontListInitFontContext(). The first call to XmFontListNextEntry() returns the first entry in the font list. Repeated calls to XmFontListNextEntry() using the same context access successive font list entries. The routine returns NULL when it has reached the end of the font list.

## Usage

The XmFontList and XmFontListEntry types are opaque, so if an application needs to perform any processing on a font list, it has to use special functions to cycle through the font list entries and retrieve information about them. These routines use a XmFontContext to maintain an arbitrary position in a font list. XmFontListInitFontContext() is called first to create the font context. XmFontListNextEntry() cycles through the font entries in a font list. XmFontListEntryGetFont() and XmFontListEntryGetTag() access the information in a font list entry. When an application is done processing the font list, it should call XmFontListFreeFontContext() with the same *context* to free the allocated data.

## See Also

*XmFontListEntryFree*(1), *XmFontListEntryGetFont*(1), *XmFontListEntryGetTag*(1), *XmFontListFreeFontContext*(1), *XmFontListInitFontContext*(1).

# XmFontListRemoveEntry

## Name

XmFontListRemoveEntry – remove a font list entry from a font list.

## Synopsis

```
XmFontList XmFontListRemoveEntry (oldlist, entry)
    XmFontList oldlist;
    XmFontListEntry entry;
```

### Inputs

| | |
|---|---|
| *oldlist* | Specifies the font list from which *entry* is removed. |
| *entry* | Specifies the font list entry. |

### Returns

The new font list, *oldlist* if *entry* is NULL or no entries are removed, or NULL if *oldlist* is NULL.

## Availability

Motif 1.2 and later.

## Description

`XmFontListRemoveEntry()` makes a new font list by removing any entries in *oldlist* that match the specified *entry*. The routine returns the new font list and deallocates *oldlist*. `XmFontListRemoveEntry()` does not deallocate the font list entry, so the application should free the storage using `XmFontListEntryFree()`.

As of Motif 1.2.1, there is a bug in `XmFontListEntryFree()` that causes it to free the font or font set, rather than the font list entry. As a workaround, you can use `XtFree()` to free the font list entry.

`XmFontListRemoveEntry()` searches the font list cache for a font list that matches the new font list. If the routine finds a matching font list, it returns that font list and increments its reference count. Otherwise, the routine allocates space for the new font list and caches it. In either case, the application is responsible for managing the memory associated with the font list. When the application is done using the font list, it should be freed using `XmFontList-Free()`.

## Usage

In Motif 1.2, a font list contains font list entries, where each entry consists of a font or font set and an associated tag. An application can use `XmFontListRemoveEntry()` to remove a font list entry from a font list. If an application needs to process the font list to determine which entries to remove, it can use `XmFontListInitFontContext()` and `XmFont-ListNextEntry()` to cycle through the entries in the font list.

## See Also

*XmFontListAppendEntry*(1), *XmFontListEntryCreate*(1), *XmFontListEntryFree*(1), *XmFontListEntryLoad*(1), *XmFontListFree*(1).

# XmGetAtomName

## Name

XmGetAtomName – get the string representation of an atom.

## Synopsis

```
#include <Xm/AtomMgr.h>
String XmGetAtomName (display, atom)
    Display *display;
    Atom atom;
```

### Inputs

| | |
|---|---|
| *display* | Specifies a connection to an X server; returned from `XOpenDisplay()` or `XtDisplay()`. |
| *atom* | Specifies the atom for the property name to be returned. |

### Returns

The string that represents *atom*.

## Description

`XmGetAtomName()` returns the string that is used to represent a given *atom*. This routine works like Xlib's `XGetAtomName()` routine, but the Motif routine provides the added feature of client-side caching. `XmGetAtomName()` allocates space for the returned string; the application is responsible for freeing this storage using `XtFree()` when the atom is no longer needed.

## Usage

An atom is a number that identifies a property. Properties also have string names. `XmGetAtomName()` returns the string name specified in the original call to `XmInternAtom()` or `XInternAtom()`, or for predefined atoms, a string version of the symbolic constant without the `XA_` attached.

## See Also

*XmInternAtom*(1).

# XmGetColorCalculation



## Name

XmGetColorCalculation – get the procedure that calculates default colors.

## Synopsis

```
XmColorProc XmGetColorCalculation ()
```

### Returns

The procedure that calculates default colors.

## Description

`XmGetColorCalculation()` returns the procedure that calculates the default foreground, top and bottom shadow, and select colors. The procedure calculates these colors based on the background color that is passed to the procedure.

## Usage

Motif widgets rely on the use of shadowed borders to create their three-dimensional appearance. The top and bottom shadow colors are lighter and darker shades of the background color; these colors are reversed to make a component appear raised out of the screen or recessed into the screen. The select color is a slightly darker shade of the background color that indicates that a component is selected. The foreground color is either black or white, depending on which color provides the most contrast with the background color. `XmGetColorCalculation()` returns the procedure that calculates these colors. Use `XmSetColorCalculation()` to change the calculation procedure.

## Procedures

The `XmColorProc` has the following syntax:

```
typedef void (*XmColorProc) (XColor, XColor, XColor, XColor, XColor)
    XColor *bg_color;   /* specifies the background color */
    XColor *fg_color;   /* returns the foreground color */
    XColor *sel_color;  /* returns the select color */
    XColor *ts_color;   /* returns the top shadow color */
    XColor *bs_color;   /* returns the bottom shadow color */
```

An `XmColorProc` takes five arguments. The first argument, *`bg_color`*, is a pointer to an `XColor` structure that specifies the background color. The `red`, `green`, `blue`, and `pixel` fields in the structure contain valid values. The rest of the arguments are pointers to `XColor` structures for the colors that are to be calculated. The procedure fills in the `red`, `green`, and `blue` fields in these structures.

## See Also

*XmChangeColor*(1), *XmGetColors*(1), *XmSetColorCalculation*(1).

## Name

XmGetColors – get the foreground, select, and shadow colors.

## Synopsis

```
void XmGetColors (screen, colormap, background, foreground, top_shadow,
        bottom_shadow, select)
    Screen *screen;
    Colormap colormap;
    Pixel background;
    Pixel *foreground;
    Pixel *top_shadow;
    Pixel *bottom_shadow;
    Pixel *select;
```

### Inputs

*screen* Specifies the screen for which the colors are to be allocated.

*colormap* Specifies the colormap from which the colors are to be allocated.

*background* Specifies the background color.

### Outputs

*foreground* Returns the foreground color.

*top_shadow* Returns the top shadow color.

*bottom_shadow*
Returns the bottom shadow color.

*select* Returns the select color.

## Description

XmGetColors() returns appropriate pixel values for the foreground, selection, and shadow colors based on the specified *screen*, *colormap*, and *background* color. If *foreground*, *top_shadow*, *bottom_shadow*, or *select* is specified as NULL, the routine does not return a pixel value for that argument. XmGetColors() uses the default color calculation procedure unless a customized color calculation procedure has been set with XmSetColorCalculation().

## Usage

XmGetColors() calculates the new colors based on a background color, but it does not set the colors for any widgets. To calculate and set the new colors for a widget in Motif 1.2, call XmChangeColor(). Alternatively, you can set the XmNforeground, XmNtopShadowColor, XmNbottomShadowColor, XmNselectColor resources for the widget with XtSetValues().

## See Also

*XmChangeColor*(1), *XmGetColorCalculation*(1), *XmSetColorCalculation*(1).

# XmGetDestination



## Name

XmGetDestination – get the current destination widget.

## Synopsis

```
Widget XmGetDestination (display)
    Display *display;
```

### Inputs

*display* Specifies a connection to an X server; returned from `XOpenDisplay()` or `XtDisplay()`.

### Returns

The widget ID of the current destination widget or `NULL` if there is no current destination widget.

## Description

`XmGetDestination()` returns the widget ID of the current destination widget for the specified *display*. The destination widget is usually the widget most recently changed by a select, edit, insert, or paste operation. `XmGetDestination()` identifies the widget that serves as the destination for quick paste operations and some clipboard routines. This routine returns `NULL` if there is no current destination, which occurs when no edit operations have been performed on a widget.

## Usage

`XmGetDestination()` provides a way for an application to retrieve the widget that would be acted on by various selection operations, so that the application can do any necessary processing before the operation occurs.

## See Also

*XmGetFocusWidget*(1), *XmGetTabGroup*(1).

# XmGetDragContext

## Name

XmGetDragContext – get information about a drag and drop operation.

## Synopsis

```
#include <Xm/DragDrop.h>
Widget XmGetDragContext (widget, timestamp)
    Widget widget;
    Time timestamp;
```

### Inputs

*widget* Specifies a widget on the display where the drag and drop operation is taking place.

*timestamp* Specifies a timestamp that identifies a DragContext.

### Returns

The ID of the DragContext object or NULL if no active DragContext is found.

## Availability

Motif 1.2 and later.

## Description

XmGetDragContext() retrieves the DragContext object associated with the display of the specified *widget* that is active at the specified *timestamp*. When more that one drag operation has been started on a disply, a timestamp can uniquely identify the active DragContext. If the specified *timestamp* corresponds to a timestamp processed between the beginning and end of a single drag and drop operation, XmGetDragContext() returns the DragContext associated with the operation. If there is no active DragContext for the *timestamp*, the routine returns NULL.

## Usage

Motif 1.2 supports the drag and drop model of selection actions. Every drag and drop operation has a DragContext object associated with it that stores information about the drag operation. Both the initiating and the receiving clients use information in the DragContext to process the drag transaction. The DragContext object is widget-like, in that it uses resources to specify its attributes. These resources can be checked using XtGetValues() and modified using XtSetValues().

XmGetDragContext() provides a way for an application to retrieve a DragContext object. The application can then use XtGetValues() and XtSetValues() to manipulate the DragContext.

## See Also

*XmDragCancel*(1), *XmDragStart*(1),
*XmDragContext*(2).

# XmGetFocusWidget

## Name

XmGetFocusWidget – get the widget that has the keyboard focus.

## Synopsis

```
Widget XmGetFocusWidget (widget)
    Widget widget;
```

### Inputs

*widget* Specifies the widget whose hierarchy is to be traversed.

### Returns

The widget ID of the widget with the keyboard focus or `NULL` if no widget has the focus.

## Availability

Motif 1.2 and later.

## Description

`XmGetFocusWidget()` returns the widget ID of the widget that has keyboard focus in the widget hierarchy that contains the specified *widget*. The routine searches the widget hierarchy that contains the specified *widget* up to the nearest shell ancestor. `XmGetFocusWidget()` returns the widget in the hierarchy that currently has the focus, or the widget that last had the focus when the user navigated to another hierarchy. If no widget in the hierarchy has the focus, the routine returns `NULL`.

## Usage

`XmGetFocusWidget()` provides a means of determining the widget that currently has the keyboard focus, which can be useful if you are trying to control keyboard navigation in an application.

## See Also

*XmGetTabGroup*(1), *XmGetVisibility*(1), *XmIsTraversable*(1), *XmProcessTraversal*(1).

## Name

XmGetMenuCursor – get the current menu cursor.

## Synopsis

```
Cursor XmGetMenuCursor (display)
    Display *display;
```

### Inputs

*display* Specifies a connection to an X server; returned from `XOpenDisplay()` or `XtDisplay()`.

### Returns

The cursor ID for the current menu cursor or `None` if no cursor has been defined.

## Availability

In Motif 1.2, `XmGetMenuCursor()` is obsolete. It has been superceded by getting the Screen resource `XmNmenuCursor`.

## Description

`XmGetMenuCursor()` returns the cursor ID of the menu cursor currently in use by the application on the specified *display*. The routine returns the cursor for the default screen of the display. If the cursor is not yet defined because the application called the routine before any menus were created, then `XmGetMenuCursor()` returns the value `None`.

## Usage

The menu cursor is the pointer shape that is used whenever a menu is posted. This cursor can be different from the normal pointer shape. In Motif 1.2, the new Screen object has a resource, `XmNmenuCursor`, that specifies the menu cursor. `XmGetMenuCursor()` is retained for compatibility with Motif 1.1 and should not be used in newer applications.

## See Also

*XmSetMenuCursor*(1),
*XmScreen*(2).

# XmGetPixmap

## Name

XmGetPixmap – create and return a pixmap.

## Synopsis

```
Pixmap XmGetPixmap (screen, image_name, foreground, background)
    Screen *screen;
    char *image_name;
    Pixel foreground;
    Pixel background;
```

### Inputs

*screen* Specifies the screen on which the pixmap is to be drawn.

*image_name* Specifies the string name of the image used to make the pixmap.

*foreground* Specifies the foreground color that is combined with the image when it is a bitmap.

*background* Specifies the background color that is combined with the image when it is a bitmap.

### Returns

A pixmap on success or XmUNSPECIFIED_PIXMAP when the specified *image_name* cannot be found.

## Description

XmGetPixmap() generates a pixmap, stores it in the pixmap cache, and returns its resource ID. Before the routine actually creates the pixmap, it checks the pixmap cache for a pixmap that matches the specified *image_name*, *screen*, *foreground*, and *background*. If a match is found, the reference count for the pixmap is incremented and the resource ID for the pixmap is returned. If no pixmap is found, XmGetPixmap() checks the image cache for a image that matches the specified *image_name*. If a matching image is found, it is used to create the pixmap that is returned.

When no matches are found, XmGetPixmap() begins a search for an X10 or X11 bitmap file, using *image_name* as the filename. If a file is found, its contents are read, converted into an image, and cached in the image cache. Then, the image is used to generate a pixmap that is subsequently cached and returned. The depth of the pixmap is the default depth of the screen. If *image_name* specifies a bitmap, the *foreground* and *background* colors are combined with the image. If no file is found, the routine returns XmUNSPECIFIED_PIXMAP.

## Usage

When *image_name* starts with a slash (/), it specifies a full pathname and XmGet-Pixmap() opens the specified file. Otherwise, *image_name* specifies a filename which causes XmGetPixmap() to look for the file using a search path. The XMLANGPATH environment variable specifies the search path for X bitmap files. This search path can contain the substitution character %B, where *image_name* is substituted for %B. The search path can also use the substitution characters accepted by `XtResolvePathname()`, where %T is mapped to `bitmaps` and %S is mapped to `NULL`.

If XMLANGPATH is not set, `XmGetPixmap()` uses a default search path. If the XAPPLRESDIR environment variable is set, the routine searches the following paths:

*%B*
$XAPPLRESDIR/*%L/bitmaps/%N/%B*
$XAPPLRESDIR/*%l/bitmaps/%N/%B*
$XAPPLRESDIR/*bitmaps/%N/%B*
$XAPPLRESDIR/*%L/bitmaps/%B*
$XAPPLRESDIR/*%l/bitmaps/%B*
$XAPPLRESDIR/*bitmaps/%B*
$HOME/*bitmaps/%B*
$HOME/*%B*
*/usr/lib/X11/%L/bitmaps/%N/%B*
*/usr/lib/X11/%l/bitmaps/%N/%B*
*/usr/lib/X11/bitmaps/%N/%B*
*/usr/lib/X11/%L/bitmaps/%B*
*/usr/lib/X11/%l/bitmaps/%B*
*/usr/lib/X11/bitmaps/%B*
*/usr/include/X11/bitmaps/%B*

If XAPPLRESDIR is not set, `XmGetPixmap()` searches the same paths, except that XAPPLRESDIR is replaced by HOME. These search paths are vendor-dependent and a vendor may use different directories for */usr/lib/X11* and */usr/include/X11*. In the search paths, the image name is substituted for %B, the class name of the application is substituted for %N, the language string of the display is substituted for %L, and the language component of the language string is substituted for %l.

## See Also

*XmDestroyPixmap*(1), *XmGetPixmapByDepth*(1), *XmInstallImage*(1), *XmUninstallImage*(1).

# XmGetPixmapByDepth

## Name

XmGetPixmapByDepth – create and return a pixmap of the specified depth.

## Synopsis

```
Pixmap XmGetPixmapByDepth (screen, image_name, foreground, background,
        depth)
    Screen *screen;
    char *image_name;
    Pixel foreground;
    Pixel background;
    int depth;
```

### Inputs

| | |
|---|---|
| *screen* | Specifies the screen on which the pixmap is to be drawn. |
| *image_name* | Specifies the string name of the image used to make the pixmap. |
| *foreground* | Specifies the foreground color that is combined with the image when it is a bitmap. |
| *background* | Specifies the background color that is combined with the image when it is a bitmap. |
| *depth* | Specifies the depth of the pixmap. |

### Returns

A pixmap on success or XmUNSPECIFIED_PIXMAP when the specified *image_name* cannot be found.

## Availability

Motif 1.2 and later.

## Description

XmGetPixmapByDepth() generates a pixmap, stores it in the pixmap cache, and returns its resource ID. Before the routine actually creates the pixmap, it checks the pixmap cache for a pixmap that matches the specified *image_name*, *screen*, *foreground*, *background*, and *depth*. If a match is found, the reference count for the pixmap is incremented and the resource ID for the pixmap is returned. If no pixmap is found, XmGetPixmapByDepth() checks the image cache for a image that matches the specified *image_name*. If a matching image is found, it is used to create the pixmap that is returned.

When no matches are found, XmGetPixmapByDepth() begins a search for an X10 or X11 bitmap file, using *image_name* as the filename. If a file is found, its contents are read, converted into an image, and cached in the image cache. Then, the image is used to generate a pixmap that is subsequently cached and returned. The depth of the pixmap is the specified *depth*. If *image_name* specifies a bitmap, the *foreground* and *background* colors are combined with the image. If no file is found, the routine returns XmUNSPECIFIED_PIXMAP.

## Usage

`XmGetPixmapByDepth()` works just like `XmGetPixmap()` except that the depth of the pixmap can be specified. With `XmGetPixmap()`, the depth of the returned pixmap is the default depth of the screen. See `XmGetPixmap()` for an explanation of the search path that is used to find the image.

## See Also

*XmDestroyPixmap*(1), *XmGetPixmap*(1), *XmInstallImage*(1), *XmUninstallImage*(1).

# XmGetPostedFromWidget



## Name

XmGetPostedFromWidget – get the widget that posted a menu.

## Synopsis

```
#include <Xm/RowColumn.h>
Widget XmGetPostedFromWidget (menu)
    Widget menu;
```

### Inputs

*menu* Specifies the menu widget.

### Returns

The widget ID of the widget that posted the menu.

## Description

`XmGetPostedFromWidget()` returns the widget from which the specified *menu* is posted. The value that is returned depends on the type of menu that is specified. For a PopupMenu, the routine returns the widget from which *menu* is popped up. For a PulldownMenu, the routine returns the RowColumn widget from which *menu* is pulled down. For cascading submenus, the returned widget is the original RowColumn widget at the top of the menu system. For tear-off menus in Motif 1.2, `XmGetPostedFromWidget()` returns the widget from which the menu is torn off.

## Usage

If an application uses the same menu in different contexts, it can use `XmGetPostedFromWidget()` in an activate callback to determine the context in which the menu callback should be interpreted.

## See Also

*XmRowColumn*(2), *XmPopupMenu*(2), *XmPulldownMenu*(2).

# XmGetSecondaryResourceData

## Name

XmGetSecondaryResourceData – retrieve secondary widget resource data.

## Synopsis

```
Cardinal XmGetSecondaryResourceData (widget_class, secondary_data_return)
     WidgetClass widget_class;
     XmSecondaryResourceData **secondary_data_return;
```

### Inputs

*widget_class*

Specifies the widget class.

### Outputs

*secondary_data_return*

Returns an array of `XmSecondaryResourceData` pointers.

### Returns

The number of secondary resource data structures associated with the widget class.

## Availability

Motif 1.2 and later.

## Description

`XmGetSecondaryResourceData()` provides access to the secondary widget resource data associated with a widget class. Some Motif widget classes have resources that are not accessible with the functions `XtGetResourceList()` and `XtGetConstraint-ResourceList()`. If the specified *widget_class* has secondary resources, `XmGet-SecondaryResourceData` provides descriptions of the resources in one or more data structures and returns the number such structures. If the *widget_class* does not have secondary resources, the routine returns 0 (zero) and the value of *secondary_data_return* is undefined.

If the *widget_class* has secondary resources, `XmGetSecondaryResourceData` allocates an array of pointers to the corresponding data structures. The application is responsible for freeing the allocated memory using `XtFree()`. The resource list in each structure (the value of the `resources` field), the structures, and the array of pointers to the structures all need to be freed.

## Usage

`XmGetSecondaryResources()` only returns the secondary resources for a widget class if the class has been initialized. You can initialize a widget class by creating an instance of the class or any of its subclass. VendorShell and Text are two Motif widget classes that have secondary resources. The two fields in the `XmSecondaryResourceData` structure that are of interest to an application are `resources` and `num_resources`. These fields contain a list of the secondary resources and the number of such resources.

Most applications do not need to query a widget class for the resources it supports. `XmGetSecondaryResourceData()` is intended to support interface builders and applications like *editres* that allow a user to view the available resources and set them interactively. Use `XtGetResourceList()` and `XtGetConstraintResourceList()` to get the regular and constraint resources for a widget class.

## Example

The following code fragment shows the use of `XmGetSecondaryResourceData()` to print the names of the secondary resources of the VendorShell widget:

```
XmSecondaryResourceData *res;
Cardinal num_res, i, j;

if (num_res = XmGetSecondaryResourceData (vendorShellWidgetClass, &res )) {
    for (i = 0; i < num_res; i++) {
        for (j = 0; j < res[i]->num_resources; j++) {
            printf("%s\n", res[i]->resources[j].resource_name);
        }
        XtFree((char*) res[i]->resources);
        XtFree((char*) res[i]);
    }
    XtFree((char*) res);
}
```

## Structures

The `XmSecondaryResourceData` structure is defined as follows:

```
typedef struct {
    XmResourceBaseProcbase_proc;
    XtPointer       client_data;
    String          name;
    String          res_class;
    XtResourceList  resources;
    Cardinal        num_resources;
} XmSecondaryResourceDataRec, *XmSecondaryResourceData;
```

## See Also

*VendorShell*(2), *XmText*(2).

# XmGetTabGroup

## Name

XmGetTabGroup – get the tab group for a widget.

## Synopsis

```
Widget XmGetTabGroup (widget)
    Widget widget;
```

### Inputs

*widget* Specifies the widget whose tab group is to be returned.

### Returns

The widget ID of the tab group of *widget*.

## Availability

Motif 1.2 and later.

## Description

`XmGetTabGroup()` returns the widget ID of the widget that is the tab group for the specified *widget*. If *widget* is a tab group or a shell, the routine returns *widget*. If *widget* is not a tab group and no ancestor up to the nearest shell ancestor is a tab group, the routine returns the nearest shell ancestor. Otherwise, `XmGetTabGroup()` returns the nearest ancestor of *widget* that is a tab group.

## Usage

`XmGetTabGroup()` provides a way to find out the tab group for a particular widget in an application. A tab group is a group of widgets that can be traversed using the keyboard rather than the mouse. Users move from widget to widget within a single tab group by pressing the arrow keys. Users move between different tab groups by pressing the Tab or Shift-Tab keys. If the *tab_group* widget is a manager, its children are all members of the tab group (unless they are made into separate tab groups). If the widget is a primitive, it is its own tab group. Certain widgets must not be included with other widgets within a tab group. For example, each List, Scrollbar, OptionMenu, or multi-line Text widget must be placed in a tab group by itself, since these widgets define special behavior for the arrow or Tab keys, which prevents the use of these keys for widget traversal.

## See Also

*XmGetFocusWidget*(1), *XmGetVisibility*(1), *XmIsTraversable*(1), *XmProcessTraversal*(1), *XmManager*(2), *XmPrimitive*(2).

# XmGetTearOffControl



## Name

XmGetTearOffControl – get the tear-off control for a menu.

## Synopsis

```
#include <Xm/RowColumn.h>
Widget XmGetTearOffControl (menu)
    Widget menu;
```

### Inputs

*menu* Specifies the RowColumn widget whose tear-off control is to be returned.

### Returns

The widget ID of the tear-off control or NULL if no tear-off control exists.

## Availability

Motif 1.2 and later.

## Description

XmGetTearOffControl() retrieves the widget ID of the widget that is the tear-off control for the specified *menu*. When the XmNtearOffModel resource of a RowColumn widget is set to XmTEAR_OFF_ENABLED for a PulldownMenu or a PopupMenu, the RowColumn creates a tear-off button for the menu. The tear-off button, which contains a dashed line by default, is the first element in the menu. When the button is activated, the menu is torn off. If the specified *menu* does not have a tear-off control, XmGetTearOffControl() returns NULL.

## Usage

In Motif 1.2, a RowColumn that is configured as a PopupMenu or a PulldownMenu supports tear-off menus. When a menu is torn off, it remains on the screen after a selection is made so that additional selections can be made. The tear-off control is a button that has a Separator-like appearance. Once you retrieve the widget ID of the tear-off control, you can set resources to specify its appearance. You can specify values for the following resources: XmNbackground, XmNbackgroundPixmap, XmNbottomShadowColor, XmNforeground, XmNheight, XmNmargin, XmNseparatorType, XmNshadowThickness, and XmNtopShadowColor. You can also set these resources in a resource file by using the name of the control, which is TearOffControl.

## See Also

*XmRepTypeInstallTearOffModelConverter*(1),
*XmPopupMenu*(2), *XmPulldownMenu*(2), *XmRowColumn*(2), *XmSeparator*(2).

# XmGetVisibility

## Name

XmGetVisibility – determine whether or not a widget is visible.

## Synopsis

```
XmVisibility XmGetVisibility (widget)
    Widget widget;
```

### Inputs

*widget* Specifies the widget whose visibility state is to be returned.

### Returns

XmVISIBILITY_UNOBSCURED if *widget* is completely visible, XmVISIBILITY_-PARTIALLY_OBSCURED if *widget* is partially visible, or XmVISIBILITY_FULLY_-OBSCURED if *widget* is not visible.

## Availability

Motif 1.2 and later.

## Description

XmGetVisibility() determines whether or not the specified *widget* is visible. The routine returns XmVISIBILITY_UNOBSCURED if the entire rectangular area of the widget is visible. It returns XmVISIBILITY_PARTIALLY_OBSCURED if a part of the rectangular area of the widget is obscured by its ancestors. XmGetVisibility() returns XmVISIBILITY_FULLY_OBSCURED if the widget is completely obscured by its ancestors or if it is not visible for some other reason, such as if it is unmapped or unrealized.

## Usage

XmGetVisibility() provides a way for an application to find out the visibility state of a particular widget. This information can be used to help determine whether or not a widget is eligible to receive the keyboard focus. In order for a widget to receive the keyboard focus, it and all of its ancestors must not be in the process of being destroyed and they must be sensitive to input. The widget and its ancestors must also have their XmNtraversalOn resources set to True. If the widget is viewable, which means that it and its ancestors are managed, mapped, and realized and some part of the widget is visible, then the widget is eligible to receive the keyboard focus. A fully-obscured widget is not eligible to receive the focus unless part of it is within the work area of a ScrolledWindow with an XmNscrollingPolicy of XmAUTOMATIC that has an XmNtraverseObscuredCallback.

## Structures

XmVisibility is defined as follows:

```
typedef enum {
    XmVISIBILITY_UNOBSCURED,
    XmVISIBILITY_PARTIALLY_OBSCURED,
    XmVISIBILITY_FULLY_OBSCURED
} XmVisibility;
```

## See Also

*XmGetFocusWidget*(1), *XmGetTabGroup*(1), *XmIsTraversable*(1), *XmProcessTraversal*(1), *XmManager*(2), *XmScrolledWindow*(2).

# XmGetXmDisplay

## Name

XmGetXmDisplay – get the Display object for a display.

## Synopsis

```
Widget XmGetXmDisplay (display)
    Display *display;
```

### Inputs

*display* Specifies a connection to an X server; returned from `XOpenDisplay()` or `XtDisplay()`.

### Returns

The Display object for the display.

## Availability

Motif 1.2 and later.

## Description

`XmGetXmDisplay()` retrieves the Display object for the specified *display*.

## Usage

In Motif 1.2, the Display object stores display-specific information for use by the toolkit. An application has a Display object for each display it accesses. When an application creates its first shell on a display, typically by calling `XtAppInitialize()` or `XtAppCreateShell()`, a Display object is created automatically. There is no way to create a Display independently. Use `XmGetXmDisplay()` to get the ID of the Display object, so that you can use `XtGetValues()` and `XtSetValues()` to access and modify Display resources.

## See Also

*XmDisplay*(2), *XmScreen*(2).

# XmGetXmScreen

## Name

XmGetXmScreen – get the Screen object for a screen.

## Synopsis

```
Widget XmGetXmScreen (screen)
    Screen *screen;
```

### Inputs

*screen* Specifies a screen on a display; returned by `XtScreen()`.

### Returns

The Screen object for the screen.

## Availability

Motif 1.2 and later.

## Description

`XmGetXmScreen()` retrieves the Screen object for the specified *screen*.

## Usage

In Motif 1.2, the Screen object stores screen-specific information for use by the toolkit. An application has a Screen object for each screen that it accesses. When an application creates its first shell on a screen, typically by calling `XtAppInitialize()` or `XtAppCreateShell()`, a Screen object is created automatically. There is no way to create a Screen independently. Use `XmGetXmScreen()` to get the ID of the Screen object, so that you can use `XtGetValues()` and `XtSetValues()` to access and modify Screen resources.

## See Also

*XmDisplay*(2), *XmScreen*(2).

# XmInstallImage

## Name

XmInstallImage – install an image in the image cache.

## Synopsis

```
Boolean XmInstallImage (image, image_name)
    XImage *image;
    char *image_name;
```

### Inputs

| | |
|---|---|
| *image* | Specifies the image to be installed. |
| *image_name* | Specifies the string name of the image. |

### Returns

`True` on success or `False` if *image* or *image_name* is NULL or *image_name* duplicates an image name already in the cache.

## Description

`XmInstallImage()` installs the specified *image* in the image cache. The image can later be used to create a pixmap. When the routine installs the image, it does not make a copy of the image, so an application should not destroy the image until it has been uninstalled. The routine also expands the resource converter that handles images so that *image_name* can be used in a resource file. In order to allow references from a resource file, `XmInstallImage()` must be called to install an image before any widgets that use the image are created.

## Usage

An application can use `XmInstallImage()` to install and cache images, so that the images can be shared throughout the application. Once an image is installed, it can be used to create a pixmap with `XmGetPixmap()`. The toolkit provides eight pre-installed images that can be referenced in a resource file or used to create a pixmap:

| Image Name | Image Description |
|---|---|
| `background` | Solid background tile |
| `25_foreground` | A 25% foreground, 75% background tile |
| `50_foreground` | A 50% foreground, 50% background tile |
| `75_foreground` | A 75% foreground, 25% background tile |
| `horizontal` | Horizontal lines tile |
| `vertical` | Vertical lines tile |
| `slant_right` | Right slanting lines tile |
| `slant_left` | Left slanting lines tile |

## Example

You might use the following code to define and install an image:

```
#define bitmap_width 16
#define bitmap_height 16
static char bitmap_bits[ ] = {
    0xFF, 0x00, 0xFF, 0x00, 0xFF, 0x00, 0xFF, 0x00,
    0xFF, 0x00, 0xFF, 0x00, 0xFF, 0x00, 0xFF, 0x00,
    0x00, 0xFF, 0x00, 0xFF, 0x00, 0xFF, 0x00, 0xFF,
    0x00, 0xFF, 0x00, 0xFF, 0x00, 0xFF, 0x00, 0xFF
};

static XImage ximage = {
    ximage.width = bitmap_width;
    ximage.height = bitmap_height;
    ximage.data = bitmap_bits;
    ximage.xoffset = 0;
    ximage.format = XYBitmap;
    ximage.byte_order = MSBFirst;
    ximage.bitmap_pad = 8;
    ximage.bitmap_bit_order = LSBFirst;
    ximage.bitmap_unit = 8;
    ximage.depth = 1;
    ximage.bytes_per_line = 2;
    ximage.obdata = NULL;
};
    .
    .
    .
XmInstallImage(&ximage, "image_name");
    .
    .
    .
```

## See Also

*XmDestroyPixmap*(1), *XmGetPixmap*(1), *XmUninstallImage*(1).

# XmInternAtom

## Name

XmInternAtom – return an atom for a given property name string.

## Synopsis

```
#include <Xm/AtomMgr.h>
Atom XmInternAtom (display, name, only_if_exists)
    Display *display;
    String name;
    Boolean only_if_exists;
```

### Inputs

*display* Specifies a connection to an X server; returned from XOpenDisplay() or XtDisplay().

*name* Specifies the string name of the property for which you want the atom.

*only_if_exists*
Specifies a Boolean value that indicates whether or not the atom is created if it does not exist.

### Returns

An atom on success or None.

## Description

XmInternAtom() returns the atom that corresponds to the given property *name*. This routine works like Xlib's XInternAtom() routine, but the Motif routine provides the added feature of client-side caching. If no atom exists with the specified *name* and *only_if_exists* is True, XmInternAtom() does not create a new atom; it simply returns None. If *only_if_exists* is False, the routine creates the atom and returns it.

## Usage

An atom is a number that identifies a property. Properties also have string names. XmInternAtom() returns the atom associated with a property if it exists, or it may create the atom if it does not exist. The atom remains defined even after the client that defined it has exited. An atom does not become undefined until the last connection to the X server closes. Predefined atoms are defined in *<X11/Xatom.h>* and begin with the prefix XA_. Predefined atoms do not need to be interned with XmInternAtom().

## See Also

*XmGetAtomName*(1).

# XmIsMotifWMRunning



## Name

XmIsMotifWMRunning – check whether the Motif Window Manager (*mwm*) is running.

## Synopsis

```
Boolean XmIsMotifWMRunning (shell)
    Widget shell;
```

### Inputs

*shell*  Specifies the shell widget whose screen is queried.

### Returns

`True` if *mwm* is running or `False` otherwise.

## Description

`XmIsMotifWMRunning()` checks for the presence of the `_MOTIF_WM_INFO` property on the root window of the screen of the specified *shell* to determine whether the Motif Window Manager (*mwm*) is running on the screen.

## Usage

*mwm* defines additional types of communication between itself and client programs. This communication is optional, so an application should not depend on the communication or the presence of *mwm* for any functionality. `XmIsMotifWMRunning()` allows an application to check if *mwm* is running and act accordingly.

## See Also

*mwm*(4).

# XmIs*Object*

## Name

XmIs*Object* – determine whether a widget is a subclass of a class.

## Synopsis

```
Boolean XmIsGadget (widget)
Boolean XmIsManager (widget)
Boolean XmIsPrimitive (widget)

#include <Xm/ArrowB.h>
Boolean XmIsArrowButton (widget)

#include <Xm/ArrowBG.h>
Boolean XmIsArrowButtonGadget (widget)

#include <Xm/BulletinB.h>
Boolean XmIsBulletinBoard (widget)

#include <Xm/CascadeB.h>
Boolean XmIsCascadeButton (widget)

#include <Xm/CascadeBG.h>
Boolean XmIsCascadeButtonGadget (widget)

#include <Xm/Command.h>
Boolean XmIsCommand (widget)

#include <Xm/DialogS.h>
Boolean XmIsDialogShell (widget)

#include <Xm/Display.h>
Boolean XmIsDisplay (widget)

#include <Xm/DragC.h>
Boolean XmIsDragContext (widget)

#include <Xm/DragIcon.h>
Boolean XmIsDragIconObjectClass (widget)

#include <Xm/DrawingA.h>
Boolean XmIsDrawingArea (widget)

#include <Xm/DrawnB.h>
Boolean XmIsDrawnButton (widget)

#include <Xm/DropSMgr.h>
Boolean XmIsDropSiteManager (widget)
```

```
#include <Xm/DropTrans.h>
Boolean XmIsDropTransfer (widget)

#include <Xm/FileSB.h>
Boolean XmIsFileSelectionBox (widget)

#include <Xm/Form.h>
Boolean XmIsForm (widget)

#include <Xm/Frame.h>
Boolean XmIsFrame (widget)

#include <Xm/Label.h>
Boolean XmIsLabel (widget)

#include <Xm/LabelG.h>
Boolean XmIsLabelGadget (widget)

#include <Xm/List.h>
Boolean XmIsList (widget)

#include <Xm/MainW.h>
Boolean XmIsMainWindow (widget)

#include <Xm/MenuShell.h>
Boolean XmIsMenuShell (widget)

#include <Xm/MessageB.h>
Boolean XmIsMessageBox (widget)

#include <Xm/PanedW.h>
Boolean XmIsPanedWindow (widget)

#include <Xm/PushB.h>
Boolean XmIsPushButton (widget)

#include <Xm/PushBG.h>
Boolean XmIsPushButtonGadget (widget)

#include <Xm/RowColumn.h>
Boolean XmIsRowColumn (widget)

#include <Xm/Scale.h>
Boolean XmIsScale (widget)

#include <Xm/Screen.h>
Boolean XmIsScreen (widget)
```

```
#include <Xm/ScrollBar.h>
Boolean XmIsScrollBar (widget)

#include <Xm/ScrolledW.h>
Boolean XmIsScrolledWindow (widget)

#include <Xm/SelectioB.h>
Boolean XmIsSelectionBox (widget)

#include <Xm/Separator.h>
Boolean XmIsSeparator (widget)

#include <Xm/SeparatoG.h>
Boolean XmIsSeparatorGadget (widget)

#include <Xm/Text.h>
Boolean XmIsText (widget)

#include <Xm/TextF.h>
Boolean XmIsTextField (widget)

#include <Xm/ToggleB.h>
Boolean XmIsToggleButton (widget)

#include <Xm/ToggleBG.h>
Boolean XmIsToggleButtonGadget (widget)

#include <Xm/VendorS.h>
Boolean XmIsVendorShell (widget)

    Widget widget;
```



### Inputs

*widget* Specifies the widget ID of the widget whose class is to be checked.

### Returns

`True` if *widget* is of the specified class or `False` otherwise.

## Availability

`XmIsDisplay()`, `XmIsDragContext()`, `XmIsDragIconObjectClass()`, `XmIs-DropSiteManager()`, `XmIsDropTransfer()`, and `XmIsScreen()` are only available in Motif 1.2 and later.

## Description

The `XmIs*()` routines are macros that check the class of the specified *widget*. The macros returns `True` if *widget* is of the specified class or a subclass of the specified class. Otherwise, the macros return `False`.

## Usage

An application can use the `XmIs*()` macros to check the class of a particular widget. All of the macros use `XtIsSubclass()` to determine the class of the widget.

## See Also

*XmCreateObject*(1),
*VendorShell*(2), *XmArrowButton*(2), *XmArrowButtonGadget*(2), *XmBulletinBoard*(2), *XmCascadeButton*(2), *XmCascadeButtonGadget*(2), *XmCommand*(2), *XmDialogShell*(2), *XmDisplay*(2), *XmDragContext*(2), *XmDragIcon*(2), *XmDrawingArea*(2), *XmDrawnButton*(2), *XmDropSite*(2), *XmDropTransfer*(2), *XmFileSelectionBox*(2), *XmForm*(2), *XmFrame*(2), *XmGadget*(2), *XmLabel*(2), *XmLabelGadget*(2), *XmList*(2), *XmMainWindow*(2), *XmManager*(2), *XmMenuShell*(2), *XmMessageBox*(2), *XmPanedWindow*(2), *XmPrimitive*(2), *XmPushButton*(2), *XmPushButtonGadget*(2), *XmRowColumn*(2), *XmScale*(2), *XmScreen*(2), *XmScrollBar*(2), *XmScrolledWindow*(2), *XmSelectionBox*(2), *XmSeparator*(2), *XmSeparatorGadget*(2), *XmText*(2), *XmTextField*(2), *XmToggleButton*(2), *XmToggleButtonGadget*(2).

## Name

XmIsTraversable – determine whether or not a widget can receive the keyboard focus.

## Synopsis

```
Boolean XmIsTraversable (widget)
    Widget widget;
```

### Inputs

*widget* Specifies the widget whose traversibility state is to be returned.

### Returns

`True` if *widget* is eligible to receive the keyboard focus or `False` otherwise.

## Availability

Motif 1.2 and later.

## Description

`XmIsTraversable()` determines whether or not the specified *widget* can receive the keyboard focus. The routine returns `True` if the widget is eligible to receive the keyboard focus; otherwise it returns `False`.

## Usage

In order for a widget to receive the keyboard focus, it and all of its ancestors must not be in the process of being destroyed and they must be sensitive to input. The widget and its ancestors must also have their `XmNtraversalOn` resources set to `True`. If the widget is viewable, which means that it and its ancestors are managed, mapped, and realized and some part of the widget is visible, then the widget is eligible to receive the keyboard focus. A fully-obscured widget is not eligible to receive the focus unless part of it is within the work area of a ScrolledWindow with an `XmNscrollingPolicy` of `XmAUTOMATIC` that has an `XmNtraverseObscuredCallback`.

Primitive widgets and gadgets can receive the keyboard focus, while most manager widgets cannot, even if they have traversable children. However, some managers may be eligible to receive the keyboard focus under certain conditions. For example, a DrawingArea can receive the keyboard focus if it meets the conditions above and it does not have any children with the `XmNtraversalOn` resource set to `True`.

## See Also

*XmGetFocusWidget*(1), *XmGetTabGroup*(1), *XmGetVisibility*(1), *XmProcessTraversal*(1), *XmManager*(2), *XmScrolledWindow*(2).

# XmListAddItem

## Name

XmListAddItem, XmListAddItems – add an item/items to a list.

## Synopsis

```
#include <Xm/List.h>
void XmListAddItem (widget, item, position)
    Widget widget;
    XmString item;
    int position;

void XmListAddItems (widget, items, item_count, position)
    Widget widget;
    XmString *items;
    int item_count;
    int position;
```

### Inputs

| | |
|---|---|
| *widget* | Specifies the List widget. |
| *item* | Specifies the item that is to be added. |
| *items* | Specifies a list of items that are to be added. |
| *item_count* | Specifies the number of items to be added. |
| *position* | Specifies the position at which to add the new item(s). |

## Description

XmListAddItem() inserts the specified *item* into the list, while XmListAddItems() inserts the specified list of *items*. If *item_count* is smaller than the number of *items*, only the first *item_count* items of the array are added. The *position* argument specifies the location of the new item(s) in the list. A *position* value of 1 indicates the first item, a *position* value of 2 indicates the second item, and so on. A value of 0 (zero) specifies the last item in the list. An inserted item appears selected if it matches an item in the XmNselectedItems list.

## Usage

XmListAddItem() and XmListAddItems() are convenience routines that allow you to add items to a list. The routines add items to the list by modifying the XmNitems and XmNitemCount resources. If an item being added to the list duplicates an item that is already selected, the new item appears as selected. You should only use these routines if the list supports multiple selections and you want to select the new items whose duplicates are already selected. In order to add items with these routines, you have to create a compound string for each item.

## See Also

*XmListAddItemUnselected*(1), *XmListReplaceItems*(1), *XmListReplaceItemsPos*(1), *XmListReplaceItemsPosUnselected*(1), *XmListReplacePositions*(1), *XmList*(2).

# XmListAddItemUnselected

## Name

XmListAddItemUnselected, XmListAddItemsUnselected – add an item/items to a list.

## Synopsis

```
#include <Xm/List.h>
void XmListAddItemUnselected (widget, item, position)
    Widget widget;
    XmString item;
    int position;

void XmListAddItemsUnselected (widget, items, item_count, position)
    Widget widget;
    XmString *items;
    int item_count;
    int position;
```

### Inputs

| | |
|---|---|
| *widget* | Specifies the List widget. |
| *item* | Specifies the item that is to be added. |
| *items* | Specifies a list of items that are to be added. |
| *item_count* | Specifies the number of items to be added. |
| *position* | Specifies the position at which to add the new item(s). |

## Availability

`XmListAddItemsUnselected()` is only available in Motif 1.2 and later.

## Description

`XmListAddItemUnselected()` inserts the specified *item* into the list, while `XmListAddItemsUnselected()` inserts the specified list of *items*. If *item_count* is smaller than the number of *items*, only the first *item_count* items of the array are added. The *position* argument specifies the location of the new item(s) in the list. A *position* value of 1 indicates the first item, a *position* value of 2 indicates the second item, and so on. A value of 0 (zero) specifies the last item in the list. An inserted item does not appear selected, even if it matches an item in the `XmNselectedItems` list.

## Usage

`XmListAddItemUnselected()` and `XmListAddItemsUnselected()` are convenience routines that allow you to add items to a list. These routines add items to the list by modifying the `XmNitems` and `XmNitemCount` resources. If an item being added to the list duplicates an item that is already selected, the new item does not appear as selected. In order to add items with these routines, you have to create a compound string for each item.

## Example

The following callback routine shows how to use of `XmListAddItemUnselected()` to insert an item into a list in alphabetical order:

```
void add_item(text_w, client_data, call_data)
Widget text_w;
XtPointer client_data;
XtPointer call_data;
{
    char *text, *newtext = XmTextFieldGetString(text_w);
    XmString str, *strlist;
    int u_bound, l_bound = 0;
    Widget list_w = (Widget) client_data;

    /* newtext is the text typed in the TextField widget */
    if (!newtext || !*newtext) {
        XtFree(newtext);
        return;
    }

    /* get the current entries (and number of entries) from the List */
    XtVaGetValues(list_w,
        XmNitemCount, &u_bound,
        XmNitems,     &strlist,
        NULL);
    u_bound--;

    /* perform binary search */
    while (u_bound >= l_bound) {
        int i = l_bound + (u_bound - l_bound)/2;
        if (!XmStringGetLtoR(strlist[i], XmFONTLIST_DEFAULT_TAG, &text))
            break;
        if (strcmp(text, newtext) > 0)
            u_bound = i-1;
        else
            l_bound = i+1;
        XtFree(text);
    }

    /* insert item at appropriate location */
    str = XmStringCreateLocalized(newtext);
    XmListAddItemUnselected(list_w, str, l_bound+1);
    XmStringFree(str);
    XtFree(newtext);
}
```

## See Also

*XmListAddItem*(1), *XmListReplaceItems*(1), *XmListReplaceItemsPos*(1), *XmListReplaceItemsPosUnselected*(1), *XmListReplaceItemsUnselected*(1), *XmListReplacePositions*(1), *XmList*(2).

## Name

XmListDeleteAllItems – delete all of the items from a list.

## Synopsis

```
#include <Xm/List.h>
void XmListDeleteAllItems (widget)
    Widget widget;
```

### Inputs

*widget*    Specifies the List widget.

## Description

`XmListDeleteAllItems()` removes all of the items from the specified List *widget*.

## Usage

`XmListDeleteAllItems()` is a convenience routine that allows you to remove all of the items from a list. The routine removes the items by modifying the `XmNitems` and `XmNitemCount` resources.

## See Also

*XmListDeleteItem*(1), *XmListDeleteItemsPos*(1), *XmListDeletePos*(1), *XmListDeletePositions*(1), *XmList*(2).

# XmListDeleteItem



## Name

XmListDeleteItem, XmListDeleteItems – delete an item/items from a list.

## Synopsis

```
#include <Xm/List.h>
void XmListDeleteItem (widget, item)
    Widget widget;
    XmString item;

void XmListDeleteItems (widget, items, item_count)
    Widget widget;
    XmString *items;
    int item_count;
```

### Inputs

| | |
|---|---|
| *widget* | Specifies the List widget. |
| *item* | Specifies the item that is to be deleted. |
| *items* | Specifies a list of items that are to be deleted. |
| *item_count* | Specifies the number of items to be deleted. |

## Description

`ListDeleteItem()` removes the first occurrence of the specified *item* from the list, while `XmListDeleteItems()` removes the first occurrence of each of the elements of *items*. If an item does not exist, a warning message is displayed.

## Usage

`XmListDeleteItem()` and `XmListDeleteItems()` are convenience routines that allow you to remove items from a list. The routines remove the items by modifying the `XmNitems` and `XmNitemCount` resources. If there is more than one occurrence of an item in the list, the routines only remove the first occurrence. In order to remove items with these routines, you have to create a compound string for each item. The routines use a linear search to locate the items to be deleted.

## See Also

*XmListDeleteAllItems*(1), *XmListDeleteItemsPos*(1), *XmListDeletePos*(1), *XmListDeletePositions*(1), *XmList*(2).

# XmListDeleteItemsPos

## Name

XmListDeleteItemsPos – delete items starting at a specified position from a list.

## Synopsis

```
#include <Xm/List.h>
void XmListDeleteItemsPos (widget, item_count, position)
    Widget widget;
    int item_count;
    int position;
```

### Inputs

| | |
|---|---|
| *widget* | Specifies the List widget. |
| *item_count* | Specifies the number of items to be deleted. |
| *position* | Specifies the position from which to delete items. |

## Description

`XmListDeleteItemsPos()` removes *item_count* items from the list, starting at the specified *position*. A *position* value of 1 indicates the first item, a *position* value of 2 indicates the second item, and so on. If the number of items between *position* and the end of the list is less than *item_count*, the routine deletes all of the items up through the last item in the list.

## Usage

`XmListDeleteItemsPos()` is a convenience routine that allows you to remove items from a list. The routine remove the items by modifying the `XmNitems` and `XmNitemCount` resources. Since you are specifying the position of the items to be removed, you do not have to create compound strings for the items. The routine does not have to search for the items, so it avoids the linear search that is used by `XmListDeleteItems()`.

## See Also

*XmListDeleteAllItems*(1), *XmListDeleteItem*(1), *XmListDeletePos*(1), *XmListDeletePositions*(1), *XmList*(2).

# XmListDeletePos

## Name

XmListDeletePos – delete an item at the specified position from a list.

## Synopsis

```
#include <Xm/List.h>
void XmListDeletePos (widget, position)
    Widget widget;
    int position;
```

### Inputs

*widget* Specifies the List widget.

*position* Specifies the position from which to delete an item.

## Description

`XmListDeletePos()` removes the item at the specified *position* from the list. A *position* value of 1 indicates the first item, a *position* value of 2 indicates the second item, and so on. A value of 0 (zero) specifies the last item in the list. If the list does not have the specified *position*, a warning message is displayed.

## Usage

`XmListDeletePos()` is a convenience routine that allows you to remove an item from a list. The routine removes the item by modifying the `XmNitems` and `XmNitemCount` resources. Since you are specifying the position of the item to be removed, you do not have to create a compound string for the item. The routine does not have to search for the item, so it avoids the linear search that is used by `XmListDeleteItem()`.

## See Also

*XmListDeleteAllItems*(1), *XmListDeleteItem*(1), *XmListDeleteItemsPos*(1), *XmListDeletePositions*(1), *XmList*(2).

# XmListDeletePositions

## Name

XmListDeletePositions – delete items at the specified positions from a list.

## Synopsis

```
#include <Xm/List.h>
void XmListDeletePositions (widget, position_list, position_count)
    Widget widget;
    int *position_list;
    int position_count;
```

### Inputs

*widget* Specifies the List widget.

*position_list*
Specifies a list of positions from which to delete items.

*position_count*
Specifies the number of positions to be deleted.

## Availability

Motif 1.2 and later.

## Description

`XmListDeletePositions()` removes the items that appear at the positions specified in *position_list* from the list. A position value of 1 indicates the first item, a value of 2 indicates the second item, and so on. If the list does not have the specified position, a warning message is displayed. If *position_count* is smaller than the number of positions in *position_list*, only the first *position_count* items of the array are deleted.

## Usage

`XmListDeletePositions()` is a convenience routine that allows you to remove items from a list. The routine remove the items by modifying the `XmNitems` and `XmNitemCount` resources. Since you are specifying the positions of the items to be removed, you do not have to create compound strings for the items. The routine does not have to search for the items, so it avoids the linear search that is used by `XmListDeleteItems()`.

## See Also

*XmListDeleteAllItems*(1), *XmListDeleteItem*(1), *XmListDeleteItemsPos*(1), *XmListDeletePos*(1), *XmList*(2).

Motif Functions and Macros

# XmListDeselectAllItems



## Name

XmListDeselectAllItems – deselect all items in a list.

## Synopsis

```
#include <Xm/List.h>
void XmListDeselectAllItems (widget)
    Widget widget;
```

### Inputs

*widget* Specifies the List widget.

## Description

`XmListDeselectAllItems()` unhighlights all of the selected items in the specified *widget* and removes these items from the `XmNselectedItems` list. If the list is in normal mode, the item with the keyboard focus remains selected; if the list is in add mode, all of the items are deselected.

## Usage

`XmListDeselectAllItems()` is a convenience routine that allows you to deselect all of the items in a list. The routine deselects the items by removing the items from the `XmNselectedItems` list and modifying the `XmNselectedItemCount` resource. This routine does not invoke any selection callbacks for the list when the items are deselected.

## See Also

*XmListDeselectItem*(1), *XmListDeselectPos*(1), *XmListSelectItem*(1), *XmListSelectPos*(1),
*XmListUpdateSelectedList*(1),
*XmList*(2).

## Name

XmListDeselectItem – deselect an item from a list.

## Synopsis

```
#include <Xm/List.h>
void XmListDeselectItem (widget, item)
    Widget widget;
    XmString item;
```

### Inputs

*widget* Specifies the List widget.

*item* Specifies the item that is to be deselected.

## Description

`XmListDeselectItem()` unhighlights and removes from the `XmNselectedItems` list the first occurrence of the specified *item*.

## Usage

`XmListDeselectItem()` is a convenience routine that allows you to deselect an item in a list. The routine deselects the item by removing the item from the `XmNselectedItems` list and modifying the `XmNselectedItemCount` resource. This routine does not invoke any selection callbacks for the list when the item is deselected. If there is more than one occurrence of an item in the list, the routine only deselects the first occurrence. In order to deselect an item with this routine, you have to create a compound string for the item. The routine uses a linear search to locate the item to be deselected.

## See Also

*XmListDeselectAllItems*(1), *XmListDeselectPos*(1), *XmListSelectItem*(1), *XmListSelectPos*(1), *XmListUpdateSelectedList*(1),
*XmList*(2).

# XmListDeselectPos

## Name

XmListDeselectPos – deselect an item at the specified position from a list.

## Synopsis

```
#include <Xm/List.h>
void XmListDeselectPos (widget, position)
    Widget widget;
    int position;
```

### Inputs

*widget* Specifies the List widget.

*position* Specifies the position at which to deselect an item.

## Description

`XmListDeselectPos()` unhighlights the item at the specified *position* in the list and remove the item from the `XmNselectedItems` list. A *position* value of 1 indicates the first item, a *position* value of 2 indicates the second item, and so on. A value of 0 (zero) specifies the last item in the list. If the list does not have the specified *position*, the routine does nothing.

## Usage

`XmListDeselectPos()` is a convenience routine that allows you to deselect an item in a list. The routine deselects the item by removing the item from the `XmNselectedItems` list and modifying the `XmNselectedItemCount` resource. This routine does not invoke any selection callbacks for the list when the item is deselected. Since you are specifying the position of the item to be deselected, you do not have to create a compound string for the item. The routine does not have to search for the item, so it avoids the linear search that is used by `XmListDeselectItem()`.

## See Also

*XmListDeselectAllItems*(1), *XmListDeselectPos*(1), *XmListGetSelectedPos*(1), *XmListPosSelected*(1), *XmListSelectItem*(1), *XmListSelectPos*(1), *XmListUpdateSelectedList*(1), *XmList*(2).

# XmListGetKbdItemPos

## Name

XmListGetKbdItemPos – get the position of the item in a list that has the location cursor.

## Synopsis

```
#include <Xm/List.h>
int XmListGetKbdItemPos (widget)
    Widget widget;
```

### Inputs

*widget* Specifies the List widget.

### Returns

The position of the item that has the location cursor.

## Availability

Motif 1.2 and later.

## Description

`XmListGetKbdItemPos()` retrieves the position of the item in the specified List *widget* that has the location cursor. A returned value of 1 indicates the first item, a value of 2 indicates the second item, and so on. The value 0 (zero) specifies that the list is empty.

## Usage

`XmListGetKbdItemPos()` provides a way to determine which item in a list has the keyboard focus. This information is useful if you need to perform actions based on the position of the location cursor in the list.

## See Also

*XmListSetAddMode*(1), *XmListSetKbdItemPos*(1),
*XmList*(2).

# XmListGetMatchPos



## Name

XmListGetMatchPos – get all occurrences of an item in a list.

## Synopsis

```
#include <Xm/List.h>
Boolean XmListGetMatchPos (widget, item, position_list, position_count)
    Widget widget;
    XmString item;
    int **position_list;
    int *position_count;
```

### Inputs

*widget* Specifies the List widget.

*item* Specifies the item whose positions are to be retrieved.

### Outputs

*position_list*
Returns a list of the positions of the item.

*position_count*
Returns the number of items in *position_list*.

### Returns

`True` if the item is in the list or `False` otherwise.

## Description

`XmListGetMatchPos()` determines whether the specified *item* exists in the list. If the list contains *item*, the routine returns `True` and *position_list* returns a list of positions that specify the location(s) of the item. A position value of 1 indicates the first item, a position value of 2 indicates the second item, and so on. `XmListGetMatchPos()` allocates storage for the *position_list* array when the item is found; the application is responsible for freeing this storage using `XtFree()`. If the list does not contain *item*, the routine returns `False` and the value of *position_list* is undefined.

## Usage

`XmListGetMatchPos()` is a convenience routine that provides a way to locate all of the occurrences of an item in a list. Alternatively, you could obtain this information yourself using the `XmNitems` resource and `XmListItemPos()`.

## Example

The following code fragments show the use of `XmListGetMatchPos()`:

```
Widget          list_w;
int            *pos_list;
int             pos_cnt, i;
char           *choice = "A Sample Text String";
XmString        str = XmStringCreateLocalized(choice);
```

```
if (!XmListGetMatchPos(list_w, str, &pos_list, &pos_cnt))
    XtWarning("Can't get items in list");
else {
    printf("%s exists at %d positions:", choice, pos_cnt);
    for (i = 0; i < pos_cnt; i++)
        printf(" %d", pos_list[i]);
    puts("");
    XtFree(pos_list);
}
XmStringFree(str);
```

## See Also

*XmListGetSelectedPos*(1),
*XmList*(2).

# XmListGetSelectedPos

## Name

XmListGetSelectedPos – get the positions of the selected items in a list.

## Synopsis

```
#include <Xm/List.h>
Boolean XmListGetSelectedPos (widget, position_list, position_count)
    Widget widget;
    int **position_list;
    int *position_count;
```

### Inputs

*widget* Specifies the List widget.

### Outputs

*position_list*
Returns a list of the positions of the selected items.

*position_count*
Returns the number of items in *position_list*.

### Returns

True if there are selected items in the list or False otherwise.

## Description

XmListGetSelectedPos() determines whether there are any selected items in the list. If the list has selected items, the routine returns True and *position_list* returns a list of positions that specify the location(s) of the items. A position value of 1 indicates the first item, a position value of 2 indicates the second item, and so on. XmListGetSelectedPos() allocates storage for the *position_list* array when there are selected items; the application is responsible for freeing this storage using XtFree(). If the list does not contain and selected items, the routine returns False and the value of *position_list* is undefined.

## Usage

XmListGetSelectedPos() is a convenience routine that provides a way to determine the positions of all of the selected items in a list. Alternatively, you could obtain this information yourself using the XmNselectedItems resource and XmListItemPos().

## See Also

*XmListGetMatchPos*(1),
*XmList*(2).

# XmListItemExists

## Name

XmListItemExists – determine if a specified item is in a list.

## Synopsis

```
#include <Xm/List.h>
Boolean XmListItemExists (widget, item)
    Widget widget;
    XmString item;
```

### Inputs

| | |
|---|---|
| *widget* | Specifies the List widget. |
| *item* | Specifies the item whose presence in the list is checked. |

### Returns

`True` if the item is in the list or `False` otherwise.

## Description

`XmListItemExists()` determines whether the list contains the specified *item*. The routine returns `True` if the item is present and `False` if it is not.

## Usage

`XmListItemExists()` is a convenience routine that determines whether or not an item is in a list. In order to use the routine, you have to create a compound string for the item. The routine uses a linear search to locate the item. You may be able to obtain this information more effectively by searching the `XmNitems` list using your own search procedure.

## See Also

*XmListGetMatchPos*(1), *XmListItemPos*(1),
*XmList*(2).

# XmListItemPos



## Name

XmListItemPos – return the position of an item in a list.

## Synopsis

```
#include <Xm/List.h>
int XmListItemPos (widget, item)
    Widget widget;
    XmString item;
```

### Inputs

| | |
|---|---|
| *widget* | Specifies the List widget. |
| *item* | Specifies the item whose position is returned. |

### Returns

The position of the item in the list or 0 (zero) if the item is not in the list.

## Description

`XmListItemPos()` returns the position of the first occurrence of the specified *item* in the list. A position value of 1 indicates the first item, a position value of 2 indicates the second item, and so on. If *item* is not in the list, `XmListItemPos()` returns 0 (zero).

## Usage

`XmListItemPos()` is a convenience routine that finds the position of an item in a list. If there is more than one occurrence of the item in the list, the routine only returns the position of the first occurrence. In order to use the routine, you have to create a compound string for the item. The routine uses a linear search to locate the item.

## Example

The following routines show how to make sure that a given item in a list is visible:

```
void MakePosVisible(list_w, item_no)
Widget list_w;
int item_no;
{
    int top, visible;

    XtVaGetValues(list_w,
        XmNtopItemPosition,  &top,
        XmNvisibleItemCount, &visible,
        NULL);
    if (item_no < top)
        XmListSetPos(list_w, item_no);
    else if (item_no >= top+visible)
        XmListSetBottomPos(list_w, item_no);
}

void MakeItemVisible(list_w, item)
Widget list_w;
```

```
XmString item;
{
    int item_no = XmListItemPos(list_w, item);

    if (item_no > 0)
        MakePosVisible(list_w, item_no);
}
```

## See Also

*XmListItemExists*(1), *XmListPosSelected*(1),
*XmList*(2).

# XmListPosSelected

## Name

XmListPosSelected – check if the item at a specified position is selected in a list.

## Synopsis

```
#include <Xm/List.h>
Boolean XmListPosSelected (widget, position)
    Widget widget;
    int position;
```

### Inputs

*widget* Specifies the List widget.

*position* Specifies the position that is checked.

### Returns

`True` if the item is selected or `False` if the item is not selected or the position is invalid.

## Availability

Motif 1.2 and later.

## Description

`XmListPosSelected()` determines whether or not the list item at the specified *position* is selected. A *position* value of 1 indicates the first item, a *position* value of 2 indicates the second item, and so on. The value 0 (zero) specifies the last item in the list. The routine returns `True` if the list item is selected. It returns `False` if the item is not selected or the list does not have the specified *position*.

## Usage

`XmListPosSelected()` is a convenience routine that lets you check if an item at a particular position is selected. Alternatively, you could check the list of positions returned by `XmListGetSelectedPos()` to see if the item at a position is selected.

## See Also

*XmListDeselectPos*(1), *XmListGetSelectedPos*(1), *XmListSelectPos*(1), *XmListUpdateSelectedList*(1), *XmList*(2).

# XmListPosToBounds

## Name

XmListPosToBounds – return the bounding box of an item at the specified position in a list.

## Synopsis

```
#include <Xm/List.h>
Boolean XmListPosToBounds (widget, position, x, y, width, height)
    Widget widget;
    int position;
    Position *x;
    Position *y;
    Dimension *width;
    Dimension *height;
```

### Inputs

| | |
|---|---|
| *widget* | Specifies the List widget. |
| *position* | Specifies the position of the item for which to return the bounding box. |

### Outputs

| | |
|---|---|
| *x* | Returns the x-coordinate of the bounding box for the item. |
| *y* | Returns the y-coordinate of the bounding box for the item. |
| *width* | Returns the width of the bounding box for the item. |
| *height* | Returns the height of the bounding box for the item. |

### Returns

`True` if item at the specified position is visible or `False` otherwise.

## Availability

Motif 1.2 and later.

## Description

`XmListPosToBounds()` returns the bounding box of the item at the specified *position* in the list. A *position* value of 1 indicates the first item, a *position* value of 2 indicates the second item, and so on. A value of 0 (zero) specifies the last item in the list. The routine returns the *x* and *y* coordinates of the upper left corner of the bounding box in relation to the upper left corner of the List widget. `XmListPosToBounds()` also returns the *width* and *height* of the bounding box. Passing a `NULL` value for any of the *x*, *y*, *width*, or *height* parameters indicates that the value for the paramater should not be returned. If the item at the specified *position* is not visible, `XmListPosToBounds()` returns `False` and the return values are undefined.

## Usage

`XmListPosToBounds()` provides a way to determine the bounding box of an item in a list. This information is useful if you want to perform additional event processing or draw special graphics for the list item.

### See Also

*XmListYToPos*(1),
*XmList*(2).

# XmListReplaceItems

## Name

XmListReplaceItems – replace specified items in a list.

## Synopsis

```
#include <Xm/List.h>
void XmListReplaceItems (widget, old_items, item_count, new_items)
    Widget widget;
    XmString *old_items;
    int item_count;
    XmString *new_items;
```

### Inputs

| | |
|---|---|
| *widget* | Specifies the List widget. |
| *old_items* | Specifies a list of the items that are to be replaced. |
| *item_count* | Specifies the number of items that are to be replaced. |
| *new_items* | Specifies a list of the new items. |

## Description

`XmListReplaceItems()` replaces the first occurrence of each item in the *old_items* list with the corresponding item from the *new_items* list. If an item in the *old_items* list does not exist in the specified List *widget*, the corresponding item in *new_list* is skipped. If *item_count* is smaller than the number of *old_items* or *new_items*, only the first *item_count* items are replaced. A new item appears selected if it matches an item in the `XmNselectedItems` list.

## Usage

`XmListReplaceItems()` is a convenience routine that allows you to replace particular items in a list. The routine replaces items by modifying the `XmNitems` resource. If a new item duplicates an item that is already selected, the new item appears as selected. You should only use this routine if the list supports multiple selections and you want to select the new items whose duplicates are already selected. In order to replace items with this routine, you have to create compound strings for all of the old and new items. The routine uses a linear search to locate the items to be replaced.

## See Also

*XmListAddItem*(1), *XmListAddItemUnselected*(1), *XmListReplaceItemsPos*(1), *XmListReplaceItemsPosUnselected*(1), *XmListReplaceItemsUnselected*(1), *XmListReplacePositions*(1), *XmList*(2).

Motif Functions and Macros

# XmListReplaceItemsPos



## Name

XmListReplaceItemsPos – replace specified items in a list.

## Synopsis

```
#include <Xm/List.h>
void XmListReplaceItemsPos (widget, new_items, item_count, position)
    Widget widget;
    XmString *new_items;
    int item_count;
    int position;
```

### Inputs

| | |
|---|---|
| *widget* | Specifies the List widget. |
| *new_items* | Specifies a list of the new items. |
| *item_count* | Specifies the number of items that are to be replaced. |
| *position* | Specifies the position at which to replace items. |

## Description

XmListReplaceItemsPos() replaces a consecutive number of items in the list with items from the *new_items* list. The first item that is replaced is located at the specified *position* and each subsequent item is replaced by the corresponding item from *new_items*. A *position* value of 1 indicates the first item, a *position* value of 2 indicates the second item, and so on. If *item_count* is smaller than the number of *new_items*, only the first *item_count* items are replaced. If the number of items between *position* and the end of the list is less than *item_count*, the routine replaces all of the items up through the last item in the list. A new item appears selected if it matches an item in the XmNselectedItems list.

## Usage

XmListReplaceItemsPos() is a convenience routine that allows you to replace a contiguous sequence of items in a list. The routine replaces items by modifying the XmNitems resource. If a new item duplicates an item that is already selected, the new item appears as selected. You should only use this routine if the list supports multiple selections and you want to select the new items whose duplicates are already selected. In order to replace items with this routine, you have to create compound strings for all of the new items. The routine does not have to search for the items, so it avoids the linear searches that are used by XmListReplaceItems().

## See Also

*XmListAddItem*(1), *XmListAddItemUnselected*(1), *XmListReplaceItems*(1), *XmListReplaceItemsPosUnselected*(1), *XmListReplaceItemsUnselected*(1), *XmListReplacePositions*(1), *XmList*(2).

# XmListReplaceItemsPosUnselected

## Name

XmListReplaceItemsPosUnselected – replace specified items in a list.

## Synopsis

```
#include <Xm/List.h>
void XmListReplaceItemsPosUnselected (widget, new_items, item_count,
        position)
    Widget widget;
    XmString *new_items;
    int item_count;
    int position;
```

### Inputs

*widget* Specifies the List widget.

*new_items* Specifies a list of the new items.

*item_count* Specifies the number of items that are to be replaced.

*position* Specifies the position at which to replace items.

## Availability

Motif 1.2 and later.

## Description

`XmListReplaceItemsPosUnselected()` replaces a consecutive number of items in the list with items from the *new_items* list. The first item that is replaced is located at the specified *position* and each subsequent item is replaced by the corresponding item from *new_items*. A *position* value of 1 indicates the first item, a *position* value of 2 indicates the second item, and so on. If *item_count* is smaller than the number of *new_items*, only the first *item_count* items are replaced. If the number of items between *position* and the end of the list is less than *item_count*, the routine replaces all of the items up through the last item in the list. A new item does not appear selected, even if it matches an item in the `XmNselectedItems` list.

## Usage

`XmListReplaceItemsPosUnselected()` is a convenience routine that allows you to replace a contiguous sequence of items in a list. The routine replaces items by modifying the `XmNitems` resource. If a new item duplicates an item that is already selected, the new item does not appear as selected. In order to replace items with this routine, you have to create compound strings for all of the new items. The routine does not have to search for the items, so it avoids the linear searches that are used by `XmListReplaceItemsUnselected()`.

## See Also

*XmListAddItem*(1), *XmListAddItemUnselected*(1), *XmListReplaceItems*(1), *XmListReplaceItemsPos*(1), *XmListReplaceItemsUnselected*(1), *XmListReplacePositions*(1), *XmList*(2).

# XmListReplaceItemsUnselected

## Name

XmListReplaceItemsUnselected – replace specified items in a list.

## Synopsis

```
#include <Xm/List.h>
void XmListReplaceItemsUnselected (widget, old_items, item_count,
        new_items)
    Widget widget;
    XmString *old_items;
    int item_count;
    XmString *new_items;
```

### Inputs

| | |
|---|---|
| *widget* | Specifies the List widget. |
| *old_items* | Specifies a list of the items that are to be replaced. |
| *item_count* | Specifies the number of items that are to be replaced. |
| *new_items* | Specifies a list of the new items. |

## Availability

Motif 1.2 and later.

## Description

XmListReplaceItemsUnselected() replaces the first occurrence of each item in the *old_items* list with the corresponding item from the *new_items* list. If an item in the *old_items* list does not exist in the specified List *widget*, the corresponding item in *new_list* is skipped. If *item_count* is smaller than the number of *old_items* or *new_items*, only the first *item_count* items are replaced. A new item does not appear selected, even if it matches an item in the XmNselectedItems list.

## Usage

XmListReplaceItemsUnselected() is a convenience routine that allows you to replace particular items in a list. The routine replaces items by modifying the XmNitems resource. If a new item duplicates an item that is already selected, the new item does not appear as selected. In order to replace items with this routine, you have to create compound strings for all of the old and new items. The routine uses a linear search to locate the items to be replaced.

## See Also

*XmListAddItem*(1), *XmListAddItemUnselected*(1), *XmListReplaceItems*(1), *XmListReplaceItemsPos*(1), *XmListReplaceItemsPosUnselected*(1), *XmListReplacePositions*(1), *XmList*(2).

# XmListReplacePositions

## Name

XmListReplacePositions – replace items at the specified postions in a list.

## Synopsis

```
#include <Xm/List.h>
void XmListReplacePositions (widget, position_list, item_list, item_count)
    Widget widget;
    int *position_list;
    XmString *item_list;
    int item_count;
```

### Inputs

*widget* Specifies the List widget.

*position_list*
Specifies a list of positions at which to replace items.

*item_list* Specifies a list of the new items.

*item_count* Specifies the number of items that are to be replaced.

## Availability

Motif 1.2 and later.

## Description

`XmListReplacePositions()` replaces the items that appear at the positions specified in *position_list* with the corresponding items from *item_list*. A position value of 1 indicates the first item, a value of 2 indicates the second item, and so on. If the list does not have the specified position, a warning message is displayed. If *item_count* is smaller than the number of positions in *position_list*, only the first *item_count* items are replaced. A new item appears selected if it matches an item in the `XmNselectedItems` list.

## Usage

`XmListReplacePositions()` is a convenience routine that allows you to replace items at particular positions in a list. The routine replaces items by modifying the `XmNitems` resource. If a new item duplicates an item that is already selected, the new item appears as selected. You should only use this routine if the list supports multiple selections and you want to select the new items whose duplicates are already selected. In order to replace items with this routine, you have to create compound strings for all of the new items. The routine does not have to search for the items, so it avoids the linear searches that are used by `XmListReplaceItems()`.

## See Also

*XmListAddItem*(1), *XmListAddItemUnselected*(1), *XmListReplaceItems*(1), *XmListReplaceItemsPos*(1), *XmListReplaceItemsPosUnselected*(1), *XmListReplaceItemsUnselected*(1), *XmList*(2).

# XmListSelectItem

## Name

XmListSelectItem – select an item from a list.

## Synopsis

```
#include <Xm/List.h>
void XmListSelectItem (widget, item, notify)
    Widget widget;
    XmString item;
    Boolean notify;
```

### Inputs

| | |
|---|---|
| *widget* | Specifies the List widget. |
| *item* | Specifies the item that is to be selected. |
| *notify* | Specifies whether or not the selection callback is invoked. |

## Description

`XmListSelectItem()` highlights and selects the first occurrence of the specified *item* in the list. If the `XmNselectionPolicy` resource of the list is `XmMULTIPLE_SELECT`, the routine toggles the selection state of *item*. For any other selection policy, `XmListSelectItem()` replaces the currently selected item(s) with *item*. The `XmNselectedItems` resource specifies the current selection of the list. If *notify* is `True`, `XmListSelectItem()` invokes the selection callback for the current selection policy.

## Usage

`XmListSelectItem()` is a convenience routine that allows you to select an item in a list. The routine selects the item by modifying the `XmNselectedItems` and `XmNselectedItemCount` resources. In order to select an item with this routine, you have to create a compound string for the item. The routine uses a linear search to locate the item to be selected. `XmListSelectItem()` only allows you to select a single item; there are no routines for selecting multiple items. If you need to select more than one item, use `XtSetValues()` to set `XmNselectedItems` and `XmNselectedItemCount`.

The *notify* parameter indicates whether or not the selection callbacks for the current selection policy are invoked. You can avoid redundant code by setting this parameter to `True`. If you are calling `XmListSelectItem()` from a selection callback routine, you probably want to set the parameter to `False` to avoid the possibility of an infinite loop. Calling `XmListSelectItem()` with *notify* set to `True` causes the callback routines to be invoked in a way that is indistinguishable from a user-initiated selection action.

## See Also

*XmListDeselectAllItems*(1), *XmListDeselectItem*(1), *XmListDeselectPos*(1), *XmListSelectPos*(1), *XmListUpdateSelectedList*(1),
*XmList*(2).

# XmListSelectPos

## Name

XmListSelectPos – select an item at the specified position from a list.

## Synopsis

```
#include <Xm/List.h>
void XmListSelectPos (widget, position, notify)
    Widget widget;
    int position;
    Boolean notify;
```

### Inputs

| | |
|---|---|
| *widget* | Specifies the List widget. |
| *position* | Specifies the position of the item that is to be selected. |
| *notify* | Specifies whether or not the selection callback is invoked. |

## Description

XmListSelectPos() highlights and selects the item at the specified *position* in the list. A *position* value of 1 indicates the first item, a *position* value of 2 indicates the second item, and so on. A value of 0 (zero) specifies the last item in the list. If the XmNselectionPolicy resource of the list is XmMULTIPLE_SELECT, the routine toggles the selection state of the item. For any other selection policy, XmListSelectPos() replaces the currently selected item with the specified item. The XmNselectedItems resource lists the current selection of the list. If *notify* is True, XmListSelectPos() invokes the selection callback for the current selection policy.

## Usage

XmListSelectPos() is a convenience routine that allows you to select an item at a particular position in a list. The routine selects the item by modifying the XmNselectedItems and XmNselectedItemCount resources. Since you are specifying the position of the item to be selected, you do not have to create a compound string for the item. The routine does not have to search for the item, so it avoids the linear search that is used by XmListSelectItem(). XmListSelectPos() only allows you to select a single item; there are no routines for selecting multiple items. If you need to select more than one item, use XtSetValues() to set XmNselectedItems and XmNselectedItemCount.

The *notify* parameter indicates whether or not the selection callbacks for the current selection policy are invoked. You can avoid redundant code by setting this parameter to True. If you are calling XmListSelectPos() from a selection callback routine, you probably want to set the parameter to False to avoid the possibility of an infinite loop. Calling XmListSelectPos() with *notify* set to True causes the callback routines to be invoked in a way that is indistinguishable from a user-initiated selection action.

### See Also

*XmListDeselectAllItems*(1), *XmListDeselectItem*(1), *XmListDeselectPos*(1), *XmListGetSelectedPos*(1), *XmListPosSelected*(1), *XmListSelectItem*(1),
*XmList*(2).

# XmListSetAddMode

## Name

XmListSetAddMode – set add mode in a list.

## Synopsis

```
#include <Xm/List.h>
void XmListSetAddMode (widget, mode)
    Widget widget;
    Boolean mode;
```

### Inputs

| | |
|---|---|
| *widget* | Specifies the List widget. |
| *mode* | Specifies whether to set add mode on or off. |

## Description

`XmListSetAddMode()` sets the state of add mode when the `XmNselectionPolicy` is `XmEXTENDED_SELECT`. If *mode* is `True`, add mode is turned on; if *mode* is `False`, add mode is turned off. When a List widget is in add mode, the user can move the location cursor without disturbing the current selection.

## Usage

`XmListSetAddMode()` provides a way to change the state of add mode in a list. The distinction between normal mode and add mode is only important for making keyboard-based selections. In normal mode, the location cursor and the selection move together, while in add mode, the location cursor and the selection can be separate.

## See Also

*XmListGetKbdItemPos*(1), *XmListSetKbdItemPos*(1),
*XmList*(2).

# XmListSetBottomItem



## Name

XmListSetBottomItem – set the last visible item in a list.

## Synopsis

```
#include <Xm/List.h>
void XmListSetBottomItem (widget, item)
    Widget widget;
    XmString item;
```

### Inputs

*widget* Specifies the List widget.

*item* Specifies the item that is made the last visible item.

## Description

XmListSetBottomItem() scrolls the List widget so that the first occurrence of the specified *item* appears as the last visible item in the list.

## Usage

XmListSetBottomItem() provides a way to make sure that a particular item is visible in a list. The routine changes the viewable portion of the list so that the specified *item* is displayed at the bottom of the viewport. If there is more than one occurrence of the item in the list, the routine uses the first occurrence. In order to use this routine, you have to create a compound string for the item. The routine uses a linear search to locate the item.

## See Also

*XmListSetBottomPos*(1), *XmListSetHorizPos*(1), *XmListSetItem*(1), *XmListSetPos*(1), *XmList*(2).

# XmListSetBottomPos

## Name

XmListSetBottomPos – set the last visible item in a list.

## Synopsis

```
#include <Xm/List.h>
void XmListSetBottomPos (widget, position)
    Widget widget;
    int position;
```

### Inputs

*widget* Specifies the List widget.

*position* Specifies the position of the item that is made the last visible item.

## Description

`XmListSetBottomPos()` scrolls the List widget so that the item at the specified *position* appears as the last visible item in the list. A *position* value of 1 indicates the first item, a *position* value of 2 indicates the second item, and so on. A value of 0 (zero) specifies the last item in the list.

## Usage

`XmListSetBottomPos()` provides a way to make sure that an item at a particular position is visible in a list. The routine changes the viewable portion of the list so that the item at the specified *position* is displayed at the bottom of the viewport. Since you are specifying the position of the item, you do not have to create a compound string for the item. The routine does not have to search for the item, so it avoids the linear search that is used by `XmListSetBottomItem()`.

## Example

The following routine shows how to make sure that an item at a given position in a list is visible:

```
void MakePosVisible(list_w, item_no)
Widget list_w;
int item_no;
{
    int top, visible;

    XtVaGetValues(list_w,
        XmNtopItemPosition,  &top,
        XmNvisibleItemCount, &visible,
        NULL);
    if (item_no < top)
        XmListSetPos(list_w, item_no);
    else if (item_no >= top+visible)
        XmListSetBottomPos(list_w, item_no);
}
```

## See Also

*XmListSetBottomItem*(1), *XmListSetHorizPos*(1), *XmListSetItem*(1), *XmListSetPos*(1), *XmList*(2).

# XmListSetHorizPos

## Name

XmListSetHorizPos – set the horizontal position of a list.

## Synopsis

```
#include <Xm/List.h>
void XmListSetHorizPos (widget, position)
    Widget widget;
    int position;
```

### Inputs

| | |
|---|---|
| *widget* | Specifies the List widget. |
| *position* | Specifies the horizontal position. |

## Description

`XmListSetHorizPos()` scrolls the list to the specified horizontal *position*. If `XmNlistSizePolicy` is set to `XmCONSTANT` or `XmRESIZE_IF_POSSIBLE` and the horizontal scroll bar is visible, `XmListSetHorizPos()` sets the `XmNvalue` resource of the horizontal scroll bar to the specified *position* and updates the visible area of the list.

## Usage

When a list item is too long to fit horizontally inside the viewing area of a List widget, the widget either expands horizontally or adds a horizontal scroll bar, depending on the value of the `XmNlistSizePolicy` resource. Calling `XmListSetHorizPos()` is equivalent to the user moving the horizontal scroll bar to the specified location.

## See Also

*XmListSetBottomItem*(1), *XmListSetBottomPos*(1), *XmListSetItem*(1), *XmListSetPos*(1), *XmList*(2).

# XmListSetItem

## Name

XmListSetItem – set the first visible item in a list.

## Synopsis

```
#include <Xm/List.h>
void XmListSetItem (widget, item)
    Widget widget;
    XmString item;
```

### Inputs

| | |
|---|---|
| *widget* | Specifies the List widget. |
| *item* | Specifies the item that is made the first visible item. |

## Description

`XmListSetItem()` scrolls the List widget so that the first occurrence of the specified *item* appears as the first visible item in the list.

## Usage

`XmListSetItem()` provides a way to make sure that a particular item is visible in a list. The routine changes the viewable portion of the list so that the specified *item* is displayed at the top of the viewport. Using this routine is equivalent to setting the `XmNtopItemPosition` resource. If there is more than one occurrence of the item in the list, the routine uses the first occurrence. In order to use this routine, you have to create a compound string for the item. The routine uses a linear search to locate the item.

## See Also

*XmListSetBottomItem*(1), *XmListSetBottomPos*(1), *XmListSetHorizPos*(1), *XmListSetPos*(1), *XmList*(2).

# XmListSetKbdItemPos

## Name

XmListSetKbdItemPos – set the position of the location cursor in a list.

## Synopsis

```
#include <Xm/List.h>
Boolean XmListSetKbdItemPos (widget, position)
    Widget widget;
    int position;
```

### Inputs

| | |
|---|---|
| *widget* | Specifies the List widget. |
| *position* | Specifies the position where the location cursor is set. |

### Returns

`True` on success or `False` if there is not item at *position* or the list is empty.

## Availability

Motif 1.2 and later.

## Description

`XmListSetKbdItemPos()` sets the location cursor at the specified *position*. A *position* value of 1 indicates the first item, a *position* value of 2 indicates the second item, and so on. A value of 0 (zero) specifies the last item in the list. The routine does not check the selection state of the item at the specified location.

## Usage

`XmListSetKbdItemPos()` provides a way to change which item in a list has the keyboard focus. The routine is useful if you need to make sure that particular item has the keyboard focus at a given time, such as when the list first receives the keyboard focus.

## See Also

*XmListGetKbdItemPos*(1), *XmListSetAddMode*(1),
*XmList*(2).

# XmListSetPos

## Name

XmListSetPos – sets the first visible item in a list.

## Synopsis

```
#include <Xm/List.h>
void XmListSetPos (widget, position)
    Widget widget;
    int position;
```

### Inputs

| | |
|---|---|
| *widget* | Specifies the List widget. |
| *position* | Specifies the position of the item that is made the first visible item. |

## Description

`XmListSetPos()` scrolls the List widget so that the item at the specified *position* appears as the first visible item in the list. A *position* value of 1 indicates the first item, a *position* value of 2 indicates the second item, and so on. A value of 0 (zero) specifies the last item in the list.

## Usage

`XmListSetPos()` provides a way to make sure that an item at a particular location is visible in a list. The routine changes the viewable portion of the list so that the item at the specified *position* is displayed at the top of the viewport. Using this routine is equivalent to setting the `XmNtopItemPosition` resource. Since you are specifying the position of the item, you do not have to create a compound string for the item. The routine does not have to search for the item, so it avoids the linear search that is used by `XmListSetItem()`.

## Example

The following routine shows how to make sure that an item at a given position in a list is visible:

```
void MakePosVisible(list_w, item_no)
Widget list_w;
int item_no;
{
    int top, visible;

    XtVaGetValues(list_w,
        XmNtopItemPosition,  &top,
        XmNvisibleItemCount, &visible,
        NULL);
    if (item_no < top)
        XmListSetPos(list_w, item_no);
    else if (item_no >= top+visible)
        XmListSetBottomPos(list_w, item_no);
}
```

## See Also

*XmListSetBottomItem*(1), *XmListSetBottomPos*(1), *XmListSetHorizPos*(1), *XmListSetItem*(1), *XmList*(2).

# XmListUpdateSelectedList

## Name

XmListUpdateSelectedList – update the list of selected items in a list.

## Synopsis

```
#include <Xm/List.h>
void XmListUpdateSelectedList (widget)
    Widget widget;
```

### Inputs

*widget*　　Specified the List widget.

## Availability

Motif 1.2 and later.

## Description

`XmListUpdateSelectedList()` updates the value of the `XmNselectedItems` resource. The routine frees the current contents of the resource and traverses the `XmNitems` list, adding each currently selected item to the `XmNselectedItems` list.

## Usage

`XmListUpdateSelectedList()` provides a way to update the list of selected items in a list. This routine is useful if the actual items that are selected get out of synch with the value of the `XmNselectedItems` resource. This situation might arise if you are using internal list functions and modifying internal data structures. If you are using the defined list routines, the situation should never occur.

## See Also

*XmListDeselectAllItems*(1), *XmListDeselectItem*(1), *XmListDeselectPos*(1), *XmListGetSelectedPos*(1), *XmListPosSelected*(1), *XmListSelectItem*(1), *XmListSelectPos*(1),
*XmList*(2).

# XmListYToPos

## Name

XmListYToPos – get the position of the item at the specified y-coordinate in a list.

## Synopsis

```
#include <Xm/List.h>
int XmListYToPos (widget, y)
    Widget widget;
    Position y;
```

### Inputs

*widget* Specifies the List widget.

*y* Specifies the y-coordinate.

### Returns

The position of the item at the specified *y*-coordinate.

## Availability

Motif 1.2 and later.

## Description

`XmListYToPos()` retrieves the position of the item at the specified *y*-coordinate in the list. The *y*-coordinate is specified in the coordinate system of the list. A returned value of 1 indicates the first item, a value of 2 indicates the second item, and so on. The value 0 (zero) specifies that there is no item at the specified location.

As of Motif 1.2, a return value of 0 (zero) indicates the first item, a value of 1 indicates the second item, and so on. The value that is returned may not be a valid position in the list, so an application should check the value with respect to the value of `XmNitemCount` before using it.

## Usage

`XmListYToPos()` provides a way to translate a y-coordinate into a list position. This routine is useful if you are processing events that report a pointer position and you need to convert the location of the event into an item position.

## See Also

*XmListPosToBounds*(1),
*XmList*(2).

# XmMainWindowSep



## Name

XmMainWindowSep1, XmMainWindowSep2, XmMainWindowSep3 – get the widget ID of a MainWindow Separator.

## Synopsis

```
#include <Xm/MainW.h>
Widget XmMainWindowSep1 (widget)

Widget XmMainWindowSep2 (widget)

Widget XmMainWindowSep3 (widget)

     Widget widget;
```

### Inputs

*widget* Specifies the MainWindow widget.

### Returns

The widget ID of the particular MainWindow Separator.

## Description

`XmMainWindowSep1()` returns the widget ID of the MainWindow widget's first Separator, which is located directly below the MenuBar. `XmMainWindowSep2()` returns the widget ID of the second Separator in the Main Window, which is between the Command and ScrolledWindow widgets. `XmMainWindowSep3()` returns the widget ID of the MainWindow's third Separator, which is located just above the message window. The three Separator widgets in a MainWindow are visible only when the `XmNshowSeparator` resource is set to `True`.

## Usage

`XmMainWindowSep1()`, `XmMainWindowSep2()`, and `XmMainWindowSep3()` provide access to the three Separator widgets that can be displayed by a MainWindow widget. With the widget IDs, you can change the visual attributes of the individual Separators.

## See Also

*XmMainWindowSetAreas*(1),
*XmMainWindow*(2), *XmScrolledWindow*(2).

## Name

XmMainWindowSetAreas – specify the children for a MainWindow.

## Synopsis

```
#include <Xm/MainW.h>
void XmMainWindowSetAreas (widget, menu_bar, command_window,
        horizontal_scrollbar, vertical_scrollbar, work_region)
    Widget widget;
    Widget menu_bar;
    Widget command_window;
    Widget horizontal_scrollbar;
    Widget vertical_scrollbar;
    Widget work_region;
```

### Inputs

*widget* Specifies the MainWindow widget.

*menu_bar* Specifies the widget ID of the MenuBar.

*command_window*
Specifies the widget ID of the command window.

*horizontal_scrollbar*
Specifies the widget ID of the horizontal ScrollBar.

*vertical_scrollbar*
Specifies the widget ID of the vertical ScrollBar.

*work_region* Specifies the widget ID of the work window.



## Description

`XmMainWindowSetAreas()` sets up the standard regions of the MainWindow widget for an application. The MainWindow must be created before the routine is called. `XmMainWindowSetAreas()` specifies the MenuBar, the work window, the command window, and the horizontal and vertical ScrollBars for the MainWindow. If an application does not have one of these regions, the corresponding argument can be specified as `NULL`. Each region may have child widgets, and this routine determines which of those children will be actively managed by the MainWindow.

## Usage

Each of the MainWindow regions is associated with a MainWindow resource; `XmMainWindowSetAreas()` sets the associated resources. The associated resources that correspond to the last five arguments to the routine are `XmNmenuBar`, `XmNcommand`, `XmNhorizontalScrollBar`, `XmNverticalScrollBar`, and `XmNworkWindow`. `XmMainWindowSetAreas()` does not provide a way to set up the message area; this region must be set up by specifying the `XmNmessageWindow` resource.

If an application does not call `XmMainWindowSetAreas()`, the widget may still set some of the standard regions. When a MenuBar child is added to a MainWindow, if `XmNmenuBar` has not been set, it is set to the MenuBar child. When a Command child is added to a MainWindow, if `XmNcommand` has not been set, it is set to the Command child. If ScrollBars are added as children, the `XmNhorizontalScrollBar` and `XmNverticalScrollBar` resources may be set if they have not already been specified. Any child that is not one of these types is used for the `XmNworkWindow`. If you want to be certain about which widgets are used for the different regions, it is wise to call `XmMainWindowSetAreas()` explicitly.

## Example

The following code fragment shows how to set some of the regions of a MainWindow:

```
Widget          top, main_w, menubar, command_w, text_w;
Arg             args[4];

main_w = XtVaCreateManagedWidget("main_w", xmMainWindowWidgetClass, top,
    NULL);

menubar = XmCreateMenuBar(main_w, "menubar", NULL, 0);
XtManageChild(menubar);

XtSetArg(args[0], XmNrows,       24);
XtSetArg(args[1], XmNcolumns,    80);
XtSetArg(args[2], XmNeditable,   False);
XtSetArg(args[3], XmNeditMode,   XmMULTI_LINE_EDIT);
text_w = XmCreateScrolledText(main_w, "text_w", args, 4);
XtManageChild(text_w);

command_w = XtVaCreateWidget("command_w", xmTextWidgetClass, main_w,
    NULL);
XtManageChild(command_w);

XmMainWindowSetAreas(main_w, menubar, command_w,
    NULL, NULL, XtParent(text_w));
```

## See Also

*XmMainWindowSep*(1),
*XmMainWindow*(2), *XmScrolledWindow*(2).

# XmMapSegmentEncoding

## Name

XmMapSegmentEncoding – get the compound text encoding format for a font list element tag.

## Synopsis

```
char * XmMapSegmentEncoding (fontlist_tag)
    char *fontlist_tag;
```

### Inputs

*fontlist_tag*
Specifies the compound string font list element tag.

### Returns

A character string that contains a copy of the compound text encoding format or NULL if the font list element tag is not found in the registry.

## Availability

Motif 1.2 and later.

## Description

XmMapSegmentEncoding() retrieves the compound text encoding format associated with the specified *fontlist_tag*. The toolkit stores the mappings between compound text encodings and font list elements tags in a registry. XmMapSegmentEncoding() searches the registry for a compound text encoding format associated with the specified *fontlist_tag* and returns a copy of the format. If *fontlist_tag* is not in the registry, the routine returns NULL. XmMapSegmentEncoding() allocates storage for the returned character string; the application is responsible for freeing the storage using XtFree().

## Usage

Compound text is an encoding that is designed to represent text from any locale. Compound text strings identify their encoding using embedded escape sequences. The compound text representation was standardized for X11R4 for use as a text interchange format for interclient communication.

XmCvtXmStringToCT() converts a compound string into compound text by using the font list tag of each compound string segment to select a compound text format from the registry for the segment. XmMapSegmentEncoding() provides a way for an application to determine the compound text format that would be used for a particular font list element tag.

## See Also

*XmCvtXmStringToCT*(1), *XmRegisterSegmentEncoding*(1).

# XmMenuPosition



## Name

XmMenuPosition – position a popup menu.

## Synopsis

```
#include <Xm/RowColumn.h>
void XmMenuPosition (menu, event)
    Widget menu;
    XButtonPressedEvent *event;
```

### Inputs

*menu* Specifies the PopupMenu.

*event* Specifies the event that was passed to the action procedure managing the PopupMenu.

## Description

`XmMenuPosition()` positions a popup menu, using the values of the `x_root` and `y_root` fields from the specified *event*. An application must call this routine before managing the popup menu, except when the application is positioning the menu itself.

## Usage

The *event* parameter for `XmMenuPosition()` is defined to be of type `XButton-PressedEvent`; using another type of event might lead to toolkit problems. The `x_root` and `y_root` fields in the event structure are used to position the menu at the location of the mouse button press. You can modify these fields to position the menu at another location.

## Example

The following routine shows the use of an event handler to post a popup menu.

```
void PostIt(pb, client_data, event)
Widget pb;
XtPointer client_data;
XEvent *event;
{
   Widget popup = (Widget) client_data;

   if (event->button != 3)
        return;

    XmMenuPosition(popup, event);
    XtManageChild(popup);
}
```

## See Also

*XmRowColumn*(2), *XmPopupMenu*(2).

# XmMessageBoxGetChild

## Name

XmMessageBoxGetChild – get the specified child of a MessageBox widget.

## Synopsis

```
#include <Xm/MessageB.h>
Widget XmMessageBoxGetChild (widget, child)
    Widget widget;
    unsigned char child;
```

### Inputs

*widget* Specifies the MessageBox widget.

*child* Specifies the child of the MessageBox widget. Pass one of the values from the list below.

### Returns

The widget ID of the specified child of the MessageBox.

## Description

`XmMessageBoxGetChild()` returns the widget ID of the specified *child* of the MessageBox widget.

## Usage

XmDIALOG_CANCEL_BUTTON, XmDIALOG_HELP_BUTTON, and XmDIALOG_OK_-BUTTON specify the action buttons in the widget. XmDIALOG_DEFAULT_BUTTON specifies the current default button. XmDIALOG_SYMBOL_LABEL specifies the label used to display the message symbol, while XmDIALOG_MESSAGE_LABEL specifies the message label. Xm-DIALOG_SEPARATOR specifies the separator that is positioned between the message and the action buttons. For more information on the different children of the MessageBox, see the manual page in Section 2, *Motif and Xt Widget Classes*.

## Structures

The possible values for *child* are:

```
XmDIALOG_CANCEL_BUTTON          XmDIALOG_OK_BUTTON
XmDIALOG_DEFAULT_BUTTON         XmDIALOG_SEPARATOR
XmDIALOG_HELP_BUTTON            XmDIALOG_SYMBOL_LABEL
XmDIALOG_MESSAGE_LABEL
```

## See Also

*XmBulletinBoard*(2), *XmErrorDialog*(2), *XmInformationDialog*(2), *XmManager*(2), *XmMessageBox*(2), *XmMessageDialog*(2), *XmQuestionDialog*(2), *XmTemplateDialog*(2), *XmWarningDialog*(2), *XmWorkingDialog*(2).

# XmOptionButtonGadget



## Name

XmOptionButtonGadget – get the CascadeButtonGadget in an option menu.

## Synopsis

```
#include <Xm/RowColumn.h>
Widget XmOptionButtonGadget (option_menu)
    Widget option_menu;
```

### Inputs

*option_menu* Specifies the option menu.

### Returns

The widget ID of the internal CascadeButtonGadget.

## Description

`XmOptionButtonGadget()` returns the widget ID for the internal CascadeButtonGadget that is created when the specified *option_menu* widget is created. An option menu is a RowColumn widget containing two gadgets: a CascadeButtonGadget that displays the current selection and posts the submenu and a LabelGadget that displays the `XmNlabelString` resource.

## Usage

`XmOptionButtonGadget()` provides a way for an application to access the internal CascadeButtonGadget that is part of an option menu. Once you have retrieved the gadget, you can alter its appearance. In Motif 1.2, you can also specify resources for the gadget using the widget name `OptionButton`.

## See Also

*XmOptionLabelGadget*(1),
*XmCascadeButtonGadget*(2), *XmLabelGadget*(2), *XmOptionMenu*(2), *XmRowColumn*(2).

# XmOptionLabelGadget

## Name

XmOptionLabelGadget – get the LabelGadget in an option menu.

## Synopsis

```
#include <Xm/RowColumn.h>
Widget XmOptionLabelGadget (option_menu)
    Widget option_menu;
```

### Inputs

*option_menu* Specifies the option menu.

## Description

`XmOptionLabelGadget()` rturns the widget ID for the internal LabelGadget that is created when the specified *option_menu* widget is created. An option menu is a Row-Column widget containing two gadgets: a LabelGadget that displays the `XmNlabelString` resource, and a CascadeButtonGadget that displays the current selection and posts the sub-menu.

## Usage

`XmOptionLabelGadget()` provides a way for an application to access the internal Label-Gadget that is part of an option menu. Once you have retrieved the gadget, you can alter its appearance. In Motif 1.2, you can also specify resources for the gadget using the widget name `OptionLabel`.

## See Also

*XmOptionButtonGadget*(1),
*XmCascadeButtonGadget*(2), *XmLabelGadget*(2), *XmOptionMenu*(2), *XmRowColumn*(2).

# XmProcessTraversal



## Name

XmProcessTraversal – set the widget that has the keyboard focus.

## Synopsis

```
Boolean XmProcessTraversal (widget, direction)
    Widget widget;
    int direction;
```

### Inputs

*widget* Specifies the widget whose hierarchy is to be traversed.

*direction* Specifies the direction in which to traverse the hierarchy. Pass one of the values from the list below.

### Returns

True on success or False otherwise.

## Description

XmProcessTraversal() causes the input focus to change to another widget under application control, rather than as a result of keyboard traversal events from a user. *widget* specifies the widget whose hierarchy is traversed up to the shell widget. If that shell has the keyboard focus, XmProcessTraversal() changes the keyboard focus immediately. If that shell does not have the focus, the routine does not have an effect until the shell receives the focus.

The *direction* argument specifies the nature of the traversal to be made. In each case, the routine locates the hierarchy that contains the specified *widget* and then performs the action that is particular to the *direction*. If the new setting succeeds, XmProcessTraversal() returns True. The routine returns False if the keyboard focus policy is not XmEXPLICIT, if no traversible items exist, or if the arguments are invalid.

## Usage

For XmTRAVERSE_CURRENT, if the tab group the contains *widget* is inactive, it is made the active tab group. If *widget* is in the active tab group, it is given the keyboard focus; if *widget* is the active tab group, the first traversable item in it is given the keyboard focus. For XmTRAVERSE_UP, XmTRAVERSE_DOWN, XmTRAVERSE_LEFT, and XmTRAVERSE_RIGHT, in the hierarchy that contains *widget*, the item in the specified direction from the active item is given the keyboard focus. For XmTRAVERSE_NEXT and XmTRAVERSE_PREV, in the hierarchy that contains *widget*, the next and previous items in child order from the active item are given keyboard focus. For XmTRAVERSE_HOME, in the hierarchy that contains *widget*, the first traversable item is given the keyboard focus. For XmTRAVERSE_NEXT_TAB_GROUP and XmTRAVERSE_PREV_TAB_GROUP, in the hierarchy that contains *widget*, the next and previous tab groups from the active tab group are given the keyboard focus.

XmProcessTraversal() does not allow traversal to widgets in different shells or widgets that are not mapped. Calling XmProcessTraversal() inside a XmNfocusCallback causes a segmentation fault.

## Example

The following code fragments shows the use of XmProcessTraversal() as a callback routine for a text widget. When the user presses the Return key, the keyboard focus is advanced to the next input area:

```
Widget form, label, text;

form = XtVaCreateWidget("form", xmFormWidgetClass, parent,
    XmNorientation,       XmHORIZONTAL,
    NULL);

label = XtVaCreateManagedWidget("label", xmLabelGadgetClass, form,
    XmNleftAttachment,    XmATTACH_FORM,
    XmNtopAttachment,     XmATTACH_FORM,
    XmNbottomAttachment,  XmATTACH_FORM,
    NULL);

text = XtVaCreateManagedWidget("text", xmTextWidgetClass, form,
    XmNleftAttachment,    XmATTACH_WIDGET,
    XmNleftWidget,        label,
    XmNtopAttachment,     XmATTACH_FORM,
    XmNrightAttachment,   XmATTACH_FORM,
    XmNbottomAttachment,  XmATTACH_FORM,
    NULL);

XtAddCallback(text, XmNactivateCallback,
    XmProcessTraversal, (XtPointer) XmTRAVERSE_NEXT_TAB_GROUP);

XtManageChild(form);
```

## Structures

The possible values for *direction* are:

```
XmTRAVERSE_CURRENT              XmTRAVERSE_NEXT
XmTRAVERSE_UP                   XmTRAVERSE_PREV
XmTRAVERSE_DOWN                 XmTRAVERSE_HOME
XmTRAVERSE_LEFT                 XmTRAVERSE_NEXT_TAB_GROUP
XmTRAVERSE_RIGHT                XmTRAVERSE_PREV_TAB_GROUP
```

## See Also

*XmGetFocusWidget*(1), *XmGetTabGroup*(1), *XmGetVisibility*(1), *XmIsTraversable*(1).

# XmRegisterSegmentEncoding

## Name

XmRegisterSegmentEncoding – register a compound text encoding format for a font list element tag.

## Synopsis

```
char * XmRegisterSegmentEncoding (fontlist_tag, ct_encoding)
    char *fontlist_tag;
    char *ct_encoding;
```

### Inputs

`fontlist_tag`
: Specifies the compound string font list element tag.

`ct_encoding`
: Specifies the compound text character set.

### Returns

The old compound text encoding format for a previously-registered font list element tag or NULL for a new font list element tag.

## Availability

Motif 1.2 and later.

## Description

`XmRegisterSegmentEncoding()` registers the specified compound text encoding format *ct_encoding* for the specified *fontlist_tag*. Both *fontlist_tag* and *ct_encoding* must be NULL-terminated ISO8859-1 strings. If the font list tag is already associated with a compound text encoding format, registering the font list tag again overwrites the previous entry and the routine returns the previous compound text format. If the font list tag is has not been registered before, the routine returns NULL. If *ct_encoding* is NULL, the font list tag is unregistered. If *ct_encoding* is XmFONTLIST_DEFAULT_TAG, the font list tag is mapped to the code set of the current locale. `XmRegisterSegmentEncoding()` allocates storage if the routine returns a character string; the application is responsible for freeing the storage using `XtFree()`.

## Usage

Compound text is an encoding that is designed to represent text from any locale. Compound text strings identify their encoding using embedded escape sequences. The compound text representation was standardized for X11R4 for use as a text interchange format for interclient communication.

`XmCvtXmStringToCT()` converts a compound string into compound text. The routine uses the font list tag of each compound string segment to select a compound text format for the segment. A mapping between font list tags and compound text encoding formats is stored in a registry. `XmRegisterSegmentEncoding()` provides a way for an application to map particular font list element tags to compound text encoding formats.

## See Also

*XmCvtXmStringToCT*(1), *XmMapSegmentEncoding*(1).

# XmRemoveProtocolCallback

## Name

XmRemoveProtocolCallback – remove client callback from a protocol.

## Synopsis

```
#include <Xm/Protocols.h>
void XmRemoveProtocolCallback (shell, property, protocol, callback,
        closure)
    Widget shell;
    Atom property;
    Atom protocol;
    XtCallbackProc callback;
    XtPointer closure;
```

### Inputs

| | |
|---|---|
| *shell* | Specifies the widget associated with the protocol property. |
| *property* | Specifies the property that holds the protocol data. |
| *protocol* | Specifies the protocol atom. |
| *callback* | Specifies the procedure that is to be removed. |
| *closure* | Specifies any client data that is passed to the *callback*. |

## Description

`XmRemoveProtocolCallback()` removes the specified *callback* from the list of callback procedures that are invoked when the client message corresponding to *protocol* is received.

## Usage

A protocol is a communication channel between applications. Protocols are simply atoms, stored in a property on the top-level shell window for the application. To communicate using a protocol, a client sends a `ClientMessage` event containing a property and protocol, and the receiving client responds by calling the associated protocol callback routine. `XmRemoveProtocolCallback()` allows you to unregister one of these callback routines. The inverse routine is `XmAddProtocolCallback()`.

## See Also

*XmAddProtocolCallback*(1), *XmInternAtom*(1), *XmRemoveWMProtocolCallback*(1), *VendorShell*(2).

# XmRemoveProtocols

## Name

XmRemoveProtocols – remove protocols from the protocol manager.

## Synopsis

```
#include <Xm/Protocols.h>
void XmRemoveProtocols (shell, property, protocols, num_protocols)
    Widget shell;
    Atom property;
    Atom *protocols;
    Cardinal num_protocols;
```

### Inputs

*shell* Specifies the widget associated with the protocol property.

*property* Specifies the property that holds the protocol data.

*protocols* Specifies a list of protocol atoms.

*num_protocols*
Specifies the number of atoms in *protocols*.

## Description

XmRemoveProtocols() removes the specified *protocols* from the protocol manager and deallocates the internal tables for the protocols. If the specified *shell* is realized and at least one of the protocols is active, the routine also updates the handlers and the property. The inverse routine is XmAddProtocols().

## Usage

A protocol is a communication channel between applications. Protocols are simply atoms, stored in a property on the top-level shell window for the application. XmRemoveProtocols() allows you eliminate protocols that can be understood by your application. The inverse routine is XmAddProtocols().

## See Also

*XmAddProtocols*(1), *XmInternAtom*(1), *XmRemoveWMProtocols*(1), *VendorShell*(2).

# XmRemoveTabGroup

## Name

XmRemoveTabGroup – remove a widget from a list of tab groups.

## Synopsis

```
void XmRemoveTabGroup (tab_group)
    Widget tab_group;
```

### Inputs

*tab_group* Specifies the widget to be removed.

## Availability

In Motif 1.1, `XmRemoveTabGroup()` is obsolete. It has been superceded by setting `XmNnavigationType` to `XmNONE`.

## Description

`XmRemoveTabGroup()` removes the specified widget from the list of tab groups associated with the widget hierarchy. This routine is retained for compatibility with Motif 1.0 and should not be used in newer applications. If traversal behavior needs to be changed, this should be done by setting the `XmNnavigationType` resource directly.

## Usage

A tab group is a group of widgets that can be traversed using the keyboard rather than the mouse. Users move from widget to widget within a single tab group by pressing the arrow keys. Users move between different tab groups by pressing the Tab or Shift-Tab keys. The inverse routine is `XmAddTabGroup()`.

## See Also

*XmAddTabGroup*(1), *XmGetTabGroup*(1),
*XmManager*(2), *XmPrimitive*(2).

## Name

XmRemoveWMProtocolCallback – remove client callbacks from a XA_WM_PROTOCOLS protocol.

## Synopsis

```
#include <Xm/Protocols.h>
void XmRemoveWMProtocolCallback (shell, protocol, callback, closure)
    Widget shell;
    Atom protocol;
    XtCallbackProc callback;
    XtPointer closure;
```

### Inputs

| | |
|---|---|
| *shell* | Specifies the widget associated with the protocol property. |
| *protocol* | Specifies the protocol atom. |
| *callback* | Specifies the procedure that is to be removed. |
| *closure* | Specifies any client data that is passed to the *callback*. |

## Description

XmRemoveWMProtocolCallback() is a convenience routine that calls XmRemoveProtocolCallback() with *property* set to XA_WM_PROTOCOL, the window manager protocol property.

## Usage

The property XA_WM_PROTOCOLS is a set of predefined protocols for communication between clients and window managers. To communicate using a protocol, a client sends a ClientMessage event containing a property and protocol, and the receiving client responds by calling the associated protocol callback routine. XmRemoveWMProtocolCallback() allows you to unregister one of these callback routines with the window manager protocol property. The inverse routine is XmAddWMProtocolCallback().

## See Also

*XmAddProtocolCallback*(1), *XmAddWMProtocolCallback*(1), *XmInternAtom*(1), *XmRemoveProtocolCallback*(1), *VendorShell*(2).

Motif Functions and Macros

# XmRemoveWMProtocols

## Name

XmRemoveWMProtocols – remove the XA_WM_PROTOCOLS protocols from the protocol manager.

## Synopsis

```
#include <Xm/Protocols.h>
void XmRemoveWMProtocols (shell, protocols, num_protocols)
    Widget shell;
    Atom *protocols;
    Cardinal num_protocols;
```

### Inputs

*shell* Specifies the widget associated with the protocol property.

*protocols* Specifies a list of protocol atoms.

*num_protocols*
Specifies the number of atoms in *protocols*.

## Description

XmRemoveWMProtocols() is a convenience routine that calls XmRemoveProtocols() with *property* set to XA_WM_PROTOCOL, the window manager protocol property. The inverse routine is XmAddWMProtocols().

## Usage

The property XA_WM_PROTOCOLS is a set of predefined protocols for communication between clients and window managers. XmRemoveWMProtocols() allows you to remove this protocol so that it is no longer understood by your application. The inverse routine is XmAddWMProtocols().

## See Also

*XmAddProtocols*(1), *XmAddWMProtocols*(1), *XmInternAtom*(1), *XmRemoveProtocols*(1), *VendorShell*(2).

# XmRepTypeAddReverse

## Name

XmRepTypeAddReverse – install the reverse converter for a representation type.

## Synopsis

```
#include <Xm/RepType.h>
void XmRepTypeAddReverse (rep_type_id)
    XmRepTypeId rep_type_id;
```

### Inputs

*rep_type_id* Specifies the ID number of the representation type.

## Availability

Motif 1.2 and later.

## Description

`XmRepTypeAddReverse()` installs a reverse converter for a previously registered representation type. The reverse converter converts numerical representation type values to string values. The *rep_type_id* argument specifies the ID number of the representation type. If the representation type contains duplicate values, the reverse converter uses the first name in the `value_names` list that matches the specified numeric value.

## Usage

In Motif 1.2, the representation type manager provides support for handling many of the tasks related to enumerated values. This facility installs resource converters that convert a string value to its numerical representation. The representation type manager can also be queried to get information about the registered types. This facility is especially useful for interface builders and applications like *editres* that allow a user to set resources interactively. `XmRepTypeAddReverse()` provides a way for an application to install a converter that converts numeric values to their string values.

## See Also

*XmRepTypeGetId*(1), *XmRepTypeRegister*(1).

# XmRepTypeGetId

## Name

XmRepTypeGetId – get the ID number of a representation type.

## Synopsis

```
#include <Xm/RepType.h>
XmRepTypeId XmRepTypeGetId (rep_type)
    String rep_type;
```

### Inputs

*rep_type* Specifies the string name of a representation type.

### Returns

The ID number of the representation type or XmREP_TYPE_INVALID if the representation type is not registered.

## Availability

Motif 1.2 and later.

## Description

XmRepTypeGetId() retrieves the ID number of the specified representation type *rep_type* from the representation type manager. The *rep_type* string is the string name of a representation type that has been registered with XmRepTypeRegister(). XmRepTypeGetId() returns the ID number if the representation type has been registered. This value is used in other representation type manager routines to identify a particular type. Otherwise, the routine returns XmREP_TYPE_INVALID.

## Usage

In Motif 1.2, the representation type manager provides support for handling many of the tasks related to enumerated values. This facility installs resource converters that convert a string value to its numerical representation. The representation type manager can also be queried to get information about the registered types. This facility is especially useful for interface builders and applications like *editres* that allow a user to set resources interactively. XmRepTypeGetId() provides a way for an application get the ID of a representation type, which can be used to identify the type to other representation mananger routine.

## See Also

*XmRepTypeGetNameList*(1), *XmRepTypeGetRecord*(1), *XmRepTypeGetRegistered*(1), *XmRepTypeRegister*(1).

# XmRepTypeGetNameList

## Name

XmRepTypeGetNameList – get the list of value names for a representation type.

## Synopsis

```
#include <Xm/RepType.h>
String * XmRepTypeGetNameList (rep_type_id, use_uppercase_format)
    XmRepTypeId rep_type_id;
    Boolean use_uppercase_format;
```

### Inputs

*rep_type_id* Specifies the ID number of the representation type.

*use_uppercase_format*
Specifies whether or not the names are in uppercase characters.

### Returns

A pointer to an array of value names.

## Availability

Motif 1.2 and later.

## Description

XmRepTypeGetNameList() retrieves the list of value names associated with the specified *rep_type_id*. The routine returns a pointer to a NULL-terminated list of value names for the representation type, where each value name is a NULL-terminated string. If *use_uppercase_format* is True, the value names are in uppercase characters with Xm prefixes. Otherwise, the value names are in lowercase characters without Xm prefixes. XmRepTypeGetNameList() allocates storage for the returned data. The application is responsible for freeing the storage using XtFree().

## Usage

In Motif 1.2, the representation type manager provides support for handling many of the tasks related to enumerated values. This facility installs resource converters that convert a string value to its numerical representation. The representation type manager can also be queried to get information about the registered types. This facility is especially useful for interface builders and applications like *editres* that allow a user to set resources interactively. XmRepTypeGetNameList() provides a way for an application to get the named values for a particular representation type.

## See Also

*XmRepTypeGetId*(1), *XmRepTypeGetRecord*(1), *XmRepTypeGetRegistered*(1), *XmRepTypeRegister*(1).

# XmRepTypeGetRecord

## Name

XmRepTypeGetRecord – get information about a representation type.

## Synopsis

```
#include <Xm/RepType.h>
XmRepTypeEntry XmRepTypeGetRecord (rep_type_id)
    XmRepTypeId rep_type_id;
```

### Inputs

*rep_type_id* Specifies the ID number of the representation type.

### Returns

A pointer to a representation type entry structure.

## Availability

Motif 1.2 and later.

## Description

`XmRepTypeGetRecord()` retrieves information about the representation type specified by *rep_type_id*. The routine returns a `XmRepTypeEntry`, which is a pointer to a representation type entry structure. This structure contains information about the value names and values for the enumerated type. `XmRepTypeGetRecord()` allocates storage for the returned data. The application is responsible for freeing the storage using `XtFree()`.

## Usage

In Motif 1.2, the representation type manager provides support for handling many of the tasks related to enumerated values. This facility installs resource converters that convert a string value to its numerical representation. The representation type manager can also be queried to get information about the registered types. This facility is especially useful for interface builders and applications like *editres* that allow a user to set resources interactively. `XmRepTypeGetRecord()` provides a way for an application to retrieve information about a particular representation type.

## Structures

The `XmRepTypeEntry` is defined as follows:

```
typedef struct {
    String         rep_type_name;      /* name of representation type */
    String         *value_names;       /* array of value names */
    unsigned char  *values;            /* array of numeric values */
    unsigned char  num_values;         /* number of values */
    Boolean        reverse_installed;  /* reverse converter installed flag */
    XmRepTypeId    rep_type_id;        /* representation type ID /*
} XmRepTypeEntryRec, *XmRepTypeEntry, XmRepTypeListRec, *XmRepTypeList;
```

## See Also

*XmRepTypeGetId*(1), *XmRepTypeGetNameList*(1), *XmRepTypeGetRegistered*(1), *XmRepTypeRegister*(1).

# XmRepTypeGetRegistered



## Name

XmRepTypeGetRegistered – get the registered representation types.

## Synopsis

```
#include <Xm/RepType.h>
XmRepTypeList XmRepTypeGetRegistered ()
```

### Returns

A pointer to the registration list of representation types.

## Availability

Motif 1.2 and later.

## Description

`XmRepTypeGetRegistered()` retrieves the whole registration list for the representation type manager. The routine returns a copy of the registration list, which contains information about all of the registered representation types. The registration list is an array of `XmRepTypeList` structures, where each structure contains information about the value names and values for a single representation type. The end of the registration list is indicated by a `NULL` pointer in the `rep_type_name` field. `XmRepTypeGetRegistered` allocates storage for the returned data. The application is responsible for freeing this storage using `XtFree()`. The list of value names (the value of the `value_names` field), the list of values (the value of the `values` field), and the array of structures all need to be freed.

## Usage

In Motif 1.2, the representation type manager provides support for handling many of the tasks related to enumerated values. This facility installs resource converters that convert a string value to its numerical representation. The representation type manager can also be queried to get information about the registered types. This facility is especially useful for interface builders and applications like *editres* that allow a user to set resources interactively. `XmRepTypeGetRegistered()` provides a way for an application to get information about all of the registered representation types.

## Example

The following code fragment shows the use of `XmRepTypeGetRegistered()` to print the value names and values of all of the registered representation types:

```
XmRepTypeList replist;
int i;

replist = XmRepTypeGetRegistered();
while (replist->rep_type_name != NULL) {
    printf("Representation type name: %s\n", replist->rep_type_name);
    printf("Value names and associated values: \n");
    for (i = 0; i < replist->num_values; i++) {
        printf("%s: ", replist->value_names[i]);
```

```
            printf("%d\n", replist->values[i]);
        }
        replist++;
        XtFree((char *)replist->values);
        XtFree((char *)replist->value_names);
    }
    XtFree((char *)replist);
```

## Structures

The XmRepTypeList is defined as follows:

```
typedef struct {
    String          rep_type_name;      /* name of representation type */
    String          *value_names;       /* array of value names */
    unsigned char   *values;            /* array of numeric values */
    unsigned char   num_values;         /* number of values */
    Boolean         reverse_installed;  /* reverse converter installed flag */
    XmRepTypeId     rep_type_id;        /* representation type ID /*
} XmRepTypeEntryRec, *XmRepTypeEntry, XmRepTypeListRec, *XmRepTypeList;
```

## See Also

*XmRepTypeGetRecord*(1), *XmRepTypeGetNameList*(1), *XmRepTypeRegister*(1).

## Name

XmRepTypeInstallTearOffModelConverter – install the resource converter for `XmNtearOffModel`.

## Synopsis

```
#include <Xm/RepType.h>
void XmRepTypeInstallTearOffModelConverter ()
```

## Availability

Motif 1.2 and later.

## Description

`XmRepTypeInstallTearOffModelConverter()` installs the resource converter for the RowColumn `XmNtearOffModel` resource. This resource controls whether or not PulldownMenus and PopupMenus in an application can be torn off. Once the converter is installed, the value of `XmNtearOffModel` can be specified in a resource file.

## Usage

In Motif 1.2, a RowColumn that is configured as a PopupMenu or a PulldownMenu supports tear-off menus. When a menu is torn off, it remains on the screen after a selection is made so that additional selections can be made. A menu pane that can be torn off contains a tear-off button at the top of the menu. The `XmNtearOffModel` resource controls whether or not tear-off functionality is available for a menu. This resource can take the values `XmTEAR_OFF_ENABLED` or `XmTEAR_OFF_DISABLED`.

The resource converter for `XmNtearOffModel` is not installed by default. Some existing applications depend on receiving a callback when a menu is mapped; since torn-off menus are always mapped, these applications might fail if a user is allowed to enable tear-off menus from a resource file. `XmRepTypeInstallTearOffModelConverter()` registers the converter that allows the resource to be set from a resource file.

## See Also

*XmRowColumn*(2).

# XmRepTypeRegister

## Name

XmRepTypeRegister – register a representation type resource.

## Synopsis

```
#include <Xm/RepType.h>
XmRepTypeId XmRepTypeRegister (rep_type, value_names, values, num_values)
    String rep_type;
    String *value_names;
    unsigned char *values;
    unsigned char num_values;
```

### Inputs

| | |
|---|---|
| *rep_type* | Specifies the string name for the representation type. |
| *value_names* | Specifies an array of value names for the representation type. |
| *values* | Specifies an array of values for the representation type. |
| *num_values* | Specifies the number of items in *value_names* and *values*. |

### Returns

The ID number of the representation type.

## Availability

Motif 1.2 and later.

## Description

XmRepTypeRegister() registers a representation type with the representation type manager. The representation type manager provides resource conversion facilities for enumerated values. XmRepTypeRegister() installs a resource converter that converts string values to numerical representation type values. The strings in the *value_names* array specify the value names for the representation type. The strings are specified in lowercase characters, with underscore characters separating words and without Xm prefixes.

If the *values* argument is NULL, the order of the strings in the *value_names* array determines the numerical values for the enumerated type. In this case, the names are assigned consecutive values starting with 0 (zero). If *values* is non-NULL, it is used to assign values to the names. Each name in the *value_names* array is assigned the corresponding value in the *values* array, so it is possible to have nonconsecutive values or duplicate names for the same value.

XmRepTypeRegister() returns the ID number that is assigned to the representation type. This value is used in other representation type manager routines to identify a particular type. A representation type can only be registered once. If a type is registered more than once, the behavior of the representation type manager is undefined.

## Usage

In Motif 1.2, the representation type manager provides support for handling many of the tasks related to enumerated values. This facility installs resource converters that convert a string value to its numerical representation. The representation type manager can also be queried to get information about the registered types. This facility is especially useful for interface builders and applications like *editres* that allow a user to set resources interactively. `XmRepTypeRegister()` provides a way for an application to register representation types for application-specific resources or for new widget classes.

## See Also

*XmRepTypeAddReverse*(1), *XmRepTypeGetId*(1), *XmRepTypeGetNameList*(1), *XmRepTypeGetRecord*(1), *XmRepTypeGetRegistered*(1), *XmRepTypeValidValue*(1).

# XmRepTypeValidValue

## Name

XmRepTypeValidValue – determine the validity of a numerical value for a representation type.

## Synopsis

```
#include <Xm/RepType.h>
Boolean XmRepTypeValidValue (rep_type_id, test_value, enable_default_-
        warning)
    XmRepTypeId rep_type_id;
    unsigned char test_value;
    Widget enable_default_warning;
```

### Inputs

*rep_type_id* Specifies the ID number of the representation type.

*test_value* Specifies the value that is to be tested.

*enable_default_warning*
Specifies a widget that is used to generate a default warning message.

### Returns

`True` if the specified value is valid or `False` otherwise.

## Availability

Motif 1.2 and later.

## Description

`XmRepTypeValidValue()` checks the validity of the specified *test_value* for the representation type specified by *rep_type_id*. The routine returns `True` if the value is valid. Otherwise, it returns `False`. If the *enable_default_warning* parameter is non-NULL, `XmRepTypeValidValue()` uses the specified widget to generate a default warning message if the value is invalid. If *enable_default_warning* is NULL, no default warning message is provided.

## Usage

In Motif 1.2, the representation type manager provides support for handling many of the tasks related to enumerated values. This facility installs resource converters that convert a string value to its numerical representation. The representation type manager can also be queried to get information about the registered types. This facility is especially useful for interface builders and applications like *editres* that allow a user to set resources interactively. `XmRepTypeValidValue()` provides a way for an application to check if a value is valid for a particular representation type.

## See Also

*XmRepTypeGetId*(1), *XmRepTypeRegister*(1).

# XmResolveAllPartOffsets



## Name

XmResolveAllPartOffsets – ensure upward-compatible widgets and applications.

## Synopsis

```
void XmResolveAllPartOffsets (widget_class, offset, constraint_offset)
    WidgetClass widget_class;
    XmOffsetPtr *offset;
    XmOffsetPtr *constraint_offset;
```

### Inputs

*widget_class*
: Specifies the widget class pointer.

### Outputs

*offset* Returns the widget offset record.

*constraint_offset*
: Returns the constraint offset record.

## Description

`XmResolveAllPartOffsets()` ensures that an application or a widget will be upwardly compatible with the records in a widget structure. In other words, if the size of a widget structure changes in the future, this routine can be used to calculate the locations of the new offsets. This routine and `XmResolvePartOffsets()` are similar. During the creation of a widget, both routines modify the widget structure by allocating an array of offset values. `XmResolvePartOffsets()` affects only the widget instance record, while `XmResolveAllPartOffsets()` affects the widget instance and constraint records.

## Usage

If you are subclassing a Motif widget, you should use `XmResolveAllPartOffsets()` and `XmResolvePartOffsets()` to ensure that your widget will be compatible with future releases of the toolkit.

## See Also

*XmResolvePartOffsets*(1).

# XmResolvePartOffsets

## Name

XmResolvePartOffsets – ensure upward-compatible widgets and applications.

## Synopsis

```
void XmResolvePartOffsets (widget_class, offset)
    WidgetClass widget_class;
    XmOffsetPtr *offset;
```

### Inputs

*widget_class*
Specifies the widget class pointer.

### Outputs

*offset* Returns the widget offset record.

## Description

`XmResolvePartOffsets()` ensures that an application or a widget will be upwardly compatible with the records in a widget structure. In other words, if the size of a widget structure changes in the future, this routine can be used to calculate the locations of the new offsets. This routine and `XmResolveAllPartOffsets()` are similar. During the creation of a widget, both routines modify the widget structure by allocating an array of offset values. `XmResolvePartOffsets()` affects only the widget instance record, while `XmResolveAllPartOffsets()` affects the widget instance and constraint records.

## Usage

If you are subclassing a Motif widget, you should use `XmResolvePartOffsets()` and `XmResolveAllPartOffsets()` to ensure that your widget will be compatible with future releases of the toolkit.

## See Also

*XmResolveAllPartOffsets*(1).

# XmScaleGetValue

## Name

XmScaleGetValue – get the slider value for a Scale widget.

## Synopsis

```
#include <Xm/Scale.h>
void XmScaleGetValue (widget, value_return)
    Widget widget;
    int *value_return;
```

### Inputs

*widget* Specifies the Scale widget.

### Outputs

*value_return*
Returns the current slider position for the Scale.

## Description

`XmScaleGetValue()` returns the current position of the slider within the specified Scale *widget*.

## Usage

`XmScaleGetValue()` is a convenience routine that returns the value of the `XmNvalue` resource for the Scale widget. Calling the routine is equivalent to calling `XtGetValues()` for that resource, although `XmScaleGetValue()` accesses the value through the widget instance structure rather than through `XtGetValues()`.

## See Also

*XmScaleSetValue*(1),
*XmScale*(2).

# XmScaleSetValue

## Name

XmScaleSetValue – set the slider value for a Scale widget.

## Synopsis

```
#include <Xm/Scale.h>
void XmScaleSetValue (widget, value)
    Widget widget;
    int value;
```

### Inputs

| | |
|---|---|
| *widget* | Specifies the Scale widget. |
| *value* | Specifies the value of the slider. |

## Description

`XmScaleSetValue()` sets the current position of the slider to *value* in the specified Scale *widget*. The *value* must be in the range `XmNminimum` to `XmNmaximum`.

## Usage

`XmScaleSetValue()` is a convenience routine that sets the value of the `XmNvalue` resource for the Scale widget. Calling the routine is equivalent to calling `XtSetValues()` for that resource, although `XmScaleSetValue()` accesses the value through the widget instance structure rather than through `XtSetValues()`.

## See Also

*XmScaleGetValue*(1),
*XmScale*(2).

# XmScrollBarGetValues

## Name

XmScrollBarGetValues – get information about the current state of a ScrollBar widget.

## Synopsis

```
#include <Xm/ScrollBar.h>
void XmScrollBarGetValues (widget, value_return, slider_size_return,
        increment_return, page_increment_return)
    Widget widget;
    int *value_return;
    int *slider_size_return;
    int *increment_return;
    int *page_increment_return;
```

### Inputs

*widget* Specifies the ScrollBar widget.

### Outputs

*value_return*
Returns the current slider position.

*slider_size_return*
Returns the current size of the slider.

*increment_return*
Returns the current increment and decrement level.

*page_increment_return*
Returns the current page increment and decrement level.

## Description

`XmScrollBarGetValues()` returns the current state information for the specified ScrollBar *widget*. This information consists of the position and size of the slider, as well as the increment and page increment values.

## Usage

`XmScrollBarGetValues()` is a convenience routine that returns the values of the `XmNvalue`, `XmNsliderSize`, `XmNincrement`, and `XmNpageIncrement` resources for the ScrollBar widget. Calling the routine is equivalent to calling `XtGetValues()` for those resources, although `XmScrollBarGetValues()` accesses the values through the widget instance structure rather than through `XtGetValues()`.

## See Also

*XmScrollBarSetValues*(1),
*XmScrollBar*(2).

# XmScrollBarSetValues

## Name

XmScrollBarSetValues – set the current state of a ScrollBar widget.

## Synopsis

```
#include <Xm/ScrollBar.h>
void XmScrollBarSetValues (widget, value, slider_size, increment,
        page_increment, notify)
    Widget widget;
    int value;
    int slider_size;
    int increment;
    int page_increment;
    Boolean notify;
```

### Inputs

*widget* Specifies the ScrollBar widget.

*value* Specifies the slider position.

*slider_size* Specifies the size of the slider.

*increment* Specifies the increment and decrement level.

*page_increment*
Specifies the page increment and decrement level.

*notify* Specifies whether or not the value changed callback is invoked.

## Description

XmScrollBarSetValues() sets the current state of the specified ScrollBar *widget*. The position of the slider is set to *value*, which must be in the range XmNminimum to XmNmaximum minus XmNsliderSize. The size of the slider is set to *slider_size*, which must be between 1 and the size of the scroll region. The increment and page increment values are set to *increment* and *page_increment*, respectively. If *notify* is True, XmScrollBarSetValues() invokes the XmNvalueChangedCallback for the ScrollBar when the state is set.

## Usage

XmScrollBarSetValues() is a convenience routine that sets the values of the XmNvalue, XmNsliderSize, XmNincrement, and XmNpageIncrement resources for the ScrollBar widget. Calling the routine is equivalent to calling XtSetValues() for those resources, although XmScrollBarSetValues() accesses the values through the widget instance structure rather than through XtSetValues().

The *notify* parameter indicates whether or not the value changed callbacks for the ScrollBar are invoked. You can avoid redundant code by setting this parameter to True. If you are calling XmScrollBarSetValues() from a value changed callback routine, you probably want to set the parameter to False to avoid the possibility of an infinite loop. Calling

`XmScrollBarSetValues()` with *notify* set to `True` causes the callback routines to be invoked in a way that is indistinguishable from a user-initiated adjustment to the ScrollBar.

## See Also

*XmScrollBarGetValues*(1),
*XmScrollBar*(2).

# XmScrollVisible

## Name

XmScrollVisible – make an obscured child of a ScrolledWindow visible.

## Synopsis

```
#include <Xm/ScrolledW.h>
void XmScrollVisible (scrollw_widget, widget, left_right_margin,
        top_bottom_margin)
    Widget scrollw_widget;
    Widget widget;
    Dimension left_right_margin;
    Dimension top_bottom_margin;
```

### Inputs

*scrollw_widget*
: Specifies the ScrolledWindow widget.

*widget*
: Specifies the widget ID of the widget that is to be made visible.

*left_right_margin*
: Specifies the distance between the *widget* and the left or right edge of the viewport if the ScrolledWindow is scrolled horizontally.

*top_bottom_margin*
: Specifies the distance between the *widget* and the top or bottom edge of the viewport if the ScrolledWindow is scrolled vertically.

## Availability

Motif 1.2 and later.

## Description

XmScrollVisible() scrolls the specified ScrolledWindow *scrollw_widget* so that the obscured or partially obscured *widget* becomes visible in the work area viewport. *widget* must be a descendent of *scrollw_widget*. The routine repositions the work area of the ScrolledWindow and sets the margins between the widget and the viewport boundaries based on *left_right_margin* and *top_bottom_margin* if necessary.

## Usage

XmScrollVisible() provides a way for an application to ensure that a particular child of a ScrolledWindow is visible. In order for the routine to work, the XmNscrollingPolicy of the ScrolledWindow widget must be set to XmAUTOMATIC. This routine is designed to be used in the XmNtraverseObscureCallback for a ScrolledWindow.

## See Also

*XmScrolledWindow*(2).

# XmScrolledWindowSetAreas



### Name

XmScrolledWindowSetAreas – specify the children for a scrolled window.

### Synopsis

```
#include <Xm/ScrolledW.h>
void XmScrolledWindowSetAreas (widget, horizontal_scrollbar,
        vertical_scrollbar, work_region)
    Widget widget;
    Widget horizontal_scrollbar;
    Widget vertical_scrollbar;
    Widget work_region;
```

#### Inputs

*widget* Specifies the ScrolledWindow widget.

*horizontal_scrollbar*
Specifies the widget ID of the horizontal ScrollBar.

*vertical_scrollbar*
Specifies the widget ID of the vertical ScrollBar.

*work_region* Specifies the widget ID of the work window.

### Description

XmScrolledWindowSetAreas() sets up the standard regions of a ScrolledWindow widget for an application. The ScrolledWindow must be created before the routine is called. XmScrolledWindowSetAreas() specifies the horizontal and vertical ScrollBars and the work window region. If a particular ScrolledWindow does not have one of these regions, the corresponding argument can be specified as NULL.

### Usage

Each of the ScrolledWindow regions is associated with a ScrolledWindow resource; XmScrolledWindowSetAreas() sets the associated resources. The resources that correspond to the last three arguments to the routine are XmNhorizontalScrollBar, XmNverticalScrollBar, and XmNworkWindow, respectively.

If an application does not call XmScrolledWindowSetAreas(), the widget may still set some of the standard regions. If ScrollBars are added as children, the XmNhorizontalScrollBar and XmNverticalScrollBar resources may be set if they have not already been specified. Any child that is not a ScrollBar is used for the XmNworkWindow. If you want to be certain about which widgets are used for the different regions, it is wise to call XmScrolledWindowSetAreas() explicitly.

### Example

The following code fragment shows how to set the regions of a ScrolledWindow:

```
Widget      toplevel, scrolled_w, drawing_a, vsb, hsb;
int         view_width, view_height;
```

```
scrolled_w = XtVaCreateManagedWidget ("scrolled_w",
    xmScrolledWindowWidgetClass, toplevel,
    XmNscrollingPolicy, XmAPPLICATION_DEFINED,
    XmNvisualPolicy,    XmVARIABLE,
    NULL);

drawing_a = XtVaCreateManagedWidget ("drawing_a",
    xmDrawingAreaWidgetClass, scrolled_w,
    XmNwidth,        view_width,
    XmNheight,       view_height,
    NULL);

vsb = XtVaCreateManagedWidget ("vsb", xmScrollBarWidgetClass, scrolled_w,
    XmNorientation, XmVERTICAL,
    NULL);

hsb = XtVaCreateManagedWidget ("hsb", xmScrollBarWidgetClass, scrolled_w,
    XmNorientation, XmHORIZONTAL,
    NULL);

XmScrolledWindowSetAreas (scrolled_w, hsb, vsb, drawing_a);
```

## See Also

*XmScrolledWindow*(2).

Motif Functions and Macros

# XmSelectionBoxGetChild

## Name

XmSelectionBoxGetChild – get the specified child of a SelectionBox widget.

## Synopsis

```
#include <Xm/SelectioB.h>
Widget XmSelectionBoxGetChild (widget, child)
    Widget widget;
    unsigned char child;
```

### Inputs

*widget* Specifies the SelectionBox widget.

*child* Specifies the child of the SelectionBox widget. Pass one of the values from the list below.

### Returns

The widget ID of the specified child of the SelectionBox.

## Description

XmSelectionBoxGetChild() returns the widget ID of the specified *child* of the SelectionBox widget.

## Usage

XmDIALOG_APPLY_BUTTON, XmDIALOG_CANCEL_BUTTON, XmDIALOG_HELP_-BUTTON, and XmDIALOG_OK_BUTTON specify the action buttons in the widget. XmDIALOG_DEFAULT_BUTTON specifies the current default button. XmDIALOG_LIST and XmDIALOG_LIST_LABEL specify the list and its label. XmDIALOG_TEXT and Xm-DIALOG_SELECTION_LABEL specify the selection text entry area and its label. XmDIALOG_SEPARATOR specifies the separator and XmDIALOG_WORK_AREA specifies any work area child that has been added to the SelectionBox. For more information on the different children of the SelectionBox, see the manual page in Section 2, *Motif and Xt Widget Classes*.

## Structures

The possible values for *child* are:

XmDIALOG_APPLY_BUTTON
XmDIALOG_CANCEL_BUTTON
XmDIALOG_DEFAULT_BUTTON
XmDIALOG_HELP_BUTTON
XmDIALOG_LIST
XmDIALOG_LIST_LABEL
XmDIALOG_OK_BUTTON
XmDIALOG_SELECTION_LABEL
XmDIALOG_SEPARATOR
XmDIALOG_TEXT
XmDIALOG_WORK_AREA

## See Also

*XmPromptDialog*(2), *XmSelectionBox*(2).

# XmSetColorCalculation

## Name

XmSetColorCalculation – set the procedure that calculates default colors.

## Synopsis

```
XmColorProc XmSetColorCalculation (color_proc)
    XmColorProc color_proc;
```

### Inputs

`color_proc` Specifies the procedure that is used for color calculation.

### Returns

The previous color calculation procedure.

## Description

`XmSetColorCalculation()` sets the procedure called by that calculates the default foreground, top and bottom shadow, and selection colors. The procedure calculates these colors based on the background color that has been passed to the procedure. If *color_proc* is `NULL`, this routine restores the default color calculation procedure. `XmSetColorCalculation()` returns the color calculation procedure that was in use when the routine was called. Both `XmGetColors()` and `XmChangeColor()` use the color calculation procedure.

## Usage

Motif widgets rely on the use of shadowed borders to create their three-dimensional appearance. The top and bottom shadow colors are lighter and darker shades of the background color; these colors are reversed to make a component appear raised out of the screen or recessed into the screen. The select color is a slightly darker shade of the background color that indicates that a component is selected. The foreground color is either black or white, depending on which color provides the most contrast with the background color. `XmSetColorCalculation()` sets the procedure that calculates these colors. Use `XmGetColorCalculation()` to get the default color calculation procedure.

## Procedures

The `XmColorProc` has the following syntax:

```
typedef void (*XmColorProc) (XColor, XColor, XColor, XColor, XColor)
    XColor *bg_color;    /* specifies the background color */
    XColor *fg_color;    /* returns the foreground color */
    XColor *sel_color;   /* returns the select color */
    XColor *ts_color;    /* returns the top shadow color */
    XColor *bs_color;    /* returns the bottom shadow color */
```

An `XmColorProc` takes five arguments. The first argument, *bg_color*, is a pointer to an `XColor` structure that specifies the background color. The `red`, `green`, `blue`, and `pixel` fields in the structure contain valid values. The rest of the arguments are pointers to `XColor` structures for the colors that are to be calculated. The procedure fills in the `red`, `green`, and `blue` fields in these structures.

## See Also

*XmChangeColor*(1), *XmGetColorCalculation*(1), *XmGetColors*(1).

# XmSetFontUnit

## Name

XmSetFontUnit – set the font unit values.

## Synopsis

```
void XmSetFontUnit (display, font_unit_value)
    Display *display;
    int font_unit_value;
```

### Inputs

*display* Specifies a connection to an X server; returned from `XOpenDisplay()` or `XtDisplay()`.

*font_unit_value*
Specifies the value for both horizontal and vertical font units.

## Availability

In Motif 1.2, `XmSetFontUnit()` is obsolete. It has been superceded by setting the Screen resources `XmNhorizontalFontUnit` and `XmNverticalFontUnit`.

## Description

`XmSetFontUnit()` sets the value of the horizontal and vertical font units for all of the screens on the display. This routine is retained for compatibility with Motif 1.1 and should not be used in newer applications.

## Usage

Font units are a resolution-independent unit of measurement that are based on the width and height characteristics of a particular font. The default horizontal and vertical font unit values are based on the `XmNfont` resource, which in Motif 1.2, is a resource of the Screen object. An application can override these default values by calling `XmSetFontUnit()`. The values should be set before any widgets that use resolution-independent data are created.

## See Also

*XmConvertUnits*(1), *XmSetFontUnits*(1),
*XmGadget*(2), *XmManager*(2), *XmPrimitive*(2), *XmScreen*(2).

# XmSetFontUnits

## Name

XmSetFontUnits – set the font unit values.

## Synopsis

```
void XmSetFontUnits (display, h_value, v_value)
    Display *display;
    int h_value;
    int v_value;
```

### Inputs

| | |
|---|---|
| *display* | Specifies a connection to an X server; returned from `XOpenDisplay()` or `XtDisplay()`. |
| *h_value* | Specifies the value for horizontal font units. |
| *v_value* | Specifies the value for vertical font units. |

## Availability

In Motif 1.2, `XmSetFontUnits()` is obsolete. It has been superceded by setting the Screen resources `XmNhorizontalFontUnit` and `XmNverticalFontUnit`.

## Description

`XmSetFontUnits()` sets the value of the horizontal and vertical font units to *h_value* and *v_value* respectively. The routine sets the font units for all of the screens on the display. This routine is retained for compatibility with Motif 1.1 and should not be used in newer applications.

## Usage

Font units are a resolution-independent unit of measurement that are based on the width and height characteristics of a particular font. The default horizontal and vertical font unit values are based on the `XmNfont` resource, which in Motif 1.2, is a resource of the Screen object. An application can override these default values by calling `XmSetFontUnits()`. The values should be set before any widgets that use resolution-independent data are created.

## See Also

*XmConvertUnits*(1), *XmSetFontUnit*(1),
*XmGadget*(2), *XmManager*(2), *XmPrimitive*(2), *XmScreen*(2).

# XmSetMenuCursor

## Name

XmSetMenuCursor – set the current menu cursor.

## Synopsis

```
void XmSetMenuCursor (display, cursorId)
    Display *display;
    Cursor cursorId;
```

### Inputs

*display* Specifies a connection to an X server; returned from `XOpenDisplay()` or `XtDisplay()`.

*cursorId* Specifies the cursor ID for the menu cursor.

## Availability

In Motif 1.2, `XmSetMenuCursor()` is obsolete. It has been superceded by setting the Screen resource `XmNmenuCursor`.

## Description

`XmSetMenuCursor()` sets the menu cursor for an application. The routine sets the cursor for all screens on the specified *display*. The specified cursor is shown whenever the application is using a Motif menu on the specified *display*. This routine is retained for compatibility with Motif 1.1 and should not be used in newer applications.

## Usage

The menu cursor is the pointer shape that is used whenever a menu is posted. This cursor can be different from the normal pointer shape. In Motif 1.2, the new Screen object has a resource, `XmNmenuCursor`, that specifies the menu cursor. `XmSetMenuCursor()` is retained for compatibility with Motif 1.1 and should not be used in newer applications.

## See Also

*XmGetMenuCursor*(1),
*XmScreen*(2).

# XmSetProtocolHooks

## Name

XmSetProtocolHooks – set prehooks and posthooks for a protocol.

## Synopsis

```
#include <Xm/Protocols.h>
void XmSetProtocolHooks (shell, property, protocol, prehook, pre_closure,
        posthook, post_closure)
    Widget shell;
    Atom property;
    Atom protocol;
    XtCallbackProc prehook;
    XtPointer pre_closure;
    XtCallbackProc posthook;
    XtPointer post_closure;
```

### Inputs

*shell* Specifies the widget associated with the protocol property.

*property* Specifies the property that holds the protocol data.

*protocol* Specifies the protocol atom.

*prehook* Specifies the procedure to invoke before the client callbacks.

*pre_closure* Specifies any client data that is passed to the *prehook*.

*posthook* Specifies the procedure to invoke after the client callbacks.

*post_closure*
Specifies any client data that is passed to the *posthook*.

## Description

`XmSetProtocolHooks()` allows pre- and post-procedures to be invoked in addition to the regular callback procedures that are performed when the Motif window mangager sends a protocol message. The *prehook* procedure is invoked before calling the procedures on the client's callback list, whereas the *posthook* procedure is invoked after calling the procedures on the client's callback list. This routine gives shells more control flow, since callback procedures aren't necessarily executed in any particular order.

## Usage

A protocol is a communication channel between applications. Protocols are simply atoms, stored in a property on the top-level shell window for the application. To communicate using a protocol, a client sends a `ClientMessage` event containing a property and protocol, and the receiving client responds by calling the associated protocol callback routine. `XmSetProtocolHooks()` gives an application more control over the flow of callback procedures, since callbacks are not necessarily invoked in any particular order.

### See Also

*XmAddProtocolCallback*(1), *XmRemoveProtocolCallback*(1), *XmSetWMProtocolHooks*(1), *VendorShell*(2).

# XmSetWMProtocolHooks

## Name

XmSetWMProtocolHooks – set prehooks and posthooks for the XA_WM_PROTOCOLS protocol.

## Synopsis

```
#include <Xm/Protocols.h>
void XmSetWMProtocolHooks (shell, protocol, prehook, pre_closure, posthook,
        post_closure)
    Widget shell;
    Atom protocol;
    XtCallbackProc prehook;
    XtPointer pre_closure;
    XtCallbackProc posthook;
    XtPointer post_closure;
```

### Inputs

*shell* Specifies the widget associated with the protocol property.

*protocol* Specifies the protocol atom.

*prehook* Specifies the procedure to invoke before the client callbacks.

*pre_closure* Specifies any client data that is passed to the *prehook*.

*posthook* Specifies the procedure to invoke after the client callbacks.

*post_closure*
Specifies any client data that is passed to the *posthook*.

## Description

XmSetXmProtocolHooks() is a convenience routine that calls XmSetProtocol-Hooks() with *property* set to XA_WM_PROTOCOL, the window manager protocol property.

## Usage

The property XA_WM_PROTOCOLS is a set of predefined protocols for communication between clients and window managers. To communicate using a protocol, a client sends a ClientMessage event containing a property and protocol, and the receiving client responds by calling the associated protocol callback routine. XmSetWMProtocolHooks() gives an application more control over the flow of callback procedures, since callbacks are not necessarily invoked in any particular order.

## See Also

*XmAddWMProtocolCallback*(1), *XmInternAtom*(1), *XmRemoveWMProtocolCallback*(1), *XmSetProtocolHooks*(1), *VendorShell*(2).

# XmStringBaseline

## Name

XmStringBaseline – get the baseline spacing for a compound string.

## Synopsis

```
Dimension XmStringBaseline (fontlist, string)
    XmFontList fontlist;
    XmString string;
```

### Inputs

*fontlist* Specifies the font list for the compound string.

*string* Specifies the compound string.

### Returns

The distance, in pixels, from the top of the character box to the baseline of the first line of text.

## Description

`XmStringBaseline()` returns the distance, in pixels, from the top of the character box to the baseline of the first line of text in *string*. If *string* is created with `XmStringCreateSimple()`, then *fontlist* must begin with the font associated with the character set from the current language environment, otherwise the result is undefined.

## Usage

A compound string is composed of one or more segments, where each segment can contain a font list element tag, a string direction, and a text component. `XmStringBaseline()` provides information that is useful if you need to render a compound string. Motif widgets render compound string automatically, so you only need to worry about rendering them yourself if you are writing your own widget. The routine is also useful if you want to get the dimensions of a compound string rendered with a particular font.

## See Also

*XmStringExtent*(1), *XmStringHeight*(1), *XmStringWidth*(1).

# XmStringByteCompare

## Name

XmStringByteCompare – compare two compound strings byte-by-byte.

## Synopsis

```
Boolean XmStringByteCompare (string1, string2)
    XmString string1;
    XmString string2;
```

### Inputs

*string1* Specifies a compound string.

*string2* Specifies another compound string.

### Returns

`True` if the two compound strings are byte-by-byte identical or `False` otherwise.

## Description

`XmStringByteCompare()` compares the compound strings *string1* and *string2* byte by byte. If the strings are equivalent, it returns `True`; otherwise it returns `False`. If two compound strings are created with `XmStringCreateLocalized()` in the same language environment, using the same character string, the strings are byte-for-byte equal. Similarly, if two compound strings are created with `XmStringCreate()` using the same font list element tag and character string, the strings are equal.

## Usage

A compound string is composed of one or more segments, where each segment can contain a font list element tag, a string direction, and a text component. `XmStringByteCompare()` is one of a number of routines that allow an application to manipulate compound strings as it would regular character strings.

When a compound string is placed into a widget, the string is sometimes converted to an internal format, which provides faster processing but strips out redundant information. As a result, when an application retrieves the compound string from the widget by calling `XtGetValues()`, the returned string does not necessarily match the original string byte-for-byte. This situation occurs most often with Label widgets and its subclasses.

## See Also

*XmStringCompare*(1).

# XmStringCompare

## Name

XmStringCompare – compare two compound strings.

## Synopsis

```
Boolean XmStringCompare (string1, string2)
    XmString string1;
    XmString string2;
```

### Inputs

*string1* Specifies a compound string.

*string2* Specifies another compound string.

### Returns

`True` if the two compound strings are semantically equivalent or `False` otherwise.

## Description

`XmStringCompare()` compares the compound strings *string1* and *string2* semantically. If the strings are equivalent, it returns `True`; otherwise it returns `False`. `XmStringCompare()` is similar to `XmStringByteCompare()` but less restrictive. Two compound string are semantically equivalent if they have the same text components, font list element tags, directions, and separators.

## Usage

A compound string is composed of one or more segments, where each segment can contain a font list element tag, a string direction, and a text component. `XmStringCompare()` is one of a number of routines that allow an application to manipulate compound strings as it would regular character strings.

## See Also

*XmStringByteCompare*(1).

# XmStringConcat

## Name

XmStringConcat – concatenate two compound strings.

## Synopsis

```
XmString XmStringConcat (string1, string2)
    XmString string1;
    XmString string2;
```

### Inputs

*string1* Specifies a compound string.

*string2* Specifies another compound string.

### Returns

A new compound string.

## Description

`XmStringConcat()` returns the compound string formed by appending *string2* to *string1*, leaving the original compound strings unchanged. Storage for the result is allocated within the routine and should be freed by calling `XmStringFree()`. Management of the allocated memory is the responsibility of the application.

## Usage

A compound string is composed of one or more segments, where each segment can contain a font list element tag, a string direction, and a text component. `XmStringConcat()` is one of a number of routines that allow an application to manipulate compound strings as it would regular character strings.

## See Also

*XmStringCopy*(1), *XmStringNConcat*(1), *XmStringNCopy*(1).

# XmStringCopy

## Name

XmStringCopy – copy a compound string.

## Synopsis

```
XmString XmStringCopy (string)
    XmString string;
```

### Inputs

*string* Specifies a compound string.

### Returns

A new compound string.

## Description

`XmStringCopy()` copies the compound string *string* and returns the copy, leaving the original compound string unchanged. Storage for the result is allocated by the routine and should be freed by calling `XmStringFree()`. Management of the allocated memory is the responsibility of the application.

## Usage

A compound string is composed of one or more segments, where each segment can contain a font list element tag, a string direction, and a text component. `XmStringCopy()` is one of a number of routines that allow an application to manipulate compound strings as it would regular character strings.

## See Also

*XmStringConcat*(1), *XmStringNConcat*(1), *XmStringNCopy*(1).

# XmStringCreate

## Name

XmStringCreate – create a compound string.

## Synopsis

```
XmString XmStringCreate (text, tag)
    char *text;
    char *tag;
```

### Inputs

| | |
|---|---|
| *text* | Specifies the text component of the compound string. |
| *tag* | Specifies the font list element tag. |

### Returns

A new compound string.

## Description

`XmStringCreate()` creates a compound string containing two components: a text component composed of *text* and the font list element tag specified by *tag*. *text* must be a NULL-terminated string. *tag* can have the value XmFONTLIST_DEFAULT_TAG, which identifies a locale-encoded text segment. Storage for the returned compound string is allocated by the routine and should be freed by calling `XmStringFree()`. Management of the allocated memory is the responsibility of the application.

## Usage

In Motif 1.2, a compound string is composed of one or more segments, where each segment can contain a font list element tag, a string direction, and a text component. `XmStringCreate()` allows you to create a compound string composed of a font list element tag and a text component.

In Motif 1.1, compound strings use character set identifiers rather than font list element tags. The character set identifier for a compound string can have the value XmSTRING_DEFAULT_CHARSET, which takes the character set from the current language environment, but this value may be removed from future versions of Motif.

`XmStringCreate()` creates a compound string with no specified direction. The default direction may be taken from the `XmNstringDirection` resource of the parent of the widget that contains the compound string. If you need a string with a direction other than the default direction, use `XmStringDirectionCreate()` to create a direction string and concatenate it with the compound string containing the text.

## Example

The following code fragment shows how to create compound strings using `XmStringCreate()`:

```
Widget          toplevel;
XmString        s1, s2, s3, text, tmp;
```

```
String              string1 = "This is a string",
                    string2 = "that contains three",
                    string3 = "separate fonts.";

s1 = XmStringCreate(string1, "tag1");
s2 = XmStringCreate(string2, "tag2");
s3 = XmStringCreate(string3, XmFONTLIST_DEFAULT_TAG);

tmp = XmStringConcat(s1, s2);
text = XmStringConcat(tmp, s3);

XtVaCreateManagedWidget("widget_name", xmLabelWidgetClass, toplevel,
    XmNlabelString,     text,
    NULL);

XmStringFree(s1);
XmStringFree(s2);
XmStringFree(s3);
XmStringFree(tmp);
XmStringFree(text);
```

## See Also

*XmStringBaseline*(1), *XmStringByteCompare*(1), *XmStringCompare*(1), *XmStringConcat*(1), *XmStringCopy*(1), *XmStringCreateLocalized*(1), *XmStringCreateLtoR*(1), *XmStringCreateSimple*(1), *XmStringDirectionCreate*(1), *XmStringDraw*(1), *XmStringDrawImage*(1), *XmStringDrawUnderline*(1), *XmStringEmpty*(1), *XmStringExtent*(1), *XmStringFree*(1), *XmStringFreeContext*(1), *XmStringGetLtoR*(1), *XmStringGetNextComponent*(1), *XmStringGetNextSegment*(1), *XmStringHasSubstring*(1), *XmStringHeight*(1), *XmStringInitContext*(1), *XmStringLength*(1), *XmStringLineCount*(1), *XmStringNConcat*(1), *XmStringNCopy*(1), *XmStringPeekNextComponent*(1), *XmStringSegmentCreate*(1), *XmStringSeparatorCreate*(1), *XmStringWidth*(1).

# XmStringCreateLocalized

## Name

XmStringCreateLocalized – create a compound string in the current locale.

## Synopsis

```
XmString XmStringCreateLocalized (text)
    char *text;
```

### Inputs

*text* Specifies the text component of the compound string.

### Returns

A new compound string.

## Availability

Motif 1.2 and later.

## Description

`XmStringCreateLocalized()` creates a compound string containing two components: a text component composed of *text* and the font list element tag XmFONTLIST_DEFAULT_TAG, which identifies a locale-encoded text segment. *text* must be a NULL-terminated string. Storage for the returned compound string is allocated by the routine and should be freed by calling `XmStringFree()`. Management of the allocated memory is the responsibility of the application.

## Usage

In Motif 1.2, a compound string is composed of one or more segments, where each segment can contain a font list element tag, a string direction, and a text component. `XmStringCreateLocalized()` creates the identical compound string that would result from calling `XmStringCreate` with XmFONTLIST_DEFAULT_TAG as the font list entry tag.

## Example

The following program shows how to create a compound string in the current locale and use it as the label for a PushButton:

```
#include <Xm/RowColumn.h>
#include <Xm/PushB.h>

String fallbacks[ ] = { "*fontList:9x15=tag", NULL };

main(argc, argv)
int argc;
char *argv[ ];
{
    Widget        toplevel, rowcol;
    XtAppContext  app;
    XmString      text;

    XtSetLanguageProc(NULL, (XtLanguageProc)NULL, NULL);
```

```
    toplevel = XtVaAppInitialize(&app, argv[0], NULL, 0,
        &argc, argv, fallbacks, NULL);

    text = XmStringCreateLocalized("Testing, testing...");

    rowcol = XtVaCreateWidget("rowcol", xmRowColumnWidgetClass, toplevel,
        NULL);

    XtVaCreateManagedWidget("pb", xmPushButtonWidgetClass, rowcol,
        XmNlabelString, text,
        NULL);

    XmStringFree(text);
    XtManageChild(rowcol);
    XtRealizeWidget(toplevel);
    XtAppMainLoop(app);
}
```

## See Also

*XmStringCreate*(1), *XmStringFree*(1).

# XmStringCreateLtoR

## Name

XmStringCreateLtoR – create a compound string.

## Synopsis

```
XmString XmStringCreateLtoR (text, tag)
    char *text;
    char *tag;
```

### Inputs

*text* Specifies the text component of the compound string.

*tag* Specifies the font list element tag.

### Returns

A new compound string.

## Description

`XmStringCreateLtoR()` creates a compound string containing two components: a text component composed of *text* and the font list element tag specified by *tag*. *text* must be a NULL-terminated string. In addition, `XmStringCreateLtoR()` searches for newline characters (\n) in *text*. Each time a newline is found, the characters up to the newline are placed into a compound string segment followed by a separator component. The routine does not add a separator component to the end of the compound string. The default direction of the string is left to right and the assumed encoding is 8-bit characters rather than 16-bit characters.

*tag* can have the value XmFONTLIST_DEFAULT_TAG, which identifies a locale-encoded text segment. Storage for the returned compound string is allocated by the routine and should be freed by calling `XmStringFree()`. Management of the allocated memory is the responsibility of the application.

## Usage

In Motif 1.2, a compound string is composed of one or more segments, where each segment can contain a font list element tag, a string direction, and a text component. `XmStringCreateLtoR()` allows you to create a compound string composed of a font list element tag and a multi-line text component.

In Motif 1.1, compound strings use character set identifiers rather than font list element tags. The character set identifier for a compound string can have the value XmSTRING_DEFAULT_CHARSET, which takes the character set from the current language environment, but this value may be removed from future versions of Motif.

## Example

The following routine shows the use of `XmStringCreateLtoR()` to read the contents of a file into a buffer and then convert the buffer into a compound string:

```
XmString ConvertFileToXmString(filename, &lines)
char *filename;
```

```
int *lines;
{
    struct stat  statb;
    int          fd, len, lines;
    char        *text;
    XmString     str;

    *lines = 0;
    if (!(fd = open(filename, O_RDONLY))) {
        XtWarning("internal error -- can't open file");
        return NULL;
    }
    if (fstat(fd, &statb) == -1 ||
            !(text = XtMalloc((len = statb.st_size) + 1))) {
        XtWarning("internal error -- can't show text");
        close(fd);
        return NULL;
    }
    (void) read(fd, text, len);
    text[len] = 0;

    str = XmStringCreateLtoR(text, XmFONTLIST_DEFAULT_TAG);

    XtFree(text);
    close(fd);

    *lines = XmStringLineCount(str);
    return str;
}
```

## See Also

*XmStringCreate*(1), *XmStringFree*(1).

# XmStringCreateSimple

## Name

XmStringCreateSimple – create a compound string in the current language environment.

## Synopsis

```
XmString XmStringCreateSimple (text)
    char *text;
```

### Inputs

*text*  Specifies the text component of the compound string.

### Returns

A new compound string.

## Availability

In Motif 1.2, `XmStringCreateSimple()` is obsolete. It has been superceded by `XmStringCreateLocalized()`.

## Description

`XmStringCreateSimple()` creates a compound string containing two components: a text component composed of *text* and a character set identifier derived from the LANG environment variable or from a vendor-specific default, which is usually ISO8859-1. *text* must be a NULL-terminated string. Storage for the returned compound string is allocated by the routine and should be freed by calling `XmStringFree()`. Management of the allocated memory is the responsibility of the application.

## Usage

In Motif 1.2, a compound string is composed of one or more segments, where each segment can contain a font list element tag, a string direction, and a text component. In Motif 1.1, compound strings use character set identifiers rather than font list element tags. `XmStringCreateSimple()` is retained for compatibility with Motif 1.1 and should not be used in newer applications.

## See Also

*XmStringCreate*(1), *XmStringCreateLocalized*(1), *XmStringFree*(1).

# XmStringDirectionCreate

## Name

XmStringDirectionCreate – create a compound string containing a direction component.

## Synopsis

```
XmString XmStringDirectionCreate (direction)
    XmStringDirection direction;
```

### Inputs

*direction* Specifies the value of the direction component. Pass either XmSTRING_DIRECTION_L_TO_R or XmSTRING_DIRECTION_R_TO_L.

### Returns

A new compound string.

## Description

XmStringDirectionCreate() creates a compound string containing a single component, which is a direction component with the specified *direction* value. Storage for the returned compound string is allocated by the routine and should be freed by calling XmStringFree(). Management of the allocated memory is the responsibility of the application.

## Usage

A compound string is composed of one or more segments, where each segment can contain a font list element tag, a string direction, and a text component. XmStringDirectionCreate() allows you to create a string direction component that can be concatenated with a compound string containing other components.

## See Also

*XmStringCreate*(1), *XmStringFree*(1).

# XmStringDraw

## Name

XmStringDraw – draw a compound string.

## Synopsis

```
void XmStringDraw (display, window, fontlist, string, gc, x, y, width,
        alignment, layout_direction, clip)
    Display *display;
    Window window;
    XmFontList fontlist;
    XmString string;
    GC gc;
    Position x;
    Position y;
    Dimension width;
    unsigned char alignment;
    unsigned char layout_direction;
    XRectangle *clip;
```

### Inputs

*display* Specifies a connection to an X server; returned from `XOpenDisplay()` or `XtDisplay()`.

*window* Specifies the window where the string is drawn.

*fontlist* Specifies the font list for drawing the string.

*string* Specifies a compound string.

*gc* Specifies the graphics context that is used to draw the string.

*x* Specifies the x-coordinate of the rectangle that will contain the string.

*y* Specifies the y-coordinate of the rectangle that will contain the string.

*width* Specifies the width of the rectangle that will contain the string.

*alignment* Specifies the alignment of the string in the rectangle. Pass one of the following values: `XmALIGNMENT_BEGINNING`, `XmALIGNMENT_CENTER`, or `XmALIGNMENT_END`.

*layout_direction*
Specifies the layout direction of the string segments. Pass either `XmSTRING_DIRECTION_L_TO_R` or `XmSTRING_DIRECTION_R_TO_L`.

*clip* Specifies an clip rectangle that restricts the area where the string will be drawn.

## Description

`XmStringDraw()` draws the compound string specified by *string* by rendering the foreground pixels for each character. If *string* is created with `XmStringCreateSimple()`, then `fontlist` must begin with the font associated with the character set from the current language environment, otherwise the result is undefined.

## Usage

A compound string is composed of one or more segments, where each segment can contain a font list element tag, a string direction, and a text component. `XmStringDraw()` provides a means of rendering a compound string that is analogous to the Xlib string rendering routines. Motif widgets render compound string automatically, so you only need to worry about rendering them yourself if you are writing your own widget.

In Motif 1.2, if a segment of a compound string is associated with a font list entry that is a font set, the font member of the *gc* is left in an undefined state by the underlying call to `XmbDrawString()`. If a segment of the compound string is not associated with a font set, the *gc* must contain a valid font member. The *gc* must be created using `XtAllocateGC()`; graphics contexts created with `XtGetGC()` are not valid.

## See Also

*XmStringDrawImage*(1), *XmStringDrawUnderline*(1).

# XmStringDrawImage

## Name

XmStringDrawImage – draw a compound string.

## Synopsis

```
void XmStringDrawImage (display, window, fontlist, string, gc, x, y, width,
        alignment, layout_direction, clip)
    Display *display;
    Window window;
    XmFontList fontlist;
    XmString string;
    GC gc;
    Position x;
    Position y;
    Dimension width;
    unsigned char alignment;
    unsigned char layout_direction;
    XRectangle *clip;
```

### Inputs

*display* — Specifies a connection to an X server; returned from `XOpenDisplay()` or `XtDisplay()`.

*window* — Specifies the window where the string is drawn.

*fontlist* — Specifies the font list for drawing the string.

*string* — Specifies a compound string.

*gc* — Specifies the graphics context that is used to draw the string.

*x* — Specifies the x-coordinate of the rectangle that will contain the string.

*y* — Specifies the y-coordinate of the rectangle that will contain the string.

*width* — Specifies the width of the rectangle that will contain the string.

*alignment* — Specifies the alignment of the string in the rectangle. Pass one of the following values: `XmALIGNMENT_BEGINNING`, `XmALIGNMENT_CENTER`, or `XmALIGNMENT_END`.

*layout_direction* — Specifies the layout direction of the string segments. Pass either `XmSTRING_DIRECTION_L_TO_R` or `XmSTRING_DIRECTION_R_TO_L`.

*clip* — Specifies an clip rectangle that restricts the area where the string will be drawn.

## Description

`XmStringDrawImage()` draws the compound string specified by *string* by painting the foreground and background pixels for each character. If *string* is created with `XmString-`

`CreateSimple()`, then *fontlist* must begin with the font associated with the character set from the current language environment, otherwise the result is undefined.

## Usage

A compound string is composed of one or more segments, where each segment can contain a font list element tag, a string direction, and a text component. `XmStringDrawImage()` provides a means of rendering a compound string that is analogous to the Xlib string rendering routines. Motif widgets render compound string automatically, so you only need to worry about rendering them yourself if you are writing your own widget.

In Motif 1.2, if a segment of a compound string is associated with a font list entry that is a font set, the font member of the *gc* is left in an undefined state by the underlying call to `XmbDrawImageString()`. If a segment of the compound string is not associated with a font set, the *gc* must contain a valid font member. The *gc* must be created using `XtAllocateGC()`; graphics contexts created with `XtGetGC()` are not valid.

## See Also

*XmStringDraw*(1), *XmStringDrawUnderline*(1).

# XmStringDrawUnderline



## Name

XmStringDrawUnderline – draw a compound string with an underlined substring.

## Synopsis

```
void XmStringDrawUnderline (display, window, fontlist, string, gc, x, y,
        width, alignment, layout_direction, clip, underline)
    Display *display;
    Window window;
    XmFontList fontlist;
    XmString string;
    GC gc;
    Position x;
    Position y;
    Dimension width;
    unsigned char alignment;
    unsigned char layout_direction;
    XRectangle *clip;
    XmString underline;
```

### Inputs

*display* Specifies a connection to an X server; returned from XOpenDisplay() or XtDisplay().

*window* Specifies the window where the string is drawn.

*fontlist* Specifies the font list for drawing the string.

*string* Specifies a compound string.

*gc* Specifies the graphics context that is used to draw the string.

*x* Specifies the x-coordinate of the rectangle that will contain the string.

*y* Specifies the y-coordinate of the rectangle that will contain the string.

*width* Specifies the width of the rectangle that will contain the string.

*alignment* Specifies the alignment of the string in the rectangle. Pass one of the following values: XmALIGNMENT_BEGINNING, XmALIGNMENT_CENTER, or XmALIGNMENT_END.

*layout_direction*
Specifies the layout direction of the string segments. Pass either XmSTRING_DIRECTION_L_TO_R or XmSTRING_DIRECTION_R_TO_L.

*clip* Specifies an clip rectangle that restricts the area where the string will be drawn.

*underline* Specifies the substring that is to be underlined.

## Description

`XmStringDrawUnderline()` is similar to `XmStringDraw()`, but it also draws an underline beneath the first matching substring *underline* that is contained within *string*. If *string* is created with `XmStringCreateSimple()`, then *fontlist* must begin with the font associated with the character set from the current language environment, otherwise the result is undefined.

## Usage

A compound string is composed of one or more segments, where each segment can contain a font list element tag, a string direction, and a text component. `XmStringDrawUnderline()` provides a means of rendering a compound string and underlining a substring within it. Motif widgets render compound string automatically, so you only need to worry about rendering them yourself if you are writing your own widget.

In Motif 1.2, if a segment of a compound string is associated with a font list entry that is a font set, the font member of the *gc* is left in an undefined state by the underlying call to `XmbDrawString()`. If a segment of the compound string is not associated with a font set, the *gc* must contain a valid font member. The *gc* must be created using `XtAllocateGC()`; graphics contexts created with `XtGetGC()` are not valid.

## See Also

*XmStringDraw*(1), *XmStringDrawImage*(1).

# XmStringEmpty



## Name

XmStringEmpty – determine whether there are text segments in a compound string.

## Synopsis

```
Boolean XmStringEmpty (string)
    XmString string;
```

### Inputs

*string*    Specifies a compound string.

### Returns

True if there are no text segments in the string or False otherwise.

## Description

XmStringEmpty() returns True if no text segments exist in the specified *string* and False otherwise. If the routine is passed NULL, it returns True.

## Usage

A compound string is composed of one or more segments, where each segment can contain a font list element tag, a string direction, and a text component. XmStringEmpty() is one of a number of routines that allow an application to manipulate compound strings as it would regular character strings.

## See Also

*XmStringLength*(1), *XmStringLineCount*(1).

# XmStringExtent

## Name

XmStringExtent – get the smallest rectangle that contains a compound string.

## Synopsis

```
void XmStringExtent (fontlist, string, width, height)
    XmFontList fontlist;
    XmString string;
    Dimension *width;
    Dimension *height;
```

### Inputs

| | |
|---|---|
| *fontlist* | Specifies the font list for the compound string. |
| *string* | Specifies the compound string. |

### Outputs

| | |
|---|---|
| *width* | Returns the width of the containing rectangle. |
| *height* | Returns the height of the containing rectangle. |

## Description

`XmStringExtent()` calculates the size of the smallest rectangle that can enclose the specified compound *string* and returns the width and height of the rectangle in pixels. If *string* is created with `XmStringCreateSimple()`, then *fontlist* must begin with the font from the character set of the current language environment, otherwise the result is undefined.

## Usage

A compound string is composed of one or more segments, where each segment can contain a font list element tag, a string direction, and a text component. `XmStringExtent()` provides information that is useful if you need to render a compound string. Motif widgets render compound string automatically, so you only need to worry about rendering them yourself if you are writing your own widget. The routine is also useful if you want to get the dimensions of a compound string rendered with a particular font.

## See Also

*XmStringBaseline*(1), *XmStringHeight*(1), *XmStringWidth*(1).

# XmStringFree



## Name

XmStringFree – free the memory used by a compound string.

## Synopsis

```
void XmStringFree (string)
    XmString string;
```

### Inputs

*string* Specifies the compound string.

## Description

`XmStringFree()` frees the memory used by the specified compound *string*.

## Usage

A compound string is composed of one or more segments, where each segment can contain a font list element tag, a string direction, and a text component. All of the routines that return a compound string allocate memory for the string. An application is responsible for this storage; `XmStringFree()` provides a way to free the memory.

When `XtGetValues()` is called for a resource that contains an `XmString`, a copy of the compound string is returned. The allocated storage is again the responsibility of the application and can be freed using `XmStringFree()`.

## Example

The following code fragment shows the use of `XmStringFree()`:

```
Widget        toplevel, rowcol, pb;
XmString      str;
char         *text;

str = XmStringCreateLocalized("Testing, testing...");

rowcol = XtVaCreateWidget("rowcol", xmRowColumnWidgetClass, toplevel,
    NULL);

pb = XtVaCreateManagedWidget("pb", xmPushButtonWidgetClass, rowcol,
    XmNlabelString, str,
    NULL);

XmStringFree(str);
.
.
.
XtVaGetValues(pb, XmNlabelString, &str, NULL);
XmStringGetLtoR(str, XmFONTLIST_DEFAULT_TAG, &text);
printf("PushButton's label is %s\n", text);
XmStringFree(str);
XtFree(text);
```

## See Also

*XmStringCreate*(1), *XmStringCreateLocalized*(1), *XmStringCreateLtoR*(1), *XmStringCreateSimple*(1), *XmStringDirectionCreate*(1), *XmStringSegmentCreate*(1), *XmStringSeparatorCreate*(1).

# XmStringFreeContext



## Name

XmStringFreeContext – free a string context.

## Synopsis

```
void XmStringFreeContext (context)
    XmStringContext context;
```

### Inputs

*context*   Specifies the string context that is to be freed.

## Description

`XmStringFreeContext()` deallocates the string context structure specified by *context*.

## Usage

The `XmString` type is opaque, so if an application needs to perform any processing on a compound string, it has to use special functions to cycle through the string. These routines use a `XmStringContext` to maintain an arbitrary position in a compound string. `XmStringFreeContext()` is the last of the string context routines that an application should call when processing a compound string, as it frees the string context data structure. An application begins by calling `XmStringInitContext()` to create a string context and then makes repeated calls to either `XmStringGetNextComponent()` or `XmStringGetNextSegment()` to cycle through the compound string.

The most common use of these routines is in converting a compound string to a regular character string when the compound string uses multiple fontlist element tags or it has a right-to-left orientation.

## Example

The following code fragment shows how to convert a compound string into a character string:

```
XmString            str;
XmStringContext     context;
char               *text, buf[128], *p;
XmStringCharSet     tag;
XmStringDirection   direction;
Boolean             separator;

XtVaGetValues(widget, XmNlabelString, &str, NULL);

if (!XmStringInitContext(&context, str)) {
    XmStringFree(str);
    XtWarning("Can't convert compound string.");
    return;
}

/* p keeps a running pointer thru buf as text is read */
p = buf;
```

```
while (XmStringGetNextSegment(context, &text, &tag, &direction, &separator)) {
    /* copy text into p and advance to the end of the string */
    p += (strlen(strcpy(p, text)));
    if (separator == True) { /* if there's a separator ... */
        *p++ = '\n';
        *p = 0;  /* add newline and null-terminate */
    }
    XtFree(text);    /* we're done with the text; free it */
}
XmStringFreeContext(context);

XmStringFree(str);

printf("Compound string:\n%s\n", buf);
```

## See Also

*XmStringInitContext*(1), *XmStringGetNextSegment*(1), *XmStringGetNextComponent*(1), *XmStringPeekNextComponent*(1).

# XmStringGetLtoR

## Name

XmStringGetLtoR – get a text segment from a compound string.

## Synopsis

```
Boolean XmStringGetLtoR (string, tag, text)
     XmString string;
     XmStringCharSet tag;
     char **text;
```

### Inputs

*string* Specifies the compound string.

*tag* Specifies the font list element tag.

### Outputs

*text* Returns the NULL-terminated character string.

### Returns

True if there is a matching text segment or False otherwise.

## Description

XmStringGetLtoR() looks for a text segment in *string* that matches the font list element tag specified by *tag*. *tag* can have the value XmFONTLIST_DEFAULT_TAG, which identifies a locale-encoded text segment. The routine returns True if a text segment is found. *text* returns a pointer to the NULL-terminated character string that contains the text from the segment. Storage for the returned character string is allocated by the routine and should be freed by calling XtFree(). Management of the allocated memory is the responsibility of the application.

## Usage

In Motif 1.2, a compound string is composed of one or more segments, where each segment can contain a font list element tag, a string direction, and a text component. XmStringGetLtoR() allows you to retrieve a character string from a compound string, so that you can use the string with the standard C string manipulation functions.

In Motif 1.1, compound strings use character set identifiers rather than font list element tags. The character set identifier for a compound string can have the value XmSTRING_DEFAULT_CHARSET, which takes the character set from the current language environment, but this value may be removed from future versions of Motif.

XmStringGetLtoR() gets the first text segment from the compound string that is associated with the specified *tag*. If the string contains multiple font list element tags, you must cycle through the compound string and retrieve each segment individually in order to retrieve the entire string. The routine only gets strings with a left-to-right orientation.

## Example

The following code fragment shows the use of `XmStringGetLtoR()`:

```
Widget        pb;
XmString      str;
char         *text;

XtVaGetValues(pb, XmNlabelString, &str, NULL);
XmStringGetLtoR(str, XmFONTLIST_DEFAULT_TAG, &text);
printf("PushButton's label is %s\n", text);
XmStringFree(str);
XtFree(text);
```

## See Also

*XmStringCreate*(1), *XmStringCreateLtoR*(1), *XmStringGetNextSegment*(1).

# XmStringGetNextComponent



## Name

XmStringGetNextComponent – retrieves information about the next compound string component.

## Synopsis

```
XmStringComponentType XmStringGetNextComponent (context, text, tag,
        direction, unknown_tag, unknown_length, unknown_value)
    XmStringContext context;
    char **text;
    XmStringCharSet *tag;
    XmStringDirection *direction;
    XmStringComponentType *unknown_tag;
    unsigned short *unknown_length;
    unsigned char **unknown_value;
```

### Inputs

*context* Specifies the string context for the compound string.

### Outputs

*text* Returns the NULL-terminated string for a text component.

*tag* Returns the font list element tag for a tag component.

*direction* Returns the string direction for a direction component.

*unknown_tag* Returns the tag of an unknown component.

*unknown_length*
Returns the length of an unknown component.

*unknown_value*
Returns the value of an unknown component.

### Returns

The type of the compound string component. The type is one of the values described below.

## Description

XmStringGetNextComponent() reads the next component in the compound string specified by *context* and returns the type of component found. The return value indicates which, if any, of the output parameters are valid. Storage for the returned values is allocated by the routine and must be freed by the application using XtFree().

For the type XmSTRING_COMPONENT_FONTLIST_ELEMENT_TAG, the font list element tag is returned in *tag*. In Motif 1.2, the type XmSTRING_COMPONENT_CHARSET is obsolete and is retained for compatibility with Motif 1.1. The type indicates that the character set identifier is returned in *tag*. XmSTRING_COMPONENT_FONTLIST_ELEMENT_TAG replaces XmSTRING_COMPONENT_CHARSET.

For the types XmSTRING_COMPONENT_TEXT and XmSTRING_COMPONENT_LOCALE_-TEXT, the text string is returned in *text*. For XmSTRING_COMPONENT_DIRECTION, the direction is returned in *direction*. Only one of *tag*, *text*, and *direction* can be valid at any one time.

The type XmSTRING_COMPONENT_SEPARATOR indicates that the next component is a separator, while XmSTRING_COMPONENT_END specifies the end of the compound string. For type XmSTRING_COMPONENT_UNKNOWN, the tag, length, and value of the unknown component are returned in the corresponding arguments.

## Usage

The XmString type is opaque, so if an application needs to perform any processing on a compound string, it has to use special functions to cycle through the string. These routines use a XmStringContext to maintain an arbitrary position in a compound string. XmStringInitContext() is called first to create the string context. XmStringGetNextComponent() cycles through the components in the compound string. When an application is done processing the string, it should call XmStringFreeContext() with the same *context* to free the allocated data.

## Structures

A XmStringComponentType can have one of the following values:

```
XmSTRING_COMPONENT_FONTLIST_ELEMENT_TAG
XmSTRING_COMPONENT_CHARSET
XmSTRING_COMPONENT_TEXT
XmSTRING_COMPONENT_LOCALE_TEXT
XmSTRING_COMPONENT_DIRECTION
XmSTRING_COMPONENT_SEPARATOR
XmSTRING_COMPONENT_END
XmSTRING_COMPONENT_UNKNOWN
```

Motif Functions and Macros

## See Also

*XmStringFreeContext*(1), *XmStringGetNextSegment*(1), *XmStringInitContext*(1), *XmStringPeekNextComponent*(1).

# XmStringGetNextSegment

## Name

XmStringGetNextSegment – retrieves information about the next compound string segment.

## Synopsis

```
Boolean XmStringGetNextSegment (context, text, tag, direction, separator)
    XmStringContext context;
    char **text;
    XmStringCharSet *charset;
    XmStringDirection *direction;
    Boolean *separator;
```

### Inputs

*context* Specifies the string context for the compound string.

### Outputs

*text* Returns the NULL-terminated string for the segment.

*tag* Returns the font list element tag for the segment.

*direction* Returns the string direction for the segment.

*separator* Returns whether or not the next component is a separator.

### Returns

True if a valid segment is located or False otherwise.

## Description

XmStringGetNextSegment() retrieves the text string, font list element tag, and direction for the next segment of the compound string specified by *context*. The routine returns True if a valid segment is retrieved; otherwise, it returns False. Storage for the returned *text* is allocated by the routine and must be freed by the application using XtFree().

## Usage

The XmString type is opaque, so if an application needs to perform any processing on a compound string, it has to use special functions to cycle through the string. These routines use a XmStringContext to maintain an arbitrary position in a compound string. XmStringInitContext() is called first to create the string context. XmStringGetNextSegment() cycles through the segments in the compound string. The *separator* boolean can be used to determine whether or not the next component in the compound string is a separator. When an application is done processing the string, it should call XmStringFreeContext() with the same *context* to free the allocated data.

The most common use of these routines is in converting a compound string to a regular character string when the compound string uses multiple fontlist element tags or it has a right-to-left orientation.

## Example

The following code fragment shows how to convert a compound string into a character string:

```
XmString            str;
XmStringContext     context;
char               *text, buf[128], *p;
XmStringCharSet     tag;
XmStringDirection   direction;
Boolean             separator;

XtVaGetValues(widget, XmNlabelString, &str, NULL);

if (!XmStringInitContext(&context, str)) {
    XmStringFree(str);
    XtWarning("Can't convert compound string.");
    return;
}

/* p keeps a running pointer thru buf as text is read */
p = buf;

while (XmStringGetNextSegment(context, &text, &tag, &direction, &separator)) {
    /* copy text into p and advance to the end of the string */
    p += (strlen(strcpy(p, text)));
    if (separator == True) { /* if there's a separator ... */
        *p++ = '\n';
        *p = 0;  /* add newline and null-terminate */
    }
    XtFree(text);   /* we're done with the text; free it */
}
XmStringFreeContext(context);

XmStringFree(str);

printf("Compound string:\n%s\n", buf);
```

## See Also

*XmStringFreeContext*(1), *XmStringGetLtoR*(1), *XmStringGetNextComponent*(1), *XmStringInitContext*(1), *XmStringPeekNextComponent*(1).

# XmStringHasSubstring

## Name

XmStringHasSubstring – determine whether a compound string contains a substring.

## Synopsis

```
Boolean XmStringHasSubstring (string, substring)
    XmString string;
    XmString substring;
```

### Inputs

*string* Specifies the compound string.

*substring* Specifies the substring.

### Returns

`True` if *string* contains *substring* or *False* otherwise.

## Description

`XmStringHasSubstring()` determines whether the compound string *substring* is contained within any single segment of the compound string *string*. *substring* must have only a single segment. The routine returns `True` if the string contains the substring and `False` otherwise.

If two compound strings are created with `XmStringCreateLocalized()` in the same language environment and they satisfy the above condition, `XmStringHasSubstring()` returns `True`. If two strings are created with `XmStringCreate()` using the same character set and they satisfy the condition, the routine also returns `True`. When comparing a compound string created by `XmStringCreate()` with a compound string created by `XmStringCreateSimple()` the result is undefined.

## Usage

A compound string is composed of one or more segments, where each segment can contain a font list element tag, a string direction, and a text component. `XmStringHasSubstring()` is one of a number of routines that allow an application to manipulate compound strings as it would regular character strings.

## See Also

*XmStringEmpty*(1), *XmStringLength*(1), *XmStringLineCount*(1).

# XmStringHeight

## Name

XmStringHeight – get the line height of a compound string.

## Synopsis

```
Dimension XmStringHeight (fontlist, string)
    XmFontList fontlist;
    XmString string;
```

### Inputs

*fontlist* Specifies the font list for the compound string.

*string* Specifies the compound string.

### Returns

The height of the compound string.

## Description

`XmStringHeight()` returns the height, in pixels, of the specified compound *string*. If *string* contains multiple lines, where a separator component delimits each line, then the total height of all of the lines is returned. If *string* is created with `XmStringCreateSimple()`, then *fontlist* must begin with the font from the character set of the current language environment, otherwise the result is undefined.

## Usage

A compound string is composed of one or more segments, where each segment can contain a font list element tag, a string direction, and a text component. `XmStringHeight()` provides information that is useful if you need to render a compound string. Motif widgets render compound string automatically, so you only need to worry about rendering them yourself if you are writing your own widget. The routine is also useful if you want to get the dimensions of a compound string rendered with a particular font.

## See Also

*XmStringBaseline*(1), *XmStringExtent*(1), *XmStringWidth*(1).

# XmStringInitContext

## Name

XmStringInitContext – create a string context.

## Synopsis

```
Boolean XmStringInitContext (context, string)
    XmStringContext *context;
    XmString string;
```

### Inputs

*string* Specifies the compound string.

### Outputs

*context* Returns the allocated string context structure.

### Returns

`True` if the string context is allocated or `False` otherwise.

## Description

`XmStringInitContext()` creates a string context for the specified compound *string*. This string *context* allows an application to access the contents of a compound string.

## Usage

The `XmString` type is opaque, so if an application needs to perform any processing on a compound string, it has to use special functions to cycle through the string. These routines use a `XmStringContext` to maintain an arbitrary position in a compound string. `XmStringInitContext()` is the first of the three string context routines that an application should call when processing a compound string, as it creates the string context data structure. The *context* is passed to `XmStringGetNextComponent()` or `XmStringGetNextSegment()` to cycle through the compound string. When an application is done processing the string, it should call `XmStringFreeContext()` with the same *context* to free the allocated data.

The most common use of these routines is in converting a compound string to a regular character string when the compound string uses multiple fontlist element tags or it has a right-to-left orientation.

## Example

The following code fragment shows how to convert a compound string into a character string:

```
XmString            str;
XmStringContext     context;
char               *text, buf[128], *p;
XmStringCharSet     tag;
XmStringDirection   direction;
Boolean             separator;

XtVaGetValues(widget, XmNlabelString, &str, NULL);
```

```
if (!XmStringInitContext(&context, str)) {
    XmStringFree(str);
    XtWarning("Can't convert compound string.");
    return;
}

/* p keeps a running pointer thru buf as text is read */
p = buf;

while (XmStringGetNextSegment(context, &text, &tag, &direction, &separator)) {
    /* copy text into p and advance to the end of the string */
    p += (strlen(strcpy(p, text)));
    if (separator == True) { /* if there's a separator ... */
        *p++ = '\n';
        *p = 0;  /* add newline and null-terminate */
    }
    XtFree(text);   /* we're done with the text; free it */
}
XmStringFreeContext(context);

XmStringFree(str);

printf("Compound string:\n%s\n", buf);
```

## See Also

*XmStringFreeContext*(1), *XmStringGetNextComponent*(1), *XmStringGetNextSegment*(1), *XmStringPeekNextComponent*(1).

# XmStringLength

## Name

XmStringLength – get the length of a compound string.

## Synopsis

```
int XmStringLength (string)
    XmString string;
```

### Inputs

*string* Specifies the compound string.

### Returns

The length of the compound string.

## Description

`XmStringLength()` returns the length, in bytes, of the specified compound *string*. The calculation includes the length of all tags, direction indicators, and separators. The routine returns 0 (zero) if the structure of *string* is invalid.

## Usage

A compound string is composed of one or more segments, where each segment can contain a font list element tag, a string direction, and a text component. `XmStringLength()` is one of a number of routines that allow an application to manipulate compound strings as it would regular character strings. However, this routine cannot be used to get the length of the text represented by the compound string; it is not the same as `strlen()`.

## See Also

*XmStringEmpty*(1), *XmStringLineCount*(1).

## Name

XmStringLineCount – get the number of lines in a compound string.

## Synopsis

```
int XmStringLineCount (string)
    XmString string;
```

### Inputs

*string* Specifies the compound string.

### Returns

The number of lines in the compound string.

## Description

`XmStringLineCount()` returns the number of lines in the specified compound *string*. The line count is determined by adding 1 to the number of separators in the string.

## Usage

A compound string is composed of one or more segments, where each segment can contain a font list element tag, a string direction, and a text component. `XmStringHeight()` provides information that is useful in laying out components that display compound strings.

## Example

The following routine shows how to read the contents of a file into a buffer and then convert the buffer into a compound string. The routine also returns the number of lines in the compound string:

```
XmString ConvertFileToXmString(filename, &lines)
char *filename;
int *lines;
{
    struct stat  statb;
    int          fd, len, lines;
    char        *text;
    XmString     str;

    *lines = 0;
    if (!(fd = open(filename, O_RDONLY))) {
        XtWarning("internal error -- can't open file");
        return NULL;
    }
    if (fstat(fd, &statb) == -1 ||
            !(text = XtMalloc((len = statb.st_size) + 1))) {
        XtWarning("internal error -- can't show text");
        close(fd);
        return NULL;
    }
    (void) read(fd, text, len);
```

Motif Functions and Macros

```
        text[len] = 0;

        str = XmStringCreateLtoR(text, XmFONTLIST_DEFAULT_TAG);

        XtFree(text);
        close(fd);

        *lines = XmStringLineCount(str);
        return str;
    }
```

## See Also

*XmStringEmpty*(1), *XmStringLength*(1).

# XmStringNConcat

## Name

XmStringNConcat – concatenate a specified portion of a compound string to another compound string.

## Synopsis

```
XmString XmStringNConcat (string1, string2, num_bytes)
    XmString string1;
    XmString string2;
    int num_bytes;
```

### Inputs

| | |
|---|---|
| *string1* | Specifies a compound string. |
| *string2* | Specifies the compound string that is appended. |
| *num_bytes* | Specifies the number of bytes of *string2* that are appended. |

### Returns

A new compound string.

## Description

`XmStringNConcat()` returns the compound string formed by appending bytes from *string2* to the end of *string1*, leaving the original compound strings unchanged. *num_bytes* of *string* are appended, which includes tags, directional indicators, and separators. Storage for the result is allocated within this routine and should be freed by calling `XmStringFree()`. Management of the allocated memory is the responsibility of the application.

If *num_bytes* is less than the length of *string2*, the resulting string could be invalid. In this case, `XmStringNConcat()` appends as many bytes as possible, up to a maximum of *num_bytes*, to ensure the creation of a valid string.

## Usage

A compound string is composed of one or more segments, where each segment can contain a font list element tag, a string direction, and a text component. `XmStringNConcat()` is one of a number of routines that allow an application to manipulate compound strings as it would regular character strings.

## See Also

*XmStringConcat*(1), *XmStringCopy*(1), *XmStringNCopy*(1).

Motif Functions and Macros

# XmStringNCopy

## Name

XmStringNCopy – copy a specified portion of a compound string.

## Synopsis

```
XmString XmStringNCopy (string, num_bytes)
    XmString string;
    int num_bytes;
```

### Inputs

*string* Specifies a compound string.

*num_bytes* Specifies the number of bytes of *string* that are copied.

### Returns

A new compound string.

## Description

`XmStringNCopy()` copies *num_bytes* bytes from the compound string *string* and returns the resulting copy, leaving the original string unchanged. The number of bytes copied includes tags, directional indicators, and separators. Storage for the result is allocated within this routine and should be freed by calling `XmStringFree()`. Management of the allocated memory is the responsibility of the application.

If *num_bytes* is less than the length of *string*, the resulting string could be invalid. In this case, `XmStringNCopy()` copies as many bytes as possible, up to a maximum of *num_bytes* to ensure the creation of a valid string.

## Usage

A compound string is composed of one or more segments, where each segment can contain a font list element tag, a string direction, and a text component. `XmStringNCopy()` is one of a number of routines that allow an application to manipulate compound strings as it would regular character strings.

## See Also

*XmStringConcat*(1), *XmStringCopy*(1), *XmStringNConcat*(1).

# XmStringPeekNextComponent

## Name

XmStringPeekNextComponent – returns the type of the next compound string component.

## Synopsis

```
XmStringComponentType XmStringPeekNextComponent (context)
    XmStringContext context;
```

### Inputs

*context* Specifies the string context for the compound string.

### Returns

The type of the compound string component. The type is one of the values described below.

## Description

`XmStringPeekNextComponent()` checks the next component in the compound string specified by *context* and returns the type of the component found. The routine shows what would be returned by a call to `XmStringGetNextComponent()`, without actually updating *context*.

The type `XmSTRING_COMPONENT_FONTLIST_ELEMENT_TAG` indicates that the next component is a font list element tag. In Motif 1.2, the type `XmSTRING_COMPONENT_CHARSET` is obsolete and is retained for compatibility with Motif 1.1. The type indicates that the next component is a character set identifier. `XmSTRING_COMPONENT_FONTLIST_ELEMENT_TAG` replaces `XmSTRING_COMPONENT_CHARSET`.

The types `XmSTRING_COMPONENT_TEXT` and `XmSTRING_COMPONENT_LOCALE_TEXT` specify that the next component is text. `XmSTRING_COMPONENT_DIRECTION` indicates that the next component is a string direction component.

The type `XmSTRING_COMPONENT_SEPARATOR` indicates that the next component is a separator, while `XmSTRING_COMPONENT_END` specifies the end of the compound string. The type `XmSTRING_COMPONENT_UNKNOWN`, indicates that the type of the next component is unknown.

## Usage

The `XmString` type is opaque, so if an application needs to perform any processing on a compound string, it has to use special functions to cycle through the string. These routines use a `XmStringContext` to maintain an arbitrary position in a compound string. `XmStringInitContext()` is called first to create the string context. `XmStringPeekNextComponent()` peeks at the next component in the compound string without cycling through the component. When an application is done processing the string, it should call `XmStringFreeContext()` with the same *context* to free the allocated data.

## Structures

A `XmStringComponentType` can have one of the following values:

```
XmSTRING_COMPONENT_FONTLIST_ELEMENT_TAG
XmSTRING_COMPONENT_CHARSET
XmSTRING_COMPONENT_TEXT
XmSTRING_COMPONENT_LOCALE_TEXT
XmSTRING_COMPONENT_DIRECTION
XmSTRING_COMPONENT_SEPARATOR
XmSTRING_COMPONENT_END
XmSTRING_COMPONENT_UNKNOWN
```

## See Also

*XmStringFreeContext*(1), *XmStringGetNextComponent*(1), *XmStringGetNextSegment*(1), *XmStringInitContext*(1).

# XmStringSegmentCreate

## Name

XmStringSegmentCreate – create a compound string segment.

## Synopsis

```
XmString XmStringSegmentCreate (text, tag, direction, separator)
    char *text;
    XmStringCharSet tag;
    XmStringDirection direction;
    Boolean separator;
```

### Inputs

| | |
|---|---|
| *text* | Specifies the text component of the compound string segment. |
| *tag* | Specifies the font list element tag. |
| *direction* | Specifies the value of the direction component. Pass either XmSTRING_DIRECTION_L_TO_R or XmSTRING_DIRECTION_R_TO_L. |
| *separator* | Specifies whether or not a separator is added to the compound string. |

### Returns

A new compound string.

## Description

XmStringSegmentCreate() creates a compound string segment that contains the specified *text*, *tag*, and *direction*. If *separator* is True, a separator is added to the segment, following the text. If *separator* is False, the compound string segment does not contain a separator. Storage for the returned compound string is allocated by the routine and should be freed by calling XmStringFree(). Management of the allocated memory is the responsibility of the application.

## Usage

A compound string is composed of one or more segments, where each segment can contain a font list element tag, a string direction, and a text component. XmStringSegmentCreate() allows you to create a single segment that can be concatenated with a compound string containing other segments.

## Example

The following code fragment shows how to create a compound string with right-to-left orientation using XmStringSegmentCreate():

```
Widget      toplevel, rowcol;
XmString    text;

text = XmStringSegmentCreate("Testing, testing...",
    XmFONTLIST_DEFAULT_TAG, XmSTRING_DIRECTION_R_TO_L, False);

rowcol = XtVaCreateWidget("rowcol", xmRowColumnWidgetClass, toplevel,
    NULL);
```

```
XtVaCreateManagedWidget ("pb", xmPushButtonWidgetClass, rowcol,
    XmNlabelString, text,
    NULL);

XmStringFree(text);
```

## See Also

*XmStringCreate*(1), *XmStringFree*(1).

# XmStringSeparatorCreate

## Name

XmStringSeparatorCreate – create a compound string containing a separator component.

## Synopsis

```
XmString XmStringSeparatorCreate ()
```

### Returns

A new compound string.

## Description

`XmStringSeparatorCreate()` creates and returns a compound string containing a separator as its only component.

## Usage

A compound string is composed of one or more segments, where each segment can contain a font list element tag, a string direction, and a text component and segments are separated by separators. `XmStringSeparatorCreate()` allows you to create a separator component that can be concatenated with a compound string containing other components.

## See Also

*XmStringCreate*(1), *XmStringFree*(1), *XmStringSegmentCreate*(1).

# XmStringWidth

## Name

XmStringWidth – get the width of the longest line of text in a compound string.

## Synopsis

```
Dimension XmStringWidth (fontlist, string)
    XmFontList fontlist;
    XmString string;
```

### Inputs

*fontlist* Specifies the font list for the compound string.

*string* Specifies the compound string.

### Returns

The width of the compound string.

## Description

`XmStringWidth()` returns the width, in pixels, of the longest line of text in the specified compound *string*. Lines in the compound string are delimited by separator components. If *string* is created with `XmStringCreateSimple()`, then *fontlist* must begin with the font from the character set of the current language environment, otherwise the result is undefined.

## Usage

A compound string is composed of one or more segments, where each segment can contain a font list element tag, a string direction, and a text component. `XmStringWidth()` provides information that is useful if you need to render a compound string. Motif widgets render compound strings automatically, so you only need to worry about rendering them yourself if you are writing your own widget. The routine is also useful if you want to get the dimensions of a compound string rendered with a particular font.

## See Also

*XmStringBaseline*(1), *XmStringExtent*(1), *XmStringHeight*(1).

# XmTargetsAreCompatible

## Name

XmTargetsAreCompatible – determine whether or not the target types of a drag source and a drop site match.

## Synopsis

```
#include <Xm/DragDrop.h>
Boolean XmTargetsAreCompatible (display, export_targets,
        num_export_targets, import_targets, num_import_targets)
    Display *display;
    Atom *export_targets;
    Cardinal num_export_targets;
    Atom *import_targets;
    Cardinal num_import_targets;
```

### Inputs

*display* Specifies a connection to an X server; returned from `XOpenDisplay()` or `XtDisplay()`.

*export_targets*
Specifies the list of target atoms to which the drag source can convert the data.

*num_export_targets*
Specifies the number of items in *export_targets*.

*import_targets*
Specifies the list of target atoms that are accepted by the drop site.

*num_import_targets*
Specifies the number of items in *import_targets*.

### Returns

`True` if there is a compatible target or `False` otherwise.

## Availability

Motif 1.2 and later.

## Description

`XmTargetsAreCompatible()` determines whether or not the import targets of a drop site match any of the export targets of a drag source. The routine returns `True` if the two objects have at least one target in common; otherwise it returns `False`.

## Usage

Motif 1.2 supports the drag and drop model of selection actions. In a widget that acts as a drag source, a user can make a selection and then drag the selection, using `BTransfer`, to other widgets that are registered as drop sites. These drop sites can be in the same application or another application. In order for a drag and drop operation to succeed, the drag source and the drop site must both be able to handle data in the same format. `XmTargetsAreCompatible()` provides a way for an application to check if a drag source and a drop site support compatible formats.

## See Also

*XmDragContext*(2), *XmDropSite*(2).

## Name

XmTextClearSelection, XmTextFieldClearSelection – clear the primary selection.

## Synopsis

```
#include <Xm/Text.h>
void XmTextClearSelection (widget, time)

#include <Xm/TextF.h>
void XmTextFieldClearSelection (widget, time)

    Widget widget;
    Time time;
```

### Inputs

*widget* Specifies the Text or TextField widget.

*time* Specifies the time of the event that caused the request.

## Description

`XmTextClearSelection()` and `XmTextFieldClearSelection()` clear the primary selection in the specified *widget*. `XmTextClearSelection()` works when *widget* is a Text widget or a TextField widget, while `XmTextFieldClearSelection()` only works for a TextField widget. For each routine, *time* specifies the server time of the event that caused the request to clear the selection.



## Usage

`XmTextClearSelection()` and `XmTextFieldClearSelection()` provide a convenient way to deselect the text selection in a Text or TextField widget. If no text is selected, the routines do nothing. Any text that is stored in the clipboard or selection properties remains; the routines affect the selected text in the widget only. If you are calling one of these routines from a callback routine, you probably want to use the `time` field from the `event` pointer in the callback structure as the value of the *time* parameter. You can also use the value `CurrentTime`, but there is no guarantee that using this time prevents race conditions between multiple clients that are trying to use the clipboard.

## Example

The following callback routine for the items on an **Edit** menu (**Cut**, **Copy**, **Paste**, and **Clear**) shows the use of `XmTextClearSelection()`:

```
Widget text_w, status;

void cut_paste(widget, client_data, call_data)
Widget widget;
XtPointer client_data;
XtPointer call_data;
{
    int num = (int) client_data;
```

```
        XmAnyCallbackStruct *cbs = (XmAnyCallbackStruct *) call_data;
        Boolean result = True;

        switch (num) {
            case 0 :
                result = XmTextCut(text_w, cbs->event->xbutton.time);
                break;
            case 1 :
                result = XmTextCopy(text_w, cbs->event->xbutton.time);
                break;
            case 2 :
                result = XmTextPaste(text_w);
                break;
            case 3 :
                XmTextClearSelection(text_w, cbs->event->xbutton.time);
                break;
        }

        if (result == False)
            XmTextSetString(status, "There is no selection.");
        else
            XmTextSetString(status, NULL);
    }
```

## See Also

*XmTextCopy*(1), *XmTextCut*(1), *XmTextGetSelection*(1), *XmTextGetSelectionPosition*(1), *XmTextGetSelectionWcs*(1), *XmTextSetSelection*(1), *XmText*(2), *XmTextField*(2).

# XmTextCopy

## Name

XmTextCopy, XmTextFieldCopy – copy the primary selection to the clipboard.

## Synopsis

```
#include <Xm/Text.h>
Boolean XmTextCopy (widget, time)

#include <Xm/TextF.h>
Boolean XmTextFieldCopy (widget, time)

    Widget widget;
    Time time;
```

### Inputs

*widget* Specifies the Text or TextField widget.

*time* Specifies the time of the event that caused the request.

### Returns

`True` on success or `False` otherwise.

## Description

`XmTextCopy()` and `XmTextFieldCopy()` copy the primary selection in the specified *widget* to the clipboard. `XmTextCopy()` works when *widget* is a Text widget or a TextField widget, while `XmTextFieldCopy()` only works for a TextField widget. For each routine, *time* specifies the server time of the event that caused the request to copy the selection. Both routines return `True` if successful. If the primary selection is `NULL`, if it is not owned by the specified *widget*, or if the function cannot obtain ownership of the clipboard selection, the routines return `False`.

## Usage

`XmTextCopy()` and `XmTextFieldCopy()` copy the text that is selected in a Text or TextField widget and place it on the clipboard. If you are calling one of these routines from a callback routine, you probably want to use the `time` field from the `event` pointer in the callback structure as the value of the *time* parameter. You can also use the value `CurrentTime`, but there is no guarantee that using this time prevents race conditions between multiple clients that are trying to use the clipboard.

## Example

The following callback routine for the items on an **Edit** menu (**Cut**, **Copy**, **Paste**, and **Clear**) shows the use of `XmTextCopy()`:

```
Widget text_w, status;

void cut_paste(widget, client_data, call_data)
Widget widget;
XtPointer client_data;
```

```
XtPointer call_data;
{
    int num = (int) client_data;
    XmAnyCallbackStruct *cbs = (XmAnyCallbackStruct *) call_data;
    Boolean result = True;

    switch (num) {
        case 0 :
            result = XmTextCut(text_w, cbs->event->xbutton.time);
            break;
        case 1 :
            result = XmTextCopy(text_w, cbs->event->xbutton.time);
            break;
        case 2 :
            result = XmTextPaste(text_w);
            break;
        case 3 :
            XmTextClearSelection(text_w, cbs->event->xbutton.time);
            break;
    }

    if (result == False)
        XmTextSetString(status, "There is no selection.");
    else
        XmTextSetString(status, NULL);
}
```

## See Also

*XmTextClearSelection*(1), *XmTextCut*(1), *XmTextGetSelection*(1), *XmTextGetSelectionWcs*(1), *XmTextPaste*(1), *XmTextRemove*(1), *XmTextSetSelection*(1), *XmText*(2), *XmTextField*(2).

# XmTextCut

## Name

XmTextCut, XmTextFieldCut – copy the primary selection to the clipboard and remove the selected text.

## Synopsis

```
#include <Xm/Text.h>
Boolean XmTextCut (widget, time)

#include <Xm/TextF.h>
Boolean XmTextFieldCut (widget, time)

    Widget widget;
    Time time;
```

### Inputs

| | |
|---|---|
| *widget* | Specifies the Text or TextField widget. |
| *time* | Specifies the time of the event that caused the request. |

### Returns

`True` on success or `False` otherwise.

## Description

`XmTextCut()` and `XmTextFieldCut()` copy the primary selection in the specified *widget* to the clipboard and then delete the primary selection. `XmTextCut()` works when *widget* is a Text widget or a TextField widget, while `XmTextFieldCut()` only works for a TextField widget. For each routine, *time* specifies the server time of the event that caused the request to cut the selection. Both routines return `True` if successful. If the *widget* is not editable, if the primary selection is `NULL` or if it is not owned by the specified *widget*, or if the function cannot obtain ownership of the clipboard selection, the routines return `False`.

`XmTextCut()` and `XmTextFieldCut()` also invoke the callback routines for the `XmNvalueChangedCallback`, the `XmNmodifyVerifyCallback`, and the `XmNmodifyVerifyCallbackWcs` callbacks for the specified *widget*. If both verification callbacks are present, the `XmNmodifyVerifyCallback` procedures are invoked first and the results are passed to the `XmNmodifyVerifyCallbackWcs` procedures.

## Usage

`XmTextCut()` and `XmTextFieldCut()` copy the text that is selected in a Text or TextField widget, place it on the clipboard, and then delete the selected text. If you are calling one of these routines from a callback routine, you probably want to use the `time` field from the `event` pointer in the callback structure as the value of the *time* parameter. You can also use the value `CurrentTime`, but there is no guarantee that using this time prevents race conditions between multiple clients that are trying to use the clipboard.

### Example

The following callback routine for the items on an **Edit** menu (**Cut**, **Copy**, **Paste**, and **Clear**) shows the use of `XmTextPaste()`:

```
Widget text_w, status;

void cut_paste(widget, client_data, call_data)
Widget widget;
XtPointer client_data;
XtPointer call_data;
{
    int num = (int) client_data;
    XmAnyCallbackStruct *cbs = (XmAnyCallbackStruct *) call_data;
    Boolean result = True;

    switch (num) {
        case 0 :
            result = XmTextCut(text_w, cbs->event->xbutton.time);
            break;
        case 1 :
            result = XmTextCopy(text_w, cbs->event->xbutton.time);
            break;
        case 2 :
            result = XmTextPaste(text_w);
            break;
        case 3 :
            XmTextClearSelection(text_w, cbs->event->xbutton.time);
            break;
    }

    if (result == False)
        XmTextSetString(status, "There is no selection.");
    else
        XmTextSetString(status, NULL);
}
```

### See Also

*XmTextClearSelection*(1), *XmTextCopy*(1), *XmTextGetSelection*(1), *XmTextGetSelectionWcs*(1), *XmTextPaste*(1), *XmTextRemove*(1), *XmTextSetSelection*(1), *XmText*(2), *XmTextField*(2).

# XmTextDisableRedisplay

## Name

XmTextDisableRedisplay – prevent visual update of a Text widget.

## Synopsis

```
#include <Xm/Text.h>
void XmTextDisableRedisplay (widget)
    Widget widget;
```

### Inputs

*widget* Specifies the Text widget.

## Availability

Motif 1.2 and later.

## Description

`XmTextDisableRedisplay()` temporarily inhibits visual update of the specified Text *widget*. Even if the visual attributes of the widget have been modified, the appearance remains unchanged until `XmTextEnableRedisplay()` is called.

## Usage

`XmTextDisableRedisplay()` and `XmTextEnableRedisplay()` allow an application to make multiple changes to a Text widget without immediate visual updates. When multiple changes are made with redisplay enabled, visual flashing often occurs. These routines eliminate this problem.

## See Also

*XmTextEnableRedisplay*(1), *XmUpdateDisplay*(1),
*XmText*(2).

# XmTextEnableRedisplay

## Name

XmTextEnableRedisplay – allow visual update of a Text widget.

## Synopsis

```
#include <Xm/Text.h>
void XmTextEnableRedisplay (widget)
    Widget widget;
```

### Inputs

*widget* Specifies the Text widget.

## Availability

Motif 1.2 and later.

## Description

`XmTextEnableRedisplay()` allows the specified Text *widget* to update its visual appearance. This routine is used in conjunction with `XmTextDisableRedisplay()`, which prevents visual update of the Text widget. When `XmTextEnableRedisplay()` is called, the widget modifies its visuals to reflect all of the changes since the last call to `XmTextDisableRedisplay()`. All future changes that affect the visual appearance are displayed immediately.

## Usage

`XmTextDisableRedisplay()` and `XmTextEnableRedisplay()` allow an application to make multiple changes to a Text widget without immediate visual updates. When multiple changes are made with redisplay enabled, visual flashing often occurs. These routines eliminate this problem.

## See Also

*XmTextDisableRedisplay*(1), *XmUpdateDisplay*(1),
*XmText*(2).

# XmTextFindString

## Name

XmTextFindString – find the beginning position of a text string.

## Synopsis

```
#include <Xm/Xm.h>
Boolean XmTextFindString (widget, start, string, direction, position)
    Widget widget;
    XmTextPosition start;
    char *string;
    XmTextDirection direction;
    XmTextPosition *position;
```

### Inputs

| | |
|---|---|
| *widget* | Specifies the Text widget. |
| *start* | Specifies the position from which the search begins. |
| *string* | Specifies the string for which to search. |
| *direction* | Specifies the direction of the search. Pass either `XmTEXT_FORWARD` or `XmTEXT_BACKWARD`. |

### Outputs

| | |
|---|---|
| *position* | Returns the position where the search string starts. |

### Returns

`True` if the string is found or `False` otherwise.

## Availability

Motif 1.2 and later.

## Description

`XmTextFindString()` finds the beginning *position* of the specified *string* in the Text *widget*. Depending on the value of *direction*, the routine searches forward or backward from the specified *start* position for the first occurrence of *string*. If `XmTextFindString()` finds a match, it returns `True` and *position* specifies the position of the first character of the string as the number of characters from the beginning of the text, where the first character position is 0 (zero). If a match is not found, the routine returns `False` and the value of *position* is undefined.

## Usage

`XmTextFindString()` is a convenience routine that searches the text in a Text widget for a particular string. Without the routine, the search must be performed using the standard string manipulation routines.

## Example

The following routine shows the use of `XmTextFindString()` to locate a string in a text editing window. The search string is specified by the user in a single-line Text widget:

```
Widget text_w, search_w;

void search_text()
{
    char *search_pat;
    XmTextPosition pos, search_pos;
    Boolean found = False;

    if (!(search_pat = XmTextGetString(search_w)) || !*search_pat) {
        XtFree(search_pat);
        return;
    }

    /* find next occurrence from current position -- wrap if necessary */
    pos = XmTextGetCursorPosition(text_w);
    found = XmTextFindString(text_w, pos, search_pat,
        XmTEXT_FORWARD, &search_pos);
    if (!found)
        found = XmTextFindString(text_w, 0, search_pat,
            XmTEXT_FORWARD, &search_pos);

    if (found)
        XmTextSetInsertionPosition(text_w, search_pos);
    XtFree(search_pat);
}
```

## See Also

*XmTextFindStringWcs*(1), *XmTextGetSubstring*(1), *XmTextGetSubstringWcs*(1), *XmText*(2).

# XmTextFindStringWcs

## Name

XmTextFindStringWcs – find the beginning position of a wide-character

## Synopsis

```
#include <Xm/Text.h>
Boolean XmTextFindStringWcs (widget, start, wcstring, direction, position)
    Widget widget;
    XmTextPosition start;
    wchar_t *wcstring;
    XmTextDirection direction;
    XmTextPosition *position;
```

### Inputs

*widget* Specifies the Text widget.

*start* Specifies the position from which the search begins.

*wcstring* Specifies the wide-character string for which to search.

*direction* Specifies the direction of the search. Pass either XmTEXT_FORWARD or XmTEXT_BACKWARD.

### Outputs

*position* Returns the position where the search string starts.

### Returns

True if the string is found or False otherwise.

## Availability

Motif 1.2 and later.

## Description

XmTextFindStringWcs() finds the beginning *position* of the specified wide-character *wcstring* in the Text *widget*. Depending on the value of *direction*, the routine searches forward or backward from the specified *start* position for the first occurrence of *wcstring*. If XmTextFindStringWcs() finds a match, it returns True and *position* specifies the position of the first character of the string as the number of characters from the beginning of the text, where the first character position is 0 (zero). If a match is not found, the routine returns False and the value of *position* is undefined.

## Usage

In Motif 1.2, the Text widget supports wide-character strings. XmTextFindStringWcs() is a convenience routine that searches the text in a Text widget for a particular wide-character string. The routine converts the wide-character string into a multi-byte string and then performs the search. Without the routine, the search must be performed using the standard string manipulation routines.

## See Also

*XmTextFindString*(1), *XmTextGetSubstring*(1), *XmTextGetSubstringWcs*(1), *XmText*(2).

# XmTextGetBaseline

## Name

XmTextGetBaseline, XmTextFieldGetBaseline – get the position of the baseline.

## Synopsis

```
#include <Xm/Text.h>
int XmTextGetBaseline (widget)

#include <Xm/TextF.h>
int XmTextFieldGetBaseline (widget)

    Widget widget;
```

### Inputs

*widget* Specifies the Text or TextField widget.

### Returns

The baseline position.

## Description

`XmTextGetBaseline()` returns the y coordinate of the baseline of the first line of text in the specified Text *widget*, while `XmTextFieldGetBaseline()` returns the y coordinate of the baseline for the text in the specified TextField *widget*. `XmTextGetBaseline()` works when *widget* is a Text widget or a TextField widget, while `XmTextFieldGetBaseline()` only works for a TextField widget. For each routine, the returned value is relative to the top of the *widget* and it accounts for the margin height, shadow thickness, highlight thickness, and font ascent of the first font in the font list.

## Usage

`XmTextGetBaseline()` and `XmTextFieldGetBaseline()` provide information that is useful when you are laying out an application and trying to align different components.

## See Also

*XmWidgetGetBaselines*(1), *XmWidgetGetDisplayRect*(1),
*XmText*(2), *XmTextField*(2).

# XmTextGetCursorPosition



## Name

XmTextGetCursorPosition, XmTextFieldGetCursorPosition – get the position of the insertion cursor.

## Synopsis

```
#include <Xm/Text.h>
XmTextPosition XmTextGetCursorPosition (widget)

#include <Xm/TextF.h>
XmTextPosition XmTextFieldGetCursorPosition (widget)

    Widget widget;
```

### Inputs

*widget* Specifies the Text or TextField widget.

### Returns

The value of the XmNcursorPosition resource.

## Description

XmTextGetCursorPosition() and XmTextFieldGetCursorPosition() return the value of the XmNcursorPosition resource for the specified *widget*. XmTextGetCursorPosition() works when *widget* is a Text widget or a TextField widget, while XmTextFieldGetCursorPosition() only works for a TextField widget. For each routine, the value specifies the location of the insertion cursor as the number of characters from the beginning of the text, where the first character position is 0 (zero).

## Usage

XmTextGetCursorPosition() and XmTextFieldGetCursorPosition() are convenience routines that return the value of the XmNcursorPosition resource for a Text or TextField widget. Calling one of the routines is equivalent to calling XtGetValues() for the resource, although the routines access the value through the widget instance structures rather than through XtGetValues().

## See Also

*XmTextGetInsertionPosition*(1), *XmTextSetCursorPosition*(1), *XmTextSetInsertionPosition*(1), *XmTextShowPosition*(1),
*XmText*(2), *XmTextField*(2).

# XmTextGetEditable

## Name

XmTextGetEditable, XmTextFieldGetEditable – get the edit permission state.

## Synopsis

```
#include <Xm/Text.h>
Boolean XmTextGetEditable (widget)

#include <Xm/TextF.h>
Boolean XmTextFieldGetEditable (widget)

    Widget widget;
```

### Inputs

| | |
|---|---|
| *widget* | Specifies the Text or TextField widget. |

### Returns

The state of the `XmNeditable` resource.

## Description

`XmTextGetEditable()` and `XmTextFieldGetEditable()` return the value of the `XmNeditable` resource for the specified Text or TextField *widget*. `XmTextGetEditable()` works when *widget* is a Text widget or a TextField widget, while `XmTextFieldGetEditable()` only works for a TextField widget.

## Usage

By default, the `XmNeditable` resource is `True`, which means that a user can edit the text string. Setting the resource to `False` makes a text area read-only. `XmTextGetEditable()` and `XmTextFieldGetEditable()` are convenience routines that return the value of the `XmNeditable` resource for a Text or TextField widget. Calling one of the routines is equivalent to calling `XtGetValues()` for the resource, although the routines access the value through the widget instance structures rather than through `XtGetValues()`.

## See Also

*XmTextSetEditable*(1),
*XmText*(2), *XmTextField*(2).

# XmTextGetInsertionPosition



## Name

XmTextGetInsertionPosition, XmTextFieldGetInsertionPosition – get the position of the insertion cursor.

## Synopsis

```
#include <Xm/Text.h>
XmTextPosition XmTextGetInsertionPosition (widget)

#include <Xm/TextF.h>
XmTextPosition XmTextFieldGetInsertionPosition (widget)

    Widget widget;
```

### Inputs

*widget* Specifies the Text or TextField widget.

### Returns

The value of the `XmNcursorPosition` resource.

## Description

The functions, `XmTextGetInsertionPosition()` and `XmTextFieldGetInsertionPosition()`, return the value of the `XmNcursorPosition` resource for the specified *widget*. `XmTextGetInsertionPosition()` works when *widget* is a Text widget or a TextField widget, while `XmTextFieldGetInsertionPosition()` only works for a TextField widget. For each routine, the value specifies the location of the insertion cursor as the number of characters from the beginning of the text, where the first character position is 0 (zero).

## Usage

The functions, `XmTextGetInsertionPosition()` and `XmTextFieldGetInsertionPosition()`, are convenience routines that return the value of the `XmNcursorPosition` resource for a Text or TextField widget. Calling one of the routines is equivalent to calling `XtGetValues()` for the resource, although the routines access the value through the widget instance structures rather than through `XtGetValues()`.

## See Also

*XmTextGetCursorPosition*(1), *XmTextSetInsertionPosition*(1), *XmTextSetCursorPosition*(1), *XmTextShowPosition*(1),
*XmText*(2), *XmTextField*(2).

# XmTextGetLastPosition

## Name

XmTextGetLastPosition, XmTextFieldGetLastPosition – get the position of the last character of text.

## Synopsis

```
#include <Xm/Text.h>
XmTextPosition XmTextGetLastPosition (widget)

#include <Xm/TextF.h>
XmTextPosition XmTextFieldGetLastPosition (widget)

    Widget widget;
```

### Inputs

*widget* Specifies the Text or TextField widget.

### Returns

The position of the last text character.

## Description

`XmTextGetLastPosition()` and `XmTextFieldGetLastPosition()` return the position of the last character of text in the specified *widget*. `XmTextGetLastPosition()` works when *widget* is a Text widget or a TextField widget, while `XmTextFieldGetLastPosition()` only works for a TextField widget. For each routine, the returned value specifies the position as the number of characters from the beginning of the text, where the first character position is 0 (zero).

## Usage

`XmTextGetLastPosition()` and `XmTextFieldGetLastPosition()` are convenience routines that return the number of characters of text in a Text or TextField widget.

## See Also

*XmTextGetCursorPosition*(1), *XmTextGetInsertionPosition*(1), *XmTextGetTopCharacter*(1), *XmTextScroll*(1), *XmTextSetCursorPosition*(1), *XmTextSetInsertionPosition*(1), *XmTextSetTopCharacter*(1), *XmTextShowPosition*(1), *XmText*(2), *XmTextField*(2).

# XmTextGetMaxLength



## Name

XmTextGetMaxLength, XmTextFieldGetMaxLength – get the maximum possible length of a text string.

## Synopsis

```
#include <Xm/Text.h>
int XmTextGetMaxLength (widget)

#include <Xm/TextF.h>
int XmTextFieldGetMaxLength (widget)

    Widget widget;
```

### Inputs

*widget* Specifies the Text or TextField widget.

### Returns

The value of the `XmNmaxLength` resource.

## Description

`XmTextGetMaxLength()` and `XmTextFieldGetMaxLength()` return the value of the `XmNmaxLength` resource for the specified Text or TextField *widget*. `XmTextGetMaxLength()` works when *widget* is a Text widget or a TextField widget, while `XmTextFieldGetMaxLength()` only works for a TextField widget. For each routine, the returned value specifies the maximum allowable length of a text string that a user can enter from the keyboard.

## Usage

`XmTextGetMaxLength()` and `XmTextFieldGetMaxLength()` are convenience routines that return the value of the `XmNmaxLength` resource for a Text or TextField widget. Calling one of the routines is equivalent to calling `XtGetValues()` for the resource, although the routines access the value through the widget instance structures rather than through `XtGetValues()`.

## See Also

*XmTextSetMaxLength*(1),
*XmText*(2), *XmTextField*(2).

# XmTextGetSelection

## Name

XmTextGetSelection, XmTextFieldGetSelection – get the value of the primary selection.

## Synopsis

```
#include <Xm/Text.h>
char * XmTextGetSelection (widget)

#include <Xm/TextF.h>
char * XmTextFieldGetSelection (widget)

    Widget widget;
```

### Inputs

*widget* Specifies the Text or TextField widget.

### Returns

A string containing the primary selection.

## Description

`XmTextGetSelection()` and `XmTextFieldGetSelection()` return a pointer to a character string containing the primary selection in the specified *widget*. `XmTextGetSelection()` works when *widget* is a Text widget or a TextField widget, while `XmTextFieldGetSelection()` only works for a TextField widget. For each routine, if no text is selected in the *widget*, the returned value is `NULL`. Storage for the returned string is allocated by the routine and should be freed by calling `XtFree()`. Management of the allocated memory is the responsibility of the application.

## Usage

`XmTextGetSelection()` and `XmTextFieldGetSelection()` provide a convenient way to get the current selection from a Text or TextField widget.

## See Also

*XmTextGetSelectionPosition*(1), *XmTextGetSelectionWcs*(1), *XmTextSetSelection*(1), *XmText*(2), *XmTextField*(2).

# XmTextGetSelectionPosition



## Name

XmTextGetSelectionPosition, XmTextFieldGetSelectionPosition – get the position of the primary selection.

## Synopsis

```
#include <Xm/Text.h>
Boolean XmTextGetSelectionPosition (widget, left, right)

#include <Xm/TextF.h>
Boolean XmTextFieldGetSelectionPosition (widget, left, right)

    Widget widget;
    XmTextPosition *left;
    XmTextPosition *right;
```

### Inputs

*widget* Specifies the Text or TextField widget.

### Outputs

*left* Returns the position of the left boundary of the primary selection.

*right* Returns the position of the right boundary of the primary selection.

### Returns

`True` if *widget* owns the primary selection or `False` otherwise.

## Description

The functions, `XmTextGetSelectionPosition()` and `XmTextFieldGetSelectionPosition()` return the left and right boundaries of the primary selection for the specified *widget*. `XmTextGetSelectionPosition()` works when *widget* is a Text widget or a TextField widget, while `XmTextFieldGetSelectionPosition()` only works for a TextField widget. Each boundary value specifies the position as the number of characters from the beginning of the text, where the first character position is 0 (zero). Each routine returns `True` if the specified Text or TextField *widget* owns the primary selection; otherwise, the routine returns `False` and the values of *left* and *right* are undefined.

## Usage

The functions, `XmTextGetSelectionPosition()` and `XmTextFieldGetSelectionPosition()`, provide a convenient way to get the position of the current selection from a Text or TextField widget.

## See Also

*XmTextGetSelection*(1), *XmTextGetSelectionWcs*(1), *XmTextSetSelection*(1), *XmText*(2), *XmTextField*(2).

# XmTextGetSelectionWcs

## Name

XmTextGetSelectionWcs, XmTextFieldGetSelectionWcs – get the wide-character value of the primary selection.

## Synopsis

```
#include <Xm/Text.h>
wchar_t * XmTextGetSelectionWcs (widget)

#include <Xm/TextF.h>
wchar_t * XmTextFieldGetSelectionWcs (widget)

    Widget widget;
```

### Inputs

*widget* Specifies the Text or TextField widget.

### Returns

A wide-character string containing the primary selection.

## Availability

Motif 1.2 and later.

## Description

`XmTextGetSelectionWcs()` and `XmTextFieldGetSelectionWcs()` return a pointer to a wide-character string containing the primary selection in the specified *widget*. `XmTextGetSelectionWcs()` works when *widget* is a Text widget or a TextField widget, while `XmTextFieldGetSelectionWcs()` only works for a TextField widget. For each routine, if no text is selected in the *widget*, the returned value is `NULL`. Storage for the returned wide-character string is allocated by the routine and should be freed by calling `XtFree()`. Management of the allocated memory is the responsibility of the application.

## Usage

In Motif 1.2, the Text and TextField widgets support wide-character strings. `XmTextGetSelectionWcs()` and `XmTextFieldGetSelectionWcs()` provide a convenient way to get the current selection in wide-character format from a Text or TextField widget.

## See Also

*XmTextGetSelection*(1), *XmTextGetSelectionPosition*(1), *XmTextSetSelection*(1), *XmText*(2), *XmTextField*(2).

# XmTextGetSource

## Name

XmTextGetSource – get the text source.

## Synopsis

```
#include <Xm/Text.h>
XmTextSource XmTextGetSource (widget)
    Widget widget;
```

### Inputs

*widget* Specifies the Text widget.

### Returns

The source of the Text widget.

## Description

`XmTextGetSource()` returns the source of the specified Text *widget*. Every Text widget has an `XmTextSource` data structure associated with it that functions as the text source and sink.

## Usage

Multiple text widgets can share the same text source, which means that editing in one of the widgets is reflected in all of the others. `XmTextGetSource()` retrieves the source for a *widget*; this source can then be used to set the source of another Text widget using `XmTextSetSource()`. `XmTextGetSource()` is a convenience routine that returns the value of the `XmNsource` resource for the Text widget. Calling the routine is equivalent to calling `XtGetValues()` for the resource, although the routine accesses the value through the widget instance structures rather than through `XtGetValues()`.

## See Also

*XmTextSetSource*(1),
*XmText*(2).

# XmTextGetString

## Name

XmTextGetString, XmTextFieldGetString – get the text string.

## Synopsis

```
#include <Xm/Text.h>
char * XmTextGetString (widget)

#include <Xm/TextF.h>
char * XmTextFieldGetString (widget)

    Widget widget;
```

### Inputs

*widget* Specifies the Text or TextField widget.

### Returns

A string containing the value of the Text or TextField *widget*.

## Description

XmTextGetString() and XmTextFieldGetString() return a pointer to a character string containing the value of the specified *widget*. XmTextGetString() works when *widget* is a Text widget or a TextField widget, while XmTextFieldGetString() only works for a TextField widget. For each routine, if the string has a length of 0 (zero), the returned value is the empty string. Storage for the returned string is allocated by the routine and should be freed by calling XtFree(). Management of the allocated memory is the responsibility of the application.



## Usage

XmTextGetString() and XmTextFieldGetString() are convenience routines that return the value of the XmNvalue resource for a Text or TextField widget. Calling one of the routines is equivalent to calling XtGetValues() for the resource, although the routines access the value through the widget instance structures rather than through XtGetValues().

In Motif 1.2, the Text and TextField widgets support wide-character strings. The resource XmNvalueWcs can be used to set the value of a Text or TextField widget to a wide-character string. Even if you set the XmNvalueWcs resource, you can still use XmTextGetString() or XmTextFieldGetString() to retrieve the value of the widget, since the value is stored internally as a multi-byte string.

## Example

The following routine shows the use of XmTextGetString() to retrieve the text from one Text widget and use the text to search for the string in another Text widget:

```
Widget text_w, search_w;

void search_text()
{
```

```
        char *search_pat;
        XmTextPosition pos, search_pos;
        Boolean found = False;

        if (!(search_pat = XmTextGetString(search_w)) || !*search_pat) {
            XtFree(search_pat);
            return;
        }

        /* find next occurrence from current position -- wrap if necessary */
        pos = XmTextGetCursorPosition(text_w);
        found = XmTextFindString(text_w, pos, search_pat,
            XmTEXT_FORWARD, &search_pos);
        if (!found)
            found = XmTextFindString(text_w, 0, search_pat,
                XmTEXT_FORWARD, &search_pos);

        if (found)
            XmTextSetInsertionPosition(text_w, search_pos);
        XtFree(search_pat);
    }
```

## See Also

*XmTextGetStringWcs*(1), *XmTextGetSubstring*(1), *XmTextGetSubstringWcs*(1), *XmTextSetString*(1), *XmTextSetStringWcs*(1),
*XmText*(2), *XmTextField*(2).

# XmTextGetStringWcs

## Name

XmTextGetStringWcs, XmTextFieldGetStringWcs – get the wide-character text string.

## Synopsis

```
#include <Xm/Text.h>
wchar_t * XmTextGetStringWcs (widget)

#include <Xm/TextF.h>
wchar_t * XmTextFieldGetStringWcs (widget) Widget

    Widget widget;
```

### Inputs

*widget* Specifies the Text or TextField widget.

### Returns

A wide-character string containing the value of the Text or TextField *widget*.

## Availability

Motif 1.2 and later.

## Description

XmTextGetStringWcs() and XmTextFieldGetStringWcs() return a pointer to a wide-character string containing the value of the specified *widget*. XmTextGetStringWcs() works when *widget* is a Text widget or a TextField widget, while XmTextFieldGetStringWcs() only works for a TextField widget. For each routine, if the string has a length of 0 (zero), the returned value is the empty string. Storage for the returned wide-character string is allocated by the routine and should be freed by calling XtFree(). Management of the allocated memory is the responsibility of the application.

## Usage

XmTextGetStringWcs() and XmTextFieldGetStringWcs() are convenience routines that return the value of the XmNvalueWcs resource for a Text or TextField widget. Calling one of the routines is equivalent to calling XtGetValues() for the resource, although the routines access the value through the widget instance structures rather than through XtGetValues().

In Motif 1.2, the Text and TextField widgets support wide-character strings. The resource XmNvalueWcs can be used to set the value of a Text or TextField widget to a wide-character string. Even if you use the XmNvalue resource to set the value of a widget, you can still use XmTextGetStringWcs() or XmTextFieldGetStringWcs() to retrieve the value of the widget, since the value can be converted to a wide-character string.

## See Also

*XmTextGetString*(1), *XmTextGetSubstring*(1), *XmTextGetSubstringWcs*(1), *XmTextSetString*(1), *XmTextSetStringWcs*(1),
*XmText*(2), *XmTextField*(2).

# XmTextGetSubstring

## Name

XmTextGetSubstring, XmTextFieldGetSubstring – get a copy of part of the text string.

## Synopsis

```
#include <Xm/Text.h>
int XmTextGetSubstring (widget, start, num_chars, buffer_size, buffer)

#include <Xm/TextF.h>
int XmTextFieldGetSubstring (widget, start, num_chars, buffer_size, buffer)

    Widget widget;
    XmTextPosition start;
    int num_chars;
    int buffer_size;
    char *buffer;
```

### Inputs

| | |
|---|---|
| *widget* | Specifies the Text or TextField widget. |
| *start* | Specifies the starting character position from which data is copied. |
| *num_chars* | Specifies the number of characters that are copied. |
| *buffer_size* | Specifies the size of *buffer*. |
| *buffer* | Specifies the character buffer where the copy is stored. |

### Returns

XmCOPY_SUCCEEDED on success, XmCOPY_TRUNCATED if fewer than *num_chars* are copied, or XmCOPY_FAILED on failure.

## Availability

Motif 1.2 and later.

## Description

XmTextGetSubstring() and XmTextFieldGetSubstring() get a copy of part of the internal text buffer for the specified *widget*. XmTextGetString() works when *widget* is a Text widget or a TextField widget, while XmTextFieldGetString() only works for a TextField widget. The routines copy *num_chars* characters starting at *start* position, which specifies the position as the number of characters from the beginning of the text, where the first character position is 0 (zero). The characters are copied into the provided *buffer* and are NULL-terminated.

XmTextGetSubstring() and XmTextFieldGetSubstring() return XmCOPY_-SUCCEEDED on success. If the specified *num_chars* does not fit in the provided *buffer*, the routines return XmCOPY_TRUNCATED. In this case, *buffer* contains as many characters as would fit plus a NULL terminator. If either of the routines fails to make the copy, it returns XmCOPY_FAILED and the contents of *buffer* are undefined.

## Usage

XmTextGetSubstring() and XmTextFieldGetSubstring() provide a convenient way to retrieve a portion of the text string in a Text or TextField widget. The routines return the specified part of the XmNvalue resource for the widget.

In Motif 1.2, the Text and TextField widgets support wide-character strings. The resource XmNvalueWcs can be used to set the value of a Text or TextField widget to a wide-character string. Even if you set the XmNvalueWcs resource, you can still use XmTextGetSubstring() or XmTextFieldGetSubstring() to retrieve part of the value of the widget, since the value is stored internally as a multi-byte string.

The necessary *buffer_size* for XmTextGetSubstring() and XmTextFieldGetSubstring() depends on the maximum number of bytes per character for the current locale. This information is stored in MB_CUR_MAX, a macro defined in *stdlib.h*. The *buffer* needs to be large enough to store the substring and a NULL terminator. You can use the following equation to calculate the necessary *buffer_size*:

```
buffer_size = (num_chars * MB_CUR_MAX) + 1
```

## See Also

*XmTextGetString*(1), *XmTextGetStringWcs*(1), *XmTextGetSubstringWcs*(1), *XmTextSetString*(1), *XmTextSetStringWcs*(1),
*XmText*(2), *XmTextField*(2).

# XmTextGetSubstringWcs

## Name

XmTextGetSubstringWcs, XmTextFieldGetSubstringWcs – get a copy of part of the wide-character text string.

## Synopsis

```
#include <Xm/Text.h>
int XmTextGetSubstringWcs (widget, start, num_chars, buffer_size,
        buffer)

#include <Xm/TextF.h>
int XmTextFieldGetSubstringWcs (widget, start, num_chars, buffer_size,
        buffer)

    Widget widget;
    XmTextPosition start;
    int num_chars;
    int buffer_size;
    wchar_t *buffer;
```

### Inputs

`widget` Specifies the Text or TextField widget.

`start` Specifies the starting character position from which data is copied.

`num_chars` Specifies the number of wide-characters that are copied.

`buffer_size` Specifies the size of `buffer`.

`buffer` Specifies the wide-character buffer where the copy is stored.

### Returns

XmCOPY_SUCCEEDED on success, XmCOPY_TRUNCATED if fewer than *num_chars* are copied, or XmCOPY_FAILED on failure.

## Availability

Motif 1.2 and later.

## Description

XmTextGetSubstringWcs() and XmTextFieldGetSubstringWcs() get a copy of part of the internal wide-character text buffer for the specified *widget*. XmTextGetSubstringWcs() works when *widget* is a Text widget or a TextField widget, while XmTextFieldGetSubstringWcs() only works for a TextField widget. The routines copy *num_chars* wide-characters starting at *start* position, which specifies the position as the number of characters from the beginning of the text, where the first character position is 0 (zero). The wide-characters are copied into the provided *buffer* and are NULL-terminated.

XmTextGetSubstringWcs() and XmTextFieldGetSubstringWcs() return XmCOPY_SUCCEEDED on success. If the specified *num_chars* does not fit in the provided *buffer*, the routines return XmCOPY_TRUNCATED. In this case, *buffer* contains as many wide-characters as would fit plus a NULL terminator. If either of the routines fails to make the copy, it returns XmCOPY_FAILED and the contents of *buffer* are undefined.

## Usage

XmTextGetSubstringWcs() and XmTextFieldGetSubstringWcs() provide a convenient way to retrieve a portion of the wide-character text string in a Text or TextField widget. The routines return the specified part of the XmNvalueWcs resource for the widget.

In Motif 1.2, the Text and TextField widgets support wide-character strings. The resource XmNvalueWcs can be used to set the value of a Text or TextField widget to a wide-character string. Even if you use the XmNvalue resource to set the value of a widget, you can still use XmTextGetSubstringWcs() or XmTextFieldGetSubstringWcs() to retrieve part of the value of the widget, since the value can be converted to a wide-character string. The necessary *buffer_size* for XmTextGetSubstringWcs() and XmTextFieldGet-SubstringWcs() is *num_chars* + 1.

## See Also

*XmTextGetString*(1), *XmTextGetStringWcs*(1), *XmTextGetSubstring*(1), *XmTextSetString*(1), *XmTextSetStringWcs*(1),
*XmText*(2), *XmTextField*(2).

# XmTextGetTopCharacter

## Name

XmTextGetTopCharacter – get the position of the first character of text that is displayed.

## Synopsis

```
#include <Xm/Text.h>
XmTextPosition XmTextGetTopCharacter (widget)
    Widget widget;
```

### Inputs

*widget* Specifies the Text widget.

### Returns

The position of the first visible character.

## Description

`XmTextGetTopCharacter()` returns the value of the `XmNtopCharacter` resource for the specified Text *widget*. The returned value specifies the position of the first visible character of text as the number of characters from the beginning of the text, where the first character position in 0 (zero).

## Usage

`XmTextGetTopCharacter()` is a convenience routine that returns the value of the `XmNtopCharacter` resource for a Text widget. Calling the routines is equivalent to calling `XtGetValues()` for the resource, although the routines accesses the value through the widget instance structures rather than through `XtGetValues()`.

## See Also

*XmTextGetCursorPosition*(1), *XmTextGetInsertionPosition*(1), *XmTextGetLastPosition*(1), *XmTextScroll*(1), *XmTextSetCursorPosition*(1), *XmTextSetInsertionPosition*(1), *XmTextSetTopCharacter*(1), *XmTextShowPosition*(1), *XmText*(2).

# XmTextInsert

## Name

XmTextInsert, XmTextFieldInsert – insert a string into the text string.

## Synopsis

```
#include <Xm/Text.h>
void XmTextInsert (widget, position, value)

#include <Xm/TextF.h>
void XmTextFieldInsert (widget, position, value)

    Widget widget;
    XmTextPosition position;
    char *string;
```

### Inputs

| | |
|---|---|
| *widget* | Specifies the Text or TextField widget. |
| *position* | Specifies the position at which the string is inserted. |
| *string* | Specifies the string to be inserted. |

## Description

`XmTextInsert()` and `XmTextFieldInsert()` insert a text string in the specified Text or TextField *widget*. `XmTextInsert()` works when *widget* is a Text widget or a TextField widget, while `XmTextFieldInsert()` only works for a TextField widget. The specified *string* is inserted at *position*, where character positions are numbered sequentially, starting with 0 (zero) at the beginning of the text. To insert a string after the *n*th character, use a *position* value of *n*.

`XmTextInsert()` and `XmTextFieldInsert()` also invoke the callback routines for the `XmNvalueChangedCallback`, the `XmNmodifyVerifyCallback`, and the `XmNmodifyVerifyCallbackWcs` callbacks for the specified *widget*. If both verification callbacks are present, the `XmNmodifyVerifyCallback` procedures are invoked first and the results are passed to the `XmNmodifyVerifyCallbackWcs` procedures.

## Usage

`XmTextInsert()` and `XmTextFieldInsert()` provide a convenient means of inserting text in a Text or TextField widget. The routines insert text by modifying the value of the `XmNvalue` resource of the widget.

## Example

The following routine shows the use of `XmTextInsert()` to insert a message into a status Text widget:

```
Widget status;

void insert_text(message)
char *message;
```

```
{
    XmTextPosition curpos;

    curpos = XmTextGetInsertionPosition(status);
    XmTextInsert(status, curpos, message);

    curpos = curpos + strlen(message);
    XmTextShowPosition(status, curpos);
    XmTextSetInsertionPosition(status, curpos);
}
```

## See Also

*XmTextInsertWcs*(1), *XmTextReplace*(1), *XmTextReplaceWcs*(1), *XmText*(2), *XmTextField*(2).

# XmTextInsertWcs



## Name

XmTextInsertWcs, XmTextFieldInsertWcs – insert a wide-character string into the text string.

## Synopsis

```
#include <Xm/Text.h>
void XmTextInsert(widget, position, wcstring)

#include <Xm/TextF.h>
void XmTextFieldInsertWcs (widget, position, wcstring)

    Widget widget;
    XmTextPosition position;
    wchar_t * wcstring;
```

### Inputs

*widget* Specifies the Text or TextField widget.

*position* Specifies the position at which the string is inserted.

*wcstring* Specifies the wide-character string to be inserted.

## Availability

Motif 1.2 and later.

## Description

XmTextInsertWcs() and XmTextFieldInsertWcs() insert a wide-character text string in the specified *widget*. XmTextInsertWcs() works when *widget* is a Text widget or a TextField widget, while XmTextFieldInsertWcs() only works for a TextField widget. The specified *string* is inserted at *position*, where character positions are numbered sequentially, starting with 0 (zero) at the beginning of the text. To insert a string after the *n*th character, use a *position* value of *n*.

XmTextInsertWcs() and XmTextFieldInsertWcs() also invoke the callback routines for the XmNvalueChangedCallback, the XmNmodifyVerifyCallback, and the XmNmodifyVerifyCallbackWcs callbacks for the specified *widget*. If both verification callbacks are present, the XmNmodifyVerifyCallback procedures are invoked first and the results are passed to the XmNmodifyVerifyCallbackWcs procedures.

## Usage

In Motif 1.2, the Text and TextField widgets support wide-character strings. XmTextInsertWcs() and XmTextFieldInsertWcs() provide a convenient means of inserting a wide-character string in a Text or TextField widget. The routines insert text by converting the wide-character string to a multi-byte string and then modifying the value of the XmNvalue resource of the widget.

## See Also

*XmTextInsert*(1), *XmTextReplace*(1), *XmTextReplaceWcs*(1), *XmText*(2), *XmTextField*(2).

# XmTextPaste



## Name

XmTextPaste, XmTextFieldPaste – insert the clipboard selection.

## Synopsis

```
#include <Xm/Text.h>
Boolean XmTextPaste (widget)

#include <Xm/TextF.h>
Boolean XmTextFieldPaste (widget)

    Widget widget;
```

### Inputs

*widget* Specifies the Text or TextField widget.

### Returns

`True` on success or `False` otherwise.

## Description

`XmTextPaste()` and `XmTextFieldPaste()` insert the clipboard selection at the current position of the insertion cursor in the specified *widget*. `XmTextPaste()` works when *widget* is a Text widget or a TextField widget, while `XmTextFieldPaste()` only works for a TextField widget. If the insertion cursor is within the current selection and the value of `XmNpendingDelete` is `True`, the current selection is replaced by the clipboard selection. Both routines return `True` if successful. If the *widget* is not editable or if the function cannot obtain ownership of the clipboard selection, the routines return `False`.

`XmTextPaste()` and `XmTextFieldPaste()` also invoke the callback routines for the `XmNvalueChangedCallback`, the `XmNmodifyVerifyCallback`, and the `XmNmodifyVerifyCallbackWcs` callbacks for the specified *widget*. If both verification callbacks are present, the `XmNmodifyVerifyCallback` procedures are invoked first and the results are passed to the `XmNmodifyVerifyCallbackWcs` procedures.

## Usage

`XmTextPaste()` and `XmTextFieldPaste()` get the current selection from the clipboard and insert it at the location of the insertion cursor in the Text or TextField widget.

## Example

The following callback routine for the items on an **Edit** menu (**Cut**, **Copy**, **Paste**, and **Clear**) shows the use of `XmTextPaste()`:

```
Widget text_w, status;

void cut_paste(widget, client_data, call_data)
Widget widget;
XtPointer client_data;
XtPointer call_data;
```

```
{
    int num = (int) client_data;
    XmAnyCallbackStruct *cbs = (XmAnyCallbackStruct *) call_data;
    Boolean result = True;

    switch (num) {
        case 0 :
         result = XmTextCut(text_w, cbs->event->xbutton.time);
         break;
        case 1 :
         result = XmTextCopy(text_w, cbs->event->xbutton.time);
         break;
        case 2 :
         result = XmTextPaste(text_w);
         break;
        case 3 :
         XmTextClearSelection(text_w, cbs->event->xbutton.time);
         break;
    }

    if (result == False)
        XmTextSetString(status, "There is no selection.");
    else
        XmTextSetString(status, NULL);
}
```

## See Also

*XmTextCopy*(1), *XmTextCut*(1),
*XmText*(2), *XmTextField*(2).

# XmTextPosToXY

## Name

XmTextPosToXY, XmTextFieldPosToXY – get the x, y position of a character position.

## Synopsis

```
#include <Xm/Text.h>
Boolean XmTextPosToXY (widget, position, x, y)

#include <Xm/TextF.h>
Boolean XmTextFieldPosToXY (widget, position, x, y)

    Widget widget;
    XmTextPosition position;
    Position *x;
    Position *y;
```

### Inputs

| | |
|---|---|
| *widget* | Specifies the Text or TextField widget. |
| *position* | Specifies the character position. |

### Outputs

| | |
|---|---|
| *x* | Returns the x-coordinate of the character position. |
| *y* | Returns the y-coordinate of the character position. |

### Returns

`True` if the character position is displayed in the *widget* or `False` otherwise.

## Description

`XmTextPosToXY()` and `XmTextFieldPosToXY()` return the x and y coordinates of the character at the specified *position* within the specified *widget*. `XmTextPosToXY()` works when *widget* is a Text widget or a TextField widget, while `XmTextFieldPosToXY()` only works for a TextField widget. Character positions are numbered sequentially, starting with 0 (zero) at the beginning of the text. The returned coordinate values are specified relative to the upper-left corner of *widget*. Both routines return `True` if the character at *position* is currently displayed in the *widget*. Otherwise, the routines return `False` and no values are returned in the *x* and *y* arguments.

## Usage

`XmTextPosToXY()` and `XmTextFieldPosToXY()` provide a way to determine the actual position of a character in a Text or TextField widget. This information is useful if you need to perform additional event processing or draw special graphics in the widget.

## See Also

*XmTextXYToPos*(1),
*XmText*(2), *XmTextField*(2).

# XmTextRemove

## Name

XmTextRemove, XmTextFieldRemove – delete the primary selection.

## Synopsis

```
#include <Xm/Text.h>
Boolean XmTextRemove (widget)

#include <Xm/TextF.h>
Boolean XmTextFieldRemove (widget)

    Widget widget;
```

### Inputs

*widget* Specifies the Text or TextField widget.

### Returns

`True` on success or `False` otherwise.

## Description

`XmTextRemove()` and `XmTextFieldRemove()` delete the primary selected text from the specified *widget*. `XmTextRemove()` works when *widget* is a Text widget or a TextField widget, while `XmTextFieldRemove()` only works for a TextField widget. Both routines return `True` if successful. If the *widget* is not editable, if the primary selection is `NULL`, or if it is not owned by the specified *widget*, the routines return `False`.

`XmTextRemove()` and `XmTextFieldRemove()` also invoke the callback routines for the `XmNvalueChangedCallback`, the `XmNmodifyVerifyCallback`, and the `XmNmodifyVerifyCallbackWcs` callbacks for the specified *widget*. If both verification callbacks are present, the `XmNmodifyVerifyCallback` procedures are invoked first and the results are passed to the `XmNmodifyVerifyCallbackWcs` procedures.

## Usage

`XmTextRemove()` and `XmTextFieldRemove()` are like `XmTextCut()` and `XmTextFieldCut()`, in that they remove selected text from a Text or TextField widget. However, the routines do not copy the selected text to the clipboard before removing it.

## See Also

*XmTextClearSelection*(1), *XmTextCut*(1), *XmTextGetSelection*(1), *XmTextGetSelectionPosition*(1), *XmTextGetSelectionWcs*(1), *XmTextSetSelection*(1), *XmText*(2), *XmTextField*(2).

# XmTextReplace



## Name

XmTextReplace, XmTextFieldReplace – replace part of the text string.

## Synopsis

```
#include <Xm/Text.h>
void XmTextReplace (widget, from_pos, to_pos, value)

#include <Xm/TextF.h>
void XmTextFieldReplace (widget, from_pos, to_pos, value)

    Widget widget;
    XmTextPosition from_pos;
    XmTextPosition to_pos;
    char *value;
```

### Inputs

*widget* Specifies the Text or TextField widget.

*from_pos* Specifies the starting position of the text that is to be replaced.

*to_pos* Specifies the ending position of the text that is to be replaced.

*value* Specifies the replacement string.

## Description

XmTextReplace() and XmTextFieldReplace() replace a portion of the text string in the specified *widget*. XmTextReplace() works when *widget* is a Text widget or a TextField widget, while XmTextFieldReplace() only works for a TextField widget. The specified *value* replaces the text starting at *from_pos* and continuing up to, but not including, *to_pos*, where character positions are numbered sequentially, starting with 0 (zero) at the beginning of the text. To replace the characters after the *n*th character up to the *m*th character, use a *from_pos* value of *n* and a *to_pos* value of *m*.

XmTextReplace() and XmTextFieldReplace() also invoke the callback routines for the XmNvalueChangedCallback, the XmNmodifyVerifyCallback, and the XmNmodifyVerifyCallbackWcs callbacks for the specified *widget*. If both verification callbacks are present, the XmNmodifyVerifyCallback procedures are invoked first and the results are passed to the XmNmodifyVerifyCallbackWcs procedures.

## Usage

XmTextReplace() and XmTextFieldReplace() provide a convenient means of replacing text in a Text or TextField widget. The routines replace text by modifying the value of the XmNvalue resource of the widget.

## Example

The following routine shows the use of `XmTextReplace()` to replace all of the occurrences of a string in a Text widget. The search and replacement strings are specified by the user in single-line Text widgets:

```
Widget text_w, search_w, replace_w;

void search_and_replace()
{
    char *search_pat, *new_pat;
    XmTextPosition curpos, searchpos;
    int search_len, pattern_len;
    Boolean found = False;

    search_len = XmTextGetLastPosition(search_w);
    if (!(search_pat = XmTextGetString(search_w)) || !*search_pat) {
        XtFree(search_pat);
        return;
    }

    pattern_len = XmTextGetLastPosition(replace_w);
    if (!(new_pat = XmTextGetString(replace_w)) || !*new_pat) {
        XtFree(search_pat);
        XtFree(new_pat);
        return;
    }

    curpos = 0;
    found = XmTextFindString(text_w, curpos, search_pat,
        XmTEXT_FORWARD, &searchpos);
    while (found) {
        XmTextReplace(text_w, searchpos, searchpos + search_len, new_pat);
        curpos = searchpos + 1;
        found = XmTextFindString(text_w, curpos, search_pat,
            XmTEXT_FORWARD, &searchpos);
    }

    XtFree(search_pat);
    XtFree(new_pat);
}
```

## See Also

*XmTextInsert*(1), *XmTextInsertWcs*(1), *XmTextReplaceWcs*(1), *XmText*(2), *XmTextField*(2).

# XmTextReplaceWcs



## Name

XmTextReplaceWcs, XmTextFieldReplaceWcs – replace part of the wide-character text string.

## Synopsis

```
#include <Xm/Text.h>
void XmTextReplaceWcs (widget, from_pos, to_pos, wcstring)

#include <Xm/TextF.h>
void XmTextFieldReplaceWcs (widget, from_pos, to_pos, wcstring)

    Widget widget;
    XmTextPosition from_pos;
    XmTextPosition to_pos;
    wchar_t *wcstring;
```

### Inputs

| | |
|---|---|
| *widget* | Specifies the Text or TextField widget. |
| *from_pos* | Specifies the starting position of the text that is to be replaced. |
| *to_pos* | Specifies the ending position of the text that is to be replaced. |
| *wcstring* | Specifies the replacement wide-character string. |

## Availability

Motif 1.2 and later.

## Description

XmTextReplaceWcs() and XmTextFieldReplaceWcs() replace a portion of the text string in the specified *widget* with the specified wide-character string *wcstring*. XmTextReplaceWcs() works when *widget* is a Text widget or a TextField widget, while XmTextFieldReplaceWcs() only works for a TextField widget. The specified *wcstring* replaces the text starting at *from_pos* and continuing up to, but not including, *to_pos*, where character positions are numbered sequentially, starting with 0 (zero) at the beginning of the text. To replace the characters after the *n*th character up to the *m*th character, use a *from_pos* value of *n* and a *to_pos* value of *m*.

XmTextReplaceWcs() and XmTextFieldReplaceWcs() also invoke the callback routines for the XmNvalueChangedCallback, the XmNmodifyVerifyCallback, and the XmNmodifyVerifyCallbackWcs callbacks for the specified *widget*. If both verification callbacks are present, the XmNmodifyVerifyCallback procedures are invoked first and the results are passed to the XmNmodifyVerifyCallbackWcs procedures.

## Usage

In Motif 1.2, the Text and TextField widgets support wide-character strings. XmTextReplaceWcs() and XmTextFieldReplaceWcs() provide a convenient means of replacing a string in a Text or TextField widget with a wide-character string. The routines convert the wide-character string to a multi-byte string and then replace the text by modifying the value of the `XmNvalue` resource of the widget.

## See Also

*XmTextInsert*(1), *XmTextInsertWcs*(1), *XmTextReplace*(1),
*XmText*(2), *XmTextField*(2).

# XmTextScroll



## Name

XmTextScroll – scroll the text.

## Synopsis

```
#include <Xm/Text.h>
void XmTextScroll (widget, lines)
    Widget widget;
    int lines;
```

### Inputs

*widget* Specifies the Text widget.

## Description

`XmTextScroll()` scrolls the text in the specified Text *widget* by the specified number of *lines*. The text is scrolled upward if *lines* is positive and downward if *lines* is negative.

## Usage

`XmTextScroll()` provides a way to perform relative scrolling in a Text widget. The Text widget does not have to be the child of a ScrolledWindow for the scrolling to occur. The routine simply changes the currently viewable region of text.

## See Also

*XmTextGetCursorPosition*(1), *XmTextGetInsertionPosition*(1), *XmTextGetLastPosition*(1), *XmTextGetTopCharacter*(1), *XmTextSetCursorPosition*(1), *XmTextSetInsertionPosition*(1), *XmTextSetTopCharacter*(1),
*XmText*(2).

# XmTextSetAddMode

## Name

XmTextSetAddMode, XmTextFieldSetAddMode – set the add mode state.

## Synopsis

```
#include <Xm/Text.h>
void XmTextSetAddMode (widget, state)

#include <Xm/TextF.h>
void XmTextFieldSetAddMode (widget, state)

    Widget widget;
    Boolean state;
```

### Inputs

| | |
|---|---|
| *widget* | Specifies the Text or TextField widget. |
| *state* | Specifies the state of add mode. |

## Description

`XmTextSetAddMode()` and `XmTextFieldSetAddMode()` set the state of add mode for the specified *widget*. `XmTextSetAddMode()` works when *widget* is a Text widget or a TextField widget, while `XmTextFieldSetAddMode()` only works for a TextField widget. If *state* is `True` add mode is turned on; if *state* is `False`, add mode is turned off. When a Text or TextField widget is in add mode, the user can move the insertion cursor without altering the primary selection.

## Usage

`XmTextSetAddMode()` and `XmTextFieldSetAddMode()` provide a way to change the state of add mode in a Text or TextField widget. The distinction between normal mode and add mode is only important for making keyboard-based selections. In normal mode, the location cursor and the selection move together, while in add mode, the location cursor and the selection can be separate.

## See Also

*XmTextSetCursorPosition*(1), *XmTextSetInsertionPosition*(1), *XmText*(2), *XmTextField*(2).

# XmTextSetCursorPosition



## Name

XmTextSetCursorPosition, XmTextFieldSetCursorPosition – set the position of the insertion cursor.

## Synopsis

```
#include <Xm/Text.h>
void XmTextSetCursorPosition (widget, position)

#include <Xm/TextF.h>
void XmTextFieldSetCursorPosition (widget, position)

    Widget widget;
    XmTextPosition position;
```

### Inputs

*widget* Specifies the Text or TextField widget.

*position* Specifies the position of the insertion cursor.

## Description

XmTextSetCursorPosition() and XmTextFieldSetCursorPosition() set the value of the XmNcursorPosition resource to *position* for the specified *widget*. XmTextSetCursorPosition() works when *widget* is a Text widget or a TextField widget, while XmTextFieldSetCursorPosition() only works for a TextField widget. This resource specifies the location of the insertion cursor as the number of characters from the beginning of the text, where the first character position is 0 (zero).

XmTextSetCursorPosition() and XmTextFieldSetCursorPosition() also invoke the callback routines for the XmNmotionVerifyCallback for the specified *widget* if the position of the insertion cursor changes.

## Usage

XmTextSetCursorPosition() and XmTextFieldSetCursorPosition() are convenience routines that set the value of the XmNcursorPosition resource for a Text or TextField widget. Calling one of the routines is equivalent to calling XtSetValues() for the resource, although the routines access the value through the widget instance structures rather than through XtSetValues().

## See Also

*XmTextGetCursorPosition*(1), *XmTextGetInsertionPosition*(1), *XmTextSetInsertionPosition*(1), *XmTextShowPosition*(1),
*XmText*(2), *XmTextField*(2).

# XmTextSetEditable

## Name

XmTextSetEditable, XmTextFieldSetEditable – set the edit permission state.

## Synopsis

```
#include <Xm/Text.h>
void XmTextSetEditable (widget, editable)

#include <Xm/TextF.h>
void XmTextFieldSetEditable (widget, editable)

    Widget widget;
    Boolean editable;
```

### Inputs

| | |
|---|---|
| *widget* | Specifies the Text or TextField widget. |
| *editable* | Specifies whether or not the text can be edited. |

## Description

`XmTextSetEditable()` and `XmTextFieldSetEditable()` set the value of the `XmNeditable` resource to *editable* for the specified *widget*. `XmTextSetEditable()` works when *widget* is a Text widget or a TextField widget, while `XmTextFieldSetEditable()` only works for a TextField widget.

## Usage

By default, the `XmNeditable` resource is `True`, which means that a user can edit the text string. Setting the resource to `False` makes a text area read-only. `XmTextSetEditable()` and `XmTextFieldSetEditable()` are convenience routines that set the value of the `XmNeditable` resource for a Text or TextField widget. Calling one of the routines is equivalent to calling `XtSetValues()` for the resource, although the routines access the value through the widget instance structures rather than through `XtSetValues()`.

## See Also

*XmTextGetEditable*(1),
*XmText*(2), *XmTextField*(2).

# XmTextSetHighlight



## Name

XmTextSetHighlight, XmTextFieldSetHighlight – highlight text.

## Synopsis

```
#include <Xm/Text.h>
void XmTextSetHighlight (widget, left, right, mode)

#include <Xm/TextF.h>
void XmTextFieldSetHighlight (widget, left, right, mode)

    Widget widget;
    XmTextPosition left;
    XmTextPosition right;
    XmHighlightMode mode;
```

### Inputs

| | |
|---|---|
| *widget* | Specifies the Text or TextField widget. |
| *left* | Specifies the left boundary position of the text to be highlighted. |
| *right* | Specifies the right boundary position of the text to be highlighted. |
| *mode* | Specifies the highlighting mode. Pass one of the following values: XmHIGHLIGHT_NORMAL, XmHIGHLIGHT_SELECTED, or XmHIGHLIGHT_SECONDARY_SELECTED. |

## Description

XmTextSetHighlight() and XmTextFieldSetHighlight() highlight text in the specified *widget* without selecting the text. XmTextSetHighlight() works when *widget* is a Text widget or a TextField widget, while XmTextFieldSetHighlight() only works for a TextField widget. The *left* and *right* arguments specify the boundary positions of the text that is to be highlighted. Each boundary value specifies the position as the number of characters from the beginning of the text, where the first character position is 0 (zero). The *mode* parameter indicates the type of highlighting that is done. XmHIGHLIGHT_NORMAL removes any highlighting, XmHIGHLIGHT_SELECTED uses reverse video highlighting, and XmHIGHLIGHT_SECONDARY_SELECTED uses underline highlighting.

## Usage

XmTextSetHighlight() and XmTextFieldSetHighlight() provide a way to highlight text in a Text or TextField widget. These routines are useful if you need to emphasize certain text in a widget. These routine only highlight text; they do not select the specified text.

## Example

The following routine shows the use of `XmTextSetHighlight()` to highlight all of the occurrences of a string in a Text widget. The search string is specified by the user in a single-line Text widget:

```
Widget text_w, search_w;

void search_text()
{
    char *search_pat;
    XmTextPosition curpos, searchpos;
    int len;
    Boolean found = False;

    len = XmTextGetLastPosition(search_w);
    if (!(search_pat = XmTextGetString(search_w)) || !*search_pat) {
        XtFree(search_pat);
        return;
    }

    curpos = 0;
    found = XmTextFindString(text_w, curpos, search_pat,
        XmTEXT_FORWARD, &searchpos);
    while (found) {
        XmTextSetHighlight(text_w, searchpos, searchpos + len,
            XmHIGHLIGHT_SECONDARY_SELECTED);
        curpos = searchpos + 1;
        found = XmTextFindString(text_w, curpos, search_pat,
            XmTEXT_FORWARD, &searchpos);
    }

    XtFree(search_pat);
}
```

## See Also

*XmTextSetSelection*(1),
*XmText*(2), *XmTextField*(2).

# XmTextSetInsertionPosition



## Name

XmTextSetInsertionPosition, XmTextFieldSetInsertionPosition – set the position of the insertion cursor.

## Synopsis

```
#include <Xm/Text.h>
void XmTextSetInsertionPosition (widget, position)

#include <Xm/TextF.h>
void XmTextFieldSetInsertionPosition (widget, position)

    Widget widget;
    XmTextPosition position;
```

### Inputs

*widget* Specifies the Text or TextField widget.

*position* Specifies the position of the insertion cursor.

## Description

The functions, `XmTextSetInsertionPosition()` and `XmTextFieldSetInsertionPosition()`, set the value of the `XmNcursorPosition` resource to *position* for the specified *widget*. `XmTextSetInsertionPosition()` works when *widget* is a Text widget or a TextField widget, while `XmTextFieldSetInsertionPosition()` only works for a TextField widget. This resource specifies the location of the insertion cursor as the number of characters from the beginning of the text, where the first character position is 0 (zero).

`XmTextSetInsertionPosition()` and `XmTextFieldSetInsertionPosition()` also invoke the callback routines for the `XmNmotionVerifyCallback` for the specified *widget* if the position of the insertion cursor changes.

## Usage

The functions, `XmTextSetInsertionPosition()` and `XmTextFieldSetInsertionPosition()`, are convenience routines that set the value of the `XmNcursorPosition` resource for a Text or TextField widget. Calling one of the routines is equivalent to calling `XtSetValues()` for the resource, although the routines access the value through the widget instance structures rather than through `XtSetValues()`.

## Example

The following code shows the use of `XmTextSetInsertionPosition()` in a routine that searches for a string in a Text widget and moves the insertion cursor to the string if it is found:

```
Widget text_w, search_w;

void search_text()
{
```

```
    char *search_pat;
    XmTextPosition pos, search_pos;
    Boolean found = False;

    if (!(search_pat = XmTextGetString(search_w)) || !*search_pat) {
        XtFree(search_pat);
        return;
    }

    /* find next occurrence from current position -- wrap if necessary */
    pos = XmTextGetCursorPosition(text_w);
    found = XmTextFindString(text_w, pos, search_pat,
        XmTEXT_FORWARD, &search_pos);
    if (!found)
        found = XmTextFindString(text_w, 0, search_pat,
            XmTEXT_FORWARD, &search_pos);

    if (found)
        XmTextSetInsertionPosition(text_w, search_pos);
    XtFree(search_pat);
}
```

## See Also

*XmTextGetCursorPosition*(1), *XmTextGetInsertionPosition*(1), *XmTextSetCursorPosition*(1), *XmTextShowPosition*(1),
*XmText*(2), *XmTextField*(2).

# XmTextSetMaxLength

## Name

XmTextSetMaxLength, XmTextFieldSetMaxLength – set the maximum possible length of a text string.

## Synopsis

```
#include <Xm/Text.h>
void XmTextSetMaxLength (widget, max_length)

#include <Xm/TextF.h>
void XmTextFieldSetMaxLength (widget, max_length)

    Widget widget;
    int max_length;
```

### Inputs

*widget* Specifies the Text or TextField widget.

*max_length* Specifies the maximum allowable length of the text string.

## Description

XmTextSetMaxLength() and XmTextFieldSetMaxLength() set the value of the XmNmaxLength resource to *max_length* for the specified *widget*. XmTextSetMaxLength() works when *widget* is a Text widget or a TextField widget, while XmTextFieldSetMaxLength() only works for a TextField widget. This resource specifies the maximum allowable length of a text string that a user can enter from the keyboard.

## Usage

XmTextSetMaxLength() and XmTextFieldSetMaxLength() are convenience routines that set the XmNmaxLength resource for a Text or TextField widget. Calling one of the routines is equivalent to calling XtSetValues() for the resource, although the routines access the value through the widget instance structures rather than through XtSetValues(). The resource limits the length of a text string that a user may type, but it does not limit the length of strings entered with the XmNvalue or XmNvalueWcs resources or the XmTextSetString(), XmTextFieldSetString(), XmTextSetStringWcs(), and XmTextFieldSetStringWcs() routines.

## See Also

*XmTextGetMaxLength*(1),
*XmText*(2), *XmTextField*(2).

# XmTextSetSelection

## Name

XmTextSetSelection, XmTextFieldSetSelection – set the value of the primary selection.

## Synopsis

```
#include <Xm/Text.h>
void XmTextSetSelection (widget, first, last, time)

#include <Xm/TextF.h>
void XmTextFieldSetSelection (widget, first, last, time)

    Widget widget;
    XmTextPosition first;
    XmTextPosition last;
    Time time;
```

### Inputs

| | |
|---|---|
| *widget* | Specifies the Text or TextField widget. |
| *first* | Specifies the first character position to be selected. |
| *last* | Specifies the last character position to be selected. |
| *time* | Specifies the time of the event that caused the request. |

## Description

`XmTextSetSelection()` and `XmTextFieldSetSelection()` set the primary selection in the specified *widget*. `XmTextSetSelection()` works when *widget* is a Text widget or a TextField widget, while `XmTextFieldSetSelection()` only works for a TextField widget. The *first* and *last* arguments specify the beginning and ending positions of the text that is to be selected. Each of these values specifies the position as the number of characters from the beginning of the text, where the first character position is 0 (zero). For each routine, *time* specifies the server time of the event that caused the request to set the selection.

`XmTextSetSelection()` and `XmTextFieldSetSelection()` change the insertion cursor for the *widget* to the *last* position of the selection. The routines also invoke the callback routines for the `XmNmotionVerifyCallback` for the specified *widget*.

## Usage

`XmTextSetSelection()` and `XmTextFieldSetSelection()` provide a convenient way to set the current selection in a Text or TextField widget.

## See Also

*XmTextClearSelection*(1), *XmTextCopy*(1), *XmTextCut*(1), *XmTextGetSelection*(1), *XmTextGetSelectionPosition*(1), *XmTextGetSelectionWcs*(1), *XmTextRemove*(1), *XmText*(2), *XmTextField*(2).

# XmTextSetSource

XmTextSetSource – set the text source.

## Synopsis

```
#include <Xm/Text.h>
void XmTextSetSource (widget, source, top_character, cursor_position)
    Widget widget;
    XmTextSource source;
    XmTextPosition top_character;
    XmTextPosition cursor_position;
```

### Inputs

*widget* Specifies the Text widget.

*source* Specifies the text source.

*top_character*
Specifies the character position to display at the top of the widget.

*cursor_position*
Specifies the position of the insertion cursor.

## Description

`XmTextSetSource()` sets the source of the specified Text *widget*. The *top_-character* and *cursor_position* values specify positions as the number of characters from the beginning of the text, where the first character position is 0 (zero). If *source* is `NULL`, the Text widget creates a default string source and displays a warning message.

## Usage

Multiple text widgets can share the same text source, which means that editing in one of the widgets is reflected in all of the others. `XmTextGetSource()` retrieves the source for a *widget*; this source can then be used to set the source of another Text widget using `XmText-SetSource()`. `XmTextSetSource()` is a convenience routine that sets the value of the `XmNsource` resource for the Text widget. Calling the routine is equivalent to calling `Xt-SetValues()` for the resource, although the routine accesses the value through the widget instance structures rather than through `XtSetValues()`.

When a new text source is set, the old text source is destroyed unless another Text widget is using the old source. If you want to replace a text source without destroying it, create an unmanaged Text widget and set its source to the text source you want to save.

## See Also

*XmTextGetSource*(1),
*XmText*(2).

# XmTextSetString

## Name

XmTextSetString, XmTextFieldSetString – set the text string.

## Synopsis

```
#include <Xm/Text.h>
void XmTextSetString (widget, value)

#include <Xm/TextF.h>
void XmTextFieldSetString (widget, value)

    Widget widget;
    char *string;
```

### Inputs

*widget* — Specifies the Text or TextField widget.

*string* — Specifies the string value.

## Description

`XmTextSetString()` and `XmTextFieldSetString()` set the current text string in the specified *widget* to the specified *string*. `XmTextSetString()` works when *widget* is a Text widget or a TextField widget, while `XmTextFieldSetString()` only works for a TextField widget. Both functions also set the position of the insertion cursor to the beginning of the new text string.

`XmTextSetString()` and `XmTextFieldSetString()` invoke the callback routines for the `XmNvalueChangedCallback`, the `XmNmodifyVerifyCallback`, and the `XmNmodifyVerifyCallbackWcs` callbacks for the specified *widget*. If both verification callbacks are present, the `XmNmodifyVerifyCallback` procedures are invoked first and the results are passed to the `XmNmodifyVerifyCallbackWcs` procedures. The routines also invoke the callback routines for the `XmNmotionVerifyCallback` for the specified *widget*.

## Usage

`XmTextSetString()` and `XmTextFieldSetString()` are convenience routines that set the value of the `XmNvalue` resource for a Text or TextField widget. Calling one of the routines is equivalent to calling `XtSetValues()` for the resource, although the routines access the value through the widget instance structures rather than through `XtSetValues()`.

## Example

The following code shows the use of `XmTextSetString()` in a routine that displays the contents of file in a Text widget. The filename is specified by the user in a TextField widget:

```
Widget text_w, file_w;

void read_file()
{
```

```
    char *filename, *text;
    struct stat statb;
    int fd, len;

    if (!(filename = XmTextFieldGetString(file_w)) || !*filename) {
        XtFree(filename);
        return;
    }

    if (!(fd = open(filename, O_RDONLY))) {
        XtWarning("internal error -- can't open file");
    }
    if (fstat(fd, &statb) == -1 ||
            !(text = XtMalloc((len = statb.st_size) + 1))) {
        XtWarning("internal error -- can't show text");
        close(fd);
    }
    (void) read(fd, text, len);
    text[len] = 0;

    XmTextSetString(text_w, text);

    XtFree(text);
    XtFree(filename);
    close(fd);
}
```

### See Also

*XmTextGetString*(1), *XmTextGetStringWcs*(1), *XmTextGetSubstring*(1), *XmTextGetSubstringWcs*(1),
*XmTextSetStringWcs*(1),
*XmText*(2), *XmTextField*(2).

# XmTextSetStringWcs

## Name

XmTextSetStringWcs, XmTextFieldSetStringWcs – set the wide-character text string.

## Synopsis

```
#include <Xm/Text.h>
void XmTextSetStringWcs (widget, wcstring)

#include <Xm/TextF.h>
void XmTextFieldSetStringWcs (widget, wcstring)

    Widget widget;
    wchar_t *wcstring;
```

### Inputs

*widget* Specifies the Text or TextField widget.

*wcstring* Specifies the wide-character string value.

## Availability

Motif 1.2 and later.

## Description

XmTextSetStringWcs() and XmTextFieldSetStringWcs() set the current wide-character text string in the specified *widget* to the specified *string*. XmTextSetStringWcs() works when *widget* is a Text widget or a TextField widget, while XmTextFieldSetStringWcs() only works for a TextField widget. Both functions also set the position of the insertion cursor to the beginning of the new text string.

XmTextSetStringWcs() and XmTextFieldSetStringWcs() invoke the callback routines for the XmNvalueChangedCallback, the XmNmodifyVerifyCallback, and the XmNmodifyVerifyCallbackWcs callbacks for the specified *widget*. If both verification callbacks are present, the XmNmodifyVerifyCallback procedures are invoked first and the results are passed to the XmNmodifyVerifyCallbackWcs procedures. The routines also invoke the callback routines for the XmNmotionVerifyCallback for the specified *widget*.

## Usage

In Motif 1.2, the Text and TextField widgets support wide-character strings. The resource XmNvalueWcs can be used to set the value of a Text or TextField widget to a wide-character string. XmTextSetStringWcs() and XmTextFieldSetStringWcs() are convenience routines that set the value of the XmNvalueWcs resource for a Text or TextField widget. Calling one of the routines is equivalent to calling XtSetValues() for the resource, although the routines access the value through the widget instance structures rather than through XtSetValues().

## See Also

*XmTextGetString*(1), *XmTextGetStringWcs*(1), *XmTextGetSubstring*(1), *XmTextGetSubstringWcs*(1), *XmTextSetString*(1),
*XmText*(2), *XmTextField*(2).

# XmTextSetTopCharacter

## Name

XmTextSetTopCharacter – set the position of the first character of text that is displayed.

## Synopsis

```
#include <Xm/Text.h>
void XmTextSetTopCharacter (widget, top_character)
    Widget widget;
    XmTextPosition top_character;
```

### Inputs

*widget* Specifies the Text widget.

*top_character*
Specifies the position that is to be displayed at the top of the widget.

## Description

`XmTextSetTopCharacter()` sets the value of the `XmNtopCharacter` resource to *top_character* for the specified Text *widget*. If the `XmNeditMode` resource is set to `XmMULTI_LINE_EDIT`, the routine scrolls the text so that the line containing the character position specified by *top_character* appears at the top of the widget, but does not shift the text left or right. Otherwise, the character position specified by *top_character* is displayed as the first visible character in the widget. *top_character* specifies a character position as the number of characters from the beginning of the text, where the first character position in 0 (zero).

## Usage

`XmTextSetTopCharacter()` is a convenience routine that sets the value of the `XmNtop-Character` resource for a Text widget. Calling the routines is equivalent to calling `XtSet-Values()` for the resource, although the routines accesses the value through the widget instance structures rather than through `XtSetValues()`.

## See Also

*XmTextGetCursorPosition*(1), *XmTextGetInsertionPosition*(1), *XmTextGetLastPosition*(1), *XmTextGetTopCharacter*(1), *XmTextScroll*(1), *XmTextSetCursorPosition*(1), *XmTextSetInsertionPosition*(1), *XmTextShowPosition*(1), *XmText*(2).

# XmTextShowPosition

## Name

XmTextShowPosition, XmTextFieldShowPosition – display the text at a specified position.

## Synopsis

```
#include <Xm/Text.h>
void XmTextShowPosition (widget, position)

#include <Xm/TextF.h>
void XmTextFieldShowPosition (widget, position)

    Widget widget;
    XmTextPosition position;
```

### Inputs

*widget* Specifies the Text or TextField widget.

*position* Specifies the character position that is to be displayed.

## Description

XmTextShowPosition() and XmTextFieldShowPosition() cause the text character at *position* to be displayed in the specified *widget*. XmTextShowPosition() works when *widget* is a Text widget or a TextField widget, while XmTextFieldShowPosition() only works for a TextField widget. The *position* argument specifies the position as the number of characters from the beginning of the text, where the first character position in 0 (zero).

## Usage

XmTextShowPosition() and XmTextFieldShowPosition() provide a way to force a Text or TextField widget to display a certain portion of its text. This routine is useful if you modify the value of widget and want the modification to be immediately visible without the user having to scroll the text. If the value of the XmNautoShowCursorPosition resource is True, you should set the insertion cursor to *position* as well. You can set the insertion cursor by setting the XmcursorPosition resource or by using XmTextSetInsertionPosition() or XmTextFieldSetInsertionPosition().

## Example

The following code shows the use of XmTextShowPosition() in a routine that inserts a message into a status Text widget:

```
Widget status;

void insert_text(message)
char *message;
{
    XmTextPosition curpos;

    curpos = XmTextGetInsertionPosition(status);
```

```
        XmTextInsert(status, curpos, message);

        curpos = curpos + strlen(message);
        XmTextShowPosition(status, curpos);
        XmTextSetInsertionPosition(status, curpos);
    }
```

## See Also

*XmTextGetCursorPosition*(1), *XmTextGetInsertionPosition*(1), *XmTextSetCursorPosition*(1), *XmTextSetInsertionPosition*(1),
*XmText*(2), *XmTextField*(2).

# XmTextXYToPos



## Name

XmTextXYToPos, XmTextFieldXYToPos – get the character position for an x, y position.

## Synopsis

```
#include <Xm/Text.h>
XmTextPosition XmTextXYToPos (widget, x, y)

#include <Xm/TextF.h>
XmTextPosition XmTextFieldXYToPos (widget, x, y)

    Widget widget;
    Position x;
    Position y;
```

### Inputs

| | |
|---|---|
| *widget* | Specifies the Text or TextField widget. |
| *x* | Specifies the x-coordinate relative to the upper-left corner of the widget. |
| *y* | Specifies the y-coordinate relative to the upper-left corner of the widget. |

### Returns

The character position that is closest to the x, y position.

## Description

`XmTextXYToPos()` and `XmTextFieldXYToPos()` return the position of the character closest to the specified *x* and *y* coordinates within the specified `widget`. `XmTextXYToPos()` works when *widget* is a Text widget or a TextField widget, while `XmTextFieldXYToPos()` only works for a TextField widget. The x and y coordinates are relative to the upper-left corner of the widget. Character positions are numbered sequentially, starting with 0 (zero) at the beginning of the text.

## Usage

`XmTextXYToPos()` and `XmTextFieldXYToPos()` provide a way to determine the character at a particular coordinate in a Text or TextField widget. This information is useful if you need to perform additional event processing or draw special graphics in the widget.

## See Also

*XmTextPosToXY*(1),
*XmText*(2), *XmTextField*(2).

# XmToggleButtonGetState

## Name

XmToggleButtonGetState, XmToggleButtonGadgetGetState – get the state of a ToggleButton.

## Synopsis

```
#include <Xm/ToggleB.h>
Boolean XmToggleButtonGetState (widget)

#include <Xm/ToggleBG.h>
Boolean XmToggleButtonGadgetGetState (widget)

    Widget widget;
```

### Inputs

*widget* Specifies the ToggleButton or ToggleButtonGadget.

### Returns

The state of the button.

## Description

XmToggleButtonGetState() and XmToggleButtonGadgetGetState() return the state of the specified *widget*. XmToggleButtonGetState() works when *widget* is a ToggleButton or a ToggleButtonGadget, while XmToggleButtonGadgetGetState() only works for a ToggleButtonGadget. Each of the routines returns True if the button is selected or False if the button is unselected.

## Usage

XmToggleButtonGetState() and XmToggleButtonGadgetGetState() are convenience routines that return the value of the XmNset resource for a ToggleButton or ToggleButtonGadget. Calling one of the routines is equivalent to calling XtGetValues() for the resource, although the routines access the value through the widget instance stuctures rather than through XtGetValues().

## See Also

*XmToggleButtonSetState*(1),
*XmToggleButton*(2).

# XmToggleButtonSetState

## Name

XmToggleButtonSetState, XmToggleButtonGadgetSetState – set the state of a ToggleButton.

## Synopsis

```
#include <Xm/ToggleB.h>
void XmToggleButtonSetState (widget, state, notify)

#include <Xm/ToggleBG.h>
void XmToggleButtonGadgetSetState (widget, state, notify)

    Widget widget;
    Boolean state;
    Boolean notify;
```

### Inputs

*widget* Specifies the ToggleButton or ToggleButtonGadget.

*state* Specifies the state of the button.

*notify* Specifies whether or not the XmNvalueChangedCallback is called.

## Description

XmToggleButtonSetState() and XmToggleButtonGadgetSetState() set the state of the specified *widget*. XmToggleButtonSetState() works when *widget* is a ToggleButton or a ToggleButtonGadget, while XmToggleButtonGadgetSetState() only works for a ToggleButtonGadget. When *state* is True, the button is selected, and when *state* is False, the button is deselected. If *notify* is True, the routines invoke the callbacks specified by the XmNvalueChangedCallback resource. If the specified *widget* is the child of a RowColumn with XmNradioBehavior set to True, the currently selected child of the RowColumn is deselected.

## Usage

XmToggleButtonSetState() and XmToggleButtonGadgetSetState() are convenience routines that return the value of the XmNset resource for a ToggleButton or Toggle-ButtonGadget. Calling one of the routines is equivalent to calling XtSetValues() for the resource, although the routines access the value through the widget instance stuctures rather than through XtSetValues().

## See Also

*XmToggleButtonGetState*(1),
*XmToggleButton*(2).

# XmTrackingEvent

## Name

XmTrackingEvent – allow for modal selection of a component.

## Synopsis

```
#include <Xm/Xm.h>
Widget XmTrackingEvent (widget, cursor, confine_to, event_return)
    Widget widget;
    Cursor cursor;
    Boolean confine_to;
    XEvent *event_return;
```

### Inputs

*widget* Specifies the widget in which the modal interaction occurs.

*cursor* Specifies the cursor that is to be used as the pointer.

*confine_to* Specifies whether or not the pointer is confined to *widget*.

### Outputs

*event_return*

Returns the ButtonRelease or KeyRelease event.

### Returns

The widget or gadget that contains the pointer or NULL if no widget or gadget contains the pointer.

## Availability

Motif 1.2 and later.

## Description

XmTrackingEvent() grabs the pointer and waits for the user to release BSelect or press and release a key, discarding all of the intervening events. The routine returns the ID of the widget or gadget containing the pointer when BSelect or the key is released and *event_return* contains the release event. If no widget or gadget contains the pointer when the release occurs, the function returns NULL. The modal interaction occurs within the specified *widget*, which is typically a top-level shell. During the interaction, *cursor* is used as the pointer shape. If *confine_to* is True, the pointer is confined to *widget* during the interaction; otherwise the pointer is not confined.

## Usage

XmTrackingEvent() provides a way to allow a user to select a component. This modal interaction is meant to support a context-sensitive help system, where the user clicks on a widget to obtain more information about it. XmTrackingEvent() returns the selected widget, so that a help callback can be invoked to provide the appropriate information.

## Example

The following code shows the use of `XmTrackingEvent()` in a routine that initiates context-sensitive help:

```
Widget toplevel, help_button;
    .
    .
    .
    XtAddCallback(help_button, XmNactivateCallback, query_for_help, toplevel);
    .
    .
    .
void query_for_help(widget, client_data, call_data)
Widget          widget;
XtPointer       client_data;
XtPointer       call_data;
{
    Cursor                  cursor;
    Widget                  top, help_widget;
    XmAnyCallbackStruct     cb;
    XtCallbackStatus        hascb;
    XEvent                  *event;

    top = (Widget) client_data;
    cursor = XCreateFontCursor(XtDisplay(top), XC_question_arrow);

    help_widget = XmTrackingEvent(top, cursor, True, &event);
    while (help_widget != NULL) {
        hascb = XtHasCallbacks (help_widget, XmNhelpCallback);
        if ( hascb == XtCallbackHasSome ) {
            cb.reason = XmCR_HELP;
            cb.event = event;
            XtCallCallbacks(help_widget, XmNhelpCallback, (XtPointer) &cb);
            help_widget = NULL;
        }
        else
            help_widget = XtParent (help_widget);
    }
}
```

## See Also

*XmTrackingLocate*(1).

# XmTrackingLocate

## Name

XmTrackingLocate – allow for modal selection of a component.

## Synopsis

```
Widget XmTrackingLocate (widget, cursor, confine_to)
    Widget widget;
    Cursor cursor;
    Boolean confine_to;
```

### Inputs

| | |
|---|---|
| *widget* | Specifies the widget in which the modal interaction occurs. |
| *cursor* | Specifies the cursor that is to be used as the pointer. |
| *confine_to* | Specifies whether or not the pointer is confined to *widget*. |

### Returns

The widget or gadget that contains the pointer or NULL if no widget or gadget contains the pointer.

## Availability

In Motif 1.2, XmTrackingLocate() is obsolete. It has been superseded by XmTrackingEvent().

## Description

XmTrackingLocate() grabs the pointer and waits for the user to release BSelect or press and release a key, discarding all of the intervening events. The routine returns the ID of the widget or gadget containing the pointer when BSelect or the key is released. If no widget or gadget contains the pointer when the release occurs, the function returns NULL. The modal interaction occurs within the specified *widget*, which is typically a top-level shell. During the interaction, *cursor* is used as the pointer shape. If *confine_to* is True, the pointer is confined to *widget* during the interaction; otherwise the pointer is not confined. XmTrackingLocate() is retained for compatibility with Motif 1.1 and should not be used in newer applications.

## Usage

XmTrackingLocate() provides a way to allow a user to select a component. This modal interaction is meant to support a context-sensitive help system, where the user clicks on a widget to obtain more information about it. XmTrackingLocate() returns the selected widget, so that a help callback can be invoked to provide the appropriate information.

## See Also

*XmTrackingEvent*(1).

# XmTranslateKey



## Name

XmTranslateKey – convert a keycode to a keysym using the default translator.

## Synopsis

```
#include <Xm/Xm.h>
void XmTranslateKey (display, keycode, modifiers, modifiers_return,
        keysym_return)
    Display *display;
    KeyCode keycode;
    Modifiers modifiers;
    Modifiers *modifiers_return;
    KeySym *keysym_return;
```

### Inputs

*display* Specifies a connection to an X server; returned from `XOpenDisplay()` or `XtDisplay()`.

*keycode* Specifies the keycode that is translated.

*modifiers* Specifies the modifier keys that are applied to the keycode.

### Outputs

*modifiers_return*
Returns the modifiers used by the key translator to generate the keysym.

*keysym_return*
Returns the resulting keysym.

## Availability

Motif 1.2 and later.

## Description

`XmTranslateKey()` is the default `XtKeyProc` translation procedure used by Motif applications. The routine takes a keycode and modifiers and returns the corresponding osf keysym.

## Usage

The Motif toolkit uses a mechanism called *virtual bindings* to map one set of keysyms to another set. This mapping permits widgets and applications to use one set of keysyms in translation tables; applications and users can then customize the keysyms used in the translations based on the particular keyboard that is being used. Keysyms that can be used in this way are called *osf keysyms*. Motif maintains a mapping between the osf keysyms and the actual keysyms that represent keys on a particular keyboard. See the introduction to Section 2, *Motif and Xt Widget Classes*, for more information about the mapping of osf keysyms to actual keysyms.

`XmTranslateKey()` is used by the X Toolkit during event processing to translate the keycode of an event to the appropriate osf keysym if there is a mapping for the keysym. The event is then dispatched to the appropriate action routine if there is a translation for the osf keysym.

If you need to provide a new translator with expanded functionality, you can call `XmTranslateKey()` to get the default translation. Use `XtSetKeyTranslator()` to register a new key translator. To reinstall the default behavior, you can call `XtSetKeyTranslator()` with `XmTranslateKey()` as the *proc* argument.

## See Also

*xmbind*(4).

# XmUninstallImage

## Name

XmUninstallImage – remove an image from the image cache.

## Synopsis

```
Boolean XmUninstallImage (image)
    XImage *image;
```

### Inputs

| | |
|---|---|
| *image* | Specifies the image structure to be removed. |

### Returns

`True` on success or `False` if *image* is `NULL` or it cannot be found.

## Description

`XmUninstallImage()` removes the specified *image* from the image cache. The routine returns `True` if it is successful. It returns `False` if *image* is `NULL` or if *image* is not found in the image cache.

## Usage

`XmUninstallImage()` removes an image from the image cache. Once an image is uninstalled, it cannot be referenced again and a new image can be installed with the same name. If you have created any pixmaps that use the image, they are not affected by the image being uninstalled, since they are based on image data, not the image itself. After an image has been uninstalled, you can safely free the image.

## See Also

*XmDestroyPixmap*(1), *XmGetPixmap*(1), *XmInstallImage*(1).

# XmUpdateDisplay

## Name

XmUpdateDisplay – update the display.

## Synopsis

```
void XmUpdateDisplay (widget)
    Widget widget;
```

### Inputs

*widget* Specifies any widget.

## Description

`XmUpdateDisplay()` causes all pending exposure events to be processed immediately, instead of having them remain in the queue until all of the callbacks have been invoked.

## Usage

`XmUpdateDisplay()` provides applications with a way to force an visual update of the display. Because callbacks are invoked before normal exposure processing occurs, when a menu or a dialog box is unposted, the display is not updated until all of the callbacks have been called. This routine is useful whenever a time-consuming action might delay the redrawing of the windows on the display.

## See Also

*XmDisplay*(2).

# XmVaCreateSimpleCheckBox

## Name

XmVaCreateSimpleCheckBox – create a CheckBox compound object.

## Synopsis

```
Widget XmVaCreateSimpleCheckBox (parent, name, callback, . . . , NULL)
    Widget parent;
    String name;
    XtCallbackProc callback;
```

### Inputs

*parent* — Specifies the widget ID of the parent of the new widget.

*name* — Specifies the string name of the new widget for resource lookup.

*callback* — Specifies the callback procedure that is called when the value of a button changes.

*. . . ,NULL* — A NULL-terminated variable-length list of resource name/value pairs.

### Returns

The widget ID of the RowColumn widget.

## Description

XmVaCreateSimpleCheckBox() is a RowColumn convenience routine that creates a CheckBox with ToggleButtonGadgets as its children. This routine is similar to XmCreate-SimpleCheckBox(), but it uses a NULL-terminated variable-length argument list in place of the *arglist* and *argcount* parameters. The variable-length argument list specifies resource name/value pairs as well as the children of the CheckBox. The *callback* argument specifies the callback routine that is added to the XmNvalueChangedCallback of each ToggleButtonGadget child of the CheckBox. When the callback is invoked, the button number of the button whose value has changed is passed to the callback in the *client_data* parameter.

The name of each ToggleButtonGadget child is button_*n*, where *n* is the number of the button, ranging from 0 (zero) to 1 less than the number of buttons in the CheckBox. The buttons are created and named in the order in which they are specified in the variable-length argument list.

## Usage

A variable-length argument list is composed of several groups of arguments. Within each group, the first argument is a constant or a string that specifies which arguments follow in the group. The first argument can be one of the following values: XmVaCHECKBUTTON, a *resource_name*, XtVaTypedList, or XtVaNestedList. The variable-length argument list must be NULL-terminated.

If the first argument in a group is XmVaCHECKBUTTON, it is followed by four arguments: *label*, *mnemonic*, *accelerator*, and *accelerator_text*. This group specifies a

ToggleButtonGadget child of the CheckBox and its associated resources. (As of Motif 1.2, all but the `label` argument are ignored.)

If the first argument in a group is a `resource_name` string, it is followed by a resource value of type `XtArgVal`. This group specifies a standard resource name/value pair for the Row-Column widget. If the first argument in a group is `XtVaTypedArg`, it is followed by four arguments: `name`, `type`, `value`, and `size`. This group specifies a resource name and value using the standard `XtVaTypedArg` format. If the first argument in a group is `XtVaNested-List`, it is followed by one argument of type `XtVarArgsList`, which is returned by `XtVa-CreateArgsList()`.

## Example

You can use `XmVaCreateSimpleCheckBox()` as in the following example:

```
Widget toplevel, check_box;
XmString normal, bold, italic;

normal  = XmStringCreateLocalized("normal");
bold  = XmStringCreateLocalized("bold");
italic  = XmStringCreateLocalized("italic");
check_box = XmVaCreateSimpleCheckBox(toplevel, "check_box", toggled,
    XmVaCHECKBUTTON, normal,  NULL, NULL, NULL,
    XmVaCHECKBUTTON, bold,  NULL, NULL, NULL,
    XmVaCHECKBUTTON, italic, NULL, NULL, NULL,
    NULL);
XmStringFree(normal);
XmStringFree(bold);
XmStringFree(italic);
```

## See Also

*XmCheckBox*(2), *XmRowColumn*(2), *XmToggleButtonGadget*(2).

# XmVaCreateSimpleMenuBar

## Name

XmVaCreateSimpleMenuBar – create a MenuBar compound object.

## Synopsis

```
Widget XmVaCreateSimpleMenuBar (parent, name, . . . , NULL)
    Widget parent;
    String name;
```

### Inputs

| | |
|---|---|
| *parent* | Specifies the widget ID of the parent of the new widget. |
| *name* | Specifies the string name of the new widget for resource lookup. |
| . . . ,NULL | A NULL-terminated variable-length list of resource name/value pairs. |

### Returns

The widget ID of the RowColumn widget.

## Description

XmVaCreateSimpleMenuBar() is a RowColumn convenience routine that creates a MenuBar with CascadeButtonGadgets as its children. This routine is similar to XmCreate-SimpleMenuBar(), but it uses a NULL-terminated variable-length argument list in place of the *arglist* and *argcount* parameters. The variable-length argument list specifies resource name/value pairs as well as the children of the MenuBar.

The name of each CascadeButtonGadget is button_*n*, where *n* is the number of the button, ranging from 0 (zero) to 1 less than the number of buttons in the MenuBar. The buttons are created and named in the order in which they are specified in the variable-length argument list.

## Usage

A variable-length argument list is composed of several groups of arguments. Within each group, the first argument is a constant or a string that specifies which arguments follow in the group. The first argument can be one of the following values: XmVaCASCADEBUTTON, a *resource_name*, XtVaTypedList, or XtVaNestedList. The variable-length argument list must be NULL-terminated.

If the first argument in a group is XmVaCASCADEBUTTON, it is followed by two arguments: *label* and*mnemonic*. This group specifies a CascadeButtonGadget child of the MenuBar and its associated resources.

If the first argument in a group is a *resource_name* string, it is followed by a resource value of type XtArgVal. This group specifies a standard resource name/value pair for the RowColumn widget. If the first argument in a group is XtVaTypedArg, it is followed by four arguments: *name*, *type*, *value*, and *size*. This group specifies a resource name and value using the standard XtVaTypedArg format. If the first argument in a group is XtVaNested-List, it is followed by one argument of type XtVarArgsList, which is returned by XtVa-CreateArgsList().

### Example

You can use `XmVaCreateSimpleMenuBar()` as in the following example:

```
Widget      top, mainw, menubar, fmenu, emenu;
XmString    file, edit, new, quit, cut, clear, copy, paste;

file = XmStringCreateLocalized("File");
edit = XmStringCreateLocalized("Edit");
menubar = XmVaCreateSimpleMenuBar(main_w, "menubar",
    XmVaCASCADEBUTTON, file, 'F',
    XmVaCASCADEBUTTON, edit, 'E',
    NULL);
XmStringFree(file);
XmStringFree(edit);

new = XmStringCreateLocalized("New");
quit = XmStringCreateLocalized("Quit");
fmenu = XmVaCreateSimplePulldownMenu(menubar, "file_menu", 0, file_cb,
    XmVaPUSHBUTTON, new, 'N', NULL, NULL,
    XmVaSEPARATOR,
    XmVaPUSHBUTTON, quit, 'Q', NULL, NULL,
    NULL);
XmStringFree(new);
XmStringFree(quit);

cut = XmStringCreateLocalized("Cut");
copy = XmStringCreateLocalized("Copy");
clear = XmStringCreateLocalized("Clear");
paste = XmStringCreateLocalized("Paste");
emenu = XmVaCreateSimplePulldownMenu(menubar, "edit_menu", 0, cut_paste,
    XmVaPUSHBUTTON, cut, 'C', NULL, NULL,
    XmVaPUSHBUTTON, copy, 'o', NULL, NULL,
    XmVaPUSHBUTTON, paste, 'P', NULL, NULL,
    XmVaSEPARATOR,
    XmVaPUSHBUTTON, clear, 'l', NULL, NULL,
    NULL);
XmStringFree(cut);
XmStringFree(clear);
XmStringFree(copy);
XmStringFree(paste);
```

### See Also

*XmCascadeButtonGadget*(2), *XmMenuBar*(2), *XmRowColumn*(2).

## Name

XmVaCreateSimpleOptionMenu – create an OptionMenu compound object.

## Synopsis

```
Widget XmVaCreateSimpleOptionMenu (parent, name, option_label,
        option_mnemonic, button_set, callback, . . . , NULL)
    Widget parent;
    String name;
    XmString option_label;
    KeySym option_mnemonic;
    int button_set;
    XtCallbackProc callback;
```

### Inputs

*parent* Specifies the widget ID of the parent of the new widget.

*name* Specifies the string name of the new widget for resource lookup.

*option_label*
Specifies the label used for the OptionMenu.

*option_mnemonic*
Specifies the mnemonic character associated with the OptionMenu.

*button_set* Specifies the initial setting of the OptionMenu.

*callback* Specifies the callback procedure that is called when a button is activated.

. . . ,NULL A NULL-terminated variable-length list of resource name/value pairs.

### Returns

The widget ID of the RowColumn widget.

## Description

`XmVaCreateSimpleOptionMenu()` is a RowColumn convenience routine that creates an OptionMenu along with its submenu of CascadeButtonGadget and/or PushButtonGadget children. This routine is similar to `XmCreateSimpleOptionMenu()`, but it uses a NULL-terminated variable-length argument list in place of the *arglist* and *argcount* parameters. The variable-length argument list specifies resource name/value pairs as well as the children of the OptionMenu.

The *option_label*, *option_mnemonic*, and *button_set* arguments are used to set the `XmNlabelString`, `XmNmnemonic`, and `XmNmenuHistory` resources of the RowColumn respectively. The *button_set* parameter specifies the *n*th button child of the OptionMenu, where the first button is button 0 (zero); the `XmNmenuHistory` resource is set to the actual widget. The *callback* argument specifies the callback routine that is added to the `XmNactivateCallback` of each CascadeButtonGadget and PushButtonGadget child in the submenu of the OptionMenu. When the callback is invoked, the button number of the button whose value has changed is passed to the callback in the *client_data* parameter.

The name of each button is `button_n`, where *n* is the number of the button, ranging from 0 (zero) to 1 less than the number of buttons in the submenu. The name of each separator is `separator_n`, where *n* is the number of the separator, ranging from 0 (zero) to 1 less than the number of separators in the submenu. The buttons are created and named in the order in which they are specified in the variable-length argument list.

## Usage

A variable-length argument list is composed of several groups of arguments. Within each group, the first argument is a constant or a string that specifies which arguments follow in the group. The first argument can be one of the following values: XmVaPUSHBUTTON, XmVaCASCADEBUTTON, XmVaSEPARATOR, XmVaDOUBLE_SEPARATOR, a *resource_name*, XtVaTypedList, or XtVaNestedList. The variable-length argument list must be NULL-terminated.

If the first argument in a group is XmVaPUSHBUTTON, it is followed by four arguments: *label*, *mnemonic*, *accelerator*, and *accelerator_text*. This group specifies a PushButtonGadget in the pulldown submenu of the OptionMenu and its associated resources. If the first argument in a group is XmVaCASCADEBUTTON, it is followed by two arguments: *label* and *mnemonic*. This group specifies a CascadeButtonGadget in the pulldown submenu of the OptionMenu and its associated resources. If the first argument in a group is XmVaSEPARATOR or XmVaDOUBLE_SEPARATOR, it is not followed by any arguments. These groups specify SeparatorGadgets in the pulldown submenu of the OptionMenu.

If the first argument in a group is a *resource_name* string, it is followed by a resource value of type XtArgVal. This group specifies a standard resource name/value pair for the RowColumn widget. If the first argument in a group is XtVaTypedArg, it is followed by four arguments: *name*, *type*, *value*, and *size*. This group specifies a resource name and value using the standard XtVaTypedArg format. If the first argument in a group is XtVaNestedList, it is followed by one argument of type XtVarArgsList, which is returned by XtVaCreateArgsList().

## Example

You can use XmVaCreateSimpleOptionMenu() as in the following example:

```
Widget rc, option_menu;
XmString draw_shape, line, square, circle;

draw_shape = XmStringCreateLocalized("Draw Mode:");
line = XmStringCreateLocalized("Line");
square = XmStringCreateLocalized("Square");
circle = XmStringCreateLocalized("Circle");
option_menu = XmVaCreateSimpleOptionMenu(rc, "option_menu",
    draw_shape, 'D', 0, option_cb,
    XmVaPUSHBUTTON, line, 'L', NULL, NULL,
    XmVaPUSHBUTTON, square, 'S', NULL, NULL,
    XmVaPUSHBUTTON, circle, 'C', NULL, NULL,
    NULL);
```

```
    XmStringFree(line);
    XmStringFree(square);
    XmStringFree(circle);
    XmStringFree(draw_shape);
```

## See Also

*XmOptionButtonGadget*(1), *XmOptionLabelGadget*(1), *XmCascadeButtonGadget*(2), *XmLabelGadget*(2), *XmOptionMenu*(2), *XmPushButtonGadget*(2), *XmRowColumn*(2), *XmSeparatorGadget*(2).

## Name

XmVaCreateSimplePopupMenu – create a PopupMenu compound object as the child of a MenuShell.

## Synopsis

```
Widget XmVaCreateSimplePopupMenu (parent, name, callback, ..., NULL)
    Widget parent;
    String name;
    XtCallbackProc callback;
```

### Inputs

*parent* Specifies the widget ID of the parent of the MenuShell.

*name* Specifies the string name of the new widget for resource lookup.

*callback* Specifies the callback procedure that is called when a button is activated or its value changes.

. . . ,NULL A NULL-terminated variable-length list of resource name/value pairs.

### Returns

The widget ID of the RowColumn widget.

## Description

XmVaCreateSimplePopupMenu() is a RowColumn convenience routine that creates a PopupMenu along with its button children. The routine creates the PopupMenu as a child of a MenuShell. This routine is similar to XmCreateSimplePopupMenu(), but it uses a NULL-terminated variable-length argument list in place of the *arglist* and *argcount* parameters. The variable-length argument list specifies resource name/value pairs as well as the children of the PopupMenu. The *callback* argument specifies the callback routine that is added to the XmNactivateCallback of each CascadeButtonGadget and PushButtonGadget child and the XmNvalueChangedCallback of each ToggleButtonGadget child in the PopupMenu. When the callback is invoked, the button number of the button whose value has changed is passed to the callback in the *client_data* parameter.

The name of each button is button_*n*, where *n* is the number of the button, ranging from 0 (zero) to 1 less than the number of buttons in the menu. The name of each separator is separator_*n*, where *n* is the number of the separator, ranging from 0 (zero) to 1 less than the number of separators in the menu. The name of each title is label_*n*, where *n* is the the number of the title, ranging from 0 (zero) to 1 less than the number of titles in the menu. The buttons are created and named in the order in which they are specified in the variable-length argument list.

## Usage

A variable-length argument list is composed of several groups of arguments. Within each group, the first argument is a constant or a string that specifies which arguments follow in the group. The first argument can be one of the following values: XmVaPUSHBUTTON,

XmVaCASCADEBUTTON, XmVaRADIOBUTTON, XmVaCHECKBUTTON, XmVaTITLE, XmVaSEPARATOR, XmVaDOUBLE_SEPARATOR, a *resource_name*, XtVaTypedList, or XtVaNestedList. The variable-length argument list must be NULL-terminated.

If the first argument in a group is XmVaPUSHBUTTON, it is followed by four arguments: *label*, *mnemonic*, *accelerator*, and *accelerator_text*. This group specifies a PushButtonGadget child of the PopupMenu and its associated resources. If the first argument in a group is XmVaCASCADEBUTTON, it is followed by two arguments: *label* and *mnemonic*. This group specifies a CascadeButtonGadget child of the PopupMenu and its associated resources. If the first argument in a group is XmVaRADIOBUTTON or XmVaCHECKBUTTON, it is followed by four arguments: *label*, *mnemonic*, *accelerator*, and *accelerator_text*. These groups specify ToggleButtonGadget children of the PopupMenu and their associated resources.

If the first argument is XmVaTITLE, it is followed by a *title* argument. This group specifies a LabelGadget title in the PopupMenu and its associated resource. If the first argument in a group is XmVaSEPARATOR or XmVaDOUBLE_SEPARATOR, it is not followed by any arguments. These groups specify SeparatorGadgets in the PopupMenu.

If the first argument in a group is a *resource_name* string, it is followed by a resource value of type XtArgVal. This group specifies a standard resource name/value pair for the RowColumn widget. If the first argument in a group is XtVaTypedArg, it is followed by four arguments: *name*, *type*, *value*, and *size*. This group specifies a resource name and value using the standard XtVaTypedArg format. If the first argument in a group is XtVaNestedList, it is followed by one argument of type XtVarArgsList, which is returned by XtVaCreateArgsList().

## Example

You can use XmVaCreateSimplePopupMenu() as in the following example:

```
Widget drawing_a, popup_menu;
XmString line, square, circle, quit, quit_acc;

line = XmStringCreateLocalized("Line");
square = XmStringCreateLocalized("Square");
circle = XmStringCreateLocalized("Circle");
quit = XmStringCreateLocalized("Quit");
quit_acc = XmStringCreateLocalized("Ctrl-C");
popup_menu = XmVaCreateSimplePopupMenu(drawing_a, "popup", popup_cb,
    XmVaPUSHBUTTON, line, NULL, NULL, NULL,
    XmVaPUSHBUTTON, square, NULL, NULL, NULL,
    XmVaPUSHBUTTON, circle, NULL, NULL, NULL,
    XmVaSEPARATOR,
    XmVaPUSHBUTTON, quit, NULL, "Ctrl<Key>c", quit_acc,
    NULL);
XmStringFree(line);
XmStringFree(square);
XmStringFree(circle);
```

```
    XmStringFree(quit);
    XmStringFree(quit_acc);
```

## See Also

*XmCascadeButtonGadget*(2), *XmLabelGadget*(2), *XmMenuShell*(2), *XmPopupMenu*(2), *XmPushButtonGadget*(2), *XmRowColumn*(2), *XmSeparatorGadget*(2), *XmToggleButtonGadget*(2).

## Name

XmVaCreateSimplePulldownMenu – create a PulldownMenu compound object as the child of a MenuShell.

## Synopsis

```
Widget XmVaCreateSimplePulldownMenu (parent, name, post_from_button,
        callback, . . . , NULL)
    Widget parent;
    String name;
    int post_from_button;
    XtCallbackProc callback;
```

### Inputs

*parent* Specifies the widget ID of the parent of the MenuShell.

*name* Specifies the string name of the new widget for resource lookup.

*post_from_button*
Specifies the CascadeButton or CascadeButtonGadget in the parent widget to which the menu is attached.

*callback* Specifies the callback procedure that is called when a button is activated or its value changes.

`. . . ,NULL` A NULL-terminated variable-length list of resource name/value pairs.

### Returns

The widget ID of the RowColumn widget.

## Description

`XmVaCreateSimplePulldownMenu()` is a RowColumn convenience routine that creates a PulldownMenu along with its button children. The routine creates the PulldownMenu as a child of a MenuShell. This routine is similar to `XmCreateSimplePulldownMenu()`, but it uses a NULL-terminated variable-length argument list in place of the *arglist* and *argcount* parameters. The variable-length argument list specifies resource name/value pairs as well as the children of the PulldownMenu.

The *post_from_button* parameter specifies the CascadeButton or CascadeButtonGadget to which the PulldownMenu is attached as a submenu. The argument specifies the *n*th CascadeButton or CascadeButtonGadget, where the first button is button 0 (zero). The *callback* argument specifies the callback routine that is added to the `XmNactivateCallback` of each CascadeButtonGadget and PushButtonGadget child and the `XmNvalueChangedCallback` of each ToggleButtonGadget child in the PulldownMenu. When the callback is invoked, the button number of the button whose value has changed is passed to the callback in the *client_data* parameter.

The name of each button is `button_`*n*, where *n* is the number of the button, ranging from 0 (zero) to 1 less than the number of buttons in the menu. The name of each separator is `separator_`*n*, where *n* is the number of the separator, ranging from 0 (zero) to 1 less than the number of separators in the menu. The name of each title is `label_n`, where *n* is the number of the title, ranging from 0 (zero) to 1 less than the number of titles in the menu. The buttons are created and named in the order in which they are specified in the variable-length argument list.

## Usage

A variable-length argument list is composed of several groups of arguments. Within each group, the first argument is a constant or a string that specifies which arguments follow in the group. The first argument can be one of the following values: XmVaPUSHBUTTON, XmVaCASCADEBUTTON, XmVaRADIOBUTTON, XmVaCHECKBUTTON, XmVaTITLE, XmVaSEPARATOR, XmVaDOUBLE_SEPARATOR, a *resource_name*, XtVaTypedList, or XtVaNestedList. The variable-length argument list must be NULL-terminated.

If the first argument in a group is XmVaPUSHBUTTON, it is followed by four arguments: *label*, *mnemonic*, *accelerator*, and *accelerator_text*. This group specifies a PushButtonGadget child of the PulldownMenu and its associated resources. If the first argument in a group is XmVaCASCADEBUTTON, it is followed by two arguments: *label* and *mnemonic*. This group specifies a CascadeButtonGadget child of the PulldownMenu and its associated resources. If the first argument in a group is XmVaRADIOBUTTON or XmVaCHECKBUTTON, it is followed by four arguments: *label*, *mnemonic*, *accelerator*, and *accelerator_text*. These groups specify ToggleButtonGadget children of the PulldownMenu and their associated resources.

If the first argument is XmVaTITLE, it is followed by a *title* argument. This group specifies a LabelGadget title in the PulldownMenu and its associated resource. If the first argument in a group is XmVaSEPARATOR or XmVaDOUBLE_SEPARATOR, it is not followed by any arguments. These groups specify SeparatorGadgets in the PulldownMenu.

If the first argument in a group is a *resource_name* string, it is followed by a resource value of type XtArgVal. This group specifies a standard resource name/value pair for the RowColumn widget. If the first argument in a group is XtVaTypedArg, it is followed by four arguments: *name*, *type*, *value*, and *size*. This group specifies a resource name and value using the standard XtVaTypedArg format. If the first argument in a group is XtVaNestedList, it is followed by one argument of type XtVarArgsList, which is returned by XtVaCreateArgsList().

## Example

You can use XmVaCreateSimplePulldownMenu() as in the following example:

```
Widget        top, mainw, menubar, fmenu, emenu;
XmString      file, edit, new, quit, cut, clear, copy, paste;

file = XmStringCreateLocalized("File");
edit = XmStringCreateLocalized("Edit");
menubar = XmVaCreateSimpleMenuBar(main_w, "menubar",
    XmVaCASCADEBUTTON, file, 'F',
    XmVaCASCADEBUTTON, edit, 'E',
```

```
        NULL);
    XmStringFree(file);
    XmStringFree(edit);

    new = XmStringCreateLocalized("New");
    quit = XmStringCreateLocalized("Quit");
    fmenu = XmVaCreateSimplePulldownMenu(menubar, "file_menu", 0, file_cb,
        XmVaPUSHBUTTON, new, 'N', NULL, NULL,
        XmVaSEPARATOR,
        XmVaPUSHBUTTON, quit, 'Q', NULL, NULL,
        NULL);
    XmStringFree(new);
    XmStringFree(quit);

    cut = XmStringCreateLocalized("Cut");
    copy = XmStringCreateLocalized("Copy");
    clear = XmStringCreateLocalized("Clear");
    paste = XmStringCreateLocalized("Paste");
    emenu = XmVaCreateSimplePulldownMenu(menubar, "edit_menu", 1, cut_paste,
        XmVaPUSHBUTTON, cut, 'C', NULL, NULL,
        XmVaPUSHBUTTON, copy, 'o', NULL, NULL,
        XmVaPUSHBUTTON, paste, 'P', NULL, NULL,
        XmVaSEPARATOR,
        XmVaPUSHBUTTON, clear, 'l', NULL, NULL,
        NULL);
    XmStringFree(cut);
    XmStringFree(clear);
    XmStringFree(copy);
    XmStringFree(paste);
```

## See Also

*XmCascadeButtonGadget*(2), *XmLabelGadget*(2), *XmMenuShell*(2), *XmPulldownMenu*(2), *XmPushButtonGadget*(2), *XmRowColumn*(2), *XmSeparatorGadget*(2), *XmToggleButtonGadget*(2).

## Name

XmVaCreateSimpleRadioBox – create a RadioBox compound object.

## Synopsis

```
Widget XmVaCreateSimpleRadioBox (parent, name, button_set, callback, ...,
        NULL)
    Widget parent;
    String name;
    int button_set;
    XtCallbackProc callback;
```

### Inputs

| | |
|---|---|
| *parent* | Specifies the widget ID of the parent of the new widget. |
| *name* | Specifies the string name of the new widget for resource lookup. |
| *button_set* | Specifies the initial setting of the RadioBox. |
| *callback* | Specifies the callback procedure that is called when the value of a button changes. |
| ..., NULL | A NULL-terminated variable-length list of resource name/value pairs. |

### Returns

The widget ID of the RowColumn widget.

## Description

XmVaCreateSimpleRadioBox() is a RowColumn convenience routine that creates a RadioBox with ToggleButtonGadgets as its children. This routine is similar to XmCreateSimpleRadioBox(), but it uses a NULL-terminated variable-length argument list in place of the *arglist* and *argcount* parameters. The variable-length argument list specifies resource name/value pairs as well as the children of the CheckBox. The *button_set* argument is used to set the XmNmenuHistory resource of the RowColumn. The parameter specifies the *n*th button child of the RadioBox, where the first button is button 0 (zero); the XmNmenuHistory resource is set to the actual widget. The *callback* argument specifies the callback routine that is added to the XmNvalueChangedCallback of each ToggleButtonGadget child of the RadioBox. When the callback is invoked, the button number of the button whose value has changed is passed to the callback in the *client_data* parameter.

The name of each ToggleButtonGadget child is button_*n*, where *n* is the number of the button, ranging from 0 (zero) to 1 less than the number of buttons in the RadioBox. The buttons are created and named in the order in which they are specified in the variable-length argument list.

## Usage

A variable-length argument list is composed of several groups of arguments. Within each group, the first argument is a constant or a string that specifies which arguments follow in the group. The first argument can be one of the following values: XmVaRADIOBUTTON, a *resource_name*, XtVaTypedList, or XtVaNestedList. The variable-length argument list must be NULL-terminated.

If the first argument in a group is XmVaRADIOBUTTON, it is followed by four arguments: *label*, *mnemonic*, *accelerator*, and *accelerator_text*. This group specifies a ToggleButtonGadget child of the RadioBox and its associated resources. (As of Motif 1.2, all but the *label* argument are ignored.)

If the first argument in a group is a *resource_name* string, it is followed by a resource value of type XtArgVal. This group specifies a standard resource name/value pair for the RowColumn widget. If the first argument in a group is XtVaTypedArg, it is followed by four arguments: *name*, *type*, *value*, and *size*. This group specifies a resource name and value using the standard XtVaTypedArg format. If the first argument in a group is XtVaNestedList, it is followed by one argument of type XtVarArgsList, which is returned by XtVaCreateArgsList().

## Example

You can use XmVaCreateSimpleRadioBox() as in the following example:

```
Widget toplevel, radio_box;
XmString one, two, three;

one   = XmStringCreateLocalized("WFNX");
two   = XmStringCreateLocalized("WMJX");
three  = XmStringCreateLocalized("WXKS");
radio_box = XmVaCreateSimpleRadioBox(toplevel, "radio_box",
    0, toggled,
    XmVaRADIOBUTTON, one,  NULL, NULL, NULL,
    XmVaRADIOBUTTON, two,  NULL, NULL, NULL,
    XmVaRADIOBUTTON, three, NULL, NULL, NULL,
    NULL);
XmStringFree(one);
XmStringFree(two);
XmStringFree(three);
```

## See Also

*XmRadioBox*(2), *XmRowColumn*(2), *XmToggleButtonGadget*(2).

# XmWidgetGetBaselines

## Name

XmWidgetGetBaselines – get the positions of the baselines in a widget.

## Synopsis

```
Boolean XmWidgetGetBaselines (widget, baselines, line_count)
    Widget widget;
    Dimension **baselines;
    int *line_count;
```

### Inputs

*widget* Specifies the widget for which to get baseline values.

### Outputs

*baselines* Returns an array containing the value of each baseline of text in the widget.

*line_count* Returns the number of lines of text in the widget.

### Returns

`True` if the widget contains at least one baseline or `False` otherwise.

## Availability

Motif 1.2 and later.

## Description

`XmWidgetGetBaselines()` returns an array that contains the baseline values for the specified *widget*. For each line of text in the widget, the baseline value is the vertical offset in pixels from the origin of the bounding box of the widget to the text baseline. The routine returns the baseline values in *baselines* and the number of lines of text in the widget in *line_count*. `XmWidgetGetBaselines()` returns `True` if the widget contains at least one line of text and therefore has a baseline. If the widget does not contain any text, the routine returns `False` and the values of *baselines* and *line_count* are undefined. The routine allocates storage for the returned values. The application is responsible for freeing this storage using `XtFree()`.

## Usage

`XmWidgetGetBaselines()` provide information that is useful when you are laying out an application and trying to align different components.

## See Also

*XmWidgetGetDisplayRect*(1).

# XmWidgetGetDisplayRect



## Name

XmWidgetGetDisplayRect – get the display rectangle for a widget.

## Synopsis

```
Boolean XmWidgetGetDisplayRect (widget, displayrect)
     Widget widget;
     XRectangle *displayrect;
```

### Inputs

*widget* Specifies the widget for which to get the display rectangle.

### Outputs

*displayrect* Returns an `XRectangle` that specifies the display rectangle of the widget.

### Returns

`True` if the widget has a display rectangle or `False` otherwise.

## Availability

Motif 1.2 and later.

## Description

`XmWidgetGetDisplayRect()` gets the display rectangle for the specified *widget*. The routine returns the width, the height, and the x and y-coordinates of the upper left corner of the display rectangle in the *displayrect* `XRectangle`. All of the values are specified as pixels. The display rectangle for a widget is the smallest rectangle that encloses the string or the pixmap in the widget. `XmWidgetGetDisplayRect()` returns `True` if the widget has a display rectangle; other it returns `False` and the value of *displayrect* is undefined.

## Usage

`XmWidgetGetDisplayRect()` provide information that is useful when you are laying out an application and trying to align different components.

## See Also

*XmWidgetGetBaselines*(1).

# Section 2

## Motif and Xt Widget Classes

*This section describes the widgets and gadgets available in the Motif toolkit, including various compound objects (such as dialogs, menu bars, and pull-down menus) that are not really separate widget or gadget classes, but can be created as if they were, with a call to a single convenience routine. Objects are presented alphabetically, starting with a brief description and then listing information in separate sections. For gadgets, we list only the information that differs from the corresponding widget; for compound objects, we present only the description and refer you to the underlying objects.*

*The first reference page,* Introduction, *explains the format and contents of each of the following pages. It also includes a diagram of the Motif widget class hierarchy and describes the Motif virtual binding mechanism.*

## In This Section:



☞

XmPopupMenu
XmPrimitive
XmPromptDialog
XmPulldownMenu
XmPushButton
XmPushButtonGadget
XmQuestionDialog
XmRadioBox
XmRowColumn
XmScale
XmScreen
XmScrollBar
XmScrolledList
XmScrolledText
XmScrolledWindow
XmSelectionBox
XmSelectionDialog
XmSeparator
XmSeparatorGadget
XmTemplateDialog
XmText
XmTextField
XmToggleButton
XmToggleButtonGadget
XmWarningDialog
XmWorkingDialog

# Introduction

This page describes the format and contents of each reference page in Section 2, which covers each of the Motif and Xt Intrinsics widget types.

## Name

Widget – a brief description of the widget.

## Synopsis

**Public Headers:** The files to include when you use this widget.

**Class Name:** The name of the widget class; used as the resource class for each instance of the widget.

**Class Hierarchy:** The superclasses of this widget, listed in superclass-to-subclass order. The arrow symbol (→) indicates a subclass.

**Class Pointer:** The global variable that points to the widget class structure. This is the value used when creating a widget.

**Instantiation:** C code that instantiates the widget, for widgets that can be instantiated. For the widgets and gadgets in the Motif toolkit, we have shown how to instantiate the widget using `XtCreateWidget()`. Each widget and gadget has a convenience creation routine of the general form:

```
Widget XmCreateobject (Widget parent, String name,
                        ArgList arglist, Cardinal argcount)
```

where *object* is the shorthand for the class.

**Functions/Macros:** Functions and/or macros specific to this widget class.

## Availability

This section appears for widget classes that were added in Motif 1.2.

## Description

This section gives an overview of the widget class and the functionality it provides.

## New Resources

This section presents a table of the resources that are newly defined by each widget class (not inherited from a superclass). In addition to the resource's name, class, data type, and default value, a fifth column lists a code consisting of one or more of the letters C, S, and G. This code indicates whether the resource can be set when the widget is created (C), whether it can be set with `XtSetValues()` (S), and whether it can be read with `XtGetValues()` (G). (We've adopted this useful convention from the *Motif Programmer's Reference Manual.*) A brief description of each new resource follows the table. For resources whose values are defined constants, these constants are listed. Unless otherwise noted, they are defined in *<Xm/Xm.h>*.

### Other New Resources

If present, these sections describe resources associated with specific uses of the widget; for example, RowColumn widget resources for use with simple creation routines, or Text widget resources for use in text input.

### Callback Resources

This section presents a table of the callback resources that are newly defined by this class. The table lists the name of each resource along with its reason constant.

### Callback Structure

This section lists the structure(s) associated with the object's callback functions.

### Default Resource Values

This section presents a table of the default resource values that are set when a compound object is created.

### Inherited Resources

This section presents an alphabetically arranged table of inherited resources, along with the superclass that defines them.

### Widget Hierarchy

This section presents the widget instance hierarchy that results from creating a compound object.

### Translations

This section presents the translations associated with each widget or gadget. Because the button events and key events used in Motif do not necessarily correspond to the events in the X Window System, the Motif toolkit has created a mechanism called *virtual bindings*. Virtual bindings link the translations used in Motif to their X event counterparts. The "Translations" sections list their events in terms of these virtual bindings. In order to understand the syntax used in the "Translations" sections of these reference pages, you must understand the correspondence between virtual bindings and actual keysyms or buttons. The following tables describe the virtual bindings of events.

***Table 2-1. Virtual Modifier Bindings***

| Virtual Modifier | Actual Modifier |
|---|---|
| MAlt | <Mod1> |
| MCtrl | <Ctrl> |
| MShift | <Shift> |
| MLink | <Ctrl><Shift> |
| MMove | <Shift> |
| MCopy | <Ctrl> |

*Table 2-2. Virtual Button Event Bindings*

| Virtual Button | Actual Button Events |
|---|---|
| BCustom | <Btn3> |
| BDrag | <Btn2> |
| BExtend | <Shift><Btn1> |
| BMenu | <Btn3> |
| BSelect | <Btn1> |
| BToggle | <Ctrl><Btn1> |

*Table 2-3. Virtual Key Event Bindings*

| Virtual Key | Actual Key Events |
|---|---|
| KActivate | <Key>Return |
| | <Ctrl><Key>Return |
| | <Key>osfActivate |
| KAddMode | <Key>osfAddMode |
| KBackSpace | <Key>osfBackSpace |
| KBackTab | <Shift><Key>Tab |
| KBeginData | <Ctrl><Key>osfBeginLine |
| KBeginLine | <Key>osfBeginLine |
| KCancel | <Key>osfCancel |
| KClear | <Key>osfClear |
| KCopy | <Key>osfCopy |
| | <Ctrl><Key>osfInsert |
| KCut | <Key>osfCut |
| | <Shift><Key>osfDelete |
| KDelete | <Key>osfDelete |
| KDeselectAll | <Ctrl><Key>backslash |
| KDown | <Key>osfDown |
| KEndData | <Ctrl><Key>osfEndLine |
| KEndLine | <Key>osfEndLine |
| KEnter | <Key>Return |
| KEscape | <Key>Escape |
| KExtend | <Ctrl><Shift><Key>space |
| | <Shift><Key>osfSelect |
| KHelp | <Key>osfHelp |
| KInsert | <Key>osfInsert |
| KLeft | <Key>osfLeft |
| KMenu | <Key>osfMenu |
| KMenuBar | <Key>osfMenuBar |

*Table 2-3. Virtual Key Event Bindings (continued)*

| Virtual Key | Actual Key Events |
|---|---|
| KNextField | <Key>Tab |
| | <Ctrl><Key>Tab |
| KNextMenu | <Ctrl><Key>osfDown |
| | <Ctrl><Key>osfRight |
| KPageDown | <Key>osfPageDown |
| KPageLeft | <Ctrl><Key>osfPageUp |
| | <Key>osfPageLeft |
| KPageRight | <Ctrl><Key>osfPageDown |
| KPageUp | <Key>osfPageUp |
| KPaste | <Key>osfPaste |
| | <Shift><Key>osfInsert |
| KPrevField | <Shift><Key>Tab |
| | <Ctrl><Shift><Key>Tab |
| KPrevMenu | <Ctrl><Key>osfUp |
| | <Ctrl><Key>osfLeft |
| KPrimaryCopy | <Ctrl><Key>osfPrimaryPaste |
| | <Mod1><Key>osfCopy |
| | <Mod1><Ctrl><Key>osfInsert |
| KPrimaryCut | <Mod1><Key><osfPrimaryPaste |
| | <Mod1><Key>osfCut |
| | <Mod1><Shift><Key>osfDelete |
| KPrimaryPaste | <Key>osfPrimaryPaste |
| KQuickCopy | <Ctrl><Key>osfQuickPaste |
| KQuickCut | <Mod1><Key>osfQuickPaste |
| KQuickExtend | <Shift><Key>osfQuickPaste |
| KQuickPaste | <Key>osfQuickPaste |
| KReselect | <Ctrl><Shift><Key>osfSelect |
| KRestore | <Ctrl><Shift><Key>osfInsert |
| KRight | <Key>osfRight |
| KSelect | <Key>space |
| | <Ctrl><Key>space |
| | <Key>osfSelect |
| KSelectAll | <Ctrl><Key>slash |
| KSpace | <Key>space |
| KTab | <Key>Tab |
| KUndo | <Key>osfUndo |
| | <Mod1><Key>osfBackSpace |
| KUp | <Key>osfUp |
| KAny | <Key> |

Keysyms that begin with the letters *osf* are not defined by the X server. These keysyms are generated at run time by a client, interpreted by `XmTranslateKey()`, and used by the translation manager when the server sends an actual key avent. An application maintains a mapping between *osf* keysyms and actual keysyms that is based on information that is retrieved at application startup. This information comes from one of the following sources, listed in order of precedence:

- The `XmNdefaultVirtualBindings` resource in a resource database. A sample specification is shown below:

```
*defaultVirtualBindings:\
osfBackSpace :          <Key>BackSpace  \n\
osfInsert :             <Key>InsertChar \n\
osfDelete :             <Key>DeleteChar
```

- A property on the root window. *mwm* sets this property on startup. It can also be set by the *xmbind* client in Motif 1.2 or the prior startup of another Motif application.
- A file named *.motifbind*, in the user's home directory. In this file, the previous specification would be typed as follows:

```
osfBackSpace :          <Key>BackSpace
osfInsert :             <Key>InsertChar
osfDelete :             <Key>DeleteChar
```

- A vendor-specific set of bindings located using the file *xmbind.alias*. If this file exists in the user's home directory, it is searched for a pathname associated with the vendor string or the vendor string and vendor release. If the search is unsuccessful, Motif continues looking for *xmbind.alias* in the directory specified by XMBINDDIR or in */usr/lib/Xm/bindings* if the variable is not set. If this file exists, it is searched for a pathname as before. If either search locates a pathname and the file exists, the bindings in that file are used. An *xmbind.alias* file contains lines of the following form:

```
"vendor_string[ vendor_release]"bindings_file
```

- Via fixed fallback defaults. *osf* keysym strings have the fixed fallback default bindings listed below:

```
osfActivate             <unbound>
osfAddMode              <Shift> F8
osfBackSpace            Backspace
osfBeginLine            Home
osfClear                Clear
osfCopy                 <unbound>
osfCut                  <unbound>
osfDelete               Delete
osfDown                 Down
osfEndLine              End
osfCancel               <Escape>
```

Motif and Xt Widget Classes

```
osfHelp            F1
osfInsert          Insert
osfLeft            Left
osfMenu            F4
osfMenuBar         F10
osfPageDown        Next
osfPageLeft        <unbound>
osfPageRight       <unbound>
osfPageUp          Prior
osfPaste           <unbound>
osfPrimaryPaste    <unbound>
osfQuickPaste      <unbound>
osfRight           Right
osfSelect          Select
osfUndo            Undo
osfUp              Up
```

### Action Routines

This section describes the action routines that are listed in the "Translations" section.

### Behavior

This section describes the keyboard and mouse events that affect gadgets, which do not have translations or actions.

### Additional Behavior

This section describes any additional widget behavior that is not provided by translations and actions.

### See Also

This section refers you to related functions and widget classes. The numbers in parentheses following each reference refer to the sections of this book in which they are found.

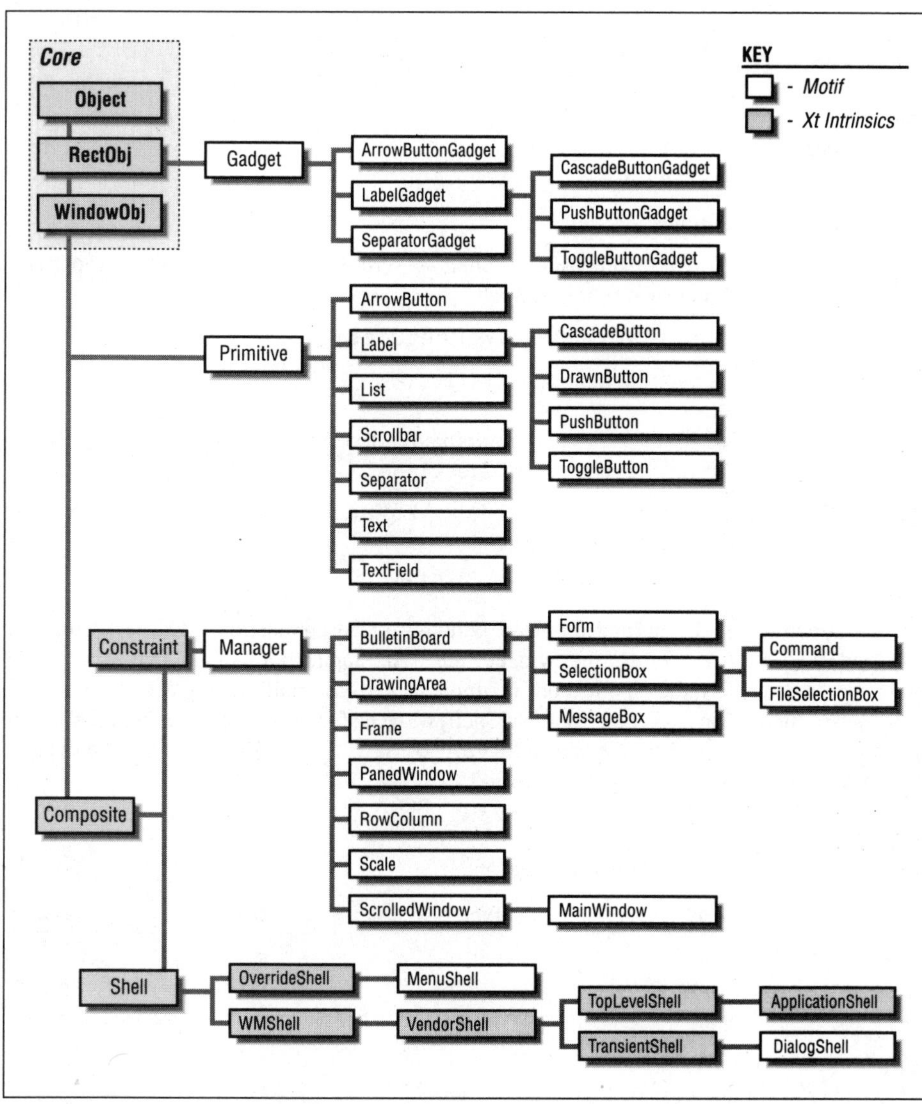


*Figure 2-1. Class hierarchy of the Motif widget set*

# ApplicationShell

## Name

ApplicationShell widget class – the main shell for an application.

## Synopsis

**Public Headers:** *<Xm/Xm.h>*
*<X11/Shell.h>*

**Class Name:** ApplicationShell

**Class Hierarchy:** Core → Composite → Shell → WMShell → VendorShell → TopLevel-Shell → ApplicationShell

**Class Pointer:** `applicationShellWidgetClass`

**Instantiation:** `widget = XtAppInitialize(...)`
or
`widget = XtAppCreateShell(app_name, app_class, applicationShellWidgetClass, ...)`

**Functions/Macros:** `XtAppCreateShell()`, `XtVaAppCreateShell()`, `XtIsApplicationShell()`

## Description

An ApplicationShell is the normal top-level window for an application. It does not have a parent and it is at the root of the widget tree. An application should have only one ApplicationShell, unless the application is implemented as multiple logical applications. Normally, an application will use TopLevelShell widgets for other top-level windows. An ApplicationShell is returned by the call to `XtVaAppInitialize()`. It can also be created explicitly with a call to `XtVaAppCreateShell()`.

## New Resources

ApplicationShell defines the following resources:

| Name | Class | Type | Default | Access |
|---|---|---|---|---|
| XmNargc | XmCArgc | int | 0 | CSG |
| XmNargv | XmCArgv | String * | NULL | CSG |

`XmNargc`
Number of arguments in `XmNargv`.

`XmNargv`
List of command-line arguments used to start the application. This is the standard C `argv`, passed in the call to `XtAppInitialize()`. It is used to set the WM_COMMAND property for this window.

## Inherited Resources

ApplicationShell inherits the following resources. The resources are listed alphabetically, along with the superclass that defines them. The default value of XmNborderWidth is reset to 0 by VendorShell.

| Resource | Inherited From | Resource | Inherited From |
|---|---|---|---|
| XmNaccelerators | Core | XmNmaxAspectX | WMShell |
| XmNallowShellResize | Shell | XmNmaxAspectY | WMShell |
| XmNancestorSensitive | Core | XmNmaxHeight | WMShell |
| XmNaudibleWarning | VendorShell | XmNmaxWidth | WMShell |
| XmNbackground | Core | XmNminAspectX | WMShell |
| XmNbackgroundPixmap | Core | XmNminAspectY | WMShell |
| XmNbaseHeight | WMShell | XmNminHeight | WMShell |
| XmNbaseWidth | WMShell | XmNminWidth | WMShell |
| XmNborderColor | Core | XmNmwmDecorations | VendorShell |
| XmNborderPixmap | Core | XmNmwmFunctions | VendorShell |
| XmNborderWidth | Core | XmNmwmInputMode | VendorShell |
| XmNbuttonFontList | VendorShell | XmNmwmMenu | VendorShell |
| XmNchildren | Composite | XmNnumChildren | Composite |
| XmNcolormap | Core | XmNoverrideRedirect | Shell |
| XmNcreatePopupChildProc | Shell | XmNpopdownCallback | Shell |
| XmNdefaultFontList | VendorShell | XmNpopupCallback | Shell |
| XmNdeleteResponse | VendorShell | XmNpreeditType | VendorShell |
| XmNdepth | Core | XmNsaveUnder | Shell |
| XmNdestroyCallback | Core | XmNscreen | Core |
| XmNgeometry | Shell | XmNsensitive | Core |
| XmNheight | Core | XmNshellUnitType | VendorShell |
| XmNheightInc | WMShell | XmNtextFontList | VendorShell |
| XmNiconic | TopLevelShell | XmNtitle | WMShell |
| XmNiconMask | WMShell | XmNtitleEncoding | WMShell |
| XmNiconName | TopLevelShell | XmNtransient | WMShell |
| XmNiconNameEncoding | TopLevelShell | XmNtranslations | Core |
| XmNiconPixmap | WMShell | XmNuseAsyncGeometry | VendorShell |
| XmNiconWindow | WMShell | XmNvisual | Shell |
| XmNiconX | WMShell | XmNwaitForWm | WMShell |
| XmNiconY | WMShell | XmNwidth | Core |
| XmNinitialResources Persistent | Core | XmNwidthInc | WMShell |
| XmNinitialState | WMShell | XmNwindowGroup | WMShell |
| XmNinput | WMShell | XmNwinGravity | WMShell |
| XmNinputMethod | VendorShell | XmNwmTimeout | WMShell |
| XmNinsertPosition | Composite | XmNx | Core |
| XmNkeyboardFocusPolicy | VendorShell | XmNy | Core |

| Resource | Inherited From | Resource | Inherited From |
|---|---|---|---|
| XmNlabelFontList | VendorShell | | |
| XmNmappedWhenManaged | Core | | |

VendorShell calls `exit()` when WM "Close" is selected and `XmNdeleteResponse` is `XmDESTROY`.

## See Also

*Composite*(2), *Core*(2), *Shell*(2), *TopLevelShell*(2), *VendorShell*(2), *WMShell*(2).

# Composite

## Name

Composite widget class – the fundamental widget that can have children.

## Synopsis

**Public Headers:** *<Xm/Xm.h>*
*<X11/Composite.h>*

**Class Name:** Composite

**Class Hierarchy:** Core → Composite

**Class Pointer:** `compositeWidgetClass`

**Instantiation:** Composite is an Intrinsics meta-class and is not normally instantiated.

**Functions/Macros:** `XtIsComposite()`

## Description

Composite is the superclass of all classes that can have children. It is a container for other widgets and can have any number of children. Composite handles the geometry management of its children. It also manages the destruction of descendants when it is destroyed.

## New Resources

Composite defines the following resources:

| Name | Class | Type | Default | Access |
|---|---|---|---|---|
| XmNchildren | XmCReadOnly | WidgetList | NULL | G |
| XmNinsertPosition | XmCInsertPosition | XtOrderProc | NULL | CSG |
| XmNnumChildren | XmCReadOnly | Cardinal | 0 | G |

`XmNchildren` List of widget's children.

`XmNinsertPosition`
Points to an `XtOrderProc()` function that is called to determine the position at which each child is inserted into the `XmNchildren` array.

`XmNnumChildren`
Length of the list in `XmNchildren`.

## Inherited Resources

Composite inherits the following resources. The resources are listed alphabetically, along with the superclass that defines them.

| Resource | Inherited From | Resource | Inherited From |
|---|---|---|---|
| XmNaccelerators | Core | XmNheight | Core |
| XmNancestorSensitive | Core | XmNinitialResourcesPersistent | Core |
| XmNbackground | Core | XmNmappedWhenManaged | Core |

| Resource | Inherited From | Resource | Inherited From |
|---|---|---|---|
| XmNbackgroundPixmap | Core | XmNscreen | Core |
| XmNborderColor | Core | XmNsensitive | Core |
| XmNborderPixmap | Core | XmNtranslations | Core |
| XmNborderWidth | Core | XmNwidth | Core |
| XmNcolormap | Core | XmNx | Core |
| XmNdepth | Core | XmNy | Core |
| XmNdestroyCallback | Core | | |

## See Also

*Core*(2).

# Constraint

## Name

Constraint widget class – a widget that provides constraint resources for its children.

## Synopsis

**Public Headers:** *<Xm/Xm.h>*
*<X11/Constraint.h>*

**Class Name:** Constraint

**Class Hierarchy:** Core → Composite → Constraint

**Class Pointer:** `constraintWidgetClass`

**Instantiation:** Constraint is an Intrinsics meta-class and is not normally instantiated.

**Functions/Macros:** `XtIsConstraint()`

## Description

Constraint widgets are so named because they may manage the geometry of their children based on constraints associated with each child. These constraints can be as simple as the maximum width and height the parent will allow the child to occupy or as complicated as how other children should change if the child is moved or resized. Constraint widgets let a parent define resources that are supplied for their children. For example, if a Constraint parent defines the maximum width and height for its children, these resources are retrieved for each child as if there were resources that were defined by the child widget.

## New Resources

Constraint does not define any new resources.

## Inherited Resources

Constraint inherits the following resources. The resources are listed alphabetically, along with the superclass that defines them.

| Resource | Inherited From | Resource | Inherited From |
|---|---|---|---|
| XmNaccelerators | Core | XmNheight | Core |
| XmNancestorSensitive | Core | XmNinitialResourcesPersistent | Core |
| XmNbackground | Core | XmNmappedWhenManaged | Core |
| XmNbackgroundPixmap | Core | XmNscreen | Core |
| XmNborderColor | Core | XmNsensitive | Core |
| XmNborderPixmap | Core | XmNtranslations | Core |
| XmNborderWidth | Core | XmNwidth | Core |
| XmNcolormap | Core | XmNx | Core |
| XmNdepth | Core | XmNy | Core |
| XmNdestroyCallback | Core | | |

## See Also

*Composite*(2), *Core*(2).

## Name

Core widget class – the fundamental class for windowed widgets.

## Synopsis

**Public Header:** *<Xm/Xm.h>*
*<X11/Core.h>*

**Class Name:** Core

**Class Hierarchy:** Object → RectObj → *unnamed* → Core

**Class Pointer:** `widgetClass` or `coreWidgetClass`

**Instantiation:** Core is an Intrinsics meta-class and is not normally instantiated.

**Functions/Macros:** `XtIsWidget()`

## Description

Core is the fundamental class for windowed widgets. All widgets with windows are subclasses of Core. The Object and RectObj classes support gadgets (windowless widgets). Core is sometimes instantiated for use as a basic drawing area.

## New Resources

Core defines the following resources (some of which are actually defined by the Object and RectObj classes):

| Name | Class | Type | Default | Access |
|---|---|---|---|---|
| XmNaccelerators | XmCAccelerators | XtAccelerators | dynamic | CSG |
| XmNancestorSensitive | XmCSensitive | Boolean | dynamic | G |
| XmNbackground | XmCBackground | Pixel | dynamic | CSG |
| XmNbackgroundPixmap | XmCPixmap | Pixmap | XmUNSPECIFIED_PIXMAP | CSG |
| XmNborderColor | XmCBorderColor | Pixel | XtDefaultForeground | CSG |
| XmNborderPixmap | XmCPixmap | Pixmap | XmUNSPECIFIED_PIXMAP | CSG |
| XmNborderWidth | XmCBorderWidth | Dimension | 1 | CSG |
| XmNcolormap | XmCColormap | Colormap | dynamic | CG |
| XmNdepth | XmCDepth | int | dynamic | CG |
| XmNdestroyCallback | XmCCallback | XtCallbackList | NULL | C |
| XmNheight | XmCHeight | Dimension | dynamic | CSG |
| XmNinitialResourcesPersistent | XmCInitialResourcesPersistent | Boolean | True | C |
| XmNmappedWhenManaged | XmCMappedWhenManaged | Boolean | True | CSG |
| XmNscreen | XmCScreen | Screen * | dynamic | CG |
| XmNsensitive | XmCSensitive | Boolean | True | CSG |

| Name | Class | Type | Default | Access |
|---|---|---|---|---|
| XmNtranslations | XmCTranslations | XtTranslations | dynamic | CSG |
| XmNwidth | XmCWidth | Dimension | dynamic | CSG |
| XmNx | XmCPosition | Position | 0 | CSG |
| XmNy | XmCPosition | Position | 0 | CSG |

`XmNaccelerators`
A translation table bound with its actions for a widget. A destination widget can be set up to use this accelerator table.

`XmNancestorSensitive`
Tells whether a widget's immediate parent should receive input. Default value is `True` if the widget is a top-level shell, copied from the `XmNancestorSensitive` resource of its parent if the widget is a popup shell, or the bitwise AND of the `XmNsensitive` and `XmNancestorSensitive` resources of the parent for other widgets.

`XmNbackground`
Widget's background color.

`XmNbackgroundPixmap`
Pixmap with which to tile the background, beginning at the upper-left corner.

`XmNborderColor`
Pixel value that defines the color of the border.

`XmNborderPixmap`
Pixmap with which to tile the border, beginning at the upper-left corner of the border.

`XmNborderWidth`
Width (in pixels) of the window's border.

`XmNcolormap`
Colormap used in converting to pixel values. Previously created pixel values are unaffected. The default value is the screen's default colormap for top-level shells or is copied from the parent for other widgets.

`XmNdepth`
Number of bits allowed for each pixel. The Xt Intrinsics set this resource when the widget is created. As with the `XmNcolormap` resource, the default value comes from the screen's default or is copied from the parent.

`XmNdestroyCallback`
List of callbacks invoked when the widget is destroyed.

`XmNheight`
Window height (in pixels), excluding the border.

`XmNinitialResourcesPersistent`
Tells whether resources should be reference counted. If `True` (default), it is assumed that the widget won't be destroyed while the application is running, and thus the widget's resources are not reference counted. Set this resource to `False` if your application might destroy the widget and will need to deallocate the resources.

`XmNmappedWhenManaged`
If `True` (default), the widget becomes visible (is mapped) as soon as it is both realized and managed. If `False`, the application performs the mapping and unmapping of the widget. If changed to `False` after the widget is realized and managed, the widget is unmapped.

`XmNscreen`
Screen location of the widget. The default value comes either from the screen's default or is copied from the parent.

`XmNsensitive`
Tells whether a widget is sensitive to input. The `XtSetSensitive()` routine can be used to change a widget's sensitivity and to guarantee that if a parent has its `XmNsensitive` resource set to `False`, then its children will have their ancestor-sensitive flag set correctly.

`XmNtranslations`
Points to a translation table; must be compiled with `XtParseTranslationTable()`.

`XmNwidth`
Window width (in pixels), excluding the border.

`XmNx`
The x-coordinate of the widget's upper-left outer corner, relative to the upper-left inner corner of its parent.

`XmNy`
The y-coordinate of the widget's upper-left outer corner, relative to the upper-left inner corner of its parent.

## See Also

*Object*(2), *RectObj*(2).

# Object



## Name

Object widget class – fundamental object class.

## Synopsis

**Public Headers:** *<Xm/Xm.h>*
*<X11/Object.h>*

**Class Name:** Object

**Class Hierarchy:** Object

**Class Pointer:** objectClass

**Instantiation:** Object is an Intrinsics meta-class and is not normally instantiated.

**Functions/Macros:** `XtIsObject()`

## Description

Object is the root of the class hierarchy; it does not have a superclass. All widgets and gadgets are subclasses of Object. Object encapsulates the mechanisms for resource management and is never instantiated.

## New Resources

Object defines the following resources:

| Name | Class | Type | Default | Access |
|---|---|---|---|---|
| `XmNdestroyCallback` | `XmCCallback` | `XtCallbackList` | NULL | C |

`XmNdestroyCallback`
List of callbacks invoked when the Object is destroyed.

## See Also

*Core*(2).

## Name

OverrideShell widget class – a popup shell that bypasses window management.

## Synopsis

**Public Header:** *<X11/Shell.h>*

**Class Name:** OverrideShell

**Class Hierarchy:** Core → Composite → Shell → OverrideShell

**Class Pointer:** `overrideShellWidgetClass`

**Instantiation:** `widget = XtCreatePopupShell(name, overrideWidgetClass, ...)`

**Functions/Macros:** `XtIsOverrideShell()`

## Description

OverrideShell is a direct subclass of Shell that performs no interaction with window managers. It is used for widgets, such as popup menus, that should bypass the window manager.

## New Resources

OverrideShell does not define any new resources.

## Inherited Resources

OverrideShell inherits the following resources. The resources are listed alphabetically, along with the superclass that defines them. OverrideShell sets the default values of both `XmNoverrideRedirect` and `XmNsaveUnder` to `True`.

| Resource | Inherited From | Resource | Inherited From |
|---|---|---|---|
| XmNaccelerators | Core | XmNinitialResourcesPersistent | Core |
| XmNallowShellResize | Shell | XmNinsertPosition | Composite |
| XmNancestorSensitive | Core | XmNmappedWhenManaged | Core |
| XmNbackground | Core | XmNnumChildren | Composite |
| XmNbackgroundPixmap | Core | XmNoverrideRedirect | Shell |
| XmNborderColor | Core | XmNpopdownCallback | Shell |
| XmNborderPixmap | Core | XmNpopupCallback | Shell |
| XmNborderWidth | Core | XmNsaveUnder | Shell |
| XmNchildren | Composite | XmNscreen | Core |
| XmNcolormap | Core | XmNsensitive | Core |
| XmNcreatePopupChildProc | Shell | XmNtranslations | Core |
| XmNdepth | Core | XmNvisual | Shell |
| XmNdestroyCallback | Core | XmNwidth | Core |

| Resource | Inherited From | Resource | Inherited From |
|---|---|---|---|
| XmNgeometry | Shell | XmNx | Core |
| XmNheight | Core | XmNy | Core |

## See Also

*Composite*(2), *Core*(2), *Shell*(2).

## Name

RectObj widget class – fundamental object class with geometry.

## Synopsis

**Public Header:** *<Xm/Xm.h>*

**Class Name:** RectObj

**Class Hierarchy:** Object → RectObj

**Class Pointer:** rectObjClass

**Instantiation:** RectObj is an Intrinsics meta-class and is not normally instantiated.

**Functions/Macros:** `XtIsRectObj()`

## Description

RectObj is a supporting superclass for widgets and gadgets. It does not have a window, but it does have a height, width, and location, and it encapsulates the mechanisms for geometry management.

## New Resources

RectObj defines the following resources:

| Name | Class | Type | Default | Access |
|---|---|---|---|---|
| XmNancestorSensitive | XmCSensitive | Boolean | dynamic | G |
| XmNborderWidth | XmCBorderWidth | Dimension | 1 | CSG |
| XmNheight | XmCHeight | Dimension | dynamic | CSG |
| XmNsensitive | XmCSensitive | Boolean | True | CSG |
| XmNwidth | XmCWidth | Dimension | dynamic | CSG |
| XmNx | XmCPosition | Position | 0 | CSG |
| XmNy | XmCPosition | Position | 0 | CSG |

`XmNancestorSensitive`
: Tells whether a gadget's immediate parent should receive input. Default value is the bitwise AND of the `XmNsensitive` and `XmNancestorSensitive` resources of the parent.

`XmNborderWidth`
: Width (in pixels) of the window's border.

`XmNheight`
: Window height (in pixels), excluding the border.

`XmNsensitive`
: Tells whether a gadget receives input (is sensitive). The `XtSetSensitive()` routine can be used to change a widget's sensitivity and to guarantee that if a parent has its

XmNsensitive resource set to False, then its children will have their ancestor-sensitive flag set correctly.

XmNwidth
Window width (in pixels), excluding the border.

XmNx
The x-coordinate of the widget's upper-left outer corner, relative to the upper-left inner corner of its parent.

XmNy
The y-coordinate of the widget's upper-left outer corner, relative to the upper-left inner corner of its parent.

## Inherited Resources

RectObj inherits the following resource:

| Resource | Inherited From |
|---|---|
| XmNdestroyCallback | Object |

## See Also

*Object*(2).

# Shell

## Name

Shell widget class – fundamental widget class that controls interaction between top-level windows and the window manager.

## Synopsis

**Public Header:** *<Xm/Xm.h>*
*<X11/Shell.h>*

**Class Name:** Shell

**Class Hierarchy:** Core → Composite → Shell

**Class Pointer:** `shellWidgetClass`

**Instantiation:** Shell is an Intrinsics meta-class and is not normally instantiated.

**Functions/Macros:** `XtIsShell()`

## Description

Shell is a subclass of Composite that handles interaction between the window manager and its single child.

## New Resources

Shell defines the following resources:

| Name | Class | Type | Default | Access |
|---|---|---|---|---|
| XmNallowShellResize | XmCAllowCWShellResize | Boolean | False | CG |
| XmNcreatePopupChildProc | XmCCreatePopupChildProc | XtCreatePopup ChildProc | NULL | CSG |
| XmNgeometry | XmCGeometry | String | NULL | CSG |
| XmNoverrideRedirect | XmCOverride Redirect | Boolean | False | CSG |
| XmNpopdownCallback | XmCCallback | XtCallbackList | NULL | C |
| XmNpopupCallback | XmCCallback | XtCallbackList | NULL | C |
| XmNsaveUnder | XmCSaveUnder | Boolean | False | CSG |
| XmNvisual | XmCVisual | Visual * | Copy From Parent | CSG |

`XmNallowShellResize`

If `False` (default), the Shell widget refuses geometry requests from its children (by returning `XtGeometryNo`).

`XmNcreatePopupChildProc`

A pointer to a procedure that creates a child widget—but only when the shell is popped up, not when the application is started. This is useful in menus, for example, since you don't need to create the menu until it is popped up. This procedure is called after those specified in the `XmNpopupCallback` resource.

XmNgeometry
: This resource specifies the values for the resources XmNx, XmNy, XmNwidth, and XmNheight in situations where an unrealized widget has added or removed some of its managed children.

XmNoverrideRedirect
: If True, the widget is considered a temporary window that redirects the keyboard focus away from the main application windows. Usually this resource shouldn't be changed.

XmNpopdownCallback
: List of callbacks that are called when the widget is popped down using XtPopdown().

XmNpopupCallback
: List of callbacks that are called when the widget is popped up using XtPopup().

XmNsaveUnder
: If True, screen contents that are obscured by a widget are saved, thereby avoiding the overhead of sending expose events after the widget is unmapped.

XmNvisual
: The visual server resource that is used when creating the widget.

## Inherited Resources

Shell inherits the following resources. The resources are listed alphabetically, along with the superclass that defines them.

| Resource | Inherited From | Resource | Inherited From |
|---|---|---|---|
| XmNaccelerators | Core | XmNheight | Core |
| XmNancestorSensitive | Core | XmNinitialResourcesPersistent | Core |
| XmNbackground | Core | XmNinsertPosition | Composite |
| XmNbackgroundPixmap | Core | XmNmappedWhenManaged | Core |
| XmNborderColor | Core | XmNnumChildren | Composite |
| XmNborderPixmap | Core | XmNscreen | Core |
| XmNborderWidth | Core | XmNsensitive | Core |
| XmNchildren | Composite | XmNtranslations | Core |
| XmNcolormap | Core | XmNwidth | Core |
| XmNdepth | Core | XmNx | Core |
| XmNdestroyCallback | Core | XmNy | Core |

## See Also

*Composite*(2), *Core*(2).

## Name

TopLevelShell widget class – additional top-level shells for an application.

## Synopsis

**Public Header:** *<Xm/Xm.h>*
*<X11/Shell.h>*

**Class Name:** TopLevelShell

**Class Hierarchy:** Core → Composite → Shell → WMShell → VendorShell → TopLevelShell

**Class Pointer:** `topLevelShellWidgetClass`

**Instantiation:** `widget = XtCreatePopupShell(name, topLevelShellWidgetClass, ...)`

**Functions/Macros:** `XtIsTopLevelShell()`

## Description

TopLevelShell is a subclass of VendorShell that is used for additional shells in applications having more than one top-level window.

## New Resources

TopLevelShell defines the following resources:

| Name | Class | Type | Default | Access |
|---|---|---|---|---|
| XmNiconic | XmCIconic | Boolean | False | CSG |
| XmNiconName | XmCIconName | String | NULL | CSG |
| XmNiconNameEncoding | XmCIconNameEncoding | Atom | dynamic | CSG |

`XmNiconic`
If `True`, the widget is realized as an icon, regardless of the value of the `XmNinitialState` resource.

`XmNiconName`
The abbreviated name that labels an iconified application.

`XmNiconNameEncoding`
The property type for encoding the `XmNiconName` resource.

Motif and Xt Widget Classes

## Inherited Resources

TopLevelShell inherits the following resources. The resources are listed alphabetically, along with the superclass that defines them. TopLevelShell resets `XmNinput` to `True`.

| Resource | Inherited From | Resource | Inherited From |
|---|---|---|---|
| XmNaccelerators | Core | XmNmaxHeight | WMShell |
| XmNallowShellResize | Shell | XmNmaxWidth | WMShell |
| XmNancestorSensitive | Core | XmNminAspectX | WMShell |
| XmNaudibleWarning | VendorShell | XmNminAspectY | WMShell |

| Resource | Inherited From |
|---|---|
| XmNbackground | Core |
| XmNbackgroundPixmap | Core |
| XmNbaseHeight | WMShell |
| XmNbaseWidth | WMShell |
| XmNborderColor | Core |
| XmNborderPixmap | Core |
| XmNborderWidth | Core |
| XmNbuttonFontList | VendorShell |
| XmNchildren | Composite |
| XmNcolormap | Core |
| XmNcreatePopupChildProc | Shell |
| XmNdefaultFontList | VendorShell |
| XmNdeleteResponse | VendorShell |
| XmNdepth | Core |
| XmNdestroyCallback | Core |
| XmNgeometry | Shell |
| XmNheight | Core |
| XmNheightInc | WMShell |
| XmNiconMask | WMShell |
| XmNiconPixmap | WMShell |
| XmNiconWindow | WMShell |
| XmNiconX | WMShell |
| XmNiconY | WMShell |
| XmNinitialResourcesPersistent | Core |
| XmNinitialState | WMShell |
| XmNinput | WMShell |
| XmNinputMethod | VendorShell |
| XmNinsertPosition | Composite |
| XmNkeyboardFocusPolicy | VendorShell |
| XmNlabelFontList | VendorShell |
| XmNmappedWhenManaged | Core |
| XmNmaxAspectX | WMShell |
| XmNmaxAspectY | WMShell |
| XmNminHeight | WMShell |
| XmNminWidth | WMShell |
| XmNmwmDecorations | VendorShell |
| XmNmwmFunctions | VendorShell |
| XmNmwmInputMode | VendorShell |
| XmNmwmMenu | VendorShell |
| XmNnumChildren | Composite |
| XmNoverrideRedirect | Shell |
| XmNpopdownCallback | Shell |
| XmNpopupCallback | Shell |
| XmNpreeditType | VendorShell |
| XmNsaveUnder | Shell |
| XmNScreen | Core |
| XmNsensitive | Core |
| XmNshellUnitType | VendorShell |
| XmNtextFontList | VendorShell |
| XmNtitle | WMShell |
| XmNtitleEncoding | WMShell |
| XmNtransient | WMShell |
| XmNtranslations | Core |
| XmNuseAsyncGeometry | VendorShell |
| XmNvisual | Shell |
| XmNwaitForWm | WMShell |
| XmNwidth | Core |
| XmNwidthInc | WMShell |
| XmNwindowGroup | WMShell |
| XmNwinGravity | WMShell |
| XmNwmTimeout | WMShell |
| XmNx | Core |
| XmNy | Core |

## See Also

*Composite*(2), *Core*(2), *Shell*(2), *VendorShell*(2), *WMShell*(2).

## Name

TransientShell widget class – popup shell that interacts with the window manager.

## Synopsis

**Public Header:** *<Xm/Xm.h>*
*<X11/Shell.h>*

**Class Name:** TransientShell

**Class Hierarchy:** Core → Composite → Shell → WMShell → VendorShell → TransientShell

**Class Pointer:** `transientShellWidgetClass`

**Instantiation:** `widget = XtCreatePopupShell(name, transientShellWidgetClass, ...)`

**Functions/Macros:** `XtIsTransientShell()`

## Description

TransientShell is a subclass of VendorShell that is used for popup shell widgets, such as dialog boxes, that interact with the window manager. Most window managers will not allow the user to iconify a TransientShell window on its own and may iconify it automatically if the window that it is transient for is iconified.

## New Resources

TransientShell defines the following resources:

| Name | Class | Type | Default | Access |
|---|---|---|---|---|
| XmNtransientFor | XmCTransientFor | Widget | NULL | CSG |

XmNtransientFor
The widget from which the TransientShell will pop up. If the value of this resource is NULL or identifies an unrealized widget, then TransientShell uses the value of the WMShell resource XmNwindowGroup.

## Inherited Resources

TransientShell inherits the following resources. The resources are listed alphabetically, along with the superclass that defines them. TransientShell resets the resources XmNinput, XmNtransient, and XmNsaveUnder to True.

| Resource | Inherited From | Resource | Inherited From |
|---|---|---|---|
| XmNaccelerators | Core | XmNmaxHeight | WMShell |
| XmNallowShellResize | Shell | XmNmaxWidth | WMShell |
| XmNancestorSensitive | Core | XmNminAspectX | WMShell |
| XmNaudibleWarning | VendorShell | XmNminAspectY | WMShell |

| Resource | Inherited From | Resource | Inherited From |
|---|---|---|---|
| XmNbackground | Core | XmNminHeight | WMShell |
| XmNbackgroundPixmap | Core | XmNminWidth | WMShell |
| XmNbaseHeight | WMShell | XmNmwmDecorations | VendorShell |
| XmNbaseWidth | WMShell | XmNmwmFunctions | VendorShell |
| XmNborderColor | Core | XmNmwmInputMode | VendorShell |
| XmNborderPixmap | Core | XmNmwmMenu | VendorShell |
| XmNborderWidth | Core | XmNnumChildren | Composite |
| XmNbuttonFontList | VendorShell | XmNoverrideRedirect | Shell |
| XmNchildren | Composite | XmNpopdownCallback | Shell |
| XmNcolormap | Core | XmNpopupCallback | Shell |
| XmNcreate PopupChildProc | Shell | XmNpreeditType | VendorShell |
| XmNdefaultFontList | VendorShell | XmNsaveUnder | Shell |
| XmNdeleteResponse | VendorShell | XmNscreen | Core |
| XmNdepth | Core | XmNsensitive | Core |
| XmNdestroyCallback | Core | XmNshellUnitType | VendorShell |
| XmNgeometry | Shell | XmNtextFontList | VendorShell |
| XmNheight | Core | XmNtitle | WMShell |
| XmNheightInc | WMShell | XmNtitleEncoding | WMShell |
| XmNiconMask | WMShell | XmNtransient | WMShell |
| XmNiconPixmap | WMShell | XmNtranslations | Core |
| XmNiconWindow | WMShell | XmNuseAsyncGeometry | VendorShell |
| XmNiconX | WMShell | XmNvisual | Shell |
| XmNiconY | WMShell | XmNwaitForWm | WMShell |
| XmNinitialResources Persistent | Core | XmNwidth | Core |
| XmNinitialState | WMShell | XmNwidthInc | WMShell |
| XmNinput | WMShell | XmNwindowGroup | WMShell |
| XmNinputMethod | VendorShell | XmNwindowGroup | WMShell |
| XmNinsertPosition | Composite | XmNwinGravity | WMShell |
| XmNkeyboardFocusPolicy | VendorShell | XmNwmTimeout | WMShell |
| XmNlabelFontList | VendorShell | XmNx | Core |
| XmNmappedWhenManaged | Core | XmNy | Core |
| XmNmaxAspectX | WMShell | | |
| XmNmaxAspectY | WMShell | | |

## See Also

*Composite*(2), *Core*(2), *Shell*(2), *VendorShell*(2), *WMShell*(2).

# VendorShell

## Name

VendorShell widget class – shell widget with Motif-specific hooks for window manager interaction.

## Synopsis

**Public Header:** *<Xm/VendorS.h>*
*<X11/Shell.h>*

**Class Name:** VendorShell

**Class Hierarchy:** Core → Composite → Shell → WMShell → VendorShell

**Class Pointer:** `vendorShellWidgetClass`

**Instantiation:** VendorShell is a meta-class and is not normally instantiated.

**Functions/Macros:** `XmIsVendorShell()`

## Description

VendorShell is a vendor-specific supporting superclass for all shell classes that are visible to the window manager and that do not have override redirection. VendorShell defines resources that provide the Motif look-and-feel and manages the specific communication needed by the Motif Window Manager (*mwm*).

## New Resources

VendorShell defines the following resources:

| Name | Class | Type | Default | Access |
|---|---|---|---|---|
| XmNaudibleWarning | XmCAudibleWarning | unsigned char | XmBELL | CSG |
| XmNbuttonFontList | XmCButtonFontList | XmFontList | dynamic | C |
| XmNdefaultFontList | XmCDefaultFontList | XmFontList | dynamic | CG |
| XmNdeleteResponse | XmCDeleteResponse | unsigned char | XmDESTROY | CSG |
| XmNinputMethod | XmCInputMethod | String | NULL | CSG |
| XmNkeyboardFocusPolicy | XmCKeyboardFocusPolicy | unsigned char | XmEXPLICIT | CSG |
| XmNlabelFontList | XmCLabelFontList | XmFontList | dynamic | C |
| XmNmwmDecorations | XmCMwmDecorations | int | -1 | CSG |
| XmNmwmFunctions | XmCMwmFunctions | int | -1 | CSG |
| XmNmwmInputMode | XmCMwmInputMode | int | -1 | CSG |
| XmNmwmMenu | XmCMwmMenu | String | NULL | CSG |
| XmNpreeditType | XmCPreeditType | String | dynamic | CSG |
| XmNshellUnitType | XmCShellUnitType | unsigned char | XmPIXELS | CSG |

| Name | Class | Type | Default | Access |
|---|---|---|---|---|
| XmNtextFontList | XmCTextFontList | XmFontList | dynamic | C |
| XmNuseAsyncGeometry | XmCUseAsyncGeometry | Boolean | False | CSG |

`XmNaudibleWarning`
: In Motif 1.2, specifies whether an action performs an associated audible cue. Possible values:

```
XmBELL              /* rings the bell */
XmNONE              /* does nothing */
```

`XmNbuttonFontList`
: In Motif 1.2, the font list used for the button children of the VendorShell widget. If this value is initially `NULL` and if the value of `XmNdefaultFontList` is not `NULL`, this value is used. Otherwise, the font list is derived from the `XmNbuttonFontList` resource found in the nearest ancestor that is a subclass of BulletinBoard, VendorShell, or MenuShell.

`XmNdefaultFontList`
: The default font list for the children of the MenuShell widget. This resource is obsolete in Motif 1.2.

`XmNdeleteResponse`
: The action to perform when the shell receives a `WM_DELETE_WINDOW` message. Possible values:

```
XmDESTROY           /* destroy window */
XmUNMAP             /* unmap window */
XmDO_NOTHING        /* leave window as is*/
```

`XmNinputMethod`
: In Motif 1.2, specifies the string that sets the locale modifier for the input method.

`XmNkeyboardFocusPolicy`
: The method of assigning keyboard focus. Possible values:

```
XmEXPLICIT          /* click-to-type policy */
XmPOINTER           /* pointer-driven policy */
```

`XmNlabelFontList`
: In Motif 1.2, the font list used for the label children of the VendorShell widget. If this value is initially `NULL` and if the value of `XmNdefaultFontList` is not `NULL`, this value is used. Otherwise, the font list is derived from the `XmNlabelFontList` resource found in the nearest ancestor that is a subclass of BulletinBoard, VendorShell, or MenuShell.

XmNmwmDecorations

This resource corresponds to the values assigned by the decorations field of the _MOTIF_WM_HINTS property. This resource determines which frame buttons and handles to include with a window. The possible values are:

```
 1   /* MWM_DECOR_ALL        remove decorations from full set */
 2   /* MWM_DECOR_BORDER     window border */
 4   /* MWM_DECOR_RESIZEH    resize handles */
 8   /* MWM_DECOR_TITLE      title bar */
16   /* MWM_DECOR_SYSTEM     window's menu button */
32   /* MWM_DECOR_MINIMIZE   minimize button */
64   /* MWM_DECOR_MAXIMIZE   maximize button */
```

XmNmwmFunctions

This resource corresponds to the values assigned by the functions field of the _MOTIF_WM_HINTS property. This resource determines which functions to include in the system menu. The possible values are:

```
 1   /* MWM_FUNC_ALL         remove functions from full set */
 2   /* MWM_FUNC_RESIZE      f.resize */
 4   /* MWM_FUNC_MOVE        f.move */
 8   /* MWM_FUNC_MINIMIZE    f.minimize */
16   /* MWM_FUNC_MAXIMIZE    f.maximize */
32   /* MWM_FUNC_CLOSE       f.kill */
```

XmNmwmInputMode

This resource corresponds to the values assigned by the input_mode field of the _MOTIF_WM_HINTS property. This resource determines the constraints on the window's keyboard focus. That is, it determines whether the application takes the keyboard focus away from the primary window or not. The possible values are:

```
1    /* INPUT_APPLICATION_MODAL  primary window does not have focus */
2    /* INPUT_SYSTEM_MODAL       primary window has keyboard focus */
```

XmNmwmMenu

The menu items to add at the bottom of the client's window menu. The string has this format:

```
label [mnemonic] [ accelerator] mwm_f.function
```

XmNpreeditType

In Motif 1.2, specifies the input method style(s) that are available. The syntax, possible values, and default value of this resource are implementation-dependent.

XmNshellUnitType

The measurement units to use in resources that specify a size or position. Possible values:

| | |
|---|---|
| XmPIXELS | Xm100TH_POINTS |
| Xm100TH_MILLIMETERS | Xm100TH_FONT_UNITS |
| Xm1000TH_INCHES | |

XmNtextFontList

In Motif 1.2, the font list used for the text children of the VendorShell widget. If this value is initially NULL and if the value of XmNdefaultFontList is not NULL, this value is used. Otherwise, the font list is derived from the XmNtextFontList resource found in the nearest ancestor that is a subclass of BulletinBoard or VendorShell.

XmNuseAsyncGeometry

If True, the geometry manager doesn't wait to confirm a geometry request that was sent to the window manager. The geometry manager performs this by setting the WMShell resource XmNwaitForWm to False and by setting the WMShell resource XmNwm-Timeout to 0. If XmNuseAsyncGeometry is False (default), the geometry manager uses synchronous notification, and so it doesn't change the resources XmNwaitForWm and XmNwmTimeout.

### Inherited Resources

VendorShell inherits the following resources. The resources are listed alphabetically, along with the superclass that defines them. VendorShell resets XmNborderWidth from 1 to 0 and resets XmNinput to True.

| Resource | Inherited From | Resource | Inherited From |
|---|---|---|---|
| XmNaccelerators | Core | XmNmaxAspectX | WMShell |
| XmNallowShellResize | Shell | XmNmaxAspectY | WMShell |
| XmNancestorSensitive | Core | XmNmaxHeight | WMShell |
| XmNbackground | Core | XmNmaxWidth | WMShell |
| XmNbackgroundPixmap | Core | XmNminAspectX | WMShell |
| XmNbaseHeight | WMShell | XmNminAspectY | WMShell |
| XmNbaseWidth | WMShell | XmNminHeight | WMShell |
| XmNborderColor | Core | XmNminWidth | WMShell |
| XmNborderPixmap | Core | XmNnumChildren | Composite |
| XmNborderWidth | Core | XmNoverrideRedirect | Shell |
| XmNchildren | Composite | XmNpopdownCallback | Shell |
| XmNcolormap | Core | XmNpopupCallback | Shell |
| XmNcreatePopupChildProc | Shell | XmNsaveUnder | Shell |
| XmNdepth | Core | XmNscreen | Core |
| XmNdestroyCallback | Core | XmNsensitive | Core |
| XmNgeometry | Shell | XmNtitle | WMShell |
| XmNheight | Core | XmNtitleEncoding | WMShell |

| Resource | Inherited From | Resource | Inherited From |
|---|---|---|---|
| XmNheightInc | WMShell | XmNtransient | WMShell |
| XmNiconMask | WMShell | XmNtranslations | Core |
| XmNiconPixmap | WMShell | XmNvisual | Shell |
| XmNiconWindow | WMShell | XmNwaitForWm | WMShell |
| XmNiconX | WMShell | XmNwidth | Core |
| XmNiconY | WMShell | XmNwidthInc | WMShell |
| XmNinitialResourcesPersistent | Core | XmNwindowGroup | WMShell |
| XmNinitialState | WMShell | XmNwinGravity | WMShell |
| XmNinput | WMShell | XmNwmTimeout | WMShell |
| XmNinsertPosition | Composite | XmNx | Core |
| XmNmappedWhenManaged | Core | XmNy | Core |

## See Also

*Composite*(2), *Core*(2), *Shell*(2), *WMShell*(2).

# WMShell



## Name

WMShell widget class – fundamental shell widget that interacts with an ICCCM-compliant window manager.

## Synopsis

**Public Header:** *<Xm/Xm.h>*
*<X11/Shell.h>*

**Class Name:** WMShell

**Class Hierarchy:** Core → Composite → Shell → WMShell

**Class Pointer:** `wmShellWidgetClass`

**Instantiation:** WMShell is an Intrinsics meta-class and is not normally instantiated.

**Functions/Macros:** `XtIsWMShell()`

## Description

WMShell is a direct subclass of Shell that provides basic window manager interaction. WMShell is not directly instantiated; it encapsulates the application resources that applications use to communicate with window managers.

## New Resources

WMShell defines the following resources:

| Name | Class | Type | Default | Access |
|---|---|---|---|---|
| XmNbaseHeight | XmCBaseHeight | int | XtUnspecifiedShellInt | CSG |
| XmNbaseWidth | XmCBaseWidth | int | XtUnspecifiedShellInt | CSG |
| XmNheightInc | XmCHeightInc | int | XtUnspecifiedShellInt | CSG |
| XmNiconMask | XmCIconMask | Pixmap | NULL | CSG |
| XmNiconPixmap | XmCIconPixmap | Pixmap | NULL | CSG |
| XmNiconWindow | XmCIconWindow | Window | NULL | CSG |
| XmNiconX | XmCIconX | int | -1 | CSG |
| XmNiconY | XmCIconY | int | -1 | CSG |
| XmNinitialState | XmCInitialState | int | NormalState | CSG |
| XmNinput | XmCInput | Boolean | False | CSG |
| XmNmaxAspectX | XmCMaxAspectX | int | XtUnspecifiedShellInt | CSG |
| XmNmaxAspectY | XmCMaxAspectY | int | XtUnspecifiedShellInt | CSG |
| XmNmaxHeight | XmCMaxHeight | int | XtUnspecifiedShellInt | CSG |
| XmNmaxWidth | XmCMaxWidth | int | XtUnspecifiedShellInt | CSG |
| XmNminAspectX | XmCMinAspectX | int | XtUnspecifiedShellInt | CSG |
| XmNminAspectY | XmCMinAspectY | int | XtUnspecifiedShellInt | CSG |
| XmNminHeight | XmCMinHeight | int | XtUnspecifiedShellInt | CSG |
| XmNminWidth | XmCMinWidth | int | XtUnspecifiedShellInt | CSG |
| XmNtitle | XmCTitle | String | dynamic | CSG |
| XmNtitleEncoding | XmCTitleEncoding | Atom | dynamic | CSG |

| Name | Class | Type | Default | Access |
|---|---|---|---|---|
| XmNtransient | XmCTransient | Boolean | False | CSG |
| XmNwaitForWm | XmCWaitForWm | Boolean | True | CSG |
| XmNwidthInc | XmCWidthInc | int | XtUnspecifiedShellInt | CSG |
| XmNwindowGroup | XmCWindowGroup | Window | dynamic | CSG |
| XmNwinGravity | XmCWinGravity | int | dynamic | CSG |
| XmNwmTimeout | XmCWmTimeout | int | 5000 | CSG |

`XmNbaseHeight`
`XmNbaseWidth`

The base dimensions from which the preferred height and width can be stepped up or down (as specified by `XmNheightInc` or `XmNwidthInc`).

`XmNheightInc`

The amount by which to increment or decrement the window's height when the window manager chooses a preferred value. The base height is `XmNbaseHeight`, and the height can decrement to the value of `XmNminHeight` or increment to the value of `XmNmaxHeight`. See also `XmNwidthInc`.

`XmNiconMask`

A bitmap that the window manager can use in order to clip the application's icon into a nonrectangular shape.

`XmNiconPixmap`

The application's icon.

`XmNiconWindow`

The ID of a window that serves as the application's icon.

`XmNiconX`
`XmNiconY`

Window manager hints for the root window coordinates of the application's icon.

`XmNinitialState`

The initial appearance of the widget instance. Possible values are defined in *<X11/Xutil.h>*:

```
NormalState     /* application starts as a window */
IconicState     /* application starts as an icon */
```

XmNinput
A Boolean that, in conjunction with the WM_TAKE_FOCUS atom in the WM_PROTOCOLS property, determines the application's keyboard focus model. The result is determined by the value of XmNinput and the existence of the atom, as described below:

| Value of XmNinput Resource | WM_TAKE_FOCUS Atom | Keyboard Focus Model |
|---|---|---|
| False | Does not exist | No input allowed |
| True | Does not exist | Passive |
| True | Exists | Locally active |
| False | Exists | Globally active |

XmNmaxAspectX
XmNmaxAspectY
The numerator and denominator, respectively, of the maximum aspect ratio requested for this widget.

XmNmaxHeight
XmNmaxWidth
The maximum dimensions for the widget's preferred height or width.

XmNminAspectX
XmNminAspectY
The numerator and denominator, respectively, of the minimum aspect ratio requested for this widget.

XmNminHeight
XmNminWidth
The minimum dimensions for the widget's preferred height or width.

XmNtitle
The string that the window manager displays as the application's name. By default, the icon name is used, but if this isn't specified, the name of the application is used.

XmNtitleEncoding
The property type for encoding the XmNtitle resource.

XmNtransient
If True, this indicates a popup window or some other transient widget. This resource is usually not changed.

XmNwaitForWm
If True (default), the X Toolkit waits for a response from the window manager before acting as if no window manager exists. The waiting time is specified by the XmNwm-Timeout resource.

XmNwidthInc

The amount by which to increment or decrement the window's width when the window manager chooses a preferred value. The base width is XmNbaseWidth, and the width can decrement to the value of XmNminWidth or increment to the value of XmNmaxWidth. See also XmNheightInc.

XmNwindowGroup

The window associated with this widget instance. This window acts as the primary window of a group of windows that have similar behavior.

XmNwinGravity

The window gravity used in positioning the widget. Unless an initial value is given, this resource will be set when the widget is realized. The default value is NorthWestGravity (if the Shell resource XmNgeometry is NULL); otherwise, XmNwinGravity assumes the value returned by the XmWMGeometry routine.

XmNwmTimeout

The number of milliseconds that the X Toolkit waits for a response from the window manager. This resource is meaningful when the XmNwaitForWm resource is set to True.

## Inherited Resources

WMShell inherits the following resources. The resources are listed alphabetically, along with the superclass that defines them.

| Resource | Inherited From | Resource | Inherited From |
|---|---|---|---|
| XmNaccelerators | Core | XmNinitialResourcesPersistent | Core |
| XmNallowShellResize | Shell | XmNinsertPosition | Composite |
| XmNancestorSensitive | Core | XmNmappedWhenManaged | Core |
| XmNbackground | Core | XmNnumChildren | Composite |
| XmNbackgroundPixmap | Core | XmNoverrideRedirect | Shell |
| XmNborderColor | Core | XmNpopdownCallback | Shell |
| XmNborderPixmap | Core | XmNpopupCallback | Shell |
| XmNborderWidth | Core | XmNsaveUnder | Shell |
| XmNchildren | Composite | XmNscreen | Core |
| XmNcolormap | Core | XmNsensitive | Core |
| XmNcreatePopupChildProc | Shell | XmNtranslations | Core |
| XmNdepth | Core | XmNvisual | Shell |
| XmNdestroyCallback | Core | XmNwidth | Core |
| XmNgeometry | Shell | XmNx | Core |
| XmNheight | Core | XmNy | Core |

## See Also

*Composite*(2), *Core*(2), *Shell*(2).

## Name

XmArrowButton widget class – a directional arrow-shaped button widget.

## Synopsis

**Public Header:** *<Xm/ArrowB.h>*

**Class Name:** XmArrowButton

**Class Hierarchy:** Core → XmPrimitive → XmArrowButton

**Class Pointer:** `xmArrowButtonWidgetClass`

**Instantiation:** `widget = XtCreateWidget(name, xmArrowButtonWidgetClass, ...)`

**Functions/Macros:** `XmCreateArrowButton(), XmIsArrowButton()`

## Description

An ArrowButton is a directional arrow-shaped button that includes a shaded border. The shading changes to make the ArrowButton appear either pressed in when selected or raised when unselected.

## New Resources

ArrowButton defines the following resources:

| Name | Class | Type | Default | Access |
|---|---|---|---|---|
| XmNarrowDirection | XmCArrowDirection | unsigned char | XmARROW_UP | CSG |
| XmNmultiClick | XmCMultiClick | unsigned char | dynamic | CSG |

`XmNarrowDirection`

Sets the arrow direction. Possible values:

```
XmARROW_UP                    XmARROW_LEFT
XmARROW_DOWN                  XmARROW_RIGHT
```

`XmNmultiClick`

A flag that determines whether successive button clicks are processed or ignored. Possible values:

```
XmMULTICLICK_DISCARD    /* ignore successive button clicks; */
                        /* default value in a menu system */
XmMULTICLICK_KEEP       /* count successive button clicks; */
                        /* default value when not in a menu */
```

Motif and Xt Widget Classes

## Callback Resources

ArrowButton defines the following callback resources:

| Callback | Reason Constant |
|---|---|
| XmNactivateCallback | XmCR_ACTIVATE |
| XmNarmCallback | XmCR_ARM |
| XmNdisarmCallback | XmCR_DISARM |

XmNactivateCallback
: List of callbacks that are called when BSelect is pressed and released inside the widget.

XmNarmCallback
: List of callbacks that are called when BSelect is pressed while the pointer is inside the widget.

XmNdisarmCallback
: List of callbacks that are called when BSelect is released after it has been pressed inside the widget.

## Callback Structure

Each callback function is passed the following structure:

```
typedef struct
{
    int     reason;       /* the reason that the callback was called */
    XEvent  *event;       /* event structure that triggered callback */
    int     click_count;  /* number of clicks in multi-click sequence */
} XmArrowButtonCallbackStruct;
```

click_count is meaningful only for XmNactivateCallback. Furthermore, if the XmN-multiClick resource is set to XmMULTICLICK_KEEP, then XmNactivateCallback is called for each click, and the value of click_count is the number of clicks that have occurred in the last sequence of multiple clicks. If the XmNmultiClick resource is set to XmMULTICLICK_DISCARD, then click_count always has a value of 1.

## Inherited Resources

ArrowButton inherits the following resources. The resources are listed alphabetically, along with the superclass that defines them. The default value of XmNborderWidth is reset to 0 by Primitive.

| Resource | Inherited From | Resource | Inherited From |
|---|---|---|---|
| XmNaccelerators | Core | XmNhighlightPixmap | Primitive |
| XmNancestorSensitive | Core | XmNhighlightThickness | Primitive |

| Resource | Inherited From | Resource | Inherited From |
|---|---|---|---|
| XmNbackground | Core | XmNinitialResources Persistent | Core |
| XmNbackgroundPixmap | Core | XmNmappedWhenManaged | Core |
| XmNborderColor | Core | XmNnavigationType | Primitive |
| XmNborderPixmap | Core | XmNscreen | Core |
| XmNborderWidth | Core | XmNsensitive | Core |
| XmNbottomShadowColor | Primitive | XmNshadowThickness | Primitive |
| XmNbottomShadowPixmap | Primitive | XmNtopShadowColor | Primitive |
| XmNcolormap | Core | XmNtopShadowPixmap | Primitive |
| XmNdepth | Core | XmNtranslations | Core |
| XmNdestroyCallback | Core | XmNtraversalOn | Primitive |
| XmNforeground | Primitive | XmNunitType | Primitive |
| XmNheight | Core | XmNuserData | Primitive |
| XmNhelpCallback | Primitive | XmNwidth | Core |
| XmNhighlightColor | Primitive | XmNx | Core |
| XmNhighlightOnEnter | Primitive | XmNy | Core |

## Translations

```
BSelect Press           Arm()
BSelect Click           Activate()
                        Disarm()
BSelect Release         Activate()
                        Disarm()
BSelect Press 2+        MultiArm()
BSelect Release 2+      MultiActivate()
KSelect                 ArmAndActivate()
KHelp                   Help()
```

## Action Routines

ArrowButton defines the following action routines:

`Activate()`
: Displays the ArrowButton as unselected, and invokes the list of callbacks specified by `XmNactivateCallback`.

`Arm()`
: Displays the ArrowButton as selected, and invokes the list of callbacks specified by `XmNarmCallback`.

`ArmAndActivate()`
: Displays the ArrowButton as selected, and invokes the list of callbacks specified by `XmNarmCallback`. After doing this, the action routine displays the ArrowButton

as unselected, and invokes the list of callbacks specified by XmNactivateCallback and XmNdisarmCallback.

Disarm()
: Displays the ArrowButton as unselected, and invokes the list of callbacks specified by XmNdisarmCallback.

Help()
: Invokes the list of callbacks specified by XmNhelpCallback. If the ArrowButton doesn't have any help callbacks, the Help() routine invokes those associated with the nearest ancestor that has them.

MultiActivate()
: Increments the click_count member of XmArrowButtonCallbackStruct, displays the ArrowButton as unselected, and invokes the list of callbacks specified by XmNactivateCallback and XmNdisarmCallback. This action routine takes effect only when the XmNmultiClick resource is set to XmMULTICLICK_KEEP.

MultiArm()
: Displays the ArrowButton as selected, and invokes the list of callbacks specified by XmNarmCallback. This action routine takes effect only when the XmNmultiClick resource is set to XmMULTICLICK_KEEP.

## Additional Behavior

ArrowButton has the following additional behavior:

<EnterWindow>
: Displays the ArrowButton as selected if the pointer leaves and re-enters the window while BSelect is pressed.

<LeaveWindow>
: Displays the ArrowButton as unselected if the pointer leaves the window while BSelect is pressed.

## See Also

*XmCreateObject*(1),
*Core*(2), *XmPrimitive*(2).

# XmArrowButtonGadget

## Name

XmArrowButtonGadget widget class – a directional arrow-shaped button gadget.

## Synopsis

**Public Header:** *<Xm/ArrowBG.h>*

**Class Name:** XmArrowButtonGadget

**Class Hierarchy:** Object → RectObj → XmGadget → XmArrowButtonGadget

**Class Pointer:** xmArrowButtonGadgetClass

**Instantiation:** `widget = XtCreateWidget(name, xmArrowButtonGadgetClass, ...)`

**Functions/Macros:** `XmCreateArrowButtonGadget()`, `XmIsArrowButtonGadget()`

## Description

ArrowButtonGadget is the gadget variant of ArrowButton.

ArrowButtonGadget's new resources, callback resources, and callback structure are the same as those for ArrowButton.

## Inherited Resources

ArrowButtonGadget inherits the following resources. The resources are listed alphabetically, along with the superclass that defines them. The default value of `XmNborderWidth` is reset to 0 by Gadget.

| Resource | Inherited From | Resource | Inherited From |
|---|---|---|---|
| XmNancestorSensitive | RectObj | XmNsensitive | RectObj |
| XmNborderWidth | RectObj | XmNshadowThickness | Gadget |
| XmNbottomShadowColor | Gadget | XmNtopShadowColor | Gadget |
| XmNdestroyCallback | Object | XmNtraversalOn | Gadget |
| XmNheight | RectObj | XmNunitType | Gadget |
| XmNhelpCallback | Gadget | XmNuserData | Gadget |
| XmNhighlightColor | Gadget | XmNwidth | RectObj |
| XmNhighlightOnEnter | Gadget | XmNx | RectObj |
| XmNhighlightThickness | Gadget | XmNy | RectObj |
| XmNnavigationType | Gadget | | |

## Behavior

As a gadget subclass, ArrowButtonGadget has no translations associated with it. However, ArrowButtonGadget behavior corresponds to the action routines of the ArrowButton widget. See the ArrowButton action routines for more information.

| Behavior | Equivalent ArrowButton Action Routine |
|---|---|
| BSelect Press | Arm() |
| BSelect Click or BSelectRelease | Activate() |
| | Disarm() |
| BSelect Press 2+ | MultiArm() |
| BSelect Release 2+ | MultiActivate() |
| KSelect | ArmAndActivate() |
| KHelp | Help() |

ArrowButtonGadget has additional behavior associated with `<Enter>` and `<Leave>`, which display the ArrowButtonGadget as selected if the pointer leaves and re-enters the gadget while `BSelect` is pressed or as unselected if the pointer leaves the gadget while `BSelect` is pressed.

## See Also

*XmCreateObject*(1),
*Object*(2), *RectObj*(2), *XmArrowButton*(2), *XmGadget*(2).

# XmBulletinBoard

## Name

XmBulletinBoard widget class – a simple geometry-managing widget.

## Synopsis

**Public Header:** *<Xm/BulletinB.h>*

**Class Name:** XmBulletinBoard

**Class Hierarchy:** Core → Composite → Constraint → XmManager → XmBulletinBoard

**Class Pointer:** `xmBulletinBoardWidgetClass`

**Instantiation:** `widget = XtCreateWidget(name, xmBulletinBoardWidgetClass, ...)`

**Functions/Macros:** `XmCreateBulletinBoard()`, `XmCreateBulletinBoardDialog()`

## Description

BulletinBoard is a general-purpose manager that allows children to be placed at arbitrary x,y positions. The simple geometry management of BulletinBoard can be used to enforce margins and to prevent child widgets from overlapping. BulletinBoard is the base widget for most dialog widgets and defines many resources that have an effect only when it is an immediate child of a DialogShell.

## New Resources

BulletinBoard defines the following resources:

| Name | Class | Type | Default | Access |
|---|---|---|---|---|
| XmNallowOverlap | XmCAllowOverlap | Boolean | True | CSG |
| XmNautoUnmanage | XmCAutoUnmanage | Boolean | True | CG |
| XmNbuttonFontList | XmCButtonFontList | XmFontList | dynamic | CSG |
| XmNcancelButton | XmCWidget | Window | NULL | SG |
| XmNdefaultButton | XmCWidget | Window | NULL | SG |
| XmNdefaultPosition | XmCDefaultPosition | Boolean | True | CSG |
| XmNdialogStyle | XmCDialogStyle | unsigned char | dynamic | CSG |
| XmNdialogTitle | XmCDialogTitle | XmString | NULL | CSG |
| XmNlabelFontList | XmCLabelFontList | XmFontList | dynamic | CSG |
| XmNmarginHeight | XmCMarginHeight | Dimension | 10 | CSG |
| XmNmarginWidth | XmCMarginWidth | Dimension | 10 | CSG |
| XmNnoResize | XmCNoResize | Boolean | False | CSG |
| XmNresizePolicy | XmCResizePolicy | unsigned char | XmRESIZE_ANY | CSG |
| XmNshadowType | XmCShadowType | unsigned char | XmSHADOW_OUT | CSG |
| XmNtextFontList | XmCTextFontList | XmFontList | dynamic | CSG |
| XmNtextTranslations | XmCTranslations | XtTranslations | NULL | C |

XmNallowOverlap
If True (default), child widgets are allowed to overlap.

XmNautoUnmanage
If True (default), the BulletinBoard is automatically unmanaged after a button is activated unless the button is an **Apply** or **Help** button.

XmNbuttonFontList
The font list used for the button children of the BulletinBoard widget. If this value is initially NULL, the font list is derived from the XmNbuttonFontList resource found in the nearest ancestor that is a subclass of BulletinBoard, VendorShell, or MenuShell.

XmNcancelButton
The widget ID of the **Cancel** button. The subclasses of BulletinBoard define a Cancel button and set this resource.

XmNdefaultButton
The widget ID of the default button. Some of the subclasses of BulletinBoard define a default button and set this resource. To indicate that it is the default, this button appears different from the others.

XmNdefaultPosition
If True (default) and if the BulletinBoard is the child of a DialogShell, then the BulletinBoard is centered relative to the DialogShell's parent.

XmNdialogStyle
The BulletinBoard's dialog style, whose value can be set only if the BulletinBoard is unmanaged. Possible values:

```
XmDIALOG_WORK_AREA    /* default when BulletinBoard's parent is not a DialogShell */
XmDIALOG_MODELESS     /* default when BulletinBoard's parent is a DialogShell */
XmDIALOG_FULL_APPLICATION_MODAL
XmDIALOG_APPLICATION_MODAL
XmDIALOG_PRIMARY_APPLICATION_MODAL
XmDIALOG_SYSTEM_MODAL
```

XmNdialogTitle
The dialog title. Setting this resource also sets the resources XmNtitle and XmN-titleEncoding in a parent that is a subclass of WMShell.

XmNlabelFontList
Like the XmNbuttonFontList resource, but for Label children.

XmNmarginHeight
Minimum spacing between a BulletinBoard's top or bottom edge and any child widget.

XmNmarginWidth
Minimum spacing between a BulletinBoard's right or left edge and any child widget.

`XmNnoResize`
If `False` (default), *mwm* includes resize controls in the window manager frame of the BulletinBoard's shell parent.

`XmNresizePolicy`
How BulletinBoard widgets are resized. Possible values:

```
XmRESIZE_NONE       /* remain at fixed size */
XmRESIZE_GROW       /* expand only */
XmRESIZE_ANY        /* shrink or expand, as needed */
```

`XmNshadowType`
The style in which shadows are drawn. Possible values:

```
XmSHADOW_IN         /* widget appears inset */
XmSHADOW_OUT        /* widget appears outset */
XmSHADOW_ETCHED_IN  /* double line; widget appears inset */
XmSHADOW_ETCHED_OUT /* double line; widget appears raised */
```

`XmNtextFontList`
Like the `XmNbuttonFontList` resource, but for Text children.

`XmNtextTranslations`
For any Text widget (or its subclass) that is a child of a BulletinBoard, this resource adds translations.

## Callback Resources

BulletinBoard defines the following callback resources:

| Callback | Reason Constant |
|---|---|
| XmNfocusCallback | XmCR_FOCUS |
| XmNmapCallback | XmCR_MAP |
| XmNunmapCallback | XmCR_UNMAP |

`XmNfocusCallback`
List of callbacks that are called when the widget or one of its descendants receives the input focus.

`XmNmapCallback`
List of callbacks that are called when the widget is mapped, if it is a child of a DialogShell.

`XmNunmapCallback`
List of callbacks that are called when the widget is unmapped, if it is a child of a DialogShell.

## Callback Structure

Each callback function is passed the following structure:

```
typedef struct
{
     int      reason;      /* the reason that the callback was called */
     XEvent  *event;       /* points to event structure that triggered callback */
} XmAnyCallbackStruct;
```

## Inherited Resources

BulletinBoard inherits the following resources. The resources are listed alphabetically, along with the superclass that defines them. BulletinBoard sets the value of `XmNinitialFocus` to the value of `XmNdefaultButton`. When it is a child of a DialogShell, BulletinBoard resets the default `XmNshadowThickness` from 0 to 1. The default value of `XmNborderWidth` is reset to 0 by Manager.

| Resource | Inherited From | Resource | Inherited From |
|---|---|---|---|
| XmNaccelerators | Core | XmNinitialResources Persistent | Core |
| XmNancestorSensitive | Core | XmNinsertPosition | Composite |
| XmNbackground | Core | XmNmappedWhenManaged | Core |
| XmNbackgroundPixmap | Core | XmNnavigationType | Manager |
| XmNborderColor | Core | XmNnumChildren | Composite |
| XmNborderPixmap | Core | XmNscreen | Core |
| XmNborderWidth | Core | XmNsensitive | Core |
| XmNbottomShadowColor | Manager | XmNshadowThickness | Manager |
| XmNbottomShadowPixmap | Manager | XmNstringDirection | Manager |
| XmNchildren | Composite | XmNtopShadowColor | Manager |
| XmNcolormap | Core | XmNtopShadowPixmap | Manager |
| XmNdepth | Core | XmNtranslations | Core |
| XmNdestroyCallback | Core | XmNtraversalOn | Manager |
| XmNforeground | Manager | XmNunitType | Manager |
| XmNheight | Core | XmNuserData | Manager |
| XmNhelpCallback | Manager | XmNwidth | Core |
| XmNhighlightColor | Manager | XmNx | Core |
| XmNhighlightPixmap | Manager | XmNy | Core |
| XmNinitialFocus | Manager | | |

## Translations

The translations for BulletinBoard include those of Manager.

## Additional Behavior

BulletinBoard has the following additional behavior:

`MAny KCancel`
For a sensitive **Cancel** button, invokes the `XmNactivateCallback` callbacks.

`KActivate`
For the button that has keyboard focus, invokes the `XmNactivateCallback` callbacks.

`<FocusIn>`
Invokes the `XmNfocusCallback` callbacks. The widget receives focus either when the user traverses to it (`XmNkeyboardFocusPolicy` is `XmEXPLICIT`) or when the pointer enters the window (`XmNkeyboardFocusPolicy` is `XmPOINTER`).

`<Map>` Invokes the `XmNmapCallback` callbacks.

`<Unmap>` Invokes the `XmNunmapCallback` callbacks.

## See Also

*XmCreateObject*(1),
*Composite*(2), *Constraint*(2), *Core*(2), *XmBulletinBoardDialog*(2), *XmDialogShell*(2), *XmManager*(2).

# XmBulletinBoardDialog

## Name

XmBulletinBoardDialog – an unmanaged BulletinBoard as a child of a DialogShell.

## Synopsis

**Public Header:** *<Xm/BulletinB.h>*

**Instantiation:** `widget = XmCreateBulletinBoardDialog(...)`

**Functions/Macros:** `XmCreateBulletinBoardDialog()`

## Description

A BulletinBoardDialog is a compound object created by a call to `XmCreateBulletinBoardDialog()` that is useful for creating custom dialogs. A BulletinBoardDialog consists of a DialogShell with an unmanaged BulletinBoard widget as its child. The BulletinBoard-Dialog does not contain any labels, buttons, or other dialog components; these components are added by the application.

## Default Resource Values

A BulletinBoardDialog sets the following default values for BulletinBoard resources:

| Name | Default |
|---|---|
| XmNdialogStyle | XmDIALOG_MODELESS |

## Widget Hierarchy

When a BulletinBoardDialog is created with a specified `name`, the DialogShell is named `name_popup` and the BulletinBoard is called `name`.

## See Also

*XmCreateObject*(1),
*XmBulletinBoard*(2), *XmDialogShell*(2).

## Name

XmCascadeButton widget class – a button widget that posts menus.

## Synopsis

**Public Header:** *<Xm/CascadeB.h>*

**Class Name:** XmCascadeButton

**Class Hierarchy:** Core → XmPrimitive → XmLabel → XmCascadeButton

**Class Pointer:** `xmCascadeButtonWidgetClass`

**Instantiation:** `widget = XtCreateWidget(name, xmCascadeButtonWidgetClass, ...)`

**Functions/Macros:** `XmCascadeButtonHighlight()`, `XmCreateCascadeButton()`, `XmIsCascadeButton()`

## Description

CascadeButtons are used in menu systems to post menus. A CascadeButton either links a menu bar to a menu pane or connects a menu pane to another menu pane. The widget can have a menu attached to it as a submenu.

## New Resources

CascadeButton defines the following resources:

| Name | Class | Type | Default | Access |
|---|---|---|---|---|
| XmNcascadePixmap | XmCPixmap | Pixmap | dynamic | CSG |
| XmNmappingDelay | XmCMappingDelay | int | 180 | CSG |
| XmNsubMenuId | XmCMenuWidget | Widget | NULL | CSG |

`XmNcascadePixmap`
: The pixmap within the CascadeButton that indicates a submenu. By default, this pixmap is an arrow pointing toward the submenu to be popped up.

`XmNmappingDelay`
: The number of milliseconds it should take for the application to display a submenu after its CascadeButton has been selected.

`XmNsubMenuId`
: The widget ID of the pulldown menu pane associated with the CascadeButton. The menu pane is displayed when the CascadeButton is selected. The pulldown menu pane and the CascadeButton must have a common parent (see discussions of `XmCreatePulldownMenu()` for clarification of the parent-child hierarchy).

## Callback Resources

CascadeButton defines the following callback resources:

| Callback | Reason Constant |
|---|---|
| XmNactivateCallback | XmCR_ACTIVATE |
| XmNcascadingCallback | XmCR_CASCADING |

XmNactivateCallback
: List of callbacks that are called when BSelect is pressed and released while the pointer is inside the widget and there is no submenu to post.

XmNcascadingCallback
: List of callbacks that are called before the submenu associated with the CascadeButton is mapped.

## Callback Structure

Each callback function is passed the following structure:

```
typedef struct
{
    int     reason;        /* the reason that the callback was called */
    XEvent  *event;        /* event structure that triggered callback */
} XmAnyCallbackStruct;
```

## Inherited Resources

CascadeButton inherits the following resources. The resources are listed alphabetically, along with the superclass that defines them. CascadeButton sets the default values of XmNmarginBottom, XmNmarginRight, XmNmarginTop, XmNmarginWidth, and XmNtraversalOn dynamically. It also sets the default value of XmNhighlightThickness to 0. The default value of XmNborderWidth is reset to 0 by Primitive.

| Resource | Inherited From | Resource | Inherited From |
|---|---|---|---|
| XmNaccelerator | Label | XmNlabelString | Label |
| XmNaccelerators | Core | XmNlabelType | Label |
| XmNacceleratorText | Label | XmNmappedWhenManaged | Core |
| XmNalignment | Label | XmNmarginBottom | Label |
| XmNancestorSensitive | Core | XmNmarginHeight | Label |
| XmNbackground | Core | XmNmarginLeft | Label |
| XmNbackgroundPixmap | Core | XmNmarginRight | Label |
| XmNborderColor | Core | XmNmarginTop | Label |
| XmNborderPixmap | Core | XmNmarginWidth | Label |
| XmNborderWidth | Core | XmNmnemonic | Label |
| XmNbottomShadowColor | Primitive | XmNmnemonicCharSet | Label |

| Resource | Inherited From | Resource | Inherited From |
|---|---|---|---|
| XmNbottomShadowPixmap | Primitive | XmNnavigationType | Primitive |
| XmNcolormap | Core | XmNrecomputeSize | Label |
| XmNdepth | Core | XmNscreen | Core |
| XmNdestroyCallback | Core | XmNsensitive | Core |
| XmNfontList | Label | XmNshadowThickness | Primitive |
| XmNforeground | Primitive | XmNstringDirection | Label |
| XmNheight | Core | XmNtopShadowColor | Primitive |
| XmNhelpCallback | Primitive | XmNtopShadowPixmap | Primitive |
| XmNhighlightColor | Primitive | XmNtranslations | Core |
| XmNhighlightOnEnter | Primitive | XmNtraversalOn | Primitive |
| XmNhighlightPixmap | Primitive | XmNunitType | Primitive |
| XmNhighlightThickness | Primitive | XmNuserData | Primitive |
| XmNinitialResourcesPersistent | Core | XmNwidth | Core |
| XmNlabelInsensitivePixmap | Label | XmNx | Core |
| XmNlabelPixmap | Label | XmNy | Core |

## Translations

| | | |
|---|---|---|
| BSelect Press | MenuBarSelect() | (in a menu bar) |
| | StartDrag() | (in a popup menu or a pulldown menu) |
| BSelect Release | DoSelect() | |
| KActivate | KeySelect() | |
| KSelect | KeySelect() | |
| KHelp | Help() | |
| MAny KCancel | CleanupMenuBar() | |

## Action Routines

CascadeButton defines the following action routines:

`CleanupMenuBar()`
: Unposts any menus and restores the keyboard focus to the group of widgets (tab group) that had the focus before the CascadeButton was armed.

`DoSelect()`
: Posts the CascadeButton's submenu and allows keyboard traversal. If there is no submenu attached to the CascadeButton, this action routine activates the CascadeButton and unposts all the menus in the cascade.

`Help()`
: Similar to `CleanupMenuBar()` in that the `Help()` routine unposts any menus and restores keyboard focus. This routine also invokes the list of callbacks specified by `XmNhelpCallback`. If the CascadeButton doesn't have any help

callbacks, the `Help()` routine invokes those associated with the nearest ancestor that has them.

`KeySelect()`
: Posts the CascadeButton's submenu, provided that keyboard traversal is allowed. If there is no submenu attached to the CascadeButton, this action routine activates the CascadeButton and unposts all the menus in the cascade.

`MenuBarSelect()`
: Unposts any previously posted menus, posts the submenu associated with the CascadeButton, and enables mouse traversal.

`StartDrag()`
: Posts the submenu associated with the CascadeButton and enables mouse traversal.

### Additional Behavior

CascadeButton has the following additional behavior:

`<EnterWindow>`
: Arms the CascadeButton and posts its submenu.

`<LeaveWindow>`
: Disarms the CascadeButton and unposts its submenu.

### See Also

*XmCascadeButtonHighlight*(1), *XmCreateObject*(1),
*Core*(2), *XmLabel*(2), *XmPrimitive*(2), *XmRowColumn*(2).

# XmCascadeButtonGadget

## Name

XmCascadeButtonGadget widget class – a button gadget that posts menus.

## Synopsis

**Public Header:** *<Xm/CascadeBG.h>*

**Class Name:** XmCascadeButtonGadget

**Class Hierarchy:** Object → RectObj → XmGadget → XmLabelGadget → XmCascadeButtonGadget

**Class Pointer:** xmCascadeButtonGadgetClass

**Instantiation:** `widget = XtCreateWidget(name, xmCascadeButtonWidgetClass, ...)`

**Functions/Macros:** `XmCascadeButtonGadgetHighlight()`, `XmCreateCascadeButtonGadget()`, `XmIsCascadeButtonGadget()`, `XmOptionButtonGadget()`

## Description

CascadeButtonGadget is the gadget variant of CascadeButton.

CascadeButtonGadget's new resources, callback resources, and callback structure are the same as those for CascadeButton.

## Inherited Resources

CascadeButtonGadget inherits the following resources. The resources are listed alphabetically, along with the superclass that defines them. CascadeButtonGadget sets the default values of `XmNmarginBotton`, `XmNmarginRight`, `XmNmarginTop`, and `XmNmarginWidth` dynamically. It also sets the default value of `XmNhighlightThickness` to 0. The default value of `XmNborderWidth` is reset to 0 by Gadget.

| Resource | Inherited From | Resource | Inherited From |
|---|---|---|---|
| XmNaccelerator | LabelGadget | XmNmarginLeft | LabelGadget |
| XmNacceleratorText | LabelGadget | XmNmarginRight | LabelGadget |
| XmNalignment | LabelGadget | XmNmarginTop | LabelGadget |
| XmNancestorSensitive | RectObj | XmNmarginWidth | LabelGadget |
| XmNborderWidth | RectObj | XmNmnemonic | LabelGadget |
| XmNbottomShadowColor | Gadget | XmNmnemonicCharSet | LabelGadget |
| XmNdestroyCallback | Object | XmNnavigationType | Gadget |
| XmNfontList | LabelGadget | XmNrecomputeSize | LabelGadget |
| XmNheight | RectObj | XmNsensitive | RectObj |
| XmNhelpCallback | Gadget | XmNshadowThickness | Gadget |
| XmNhighlightColor | Gadget | XmNstringDirection | LabelGadget |
| XmNhighlightOnEnter | Gadget | XmNtopShadowColor | Gadget |
| XmNhighlightThickness | Gadget | XmNtraversalOn | Gadget |

| Resource | Inherited From | Resource | Inherited From |
|---|---|---|---|
| XmNlabelInsensitivePixmap | LabelGadget | XmNunitType | Gadget |
| XmNlabelPixmap | LabelGadget | XmNuserData | Gadget |
| XmNlabelString | LabelGadget | XmNwidth | RectObj |
| XmNlabelType | LabelGadget | XmNx | RectObj |
| XmNmarginBottom | LabelGadget | XmNy | RectObj |
| XmNmarginHeight | LabelGadget | | |

## Behavior

As a gadget subclass, CascadeButtonGadget has no translations associated with it. However, CascadeButtonGadget behavior corresponds to the action routines of the CascadeButton widget. See the CascadeButton action routines for more information.

| Behavior | Equivalent CascadeButton Action Routine |
|---|---|
| BSelect Press | MenuBarSelect() or StartDrag() |
| BSelect Release | DoSelect() |
| KActivate or KSelect | KeySelect() |
| KHelp | Help() |
| MAny KCancel | CleanupMenuBar() |

In a menu bar that is armed, CascadeButtonGadget has additional behavior associated with `<Enter>`, which arms the CascadeButtonGadget and posts its submenu, and with `<Leave>`, which disarms the CascadeButtonGadget and unposts its submenu.

## See Also

*XmCascadeButtonHighlight*(1), *XmCreateObject*(1), *XmOptionButtonGadget*(1), *Object*(2), *RectObj*(2), *XmCascadeButton*(2), *XmGadget*(2), *XmLabelGadget*(2), *XmRowColumn*(2).

# XmCheckBox

## Name

XmCheckBox – a RowColumn that contains ToggleButtons.

## Synopsis

**Public Header:** *<Xm/RowColumn.h>*

**Class Name:** XmRowColumn

**Class Hierarchy:** Core → Composite → Constraint → XmManager → XmRowColumn

**Class Pointer:** `xmRowColumnWidgetClass`

**Instantiation:** *widget* = `XmCreateSimpleCheckBox(...)`

**Functions/Macros:** `XmCreateRowColumn()`, `XmCreateSimpleCheckBox()`, `XmIsRowColumn()`, `XmVaCreateSimpleCheckBox()`

## Description

A CheckBox is an instance of a RowColumn widget that contains ToggleButton or ToggleButtonGadget children, any number of which may be selected at a given time. A CheckBox is a RowColumn widget with its `XmNrowColumnType` resource set to `XmWORK_AREA` and `XmNradioAlwaysOne` set to `False`.

A CheckBox can be created by making a RowColumn with these resource values. When it is created in this way, a CheckBox does not automatically contain ToggleButton children; they are added by the application.

A CheckBox can also be created by a call to `XmCreateSimpleCheckBox()` or `XmVaCreateSimpleCheckBox()`. These routines automatically create the CheckBox with ToggleButtonGadgets as children. The routines use the RowColumn resources associated with the creation of simple menus. For a CheckBox, the only type allowed in the `XmNbuttonType` resource is `XmCHECKBUTTON`. The name of each ToggleButtonGadget is `button_`*n*, where *n* is the number of the button, ranging from 0 to 1 less than the number of buttons in the CheckBox.

## Default Resource Values

A CheckBox sets the following default values for its resources:

| Name | Default |
|---|---|
| `XmNnavigationType` | `XmTAB_GROUP` |
| `XmNradioBehavior` | `False` |
| `XmNrowColumnType` | `XmWORK_AREA` |
| `XmNtraversalOn` | `True` |

## See Also

*XmCreateObject*(1), *XmVaCreateSimpleCheckBox*(1), *XmRowColumn*(2), *XmToggleButton*(2), *XmToggleButtonGadget*(2).

## Name

XmCommand widget class – a composite widget for command entry.

## Synopsis

**Public Header:** *<Xm/Command.h>*

**Class Name:** XmCommand

**Class Hierarchy:** Core → Composite → Constraint → XmManager → XmBulletinBoard → XmSelectionBox → XmCommand

**Class Pointer:** `xmCommandWidgetClass`

**Instantiation:** `widget = XtCreateWidget(name, xmCommandWidgetClass, ...)`

**Functions/Macros:** `XmCommandAppendValue()`, `XmCommandError()`, `XmCommandGetChild()`, `XmCommandSetValue()`, `XmCreateCommand()`, `XmIsCommand()`

## Description

Command is a composite widget that handles command entry by providing a prompt, a command input field, and a history list region. Many of the Command widget's new resources are in fact renamed resources from SelectionBox.

## New Resources

Command defines the following resources:

| Name | Class | Type | Default | Access |
|---|---|---|---|---|
| XmNcommand | XmCTextString | XmString | "" | CSG |
| XmNhistoryItems | XmCItems | XmStringTable | NULL | CSG |
| XmNhistory ItemCount | XmCItemCount | int | 0 | CSG |
| XmNhistoryMaxItems | XmCMaxItems | int | 100 | CSG |
| XmNhistoryVisible ItemCount | XmCVisibleItemCount | int | dynamic | CSG |
| XmNpromptString | XmCPromptString | XmString | dynamic | CSG |

`XmNcommand`

The text currently displayed on the command line. Synonymous with the `XmNtextString` resource in SelectionBox. `XmNcommand` can be changed using the routines `XmCommandSetValue()` and `XmCommandAppendValue()`.

`XmNhistoryItems`

The items in the history list. Synonymous with the `XmNlistItems` resource in SelectionBox. A call to `XtGetValues()` returns the actual list items (not a copy), so don't have your application free these items.

XmNhistoryItemCount
: The number of strings in XmNhistoryItems. Synonymous with the XmNlistItemCount resource in SelectionBox.

XmNhistoryMaxItems
: The history list's maximum number of items. When this number is reached, the first history item is removed before the new command is added to the list.

XmNhistoryVisibleItemCount
: The number of history list commands that will display at one time. Synonymous with the XmNvisibleItemCount resource in SelectionBox.

XmNpromptString
: The command-line prompt. Synonymous with the XmNselectionLabelString resource in SelectionBox.

### Callback Resources

Command defines the following callback resources:

| Callback | Reason Constant |
|---|---|
| XmNcommandEnteredCallback | XmCR_COMMAND_ENTERED |
| XmNcommandChangedCallback | XmCR_COMMAND_CHANGED |

XmNcommandChangedCallback
: List of callbacks that are called when the value of the command changes.

XmNcommandEnteredCallback
: List of callbacks that are called when a command is entered in the widget.

### Callback Structure

Each callback function is passed the following structure:

```
typedef struct
{
    int       reason;   /* the reason that the callback was called */
    XEvent    *event;   /* points to event structure that triggered callback */
    XmString  value;    /* the string contained in the command area */
    int       length;   /* the size of this string */
} XmCommandCallbackStruct;
```

### Inherited Resources

Command inherits the resources shown below. The resources are listed alphabetically, along with the superclass that defines them. Command sets the default values of XmNautoUnmanage and XmNdefaultPosition to False, XmNdialogType to XmDIALOG_COMMAND, XmNlistLabelString to NULL, and XmNresizePolicy to XmRESIZE_NONE. The default value of XmNborderWidth is reset to 0 by Manager.

BulletinBoard sets the value of XmNinitialFocus to XmNdefaultButton and resets the default XmNshadowThickness from 0 to 1 if the Command widget is a child of a DialogShell.

| Resource | Inherited From | Resource | Inherited From |
|---|---|---|---|
| XmNaccelerators | Core | XmNlistItems | SelectionBox |
| XmNallowOverlap | BulletinBoard | XmNlistLabelString | SelectionBox |
| XmNancestorSensitive | Core | XmNlistVisibleItemCount | SelectionBox |
| XmNapplyCallback | SelectionBox | XmNmapCallback | BulletinBoard |
| XmNapplyLabelString | SelectionBox | XmNmappedWhenManaged | Core |
| XmNautoUnmanage | BulletinBoard | XmNmarginHeight | BulletinBoard |
| XmNbackground | Core | XmNmarginWidth | BulletinBoard |
| XmNbackgroundPixmap | Core | XmNminimizeButtons | SelectionBox |
| XmNborderColor | Core | XmNmustMatch | SelectionBox |
| XmNborderPixmap | Core | XmNnavigationType | Manager |
| XmNborderWidth | Core | XmNnoMatchCallback | SelectionBox |
| XmNbottomShadowColor | Manager | XmNnoResize | BulletinBoard |
| XmNbottomShadowPixmap | Manager | XmNnumChildren | Composite |
| XmNbuttonFontList | BulletinBoard | XmNokCallback | SelectionBox |
| XmNcancelButton | BulletinBoard | XmNokLabelString | SelectionBox |
| XmNcancelCallback | SelectionBox | XmNresizePolicy | BulletinBoard |
| XmNcancelLabelString | SelectionBox | XmNscreen | Core |
| XmNchildren | Composite | XmNselectionLabelString | SelectionBox |
| XmNcolormap | Core | XmNsensitive | Core |
| XmNdefaultButton | BulletinBoard | XmNshadowThickness | Manager |
| XmNdefaultPosition | BulletinBoard | XmNshadowType | BulletinBoard |
| XmNdepth | Core | XmNstringDirection | Manager |
| XmNdestroyCallback | Core | XmNtextAccelerators | SelectionBox |
| XmNdialogStyle | BulletinBoard | XmNtextColumns | SelectionBox |
| XmNdialogTitle | BulletinBoard | XmNtextFontList | BulletinBoard |
| XmNdialogType | SelectionBox | XmNtextString | SelectionBox |
| XmNfocusCallback | BulletinBoard | XmNtextTranslations | BulletinBoard |
| XmNforeground | Manager | XmNtopShadowColor | Manager |
| XmNheight | Core | XmNtopShadowPixmap | Manager |
| XmNhelpCallback | Manager | XmNtranslations | Core |
| XmNhelpLabelString | SelectionBox | XmNtraversalOn | Manager |
| XmNhighlightColor | Manager | XmNunitType | Manager |
| XmNhighlightPixmap | Manager | XmNunmapCallback | BulletinBoard |
| XmNinitialFocus | Manager | XmNuserData | Manager |
| XmNinitialResourcesPersistent | Core | XmNwidth | Core |
| XmNinsertPosition | Composite | XmNx | Core |

| Resource | Inherited From | Resource | Inherited From |
|---|---|---|---|
| `XmNlabelFontList` | `BulletinBoard` | `XmNy` | `Core` |
| `XmNlistItemCount` | `SelectionBox` | | |

## Translations

The translations for Command are inherited from SelectionBox.

## Action Routines

Command defines the following action routines:

`SelectionBoxUpOrDown(`*`flag`*`)`
: Selects a command from the history list, replaces the current command-line text with this list item, and invokes the callbacks specified by `XmNcommand-ChangedCallback`. The value of *`flag`* determines which history list command is selected. With a *`flag`* value of 0, 1, 2, or 3, this action routine selects the list's previous, next, first, or last item, respectively.

## Additional Behavior

Command has the following additional behavior:

`MAny KCancel`
: The event is passed to the parent if it is a manager widget.

`KActivate`
: In the Text widget, invokes the `XmNactivateCallback` callbacks, appends the text to the history list, and invokes the `XmNcommandEnteredCallback` callbacks.

`<Key>`
: In the Text widget, any keystroke that changes text invokes the `XmNcommand-ChangedCallback` callbacks.

`KActivate` or `<DoubleClick>`
: In the List widget, invokes the `XmNdefaultActionCallback` callbacks, appends the selected item to the history list, and invokes the `XmNcommand-EnteredCallback` callbacks.

`<FocusIn>`
: Invokes the `XmNfocusCallback` callbacks.

`<MapWindow>`
: If the widget is a child of a DialogShell, invokes the `XmNmapCallback` callbacks when the widget is mapped.

`<UnmapWindow>`
: If the widget is a child of a DialogShell, invokes the `XmNunmapCallback` callbacks when the widget is unmapped.

## See Also

*XmCommandAppendValue*(1), *XmCommandError*(1), *XmCommandGetChild*(1), *XmCommandSetValue*(1), *XmCreateObject*(1), *Composite*(2), *Constraint*(2), *Core*(2), *XmBulletinBoard*(2), *XmManager*(2), *XmSelectionBox*(2).

# XmDialogShell

## Name

XmDialogShell widget class – the Shell parent for dialog boxes.

## Synopsis

**Public Header:** *<Xm/DialogS.h>*

**Class Name:** XmDialogShell

**Class Hierarchy:** Core → Composite → Shell → WMShell → VendorShell → TransientShell → XmDialogShell

**Class Pointer:** `xmDialogShellWidgetClass`

**Instantiation:** `widget = XtCreateWidget(name, xmDialogShellWidgetClass, ...)`

**Functions/Macros:** `XmCreateDialogShell()`, `XmIsDialogShell()`

## Description

DialogShell is the parent for dialog boxes. A DialogShell cannot be iconified separately, but only when the main application shell is iconified. The child of a DialogShell is typically a subclass of BulletinBoard and much of the functionality of DialogShell is based on this assumption.

## New Resources

DialogShell does not define any new resources.

## Inherited Resources

DialogShell inherits the following resources. The resources are listed alphabetically, along with the superclass that defines them. DialogShell sets the default values of `XmNdeleteResponse` to `XmUNMAP` and `XmNinput` and `XmNtransient` to `True`. The default value of `XmNborderWidth` is reset to 0 by VendorShell.

| Resource | Inherited From | Resource | Inherited From |
|---|---|---|---|
| XmNaccelerators | Core | XmNmaxHeight | WMShell |
| XmNallowShellResize | Shell | XmNmaxWidth | WMShell |
| XmNancestorSensitive | Core | XmNminAspectX | WMShell |
| XmNaudibleWarning | VendorShell | XmNminAspectY | WMShell |
| XmNbackground | Core | XmNminHeight | WMShell |
| XmNbackgroundPixmap | Core | XmNminWidth | WMShell |
| XmNbaseHeight | WMShell | XmNmwmDecorations | VendorShell |
| XmNbaseWidth | WMShell | XmNmwmFunctions | VendorShell |
| XmNborderColor | Core | XmNmwmInputMode | VendorShell |
| XmNborderPixmap | Core | XmNmwmMenu | VendorShell |
| XmNborderWidth | Core | XmNnumChildren | Composite |
| XmNbuttonFontList | VendorShell | XmNoverrideRedirect | Shell |
| XmNchildren | Composite | XmNpopdownCallback | Shell |

| Resource | Inherited From | Resource | Inherited From |
|---|---|---|---|
| XmNcolormap | Core | XmNpopupCallback | Shell |
| XmNcreatePopupChildProc | Shell | XmNpreeditType | VendorShell |
| XmNdefaultFontList | VendorShell | XmNsaveUnder | Shell |
| XmNdeleteResponse | VendorShell | XmNscreen | Core |
| XmNdepth | Core | XmNsensitive | Core |
| XmNdestroyCallback | Core | XmNshellUnitType | VendorShell |
| XmNgeometry | Shell | XmNtextFontList | VendorShell |
| XmNheight | Core | XmNtitle | WMShell |
| XmNheightInc | WMShell | XmNtitleEncoding | WMShell |
| XmNiconMask | WMShell | XmNtransient | WMShell |
| XmNiconPixmap | WMShell | XmNtransientFor | TransientShell |
| XmNiconWindow | WMShell | XmNtranslations | Core |
| XmNiconX | WMShell | XmNuseAsyncGeometry | VendorShell |
| XmNiconY | WMShell | XmNvisual | Shell |
| XmNinitialResources Persistent | Core | XmNwaitForWm | WMShell |
| XmNinitialState | WMShell | XmNwidth | Core |
| XmNinput | WMShell | XmNwidthInc | WMShell |
| XmNinputMethod | VendorShell | XmNwindowGroup | WMShell |
| XmNinsertPosition | Composite | XmNwindowGroup | WMShell |
| XmNkeyboardFocusPolicy | VendorShell | XmNwinGravity | WMShell |
| XmNlabelFontList | VendorShell | XmNwmTimeout | WMShell |
| XmNlmappedWhenManaged | Core | XmNx | Core |
| XmNmaxAspectX | WMShell | XmNy | Core |
| XmNmaxAspectY | WMShell | | |

## See Also

*XmCreateObject*(1),
*Composite*(2), *Core*(2), *Shell*(2), *TransientShell*(2), *VendorShell*(2), *WMShell*(2),
*XmBulletinBoardDialog*(2), *XmErrorDialog*(2), *XmFileSelectionDialog*(2), *XmFormDialog*(2),
*XmInformationDialog*(2), *XmMessageDialog*(2), *XmPromptDialog*(2), *XmQuestionDialog*(2),
*XmSelectionDialog*(2), *XmTemplateDialog*(2), *XmWarningDialog*(2), *XmWorkingDialog*(2).

# XmDisplay



## Name

XmDisplay widget class – an object to store display-specific information.

## Synopsis

**Public Header:** *<Xm/Display.h>*

**Class Name:** XmDisplay

**Class Hierarchy:** Core → Composite → Shell → WMShell → VendorShell → TopLevel-Shell → ApplicationShell → XmDisplay

**Class Pointer:** xmDisplayClass

**Instantiation:** `widget = XtAppInitialize(...)`

**Functions/Macros:** `XmGetXmDisplay()`, `XmIsDisplay()`

## Availability

Motif 1.2 and later.

## Description

The Display object stores display-specific information for use by the toolkit. An application has a Display object for each display it accesses. When an application creates its first shell on a display, typically by calling `XtAppInitialize()` or `XtAppCreateShell()`, a Display object is created automatically. There is no way to create a Display independently. The function `XmGetXmDisplay()` can be used to get the widget ID of the Display object.

The `XmNdragInitiatorProtocolStyle` and `XmNdragReceiverProtocolStyle` resources specify the drag protocol for an application that performs drag and drop operations. The two protocol styles are dynamic and preregister. Under the dynamic protocol, the initiator and receiver pass messages back and forth to handle drag and drop visuals. Under the preregister protocol, the initiator handles drag and drop visuals by reading information that is preregistered and stored in properties. The actual protocol that is used by a specific initiator and receiver is based on the requested protocol styles of the receiver and initiator:

| Drag Initiator Protocol Style | Drag Receiver Protocol Style | | | |
|---|---|---|---|---|
| | Preregister | Prefer Preregister | Prefer Dynamic | Dynamic |
| Preregister | PREREGISTER | PREREGISTER | PREREGISTER | DROP_ONLY |
| Prefer Preregister | PREREGISTER | PREREGISTER | PREREGISTER | DYNAMIC |
| Prefer Receiver | PREREGISTER | PREREGISTER | DYNAMIC | DYNAMIC |
| Prefer Dynamic | PREREGISTER | DYNAMIC | DYNAMIC | DYNAMIC |
| Dynamic | DROP_ONLY | DYNAMIC | DYNAMIC | DYNAMIC |

## New Resources

Display defines the following resources:

| Name | Class | Type | Default | Access |
|---|---|---|---|---|
| XmNdefault VirtualBindings | XmCDefault VirtualBindings | String | dynamic | SG |
| XmNdragInitiator ProtocolStyle | XmCDragInitiator ProtocolStyle | unsigned char | XmDRAG_PREFER_ RECEIVER | SG |
| XmNdragReceiver ProtocolStyle | XmCDragReceiver ProtocolStyle | unsigned char | XmDRAG_PREFER_ PREREGISTER | SG |

`XmNdefaultVirtualBindings`

The default virtual bindings for the display.

`XmNdragInitiatorProtocolStyle`

The client's drag and drop protocol requirements or preference when it is the initiator of a drag and drop operation. Possible values:

```
XmDRAG_PREREGISTER          /* can only use preregister protocol */
XmDRAG_DYNAMIC              /* can only use dynamic protocol */
XmDRAG_NONE                 /* drag and drop disabled */
XmDRAG_DROP_ONLY            /* only supports dragging */
XmDRAG_PREFER_DYNAMIC       /* supports both but prefers dynamic */
XmDRAG_PREFER_PREREGISTER /* supports both but prefers preregister */
XmDRAG_PREFER_RECEIVER      /* supports both; prefers receiver's protocol */
```

`XmNdragReceiverProtocolStyle`

The client's drag and drop protocol requirements or preference when it is the receiver. Possible values:

```
XmDRAG_PREREGISTER          /* can only use preregister protocol */
XmDRAG_DYNAMIC              /* can only use dynamic protocol */
XmDRAG_NONE                 /* drag and drop disabled */
XmDRAG_DROP_ONLY            /* only supports dropping */
XmDRAG_PREFER_DYNAMIC       /* supports both but prefers dynamic */
XmDRAG_PREFER_PREREGISTER /* supports both but prefers preregister */
```

## Inherited Resources

All of the resources inherited by Display are not applicable.

## See Also

*XmGetXmDisplay*(1),
*ApplicationShell*(2), *Composite*(2), *Core*(2), *Shell*(2), *TopLevelShell*(2), *VendorShell*(2), *WMShell*(2), *XmScreen*(2).

# XmDragContext



## Name

XmDragContext widget class – an object used to store information about a drag transaction.

## Synopsis

**Public Header:** <*Xm/DragDrop.h*>

**Class Name:** XmDragContext

**Class Pointer:** xmDragContextClass

**Class Hierarchy:** Core → DragContext

**Instantiation:** `widget = XmDragStart(...)`

**Functions/Macros:** `XmDragCancel()`, `XmDragStart()`

## Availability

Motif 1.2 and later.

## Description

The DragContext object stores information that the toolkit needs to process a drag transaction. An application does not explicitly create a DragContext widget, but instead initiates a drag and drop operation by calling `XmDragStart()`, which initializes and returns a DragContext widget. The DragContext stores information about the types of data and operations of the drag source, the drag icons that are used during the drag, and the callbacks that are called during different parts of the drag. These characteristics can be specified as resources when the DragContext is created using `XmDragStart()`.

Each drag operation has a unique DragContext that is freed by the toolkit when the operation is complete. The initiating and receiving clients in a drag and drop operation both use the DragContext to keep track of the state of the operation. The drag-over visual effects that are used during a drag operation depend on the drag protocol that is being used. Under the preregister protocol, either a cursor or a pixmap can be used, since the server is grabbed. Under the dynamic protocol, the X cursor is used.

## New Resources

DragContext defines the following resources:

| Name | Class | Type | Default | Access |
|---|---|---|---|---|
| XmNblendModel | XmCBlendModel | unsigned char | XmBLEND_ALL | CG |
| XmNclientData | XmCClientData | XtPointer | NULL | CSG |
| XmNconvertProc | XmCConvertProc | XtConvertSelectionIncrProc | NULL | CSG |
| XmNcursorBackground | XmCCursorBackground | Pixel | dynamic | CSG |

| Name | Class | Type | Default | Access |
|---|---|---|---|---|
| XmNcursor Foreground | XmCCursor Foreground | Pixel | dynamic | CSG |
| XmNdrag Operations | XmCDrag Operations | unsigned char | XmDROP_COPY \| XmDROP_MOVE | C |
| XmNexport Targets | XmCExport Targets | Atom * | NULL | CSG |
| XmNincremental | XmCIncremental | Boolean | False | CSG |
| XmNinvalidCursor Foreground | XmCCursor Foreground | Pixel | dynamic | CSG |
| XmNnoneCursor Foreground | XmCCursor Foreground | Pixel | dynamic | CSG |
| XmNnumExport Targets | XmCNumExport Targets | Cardinal | 0 | CSG |
| XmNoperation CursorIcon | XmCOperation CursorIcon | Widget | dynamic | CSG |
| XmNsource CursorIcon | XmCSource CursorIcon | Widget | dynamic | CSG |
| XmNsource PixmapIcon | XmCSource PixmapIcon | Widget | dynamic | CSG |
| XmNstate CursorIcon | XmCState CursorIcon | Widget | dynamic | CSG |
| XmNvalidCursor Foreground | XmCCursor Foreground | Pixel | dynamic | CSG |

`XmNblendModel`

The combination of DragIcons that are blended to produce a drag-over visual. Possible values:

```
XmBLEND_ALL                /* source, state, and operation */
XmBLEND_STATE_SOURCE       /* source and state */
XmBLEND_JUST_SOURCE        /* source only */
XmBLEND_NONE               /* no drag-over visual */
```

`XmNclientData`

The client data that is passed to the `XmNconvertProc`.

`XmNconvertProc`

A procedure of type `XtConvertSelectionIncrProc` that converts the data to the format(s) specified by the receiving client. The *`widget`* argument passed to this procedure is the DragContext widget and the selection atom is `_MOTIF_DROP`. If `XmNincremental` is `False`, the conversion procedure should process the conversion atomically and ignore the *`max_length`*, *`client_data`*, and *`request_id`* arguments. Allocate any data returned by `XmNconvertProc` using `XtMalloc()` and it will be freed automatically by the toolkit after the transfer.

`XmNcursorBackground`
The background color of the cursor.

`XmNcursorForeground`
The foreground color of the cursor when the state icon is not blended. The default value is the foreground color of the widget passed to `XmDragStart()`.

`XmNdragOperations`
The valid operations for the drag. The value is a bit mask that is formed by combining one or more of these possible values:

```
XmDROP_COPY      /* copy operations are valid */
XmDROP_LINK      /* link operations are valid */
XmDROP_MOVE      /* move operations are valid */
XmDROP_NOOP      /* no operations are valid */
```

For Text and TextField widgets, the default value is `XmDROP_COPY | XmDROP_MOVE`. For List widgets and Label and subclasses, the default is `XmDROP_COPY`.

`XmNexportTargets`
The list of target atoms that the source data can be converted to.

`XmNincremental`
If `True`, the initiator uses the Xt incremental selection transfer mechanism. If `False` (default), the initiator uses atomic transfer.

`XmNinvalidCursorForeground`
The foreground color of the cursor when the state is invalid. The default value is the value of the `XmNcursorForeground` resource.

`XmNnoneCursorForeground`
The foreground color of the cursor when the state is none. The default value is the value of the `XmNcursorForeground` resource.

`XmNnumExportTargets`
The number of atoms in the `XmNexportTargets` list.

`XmNoperationCursorIcon`
The drag icon used to show the type of drag operation being performed. If the value is `NULL`, the default Screen icons are used.

`XmNsourceCursorIcon`
The drag icon used to represent the source data under the dynamic protocol. If the value is `NULL`, the default Screen icon is used.

`XmNsourcePixmapIcon`
The drag icon used to represent the source data under the preregister protocol. If the value is `NULL`, `XmNsourceCursorIcon` is used.

`XmNstateCursorIcon`
The drag icon used to show the state of a drop site. If the value is `NULL`, the default Screen icons are used.

`XmNvalidCursorForeground`

The foreground color of the cursor when the state is valid. The default value is the value of the `XmNcursorForeground` resource.

### Callback Resources

DragContext defines the following callback resources:

| Callback | Reason Constant |
|---|---|
| XmNdragDropFinishCallback | XmCR_DRAG_DROP_FINISH |
| XmNdragMotionCallback | XmCR_DRAG_MOTION |
| XmNdropFinishCallback | XmCR_DROP_FINISH |
| XmNdropSiteEnterCallback | XmCR_DROP_SITE_ENTER |
| XmNdropSiteLeaveCallback | XmCR_DROP_SITE_LEAVE |
| XmNdropStartCallback | XmCR_DROP_START |
| XmNoperationChanged | XmCR_OPERATION_CHANGED |
| XmNtopLevelEnter | XmCR_TOP_LEVEL_ENTER |
| XmNtopLevelLeave | XmCR_TOP_LEVEL_LEAVE |

`XmNdragDropFinishCallback`

List of callbacks that are called when the entire transaction is finished.

`XmNdragMotionCallback`

List of callbacks that are called when the pointer moves during a drag.

`XmNdropFinishCallback`

List of callbacks that are called when the drop is finished.

`XmNdropSiteEnterCallback`

List of callbacks that are called when the pointer enters a drop site.

`XmNdropSiteLeaveCallback`

List of callbacks that are called when the pointer leaves a drop site.

`XmNdropStartCallback`

List of callbacks that are called when a drop is started

`XmNoperationChangedCallback`

List of callbacks that are called when the user changes the operation during a drag.

`XmNtopLevelEnterCallback`

List of callbacks that are called when the pointer enters a top-level window or root window.

`XmNtopLevelLeaveCallback`

List of callbacks that are called when the pointer leaves a top-level window or the root window.

### Callback Structures

The XmNdragDropFinishCallback is passed the following structure:

```
typedef struct
{
    int     reason;         /* the reason the callback was called */
    XEvent  *event;         /* event structure that triggered callback */
    Time    timeStamp;      /* time at which operation completed */
}XmDragDropFinishCallbackStruct, *XmDragDropFinishCallback;
```

The XmNdragMotionCallback is passed the following structure:

```
typedef struct
{
    int           reason;         /* the reason the callback was called */
    XEvent        *event;         /* event structure that triggered callback */
    Time          timeStamp;      /* timestamp of logical event */
    unsigned char operation;      /* current operation */
    unsigned char operations;     /* supported operations */
    unsigned char dropSiteStatus;/* valid, invalid, or none */
    Position      x;              /* x-coordinate of pointer */
    Position      y;              /* y-coordinate of pointer */
}XmDragMotionCallbackStruct, *XmDragMotionCallback;
```

The XmNdropFinishCallback is passed the following structure:

```
typedef struct
{
    int           reason;         /* the reason the callback was called */
    XEvent        *event;         /* event structure that triggered callback */
    Time          timeStamp;      /* time at which drop completed */
    unsigned char operation;      /* current operation */
    unsigned char operations;     /* supported operations */
    unsigned char dropSiteStatus;/* valid, invalid, or none */
    unsigned char dropAction;     /* drop, cancel, help, or interrupt */
    unsigned char completionStatus;/* s-1success or failure */
}XmDropFinishCallbackStruct, *XmDropFinishCallback;
```

The XmNdropSiteEnterCallback is passed the following structure:

```
typedef struct
{
    int           reason;         /* the reason the callback was called */
    XEvent        *event;         /* event structure that triggered callback */
    Time          timeStamp;      /* time of crossing event */
    unsigned char operation;      /* current operation */
    unsigned char operations;     /* supported operations */
    unsigned char dropSiteStatus;/* valid, invalid, or none */
    Position      x;              /* x-coordinate of pointer */
```

```
    Position      y;              /* y-coordinate of pointer */
}XmDropSiteEnterCallbackStruct, *XmDropSiteEnterCallback;
```

The `XmNdropSiteLeaveCallback` is passed the follwing structure:

```
typedef struct
{
    int      reason;         /* the reason the callback was called */
    XEvent   *event;         /* event structure that triggered callback */
    Time     timeStamp;      /* time of crossing event */
}XmDropSiteLeaveCallbackStruct, *XmDropSiteLeaveCallback;
```

The `XmNdropStartCallback` is passed the following structure:

```
typedef struct
{
    int             reason;         /* the reason the callback was called */
    XEvent          *event;         /* the event structure that triggered callback */
    Time            timeStamp;      /*time at which drag completed */
    unsigned char operation;        /* current operation */
    unsigned char operations;       /* supported operations */
    unsigned char dropSiteStatus;/* valid, invalid, or none */
    unsigned char dropAction;       /* drop, cancel, help, or interrupt */
    Position        x;              /* x-coordinate of pointer */
    Position        y;              /* y-coordinate of pointer */
}XmDropStartCallbackStruct, *XmDropStartCallback;
```

The `XmNoperationChangedCallback` is passed the following structure:

```
typedef struct
{
    int             reason;         /* the reason the callback was called */
    XEvent          *event;         /* event structure that triggered callback */
    Time            timeStamp;      /* timestamp of logical event */
    unsigned char operation;        /* current operation */
    unsigned char operations;       /* supported operations */
    unsigned char dropSiteStatus;/* valid, invalid, or none */
}XmOperationChangedCallbackStruct, *XmOperationChangedCallback;
```

The `XmNtopLevelEnterCallback` is passed the following structure:

```
typedef struct
{
    int             reason;         /* the reason the callback was called */
    XEvent          *event;         /* event structure that triggered callback */
    Time            timestamp;      /* timestamp of logical event */
    Screen          screen;         /* screen of top-level window */
    Window          window;         /* window being entered */
    Position        x;              /* x-coordinate of pointer */
    Position        y;              /* y-coordinate of pointer */
```

```
    unsigned char dragProtocolStyle;/* drag protocol of initiator */
}XmTopLevelEnterCallbackStruct, *XmTopLevelEnterCallback;
```

The `XmNtopLevelLeaveCallback` is passed the following structure:

```
typedef struct
{
    int     reason;         /* the reason the callback was called */
    XEvent  *event;         /* event structure that triggered callback */
    Time    timestamp;      /* timestamp of logical event */
    Screen  screen;         /* screen of top-level window */
    Window  window;         /* window being left */
}XmTopLevelLeaveCallbackStruct, *XmTopLevelLeaveCallback;
```

The `operations` field in these structures specifies the set of operations supported for the data being dragged. The toolkit initializes the value based on the `operations` field of the `XmDragProcCallbackStruct`, the `XmNdropSiteOperations` resource of the DropSite, the `XmNdragOperations` resource of the DragContext and the operation selected by the user. The `operation` field in these structures specifies the current operation. The toolkit initializes the value based on the value of the `operation` field of the `XmDragProcCallbackStruct`, `operations`, and the `XmNdropSiteOperations` resource of the Drop Site.

The `dropSiteStatus` field in these structures specifies whether or not the drop site is valid. The toolkit initializes the value based on the `XmNimportTargets` resource of the DropSite and the `XmNexportTargets` resource of the DragContext and the location of the pointer. The possible values are `XmDROP_SITE_VALID`, `XmDROP_SITE_INVALID`, and `XmNO_DROP_SITE`.

The `dropAction` field in these structures specifies the action associated with the drop. The possible values are `XmDROP`, `XmDROP_CANCEL`, `XmDROP_INTERRUPT`, and `DROP_HELP`. `XmDROP_INTERRUPT` is unsupported and is interpreted as `XmDROP_CANCEL`.

The `completionStatus` field in the `XmDropFinishCallbackStruct` specifies the status of the drop transaction, which determines the drop visual effect. The value of this field can be changed by the `XmNdropFinishCallbackStruct`. The possible values are `XmSUCCESS` and `XmFAILURE`.

## Inherited Resources

DragContext inherits the following resources. The resources are listed alphabetically, along with the superclass that defines them. DragContext sets the default value of `XmNborderWidth` to 0.

| Resource | Inherited From | Resource | Inherited From |
|---|---|---|---|
| XmNaccelerators | Core | XmNheight | Core |
| XmNancestorSensitive | Core | XmNinitialResourcesPersistent | Core |

| Resource | Inherited From | Resource | Inherited From |
|---|---|---|---|
| XmNbackground | Core | XmNmappedWhenManaged | Core |
| XmNbackgroundPixmap | Core | XmNscreen | Core |
| XmNborderColor | Core | XmNsensitive | Core |
| XmNborderPixmap | Core | XmNtranslations | Core |
| XmNborderWidth | Core | XmNwidth | Core |
| XmNcolormap | Core | XmNx | Core |
| XmNdepth | Core | XmNy | Core |
| XmNdestroyCallback | Core | | |

## Translations

```
BDrag Motion          DragMotion()
BDrag Release         FinishDrag()
KCancel               CancelDrag()
KHelp                 HelpDrag()
```

## Action Routines

DragContext defines the following action routines:

`CancelDrag()`
: Cancels the drag operation and frees the associated DragContext.

`DragMotion()`
: Drags the selected data as the pointer is moved.

`FinishDrag()`
: Completes the drag operation and initiates the drop operation.

`HelpDrag()`
: Starts a conditional drop that allows the receiving client to provide help information to the user. The user can cancel or continue the drop operation in response to this information.

## See Also

*XmDragCancel*(1), *XmDragStart*(1), *XmGetDragContext*(1),
*Core*(2), *XmDisplay*(2), *XmDragIcon*(2), *XmDropSite*(2), *XmDropTransfer*(2), *XmScreen*(2).

# XmDragIcon

## Name

XmDragIcon widget class – an object used to represent the data in a drag and drop operation.

## Synopsis

**Public Header:** *<Xm/DragDrop.h>*

**Class Name:** XmDragIcon

**Class Pointer:** xmDragIconObjectClass

**Class Hierarchy:** Object → DragIcon

**Instantiation:** `widget = XmCreateDragIcon(...)`

**Functions/Macros:** `XmCreateDragIcon()`, `XmIsDragIconObjectClass()`

## Availability

Motif 1.2 and later.

## Description

A DragIcon is an object that represents the source data in a drag and drop transaction. During a drag operation, the cursor changes into a visual that is created by combining the various DragIcons specified in the DragContext associated with the operation. A DragIcon is created using the `XmCreateDragIcon()` function or from entries in the resource database.

A drag-over visual can have both a static and a dynamic part. The static part of the visual is the DragIcon that represents the source data. The dynamic parts can be DragIcons that change to indicate the type of operation that is being performed and whether the pointer is over a valid or an invalid drop site. The `XmNblendModel` resource of the DragContext for a drag and drop operation specifies which icons are blended to produce the drag-over visual. DragIcon resources specify the relative positions of the operation and state icons if they are used. When a DragIcon is not specified, the default DragIcons from the appropriate Screen object are used.

## New Resources

DragIcon defines the following resources:

| Name | Class | Type | Default | Access |
|---|---|---|---|---|
| XmNattachment | XmCAttachment | unsigned char | XmATTACH_NORTH_WEST | CSG |
| XmNdepth | XmCDepth | int | 1 | CSG |
| XmNheight | XmCHeight | Dimension | 0 | CSG |
| XmNhotX | XmCHot | Position | 0 | CSG |
| XmNhotY | XmCHot | Position | 0 | CSG |
| XmNmask | XmCPixmap | Pixmap | XmUNSPECIFIED_PIXMAP | CSG |
| XmNoffsetX | XmCOffset | Position | 0 | CSG |
| XmNoffsetY | XmCOffset | Position | 0 | CSG |

| Name | Class | Type | Default | Access |
|---|---|---|---|---|
| XmNpixmap | XmCPixmap | Pixmap | XmUNSPECIFIED_PIXMAP | CSG |
| XmNwidth | XmCWidth | Dimension | 0 | CSG |

XmNattachment
: The relative location on the source icon where the state or operation icon is attached. Possible values:

| | |
|---|---|
| XmATTACH_NORTH_WEST | XmATTACH_NORTH |
| XmATTACH_NORTH_EAST | XmATTACH_EAST |
| XmATTACH_SOUTH_EAST | XmATTACH_SOUTH |
| XmATTACH_SOUTH_WEST | XmATTACH_WEST |
| XmATTACH_CENTER | XmATTACH_HOT |

XmNdepth
: The depth of the pixmap.

XmNheight
: The height of the pixmap.

XmNhotX
: The x-coordinate of the hotspot of the cursor.

XmNhotY
: The y-coordinate of the hotspot of the cursor.

XmNmask
: The mask for the DragIcon pixmap.

XmNoffsetX
: The horizontal offset in pixels of the origin of the state or operation icon relative to the attachment point on the source icon.

XmNoffsetY
: The vertical offset in pixels of the origin of the state or operation icon relative to the attachment point on the source icon.

XmNpixmap
: The pixmap for the DragIcon.

XmNwidth
: The width of the pixmap.

## Inherited Resources

DragIcon inherits the following resource:

| Resource | Inherited From |
|---|---|
| `XmNdestroyCallback` | `Object` |

## See Also

*XmCreateObject*(1),
*Object*(2), *XmDisplay*(2), *XmDragContext*(2), *XmDropSite*(2), *XmDropTransfer*(2), *XmScreen*(2).

## Name

XmDrawingArea widget class – a simple manager widget for interactive drawing.

## Synopsis

**Public Header:** *<Xm/DrawingA.h>*

**Class Name:** XmDrawingArea

**Class Hierarchy:** Core → Composite → Constraint → XmManager → XmDrawingArea

**Class Pointer:** `xmDrawingAreaWidgetClass`

**Instantiation:** `widget = XtCreateWidget(name, xmDrawingAreaWidgetClass, ...)`

**Functions/Macros:** `XmCreateDrawingArea(), XmIsDrawingArea()`

## Description

DrawingArea provides a blank canvas for interactive drawing. The widget does not do any drawing of its own. Since DrawingArea is a subclass of Manager, it can provide simple geometry management of multiple widget or gadget children. The widget does not define any behavior except for invoking callbacks that notify an application when it receives input events, exposure events, and resize events.

## New Resources

DrawingArea defines the following resources:

| Name | Class | Type | Default | Access |
|---|---|---|---|---|
| XmNmarginHeight | XmCMarginHeight | Dimension | 10 | CSG |
| XmNmarginWidth | XmCMarginWidth | Dimension | 10 | CSG |
| XmNresizePolicy | XmCResizePolicy | unsigned char | XmRESIZE_ANY | CSG |

`XmNmarginHeight`

The spacing between a DrawingArea's top or bottom edge and any child widget.

`XmNmarginWidth`

The spacing between a DrawingArea's right or left edge and any child widget.

`XmNresizePolicy`

How DrawingArea widgets are resized. Possible values:

```
XmRESIZE_NONE    /* remain at fixed size */
XmRESIZE_GROW    /* expand only */
XmRESIZE_ANY     /* shrink or expand, as needed */
```

## Callback Resources

DrawingArea defines the following callback resources:

| Callback | Reason Constant |
|---|---|
| XmNexposeCallback | XmCR_EXPOSE |
| XmNinputCallback | XmCR_INPUT |
| XmNresizeCallback | XmCR_RESIZE |

XmNexposeCallback
: List of callbacks that are called when the DrawingArea receives an exposure event.

XmNinputCallback
: List of callbacks that are called when the DrawingArea receives a keyboard or mouse event.

XmNresizeCallback
: List of callbacks that are called when the DrawingArea receives a resize event.

## Callback Structure

Each callback function is passed the following structure:

```
typedef struct
{
    int     reason;          /* the reason that the callback was called */
    XEvent  *event;          /* event structure that triggered callback; */
                             /* for XmNresizeCallback, this is NULL */
    Window  window;          /* the widget's window */
} XmDrawingAreaCallbackStruct;
```

## Inherited Resources

DrawingArea inherits the following resources. The resources are listed alphabetically, along with the superclass that defines them. The default value of XmNborderWidth is reset to 0 by Manager.

| Resource | Inherited From | Resource | Inherited From |
|---|---|---|---|
| XmNaccelerators | Core | XmNinitialResourcesPersistent | Core |
| XmNancestorSensitive | Core | XmNinsertPosition | Composite |
| XmNbackground | Core | XmNmappedWhenManaged | Core |
| XmNbackgroundPixmap | Core | XmNnavigationType | Manager |
| XmNborderColor | Core | XmNnumChildren | Composite |
| XmNborderPixmap | Core | XmNscreen | Core |
| XmNborderWidth | Core | XmNsensitive | Core |
| XmNbottomShadowColor | Manager | XmNshadowThickness | Manager |
| XmNbottomShadowPixmap | Manager | XmNstringDirection | Manager |

| Resource | Inherited From | Resource | Inherited From |
|---|---|---|---|
| XmNchildren | Composite | XmNtopShadowColor | Manager |
| XmNcolormap | Core | XmNtopShadowPixmap | Manager |
| XmNdepth | Core | XmNtranslations | Core |
| XmNdestroyCallback | Core | XmNtraversalOn | Manager |
| XmNforeground | Manager | XmNunitType | Manager |
| XmNheight | Core | XmNuserData | Manager |
| XmNhelpCallback | Manager | XmNwidth | Core |
| XmNhighlightColor | Manager | XmNx | Core |
| XmNhighlightPixmap | Manager | XmNy | Core |
| XmNinitialFocus | Manager | | |

## Translations

The translations for DrawingArea include those of Manager. All of the events in the inherited translations except `<BtnMotion>`, `<EnterWindow>`, `<LeaveWindow>`, `<FocusIn>`, and `<FocusOut>` call the `DrawingAreaInput()` action before calling the Manager actions.

DrawingArea has the following additional translations:

```
MAny BAny Press          DrawingAreaInput()
MAny BAny Release        DrawingAreaInput()
MAny KAny Press          DrawingAreaInput()
                         ManagerGadgetKeyInput()
MAny KAny Release        DrawingAreaInput()
```

## Action Routines

DrawingArea defines the following action routines:

`DrawingAreaInput()`
: When a widget child of a DrawingArea receives a keyboard or mouse event, this action routine invokes the list of callbacks specified by `XmNinputCallback`.

`ManagerGadgetKeyInput()`
: When a gadget child of a DrawingArea receives a keyboard or mouse event, this action routine processes the event.

## Additional Behavior

DrawingArea has the following additional behavior:

`<Expose>`
: Invokes the `XmNexposeCallback` callbacks.

`<WidgetResize>`
Invokes the `XmNresizeCallback` callbacks.

## See Also

*XmCreateObject*(1),
*Composite*(2), *Constraint*(2), *Core*(2), *XmManager*(2).

# XmDrawnButton

## Name

XmDrawnButton widget class – a button widget that provides a graphics area.

## Synopsis

**Public Header:** *<Xm/DrawnB.h>*

**Class Name:** XmDrawnButton

**Class Hierarchy:** Core → XmPrimitive → XmLabel → XmDrawnButton

**Class Pointer:** `xmDrawnButtonWidgetClass`

**Instantiation:** `widget = XtCreateWidget(name, xmDrawnButtonWidgetClass, ...)`

**Functions/Macros:** `XmCreateDrawnButton(), XmIsDrawnButton()`

## Description

DrawnButton is an empty widget window, surrounded by a shaded border. The widget provides a graphics area that can act like a PushButton. The graphics can be dynamically updated by the application.

## New Resources

DrawnButton defines the following resources:

| Name | Class | Type | Default | Access |
|---|---|---|---|---|
| XmNmultiClick | XmCMultiClick | unsigned char | dynamic | CSG |
| XmNpushButtonEnabled | XmCPushButtonEnabled | Boolean | False | CSG |
| XmNshadowType | XmCShadowType | unsigned char | XmSHADOW_ETCHED_IN | CSG |

`XmNmultiClick`

A flag that determines whether successive button clicks are processed or ignored. Possible values:

```
XmMULTICLICK_DISCARD    /* ignore successive button clicks; */
                        /* default value in a menu system */
XmMULTICLICK_KEEP       /* count successive button clicks; */
                        /* default value when not in a menu */
```

`XmNpushButtonEnabled`

If `False` (default), the shadow drawing doesn't appear three dimensional; if `True`, the shading provides a pushed in or raised appearance as for the PushButton widget.

XmNshadowType

The style in which shadows are drawn. Possible values:

```
XmSHADOW_IN              /* widget appears inset */
XmSHADOW_OUT             /* widget appears outset */
XmSHADOW_ETCHED_IN       /* double line; widget appears inset */
XmSHADOW_ETCHED_OUT      /* double line; widget appears raised */
```

## Callback Resources

DrawnButton defines the following callback resources:

| Callback | Reason Constant |
|---|---|
| XmNactivateCallback | XmCR_ACTIVATE |
| XmNarmCallback | XmCR_ARM |
| XmNdisarmCallback | XmCR_DISARM |
| XmNexposeCallback | XmCR_EXPOSE |
| XmNresizeCallback | XmCR_RESIZE |

XmNactivateCallback

List of callbacks that are called when BSelect is pressed and released inside of the widget.

XmNarmCallback

List of callbacks that are called when BSelect is pressed while the pointer is inside the widget.

XmNdisarmCallback

List of callbacks that are called when BSelect is released after it has been pressed inside of the widget.

XmNexposeCallback

List of callbacks that are called when the widget receives an exposure event.

XmNresizeCallback

List of callbacks that are called when the widget receives a resize event.

## Callback Structure

Each callback function is passed the following structure:

```
typedef struct
{
    int     reason;         /* the reason that the callback was called */
    XEvent  *event;         /* event structure that triggered callback */
    Window  window;         /* ID of window in which the event occurred */
    int     click_count;    /* number of multi-clicks */
} XmDrawnButtonCallbackStruct;
```

event is NULL for XmNresizeCallback and is sometimes NULL for XmNactivate-Callback.

click_count is meaningful only for XmNactivateCallback. Furthermore, if the XmN-multiClick resource is set to XmMULTICLICK_KEEP, then XmNactivateCallback is called for each click, and the value of click_count is the number of clicks that have occurred in the last sequence of multiple clicks. If the XmNmultiClick resource is set to XmMULTICLICK_DISCARD, then click_count always has a value of 1.

## Inherited Resources

DrawnButton inherits the following resources. The resources are listed alphabetically, along with the superclass that defines them. DrawnButton sets default value of XmNlabelString to "\0". The default value of XmNborderWidth is reset to 0 by Primitive.

| Resource | Inherited From | Resource | Inherited From |
|---|---|---|---|
| XmNaccelerator | Label | XmNlabelString | Label |
| XmNaccelerators | Core | XmNlabelType | Label |
| XmNacceleratorText | Label | XmNmappedWhenManaged | Core |
| XmNalignment | Label | XmNmarginBottom | Label |
| XmNancestorSensitive | Core | XmNmarginHeight | Label |
| XmNbackground | Core | XmNmarginLeft | Label |
| XmNbackgroundPixmap | Core | XmNmarginRight | Label |
| XmNborderColor | Core | XmNmarginTop | Label |
| XmNborderPixmap | Core | XmNmarginWidth | Label |
| XmNborderWidth | Core | XmNmnemonic | Label |
| XmNbottomShadowColor | Primitive | XmNmnemonicCharSet | Label |
| XmNbottomShadowPixmap | Primitive | XmNnavigationType | Primitive |
| XmNcolormap | Core | XmNrecomputeSize | Label |
| XmNdepth | Core | XmNscreen | Core |
| XmNdestroyCallback | Core | XmNsensitive | Core |
| XmNfontList | Label | XmNshadowThickness | Primitive |
| XmNforeground | Primitive | XmNstringDirection | Label |
| XmNheight | Core | XmNtopShadowColor | Primitive |
| XmNhelpCallback | Primitive | XmNtopShadowPixmap | Primitive |
| XmNhighlightColor | Primitive | XmNtranslations | Core |
| XmNhighlightOnEnter | Primitive | XmNtraversalOn | Primitive |
| XmNhighlightPixmap | Primitive | XmNunitType | Primitive |
| XmNhighlightThickness | Primitive | XmNuserData | Primitive |
| XmNinitialResources Persistent | Core | XmNwidth | Core |
| XmNlabelInsensitivePixmap | Label | XmNx | Core |
| XmNlabelPixmap | Label | XmNy | Core |

Motif and Xt Widget Classes

### Translations

```
BSelect Press        Arm()
BSelect Click        Activate()
                     Disarm()
BSelect Release      Activate()
                     Disarm()
BSelect Press 2+     MultiArm()
BSelect Release 2+   MultiActivate()
KSelect              ArmAndActivate()
KHelp                Help()
```

### Action Routines

DrawnButton defines the following action routines:

`Activate()`
: Displays the DrawnButton as unselected if `XmNpushButtonEnabled` is `True` or displays the shadow according to `XmNshadowType`. Invokes the list of callbacks specified by `XmNactivateCallback`.

`Arm()`
: Displays the DrawnButton as selected if `XmNpushButtonEnabled` is `True` or displays the shadow according to `XmNshadowType`. Invokes the list of callbacks specified by `XmNarmCallback`.

`ArmAndActivate()`
: Displays the DrawnButton as selected if `XmNpushButtonEnabled` is `True` or displays the shadow according to `XmNshadowType`. Invokes the list of callbacks specified by `XmNarmCallback`. After doing this, the action routine displays the DrawnButton as unselected if `XmNpushButtonEnabled` is `True` or displays the shadow according to `XmNshadowType` and invokes the list of callbacks specified by `XmNactivateCallback` and `XmNdisarmCallback`.

`Disarm()`
: Displays the DrawnButton as unselected and invokes the list of callbacks specified by `XmNdisarmCallback`.

`Help()`
: Invokes the list of callbacks specified by `XmNhelpCallback`. If the DrawnButton doesn't have any help callbacks, the `Help()` routine invokes those associated with the nearest ancestor that has them.

`MultiActivate()`
: Increments the `click_count` member of `XmDrawnButtonCallbackStruct`, displays the DrawnButton as unselected if `XmNpushButtonEnabled` is `True` or displays the shadow according to `XmNshadowType`, and invokes the list of callbacks specified by `XmNactivateCallback` and `XmNdisarmCallback`. This action routine takes effect only when the `XmNmultiClick` resource is set to `XmMULTICLICK_KEEP`.

`MultiArm()`

Displays the DrawnButton as selected if `XmNpushButtonEnabled` is `True` or displays the shadow according to `XmNshadowType`, and invokes the list of callbacks specified by `XmNarmCallback`. This action routine takes effect only when the `XmNmultiClick` resource is set to `XmMULTICLICK_KEEP`.

## Additional Behavior

DrawnButton has the following additional behavior:

`<EnterWindow>`

Displays the DrawnButton as selected if `XmNpushButtonEnabled` is `True` and the pointer leaves and re-enters the window while `BSelect` is pressed.

`<LeaveWindow>`

Displays the DrawnButton as unselected if `XmNpushButtonEnabled` is `True` and the pointer leaves the window while `BSelect` is pressed.

## See Also

*XmCreateObject*(1),
*Core*(2), *XmLabel*(2), *XmPrimitive*(2), *XmPushButton*(2).

# XmDropSite

## Name

XmDropSite registry – an object that defines the characteristics of a drop site.

## Synopsis

**Public Header:** *<Xm/DragDrop.h>*

**Class Hierarchy:** DropSite does not inherit from any widget class.

**Instantiation:** `XmDropSiteRegister(...)`

**Functions/Macros:**

`XmDropSiteConfigureStackingOrder(), XmDropSiteEndUpdate(), XmDropSiteQueryStackingOrder(), XmDropSiteRegister(), XmDropSiteRetrieve(), XmDropSiteStartUpdate(), XmDropSiteUpdate(), XmDropSiteUnregister()`

## Availability

Motif 1.2 and later.

## Description

A DropSite is an object that stores data about a drop site for drag and drop operations. A DropSite is associated with a particular widget or gadget in an application. An application registers a widget or gadget as a DropSite using `XmDropSiteRegister()`. The DropSite stores information about the shape of the drop site, the animation effects used when the pointer enters the drop site, the types of data supported by the drop site, and the callback that is activated when a drop occurs. These characteristics can be specified as resources when the DropSite is created.

The functions `XmDropSiteUpdate()` and `XmDropSiteRetrieve()` set and get the drop site resources for a widget that is registered as a DropSite. Use these routines instead of `XtSetValues()` and `XtGetValues()`.

## New Resources

DropSite defines the following resources:

| Name | Class | Type | Default | Access |
|---|---|---|---|---|
| XmNanimationMask | XmCAnimationMask | Pixmap | XmUNSPECIFIED_PIXMAP | CSG |
| XmNanimationPixmap | XmCAnimationPixmap | Pixmap | XmUNSPECIFIED_PIXMAP | CSG |
| XmNanimationPixmapDepth | XmCAnimationPixmapDepth | int | 0 | CSG |

| Name | Class | Type | Default | Access |
|---|---|---|---|---|
| XmNanimation Style | XmCAnimationStyle | unsigned char | XmDRAG_UNDER_ HIGHLIGHT | CSG |
| XmNdrop Rectangles | XmCDropRectangles | XRectangle * | dynamic | CSG |
| XmNdropSite Activity | XmCDropSiteActivity | unsigned char | XmDROP_SITE_ ACTIVE | CSG |
| XmNdropSite Operations | XmCDropSiteOperations | unsigned char | XmDROP_MOVE \| XmDROP_COPY | CSG |
| XmNdrop SiteType | XmCDropSiteType | unsigned char | XmDROP_SITE_ SIMPLE | CG |
| XmNimport Targets | XmCImportTargets | Atom * | NULL | CSG |
| XmNnumDrop Rectangles | XmCNumDropRectangles | Cardinal | 1 | CSG |
| XmNnumImport Targets | XmCNumImportTargets | Cardinal | 0 | CSG |

XmNanimationMask

The mask for the XmNanimationPixmap when the animation style is XmDRAG_UNDER_PIXMAP.

XmNanimationPixmap

The pixmap used for drag-under animation when the animation style is XmDRAG_UNDER_PIXMAP.

XmNanimationPixmapDepth

The depth of the pixmap specified by XmNanimationPixmap.

XmNanimationStyle

The style of drag-under animation used when the pointer enters a valid drop site during a drag operation. Possible values:

```
XmDRAG_UNDER_HIGHLIGHT      /* drop site highlighted */
XmDRAG_UNDER_SHADOW_OUT     /* drop site shown with outset shadow */
XmDRAG_UNDER_SHADOW_IN      /* drop site shown with inset shadow */
XmDRAG_UNDER_PIXMAP         /* drop site displays pixmap */
XmDRAG_UNDER_NONE           /* no animation effects unless in XmNdragProc */
```

XmNdropRectangles

A list of rectangles that specify the shape of the drop site. When the value is NULL, the drop site is the entire widget.

XmNdropSiteActivity

Specifies the state of the drop site. Possible values:

```
XmDROP_SITE_ACTIVE      /* participates in drop operations */
XmDROP_SITE_INACTIVE    /* does not participate in drop operations */
```

`XmNdropSiteOperations`
The valid operations for a drop site. The value is a bit mask that is formed by combining one or more of these possible values:

```
XmDROP_COPY      /* copy operations are valid */
XmDROP_LINK      /* link operations are valid */
XmDROP_MOVE      /* move operations are valid */
XmDROP_NOOP      /* no operations are valid */
```

`XmNdropSiteType`
The type of the drop site. Possible values:

```
XmDROP_SITE_SIMPLE        /* no children are registered as drop sites */
XmDROP_SITE_COMPOSITE     /* has children registered as drop sites */
```

`XmNimportTargets`
The list of target atoms that the drop site accepts.

`XmNnumDropRectangles`
The number of rectangles in the `XmNdropRectangles` list.

`XmNnumImportTargets`
The number of atoms in the `XmNimportTargets` list.

## Callback Resources

DropSite defines the following callback resources:

| Callback | Reason Constant |
|---|---|
| XmNdragProc | XmCR_DROP_SITE_ENTER_MESSAGE |
| | XmCR_DROP_SITE_LEAVE_MESSAGE |
| | XmCR_DRAG_MOTION_MESSAGE |
| | XmCR_OPERATION_CHANGED_MESSAGE |
| XmNdropProc | XmCR_DROP_MESSAGE |

`XmNdragProc`
The procedure that is called when the drop site receives a crossing, motion, or operation changed message under the dynamic protocol. The reason passed to the procedure depends on the type of message that is received.

`XmNdropProc`
The procedure that is called when a drop operation occurs on the drop site.

## Callback Structures

The XmNdragProc is passed the following structure:

```
typedef struct
{
    int            reason;         /* the reason the callback was called */
    XEvent         *event;         /* event structure that triggered callback */
    Time           timeStamp;      /* timestamp of logical event */
    Widget         dragContext;    /* DragContext widget associated with operation */
    Position       x;              /* x-coordinate of pointer */
    Position       y;              /* y-coordinate of pointer */
    unsigned char  dropSiteStatus;/* valid or invalid */
    unsigned char  operation;      /* current operation */
    unsigned char  operations;     /* supported operations */
    Boolean        animate;        /* toolkit or receiver does animation */
} XmDragProcCallbackStruct, *XmDragProcCallback;
```

The XmNdragProc can change the value of the dropSiteStatus, operation, and operations fields in this structure. When the drag procedure completes, the toolkit uses the resulting values to initialize the corresponding fields in the callback structure passed to the initiating client's callbacks.

The XmNdropProc is passed the following structure:

```
typedef struct
{
        int        reason;         /* the reason the callback was called */
    XEvent         *event;         /* event structure that triggered callback */
    Time           timeStamp;      /* timestamp of logical event */
    Widget         dragContext;    /* DragContext widget associated with operation */
    Position       x;              /* x-coordinate of pointer */
    Position       y;              /* y-coordinate of pointer */
    unsigned char  dropSiteStatus;/* valid or invalid */
    unsigned char  operation;      /* current operation */
    unsigned char  operations;     /* supported operations */
    unsigned char  dropAction;     /* drop or help */
} XmDropProcCallbackStruct, *XmDropProcCallback;
```

The XmNdropProc can change the value of the dropSiteStatus, operation, operations, and dropAction fields in this structure. When the drop procedure completes, the toolkit uses the resulting values to initialize the corresponding fields in the XmDropProcCallbackStruct callback structure passed to the initiating client's drop start callbacks.

The dropSiteStatus field in these structures specifies whether or not the drop site is valid. The toolkit initializes the value based on the XmNimportTargets resource of the DropSite and the XmNexportTargets resource of the DragContext. The possible values are XmDROP_SITE_VALID and XmDROP_SITE_INVALID.

The operations field in these structure specifies the set of operations supported for the data being dragged. The toolkit initializes the value based on the XmNdragOperations resource of the DragContext and the operation selected by the user. The operation field in these structures specifies the current operation. The toolkit initializes the value based on the value of operations and the XmNdropSiteOperations resource.

The animate field in the XmDragProcCallbackStruct specifies whether the toolkit or the receiving client handles the drag-under effects for the drop site. If the value is True, the toolkit handles the effects based on the XmNanimationStyle resource. Otherwise the receiver is responsible for providing drag-under effects.

The dropAction field in the XmDropProcCallbackStruct specifies the action associated with the drop, which is either a normal drop or a help action. The possible values are XmDROP and DROP_HELP.

## See Also

*XmDropSiteConfigureStackingOrder*(1), *XmDropSiteEndUpdate*(1), *XmDropSiteQueryStackingOrder*(1), *XmDropSiteRegister*(1), *XmDropSiteRetrieve*(1), *XmDropSiteStartUpdate*(1), *XmDropSiteUnregister*(1), *XmDropSiteUpdate*(1), *XmDisplay*(2), *XmDragContext*(2), *XmDragIcon*(2), *XmDropTransfer*(2), *XmScreen*(2).

## Name

XmDropTransfer widget class – an object used to store information about a drop transaction.

## Synopsis

**Public Header:** *<Xm/DragDrop.h>*

**Class Name:** XmDropTransfer

**Class Pointer:** xmDropTransferObjectClass

**Class Hierarchy:** Object → DropTransfer

**Instantiation:** `widget = XmDropTransferStart(...)`

**Functions/Macros:** `XmDropTransferAdd()`, `XmDropTransferStart()`

## Availability

Motif 1.2 and later.

## Description

The DropTransfer object stores information that the toolkit needs to process a drop transaction. An application does not explicitly create a DropTransfer widget, but instead initiates a data transfer by calling `XmDropTransferStart()`, which initializes and returns a DropTransfer widget. If `XmDropTransferStart()` is called within an `XmNdropProc`, the data transfer starts after the callback returns. If no data needs to be transferred or the drop transaction is a failure, an application still needs to call `XmDropTransferStart()` with a failure status, so that the toolkit can complete the drag and drop operation.

The `XmNtransferProc` resource specifies a procedure of type XtSelectionCallbackProc that handles transferring the requested selection data. This procedure performs in conjunction with the underlying Xt selection mechanisms and is called for each type of data being transferred. Target types can be added after a transfer has started by calling the `XmDropTransferAdd()`.

## New Resources

DropTransfer defines the following resources:

| Name | Class | Type | Default | Access |
|---|---|---|---|---|
| XmNdropTransfers | XmCDropTransfers | XmDropTransferEntryRec * | NULL | CG |
| XmNincremental | XmCIncremental | Boolean | False | CSG |
| XmNnumDropTransfers | XmCNumDropTransfers | Cardinal | 0 | CSG |
| XmNtransferProc | XmCTransferProc | XtSelectionCallbackProc | NULL | CSG |
| XmNtransferStatus | XmCTransferStatus | unsigned char | XmTRANSFER_SUCCESS | CSG |

XmNdropTransfers

Pointer to an array of XmDropTransferEntryRec structures, which specifies the requested target data types for the source data. A XmDropTransferEntryRec is defined as follows:

```
typedef struct
{
    XtPointer   client_data;   /* any additional information necessary */
    Atom        target;        /* selection target type */
} XmDropTransferEntryRec, *XmDropTransferEntry;
```

The drop transfer is done when all of the entries have been processed.

XmNincremental

If True, the receiver uses the Xt incremental selection transfer mechanism. If False (default), the receiver uses atomic transfer.

XmNnumDropTransfers

The number of entries in XmNdropTransfers. The transfer is complete if the value is set to 0 at any time.

XmNtransferProc

A procedure of type XtSelectionCallbackProc that provides the requested selection values. The *widget* argument passed to this procedure is the DropTransfer widget and the selection atom is _MOTIF_DROP.

XmNtransferStatus

The current status of the drop transfer. The receiving client updates this value when the transfer ends and the value is communicated to the initiator. Possible values:

```
XmTRANSFER_SUCCESS
XmTRANSFER_FAILURE
```

## Inherited Resources

DropTransfer inherits the following resource:

| Resource | Inherited From |
|---|---|
| XmNdestroyCallback | Object |

## See Also

*XmDropTransferAdd*(1), *XmDropTransferStart*(1), *XmTargetsAreCompatible*(1), *Object*(2), *XmDisplay*(2), *XmDragContext*(2), *XmDragIcon*(2), *XmDropTransfer*(2), *XmScreen*(2).

# XmErrorDialog

## Name

XmErrorDialog – an unmanaged MessageBox as a child of a DialogShell.

## Synopsis

**Public Header:** *<Xm/MessageB.h>*

**Instantiation:** `widget = XmCreateErrorDialog(...)`

**Functions/Macros:** `XmCreateErrorDialog()`, `XmMessageBoxGetChild()`

## Description

An ErrorDialog is a compound object created by a call to `XmCreateErrorDialog()` that an application can use to inform the user about any type of error. An ErrorDialog consists of a DialogShell with an unmanaged MessageBox widget as its child. The MessageBox resource `XmNdialogType` is set to `XmDIALOG_ERROR`. An ErrorDialog includes four components: a symbol, a message, three buttons, and a separator between the message and the buttons. By default, the symbol is an octagon with a diagonal slash. In Motif 1.2, the default button labels can be localized. In the C locale, and in Motif 1.1, the PushButtons are labeled **OK**, **Cancel**, and **Help** by default.

## Default Resource Values

An ErrorDialog sets the following default values for MessageBox resources:

| Name | Default |
|---|---|
| XmNdialogType | XmDIALOG_ERROR |
| XmNsymbolPixmap | xm_error |

## Widget Hierarchy

When an ErrorDialog is created with a specified `name`, the DialogShell is named `name_popup` and the MessageBox is called `name`.

## See Also

*XmCreateObject*(1), *XmMessageBoxGetChild*(1),
*XmDialogShell*(2), *XmMessageBox*(2).

# XmFileSelectionBox

## Name

XmFileSelectionBox widget class – a widget for selecting files.

## Synopsis

**Public Header:** *<Xm/FileSB.h>*

**Class Name:** XmFileSelectionBox

**Class Hierarchy:** Core → Composite → Constraint → XmManager → XmBulletinBoard → XmSelectionBox → XmFileSelectionBox

**Class Pointer:** `xmFileSelectionBoxWidgetClass`

**Instantiation:** `widget = XtCreateWidget(name, xmFileSelectionBoxWidgetClass, ...)`

**Functions/Macros:** `XmCreateFileSelectionBox()`, `XmCreateFileSelectionDialog()`, `XmFileSelectionBoxGetChild()`, `XmFileSelectionDoSearch()`, `XmIsFileSelectionBox()`

## Description

FileSelectionBox is a composite widget that is used to traverse a directory hierarchy and select files. FileSelectionBox provides a directory mask input field, a scrollable list of subdirectories, a scrollable list of filenames, a filename input field, and a group of four PushButtons. The names for the filter text, directory list, and directory list label are `Text`, `DirList`, and `Dir` respectively. The other components have the same names as the components in a SelectionBox.

In Motif 1.2, the button labels can be localized. In the C locale, and in Motif 1.1, the PushButtons are labeled **OK**, **Filter**, **Cancel**, and **Help** by default.

You can customize a FileSelectionBox by removing existing children or adding new children. Use `XmFileSelectionBoxGetChild()` to retrieve the widget ID of an existing child and then unmanage the child. With Motif 1.2, multiple widgets can be added as children of a FileSelectionBox. Additional children are added in the same way as for a SelectionBox. In Motif 1.1, only a single widget can be added as a child of a FileSelectionBox. This child is placed below the filename input field and acts as a work area.

## New Resources

FileSelectionBox defines the following resources:

| Name | Class | Type | Default | Access |
|---|---|---|---|---|
| `XmNdirectory` | `XmCDirectory` | `XmString` | dynamic | CSG |
| `XmNdirectoryValid` | `XmCDirectoryValid` | `Boolean` | dynamic | SG |
| `XmNdirListItems` | `XmCDirListItems` | `XmStringTable` | dynamic | SG |

| Name | Class | Type | Default | Access |
|---|---|---|---|---|
| XmNdirListItemCount | XmCDirList ItemCount | int | dynamic | SG |
| XmNdirListLabelString | XmCDirList LabelString | XmString | dynamic | CSG |
| XmNdirMask | XmCDirMask | XmString | dynamic | CSG |
| XmNdirSearchProc | XmCDirSearchProc | XmSearch Proc | default procedure | CSG |
| XmNdirSpec | XmCDirSpec | XmString | dynamic | CSG |
| XmNfileListItems | XmCItems | XmString Table | dynamic | SG |
| XmNfileListItemCount | XmCItemCount | int | dynamic | SG |
| XmNfileListLabelString | XmCFileList LabelString | XmString | dynamic | CSG |
| XmNfileSearchProc | XmCFile SearchProc | XmSearchProc | default procedure | CSG |
| XmNfileTypeMask | XmCFile TypeMask | unsigned char | XmFILE_ REGULAR | CSG |
| XmNfilterLabelString | XmCFilter LabelString | XmString | dynamic | CSG |
| XmNlistUpdated | XmCList Updated | Boolean | dynamic | SG |
| XmNnoMatchString | XmCNo MatchString | XmString | "[ ]" | CSG |
| XmNpattern | XmCPattern | XmString | dynamic | CSG |
| XmNqualifySearchDataProc | XmCQualify SearchDataProc | XmQualifyProc | default procedure | CSG |

`XmNdirectory`
: The base directory that, in combination with `XmNpattern`, forms the directory mask (the `XmNdirMask` resource). The directory mask determines which files and directories to display.

`XmNdirectoryValid`
: A resource that can be set only by the directory search procedure (as specified by the `XmNdirSearchProc` resource). If the directory search procedure is unable to search the directory that was passed to it, then it will set `XmNdirectoryValid` to `False`, and as a result, the file search procedure won't be called.

`XmNdirListItems`
: The items in the directory list. This resource is set only by the directory search procedure. A call to `XtGetValues()` returns the actual list items (not a copy), so don't have your application free these items.

XmNdirListItemCount
: The number of items in XmNdirListItems. This resource is set only by the directory search procedure.

XmNdirListLabelString
: The string that labels the directory list. In Motif 1.2, the default value is locale-dependent. In the C locale, and in Motif 1.1, the default value is "Directories".

XmNdirMask
: The directory mask that determines which files and directories to display. This value combines the values of the resources XmNdirectory and XmNpattern.

XmNdirSearchProc
: The procedure that performs directory searches. For most applications, the default procedure works just fine. The call to this procedure contains two arguments: the widget ID of the FileSelectionBox and a pointer to an XmFileSelection-CallbackStruct.

XmNdirSpec
: The complete specification of the file path. Synonymous with the XmNtextString resource in SelectionBox. It is the initial directory and file search that determines the default value for this resource.

XmNfileListItems
: The items in the file list. Synonymous with the XmNlistItems resource in Selection-Box. This resource is set only by the file search procedure. A call to XtGetValues() returns the actual list items (not a copy), so don't have your application free these items.

XmNfileListItemCount
: The number of items in XmNfileListItems. Synonymous with the XmNlist-ItemCount resource in SelectionBox. This resource is set only by the file search procedure.

XmNfileListLabelString
: The string that labels the file list. Synonymous with the XmNlistLabelString resource in SelectionBox. In Motif 1.2, the default value is locale-dependent. In the C locale, and in Motif 1.1, the default value is "Files".

XmNfileSearchProc
: The procedure that performs file searches. For most applications, the default procedure works just fine. The call to this procedure contains two arguments: the widget ID of the FileSelectionBox and a pointer to an XmFileSelectionCallbackStruct.

XmNfileTypeMask
: Determines whether the file list will display only regular files, only directories, or any type of file. Possible values are XmFILE_DIRECTORY, XmFILE_REGULAR, and Xm-FILE_ANY_TYPE.

`XmNfilterLabelString`
: The string that labels the field in which the directory mask is typed in by the user. In Motif 1.2, the default value is locale-dependent. In the C locale, and in Motif 1.1, the default value is `"Filter"`.

`XmNlistUpdated`
: A resource that can be set only by the directory search procedure or by the file search procedure. This resource is set to `True` if the directory or file list was updated by a search procedure.

`XmNnoMatchString`
: A string that displays in the file list when there are no filenames to display.

`XmNpattern`
: The file search pattern that, in combination with `XmNdirectory`, forms the directory mask (the `XmNdirMask` resource). The directory mask determines which files and directories to display. If the `XmNpattern` resource defaults to `NULL` or is empty, a pattern for matching all files will be used.

`XmNqualifySearchDataProc`
: The procedure that generates a valid directory mask, base directory, and search pattern to be used by `XmNdirSearchProc` and `XmNfileSearchProc` (the search procedures for directories and files). For most applications, the default procedure works just fine. The call to this procedure contains three arguments: the widget ID of the FileSelection-Box, a pointer to an `XmFileSelectionCallbackStruct` containing the input data, and a pointer to an `XmFileSelectionCallbackStruct` that will contain the output data.

### Callback Structure

Each callback function is passed the following structure:

```
typedef struct
{
    int       reason;         /* the reason that the callback was called */
    XEvent    *event;         /* event structure that triggered callback */
    XmString  value;          /* current value of XmNdirSpec resource */
    int       length;         /* number of bytes in value member */
    XmString  mask;           /* current value of XmNdirMask resource */
    int       mask_length;    /* number of bytes in mask member */
    XmString  dir;            /* current base directory */
    int       dir_length;     /* number of bytes in dir member */
    XmString  pattern;        /* current search pattern */
    int       pattern_length; /* number of bytes in pattern member */
} XmFileSelectionBoxCallbackStruct;
```

## Inherited Resources

FileSelectionBox inherits the following resources. The resources are listed alphabetically, along with the superclass that defines them. FileSelectionBox sets the default values of XmNautoUnmanage to False and XmNdialogType to XmDIALOG_FILE_SELECTION. It also sets the default values of XmNlistItems and XmNlistItemCount dynamically. The default value of XmNborderWidth is reset to 0 by Manager. BulletinBoard sets the value of XmNinitialFocus to XmNdefaultButton and resets the default XmNshadowThickness from 0 to 1 if the FileSelectionBox is a child of a DialogShell.

| Resource | Inherited From | Resource | Inherited From |
|---|---|---|---|
| XmNaccelerators | Core | XmNlistItems | SelectionBox |
| XmNallowOverlap | BulletinBoard | XmNlistLabelString | SelectionBox |
| XmNancestorSensitive | Core | XmNlistVisibleItemCount | SelectionBox |
| XmNapplyCallback | SelectionBox | XmNmapCallback | BulletinBoard |
| XmNapplyLabelString | SelectionBox | XmNmappedWhenManaged | Core |
| XmNautoUnmanage | BulletinBoard | XmNmarginHeight | BulletinBoard |
| XmNbackground | Core | XmNmarginWidth | BulletinBoard |
| XmNbackgroundPixmap | Core | XmNminimizeButtons | SelectionBox |
| XmNborderColor | Core | XmNmustMatch | SelectionBox |
| XmNborderPixmap | Core | XmNnavigationType | Manager |
| XmNborderWidth | Core | XmNnoMatchCallback | SelectionBox |
| XmNbottomShadowColor | Manager | XmNnoResize | BulletinBoard |
| XmNbottomShadowPixmap | Manager | XmNnumChildren | Composite |
| XmNbuttonFontList | BulletinBoard | XmNokCallback | SelectionBox |
| XmNcancelButton | BulletinBoard | XmNokLabelString | SelectionBox |
| XmNcancelCallback | SelectionBox | XmNresizePolicy | BulletinBoard |
| XmNcancelLabelString | SelectionBox | XmNscreen | Core |
| XmNchildren | Composite | XmNselectionLabelString | SelectionBox |
| XmNcolormap | Core | XmNsensitive | Core |
| XmNdefaultButton | BulletinBoard | XmNshadowThickness | Manager |
| XmNdefaultPosition | BulletinBoard | XmNshadowType | BulletinBoard |
| XmNdepth | Core | XmNstringDirection | Manager |
| XmNdestroyCallback | Core | XmNtextAccelerators | SelectionBox |
| XmNdialogStyle | BulletinBoard | XmNtextColumns | SelectionBox |
| XmNdialogTitle | BulletinBoard | XmNtextFontList | BulletinBoard |
| XmNdialogType | SelectionBox | XmNtextString | SelectionBox |
| XmNfocusCallback | BulletinBoard | XmNtextTranslations | BulletinBoard |
| XmNforeground | Manager | XmNtopShadowColor | Manager |
| XmNheight | Core | XmNtopShadowPixmap | Manager |
| XmNhelpCallback | Manager | XmNtranslations | Core |
| XmNhelpLabelString | SelectionBox | XmNtraversalOn | Manager |
| XmNhighlightColor | Manager | XmNunitType | Manager |

| Resource | Inherited From | Resource | Inherited From |
|---|---|---|---|
| XmNhighlightPixmap | Manager | XmNunmapCallback | BulletinBoard |
| XmNinitialFocus | Manager | XmNuserData | Manager |
| XmNinitialResources Persistent | Core | XmNwidth | Core |
| XmNinsertPosition | Composite | XmNx | Core |
| XmNlabelFontList | BulletinBoard | XmNy | Core |
| XmNlistItemCount | SelectionBox | | |

## Translations

The translations for FileSelectionBox are inherited from SelectionBox.

## Action Routines

FileSelectionBox defines the following action routines:

`SelectionBoxUpOrDown(`*`flag`*`)`

Replaces the selection text or the filter text, depending on which one has the keyboard focus. That is, this action replaces either: the text string in the selection area with an item from the file list, or the text string in the directory mask (filter) area with an item from the directory list.

The value of *flag* determines which file list item or which directory list item is selected as the replacement string. A *flag* value of 0, 1, 2, or 3 selects the previous, next, first, or last item, respectively, of the appropriate list.

`SelectionBoxRestore()`

Replaces the selection text or the filter text, depending on which one has the keyboard focus. That is, this action replaces either: the text string in the selection area with the currently selected item in the file list (clearing the selection area if no list item is selected), or the text string in the filter area with a new directory mask (which is formed by combining the values of the `XmNdirectory` and `XmNpattern` resources).

## Additional Behavior

FileSelectionBox has the following additional behavior:

`MAny KCancel`

If the **Cancel** button is sensitive, invokes its `XmNactivateCallback` callbacks. If there is no **Cancel** button, the event is passed to the parent if it is a manager.

`KActivate`

In the filename text input area, first invokes the `XmNactivateCallback` callbacks for the text and then invokes either the `XmNnoMatchCallback` or the `XmNokCallback` callbacks based on the value of `XmNmustMatch`.

In the directory mask text input area, first invokes the XmNactivateCallback callbacks for the text and then starts a directory and file search and invokes the XmNapplyCallback callbacks.

In the directory list, invokes the XmNdefaultActionCallback callback, begins a directory and file search, and invokes the XmNapplyCallback callbacks.

In the file list, invokes XmNdefaultActionCallback and XmNokCallback callbacks.

When none of these areas nor any button has the keyboard focus, invokes the callbacks in either XmNnoMatchCallback or XmNokCallback depending on the value of XmNmustMatch and whether or not the selection text matches a file in the file list.

<DoubleClick>
In the directory or file list, has the same behavior as KActivate.

<Single Select> or <Browse Select>
In the directory list, composes a directory mask using the selected directory item and the current pattern. In the file list, uses the selected file item to replace the selection text.

BTransfer
In Motif 1.2, in the file or directory list, starts a drag and drop operation using the selected items in the list. If BTransfer is pressed over an unselected item, only that item is used in the drag and drop operation.

<Apply Button Activated>
Starts a directory and file search and invokes the XmNapplyCallback callbacks.

<Ok Button Activated>
Invokes either the XmNnoMatchCallback or XmNokCallback callbacks based on the value of XmNmustMatch and whether or not the selection text matches a file in the file list.

<Cancel Button Activated>
Invokes the XmNcancelCallback callbacks.

<Help Button Activated>
Invokes the XmNhelpCallback callbacks.

## See Also

*XmCreateObject*(1), *XmFileSelectionBoxGetChild*(1), *XmFileSelectionDoSearch*(1), *Composite*(2), *Constraint*(2), *Core*(2), *XmBulletinBoard*(2), *XmFileSelectionDialog*(2), *XmManager*(2), *XmSelectionBox*(2).

# XmFileSelectionDialog

## Name

XmFileSelectionDialog – an unmanaged FileSelectionBox as a child of a Dialog Shell.

## Synopsis

**Public Header:** *<Xm/FileSB.h>*

**Instantiation:** `widget = XmCreateFileSelectionDialog(...)`

**Functions/Macros:** `XmCreateFileSelectionBox()`, `XmFileSelectionBoxGetChild()`, `XmCreateFileSelectionDialog()`, `XmFileSelectionDoSearch()`, `XmIsFileSelectionBox()`

## Description

FileSelectionDialog is a compound object created by a call to `XmCreateFileSelectionDialog()` that an application can use to allow a user to select a file from a dialog box. A FileSelectionDialog consists of a DialogShell with an unmanaged FileSelectionBox widget as its child. The SelectionBox resource `XmNdialogType` is set to `XmDIALOG_FILE_SELECTION`.

A FileSelectionDialog provides a directory mask input field, a scrollable list of subdirectories, a scrollable list of filenames, a filename input field, and a group of four PushButtons. In Motif 1.2, the button labels can be localized. In the C locale, and in Motif 1.1, the PushButtons are labeled **OK**, **Filter**, **Cancel**, and **Help** by default.

## Default Resource Values

A FileSelectionDialog sets the following default values for its resources:

| Name | Default |
|---|---|
| `XmNdialogType` | `XmDIALOG_FILE_SELECTION` |

## Widget Hierarchy

When a FileSelectionDialog is created with a specified `name`, the DialogShell is named `name_popup` and the FileSelectionBox is called `name`.

## See Also

*XmCreateObject*(1), *XmFileSelectionBoxGetChild*(1), *XmFileSelectionDoSearch*(1), *XmFileSelectionBox*(2), *XmDialogShell*(2).

# XmForm

## Name

XmForm widget class – a container widget that constrains its children.

## Synopsis

**Public Header:** *<Xm/Form.h>*

**Class Name:** XmForm

**Class Hierarchy:** Core → Composite → Constraint → XmManager → XmBulletinBoard → XmForm

**Class Pointer:** `xmFormWidgetClass`

**Instantiation:** `widget = XtCreateWidget(name, xmFormWidgetClass, ...)`

**Functions/Macros:** `XmCreateForm(), XmCreateFormDialog(), XmIsForm()`

## Description

Form is a container widget that constrains its children so as to define their layout when the Form is resized. Constraints on the children of a Form specify the attachments for each of the four sides of a child. Children may be attached to each other, to edges of the Form, or to relative positions within the Form.

## New Resources

Form defines the following resources:

| Name | Class | Type | Default | Access |
|---|---|---|---|---|
| XmNfractionBase | XmCMaxValue | int | 100 | CSG |
| XmNhorizontalSpacing | XmCSpacing | Dimension | 0 | CSG |
| XmNrubberPositioning | XmCRubberPositioning | Boolean | False | CSG |
| XmNverticalSpacing | XmCSpacing | Dimension | 0 | CSG |

`XmNfractionBase`

The denominator part of the fraction that describes a child's relative position within a Form. The numerator of this fraction is one of the four positional constraint resources: `XmNbottomPosition`, `XmNleftPosition`, `XmNrightPosition`, or `XmNtopPosition`. For example, suppose you use the default `XmNfractionBase` of 100. Then, if you specify `XmNtopPosition` as 30, the top of the child will remain invariably attached to a location that is 30/100 (or 30 percent) from the top of the Form. (In other words, resizing the Form's height might change the absolute position of the child's top, but not its position relative to the top of the Form.) Similarly, a value of 50 for `XmNleftPosition` ensures that the left side of the child is attached 50/100 from the left of the Form (or in this case, halfway between the left and right side). Note that these fractions are implemented only when the child's corresponding attachment constraint is set to XmATTACH_POSITION. (The attachment constraints are XmNbottomAttachment, XmNleftAttachment, XmNrightAttachment, and XmNtopAttachment.)

XmNhorizontalSpacing
The offset for right and left attachments.

XmNrubberPositioning
Defines the default behavior of a child's top and left side, in the absence of other settings. If this resource is False (default), the child's top and left sides are positioned using absolute values. If True, the child's top and left sides are positioned relative to the size of the Form.

XmNverticalSpacing
The offset for top and bottom attachments.

## New Constraint Resources

Form defines the following constraint resources for its children:

| Name | Class | Type | Default | Access |
|---|---|---|---|---|
| XmNbottomAttachment | XmCAttachment | unsigned char | XmATTACH_NONE | CSG |
| XmNbottomOffset | XmCOffset | int | 0 | CSG |
| XmNbottomPosition | XmCAttachment | int | 0 | CSG |
| XmNbottomWidget | XmCWidget | Window | NULL | CSG |
| XmNleftAttachment | XmCAttachment | unsigned char | XmATTACH_NONE | CSG |
| XmNleftOffset | XmCOffset | int | 0 | CSG |
| XmNleftPosition | XmCAttachment | int | 0 | CSG |
| XmNleftWidget | XmCWidget | Window | NULL | CSG |
| XmNresizable | XmCBoolean | Boolean | True | CSG |
| XmNrightAttachment | XmCAttachment | unsigned char | XmATTACH_NONE | CSG |
| XmNrightOffset | XmCOffset | int | 0 | CSG |
| XmNrightPosition | XmCAttachment | int | 0 | CSG |
| XmNrightWidget | XmCWidget | Window | NULL | CSG |
| XmNtopAttachment | XmCAttachment | unsigned char | XmATTACH_NONE | CSG |
| XmNtopOffset | XmCOffset | int | 0 | CSG |
| XmNtopPosition | XmCAttachment | int | 0 | CSG |
| XmNtopWidget | XmCWidget | Window | NULL | CSG |

XmNbottomAttachment
The method of attachment for the child's bottom side. Each of the four attachment resources (XmNtopAttachment, XmNbottomAttachment, XmNleft-Attachment, and XmNrightAttachment) has the following possible values. The

comments below refer to a corresponding edge (top, bottom, left, or right) of the child widget within the Form.

```
XmATTACH_NONE                 /* remains unattached */
XmATTACH_FORM                 /* attached to same edge of Form */
XmATTACH_OPPOSITE_FORM        /* attached to other edge of Form */
XmATTACH_WIDGET               /* abuts an adjacent widget */
XmATTACH_OPPOSITE_WIDGET      /* attached to other edge of adjacent widget */
XmATTACH_POSITION             /* relative to a dimension of Form */
XmATTACH_SELF                 /* relative to its current position & to Form */
```

`XmNbottomOffset`
The distance between the child's bottom side and the object it's attached to. Offsets are absolute. A nonzero offset is ignored when `XmNbottomAttachment` is set to `XmATTACH_POSITION`, because a resize operation applies relative positioning in this case. Offsets are of type `int` and may not be resolution-independent.

`XmNbottomPosition`
Used in conjunction with `XmNfractionBase` to calculate the position of the bottom of a child, relative to the bottom of the Form. This resource has no effect unless the child's `XmNbottomAttachment` resource is set to `XmATTACH_POSITION`. (See `XmNfractionBase` for details.)

`XmNbottomWidget`
The name of the widget or gadget that serves as the attachment point for the bottom of the child. To use this resource, set the `XmNbottomAttachment` resource to either `XmATTACH_WIDGET` or `XmATTACH_OPPOSITE_WIDGET`.

`XmNleftAttachment`
The method of attachment for the child's left side.

`XmNleftOffset`
The distance between the child's left side and the object it's attached to. Offsets are absolute. A nonzero offset is ignored when `XmNleftAttachment` is set to `XmATTACH_POSITION`, because a resize operation applies relative positioning in this case. Offsets are of type `int` and may not be resolution-independent.

`XmNleftPosition`
Used in conjunction with `XmNfractionBase` to calculate the position of the left side of a child, relative to the left side of the Form. This resource has no effect unless the child's `XmNleftAttachment` resource is set to `XmATTACH_POSITION`. (See `XmNfractionBase` for details.)

`XmNleftWidget`
The name of the widget or gadget that serves as the attachment point for the left side of the child. To use this resource, set the `XmNleftAttachment` resource to either `XmATTACH_WIDGET` or `XmATTACH_OPPOSITE_WIDGET`.

`XmNresizable`
If `True` (default), a child's resize request is accepted by the Form, provided that the child isn't constrained by its attachments. That is, if both the left and right sides of a child are attached, or if both the top and bottom are attached, the resize request fails, whereas if the child has only one horizontal or one vertical attachment, the resize request is granted. If this resource is `False`, the child is never resized.

`XmNrightAttachment`
The method of attachment for the child's right side.

`XmNrightOffset`
The distance between the child's right side and the object it's attached to. Offsets are absolute. A nonzero offset is ignored when `XmNrightAttachment` is set to `XmATTACH_POSITION`, because a resize operation applies relative positioning in this case. Offsets are of type `int` and may not be resolution-independent.

`XmNrightPosition`
Used in conjunction with `XmNfractionBase` to calculate the position of the right side of a child, relative to the right side of the Form. This resource has no effect unless the child's `XmNrightAttachment` resource is set to `XmATTACH_POSITION`. (See `XmNfractionBase` for details.)

`XmNrightWidget`
The name of the widget or gadget that serves as the attachment point for the right side of the child. To use this resource, set the `XmNrightAttachment` resource to either `XmATTACH_WIDGET` or `XmATTACH_OPPOSITE_WIDGET`.

`XmNtopAttachment`
The method of attachment for the child's top side.

`XmNtopOffset`
The distance between the child's top side and the object it's attached to. Offsets are absolute. A nonzero offset is ignored when `XmNtopAttachment` is set to `XmATTACH_POSITION`, because a resize operation applies relative positioning in this case. Offsets are of type `int` and may not be resolution-independent.

`XmNtopPosition`
Used in conjunction with `XmNfractionBase` to calculate the position of the top of a child, relative to the top of the Form. This resource has no effect unless the child's `XmNtopAttachment` resource is set to `XmATTACH_POSITION`. (See `XmNfractionBase` for details.)

`XmNtopWidget`
The name of the widget or gadget that serves as the attachment point for the top of the child. To use this resource, set the `XmNtopAttachment` resource to either `XmATTACH_WIDGET` or `XmATTACH_OPPOSITE_WIDGET`.

## Inherited Resources

Form inherits the following resources. The resources are listed alphabetically, along with the superclass that defines them. Form sets the default values of XmNmarginWidth and XmN-marginHeight to 0. The default value of XmNborderWidth is reset to 0 by Manager. BulletinBoard sets the value of XmNinitialFocus to XmNdefaultButton and resets the default XmNshadowThickness from 0 to 1 if the Form widget is a child of DialogShell.

| Resource | Inherited From | Resource | Inherited From |
|---|---|---|---|
| XmNaccelerators | Core | XmNinsertPosition | Composite |
| XmNallowOverlap | Bulletin Board | XmNlabelFontList | Bulletin Board |
| XmNancestorSensitive | Core | XmNmapCallback | Bulletin Board |
| XmNautoUnmanage | Bulletin Board | XmNmappedWhenManaged | Core |
| XmNbackground | Core | XmNmarginHeight | Bulletin Board |
| XmNbackgroundPixmap | Core | XmNmarginWidth | Bulletin Board |
| XmNborderColor | Core | XmNnavigationType | Manager |
| XmNborderPixmap | Core | XmNnoResize | Bulletin Board |
| XmNborderWidth | Core | XmNnumChildren | Composite |
| XmNbottomShadowColor | Manager | XmNresizePolicy | Bulletin Board |
| XmNbottomShadowPixmap | Manager | XmNscreen | Core |
| XmNbuttonFontList | Bulletin Board | XmNsensitive | Core |
| XmNcancelButton | Bulletin Board | XmNshadowThickness | Manager |
| XmNchildren | Composite | XmNshadowType | Bulletin Board |
| XmNcolormap | Core | XmNstringDirection | Manager |
| XmNdefaultButton | Bulletin Board | XmNtextFontList | Bulletin Board |
| XmNdefaultPosition | Bulletin Board | XmNtextTranslations | Bulletin Board |
| XmNdepth | Core | XmNtopShadowColor | Manager |
| XmNdestroyCallback | Core | XmNtopShadowPixmap | Manager |
| XmNdialogStyle | Bulletin Board | XmNtranslations | Core |
| XmNdialogTitle | Bulletin Board | XmNtraversalOn | Manager |

| Resource | Inherited From | Resource | Inherited From |
|---|---|---|---|
| XmNfocusCallback | BulletinBoard | XmNunitType | Manager |
| XmNforeground | Manager | XmNunmapCallback | BulletinBoard |
| XmNheight | Core | XmNuserData | Manager |
| XmNhelpCallback | Manager | XmNwidth | Core |
| XmNhighlightColor | Manager | XmNx | Core |
| XmNhighlightPixmap | Manager | XmNy | Core |
| XmNinitialFocus | Manager | | |
| XmNinitialResourcesPersistent | Core | | |

## Translations

The translations for Form are inherited from BulletinBoard.

## See Also

*XmCreateObject(1),*
*Composite(2), Constraint(2), Core(2), XmBulletinBoard(2), XmFormDialog(2), XmManager(2).*

# XmFormDialog



## Name

XmFormDialog – an unmanaged Form as a child of a DialogShell.

## Synopsis

**Public Header:** *<Xm/Form.h>*

**Instantiation:** `widget = XmCreateFormDialog(...)`

**Functions/Macros:** `XmCreateFormDialog()`

## Description

A FormDialog is a compound object created by a call to `XmCreateFormDialog()` that is useful for creating custom dialogs. A FormDialog consists of a DialogShell with an unmanaged Form widget as its child. The FormDialog does not contain any labels, buttons, or other dialog components; these components are added by the application.

## Widget Hierarchy

When a FormDialog is created with a specified `name`, the DialogShell is named `name_popup` and the Form is called `name`.

## See Also

*XmCreateObject*(1),
*XmDialogShell*(2), *XmForm*(2).

# XmFrame

## Name

XmFrame widget class – a manager widget that places a border around a single child.

## Synopsis

**Public Header:** *<Xm/Frame.h>*

**Class Name:** XmFrame

**Class Hierarchy:** Core → Composite → Constraint → XmManager → XmFrame

**Class Pointer:** `xmFrameWidgetClass`

**Instantiation:** `widget = XtCreateWidget(name, xmFrameWidgetClass, ...)`

**Functions/Macros:** `XmCreateFrame()`, `XmIsFrame()`

## Description

Frame is a simple subclass of Manager that places a three-dimensional border around a single child. Frame is used to provide the typical Motif-style appearance for widget classes that do not have a visible frame, such as RowColumn.

As of Motif 1.2, a Frame can have two children: a work area child and a title child. The widget uses constraint resources to indicate the type of each child and to specify the alignment of the title child.

## New Resources

Frame defines the following resources:

| Name | Class | Type | Default | Access |
|---|---|---|---|---|
| XmNmarginWidth | XmCMarginWidth | Dimension | 0 | CSG |
| XmNmarginHeight | XmCMarginHeight | Dimension | 0 | CSG |
| XmNshadowType | XmCShadowType | unsigned char | dynamic | CSG |

`XmNmarginHeight`

The spacing between the top or bottom of a Frame widget's child and the shadow of the Frame widget.

`XmNmarginWidth`

The spacing between the right or left side of a Frame widget's child and the shadow of the Frame widget.

`XmNshadowType`

The style in which Frame widgets are drawn. Possible values:

```
XmSHADOW_IN              /* widget appears inset */
XmSHADOW_OUT             /* widget appears outset */
XmSHADOW_ETCHED_IN       /* double line; widget appears inset */
XmSHADOW_ETCHED_OUT      /* double line; widget appears raised */
```

### New Constraint Resources

As of Motif 1.2, Frame defines the following constraint resources for its children:

| Name | Class | Type | Default | Access |
|---|---|---|---|---|
| XmNchildType | XmCChildType | unsigned char | XmFRAME_ WORKAREA_CHILD | CSG |
| XmNchildHorizontal Alignment | XmCChildHorizontal Alignment | unsigned char | XmALIGNMENT_ BEGINNING | CSG |
| XmNchildHorizontal Spacing | XmCChildHorizontal Spacing | Dimension | dynamic | CSG |
| XmNchildVertical Alignment | XmCChildVertical Alignment | unsigned char | XmALIGNMENT_ CENTER | CSG |

XmNchildType

The type of the child. Frame supports one title and one work area child. Possible values:

```
XmFRAME_TITLE_CHILD          /* child is the title */
XmFRAME_WORKAREA_CHILD       /* child is the work area */
XmFRAME_GENERIC_CHILD        /* child is ignored */
```

XmNchildHorizontalAlignment

The alignment (left to right) for a Frame's title. Possible values are XmALIGNMENT_BEGINNING, XmALIGNMENT_CENTER, and XmALIGNMENT_END.

XmNchildHorizontalSpacing

The minimum distance between the title text and the Frame shadow. The title is clipped to maintain this distance. The value of XmNmarginWidth is used as the default value.

XmNchildVerticalPlacement

The alignment of the Frame's title relative to the top shadow of the Frame. Possible values:

```
XmALIGNMENT_BASELINE_BOTTOM
XmALIGNMENT_BASELINE_TOP
XmALIGNMENT_WIDGET_TOP
XmALIGNMENT_CENTER
XmALIGNMENT_WIDGET_BOTTOM
```

### Inherited Resources

Frame inherits the following resources. The resources are listed alphabetically, along with the superclass that defines them. Frame sets the default value of XmNshadowThickness to 1 if the Frame is a child of a Shell and 2 otherwise. The default value of XmNborderWidth is reset to 0 by Manager.

| Resource | Inherited From | Resource | Inherited From |
|---|---|---|---|
| XmNaccelerators | Core | XmNinitialResources Persistent | Core |
| XmNancestorSensitive | Core | XmNinsertPosition | Composite |
| XmNbackground | Core | XmNmappedWhenManaged | Core |
| XmNbackgroundPixmap | Core | XmNnavigationType | Manager |
| XmNborderColor | Core | XmNnumChildren | Composite |
| XmNborderPixmap | Core | XmNscreen | Core |
| XmNborderWidth | Core | XmNsensitive | Core |
| XmNbottomShadowColor | Manager | XmNshadowThickness | Manager |
| XmNbottomShadowPixmap | Manager | XmNstringDirection | Manager |
| XmNchildren | Composite | XmNtopShadowColor | Manager |
| XmNcolormap | Core | XmNtopShadowPixmap | Manager |
| XmNdepth | Core | XmNtranslations | Core |
| XmNdestroyCallback | Core | XmNtraversalOn | Manager |
| XmNforeground | Manager | XmNunitType | Manager |
| XmNheight | Core | XmNuserData | Manager |
| XmNhelpCallback | Manager | XmNwidth | Core |
| XmNhighlightColor | Manager | XmNx | Core |
| XmNhighlightPixmap | Manager | XmNy | Core |
| XmNinitialFocus | Manager | | |

## Translations

The translations for Frame are inherited from Manager.

## See Also

*XmCreateObject*(1),
*Composite*(2), *Constraint*(2), *Core*(2), *XmManager*(2).

# XmGadget



## Name

XmGadget widget class – the fundamental class for windowless widgets.

## Synopsis

**Public Header:** *<Xm/Xm.h>*

**Class Name:** XmGadget

**Class Hierarchy:** Object → RectObj → XmGadget

**Class Pointer:** `xmGadgetClass`

**Instantiation:** Gadget is a meta-class and is not normally instantiated.

**Functions/Macros:** `XmIsGadget()`

## Description

Gadget is a supporting superclass for other gadget classes. Gadget takes care of drawing and highlighting border shadows as well as managing traversal. A gadget uses its Manager widget parent's pixmap and color resources (e.g. `XmNforeground`) so take care when setting these resources via `XtSetValues()`. If you change such a resource in a manager widget, all of its gadget children are affected as well.

## New Resources

Gadget defines the following resources:

| Name | Class | Type | Default | Access |
|---|---|---|---|---|
| XmNbottomShadowColor | XmCBottomShadowColor | Pixel | dynamic | G |
| XmNhighlightColor | XmCHighlightColor | Pixel | dynamic | G |
| XmNhighlightOnEnter | XmCHighlightOnEnter | Boolean | False | CSG |
| XmNhighlightThickness | XmCHighlightThickness | Dimension | 2 | CSG |
| XmNnavigationType | XmCNavigationType | XmNavigation Type | XmNONE | CSG |
| XmNshadowThickness | XmCShadowThickness | Dimension | 2 | CSG |
| XmNtopShadowColor | XmCTopShadowColor | Pixel | dynamic | G |
| XmNtraversalOn | XmCTraversalOn | Boolean | True | CSG |
| XmNunitType | XmCUnitType | unsigned char | dynamic | CSG |
| XmNuserData | XmCUserData | XtPointer | NULL | CSG |

`XmNbottomShadowColor`

In Motif 1.2, the color used in drawing the border shadow's bottom and right sides.

`XmNhighlightColor`

In Motif 1.2, the color used in drawing the highlighting rectangle.

XmNhighlightOnEnter

Determines whether to draw a gadget's highlighting rectangle whenever the cursor moves into the gadget. This resource applies only when the shell has a focus policy of XmPOINTER. If the XmNhighlightOnEnter resource is True, highlighting is drawn; if False (default), highlighting is not drawn.

XmNhighlightThickness

The thickness of the highlighting rectangle.

XmNnavigationType

Determines the way in which gadgets are to be traversed during keyboard navigation. Possible values:

```
XmNONE                  /* exclude from keyboard navigation (default for */
                        /* non-shell parent ) */
XmTAB_GROUP             /* include in keyboard navigation (default when */
                        /* parent is a shell) */
XmSTICKY_TAB_GROUP      /* include in keyboard navigation, even if */
                        /* XmAddTabGroup() was called */
XmEXCLUSIVE_TAB_GROUP   /* application defines order of navigation */
```

XmNshadowThickness

The thickness of the shadow border.

XmNtopShadowColor

In Motif 1.2, the color used in drawing the border shadow's top and left sides.

XmNtraversalOn

If True (default), traversal of this gadget is made possible.

XmNunitType

The measurement units to use in resources that specify a size or position—for example, any resources of data type Dimension (whose names generally include one of the words "Margin" or "Thickness"). For a gadget whose parent is a Manager subclass, the default value is copied from this parent (provided the value hasn't been explicitly set by the application); otherwise, the default is XmPIXELS. Possible values:

```
XmPIXELS                Xm100TH_POINTS
Xm100TH_MILLIMETERS     Xm100TH_FONT_UNITS
Xm1000TH_INCHES
```

XmNuserData

A pointer to data that the application can attach to the gadget. This resource is unused internally.

## Callback Resources

Gadget defines the following callback resources:

| Callback | Reason Constant |
|---|---|
| XmNhelpCallback | XmCR_HELP |

XmNhelpCallback
List of callbacks that are called when help is requested.

## Callback Structure

Each callback function is passed the following structure:

```
typedef struct
{
        int      reason;     /* the reason that the callback was called */
        XEvent   *event;     /* event structure that triggered callback */
} XmAnyCallbackStruct;
```

## Inherited Resources

Gadget inherits the following resources. The resources are listed alphabetically, along with the superclass that defines them. Gadget resets the default value of XmNborderWidth from 1 to 0.

| Resource | Inherited From | Resource | Inherited From |
|---|---|---|---|
| XmNancestorSensitive | RectObj | XmNsensitive | RectObj |
| XmNborderWidth | RectObj | XmNwidth | RectObj |
| XmNdestroyCallback | Object | XmNx | RectObj |
| XmNheight | RectObj | XmNy | RectObj |

## Behavior

Since Gadgets cannot have translations associated with them, a Gadget's behavior is controlled by the Manager widget that contains the Gadget. If a Gadget has the keyboard focus, the Manager handles passing events to the Gadget.

## See Also

*Object*(2), *RectObj*(2), *XmManager*(2), *XmScreen*(2).

# XmInformationDialog

## Name

XmInformationDialog – an unmanaged MessageBox as a child of a DialogShell.

## Synopsis

**Public Header:** *<Xm/MessageB.h>*

**Instantiation:** `widget = XmCreateInformationDialog(...)`

**Functions/Macros:** `XmCreateInformationDialog()`, `XmMessageBoxGetChild()`

## Description

An InformationDialog is a compound object created by a call to `XmCreateInformationDialog()` that an application can use to provide the user with information. An InformationDialog consists of a DialogShell with an unmanaged MessageBox widget as its child. The MessageBox resource `XmNdialogType` is set to `XmDIALOG_INFORMATION`. An InformationDialog includes four components: a symbol, a message, three buttons, and a separator between the message and the buttons. By default, the symbol is a lowercase *i*. In Motif 1.2, the default button labels can be localized. In the C locale, and in Motif 1.1, the PushButtons are labeled **OK**, **Cancel**, and **Help** by default.

## Default Resource Values

An InformationDialog sets the following default values for MessageBox resources:

| Name | Default |
|---|---|
| XmNdialogType | XmDIALOG_INFORMATION |
| XmNsymbolPixmap | Xm_information |

## Widget Hierarchy

When an InformationDialog is created with a specified `name`, the DialogShell is named `name_popup` and the MessageBox is called `name`.

## See Also

*XmCreateObject*(1), *XmMessageBoxGetChild*(1), *XmDialogShell*(2), *XmMessageBox*(2).

# XmLabel

## Name

XmLabel widget class – a simple widget that displays a non-editable label.

## Synopsis

**Public Header:** *<Xm/Label.h>*

**Class Name:** XmLabel

**Class Hierarchy:** Core → XmPrimitive → XmLabel

**Class Pointer:** `xmLabelWidgetClass`

**Instantiation:** `widget = XtCreateWidget(name, xmLabelWidgetClass, ...)`

**Functions/Macros:** `XmCreateLabel(), XmIsLabel()`

## Description

Label provides a text string or a pixmap for labeling other widgets in an application. Label is also a superclass for the various button widgets. Label does not accept any button or key events, but it does receive enter and leave events.

## New Resources

Label defines the following resources:

| Name | Class | Type | Default | Access |
|---|---|---|---|---|
| XmNaccelerator | XmCAccelerator | String | NULL | CSG |
| XmNacceleratorText | XmCAcceleratorText | XmString | NULL | CSG |
| XmNalignment | XmCAlignment | unsigned char | dynamic | CSG |
| XmNfontList | XmCFontList | XmFontList | dynamic | CSG |
| XmNlabel InsensitivePixmap | XmCLabel InsensitivePixmap | Pixmap | XmUNSPECIFIED_ PIXMAP | CSG |
| XmNlabelPixmap | XmCLabelPixmap | Pixmap | XmUNSPECIFIED_ PIXMAP | CSG |
| XmNlabelString | XmCXmString | XmString | dynamic | CSG |
| XmNlabelType | XmCLabelType | unsigned char | XmSTRING | CSG |
| XmNmarginBottom | XmCMarginBottom | Dimension | 0 | CSG |
| XmNmarginHeight | XmCMarginHeight | Dimension | 2 | CSG |
| XmNmarginLeft | XmCMarginLeft | Dimension | 0 | CSG |
| XmNmarginRight | XmCMarginRight | Dimension | 0 | CSG |
| XmNmarginTop | XmCMarginTop | Dimension | 0 | CSG |
| XmNmarginWidth | XmCMarginWidth | Dimension | 2 | CSG |
| XmNmnemonic | XmCMnemonic | KeySym | NULL | CSG |
| XmNmnemonicCharSet | XmCMnemonicCharSet | String | XmFONTLIST_ DEFAULT_TAG | CSG |
| XmNrecomputeSize | XmCRecomputeSize | Boolean | True | CSG |

| Name | Class | Type | Default | Access |
|---|---|---|---|---|
| XmNstringDirection | XmCStringDirection | XmString Direction | dynamic | CSG |

`XmNaccelerator`
A string that describes a button widget's accelerator (the modifiers and key to use as a shortcut in selecting the button). The string's format is like that of a translation but allows only a single key press event to be specified.

`XmNacceleratorText`
The text that is displayed for an accelerator.

`XmNalignment`
The alignment (left to right) for a label's text or pixmap. Possible values are `XmALIGNMENT_BEGINNING`, `XmALIGNMENT_CENTER`, and `XmALIGNMENT_END`.

`XmNfontList`
The font list used for the widget's text. If this value is initially `NULL`, the font list is derived from the `XmNlabelFontList` or `buttonFontList` resource from the nearest parent that is a subclass of BulletinBoard, MenuShell, or VendorShell.

`XmNlabelInsensitivePixmap`
The pixmap label for an insensitive button (when `XmNlabelType` is `XmPIXMAP`).

`XmNlabelPixmap`
The pixmap used when `XmNlabelType` is `XmPIXMAP`.

`XmNlabelString`
The compound string used when `XmNlabelType` is `XmSTRING`. If this resource is `NULL`, the application uses the widget's name (converted to compound string format).

`XmNlabelType`
The type of label (either string or pixmap). Possible values:

```
XmPIXMAP     /* use XmNlabelPixmap or XmNlabelInsensitvePixmap */
XmSTRING     /* use XmNlabelString */
```

`XmNmarginTop`, `XmNmarginBottom`,
`XmNmarginLeft`, `XmNmarginRight`
The amount of space between one side of the label text and the nearest margin.

`XmNmarginHeight`
`XmNmarginWidth`
The spacing between one side of the label and the nearest edge of a shadow.

`XmNmnemonic`
A keysym that gives the user another way to select a button. In the label string, the first character matching this keysym will be underlined.

XmNmnemonicCharSet
The character set for the label's mnemonic.

XmNrecomputeSize
If True (default), the Label widget changes its size so that the string or pixmap fits exactly.

XmNstringDirection
The direction in which to draw the string. Possible values are XmSTRING_DIRECTION_L_TO_R and XmSTRING_DIRECTION_R_TO_L.

## Callback Structure

Each callback function is passed the following structure:

```
typedef struct
{
    int     reason;      /* set to XmCR_HELP */
    XEvent *event;       /* points to event structure that triggered callback */
} XmAnyCallbackStruct;
```

## Inherited Resources

Label inherits the following resources. The resources are listed alphabetically, along with the superclass that defines them. Label sets the default values of XmNhighlightThickness and XmNshadowThickness to 0 and XmNtraversalOn to False. The default value of XmNborderWidth is reset to 0 by Primitive.

| Resource | Inherited From | Resource | Inherited From |
|---|---|---|---|
| XmNaccelerators | Core | XmNhighlightPixmap | Primitive |
| XmNancestorSensitive | Core | XmNhighlightThickness | Primitive |
| XmNbackground | Core | XmNinitialResources Persistent | Core |
| XmNbackgroundPixmap | Core | XmNmappedWhenManaged | Core |
| XmNborderColor | Core | XmNnavigationType | Primitive |
| XmNborderPixmap | Core | XmNscreen | Core |
| XmNborderWidth | Core | XmNsensitive | Core |
| XmNbottomShadowColor | Primitive | XmNshadowThickness | Primitive |
| XmNbottomShadowPixmap | Primitive | XmNtopShadowColor | Primitive |
| XmNcolormap | Core | XmNtopShadowPixmap | Primitive |
| XmNdepth | Core | XmNtranslations | Core |
| XmNdestroyCallback | Core | XmNtraversalOn | Primitive |
| XmNforeground | Primitive | XmNunitType | Primitive |
| XmNheight | Core | XmNuserData | Primitive |
| XmNhelpCallback | Primitive | XmNwidth | Core |

| Resource | Inherited From | Resource | Inherited From |
|---|---|---|---|
| XmNhighlightColor | Primitive | XmNx | Core |
| XmNhighlightOnEnter | Primitive | XmNy | Core |

## Translations

```
BTransfer Press   ProcessDrag()
KHelp             Help()
```

For subclasses of Label:

```
KLeft          MenuTraverseLeft()
KRight         MenuTraverseRight()
KUp            MenuTraverseUp()
KDown          MenuTraverseDown()
MAny KCancel   MenuEscape()
```

## Action Routines

Label defines the following action routines:

`Help()` Unposts menus, restores keyboard focus, and invokes the callbacks from `XmNhelpCallback`, if there are any.

`MenuEscape()`
Unposts the menu, disarms the associated CascadeButton, and restores keyboard focus.

`MenuTraverseDown()`
In a MenuBar, if the current menu item has a submenu, posts the submenu, disarms the current menu item, and arms the first item in the submenu. In a menu pane, disarms the current menu item and arms the item below it, wrapping around to the top if necessary.

`MenuTraverseLeft()`
In a MenuBar, disarms the current menu item and arms the next item to the left, wrapping if necessary. In a menu pane, disarms the current item and arms the item to the left if there is such an item. Otherwise, unposts the current submenu and, if that submenu is attached to a MenuBar item, traverses to the MenuBar item to the left (wrapping if necessary), posts the submenu, and arms the first item in the submenu. In a PopupMenu or a torn-off menu pane, traverses to the menu item to the left, wrapping to the right if necessary.

`MenuTraverseRight()`
In a MenuBar, disarms the current menu item and arms the next item to the right, wrapping if necessary. In a menu pane, if the current item is a CascadeButton, posts the associated submenu. Otherwise, disarms the current item and arms the item to the right if there is such an item or unposts all submenus, traverses to the

MenuBar item to the right (wrapping if necessary), posts the submenu, and arms the first item in the submenu. In a PopupMenu or a torn-off menu pane, traverses to the menu item to the right, wrapping to the left if necessary.

`MenuTraverseUp()`
: In a menu pane, disarms the current menu item and arms the item above it, wrapping around to the bottom if necessary.

`ProcessDrag()`
: In Motif 1.2, initiates a drag and drop operation using the contents of the Label.

## See Also

*XmCreateObject*(1),
*Core*(2), *XmPrimitive*(2).

# XmLabelGadget

## Name

XmLabelGadget widget class – a simple gadget that displays a non-editable label.

## Synopsis

**Public Header:** *<Xm/LabelG.h>*

**Class Name:** XmLabelGadget

**Class Hierarchy:** Object → RectObj → XmGadget → XmLabelGadget

**Class Pointer:** xmLabelGadgetClass

**Instantiation:** `widget = XtCreateWidget(name, xmLabelWGadgetClass, ...)`

**Functions/Macros:** `XmCreateLabelGadget()`, `XmOptionLabelGadget()`, `XmIsLabelGadget()`

## Description

LabelGadget is the gadget variant of Label.

LabelGadget's new resources and callback structure are the same as those for Label.

## Inherited Resources

LabelGadget inherits the following resources. The resources are listed alphabetically, along with the superclass that defines them. LabelGadget sets the default values of `XmNhighlightThickness` and `XmNshadowThickness` to 0 and `XmNtraversalOn` to `False`. The default value of `XmNborderWidth` is reset to 0 by Gadget.

| Resource | Inherited From | Resource | Inherited From |
|---|---|---|---|
| XmNancestorSensitive | RectObj | XmNsensitive | RectObj |
| XmNborderWidth | RectObj | XmNshadowThickness | Gadget |
| XmNbottomShadowColor | Gadget | XmNtopShadowColor | Gadget |
| XmNdestroyCallback | Object | XmNtraversalOn | Gadget |
| XmNheight | RectObj | XmNunitType | Gadget |
| XmNhelpCallback | Gadget | XmNuserData | Gadget |
| XmNhighlightColor | Gadget | XmNwidth | RectObj |
| XmNhighlightOnEnter | Gadget | XmNx | RectObj |
| XmNhighlightThickness | Gadget | XmNy | RectObj |
| XmNnavigationType | Gadget | | |

## Behavior

As a Gadget subclass, LabelGadget has no translations associated with it. However, LabelGadget behavior corresponds to the action routines of the Label widget. See the Label action routines for more information.

| Behavior | Equivalent Label Action Routine |
|---|---|
| BTransfer Press | ProcessDrag() |
| KHelp | Help() |
| KLeft | MenuTraverseLeft() |
| KRight | MenuTraverseRight() |
| KUp | MenuTraverseUp() |
| KDown | MenuTraverseDown() |
| MAny KCancel | MenuEscape() |

## See Also

*XmCreateObject*(1), *XmOptionLabelGadget*(1),
*Object*(2), *RectObj*(2), *XmGadget*(2), *XmLabel*(2).

## Name

XmList widget class – a widget that allows a user to select from a list of choices.

## Synopsis

**Public Header:** *<Xm/List.h>*

**Class Name:** XmList

**Class Hierarchy:** Core → XmPrimitive → XmList

**Class Pointer:** `xmListWidgetClass`

**Instantiation:** `widget = XtCreateWidget(name, xmListWidgetClass, ...)`

**Functions/Macros:** `XmCreateList()`, `XmCreateScrolledList()`, `XmList...` routines, `XmIsList()`

## Description

List provides a list of choices from which a user can select one or more items, based on the selection policy. List supports four selection policies: single select, browse select, multiple select, and extended select.

In single select mode, only one item can be selected at a time; a button press on an item selects it and deselects the previously selected item. In browse select mode, only one item can be selected at a time; a button press works as in single select mode and, additionally, a button drag moves the selection with the pointer. In multiple select mode, any number of items can be selected at a time; a button press toggles the selection state of an item and does not change the selection state of any other items. In extended select mode, any number of items can be selected at a time; discontiguous ranges of items can be selected by combining button presses and button drags.

Selections can be made by using either the pointer or the keyboard. Keyboard selection has two modes: normal mode and add mode. In normal mode, keyboard navigation operations affect the selection; the item with the keyboard focus is always selected. In add mode, keyboard navigation operations are distinct from selection operations; the item with the keyboard focus can be disjoint from the selection. Browse select operates in normal mode; single select and multiple select operate in add mode; extended select can be made to operate in either mode. Normal mode uses a solid location cursor while add mode uses a dashed location cursor.

In Motif 1.2, List is a supported drag source for drag and drop operations. `BTransfer Press` starts a drag and drop operation using the selected items in the list. If `BTransfer` is pressed over an unselected item, that item is dragged instead of the selected items.

## New Resources

List defines the following resources:

| Name | Class | Type | Default | Access |
|---|---|---|---|---|
| XmNautomatic Selection | XmCAutomatic Selection | Boolean | False | CSG |
| XmNdoubleClick Interval | XmCDoubleClick Interval | int | dynamic | CSG |
| XmNfontList | XmCFontList | XmFontList | dynamic | CSG |
| XmNitemCount | XmCItemCount | int | 0 | CSG |
| XmNitems | XmCItems | XmString Table | NULL | CSG |
| XmNlistMarginHeight | XmCListMarginHeight | Dimension | 0 | CSG |
| XmNlistMarginWidth | XmCListMarginWidth | Dimension | 0 | CSG |
| XmNlistSizePolicy | XmCListSizePolicy | unsigned char | XmVARIABLE | CG |
| XmNlistSpacing | XmCListSpacing | Dimension | 0 | CSG |
| XmNscrollBar DisplayPolicy | XmCScrollBar DisplayPolicy | unsigned char | XmAS_NEEDED | CSG |
| XmNselectedItemCount | XmCSelectedItemCount | int | 0 | CSG |
| XmNselectedItems | XmCSelectedItems | XmString Table | NULL | CSG |
| XmNselectionPolicy | XmCSelectionPolicy | unsigned char | XmBROWSE_ SELECT | CSG |
| XmNstringDirection | XmCStringDirection | XmString Direction | dynamic | CSG |
| XmNtopItemPosition | XmCTopItemPosition | int | 1 | CSG |
| XmNvisibleItemCount | XmCVisibleItemCount | int | dynamic | CSG |

XmNautomaticSelection

If True (and the widget's XmNselectionPolicy is either XmBROWSE_SELECT or XmEXTENDED_SELECT), then this resource calls XmNsingleSelection-Callback whenever the user moves into a new item. If False, then the user must release the mouse button before any selection callbacks are called.

XmNdoubleClickInterval

The time span (in milliseconds) within which two button clicks must occur to be considered a double click rather than two single clicks. By default, this value is the multiclick time of the display.

XmNfontList

The font list used for the items in the list. If this value is initially NULL, the font list is derived from the XmNtextFontList resource from the nearest parent that is a subclass of BulletinBoard or VendorShell. This resource, together with the XmNvisibleItemsCount resource, is used to calculate the List widget's height.

`XmNitemCount`

The total number of items. The widget updates this resource every time a list item is added or removed.

`XmNitems`

A pointer to an array of compound strings. The compound strings are the list items to display. A call to `XtGetValues()` returns the actual list items (not a copy), so don't have your application free these items.

`XmNlistMarginHeight`
`XmNlistMarginWidth`

The height or width of the margin between the border of the list and the items in the list.

`XmNlistSizePolicy`

The method for resizing the widget when a list item exceeds the width of the work area. This resizing policy must be set at creation time. Possible values:

```
XmVARIABLE              /* grow to fit; don't add ScrollBar */
XmCONSTANT              /* don't grow to fit; add ScrollBar */
XmRESIZE_IF_POSSIBLE    /* grow or shrink; add ScrollBar if too large */
```

`XmNlistSpacing`

The spacing between items.

`XmNscrollBarDisplayPolicy`

Determines when to display vertical scrollbars in a ScrolledList widget. Possible values:

```
XmSTATIC                /* vertical ScrollBar always displays */
XmAS_NEEDED             /* add ScrollBar when list is too large */
```

`XmNselectedItemCount`

The number of items in the list of selected items.

`XmNselectedItems`

A pointer to an array of compound strings. The compound strings represent the currently selected list items. A call to `XtGetValues()` returns the actual list items (not a copy), so don't have your application free these items.

`XmNselectionPolicy`

Determines the effect of a selection action. Possible values:

```
XmSINGLE_SELECT         XmBROWSE_SELECT
XmMULTIPLE_SELECT       XmEXTENDED_SELECT
```

`XmNstringDirection`

The direction in which to draw the string. Possible values are `XmSTRING_DIRECTION_L_TO_R` and `XmSTRING_DIRECTION_R_TO_L`.

`XmNtopItemPosition`
The position of the first item that will be visible in the list. Calling the `XmListSetPos()` routine is the same as setting this resource. In both cases, the first position is specified as 1 and the last position is specified as 0.

`XmNvisibleItemCount`
The number of items to display in the work area of the list. This value affects the widget's height. In Motif 1.2, the default value of this resource is dynamic and based on the height of the List, while in Motif 1.1, the default value is 1.

## Callback Resources

List defines the following callback resources:

| Callback | Reason Constant |
|---|---|
| XmNbrowseSelectionCallback | XmCR_BROWSE_SELECT |
| XmNdefaultActionCallback | XmCR_DEFAULT_ACTION |
| XmNextendedSelectionCallback | XmCR_EXTENDED_SELECT |
| XmNmultipleSelectionCallback | XmCR_MULTIPLE_SELECT |
| XmNsingleSelectionCallback | XmCR_SINGLE_SELECT |

`XmNbrowseSelectionCallback`
List of callbacks that are called when a list item is selected using the browse selection policy.

`XmNdefaultActionCallback`
List of callbacks that are called when a list item is double clicked or `KActivate` is pressed.

`XmNextendedSelectionCallback`
List of callbacks that are called when list items are selected using the extended selection policy.

`XmNmultipleSelectionCallback`
List of callbacks that are called when a list item is selected using the multiple selection policy.

`XmNsingleSelectionCallback`
List of callbacks that are called when a list item is selected using the single selection policy.

## Callback Structure

Each callback function is passed the structure below; however, some structure members might be unused because they aren't meaningful for particular callback reasons.

```
typedef struct
{
   int        reason;              /* the reason that the callback was called */
```

```
   XEvent    *event;             /* points to event structure that triggered callback */
   XmString  item;               /* item that was most recently selected at */
                                 /* the time event occurred */
   int       item_length;        /* number of bytes in item member */
   int       item_position;      /* item's position within the XmNitems array */
   XmString  *selected_items;    /* list of items selected at the time */
                                 /* event occurred */
   int       selected_item_count;/* number of items in selected_items */
   int       *selected_item_positions;/* array of integers that mark  */
                                 /* selected items */
   int       selection_type;     /* type of the most recent selection */
} XmListCallbackStruct;
```

The structure members event, item, item_length, and item_position are valid for any value of reason. The structure members selected_items, selected_item_count, and selected_item_ positions are valid when the reason field has a value of XmCR_MULTIPLE_SELECT or XmCR_EXTENDED_SELECT. The structure member selection_type is valid only when the reason field is XmCR_EXTENDED_SELECT.

For the strings pointed to by item and selected_items, as well as for the integers pointed to by selected_item_positions, storage is overwritten each time the callback is invoked. Applications that need to save this data should make their own copies of it.

selected_item_positions is an integer array. The elements of the array indicate the positions of each selected item within the List widget's XmNitems array.

selection_type specifies what kind of extended selection was most recently made. One of three values is possible:

```
XmINITIAL         /* selection was the initial selection */
XmMODIFICATION    /* selection changed an existing selection */
XmADDITION        /* selection added non-adjacent items to existing selection */
```

## Inherited Resources

List inherits the following resources. The resources are listed alphabetically, along with the superclass that defines them. List sets the default value of XmNnavigationType to Xm-TAB_GROUP. The default value of XmNborderWidth is reset to 0 by Primitive.

| Resource | Inherited From | Resource | Inherited From |
|---|---|---|---|
| XmNaccelerators | Core | XmNhighlightPixmap | Primitive |
| XmNancestorSensitive | Core | XmNhighlightThickness | Primitive |
| XmNbackground | Core | XmNinitialResourcesPersistent | Core |
| XmNbackgroundPixmap | Core | XmNmappedWhenManaged | Core |
| XmNborderColor | Core | XmNnavigationType | Primitive |
| XmNborderPixmap | Core | XmNscreen | Core |
| XmNborderWidth | Core | XmNsensitive | Core |

Motif and Xt Widget Classes

| Resource | Inherited From | Resource | Inherited From |
|---|---|---|---|
| XmNbottomShadowColor | Primitive | XmNshadowThickness | Primitive |
| XmNbottomShadowPixmap | Primitive | XmNtopShadowColor | Primitive |
| XmNcolormap | Core | XmNtopShadowPixmap | Primitive |
| XmNdepth | Core | XmNtranslations | Core |
| XmNdestroyCallback | Core | XmNtraversalOn | Primitive |
| XmNforeground | Primitive | XmNunitType | Primitive |
| XmNheight | Core | XmNuserData | Primitive |
| XmNhelpCallback | Primitive | XmNwidth | Core |
| XmNhighlightColor | Primitive | XmNx | Core |
| XmNhighlightOnEnter | Primitive | XmNy | Core |

## Translations

| Event | Action | Event | Action |
|---|---|---|---|
| BSelect Press | ListBeginSelect() | KBeginLine | ListBeginLine() |
| BSelect Motion | ListButtonMotion() | KEndLine | ListEndLine() |
| BSelect Release | ListEndSelect() | KBeginData | ListBeginData() |
| BExtend Press | ListBeginExtend() | MShift KBeginData | ListBeginDataExtend() |
| BExtend Motion | ListButtonMotion() | KEndData | ListEndData() |
| BExtend Release | ListEndExtend() | MShift KEndData | ListEndDataExtend() |
| BToggle Press | ListBeginToggle() | KAddMode | ListAddMode() |
| BToggle Motion | ListButtonMotion() | KActivate | ListKbdActivate() |
| BToggle Release | ListEndToggle() | KCopy Press | ListCopyToClipboard() |
| BTransfer Press | ListProcessDrag() | KSelect Press | ListKbdBeginSelect() |
| KUp | ListPrevItem() | KSelect Release | ListKbdEndSelect() |
| MShift KUp | ListExtend PrevItem() | KExtend Press | ListKbdBeginExtend() |
| KDown | ListNextItem() | KExtend Release | ListKbdEndExtend() |
| MShift KDown | ListExtend NextItem() | MAny KCancel | ListKbdCancel() |
| KLeft | ListLeftChar() | KSelectAll | ListKbdSelectAll() |
| MCtrl KLeft | ListLeftPage() | KDeselectAll | ListKbdDeSelectAll() |
| KRight | ListRightChar() | KHelp | PrimitiveHelp() |
| MCtrl KRight | ListRightPage() | KNextField | PrimitiveNextTabGroup() |
| KPageUp | ListPrevPage() | KPrevField | PrimitivePrevTabGroup() |
| KPageDown | ListNextPage() | | |
| KPageLeft | ListLeftPage() | | |
| KPageRight | ListRightPage() | | |

## Action Routines

List defines the action routines below. The current selection always appears with its foreground and background colors reversed. Note that many List actions have different effects depending on the selection policy and also that some actions apply only for a particular selection policy.

`ListAddMode()`
: Turns add mode on or off.

`ListBeginData()`
: Moves the cursor to the first list item. If keyboard selection is in normal mode, this action also selects the first item after deselecting any earlier selection and invokes the callbacks specified either by `XmNbrowseSelectionCallback` or by `XmNextendedSelectionCallback` (as dictated by the selection policy).

`ListBeginDataExtend()`
: *Multiple selection*: moves the cursor to the first list item.
: *Extended selection*: moves the cursor to the first list item, cancels any current extended selection, selects (or deselects) all items from the first item to the current anchor, and invokes the callbacks specified by `XmNextendedSelectionCallback`.

`ListBeginExtend()`
: *Extended selection*: cancels any current extended selection, selects (or deselects) all items from the pointer location to the current anchor, and invokes the callbacks specified by `XmNextendedSelectionCallback` (if the `XmNautomaticSelection` resource is `True`).

`ListBeginLine()`
: Scrolls the List's viewing area horizontally to its beginning.

`ListBeginSelect()`
: *Single selection*: selects or deselects the item under the pointer after deselecting any previous selection.
: *Browse selection*: selects the item under the pointer after deselecting any previous selection and invokes the callbacks specified by `XmNbrowseSelectionCallback` if the `XmNautomaticSelection` resource is `True`.
: *Multiple selection*: selects or deselects the item under the pointer, leaving previous selections unaffected.
: *Extended selection*: selects the item under the pointer after deselecting any previous selection, marks this item as the current anchor, and invokes the callbacks specified by `XmNextendedSelectionCallback` if the `XmNautomaticSelection` resource is `True`.

`ListBeginToggle()`
: *Extended selection*: keeps the current selection but shifts the anchor to the item under the pointer. This item's selection state is toggled, and if `XmNautomaticSelection` is `True`, the extended selection callbacks are invoked.

`ListButtonMotion()`
: *Browse selection*: selects the item under the pointer after deselecting any previous selection and invokes the browse selection callbacks if `XmNautomaticSelection` is `True` and the pointer moved over a new item.
*Extended selection*: cancels any current extended selection, selects (or deselects) all items from the pointer location to the current anchor, and invokes the extended selection callbacks if `XmNautomaticSelection` is `True` and the pointer moved over a new item.
In addition, when the pointer moves outside a ScrolledList widget, the list scrolls in sync with the pointer motion.

`ListCopyToClipboard()`
: In Motif 1.2, this action copies the selected list items to the clipboard. The items are copied as a single compound string, with a newline between each item.

`ListEndData()`
: Moves the cursor to the last list item. If keyboard selection is in normal mode, this action also selects the last item after deselecting any earlier selection and invokes the appropriate callbacks (browse selection or extended selection).

`ListEndDataExtend()`
: *Multiple selection*: moves the cursor to the last list item.
*Extended selection*: moves the cursor to the last list item, cancels any current extended selection, selects (or deselects) all items from the last item to the current anchor, and invokes the extended selection callbacks.

`ListEndExtend()`
: *Extended selection*: moves the cursor to the last item whose selection state was switched, and invokes the extended selection callbacks if `XmNautomaticSelection` is `False`.

`ListEndLine()`
: Scrolls the List's viewing area horizontally to its beginning.

`ListEndSelect()`
: *Single selection or multiple selection*: moves the cursor to the last item whose selection state was switched, and invokes the appropriate selection callbacks.
*Browse selection or extended selection*: same as above, except that the appropriate callbacks are called only if `XmNautomaticSelection` is `False`.

`ListEndToggle()`

*Extended selection*: moves the cursor to the last item whose selection state was switched, and invokes the extended selection callbacks if `XmNautomatic-Selection` is `False`.

`ListExtendNextItem()`
`ListExtendPrevItem()`

*Extended selection*: adds the next/previous item to an extended selection and invokes the extended selection callbacks.

`ListKbdActivate()`

Invokes the default action callbacks.

`ListKbdBeginExtend()`

This action is the keyboard's complement to the mouse-activated `ListBegin-Extend()` action.

*Extended selection*: cancels any current extended selection and selects (or deselects) all items from the cursor to the current anchor.

`ListKbdBeginSelect()`

This action is the keyboard's complement to the mouse-activated `ListBegin-Select()` action.

*Single selection*: selects or deselects the item at the cursor after deselecting any previous selection.

*Browse selection*: selects the item at the cursor after deselecting any previous selection and invokes the browse selection callbacks if `XmNautomatic-Selection` is `True`.

*Multiple selection*: selects or deselects the item at the cursor, leaving previous selections unaffected.

*Extended selection*: shifts the anchor to the item at the cursor. In normal mode, this item is selected after any previous selection is deselected; in add mode, this item's state is toggled, and the current selection remains unaffected. This action calls the extended selection callbacks if `XmNautomaticSelection` is `True`.

`ListKbdCancel()`

*Extended selection*: cancels an extended selection and restores the items to their previous selection state.

`ListKbdDeSelectAll()`

Deselects all list items and calls the appropriate selection callbacks. This action applies to all selection modes except browse selection because this mode requires one item to remain selected at all times. In extended selection with keyboard Normal Mode and an `XmNkeyboardFocusPolicy` of `XmEXPLICIT`, the item at the cursor remains selected after this action is applied.

`ListKbdEndExtend()`

*Extended selection*: calls the extended selection callbacks if `XmNautomatic-Selection` is `False`.

`ListKbdEndSelect()`
: *Single selection or multiple selection*: calls the appropriate selection callbacks. If `XmNautomaticSelection` is `False`, this action applies under any of the four selection policies.

`ListKbdSelectAll()`
: *Single selection or browse selection*: selects the item at the cursor and calls the appropriate selection callbacks.
*Multiple selection or extended selection*: selects all list items and calls the appropriate selection callbacks.

`ListLeftChar()`
`ListLeftPage()`
: Scrolls the list either one character or one page to the left.

`ListNextItem()`
: Moves the cursor to the next list item and has the following additional operations:
*Browse selection*: selects this item, deselects any previously selected item(s), and calls the browse selection callbacks.
*Extended selection*: in normal mode, selects this item and moves the anchor there, deselects any previously selected item(s), and calls the extended selection callbacks. In add mode, neither the selection nor the anchor is affected.

`ListNextPage()`
: Moves the cursor by scrolling the list to the list item at the top of the next page and has the same additional operations as `ListNextItem()`.

`ListPrevItem()`
: Same as `ListNextItem()`, going back one item instead.

`ListPrevPage()`
: Same as `ListNextPage()`, going back one page instead.

`ListProcessDrag()`
: In Motif 1.2, this action initiates a drag and drop operation using the selected items, where each item is separated by a newline. If `BTransfer` is pressed over an unselected item, only that item is used in the drag and drop operation.

`ListRightChar()`
`ListRightPage()`
: Scrolls the list either one character or one page to the right.

`PrimitiveHelp()`
: Calls the help callbacks for this widget.

`PrimitiveNextTabGroup()`
`PrimitivePrevTabGroup()`
: Moves the keyboard focus to the beginning of the next or previous tab group, wrapping around if necessary.

### Additional Behavior

List has the following additional behavior:

`<Double Click>`
: Calls the `XmNdefaultActionCallback` callbacks.

`<FocusIn>`
: Sets the keyboard focus and draws a location cursor under the explicit keyboard focus policy.

`<FocusOut>`
: Removes the keyboard focus and erases the location cursor under the explicit keyboard focus policy.

### See Also

*XmCreateObject*(1), *XmListAddItem*(1), *XmListAddItemUnselected*(1), *XmListDeleteAllItems*(1), *XmListDeleteItem*(1), *XmListDeleteItemsPos*(1), *XmListDeletePos*(1), *XmListDeletePositions*(1), *XmListDeselectAllItems*(1), *XmListDeselectItem*(1), *XmListDeselectPos*(1), *XmListGetKbdItemPos*(1), *XmListGetMatchPos*(1), *XmListGetSelectedPos*(1), *XmListItemExists*(1), *XmListItemPos*(1), *XmListPosSelected*(1), *XmListPosToBounds*(1), *XmListReplaceItems*(1), *XmListReplaceItemsPos*(1), *XmListReplaceItemsPosUnselected*(1), *XmListReplaceItemsUnselected*(1), *XmListReplacePositions*(1), *XmListSelectItem*(1), *XmListSelectPos*(1), *XmListSetAddMode*(1), *XmListSetBottomItem*(1), *XmListSetBottomPos*(1), *XmListSetHorizPos*(1), *XmListSetItem*(1), *XmListSetKbdItemPos*(1), *XmListSetPos*(1), *XmListUpdateSelectedList*(1), *XmListYToPos*(1), *Core*(2), *XmPrimitive*(2).

# XmMainWindow

## Name

XmMainWindow widget class – the standard layout widget for an application's primary window.

## Synopsis

**Public Header:** *<Xm/MainW.h>*

**Class Name:** XmMainWindow

**Class Hierarchy:** Core → Composite → Constraint → XmManager → XmScrolledWindow → XmMainWindow

**Class Pointer:** `xmMainWindowWidgetClass`

**Instantiation:** `widget = XtCreateWidget(name, xmMainWindowWidgetClass, ...)`

**Functions/Macros:** `XmCreateMainWindow()`, `XmMainWindowSep1()`, `XmMainWindowSep2()`, `XmMainWindowSep3()`, `XmMainWindowSetAreas()`, `XmIsMainWindow()`

## Description

MainWindow provides the standard appearance for the primary window of an application. MainWindow supports five standard areas: a MenuBar, a command window, a work region, a message window, and two ScrollBars (one horizontal and one vertical). An application can use as many or as few of these areas as necessary; they are all optional. A MainWindow can also display three Separator widgets for dividing one area from another.

Each of the MainWindow regions is associated with a MainWindow resource; `XmMainWindowSetAreas()` sets the associated resources. If an application does not call `XmMainWindowSetAreas()`, the widget may still set some of the standard regions. When a MenuBar child is added to a MainWindow, if `XmNmenuBar` has not been set, it is set to the MenuBar child. When a Command child is added to a MainWindow, if `XmNcommand` has not been set, it is set to the Command child. If ScrollBars are added as children, the `XmNhorizontalScrollBar` and `XmNverticalScrollBar` resources may be set if they have not already been specified. Any child that is not one of these types is used for the `XmNworkWindow`. If you want to be certain about which widgets are used for the different regions, it is wise to call `XmMainWindowSetAreas()` explicitly.

## New Resources

MainWindow defines the following resources:

| Name | Class | Type | Default | Access |
|---|---|---|---|---|
| XmNcommandWindow | XmCCommandWindow | Window | NULL | CSG |
| XmNcommandWindowLocation | XmCCommandWindowLocation | unsigned char | XmCOMMAND_ABOVE_WORKSPACE | CG |

| Name | Class | Type | Default | Access |
|---|---|---|---|---|
| XmNmainWindow MarginHeight | XmCMainWindow MarginHeight | Dimension | 0 | CSG |
| XmNmainWindow MarginWidth | XmCMainWindow MarginWidth | Dimension | 0 | CSG |
| XmNmenuBar | XmCMenuBar | Window | NULL | CSG |
| XmNmessage Window | XmCMessage Window | Window | NULL | CSG |
| XmNshow Separator | XmCShow Separator | Boolean | False | CSG |

XmNcommandWindow
: The widget ID of the command window child.

XmNcommandWindowLocation
: One of two positions for the command window. Possible values:

```
XmCOMMAND_ABOVE_WORKSPACE  /* default; appears below menu bar */
XmCOMMAND_BELOW_WORKSPACE  /* appears between work window and message window */
```

XmNmainWindowMarginHeight
: The margin on the top and bottom of the MainWindow widget. This resource overrides the corresponding margin resource in the ScrolledWindow widget.

XmNmainWindowMarginWidth
: The margin on the right and left of the MainWindow widget. This resource overrides the corresponding margin resource in the ScrolledWindow widget.

XmNmenuBar
: The widget ID of the menu bar child.

XmNmessageWindow
: The widget ID of the message window child.

XmNshowSeparator
: If True, separators are displayed between components of the MainWindow widget. If False (default), separators are not displayed.

### Inherited Resources

MainWindow inherits the following resources. The resources are listed alphabetically, along with the superclass that defines them. The default value of XmNborderWidth is reset to 0 by Manager.

| Resource | Inherited From | Resource | Inherited From |
|---|---|---|---|
| XmNaccelerators | Core | XmNnumChildren | Composite |
| XmNancestorSensitive | Core | XmNscreen | Core |

Motif and Xt Widget Classes

| Resource | Inherited From | Resource | Inherited From |
|---|---|---|---|
| XmNbackground | Core | XmNscrollBar DisplayPolicy | Scrolled Window |
| XmNbackgroundPixmap | Core | XmNscrollBar Placement | Scrolled Window |
| XmNborderColor | Core | XmNscrolledWindow MarginHeight | Scrolled Window |
| XmNborderPixmap | Core | XmNscrolledWindow MarginWidth | Scrolled Window |
| XmNborderWidth | Core | XmNscrollingPolicy | Scrolled Window |
| XmNbottomShadowColor | Manager | XmNsensitive | Core |
| XmNbottomShadowPixmap | Manager | XmNshadowThickness | Manager |
| XmNchildren | Composite | XmNspacing | Scrolled Window |
| XmNclipWindow | Scrolled Window | XmNstringDirection | Manager |
| XmNcolormap | Core | XmNtopShadowColor | Manager |
| XmNdepth | Core | XmNtopShadowPixmap | Manager |
| XmNdestroyCallback | Core | XmNtranslations | Core |
| XmNforeground | Manager | XmNtraversalOn | Manager |
| XmNheight | Core | XmNunitType | Manager |
| XmNhelpCallback | Manager | XmNuserData | Manager |
| XmNhighlightColor | Manager | XmNvertical ScrollBar | Scrolled Window |
| XmNhighlightPixmap | Manager | XmNvisualPolicy | Scrolled Window |
| XmNhorizontal ScrollBar | Scrolled Window | XmNwidth | Core |
| XmNinitialFocus | Manager | XmNworkWindow | Scrolled Window |
| XmNinitialResources Persistent | Core | XmNx | Core |
| XmNinsertPosition | Composite | XmNy | Core |
| XmNmappedWhenManaged | Core | | |
| XmNnavigationType | Manager | | |

## Translations

The translations for MainWindow are inherited from ScrolledWindow.

## See Also

*XmCreateObject*(1), *XmMainWindowSep*(1), *XmMainWindowSetAreas*(1), *Composite*(2), *Constraint*(2), *Core*(2), *XmManager*(2), *XmScrolledWindow*(2).

# XmManager

## Name

XmManager widget class – the fundamental class for Motif widgets that manage children.

## Synopsis

**Public Header:** *<Xm/Xm.h>*

**Class Name:** XmManager

**Class Hierarchy:** Core → Composite → Constraint → XmManager

**Class Pointer:** `xmManagerWidgetClass`

**Instantiation:** Manager is a meta-class and is not normally instantiated.

**Functions/Macros:** `XmIsManager()`

## Description

Manager is a superclass for Motif widget classes that contain children. Manager supports geometry management by providing resources for visual shadows and highlights and for keyboard traversal mechanisms.

The default values of the color resources for the foreground, background, top and bottom shadows, and highlighting are set dynamically. If no colors are specified, they are generated automatically. On a monochrome system, black and white colors are selected. On a color system, four colors are selected that provide the appropriate shading for the 3-D visuals. When the background color is specified, the shadow colors are selected to provide the appropriate 3-D appearance and foreground and highlight colors are selected to provide the necessary contrast. The colors are generated when the widget is created; using `XtSetValues()` to change the background does not change the other colors. With Motif 1.2, use `XmChangeColor()` to change the associated colors when the background color is changed.

## New Resources

Manager defines the following resources:

| Name | Class | Type | Default | Access |
|---|---|---|---|---|
| XmNbottomShadowColor | XmCBottomShadowColor | Pixel | dynamic | CSG |
| XmNbottomShadowPixmap | XmCBottomShadowPixmap | Pixmap | XmUNSPECIFIED_PIXMAP | CSG |
| XmNforeground | XmCForeground | Pixel | dynamic | CSG |
| XmNhighlightColor | XmCHighlightColor | Pixel | dynamic | CSG |
| XmNhighlightPixmap | XmCHighlightPixmap | Pixmap | dynamic | CSG |
| XmNinitialFocus | XmCInitialFocus | Widget | NULL | CSG |
| XmNnavigationType | XmCNavigationType | XmNavigationType | XmTAB_GROUP | CSG |
| XmNshadowThickness | XmCShadowThickness | Dimension | 0 | CSG |
| XmNstringDirection | XmCStringDirection | XmStringDirection | dynamic | CG |

| Name | Class | Type | Default | Access |
|---|---|---|---|---|
| XmNtopShadowColor | XmCBackgroundTopShadowColor | Pixel | dynamic | CSG |
| XmNtopShadowPixmap | XmCTopShadowPixmap | Pixmap | dynamic | CSG |
| XmNtraversalOn | XmCTraversalOn | Boolean | True | CSG |
| XmNunitType | XmCUnitType | unsigned char | dynamic | CSG |
| XmNuserData | XmCUserData | XtPointer | NULL | CSG |

XmNbottomShadowColor
: The color used in drawing the border shadow's bottom and right sides. (Used only if XmNbottomShadowPixmap is NULL.)

XmNbottomShadowPixmap
: The pixmap used in drawing the border shadow's bottom and right sides.

XmNforeground
: The foreground color used by Manager widgets.

XmNhighlightColor
: The color used in drawing the highlighting rectangle. (Used only if XmNhighlightPixmap is XmUNSPECIFIED_PIXMAP.)

XmNhighlightPixmap
: The pixmap used in drawing the highlighting rectangle.

XmNinitialFocus
: In Motif 1.2, the widget ID of the widget that receives the keyboard focus when the manager is a child of a shell and the shell receives the keyboard focus for the first time.

XmNnavigationType
: Determines the way in which a Manager widget is traversed during keyboard navigation. Possible values:

```
XmNONE                 /* exclude from keyboard navigation */
XmTAB_GROUP            /* include in keyboard navigation */
XmSTICKY_TAB_GROUP     /* include in keyboard navigation, */
                       /* even if XmAddTabGroup() was called */
XmEXCLUSIVE_TAB_GROUP  /* application defines order of navigation */
```

XmNshadowThickness
: The thickness of the shadow border. This resource is dynamically set to 1 in a top-level window and 0 otherwise.

XmNstringDirection
: The direction in which to draw the string. Possible values are XmSTRING_DIRECTION_L_TO_R and XmSTRING_DIRECTION_R_TO_L.

XmNtopShadowColor
The color used in drawing the border shadow's top and left sides. (Used only if XmNtopShadowPixmap is NULL.)

XmNtopShadowPixmap
The pixmap used in drawing the border shadow's top and left sides.

XmNtraversalOn
If True (default), traversal of this widget is made possible.

XmNunitType
The measurement units to use in resources that specify a size or position—for example, any resources of data type Dimension (whose names generally include one of the words "Margin", "Height", "Width", "Thickness", or "Spacing"), as well as the offset resources defined by Form. For a widget whose parent is a manager, the default value is copied from this parent (provided the value hasn't been explicitly set by the application); otherwise, the default is XmPIXELS. Possible values:

```
XmPIXELS                Xm100TH_POINTS
Xm100TH_MILLIMETERS     Xm100TH_FONT_UNITS
Xm1000TH_INCHES
```

XmNuserData
A pointer to data that the application can attach to the widget. This resource is unused internally.

## Callback Resources

Manager defines the following callback resources:

| Callback | Reason Constant |
|---|---|
| XmNhelpCallback | XmCR_HELP |

XmNhelpCallback
List of callbacks that are called when help is requested.

## Callback Structure

Each callback function is passed the following structure:

```
typedef struct
{
    int     reason;         /* set to XmCR_HELP */
    XEvent  *event;         /* event structure that triggered callback */
} XmAnyCallbackStruct;
```

## Inherited Resources

Manager inherits the following resources. The resources are listed alphabetically, along with the superclass that defines them. Manager resets the default value of `XmNborderWidth` from 1 to 0.

| Resource | Inherited From | Resource | Inherited From |
|---|---|---|---|
| XmNaccelerators | Core | XmNheight | Core |
| XmNancestorSensitive | Core | XmNinitialResources Persistent | Core |
| XmNbackground | Core | XmNinsertPosition | Composite |
| XmNbackgroundPixmap | Core | XmNmappedWhen Managed | Core |
| XmNborderColor | Core | XmNnumChildren | Composite |
| XmNborderPixmap | Core | XmNscreen | Core |
| XmNborderWidth | Core | XmNsensitive | Core |
| XmNchildren | Composite | XmNtranslations | Core |
| XmNcolormap | Core | XmNwidth | Core |
| XmNdepth | Core | XmNx | Core |
| XmNdestroyCallback | Core | XmNy | Core |

## Translations

For Manager widgets that have gadget children:

| Event | Action | Event | Action |
|---|---|---|---|
| BAny Motion | ManagerGadget ButtonMotion() | KCancel | ManagerParentCancel() |
| BSelect Press | ManagerGadgetArm() | KPrevField | ManagerGadget PrevTabGroup() |
| BSelect Click | ManagerGadgetActivate() | KNextField | ManagerGadget NextTabGroup() |
| BSelect Release | ManagerGadgetActivate() | KUp | ManagerGadget TraverseUp() |
| BSelect Press 2+ | ManagerGadgetMultiArm() | KDown | ManagerGadget TraverseDown() |
| BSelect Release 2+ | ManagerGadget MultiActivate() | KLeft | ManagerGadget TraverseLeft() |
| BTransfer Press | ManagerGadgetDrag() | KRight | ManagerGadget TraverseRight() |
| KSelect | ManagerGadgetSelect() | KBeginLine | ManagerGadget TraverseHome() |

| Event | Action | Event | Action |
|---|---|---|---|
| `KActivate` | `ManagerParentActivate()` (1.2)<br>`ManagerGadgetSelect()` (1.1) | `KHelp`<br>`KAny` | `ManagerGadgetHelp()`<br>`ManagerGadgetKeyInput()` |

## Action Routines

The action routines for a Manager widget affect the gadget child that has the keyboard focus. The descriptions below refer to the gadget that has the focus.

`ManagerGadgetActivate()`
: Activates the gadget.

`ManagerGadgetArm()`
: Arms the gadget.

`ManagerGadgetButtonMotion()`
: Triggers the mouse motion event that the gadget received.

`ManagerGadgetDrag()`
: In Motif 1.2, initiates a drag and drop operation using the contents of a gadget's label.

`ManagerGadgetHelp()`
: Invokes the list of callbacks specified by the gadget's `XmNhelpCallback` resource. If the gadget doesn't have any help callbacks, the `ManagerGadgetHelp()` routine invokes those associated with the nearest ancestor that has them.

`ManagerGadgetKeyInput()`
: Triggers the keyboard event that the gadget received.

`ManagerGadgetMultiActivate()`
: Processes a multiple click of the mouse.

`ManagerGadgetMultiArm()`
: Processes a multiple press of the mouse button.

`ManagerGadgetNextTabGroup()`
`ManagerGadgetPrevTabGroup()`
: Traverses to the beginning of the next/previous tab group, wrapping if necessary.

`ManagerGadgetSelect()`
: Arms and activates the gadget.

`ManagerGadgetTraverseDown()`
`ManagerGadgetTraverseUp()`
: Within the same tab group, descends/ascends to the item below/above the gadget, wrapping if necessary.

`ManagerGadgetTraverseHome()`
Changes the focus to the first item in the tab group.

`ManagerGadgetTraverseLeft()`
`ManagerGadgetTraverseRight()`
Within the same tab group, traverses to the item on the left/right of the gadget, wrapping if necessary.

`ManagerGadgetTraverseNext()`
`ManagerGadgetTraversePrev()`
Within the same tab group, traverses to the next/previous item, wrapping if necessary.

`ManagerParentActivate()`
In Motif 1.2, passes the `KActivate` event to the parent if it is a manager.

`ManagerParentCancel()`
In Motif 1.2, passes the `KCancel` event to the parent if it is a manager.

## Additional Behavior

Manager has the following additional behavior:

`<FocusIn>`
If the event occurs in a gadget, highlights the gadget and gives it the focus under the explicit keyboard focus policy.

`<FocusOut>`
If the event occurs in a gadget, unhighlights the gadget and removes the focus under the explicit keyboard focus policy.

## See Also

*Composite*(2), *Constraint*(2), *Core*(2), *XmGadget*(2).

# XmMenuBar

## Name

XmMenuBar – a type of RowColumn widget used as a menu bar.

## Synopsis

**Public Header:** *<Xm/RowColumn.h>*

**Class Name:** XmRowColumn

**Class Hierarchy:** Core → Composite → Constraint → XmManager → XmRowColumn

**Class Pointer:** `xmRowColumnWidgetClass`

**Instantiation:** `widget = XmCreateMenuBar(...)`

**Functions/Macros:** `XmCreateMenuBar()`, `XmCreateSimpleMenuBar()`, `XmVaCreateSimpleMenuBar()`, `XmIsRowColumn()`

## Description

A MenuBar is an instance of a RowColumn widget that is normally used for constructing a pulldown menu system. An application typically places a MenuBar across the top of the main application window. CascadeButtons are added to the MenuBar and pulldown menus are associated with each of the CascadeButtons.

MenuBar is a RowColumn widget whose `XmNrowColumnType` resource is set to `XmMENU_BAR`. The `XmNentryClass` resource is set to `xmCascadeButtonWidgetClass` and `XmNisHomogeneous` is set to `True`, so that only CascadeButtons can be added to the widget. The `XmNmenuAccelerator` resource is set to `KMenuBar` and `XmNmenuPost` is set to `BSelect Press`. The `XmNmenuHelpWidget` resource can be set to specify the CascadeButton for the Help menu. The `XmNorientation` resource is set to `XmHORIZONTAL`.

A MenuBar can be created using `XmCreateMenuBar()`. In this case, the MenuBar does not automatically contain any CascadeButtons; they are added by the application.

A MenuBar can also be created by `XmCreateSimpleMenuBar()`, which automatically creates the MenuBar with the specified CascadeButtonGadgets as children. This routine uses the RowColumn resources associated with the creation of simple menus. For a MenuBar, the only type allowed in the `XmNbuttonType` resource is `XmCASCADEBUTTON`. The name of each CascadeButtonGadget is `button_n`, where *n* is the number of the button, ranging from 0 to 1 less than the number of buttons in the MenuBar.

## Default Resource Values

A MenuBar sets the following default values for RowColumn resources:

| Name | Default |
|---|---|
| `XmNentryClass` | `xmCascadeButtonWidgetClass` |
| `XmNisHomogeneous` | `True` |
| `XmNmenuAccelerator` | `KMenuBar` |
| `XmNmenuPost` | `BSelect Press` |

| Name | Default |
| --- | --- |
| XmNorientation | XmHORIZONTAL |
| XmNrowColumnType | XmMENU_BAR |

## See Also

*XmCreateObject*(1), *XmVaCreateSimpleMenuBar*(1), *XmCascadeButton*(2), *XmRowColumn*(2).

# XmMenuShell

## Name

XmMenuShell widget class – a shell widget meant to contain popup and pulldown menu panes.

## Synopsis

**Public Header:** *<Xm/MenuShell.h>*

**Class Name:** XmMenuShell

**Class Hierarchy:** Core → Composite → Shell → OverrideShell → XmMenuShell

**Class Pointer:** `xmMenuShellWidgetClass`

**Instantiation:** `widget = XtCreateWidget(name, xmMenuShellWidgetClass, ...)`

**Functions/Macros:** `XmCreateMenuShell()`, `XmCreatePopupMenu()`, `XmCreatePulldownMenu()`, `XmIsMenuShell()`

## Description

MenuShell is a subclass of OverrideShell that is meant to contain only popup or pulldown menu panes. Most application writers do not need to create MenuShell widgets explicitly because they are created automatically by the convenience routines `XmCreatePopupMenu()` and `XmCreatePulldownMenu()`.

If you do not use the convenience functions and create your own MenuShell widgets, the type of menu system being built determines the parent to specify for the MenuShell. For a top-level popup menu, specify the widget from which it will pop up. For a pulldown menu pane from the menu bar, specify the menu bar. For a pulldown menu pane from another pulldown menu or a popup menu, specify the menu pane from which it is pulled down. For pulldown menu in an option menu, specify the option menu's parent.

## New Resources

MenuShell defines the following resource:

| Name | Class | Type | Default | Access |
|---|---|---|---|---|
| `XmNbuttonFontList` | `XmCButtonFontList` | `XmFontList` | dynamic | CSG |
| `XmNdefaultFontList` | `XmCDefaultFontList` | `XmFontList` | dynamic | CG |
| `XmNlabelFontList` | `XmCLabelFontList` | `XmFontList` | dynamic | CSG |

`XmNbuttonFontList`

In Motif 1.2, the font list used for the button children of the MenuShell widget. If this value is initially `NULL` and if the value of `XmNdefaultFontList` is not `NULL`, this value is used. Otherwise, the font list is derived from the `XmNbuttonFontList` resource found in the nearest ancestor that is a subclass of BulletinBoard, VendorShell, or MenuShell.

`XmNdefaultFontList`
The default font list for the children of the MenuShell widget. This resource is obsolete in Motif 1.2.

`XmNlabelFontList`
In Motif 1.2, the font list used for the label children of the MenuShell widget. If this value is initially `NULL` and if the value of `XmNdefaultFontList` is not `NULL`, this value is used. Otherwise, the font list is derived from the `XmNlabelFontList` resource found in the nearest ancestor that is a subclass of BulletinBoard, VendorShell, or MenuShell.

## Inherited Resources

MenuShell inherits the following resources. The resources are listed alphabetically, along with the superclass that defines them. MenuShell sets the default value of `XmNallowShellResize` to `True` and `XmNborderWidth` to 0. The default values of `XmNoverrideRedirect` and `XmNsaveUnder` are set to `True` by OverrideShell.

| Resource | Inherited From | Resource | Inherited From |
|---|---|---|---|
| XmNaccelerators | Core | XmNinitialResourcesPersistent | Core |
| XmNallowShellResize | Shell | XmNinsertPosition | Composite |
| XmNancestorSensitive | Core | XmNmappedWhenManaged | Core |
| XmNbackground | Core | XmNnumChildren | Composite |
| XmNbackgroundPixmap | Core | XmNoverrideRedirect | Shell |
| XmNborderColor | Core | XmNpopdownCallback | Shell |
| XmNborderPixmap | Core | XmNpopupCallback | Shell |
| XmNborderWidth | Core | XmNsaveUnder | Shell |
| XmNchildren | Composite | XmNscreen | Core |
| XmNcolormap | Core | XmNsensitive | Core |
| XmNcreatePopupChildProc | Shell | XmNtranslations | Core |
| XmNdepth | Core | XmNvisual | Shell |
| XmNdestroyCallback | Core | XmNwidth | Core |
| XmNgeometry | Shell | XmNx | Core |
| XmNheight | Core | XmNy | Core |

## Translations

| | |
|---|---|
| BSelect Press | ClearTraversal() |
| BSelect Release | MenuShellPopdownDone() |

## Action Routines

MenuShell defines the following action routines:

`ClearTraversal()`
Shuts off keyboard traversal within this menu, turns on mouse traversal, and unposts any submenus that this menu posted.

`MenuShellPopdownDone()`
Unposts the menu tree and restores the previous focus.

`MenuShellPopdownOne()`
Like `MenuShellPopdownDone()` except that it unposts only one level of the menu tree. In a top-level pulldown menu pane attached to a menu bar, this action routine disarms the cascade button and the menu bar.

## See Also

*XmCreateObject*(1),
*Composite*(2), *Core*(2), *OverrideShell*(2), *Shell*(2), *XmRowColumn*(2).

# XmMessageBox

## Name

XmMessageBox widget class – a composite widget used for creating message dialogs.

## Synopsis

**Public Header:** *<Xm/MessageB.h>*

**Class Name:** XmMessageBox

**Class Hierarchy:** Core → Composite → Constraint → XmManager → XmBulletinBoard → XmMessageBox

**Class Pointer:** `xmMessageBoxWidgetClass`

**Instantiation:** `widget = XtCreateWidget(name, xmMessageBoxWidgetClass, ...)`

**Functions/Macros:** `XmCreateErrorDialog()`, `XmCreateInformationDialog()`, `XmCreateMessageBox()`, `XmCreateMessageDialog()`, `XmCreateQuestionDialog()`, `XmCreateTemplateDialog()`, `XmCreateWarningDialog()`, `XmCreateWorkingDialog()`, `XmIsMessageBox()`, `XmMessageBoxGetChild()`

## Description

MessageBox is composite widget that is used for creating simple message dialog boxes, which normally present transient messages. A MessageBox usually contains a message symbol, a message, three PushButtons, and a separator between the message and the buttons. The names of the symbol and the separator gadgets are `Symbol` and `Separator`. In Motif 1.2, the default symbols and button labels can be localized. The `XmNdialogType` resource controls the type of message symbol that is displayed. In the C locale, and in Motif 1.1, the PushButtons are labeled **OK**, **Cancel**, and **Help** by default.

You can customize a MessageBox by removing existing children or adding new children. Use `XmMessageBoxGetChild()` to retrieve the widget ID of an existing child and then unmanage the child. With Motif 1.2, multiple widgets can be added as children of a MessageBox. If a menu bar is added, it is placed at the top of the window. Any buttons are placed after the **OK** button. Any additional children are placed below the message. In Motif 1.1, only a single widget can be added as a child of a MessageBox. This child is placed below the message and acts as a work area.

In Motif 1.2, `XmDIALOG_TEMPLATE` is a new value for `XmNdialogType`. A TemplateDialog contains nothing but a separator by default. Specifying callback, label string, or pixmap symbol resources causes the appropriate children to be created.

## New Resources

MessageBox defines the following resources:

| Name | Class | Type | Default | Access |
|---|---|---|---|---|
| XmNcancelLabelString | XmCCancelLabelString | XmString | dynamic | CSG |
| XmNdefaultButtonType | XmCDefaultButtonType | unsigned char | XmDIALOG_OK_BUTTON | CSG |
| XmNdialogType | XmCDialogType | unsigned char | XmDIALOG_MESSAGE | CSG |
| XmNhelpLabelString | XmCHelpLabelString | XmString | dynamic | CSG |
| XmNmessageAlignment | XmCAlignment | unsigned char | XmALIGNMENT_BEGINNING | CSG |
| XmNmessageString | XmCMessageString | XmString | "" | CSG |
| XmNminimizeButtons | XmCMinimizeButtons | Boolean | False | CSG |
| XmNokLabelString | XmCOkLabelString | XmString | dynamic | CSG |
| XmNsymbolPixmap | XmCPixmap | Pixmap | dynamic | CSG |

XmNcancelLabelString

The string that labels the **Cancel** button. In Motif 1.2, the default value is locale-dependent. In the C locale, and in Motif 1.1, the default value is "Cancel".

XmNdefaultButtonType

Specifies which PushButton provides the default action. Possible values:

XmDIALOG_CANCEL_BUTTON
XmDIALOG_OK_BUTTON
XmDIALOG_HELP_BUTTON

XmNdialogType

The type of MessageBox dialog, which also indicates the message symbol that displays by default. Possible values:

XmDIALOG_ERROR
XmDIALOG_INFORMATION
XmDIALOG_MESSAGE
XmDIALOG_QUESTION
XmDIALOG_TEMPLATE /* new in Motif 1.2 */
XmDIALOG_WARNING
XmDIALOG_WORKING

XmNhelpLabelString

The string that labels the **Help** button. In Motif 1.2, the default value is locale-dependent. In the C locale, and in Motif 1.1, the default value is "Help".

XmNmessageAlignment

The type of alignment for the message label. Possible values:

XmALIGNMENT_BEGINNING
XmALIGNMENT_CENTER
XmALIGNMENT_END

`XmNmessageString`
The string to use as the message label.

`XmNminimizeButtons`
If `False` (default), all buttons are standardized to be as wide as the widest button and as high as the highest button. If `True`, buttons will keep their preferred size.

`XmNokLabelString`
The string that labels the **OK** button. In Motif 1.2, the default value is locale-dependent. In the C locale, and in Motif 1.1, the default value is `"OK"`.

`XmNsymbolPixmap`
The pixmap label to use as the message symbol.

## Callback Resources

MessageBox defines the following callback resources:

| Callback | Reason Constant |
|---|---|
| XmNcancelCallback | XmCR_CANCEL |
| XmNokCallback | XmCR_OK |

`XmNcancelCallback`
List of callbacks that are called when the user selects the **Cancel** button.

`XmNokCallback`
List of callbacks that are called when the user selects the **OK** button.

## Callback Structure

Each callback function is passed the following structure:

```
typedef struct
{
    int     reason;          /* the reason that the callback was called */
    XEvent  *event;          /* event structure that triggered callback */
} XmAnyCallbackStruct;
```

## Inherited Resources

MessageBox inherits the following resources. The resources are listed alphabetically, along with the superclass that defines them. The default value of `XmNborderWidth` is reset to 0 by Manager. BulletinBoard sets the value of `XmNinitialFocus` to `XmNdefaultButton` and resets the default `XmNshadowThickness` from 0 to 1 if the MessageBox is a child of a DialogShell.

| Resource | Inherited From | Resource | Inherited From |
|---|---|---|---|
| XmNaccelerators | Core | XmNinsertPosition | Composite |
| XmNallowOverlap | BulletinBoard | XmNlabelFontList | BulletinBoard |
| XmNancestorSensitive | Core | XmNmapCallback | BulletinBoard |

| Resource | Inherited From | Resource | Inherited From |
|---|---|---|---|
| XmNautoUnmanage | BulletinBoard | XmNmappedWhenManaged | Core |
| XmNbackground | Core | XmNmarginHeight | BulletinBoard |
| XmNbackgroundPixmap | Core | XmNmarginWidth | BulletinBoard |
| XmNborderColor | Core | XmNnavigationType | Manager |
| XmNborderPixmap | Core | XmNnoResize | BulletinBoard |
| XmNborderWidth | Core | XmNnumChildren | Composite |
| XmNbottomShadowColor | Manager | XmNresizePolicy | BulletinBoard |
| XmNbottomShadowPixmap | Manager | XmNscreen | Core |
| XmNbuttonFontList | BulletinBoard | XmNsensitive | Core |
| XmNcancelButton | BulletinBoard | XmNshadowThickness | Manager |
| XmNchildren | Composite | XmNshadowType | BulletinBoard |
| XmNcolormap | Core | XmNstringDirection | Manager |
| XmNdefaultButton | BulletinBoard | XmNtextFontList | BulletinBoard |
| XmNdefaultPosition | BulletinBoard | XmNtextTranslations | BulletinBoard |
| XmNdepth | Core | XmNtopShadowColor | Manager |
| XmNdestroyCallback | Core | XmNtopShadowPixmap | Manager |
| XmNdialogStyle | BulletinBoard | XmNtranslations | Core |
| XmNdialogTitle | BulletinBoard | XmNtraversalOn | Manager |
| XmNfocusCallback | BulletinBoard | XmNunitType | Manager |
| XmNforeground | Manager | XmNunmapCallback | BulletinBoard |
| XmNheight | Core | XmNuserData | Manager |
| XmNhelpCallback | Manager | XmNwidth | Core |
| XmNhighlightColor | Manager | XmNx | Core |
| XmNhighlightPixmap | Manager | XmNy | Core |
| XmNinitialFocus | Manager | | |
| XmNinitialResources Persistent | Core | | |

## Translations

The translations for MessageBox include those from Manager.

## Additional Behavior

MessageBox has the following additional behavior:

`MAny KCancel`
: For a sensitive **Cancel** button, invokes the callbacks in `XmNactivate-Callback`.

`KActivate`
: For the button that has keyboard focus, or the default button, invokes the callbacks in `XmNactivateCallback`.

`<OK Button Activated>`
: Invokes the callbacks for `XmNokCallback`.

`<Cancel Button Activated>`
Invokes the callbacks for `XmNcancelCallback`.

`<Help Button Activated>`
Invokes the callbacks for `XmNhelpCallback`.

`<FocusIn>` Invokes the callbacks for `XmNfocusCallback`.

`<Map>` Invokes the callbacks for `XmNmapCallback` if the parent is a DialogShell.

`<Unmap>` Invokes the callbacks for `XmNunmapCallback` if the parent is a DialogShell.

## See Also

*XmCreateObject*(1), *XmMessageBoxGetChild*(1),
*Composite*(2), *Constraint*(2), *Core*(2), *XmBulletinBoard*(2), *XmErrorDialog*(2),
*XmInformationDialog*(2), *XmManager*(2), *XmQuestionDialog*(2), *XmTemplateDialog*(2),
*XmWarningDialog*(2), *XmWorkingDialog*(2),

# XmMessageDialog

## Name

XmMessageDialog – an unmanaged MessageBox as a child of DialogShell.

## Synopsis

**Public Header:** *<Xm/MessageB.h>*

**Instantiation:** `widget = XmCreateMessageDialog(...)`

**Functions/Macros:** `XmCreateMessageDialog()`, `XmMessageBoxGetChild()`

## Description

A MessageDialog is a compound object created by a call to `XmCreateMessageDialog()` that an application can use to present a message to the user. A MessageDialog consists of a DialogShell with an unmanaged MessageBox widget as its child. The MessageBox resource `XmNdialogType` is set to `XmDIALOG_MESSAGE`. A MessageDialog includes four components: a symbol, a message, three buttons, and a separator between the message and the buttons. By default, there is no symbol. In Motif 1.2, the default button labels can be localized. In the C locale, and in Motif 1.1, the PushButtons are labeled **OK**, **Cancel**, and **Help** by default.

## Default Resource Values

A MessageDialog sets the following default values for MessageBox resources:

| Name | Default |
|---|---|
| XmNdialogType | XmDIALOG_MESSAGE |

## Widget Hierarchy

When a MessageDialog is created with a specified `name`, the DialogShell is named `name_popup` and the MessageBox is called `name`.

## See Also

*XmCreateObject*(1), *XmMessageBoxGetChild*(1),
*XmDialogShell*(2), *XmMessageBox*(2).

# XmOptionMenu

## Name

XmOptionMenu – a type of RowColumn widget used as an option menu.

## Synopsis

**Public Header:** *<Xm/RowColumn.h>*

**Class Name:** XmRowColumn

**Class Hierarchy:** Core → Composite → Constraint → XmManager → XmRowColumn

**Class Pointer:** `xmRowColumnWidgetClass`

**Instantiation:** *widget* = `XmCreateOptionMenu(...)`

**Functions/Macros:** `XmCreateOptionMenu()`, `XmCreateSimpleOptionMenu()`, `XmVaCreateSimpleOptionMenu()`, `XmIsRowColumn()`, `XmOptionButtonGadget()`, `XmOptionLabelGadget()`

## Description

An OptionMenu is an instance of a RowColumn widget that is used as a menu that allows a user to select one of several choices. An OptionMenu consists of a label, a selection area, and pulldown menu pane. When you create an OptionMenu, you must supply the pulldown menu pane via the `XmNsubMenuId` resource. The menu pane must already exist and it must be a child of of the OptionMenu's parent. The label (a LabelGadget) and the selection area (a CascadeButtonGadget) are created by the OptionMenu. You can specify the label string with the `XmNlabelString` resource.

OptionMenu is a RowColumn widget whose `XmNrowColumnType` resource is set to `XmMENU_OPTION`. The `XmNorientation` resource defaults to `XmHORIZONTAL`, which means that the label is displayed to the left of the selection area. If the resource is set to `XmVERTICAL`, the label is placed above the selection area. The selection area posts the menu pane, as well as displays the label of the current selection. The `XmNmenuPost` resource is set to `BSelect Press`. The `XmNmenuHistory` resource can be used to specify which item in the pulldown menu is the current choice. The `XmNmnemonic` and `XmNmnemonicCharSet` resources can be set to specify a mnemonic for the OptionMenu.

An OptionMenu can be created using `XmCreateOptionMenu()`. In this case, the OptionMenu does not automatically create its submenu; it must be added by the application.

An OptionMenu can also be created by `XmCreateSimpleOptionMenu()`, which automatically creates the OptionMenu and its submenu with the specified children. This routine uses the RowColumn resources associated with the creation of simple menus. For an OptionMenu, the only types allowed in the `XmNbuttonType` resource are `XmCASCADEBUTTON`, `XmPUSHBUTTON`, `XmSEPARATOR`, and `XmDOUBLE_SEPARATOR`. The name of each button is `button_`*n*, where *n* is the number of the button, ranging from 0 to 1 less than the number of buttons in the submenu. The name of each separator is `separator_`*n*, where *n* is the number of the separator, ranging from 0 to 1 less than the number of separators in the submenu.

### Default Resource Values

An OptionMenu sets the following default values for RowColumn resources:

| Name | Default |
|---|---|
| `XmNmenuPost` | `BSelect Press` |
| `XmNorientation` | `XmHORIZONTAL` |
| `XmNrowColumnType` | `XmMENU_OPTION` |

### Widget Hierarchy

When an OptionMenu is created, the LabelGadget is named `OptionLabel` and the Cascade-ButtonGadget is named `OptionButton`.

### See Also

*XmCreateObject*(1), *XmOptionButtonGadget*(1), *XmOptionLabelGadget*(1), *XmVaCreateSimpleOptionMenu*(1), *XmCascadeButtonGadget*(2), *XmLabelGadget*(2), *XmRowColumn*(2).

## Name

XmPanedWindow widget class – a constraint widget that tiles its children vertically.

## Synopsis

**Public Header:** *<Xm/PanedW.h>*

**Class Name:** XmPanedWindow

**Class Hierarchy:** Core → Composite → Constraint → XmManager → XmPanedWindow

**Class Pointer:** `xmPanedWindowWidgetClass`

**Instantiation:** `widget = XtCreateWidget(name, xmPanedWindowWidgetClass, ...)`

**Functions/Macros:** `XmCreatePanedWindow()`, `XmIsPanedWindow()`

## Description

PanedWindow is a constraint widget that tiles its children vertically. In Motif 1.1, the children are laid out from top to bottom, in the order that they are added to the PanedWindow. In Motif 1.2, the position of each child is controlled by the `XmNpositionIndex` resource. A PanedWindow is as wide as its widest child and all children are made that width. Users can adjust the height of a pane using a sash that appears below the corresponding pane.

## New Resources

PanedWindow defines the following resources:

| Name | Class | Type | Default | Access |
|---|---|---|---|---|
| XmNmarginHeight | XmCMarginHeight | Dimension | 3 | CSG |
| XmNmarginWidth | XmCMarginWidth | Dimension | 3 | CSG |
| XmNrefigureMode | XmCBoolean | Boolean | True | CSG |
| XmNsashHeight | XmCSashHeight | Dimension | 10 | CSG |
| XmNsashIndent | XmCSashIndent | Position | -10 | CSG |
| XmNsashShadowThickness | XmCShadowThickness | Dimension | dynamic | CSG |
| XmNsashWidth | XmCSashWidth | Dimension | 10 | CSG |
| XmNseparatorOn | XmCSeparatorOn | Boolean | True | CSG |
| XmNspacing | XmCSpacing | Dimension | 8 | CSG |

`XmNmarginHeight`
The spacing between a PanedWindow widget's top or bottom edge and any child widget.

`XmNmarginWidth`
The spacing between a PanedWindow widget's right or left edge and any child widget.

`XmNrefigureMode`
If `True` (default), children are reset to their appropriate positions following a change in the PanedWindow widget.

XmNsashHeight
XmNsashWidth
The height and width of the sash.

XmNsashIndent
The horizontal position of the sash along each pane. Positive values specify the indent from the left edge; negative values, from the right edge (assuming the default value of XmNstringDirection). If the value is too large, the sash is placed flush with the edge of the PanedWindow.

XmNsashShadowThickness
The thickness of shadows drawn on each sash.

XmNseparatorOn
If True, the widget places a Separator or SeparatorGadget between each pane.

XmNspacing
The distance between each child pane.

## New Constraint Resources

PanedWindow defines the following constraint resources for its children:

| Name | Class | Type | Default | Access |
|---|---|---|---|---|
| XmNallowResize | XmCBoolean | Boolean | False | CSG |
| XmNpaneMaximum | XmCPaneMaximum | Dimension | 1000 | CSG |
| XmNpaneMinimum | XmCPaneMinimum | Dimension | 1 | CSG |
| XmNpositionIndex | XmCPositionIndex | short | XmLAST_POSITION | CSG |
| XmNskipAdjust | XmCBoolean | Boolean | False | CSG |

XmNallowResize
If False (default), the PanedWindow widget always refuses resize requests from its children. If True, the PanedWindow widget tries to grant requests to change a child's height.

XmNpaneMaximum
XmNpaneMinimum
The values of a pane's maximum and minimum dimensions for resizing. You can prevent a sash from being drawn by setting these values to be equal.

XmNpositionIndex
In Motif 1.2, the position of the widget in the PanedWindow's list of children, not including sashes. A value of 0 indicates the beginning of the list, while Xm-LAST_POSITION places the child at the end of the list.

XmNskipAdjust

If False (default), the PanedWindow widget automatically resizes this pane child. If True, resizing is not automatic, and the PanedWindow may choose to skip the adjustment of this pane.

## Inherited Resources

PanedWindow inherits the following resources. The resources are listed alphabetically, along with the superclass that defines them. PanedWindow sets the default value of XmNshadow-Thickness to 2. The default value of XmNborderWidth is reset to 0 by Manager.

| Resource | Inherited From | Resource | Inherited From |
|---|---|---|---|
| XmNaccelerators | Core | XmNinitialResources Persistent | Core |
| XmNancestorSensitive | Core | XmNinsertPosition | Composite |
| XmNbackground | Core | XmNmappedWhenManaged | Core |
| XmNbackgroundPixmap | Core | XmNnavigationType | Manager |
| XmNborderColor | Core | XmNnumChildren | Composite |
| XmNborderPixmap | Core | XmNscreen | Core |
| XmNborderWidth | Core | XmNsensitive | Core |
| XmNbottomShadowColor | Manager | XmNshadowThickness | Manager |
| XmNbottomShadowPixmap | Manager | XmNstringDirection | Manager |
| XmNchildren | Composite | XmNtopShadowColor | Manager |
| XmNcolormap | Core | XmNtopShadowPixmap | Manager |
| XmNdepth | Core | XmNtranslations | Core |
| XmNdestroyCallback | Core | XmNtraversalOn | Manager |
| XmNforeground | Manager | XmNunitType | Manager |
| XmNheight | Core | XmNuserData | Manager |
| XmNhelpCallback | Manager | XmNwidth | Core |
| XmNhighlightColor | Manager | XmNx | Core |
| XmNhighlightPixmap | Manager | XmNy | Core |
| XmNinitialFocus | Manager | | |

## Translations

The translations for PanedWindow are inherited from Manager. Additional translations are defined for sashes within a PanedWindow widget:

| Event | Action | Event | Action |
|---|---|---|---|
| BSelect Press | SashAction (Start) | KUp | SashAction (Key,DefaultIncr,Up) |
| BSelect Motion | SashAction (Move) | MCtrl KUp | SashAction (Key,LargeIncr,Up) |

| Event | Action | Event | Action |
|---|---|---|---|
| BSelect Release | SashAction (Commit) | KDown | SashAction (Key,DefaultIncr,Down) |
| BTransfer Press | SashAction (Start) | MCtrl KDown | SashAction (Key,LargeIncr,Down) |
| BTransfer Motion | SashAction (Move) | KNextField | NextTabGroup() |
| BTransfer Release | SashAction (Commit) | KPrevField | PrevTabGroup() |
| KHelp | Help() | | |

## Action Routines

PanedWindow defines the following action routines:

`Help()` Invokes the list of callbacks specified by `XmNhelpCallback`. If the PanedWindow doesn't have any help callbacks, the `Help()` routine invokes those associated with the nearest ancestor that has them.

`NextTabGroup()`
Traverses to the next tab group. Normally a tab group consists of a pane and its sash.

`PrevTabGroup()`
Traverses to the previous tab group. Normally a tab group consists of a pane and its sash.

`SashAction(`*`action`*`)`
Controls the interactive placement of the sash using the mouse. *`action`* can have one of three values:

`Start` Begins the placement operation.

`Move` Causes the sash to move as the mouse moves.

`Commit` Ends the placement operation.

`SashAction(Key,`*`increment`*`,`*`direction`*`)`
Controls the placement of the sash when it is moved using the keyboard. *`increment`* is either `DefaultIncr`, which moves the sash's position by one line or `LargeIncr`, which moves the sash's position by one viewing region. *`direction`* is either `Up` or `Down`.

## Additional Behavior

PanedWindow has the following additional behavior:

`<FocusIn>`
Highlights the sash and gives it keyboard focus.

<FocusOut>
Unhighlights the sash and removes its keyboard focus.

## See Also

*XmCreateObject*(1),
*Composite*(2), *Constraint*(2), *Core*(2), *XmManager*(2).

# XmPopupMenu

## Name

XmPopupMenu – a type of RowColumn widget used as a popup menu pane.

## Synopsis

**Public Header:** *<Xm/RowColumn.h>*

**Instantiation:** `widget = XmCreatePopupMenu(...)`

**Functions/Macros:** `XmCreatePopupMenu()`, `XmCreateSimplePopupMenu()`, `XmMenuPosition()`, `XmVaCreateSimplePopupMenu()`

## Description

A PopupMenu is the first menu pane in a popup menu system. All other menu panes in the menu system are pulldown panes. A PopupMenu can contain Labels, Separators, PushButtons, ToggleButtons, and CascadeButtons.

A PopupMenu is a RowColumn widget whose `XmNrowColumnType` resource is set to `XmMENU_POPUP`. The `XmNmenuAccelerator` resource is set to `KMenu` and `XmNmenuPost` is set to `BMenu Press`. The `XmNpopupEnabled` resource controls whether or not keyboard accelerators and mnemonics are enabled for a PopupMenu. A PopupMenu needs to be the child of a MenuShell widget to function properly. Use `XmMenuPosition()` to place a PopupMenu.

A PopupMenu can be created using `XmCreatePopupMenu()`. In this case, the PopupMenu does not automatically contain any components; they are added by the application. The PopupMenu created by this routine is a compound object consisting of a MenuShell widget and a RowColumn child.

A PopupMenu can also be created by `XmCreateSimplePopupMenu()`, which automatically creates the PopupMenu with the specified children and makes it the child of a MenuShell. This routine uses the RowColumn resources associated with the creation of simple menus. For a PopupMenu, any type is allowed in the `XmNbuttonType` resource. The name of each button is `button_`*n*, where *n* is the number of the button, ranging from 0 to 1 less than the number of buttons in the menu. The name of each separator is `separator_`*n*, where *n* is the number of the separator, ranging from 0 to 1 less than the number of separators in the menu. The name of each title is `label_`*n*, where *n* is the number of the title, ranging from 0 to 1 less than the number of titles in the menu.

## Default Resource Values

A PopupMenu sets the following default values for RowColumn resources:

| Name | Default |
|---|---|
| `XmNmenuAccelerator` | `KMenu` |
| `XmNmenuPost` | `BMenu Press` |

| Name | Default |
|---|---|
| XmNpopupEnabled | True |
| XmNrowColumnType | XmMENU_POPUP |

## Widget Hierarchy

When a PopupMenu is created with a specified name, the MenuShell is named popup_name and the RowColumn is called name.

## See Also

*XmCreateObject*(1), *XmMenuPosition*(1), *XmVaCreateSimplePopupMenu*(1), *XmMenuShell*(2), *XmRowColumn*(2).

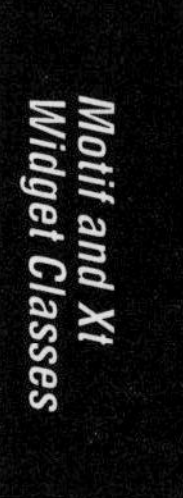

# XmPrimitive

## Name

XmPrimitive widget class – the fundamental class for simple Motif widgets.

## Synopsis

**Public Header:** *<Xm/Xm.h>*

**Class Name:** XmPrimitive

**Class Hierarchy:** Core → XmPrimitive

**Class Pointer:** `xmPrimitiveWidgetClass`

**Instantiation:** Primitive is a meta-class and is not normally instantiated.

**Functions/Macros:** `XmIsPrimitive()`

## Description

Primitive is a supporting superclass that provides Motif-specific resources for border drawing, highlighting, and keyboard traversal mechanisms. Primitive supports widget subclasses that handle elementary graphic elements such as buttons, labels, and separators.

The default values of the color resources for the foreground, background, top and bottom shadows, and highlighting are set dynamically. If no colors are specified, they are generated automatically. On a monochrome system, black and white colors are selected. On a color system, four colors are selected that provide the appropriate shading for the 3-D visuals. When the background color is specified, the shadow colors are selected to provide the appropriate 3-D appearance and foreground and highlight colors are selected to provide the necessary contrast. The colors are generated when the widget is created; using `XtSetValues()` to change the background does not change the other colors. With Motif 1.2, use `XmChangeColor()` to change the associated colors when the background color is changed.

## New Resources

Primitive defines the following resources.

| Name | Class | Type | Default | Access |
|---|---|---|---|---|
| XmNbottomShadowColor | XmCBottomShadowColor | Pixel | dynamic | CSG |
| XmNbottomShadowPixmap | XmCBottomShadowPixmap | Pixmap | XmUNSPECIFIED_PIXMAP | CSG |
| XmNforeground | XmCForeground | Pixel | dynamic | CSG |
| XmNhighlightColor | XmCHighlightColor | Pixel | dynamic | CSG |
| XmNhighlightOnEnter | XmCHighlightOnEnter | Boolean | False | CSG |
| XmNhighlightPixmap | XmCHighlightPixmap | Pixmap | dynamic | CSG |
| XmNhighlightThickness | XmCHighlightThickness | Dimension | 2 | CSG |
| XmNnavigationType | XmCNavigationType | XmNavigationType | XmNONE | CSG |
| XmNshadowThickness | XmCShadowThickness | Dimension | 2 | CSG |
| XmNtopShadowColor | XmCTopShadowColor | Pixel | dynamic | CSG |
| XmNtopShadowPixmap | XmCTopShadowPixmap | Pixmap | dynamic | CSG |

| Name | Class | Type | Default | Access |
|---|---|---|---|---|
| XmNtraversalOn | XmCTraversalOn | Boolean | True | CSG |
| XmNunitType | XmCUnitType | unsigned char | dynamic | CSG |
| XmNuserData | XmCUserData | XtPointer | NULL | CSG |

`XmNbottomShadowColor`
The color used in drawing the border shadow's bottom and right sides. (Used only if `XmNbottomShadowPixmap` is NULL.)

`XmNbottomShadowPixmap`
The pixmap used in drawing the border shadow's bottom and right sides.

`XmNforeground`
The foreground color used by Primitive widgets.

`XmNhighlightColor`
The color used in drawing the highlighting rectangle. (Used only if `XmNhighlightPixmap` is `XmUNSPECIFIED_PIXMAP`.)

`XmNhighlightOnEnter`
Determines whether to draw the widget's highlighting rectangle whenever the cursor moves into the widget. This resource applies only when the shell has a focus policy of `XmPOINTER`. If the `XmNhighlightOnEnter` resource is `True`, highlighting is drawn; if `False` (default), highlighting is not drawn.

`XmNhighlightPixmap`
The pixmap used in drawing the highlighting rectangle.

`XmNhighlightThickness`
The thickness of the highlighting rectangle.

`XmNnavigationType`
Determines the way in which a Primitive widget is traversed during keyboard navigation. Possible values:

```
XmNONE                  /* exclude from keyboard navigation */
XmTAB_GROUP             /* include in keyboard navigation */
XmSTICKY_TAB_GROUP      /* include in keyboard navigation, */
                        /* even if XmAddTabGroup() was called */
XmEXCLUSIVE_TAB_GROUP   /* application defines order of navigation */
```

`XmNshadowThickness`
The thickness of the shadow border.

`XmNtopShadowColor`
The color used in drawing the border shadow's top and left sides. (Used only if `XmNtopShadowPixmap` is NULL.)

XmNtopShadowPixmap
The pixmap used in drawing the border shadow's top and left sides.

XmNtraversalOn
If True (default), traversal of this widget is made possible.

XmNunitType
The measurement units to use in resources that specify a size or position—for example, any resources of data type Dimension (whose names generally include one of the words "Margin", "Thickness", or "Spacing"). For a widget whose parent is a manager, the default value is copied from this parent (provided the value hasn't been explicitly set by the application); otherwise, the default is XmPIXELS. Possible values:

| | |
|---|---|
| XmPIXELS | Xm100TH_POINTS |
| Xm100TH_MILLIMETERS | Xm100TH_FONT_UNITS |
| Xm1000TH_INCHES | |

XmNuserData
A pointer to data that the application can attach to the widget. This resource is unused internally.

## Callback Resources

Primitive defines the following callback resources:

| Callback | Reason Constant |
|---|---|
| XmNhelpCallback | XmCR_HELP |

XmNhelpCallback
List of callbacks that are called when help is requested.

## Inherited Resources

Primitive inherits the following resources. The resources are listed alphabetically, along with the superclass that defines them. Primitive resets the default value of XmNborderWidth from 1 to 0.

| Resource | Inherited From | Resource | Inherited From |
|---|---|---|---|
| XmNaccelerators | Core | XmNheight | Core |
| XmNancestorSensitive | Core | XmNinitialResourcesPersistent | Core |
| XmNbackground | Core | XmNmappedWhenManaged | Core |
| XmNbackgroundPixmap | Core | XmNscreen | Core |
| XmNborderColor | Core | XmNsensitive | Core |
| XmNborderPixmap | Core | XmNtranslations | Core |
| XmNborderWidth | Core | XmNwidth | Core |
| XmNcolormap | Core | XmNx | Core |

| Resource | Inherited From | Resource | Inherited From |
|---|---|---|---|
| XmNdepth | Core | XmNy | Core |
| XmNdestroyCallback | Core | | |

## Translations

| Event | Action | Event | Action |
|---|---|---|---|
| KUp | PrimitiveTraverseUp() | KNextField | PrimitiveNextTabGroup() |
| KDown | PrimitiveTraverseDown() | KPrevField | PrimitivePrevTabGroup() |
| KLeft | PrimitiveTraverseLeft() | KActivate | PrimitiveParentActivate() |
| KRight | PrimitiveTraverseRight() | KCancel | PrimitiveParentCancel() |
| KBeginLine | PrimitiveTraverseHome() | KHelp | PrimitiveHelp() |

## Action Routines

Primitive defines the following action routines:

`PrimitiveHelp()`
: Invokes the list of callbacks specified by the Primitive widget's `XmNhelpCallback` resource. If the Primitive widget doesn't have any help callbacks, this action routine invokes those associated with the nearest ancestor that has them.

`PrimitiveNextTabGroup()`
`PrimitivePrevTabGroup()`
: Traverses to the first item in the next/previous tab group, wrapping if necessary.

`PrimitiveParentActivate()`
: In Motif 1.2, passes the `KActivate` event to the parent if it is a manager.

`PrimitiveParentCancel()`
: In Motif 1.2, passes the `KCancel` event to the parent if it is a manager.

`PrimitiveTraverseDown()`
`PrimitiveTraverseUp()`
: Within the same tab group, descends/ascends to the item below/above the widget, wrapping if necessary.

`PrimitiveTraverseHome()`
: Changes the focus to the first item in the tab group.

`PrimitiveTraverseLeft()`
`PrimitiveTraverseRight()`
: Within the same tab group, traverses to the item on the left/right of the widget, wrapping if necessary.

`PrimitiveTraverseNext()`
`PrimitiveTraversePrev()`
Within the same tab group, traverses to the next/previous item, wrapping if necessary.

## Additional Behavior

Primitive has the following additional behavior:

`<FocusIn>`
Highlights the widget and gives it the focus under the explicit keyboard focus policy.

`<FocusOut>`
Unhighlights the widget and removes the focus under the explicit keyboard focus policy.

## See Also

*Core*(2).

# XmPromptDialog

## Name

XmPromptDialog – an unmanaged SelectionBox as a child of a Dialog Shell.

## Synopsis

**Public Header:** *<Xm/SelectioB.h>*

**Instantiation:** `widget = XmCreatePromptDialog(...)`

**Functions/Macros:** `XmCreatePromptDialog()`, `XmSelectionBoxGetChild()`, `XmIsSelectionBox()`

## Description

PromptDialog is a compound object created by a call to `XmCreatePromptDialog()` that an application can use to prompt the user for textual input. A PromptDialog consists of a DialogShell with an unmanaged SelectionBox widget as its child. The SelectionBox resource `XmNdialogType` is set to `XmDIALOG_PROMPT`.

A PromptDialog contains a message, a region for text input, and three managed buttons. A fourth button is created but not managed; you can manage it explicitly if necessary. In Motif 1.2, the default button labels can be localized. In the C locale, and in Motif 1.1, the PushButtons are labeled **OK**, **Apply**, **Cancel**, and **Help** by default. The **Apply** button is the unmanaged button.

## Default Resource Values

A PromptDialog sets the following default values for SelectionBox resources:

| Name | Default |
|---|---|
| XmNdialogType | XmDIALOG_PROMPT |
| XmNlistLabelString | NULL |
| XmNlistVisibleItemCount | 0 |

## Widget Hierarchy

When a PromptDialog is created with a specified `name`, the DialogShell is named `name_popup` and the SelectionBox is called `name`.

## See Also

*XmCreateObject*(1), *XmSelectionBoxGetChild*(1), *XmDialogShell*(2), *XmSelectionBox*(2).

# XmPulldownMenu

## Name

XmPulldownMenu – a type of RowColumn used as a pulldown menu pane.

## Synopsis

**Public Header:** *<Xm/RowColumn.h>*

**Instantiation:** `widget = XmCreatePulldownMenu(...)`

**Functions/Macros:**

`XmCreatePulldownMenu()`, `XmCreateSimplePulldownMenu()`, `XmVaCreateSimplePulldownMenu()`

## Description

A PulldownMenu is a menu pane for all types of pulldown menu systems, including menus off of a menu bar, cascading submenus, and the menu associated with an option menu. A PulldownMenu is associated with a CascadeButton. A PulldownMenu can contain Separators, PushButtons, ToggleButtons, and CascadeButtons.

A PulldownMenu is a RowColumn widget whose `XmNrowColumnType` resource is set to `XmMENU_PULLDOWN`. A PulldownMenu needs to be the child of a MenuShell widget to function properly.

A PulldownMenu can be created using `XmCreatePulldownMenu()`. In this case, the PulldownMenu does not automatically contain any components; they are added by the application. The PulldownMenu created by this routine is a compound object consisting of a MenuShell widget and a RowColumn child.

A PulldownMenu can also be created by `XmCreateSimplePulldownMenu()`, which automatically creates the PulldownMenu with the specified children and makes it the child of a MenuShell. This routine uses the RowColumn resources associated with the creation of simple menus. For a PulldownMenu, any type is allowed in the `XmNbuttonType` resource. The name of each button is `button_`*n*, where *n* is the number of the button, ranging from 0 to 1 less than the number of buttons in the menu. The name of each separator is `separator_`*n*, where *n* is the number of the separator, ranging from 0 to 1 less than the number of separators in the menu. The name of each title is `label_`*n*, where *n* is the number of the title, ranging from 0 to 1 less than the number of titles in the menu.

## Default Resource Values

A PulldownMenu sets the following default values for RowColumn resources:

| Name | Default |
|---|---|
| XmNrowColumnType | XmMENU_POPUP |

## Widget Hierarchy

When a PulldownMenu is created with a specified `name`, the MenuShell is named `popup_name` and the RowColumn is called `name`.

## See Also

*XmCreateObject*(1), *XmVaCreateSimplePulldownMenu*(1), *XmCascadeButton*(2), *XmMenuShell*(2), *XmRowColumn*(2).

# XmPushButton

## Name

XmPushButton widget class – a widget that starts an operation when it is pressed.

## Synopsis

**Public Header:** *<Xm/PushB.h>*

**Class Name:** XmPushButton

**Class Hierarchy:** Core → XmPrimitive → XmLabel → XmPushButton

**Class Pointer:** `xmPushButtonWidgetClass`

**Instantiation:** `widget = XtCreateWidget(name, xmPushButtonWidgetClass, ...)`

**Functions/Macros:** `XmCreatePushButton()`, `XmIsPushButton()`

## Description

A PushButton is a widget that causes something to happen in an application. A PushButton displays a textual or graphics label. It invokes an application callback when it is clicked on with the mouse. The shading of the PushButton changes to make it appear either pressed in when selected or raised when unselected.

## New Resources

PushButton defines the following resources:

| Name | Class | Type | Default | Access |
|---|---|---|---|---|
| XmNarmColor | XmCArmColor | Pixel | dynamic | CSG |
| XmNarmPixmap | XmCArmPixmap | Pixmap | XmUNSPECIFIED_PIXMAP | CSG |
| XmNdefaultButtonShadowThickness | XmCDefaultButtonShadowThickness | Dimension | dynamic | CSG |
| XmNfillOnArm | XmCFillOnArm | Boolean | True | CSG |
| XmNmultiClick | XmCMultiClick | unsigned char | dynamic | CSG |
| XmNshowAsDefault | XmCShowAsDefault | Dimension | 0 | CSG |

`XmNarmColor`

The color with which the armed button is filled. For a color display, the default color is a shade between the bottom shadow color and the background color. For a monochrome display, the default is the foreground color, and label text is switched to the background color. This resource is in effect only when `XmNfillOnArm` is set to `True`.

`XmNarmPixmap`

The pixmap that identifies the button when it is armed (and when its `XmNlabelType` is `XmPIXMAP`). For a PushButton in a menu, this resource is disabled.

`XmNdefaultButtonShadowThickness`

The width of the shadow used to indicate a default PushButton.

`XmNfillOnArm`

If `True` (default), the PushButton widget fills the button (when armed) with the color specified by `XmNarmColor`. If `False`, the PushButton widget only switches the top and bottom shadow colors. For a PushButton in a menu, this resource is disabled (and assumed to be `False`).

`XmNmultiClick`

A flag that determines whether successive button clicks are processed or ignored. Possible values:

```
XmMULTICLICK_DISCARD   /* ignore successive button clicks; */
                       /* default value in a menu system */
XmMULTICLICK_KEEP      /* count successive button clicks; */
                       /* default value when not in a menu */
```

`XmNshowAsDefault`

Indicates the default PushButton by displaying a shadow. (In a menu, this resource is disabled.) This resource works in different ways: If the width of the shadow is already set in the `XmNdefaultButtonShadowThickness` resource, then `XmNshowAsDefault` behaves like a Boolean: that is, with a value of 0, no shadow is displayed; with a value greater than 0, a shadow is displayed. If the width of the shadow has *not* been set in the `XmNdefaultButtonShadowThickness` resource (i.e., it has a value of 0), then `XmNshowAsDefault` performs double duty: that is, a value greater than 0 says to highlight the PushButton as the default button *and* to use this value as the thickness of the shadow.

## Callback Resources

PushButton defines the following callback resources:

| Callback | Reason Constant |
|---|---|
| XmNactivateCallback | XmCR_ACTIVATE |
| XmNarmCallback | XmCR_ARM |
| XmNdisarmCallback | XmCR_DISARM |

`XmNactivateCallback`

List of callbacks that are called when `BSelect` is pressed and released inside the widget.

`XmNarmCallback`

List of callbacks that are called when `BSelect` is pressed while the pointer is inside the widget.

XmNdisarmCallback
: List of callbacks that are called when BSelect is released after it has been pressed inside the widget.

## Callback Structure

Each callback function is passed the following structure:

```
typedef struct
{
    int     reason;        /* the reason that the callback was called */
    XEvent  *event;        /* event structure that triggered callback */
    int     click_count;   /* number of multi-clicks */
} XmPushButtonCallbackStruct;
```

click_count is meaningful only for XmNactivateCallback. Furthermore, if the XmNmultiClick resource is set to XmMULTICLICK_KEEP, then XmNactivateCallback is called for each click, and the value of click_count is the number of clicks that have occurred in the last sequence of multiple clicks. If the XmNmultiClick resource is set to XmMULTICLICK_DISCARD, then click_count always has a value of 1.

## Inherited Resources

PushButton inherits the following resources. The resources are listed alphabetically, along with the superclass that defines them. PushButton sets the default values of XmNmarginBottom, XmNmarginLeft, XmNmarginRight, and XmNmarginTop dynamically based on the value of XmNshowAsDefault. If XmNarmPixmap is specified but XmNlabelPixmap is not, the default value of XmNlabelPixmap is set to the value of XmNarmPixmap. The default value of XmNborderWidth is reset to 0 by Primitive.

| Resource | Inherited From | Resource | Inherited From |
|---|---|---|---|
| XmNaccelerator | Label | XmNlabelString | Label |
| XmNaccelerators | Core | XmNlabelType | Label |
| XmNacceleratorText | Label | XmNmappedWhenManaged | Core |
| XmNalignment | Label | XmNmarginBottom | Label |
| XmNancestorSensitive | Core | XmNmarginHeight | Label |
| XmNbackground | Core | XmNmarginLeft | Label |
| XmNbackgroundPixmap | Core | XmNmarginRight | Label |
| XmNborderColor | Core | XmNmarginTop | Label |
| XmNborderPixmap | Core | XmNmarginWidth | Label |
| XmNborderWidth | Core | XmNmnemonic | Label |
| XmNbottomShadowColor | Primitive | XmNmnemonicCharSet | Label |
| XmNbottomShadowPixmap | Primitive | XmNnavigationType | Primitive |
| XmNcolormap | Core | XmNrecomputeSize | Label |
| XmNdepth | Core | XmNscreen | Core |
| XmNdestroyCallback | Core | XmNsensitive | Core |
| XmNfontList | Label | XmNshadowThickness | Primitive |

| Resource | Inherited From | Resource | Inherited From |
|---|---|---|---|
| XmNforeground | Primitive | XmNstringDirection | Label |
| XmNheight | Core | XmNtopShadowColor | Primitive |
| XmNhelpCallback | Primitive | XmNtopShadowPixmap | Primitive |
| XmNhighlightColor | Primitive | XmNtranslations | Core |
| XmNhighlightOnEnter | Primitive | XmNtraversalOn | Primitive |
| XmNhighlightPixmap | Primitive | XmNunitType | Primitive |
| XmNhighlightThickness | Primitive | XmNuserData | Primitive |
| XmNinitialResources-Persistent | Core | XmNwidth | Core |
| XmNlabelInsensitive-Pixmap | Label | XmNx | Core |
| XmNlabelPixmap | Label | XmNy | Core |

## Translations

| For PushButtons Outside a Menu System: | | For PushButtons in a Menu System: | |
|---|---|---|---|
| BSelect Press | Arm() | BSelect Press | BtnDown() |
| BSelect Click | Activate()<br>Disarm() | | |
| BSelect Release | Activate()<br>Disarm() | BMenu Press<br>BMenu Release | BtnDown()<br>BtnUp() |
| BSelect Press 2+ | MultiArm() | | |
| BSelect Release 2+ | MultiActivate()<br>Disarm() | | |
| BTransfer Press | ProcessDrag() | KActivate | ArmAndActivate() |
| KSelect | ArmAndActivate() | KSelect | ArmAndActivate() |
| KHelp | Help() | MAny KCancel | MenuShellPopdownOne() |

## Action Routines

PushButton defines the following action routines:

`Activate()`
: Displays the PushButton as unarmed, and invokes the list of callbacks specified by `XmNactivateCallback`. The button's appearance may depend on the values of the resources `XmNfillOnArm` and `XmNlabelPixmap`.

`Arm()`
: Displays the PushButton as armed, and invokes the list of callbacks specified by `XmNarmCallback`. The button's appearance may depend on the values of the resources `XmNarmColor` and `XmNarmPixmap`.

`ArmAndActivate()`
: When the PushButton is in a menu, this action unposts the menu hierarchy and invokes the callbacks specified by the resources `XmNarmCallback`, `XmNactivateCallback`, and finally, `XmNdisarmCallback`.

  When the PushButton is not in a menu, this action displays the PushButton as armed (as determined by the values of the resources `XmNarmColor` and `XmNarmPixmap`) and (assuming the button is not yet armed) invokes the list of callbacks specified by `XmNarmCallback`. After this occurs, the action displays the PushButton as unarmed and invokes the callbacks specified in `XmNactivateCallback` and `XmNdisarmCallback`.

`BtnDown()`
: Unposts any menus that were posted by the parent menu of the PushButton, changes from keyboard traversal to mouse traversal, displays the PushButton as armed, and (assuming the button is not yet armed) invokes the callbacks specified by `XmNarmCallback`.

`BtnUp()` Unposts the menu hierarchy, activates the PushButton, and invokes first the callbacks specified by `XmNactivateCallback` and then those specified by `XmNdisarmCallback`.

`Disarm()`
: Invokes the callbacks specified by `XmNdisarmCallback`.

`Help()` Unposts the menu hierarchy, restores the previous keyboard focus, and invokes the callbacks specified by the `XmNhelpCallback` resource.

`MenuShellPopdownOne()`
: Unposts the current menu and (unless the menu is a pulldown submenu) restores keyboard focus to the tab group or widget that previously had it. In a top-level pulldown menu pane attached to a menu bar, this action routine also disarms the cascade button and the menu bar.

`MultiActivate()`
: Increments the `click_count` member of `XmPushButtonCallbackStruct`, displays the PushButton as unarmed (as determined by the resources `XmNfill-OnArm` and `XmNlabelPixmap`), and invokes first the callbacks specified by `XmNactivateCallback` and then those specified by `XmNdisarmCallback`. This action routine takes effect only when the `XmNmultiClick` resource is set to `XmMULTICLICK_KEEP`.

`MultiArm()`
: Displays the PushButton as armed (as determined by the resources `XmNarmColor` and `XmNarmPixmap`) and invokes the list of callbacks specified by `XmNarmCallback`. This action routine takes effect only when the `XmNmulti-Click` resource is set to `XmMULTICLICK_KEEP`.

`ProcessDrag()`
In Motif 1.2, initiates a drag and drop operation using the label of the PushButton.

## Additional Behavior

PushButton has the following additional behavior:

`<EnterWindow>`
Displays the PushButton as armed.

`<LeaveWindow>`
Displays the PushButton as unarmed.

## See Also

*XmCreateObject*(1),
*Core*(2), *XmLabel*(2), *XmPrimitive*(2).

# XmPushButtonGadget

## Name

XmPushButtonGadget widget class – a gadget that starts an operation when it is pressed.

## Synopsis

**Public Header:** *<Xm/PushBG.h>*

**Class Name:** XmPushButtonGadget

**Class Hierarchy:** Object → RectObj → XmGadget → XmLabelGadget → XmPushButtonGadget

**Class Pointer:** xmPushButtonGadgetClass

**Instantiation:** `widget = XtCreateWidget(name, xmPushButtonGadgetClass, ...)`

**Functions/Macros:** `XmCreatePushButtonGadget()`, `XmIsPushButtonGadget()`

## Description

PushButtonGadget is the gadget variant of PushButton.

PushButtonGadget's new resources, callback resources, and callback structure are the same as those for PushButton.

## Inherited Resources

PushButtonGadget inherits the following resources. The resources are listed alphabetically, along with the superclass that defines them. PushButtonGadget sets the default values of `XmNmarginBottom`, `XmNmarginLeft`, `XmNmarginRight`, and `XmNmarginTop` dynamically based on the value of `XmNshowAsDefault`. If `XmNarmPixmap` is specified but `XmNlabelPixmap` is not, the default value of `XmNlabelPixmap` is set to the value of `XmNarmPixmap`. The default value of `XmNborderWidth` is reset to 0 by Gadget.

| Resource | Inherited From | Resource | Inherited From |
|---|---|---|---|
| XmNaccelerator | LabelGadget | XmNmarginLeft | LabelGadget |
| XmNacceleratorText | LabelGadget | XmNmarginRight | LabelGadget |
| XmNalignment | LabelGadget | XmNmarginTop | LabelGadget |
| XmNancestorSensitive | RectObj | XmNmarginWidth | LabelGadget |
| XmNborderWidth | RectObj | XmNmnemonic | LabelGadget |
| XmNbottomShadowColor | Gadget | XmNmnemonicCharSet | LabelGadget |
| XmNdestroyCallback | Object | XmNnavigationType | Gadget |
| XmNfontList | LabelGadget | XmNrecomputeSize | LabelGadget |
| XmNheight | RectObj | XmNsensitive | RectObj |
| XmNhelpCallback | Gadget | XmNshadowThickness | Gadget |
| XmNhighlightColor | Gadget | XmNstringDirection | LabelGadget |
| XmNhighlightOnEnter | Gadget | XmNtopShadowColor | Gadget |
| XmNhighlightThickness | Gadget | XmNtraversalOn | Gadget |
| XmNlabelInsensitivePixmap | LabelGadget | XmNunitType | Gadget |
| XmNlabelPixmap | LabelGadget | XmNuserData | Gadget |

| Resource | Inherited From | Resource | Inherited From |
|---|---|---|---|
| XmNlabelString | LabelGadget | XmNwidth | RectObj |
| XmNlabelType | LabelGadget | XmNx | RectObj |
| XmNmarginBottom | LabelGadget | XmNy | RectObj |
| XmNmarginHeight | LabelGadget | | |

## Behavior

As a gadget subclass, PushButtonGadget has no translations associated with it. However, PushButtonGadget behavior corresponds to the action routines of the PushButton widget. See the PushButton action routines for more information.

| Behavior | Equivalent PushButton Action Routine |
|---|---|
| BTransfer Press | ProcessDrag() |
| BSelect Press | Arm() |
| | BtnDown() (in a menu) |
| BSelect Click | Activate(), Disarm() |
| | BtnUp() (in a menu) |
| BSelect Release | Activate(), Disarm() |
| | BtnUp() (in a menu) |
| BSelect Press 2+ | MultiArm() |
| BSelect Release 2+ | MultiActivate(), Disarm() |
| BTransfer Press | ProcessDrag() |
| KSelect | ArmAndActivate() |
| KActivate | ArmAndActivate() (in a menu) |
| KHelp | Help() |
| MAny KCancel | MenuShellPopdownOne() |

PushButtonGadget has additional behavior associated with <Enter> and <Leave>, which draw the shadow in the armed or unarmed state, respectively.

## See Also

*XmCreateObject*(1),
*Object*(2), *RectObj*(2), *XmGadget*(2), *XmLabelGadget*(2), *XmPushButton*(2).

# XmQuestionDialog

## Name

XmQuestionDialog – an unmanaged MessageBox as a child of a DialogShell.

## Synopsis

**Public Header:** *<Xm/MessageB.h>*

**Instantiation:** `widget = XmCreateQuestionDialog(...)`

**Functions/Macros:** `XmCreateQuestionDialog()`, `XmMessageBoxGetChild()`

## Description

A QuestionDialog is a compound object created by a call to `XmCreateQuestionDialog()` that an application can use to ask the user a question. A QuestionDialog consists of a DialogShell with a MessageBox widget as its child. The MessageBox resource `XmNdialogType` is set to `XmDIALOG_QUESTION`.

A QuestionDialog includes four components: a symbol, a message, three buttons, and a separator between the message and the buttons. By default, the symbol is a question mark. In Motif 1.2, the default button labels can be localized. In the C locale, and in Motif 1.1, the PushButtons are labeled **OK**, **Cancel**, and **Help** by default.

## Default Resource Values

A QuestionDialog sets the following default values for MessageBox resources:

| Name | Default |
|---|---|
| XmNdialogType | XmDIALOG_QUESTION |
| XmNsymbolPixmap | xm_question |

## Widget Hierarchy

When a QuestionDialog is created with a specified `name`, the DialogShell is named `name_popup` and the MessageBox is called `name`.

## See Also

*XmCreateObject*(1), *XmMessageBoxGetChild*(1), *XmDialogShell*(2), *XmMessageBox*(2).

# XmRadioBox

## Name

XmRadioBox – a RowColumn that contains ToggleButtons.

## Synopsis

**Public Header:** *<Xm/RowColumn.h>*

**Class Name:** XmRowColumn

**Class Hierarchy:** Core → Composite → Constraint → XmManager → XmRowColumn

**Class Pointer:** `xmRowColumnWidgetClass`

**Instantiation:** *`widget`* `= XmCreateRadioBox(...)`

**Functions/Macros:** `XmCreateRadioBox()`, `XmCreateSimpleRadioBox()`, `XmVaCreateSimpleRadioBox()`, `XmIsRowColumn()`

## Description

A RadioBox is an instance of a RowColumn widget that contains ToggleButtons, only one of which can be selected at a given time. When a RadioBox is created with XmCreateRadioBox(), it does not automatically contain ToggleButton children; they are added by the application developer. A RadioBox can also be created by a call to XmCreateSimpleRadioBox(), which automatically creates the specified ToggleButton widgets as children.

A RadioBox is a RowColumn widget with its `XmNrowColumnType` resource set to `XmWORK_AREA` and `XmNradioAlwaysOne` set to `True`, which means that one button is always selected. The `XmNradioBehavior` resource is set to `True`. The `XmNmenuHistory` resource indicates the last ToggleButton that was selected. The `XmNisHomogenous` resource is set to `True` and `XmNentryClass` is set to ToggleButton, to ensure that only ToggleButtons are added as children. RadioBox sets `XmNvisibleWhenOff` to `True` and `XmNindicatorType` to `XmONE_OF_MANY` for all of its ToggleButton children.

A RadioBox can be created by making a RowColumn with these resource values. When it is created in this way, a RadioBox does not automatically contain ToggleButton children; they are added by the application.

A RadioBox can also be created by a call to `XmCreateSimpleRadioBox()` or `XmVaCreateSimpleRadioBox()`. These routines automatically create the RadioBox with ToggleButtonGadgets as children. The routines use the RowColumn resources associated with the creation of simple menus. For a RadioBox, the only type allowed in the `XmNbuttonType` resource is `XmRADIOBUTTON`. The name of each ToggleButtonGadget is `button_`*n*, where *n* is the number of the button, ranging from 0 to 1 less than the number of buttons in the RadioBox.

## Default Resource Values

A RadioBox sets the following default values for its resources:

| Name | Default |
|---|---|
| XmNentryClass | xmToggleButtonWidgetClass |
| XmNisHomogeneous | True |
| XmNnavigationType | XmTAB_GROUP |
| XmNradioAlwaysOne | True |
| XmNradioBehavior | True |
| XmNrowColumnType | XmWORK_AREA |
| XmNtraversalOn | True |

## See Also

*XmCreateObject*(1), *XmVaCreateSimpleRadioBox*(1), *XmRowColumn*(2), *XmToggleButton*(2).

# XmRowColumn

## Name

XmRowColumn widget class – a manager widget that arranges its children in rows and columns.

## Synopsis

**Public Header:** *<Xm/RowColumn.h>*

**Class Name:** XmRowColumn

**Class Hierarchy:** Core → Composite → Constraint → XmManager → XmRowColumn

**Class Pointer:** `xmRowColumnWidgetClass`

**Instantiation:** `widget = XtCreateWidget(name, xmRowColumnWidgetClass, ...)`

**Functions/Macros:** `XmCreateMenuBar()`, `XmCreateOptionMenu()`, `XmCreatePopupMenu()`, `XmCreatePulldownMenu()`, `XmCreateRadioBox()`, `XmCreateRowColumn()`, `XmCreateSimpleCheckBox()`, `XmCreateSimpleMenuBar()`, `XmCreateSimpleOptionMenu()`, `XmCreateSimplePopupMenu()`, `XmCreateSimplePulldownMenu()`, `XmCreateSimpleRadioBox()`, `XmCreateWorkArea()`, `XmIsRowColumn()`, `XmVaCreateSimpleCheckBox()`, `XmVaCreateSimpleMenuBar()`, `XmVaCreateSimpleOptionMenu()`, `XmVaCreateSimplePopupMenu()`, `XmVaCreateSimplePulldownMenu()`, `XmVaCreateSimpleRadioBox()`

## Description

RowColumn provides an area in which children belonging to any widget type are displayed in rows and columns. RowColumn is a general-purpose manager widget class that can be configured into many layouts, such as a MenuBar, PopupMenu, PulldownMenu, OptionMenu, CheckBox, or RadioBox. Many of RowColumn's resources pertain only to a specific layout type.

In Motif 1.2, a RowColumn that is configured as a PopupMenu or a PulldownMenu supports tear-off menus. When a menu is torn off, it remains on the screen after a selection is made so that additional selections can be made. A menu pane that can be torn off contains a tear-off button at the top of the menu. A tear-off button is a button that has a Separator-like appearance. The name of a tear-off button in a menu pane is `TearOffControl`. An application can set the following resources for a tear-off button: `XmNbackground`, `XmNbackgroundPixmap`, `XmNbottomShadowColor`, `XmNforeground`, `XmNheight`, `XmNmargin`, `XmNseparatorType`, `XmNshadowThickness`, and `XmNtopShadowColor`.

## New Resources

RowColumn defines the following resources, which are all CSG access, except for XmN-labelString (C) and XmNrowColumnType (CG):

| Name | Class | Type | Default |
|---|---|---|---|
| XmNadjustLast | XmCAdjustLast | Boolean | True |
| XmNadjustLast | XmCAdjustLast | Boolean | True |
| XmNadjustMargin | XmCAdjustMargin | Boolean | True |
| XmNentryAlignment | XmCAlignment | unsigned char | XmALIGNMENT_ BEGINNING |
| XmNentryBorder | XmCEntryBorder | Dimension | 0 |
| XmNentryClass | XmCEntryClass | WidgetClass | dynamic |
| XmNentryVertical- Alignment | XmCVerticalAlignment | unsigned char | XmALIGNMENT_ CENTER |
| XmNisAligned | XmCIsAligned | Boolean | True |
| XmNisHomogeneous | XmCIsHomogeneous | Boolean | dynamic |
| XmNlabelString | XmCXmString | XmString | NULL |
| XmNmarginHeight | XmCMarginHeight | Dimension | dynamic |
| XmNmarginWidth | XmCMarginWidth | Dimension | dynamic |
| XmNmenuAccelerator | XmCAccelerators | String | dynamic |
| XmNmenuHelpWidget | XmCMenuWidget | Widget | NULL |
| XmNmenuHistory | XmCMenuWidget | Widget | NULL |
| XmNmenuPost | XmCMenuPost | String | NULL |
| XmNmnemonic | XmCMnemonic | KeySym | NULL |
| XmNmnemonicCharSet | XmCMnemonicCharSet | String | XmFONTLIST_ DEFAULT_TAG |
| XmNnumColumns | XmCNumColumns | short | 1 |
| XmNorientation | XmCOrientation | unsigned char | dynamic |
| XmNpacking | XmCPacking | unsigned char | dynamic |
| XmNpopupEnabled | XmCPopupEnabled | Boolean | True |
| XmNradioAlwaysOne | XmCRadioAlwaysOne | Boolean | True |
| XmNradioBehavior | XmCRadioBehavior | Boolean | False |
| XmNresizeHeight | XmCResizeHeight | Boolean | True |
| XmNresizeWidth | XmCResizeWidth | Boolean | True |
| XmNrowColumnType | XmCRowColumnType | unsigned char | XmWORK_AREA |
| XmNspacing | XmCSpacing | Dimension | dynamic |
| XmNsubMenuId | XmCMenuWidget | Widget | NULL |
| XmNtearOffModel | XmCTearOffModel | unsigned char | XmTEAR_OFF_ DISABLED |
| XmNwhichButton | XmCWhichButton | unsigned int | dynamic |

XmNadjustLast

If True (default), the last row (or column) in the RowColumn widget is expanded so as to be flush with the edge.

XmNadjustMargin
: If True (default), text in each row (or column) will align with other text in its row (or column). This is done by forcing the margin resources (defined by the Label widget) to have the same value. For example, in a horizontally-oriented RowColumn widget, all items will have the same value for XmNmarginTop and XmNmarginBottom; in a vertically-oriented RowColumn widget, all items will have the same value for XmNmarginLeft and XmNmarginRight.

XmNentryAlignment
: When XmNisAligned is True, this resource tells RowColumn children how to align. The children must be subclasses of XmLabel or XmLabelGadget. If XmNrowColumnType is XmMENU_OPTION, the resource is forced to XmALIGNMENT_CENTER and cannot be changed. Possible values:

```
XmALIGNMENT_BEGINNING
XmALIGNMENT_CENTER
XmALIGNMENT_END
```

XmNentryBorder
: The border width of a RowColumn widget's children.

XmNentryClass
: The widget class to which children must belong when being added to a RowColumn widget. This resource is used only when the XmNisHomogeneous resource is set to True. XmNentryClass ensures that a MenuBar will have only cascade button children and that a RadioBox will have only toggle button children (or gadget variants of each class). XmNentryClass can have one of two default values. For a MenuBar, the default value is xmCascadeButtonWidgetClass. For a RadioBox, the default value is xmToggleButtonGadgetClass. Possible values:

```
xmToggleButtonGadgetClass/* XmWORK_AREA with XmNradioBehavior True */
xmCascadeButtonWidgetClass/* XmMENU_BAR */
```

XmNentryVerticalAlignment
: In Motif 1.2, specifies how children that are subclasses of Label, Text, and TextField are aligned vertically. The resource has no effect if XmNorientation is XmVERTICAL or XmNpacking is XmPACK_TIGHT. Possible values:

```
XmALIGNMENT_BASELINE_BOTTOM
XmALIGNMENT_BASELINE_TOP
XmALIGNMENT_CONTENTS_BOTTOM
XmALIGNMENT_CENTER
XmALIGNMENT_CONTENTS_TOP
```

XmNisAligned
: If True, enable the alignment specified in the XmNentryAlignment resource. Alignment is ignored in a label whose parent is a popup or pulldown MenuPane.

`XmNisHomogeneous`
If `True`, enforce the condition that all RowColumn children belong to the same class (the class specified by the `XmNentryClass` resource). When creating a RadioBox or a MenuBar, the default value of this resource is `True`; otherwise, it's `False`.

`XmNlabelString`
A label used only in option menus. A text string displays beside the selection area. By default, there is no label.

`XmNmarginHeight`
`XmNmarginWidth`
The spacing between an edge of the RowColumn widget and its nearest child. In popup and pulldown menus, the default is 0; in other types of RowColumn widgets, the default is 3 pixels.

`XmNmenuAccelerator`
A pointer to a string that specifies an accelerator (keyboard shortcut) for use only in RowColumn widgets of type `XmMENU_POPUP` or `XmMENU_BAR`. In a popup menu, typing the accelerator posts the menu; in a menu bar, typing the accelerator highlights the first item and enables traversal in the menu bar. The string's format is like that of a translation but allows only a single key press event to be specified. The default value of this resource is `KMenu` (for popup menus) and `KMenuBar` (for menu bars).

`XmNmenuHelpWidget`
The widget ID of the CascadeButton widget that serves as the `Help` button. This resource is meaningful only in RowColumn widgets of type `XmMENU_BAR`.

`XmNmenuHistory`
The widget ID of the most recently activated menu entry. Since the most recently activated menu entry is also the choice that displays in an OptionMenu, this resource is useful for indicating the current selection in a RowColumn widget of type `XmMENU_OPTION`. In a RowColumn widget whose `XmNradioBehavior` resource is set to `True`, the `XmNmenuHistory` resource indicates the last toggle button to change from unselected to selected.

`XmNmenuPost`
The string that describes the event for posting a menu. The default value depends on the type of RowColumn widget: for `XmMENU_POPUP`, the default is `BMenu Press`; for `XmMENU_OPTION`, `XmMENU_BAR`, and `XmWORK_AREA` the default is `BSelect Press`; for `XmMENU_PULLDOWN`, this resource isn't meaningful.

`XmNmnemonic`
The keysym of the key to press (in combination with the `MAlt` modifier) in order to post the pulldown menu associated with an option menu. This resource is meaningful only in option menus. In the label string, the first character matching this keysym will be underlined.

XmNmnemonicCharSet
: The character set for the option menu's mnemonic. The default value depends on the current language environment.

XmNnumColumns
: The number of columns (in a vertically-oriented RowColumn widget) or the number of rows (in a horizontally-oriented RowColumn widget). This resource is meaningful only when the XmNpacking resource is set to XmPACK_COLUMN.

XmNorientation
: The direction for laying out the rows and columns of children of a RowColumn widget. For all RowColumn widgets except a MenuBar, the default value is XmVERTICAL. Possible values:

```
XmVERTICAL           /* top-to-bottom creation */
XmHORIZONTAL         /* left-to-right creation */
```

XmNpacking
: The method of spacing the items placed within a RowColumn widget. The default value is XmPACK_COLUMN for a RadioBox, and XmPACK_TIGHT for other types of Row-Column widget. Possible values:

```
XmPACK_TIGHT         /* give each box minimum sizing */
XmPACK_COLUMN        /* pad boxes to align if needed */
XmPACK_NONE          /* widget accommodates placement */
```

XmNpopupEnabled
: If True (default), keyboard shortcuts are in effect for popup menus. Set this resource to False if you want to disable accelerators and mnemonics in popup menus.

XmNradioAlwaysOne
: This resource is effective only when the XmNradioBehavior resource is True. XmNradioAlwaysOne, when set to True (default), ensures that one of the toggle buttons is always selected. Once this button is selected, clicking on it will not deselect it; it can be deselected only by selecting another toggle button. If XmNradioAlways-One is False, a selected toggle button can be deselected by clicking on it or by selecting another button.

XmNradioBehavior
: If True, the RowColumn widget acts like a RadioBox by setting two of the resources for its toggle button children. Namely, the XmNindicatorType resource defaults to XmONE_OF_MANY, and the XmNvisibleWhenOff resource defaults to True. The default value of the XmNradioBehavior resource is False, unless the RowColumn widget was created with the XmCreateRadioBox() routine.

XmNresizeHeight
XmNresizeWidth

If True (default), the widget requests a new height or width when necessary. If False, no resize requests are made.

XmNrowColumnType

The type of RowColumn widget to create. You can't change this resource after it's set. Convenience routines create a RowColumn widget of the appropriate type. Possible values:

XmWORK_AREA
XmMENU_BAR
XmMENU_POPUP
XmMENU_PULLDOWN
XmMENU_OPTION

XmNspacing

The horizontal and vertical spacing between children in the RowColumn widget. For RowColumn widgets of type XmOPTION_MENU or XmWORK_AREA, the default value is 3 pixels; for other RowColumn types, the default is 0.

XmNsubMenuId

The widget ID for the pulldown menu pane to be associated with an OptionMenu. This resource is meaningful only in RowColumn widgets of type xmMENU_OPTION.

XmNtearOffModel

In Motif 1.2, specifies whether tear-off behavior is enabled for a RowColumn with XmNrowColumnType set to XmMENU_PULLDOWN or XmMENU_POPUP. This resource cannot be set from a resource file unless a converter is installed with XmRepTypeInstallTearOffModelConverter(). Possible values:

XmTEAR_OFF_DISABLED
XmTEAR_OFF_ENABLED

XmNwhichButton

This resource has been superceded by the XmNmenuPost resource but is retained for compatibility with older releases of Motif.

### New Constraint Resources

RowColumn defines the following constraint resources for its children:

| Name | Class | Type | Default | Access |
|---|---|---|---|---|
| XmNpositionIndex | XmCPositionIndex | short | XmLAST_POSITION | CSG |

XmNpositionIndex

In Motif 1.2, the position of the widget in the RowColumn's list of children. A value of 0 indicates the beginning of the list, while XmLAST_POSITION places the child at the end of the list.

## Simple Menu Creation Resources

The following resources are used with the simple menu creation routines.

| Name | Class | Type | Default | Access |
|---|---|---|---|---|
| XmNbuttonAccelerators | XmCButtonAccelerators | StringTable | NULL | C |
| XmNbuttonAccelerator-Text | XmCButtonAccelerator-Text | XmStringTable | NULL | C |
| XmNbuttonCount | XmCButtonCount | int | 0 | C |
| XmNbuttonMnemonic-CharSets | XmCButtonMnemonic-CharSets | XmStringCharSetTable | NULL | C |
| XmNbuttonMnemonics | XmCButtonMnemonics | XmKeySymTable | NULL | C |
| XmNbuttons | XmCButtons | XmStringTable | NULL | C |
| XmNbuttonSet | XmCButtonSet | int | -1 | C |
| XmNbuttonType | XmCButtonType | XmButtonTypeTable | NULL | C |
| XmNoptionLabel | XmCOptionLabel | XmString | NULL | C |
| XmNoptionMnemonic | XmCOptionMnemonic | KeySym | NULL | C |
| XmNpostFromButton | XmCPostFromButton | int | -1 | C |
| XmNsimpleCallback | XmCCallback | XtCallbackProc | NULL | C |

`XmNbuttonAccelerators`
: A list of accelerators, containing one item for each created title, separator, and button.

`XmNbuttonAcceleratorText`
: A list of compound strings that represent the accelerators for the created buttons. The list contains one item for each created title, separator, and button.

`XmNbuttonCount`
: The number of titles, separators, and menu buttons to create.

`XmNbuttonMnemonicCharSets`
: A list of character sets to use for displaying button mnemonics. The list contains an item for each created title, separator, and button.

`XmNbuttonMnemonics`
: A list of mnemonics associated with the buttons created. The list contains one item for each created title, separator, and button.

`XmNbuttons`
: A list of compound strings that will serve as labels for the created buttons. The list contains one item for each created title, separator, and button.

`XmNbuttonSet`
: The numeric position of the button to be initially set within a RadioBox or within an OptionMenu's pulldown submenu. The first button is specified as 0.

`XmNbuttonType`
: A list of button types for the created buttons. The list contains one item for each created title, separator, and button. If this resource is not set, the buttons created will be

CascadeButtonGadgets in a MenuBar and PushButtonGadgets in other types of Row-Column widget. The XmNbuttonType resource is an enumerated type whose possible values are:

| | | |
|---|---|---|
| XmPUSHBUTTON | XmCASCADEBUTTON | XmDOUBLE_SEPARATOR |
| XmCHECKBUTTON | XmRADIOBUTTON | XmSEPARATOR |
| XmTITLE | | |

XmNoptionLabel
: A compound string with which to label the left side of an option menu.

XmNoptionMnemonic
: The keysym of the key to press (in combination with the MAlt modifier) in order to post the pulldown menu associated with an option menu.

XmNpostFromButton
: The numeric position of the cascade button (in the parent) from which the pulldown submenu is attached and subsequently posted. The first button is specified as 0.

XmNsimpleCallback
: List of callbacks that are called when a button is pressed or when its value changes. For PushButtons and CascadeButtons, the callbacks are added to the XmNactivate-Callback and for ToggleButtons they are added to the XmNvalueChanged-Callback.

### Callback Resources

RowColumn defines the following callback resources:

| Callback | Reason Constant |
|---|---|
| XmNentryCallback | XmCR_ACTIVATE |
| XmNmapCallback | XmCR_MAP |
| XmNtearOffMenuActivateCallback | XmCR_TEAR_OFF_ACTIVATE |
| XmNtearOffMenuDeactivateCallback | XmCR_TEAR_OFF_DEACTIVATE |
| XmNunmapCallback | XmCR_UNMAP |

XmNentryCallback
: List of callbacks that are called when any button is pressed or when its value changes. When this resource is specified, the XmNactivateCallback and XmNvalue-ChangedCallback callbacks for all PushButtons, ToggleButtons, DrawnButtons, and CascadeButtons are disabled and instead call this callback. This resource must be specified when the RowColumn is created.

XmNmapCallback
: List of callbacks that are called when the window associated with a RowColumn is going to be mapped.

`XmNtearOffMenuActivateCallback`
List of callbacks that are called when a tear-off menu pane is going to be torn off.

`XmNtearOffMenuDeactivateCallback`
List of callbacks that are called when a torn-off menu pane is going to be deactivated.

`XmNunmapCallback`
List of callbacks that are called when the window associated with a RowColumn is going to be unmapped.

## Callback Structure

Each callback function is passed the following structure:

```
typedef struct
{
   int      reason;           /* the reason that the callback was called */
   XEvent   *event;           /* event structure that triggered callback */
   Widget   widget;           /* ID of activated RowColumn item */
   char     *data;            /* value of application's client data */
   char     *callbackstruct;  /* created when item is activated */
} XmRowColumnCallbackStruct;
```

The structure members `widget`, `data`, and `callbackstruct` are meaningful only when the callback reason is `XmCR_ACTIVATE`; otherwise, these structure members are set to `NULL`.

`callbackstruct` points to a structure that is created by the activation callback of the Row-Column item.

## Inherited Resources

RowColumn inherits the following resources. The resources are listed alphabetically, along with the superclass that defines them. RowColumn sets the default value of `XmNshadowThickness` to 2 if `XmNrowColumnType` is `XmMENU_BAR`, `XmMENU_POPUP`, or `XmMENU_PULLDOWN`; the resource is undefined when `XmNrowColumnType` is `XmMENU_OPTION` or `XmWORK_AREA`. The default value of `XmNnavigationType` is set to `XmTAB_GROUP` for a work area and `XmNONE` for an option menu; the resource is undefined for the other row column types. The default value of `XmNtraversalOn` is set to `True` for a work area or an option menu; the resource is undefined for the other row column types. The default value of `XmNborderWidth` is reset to 0 by Manager.

| Resource | Inherited From | Resource | Inherited From |
|---|---|---|---|
| XmNaccelerators | Core | XmNinitialResourcesPersistent | Core |
| XmNancestorSensitive | Core | XmNinsertPosition | Composite |
| XmNbackground | Core | XmNmappedWhenManaged | Core |
| XmNbackgroundPixmap | Core | XmNnavigationType | Manager |
| XmNborderColor | Core | XmNnumChildren | Composite |
| XmNborderPixmap | Core | XmNscreen | Core |
| XmNborderWidth | Core | XmNsensitive | Core |

| Resource | Inherited From | Resource | Inherited From |
|---|---|---|---|
| XmNbottomShadowColor | Manager | XmNshadowThickness | Manager |
| XmNbottomShadowPixmap | Manager | XmNstringDirection | Manager |
| XmNchildren | Composite | XmNtopShadowColor | Manager |
| XmNcolormap | Core | XmNtopShadowPixmap | Manager |
| XmNdepth | Core | XmNtranslations | Core |
| XmNdestroyCallback | Core | XmNtraversalOn | Manager |
| XmNforeground | Manager | XmNunitType | Manager |
| XmNheight | Core | XmNuserData | Manager |
| XmNhelpCallback | Manager | XmNwidth | Core |
| XmNhighlightColor | Manager | XmNx | Core |
| XmNhighlightPixmap | Manager | XmNy | Core |
| XmNinitialFocus | Manager | | |

## Translations

The value of the XmNrowColumnType resource determines the available translations.

When XmNrowColumnType is XmWORK_AREA, RowColumn's translations are inherited from Manager.

When XmNrowColumnType is XmMENU_OPTION, RowColumn's translations are the traversal, KActivate, and KCancel translations inherited from Manager, as well as the following:

```
BSelect Press      MenuBtnDown()
BSelect Release    MenuBtnUp()
KSelect            ManagerGadgetSelect()
KHelp              Help()
```

When XmNrowColumnType is XmMENU_BAR, XmMENU_PULLDOWN, or XmMENU_POPUP, RowColumn has the following translations (in PopupMenu systems, BMenu performs the BSelect actions as well): following:

```
BSelect Press      MenuBtnDown()
BSelect Release    MenuBtnUp()
KActivate          ManagerGadgetSelect()
KSelect            ManagerGadgetSelect()
MAny KCancel       MenuGadgetEscape()
KHelp              Help()
KLeft              MenuGadgetTraverseLeft()
KRight             MenuGadgetTraverseRight()
KUp                MenuGadgetTraverseUp()
KDown              MenuGadgetTraverseDown()
```

### Action Routines

RowColumn defines the following action routines:

`Help()` Invokes any callbacks specified by the `XmNhelpCallback` resource.

`ManagerGadgetSelect()`
Arms and activates the gadget child (in a menu) that has focus. For a CascadeButtonGadget, its submenu is posted; for other gadget children, the menu hierarchy is unposted.

`MenuBtnDown()`
In a gadget child (in a menu), unposts any menus that were posted by the gadget's parent menu, turns mouse traversal on, and arms the gadget. If the child is a CascadeButtonGadget, its submenu is posted.

`MenuBtnUp()`
In a gadget child (in a menu), unposts the menu hierarchy and activates the gadget. If the child is a CascadeButtonGadget, this action posts the submenu and turns on keyboard traversal in the submenu.

`MenuGadgetEscape()`
Unposts the current menu and (unless the menu is a pulldown submenu) restores keyboard focus to the tab group or widget that previously had it (assuming an explicit focus policy). In a top-level pulldown menu pane attached to a menu bar, this action routine also disarms the cascade button and the menu bar.

`MenuGadgetTraverseDown()`
When the current menu item has a submenu and is in a MenuBar, disarms the current menu item, posts the submenu, and arms the first item in it. When the current menu item is in a menu pane, disarms the current menu item and arms the item below it, wrapping around to the top if necessary.

`MenuGadgetTraverseLeft()`
If the current menu item is in a MenuBar, disarms the current item and arms the MenuBar item to the left, wrapping around to the right if necessary. When the current item is in a menu pane, if the item is not at the left edge of the pane, disarms the current menu item and arms the item to its left. If the item is at the left edge of a submenu attached to the MenuBar, unposts the submenu, traverses to the MenuBar item to the left, and posts its submenu, wrapping if necessary.

`MenuGadgetTraverseRight()`
If the current menu item is in a MenuBar, disarms the current item and arms the MenuBar item to the right, wrapping around to the left if necessary. When the current item is in a menu pane, if the item is a CascadeButton, posts the associated submenu. If the current item is not at the right edge of the pane, disarms the current item and arms the item to the right, wrapping if necessary. Otherwise, unposts all submenus, traverses to the MenuBar item to the right, and posts its submenu, wrapping if necessary.

`MenuGadgetTraverseUp()`
Disarms the current menu item and arms the item above it, wrapping around to the bottom if necessary.

### Additional Behavior

RowColumn has additional menu behavior:

`KMenuBar`
In a menu bar or in any menu pane cascaded from it, unposts the menu tree and (under an explicit focus policy) returns keyboard focus to the tab group that had it before entering the menu tree. In other non-popup menu panes, turns on keyboard traversal and sets the focus to the first menu bar item.

`KMenu`
Pops up the menu associated with the component with the keyboard focus and turns on keyboard traversal. In a popup menu system, unposts the menu tree and (under an explicit focus policy) returns keyboard focus to the tab group that had it before entering the menu tree.

### See Also

*XmCreateObject*(1), *XmGetMenuCursor*(1), *XmGetPostedFromWidget*(1), *XmGetTearOffControl*(1), *XmMenuPosition*(1), *XmOptionButtonGadget*(1), *XmOptionLabelGadget*(1), *XmRepTypeInstallTearOffModelConverter*(1), *XmSetMenuCursor*(1), *XmVaCreateSimpleCheckBox*(1), *XmVaCreateSimpleMenuBar*(1), *XmVaCreateSimpleOptionMenu*(1), *XmVaCreateSimplePopupMenu*(1), *XmVaCreateSimplePulldownMenu*(1), *XmVaCreateSimpleRadioBox*(1), *Composite*(2), *Constraint*(2), *Core*(2), *XmCascadeButton*(2), *XmCheckBox*(2), *XmManager*(2), *XmMenuBar*(2), *XmOptionMenu*(2), *XmPopupMenu*(2), *XmPulldownMenu*(2), *XmRadioBox*(2).

## Name

XmScale widget class – a manager widget that allows selection from a range of values.

## Synopsis

**Public Header:** *<Xm/Scale.h>*

**Class Name:** XmScale

**Class Hierarchy:** Core → Composite → Constraint → XmManager → XmScale

**Class Pointer:** `xmScaleWidgetClass`

**Instantiation:** `widget = XtCreateWidget(name, xmScaleWidgetClass, ...)`

**Functions/Macros:** `XmCreateScale()`, `XmIsScale()`, `XmScaleGetValue()`, `XmScaleSetValue()`

## Description

A Scale displays a value from a range of values and allows a user to adjust the value. A Scale consists of a narrow, rectangular trough that contains a slider. The slider's position marks the current value within the range of values. Scale is a manager widget that orients its children along its axis. These children, typically labels, can be used as tick marks. If the Scale widget is an input-output type (`XmNsensitive is True`), a user can change the value by moving the slider. An output-only Scale displays a value but does not allow a user to modify it.

## New Resources

Scale defines the following resources:

| Name | Class | Type | Default | Access |
|---|---|---|---|---|
| XmNdecimalPoints | XmCDecimalPoints | short | 0 | CSG |
| XmNfontList | XmCFontList | XmFontList | dynamic | CSG |
| XmNhighlightOnEnter | XmCHighlight-OnEnter | Boolean | False | CSG |
| XmNhighlightThickness | XmCHighlight-Thickness | Dimension | 2 | CSG |
| XmNmaximum | XmCMaximum | int | 100 | CSG |
| XmNminimum | XmCMinimum | int | 0 | CSG |
| XmNorientation | XmCOrientation | unsigned char | XmVERTICAL | CSG |
| XmNprocessingDirection | XmCProcessing Direction | unsigned char | dynamic | CSG |
| XmNscaleHeight | XmCScaleHeight | Dimension | 0 | CSG |
| XmNscaleMultiple | XmCScaleMultiple | int | dynamic | CSG |
| XmNscaleWidth | XmCScaleWidth | Dimension | 0 | CSG |
| XmNshowValue | XmCShowValue | Boolean | False | CSG |
| XmNtitleString | XmCTitleString | XmString | NULL | CSG |
| XmNvalue | XmCValue | int | dynamic | CSG |

`XmNdecimalPoints`

A positive integer that determines how the slider's value will be displayed. The decimal point in the slider's value gets shifted to the right, and this resource specifies the number of decimal places to shift. For example, if the slider's value is 1234, then setting the `XmdecimalPoints` resource to 2 causes the widget to display the value as 12.34.

`XmNfontList`

The font list used for the text specified by the `XmNtitleString` resource. If this value is initially `NULL`, the font list is derived from the font list resource from the nearest parent that is a subclass of BulletinBoard, MenuShell, or VendorShell.

`XmNhighlightOnEnter`

Determines whether to draw the widget's highlighting rectangle whenever the cursor moves into the widget. This resource applies only when the shell has a focus policy of `XmPOINTER`. If the `XmNhighlightOnEnter` resource is `True`, highlighting is drawn; if `False` (default), highlighting is not drawn.

`XmNhighlightThickness`

The thickness of the highlighting rectangle.

`XmNmaximum`

`XmNminimum`

The maximum/minimum value of the slider.

`XmNorientation`

The direction in which the scale is displayed. Possible values:

```
XmVERTICAL          /* top-to-bottom creation */
XmHORIZONTAL        /* left-to-right creation */
```

`XmNprocessingDirection`

Determines the position at which to display the slider's maximum and minimum values, with respect to the slider. Possible values:

```
XmMAX_ON_TOP        /* scale increases toward top */
XmMAX_ON_BOTTOM     /* scale increases toward bottom */
XmMAX_ON_LEFT       /* scale increases toward left */
XmMAX_ON_RIGHT      /* scale increases toward right */
```

For vertically-oriented Scale widgets, the default value is `XmMAX_ON_TOP`. For horizontally-oriented Scale widgets, the default value is usually `XmMAX_ON_RIGHT` (depending on the value of the `XmNstringDirection` resource).

`XmNscaleHeight`
`XmNscaleWidth`

The height or width of the slider area.

`XmNscaleMultiple`

The distance to move the slider when the user moves it by a multiple increment. The default value is calculated as (`XmNmaximum` – `XmNminimum`) / 10.

`XmNshowValue`
If `True`, the label specifying the slider's current value will be displayed beside the slider. If `False`, the label isn't displayed.

`XmNtitleString`
The text string that appears as the title in the Scale widget.

`XmNvalue`
The current position of the slider along the scale. This resource must have a value between the values of `XmNminimum` and `XmNmaximum`.

### Callback Resources

Scale defines the following callback resources:

| Callback | Reason Constant |
|---|---|
| XmNdragCallback | XmCR_DRAG |
| XmNvalueChangedCallback | XmCR_VALUE_CHANGED |

`XmNdragCallback`
List of callbacks that are called when the slider is being dragged.

`XmNvalueChangedCallback`
List of callbacks that are called when the position of the slider has changed.

### Callback Structure

Each callback function is passed the following structure:

```
typedef struct
{
    int     reason;        /* the reason that the callback was called */
    XEvent  *event;        /* event structure that triggered callback */
    int     value;         /* new value of the slider */
} XmScaleCallbackStruct;
```

### Inherited Resources

Scale inherits the following resources. The resources are listed alphabetically, along with the superclass that defines them. Scale sets the default value of `XmNshadowThickness` to 0. The default value of `XmNborderWidth` is reset to 0 by Manager.

| Resource | Inherited From | Resource | Inherited From |
|---|---|---|---|
| XmNaccelerators | Core | XmNinitialResourcesPersistent | Core |
| XmNancestorSensitive | Core | XmNinsertPosition | Composite |
| XmNbackground | Core | XmNmappedWhenManaged | Core |
| XmNbackgroundPixmap | Core | XmNnavigationType | Manager |
| XmNborderColor | Core | XmNnumChildren | Composite |

| Resource | Inherited From | Resource | Inherited From |
|---|---|---|---|
| XmNborderPixmap | Core | XmNscreen | Core |
| XmNborderWidth | Core | XmNsensitive | Core |
| XmNbottomShadowColor | Manager | XmNshadowThickness | Manager |
| XmNbottomShadowPixmap | Manager | XmNstringDirection | Manager |
| XmNchildren | Composite | XmNtopShadowColor | Manager |
| XmNcolormap | Core | XmNtopShadowPixmap | Manager |
| XmNdepth | Core | XmNtranslations | Core |
| XmNdestroyCallback | Core | XmNtraversalOn | Manager |
| XmNforeground | Manager | XmNunitType | Manager |
| XmNheight | Core | XmNuserData | Manager |
| XmNhelpCallback | Manager | XmNwidth | Core |
| XmNhighlightColor | Manager | XmNx | Core |
| XmNhighlightPixmap | Manager | XmNy | Core |
| XmNinitialFocus | Manager | | |

## Translations

Scale does not define any new translations.

## Behavior

Scale has the following behavior:

`BSelect Press` or `BTransfer Press`
: In the trough between the slider and an end of the Scale, moves the slider by one multiple increment in the direction of the end of the Scale. Calls the `XmNvalueChangedCallback` callbacks. Whether the value of the Scale is incremented or decremented depends on the value of `XmNprocessingDirection`. In the slider, starts interactive dragging of the slider.

`BSelect Motion` or `BTransfer Motion`
: If the button press occured within the slider, causes the slider to track the pointer and calls the `XmNdragCallback` callbacks.

`BSelect Release` or `BTransfer Release`
: If the button press occured within the slider and the position of the slider has changed, calls the `XmNvalueChangedCallback` callbacks.

`MCtrl BSelect Press`
: In the trough between the slider and an end of the Scale, moves the slider to that end of the Scale and calls the `XmNvalueChangedCallback` callbacks. Whether the value of the Scale is incremented or decremented depends on the value of the `XmNprocessingDirection` resource.

KUp
KDown In a vertical Scale, moves the slider up or down one increment and calls the XmN-valueChangedCallback callbacks. Whether the value of the Scale is incremented or decremented depends on the value of the XmNprocessing-Direction resource.

KLeft
KRight In a horizontal Scale, moves the slider left or right one increment and calls the XmNvalueChangedCallback callbacks. Whether the value of the Scale is incremented or decremented depends on the value of the XmNprocessing-Direction resource.

MCtrl KUp or KPageUp
MCtrl KDown or KPageDown
In a vertical Scale, moves the slider up or down one multiple increment and calls the XmNvalueChangedCallback callbacks. Whether the value of the Scale is incremented or decremented depends on the value of the XmNprocessing-Direction resource.

MCtrl KLeft or KPageLeft
MCtrl KRight or KPageRight
In a horizontal Scale, moves the slider left or right one multiple increment and calls the XmNvalueChangedCallback callbacks. Whether the value of the Scale is incremented or decremented depends on the value of the XmNprocessing-Direction resource.

KBeginLine or KBeginData
Moves the slider to the Scale's minimum value and calls the XmNvalue-ChangedCallback callbacks.

KEndLine or KEndData
Moves the slider to the Scale's maximum value and calls the XmNvalue-ChangedCallback callbacks.

KNextField
KPrevField
Moves the keyboard focus to the first item in the next or previous tab group, wrapping if necessary.

KHelp Invokes the list of callbacks specified by XmNhelpCallback. If the Scale does not have any help callbacks, invokes those associated with the nearest ancestor that has them.

## See Also

*XmCreateObject*(1), *XmScaleGetValue*(1), *XmScaleSetValue*(1), *Composite*(2), *Constraint*(2), *Core*(2), *XmManager*(2).

# XmScreen

## Name

XmScreen widget class – an object used to store screen-specific information.

## Synopsis

**Public Header:** *<Xm/Screen.h>*

**Class Name:** XmScreen

**Class Pointer:** xmScreenClass

**Class Hierarchy:** Core → XmScreen

**Instantiation:** `widget = XtAppInitialize(...)`

**Functions/Macros:** `XmGetXmScreen()`, `XmIsScreen()`

## Availability

Motif 1.2 and later.

## Description

The Screen object stores screen-specific information for use by the toolkit. An application has a Screen object for each screen that it accesses. When an application creates its first shell on a screen, typically by calling `XtAppInitialize()` or `XtAppCreateShell()`, a Screen object is created automatically. There is no way to create a Screen independently. The function `XmGetXmScreen()` can be used to get the widget ID of the Screen object.

## New Resources

Screen defines the following resources:

| Name | Class | Type | Default | Access |
|---|---|---|---|---|
| XmNdarkThreshold | XmCDarkThreshold | int | dynamic | C |
| XmNdefaultCopy-CursorIcon | XmCDefaultCopy-CursorIcon | Widget | NULL | CSG |
| XmNdefaultInvalid-CursorIcon | XmCDefaultInvalid-CursorIcon | Widget | NULL | CSG |
| XmNdefaultLink-CursorIcon | XmCDefaultLink-CursorIcon | Widget | NULL | CSG |
| XmNdefaultMove-CursorIcon | XmCDefaultMove-CursorIcon | Widget | NULL | CSG |
| XmNdefaultNone-CursorIcon | XmCDefaultNone-CursorIcon | Widget | NULL | CSG |
| XmNdefaultSource-CursorIcon | XmCDefaultSource-CursorIcon | Widget | NULL | CSG |
| XmNdefaultValid-CursorIcon | XmCDefaultValid-CursorIcon | Widget | NULL | CSG |
| XmNfont | XmCFont | XFont-Struct * | NULL | CSG |

| Name | Class | Type | Default | Access |
|---|---|---|---|---|
| XmNforeground-Threshold | XmCForeground-Threshold | int | dynamic | C |
| XmNhorizontal-FontUnit | XmCHorizontal-FontUnit | int | dynamic | CSG |
| XmNlightThreshold | XmCLightThreshold | int | dynamic | C |
| XmNmenuCursor | XmCCursor | String | arrow | C |
| XmNmoveOpaque | XmCMoveOpaque | Boolean | False | CSG |
| XmNunpostBehavior | XmCUnpostBehavior | unsigned char | XmUNPOST_AND_REPLAY | CSG |
| XmNverticalFontUnit | XmCVerticalFontUnit | int | dynamic | CSG |

XmNdarkThreshold
: The level of perceived brightness (between 0 and 100) that is treated as a "dark" background color when computing default shadow and select colors.

XmNdefaultCopyCursorIcon
: The DragIcon used during a copy operation. When the value is NULL, a default system icon is used.

XmNdefaultInvalidCursorIcon
: The DragIcon used when the pointer is over an invalid drop site. When the value is NULL, a default system icon is used.

XmNdefaultLinkCursorIcon
: The DragIcon used during a link operation. When the value is NULL, a default system icon is used.

XmNdefaultMoveCursorIcon
: The DragIcon used during a move operation. When the value is NULL, a default system icon is used.

XmNdefaultNoneCursorIcon
: The DragIcon used when the pointer is not over a drop site. When the value is NULL, a default system icon is used.

XmNdefaultSourceCursorIcon
: The bitmap used as a cursor when an XmNsourceCursorIcon is not provided by the DragContext. When the value is NULL, a default system icon is used.

XmNdefaultValidCursorIcon
: The DragIcon used when the pointer is over a valid drop site. When the value is NULL, a default system icon is used.

XmNfont
: The font used in computing values for XmNhorizontalFontUnit and XmNverticalFontUnit.

`XmNforegroundThreshold`
The level of perceived brightness (between 0 and 100) that distinguishes between a "dark" and "light" background when computing the default foreground and highlight colors.

`XmNhorizontalFontUnit`
The horizontal component of the font units that are used to convert geometry values when `XmNshellUnitType` or `XmNunitType` is set to `Xm100TH_FONT_UNITS`. If a value is not specified, the default is computed from the `XmNfont` resource.

`XmNlightThreshold`
The level of perceived brightness (between 0 and 100) that is treated as a "light" background color when computing default shadow and select colors.

`XmNmenuCursor`
The cursor that is used when the application posts a menu. Possible values include all of the cursor in the X cursor font.

`XmNmoveOpaque`
If `False` (default), an operation that moves a window displays an outline of the window during the operation. If `True`, a move operation displays a representation of the window.

`XmNunpostBehavior`
The behavior of a posted menu when the pointer button is pressed outside of the menu. Possible values:

```
XmUNPOST_AND_REPLAY    /* unposts the menu hierarchy and replays event */
XmUNPOST               /* unposts the menu hierarchy */
```

`XmNverticalFontUnit`
The vertical component of the font units that are used to convert geometry values when `XmNshellUnitType` or `XmNunitType` is set to `Xm100TH_FONT_UNITS`. If a value is not specified, the default is computed from the `XmNfont` resource.

## Inherited Resources

All of the resources inherited by Screen are not applicable.

## See Also

*XmGetXmScreen*(1), *XmGetXmScreen*(1), *XmGetXmScreen*(1), *XmGetXmScreen*(1), *XmGet-XmScreen*(1), *XmGetXmScreen*(1),
*Core*(2), *XmDisplay*(2).

# XmScrollBar

## Name

XmScrollBar widget class – a widget to control the scrolling of the viewing area in another widget.

## Synopsis

**Public Header:** *<Xm/ScrollBar.h>*

**Class Name:** XmScrollBar

**Class Hierarchy:** Core → XmPrimitive → XmScrollBar

**Class Pointer:** `xmScrollBarWidgetClass`

**Instantiation:** `widget = XtCreateWidget(name, xmScrollBarWidgetClass, ...)`

**Functions/Macros:** `XmCreateScrollBar()`, `XmIsScrollBar()`, `XmScrollBarGetValues()`, `XmScrollBarSetValues()`

## Description

A ScrollBar allows users to reposition data that is too large to fit in the viewing window. Although a ScrollBar can be used as a standalone widget, it is normally used in a ScrolledWindow. A ScrollBar consists of a rectangular strip, called the scroll region or trough, and two arrows placed on either end of the scroll region. Within the scroll region is a smaller, movable rectangle called the slider. To scroll the data, users can click on one of the arrows, click in the scroll region, or drag the slider. The application typically sets the `XmNsliderSize` resource such that the size of the slider relative to the size of the scroll region corresponds to the percentage of total data that is currently displayed.

## New Resources

ScrollBar defines the following resources:

| Name | Class | Type | Default | Access |
|---|---|---|---|---|
| XmNincrement | XmCIncrement | int | 1 | CSG |
| XmNinitialDelay | XmCInitialDelay | int | 250 | CSG |
| XmNmaximum | XmCMaximum | int | dynamic | CSG |
| XmNminimum | XmCMinimum | int | 0 | CSG |
| XmNorientation | XmCOrientation | unsigned char | XmVERTICAL | CSG |
| XmNpageIncrement | XmCPageIncrement | int | 10 | C |
| XmNprocessing-Direction | XmCProcessing-Direction | unsigned char | dynamic | CSG |
| XmNrepeatDelay | XmCRepeatDelay | int | 50 | CSG |
| XmNshowArrows | XmCShowArrows | Boolean | True | CSG |
| XmNsliderSize | XmCSliderSize | int | dynamic | CSG |

Motif and Xt Widget Classes

| Name | Class | Type | Default | Access |
|---|---|---|---|---|
| XmNtroughColor | XmCTroughColor | Pixel | dynamic | CSG |
| XmNvalue | XmCValue | int | dynamic | CSG |

`XmNincrement`
: The amount the value changes due to the user's moving the slider one increment.

`XmNinitialDelay`
: The number of milliseconds a button must remain pressed before triggering continuous slider movement.

`XmNmaximum`

`XmNminimum`
: The maximum/minimum value of the slider.

`XmNorientation`
: The direction in which the scale is displayed. Possible values:

```
XmVERTICAL        /* top-to-bottom creation */
XmHORIZONTAL      /* left-to-right creation */
```

`XmNpageIncrement`
: The amount the value changes due to the user's moving the slider one page increment.

`XmNprocessingDirection`
: Determines the position at which to display the slider's maximum and minimum values, with respect to the slider. Possible values:

```
XmMAX_ON_TOP        /* scale increases toward top */
XmMAX_ON_BOTTOM     /* scale increases toward bottom */
XmMAX_ON_LEFT       /* scale increases toward left */
XmMAX_ON_RIGHT      /* scale increases toward right */
```

For vertically oriented ScrollBar widgets, the default value is `XmMAX_ON_TOP`. For horizontally oriented ScrollBar widgets, the default value is usually `XmMAX_ON_RIGHT` (depending on the value of the `XmNstringDirection` resource).

`XmNrepeatDelay`
: The number of milliseconds a button must remain pressed before continuing further slider motions, once the `XmNinitialDelay` time has been triggered.

`XmNshowArrows`
: If `True`, arrows are displayed; if `False`, they are not.

`XmNsliderSize`
: The slider's length. The length ranges from 1 to the value of `XmNmaximum` – `XmNminimum`. By default, the value is computed to be:

(`XmNmaximum` – `XmNminimum`) / 10.

XmNtroughColor
The color of the slider's trough.

XmNvalue
The slider's position. The position ranges from the value of XmNminimum to the value of (XmNmaximum – XmNsliderSize).

## Callback Resources

ScrollBar defines the following callback resources:

| Callback | Reason Constant |
|---|---|
| XmNdecrementCallback | XmCR_DECREMENT |
| XmNdragCallback | XmCR_DRAG |
| XmNincrementCallback | XmCR_INCREMENT |
| XmNpageDecrementCallback | XmCR_PAGE_DECREMENT |
| XmNpageIncrementCallback | XmCR_PAGE_INCREMENT |
| XmNtoBottomCallback | XmCR_TO_BOTTOM |
| XmNtoTopCallback | XmCR_TO_TOP |
| XmNvalueChangedCallback | XmCR_VALUE_CHANGED |

XmNdecrementCallback
List of callbacks that are called when the value of the ScrollBar decreases by one increment.

XmNdragCallback
List of callbacks that are called for each change in position when the slider is being dragged.

XmNincrementCallback
List of callbacks that are called when the value of the ScrollBar increases by one increment.

XmNpageDecrementCallback
List of callbacks that are called when the value of the ScrollBar decreases by one page increment.

XmNpageIncrementCallback
List of callbacks that are called when the value of the ScrollBar increases by one page increment.

XmNtoBottomCallback
List of callbacks that are called when the slider is moved to the maximum value of the ScrollBar.

XmNtoTopCallback
List of callbacks that are called when the slider is moved to the minimum value of the ScrollBar.

`XmNvalueChangedCallback`
List of callbacks that are called at the end of a slider drag operation. These callbacks are also called in place of each of the other ScrollBar callbacks that reports a value change when the callback resource is `NULL`.

## Callback Structure

Each callback function is passed the following structure:

```
typedef struct
{
    int     reason;       /* the reason that the callback was called */
    XEvent  *event;       /* event structure that triggered callback */
    int     value;        /* value of the slider's new location */
    int     pixel;        /* coordinate where selection occurred */
} XmScrollBarCallbackStruct;
```

`pixel` is meaningful only when the callback reason is `XmCR_TO_TOP` or `XmCR_TO_BOTTOM`. The `pixel` member specifies the location at which the mouse button selection occurred, giving the x-coordinate in the case of a horizontal ScrollBar and the y-coordinate in the case of a vertical ScrollBar.

## Inherited Resources

ScrollBar inherits the following resources. The resources are listed alphabetically, along with the superclass that defines them. ScrollBar sets the default values of `XmNhighlightThickness` to 0, `XmNnavigationType` to `XmSTICKY_TAB_GROUP`, and `XmNtraversalOn` to `False`. The default value of `XmNborderWidth` is reset to 0 by Manager.

| Resource | Inherited From | Resource | Inherited From |
|---|---|---|---|
| XmNaccelerators | Core | XmNhighlightPixmap | Primitive |
| XmNancestorSensitive | Core | XmNhighlightThickness | Primitive |
| XmNbackground | Core | XmNinitialResourcesPersistent | Core |
| XmNbackgroundPixmap | Core | XmNmappedWhenManaged | Core |
| XmNborderColor | Core | XmNnavigationType | Primitive |
| XmNborderPixmap | Core | XmNscreen | Core |
| XmNborderWidth | Core | XmNsensitive | Core |
| XmNbottomShadowColor | Primitive | XmNshadowThickness | Primitive |
| XmNbottomShadowPixmap | Primitive | XmNtopShadowColor | Primitive |
| XmNcolormap | Core | XmNtopShadowPixmap | Primitive |
| XmNdepth | Core | XmNtranslations | Core |
| XmNdestroyCallback | Core | XmNtraversalOn | Primitive |
| XmNforeground | Primitive | XmNunitType | Primitive |
| XmNheight | Core | XmNuserData | Primitive |
| XmNhelpCallback | Primitive | XmNwidth | Core |

| Resource | Inherited From | Resource | Inherited From |
|---|---|---|---|
| XmNhighlightColor | Primitive | XmNx | Core |
| XmNhighlightOnEnter | Primitive | XmNy | Core |

## Translations

The translations for ScrollBar include those from Primitive, plus the following:

| Event | Action |
|---|---|
| BSelect Press | Select() |
| BSelect Release | Release() |
| BSelect Press Moved | Moved() |
| BTransfer Press | Select() |
| BTransfer Release | Release() |
| BTransfer Press Moved | Moved() |
| MCtrl BSelect Press | TopOrBottom() |
| MCtrl BSelect Release | Release() |
| KUp | IncrementUpOrLeft(0) |
| MCtrl KUp | PageUpOrLeft(0) |
| KDown | IncrementDownOrRight(0) |
| MCtrl KDown | PageDownOrRight(0) |
| KLeft | IncrementUpOrLeft(1) |
| MCtrl KLeft | PageUpOrLeft(1) |
| KRight | IncrementDownOrRight(1) |
| MCtrl KRight | PageDownOrRight(1) |
| KPageUp | PageUpOrLeft(0) |
| KPageDown | PageDownOrRight(0) |
| KPageLeft | PageUpOrLeft(1) |
| KPageRight | PageDownOrRight(1) |
| KBeginLine | TopOrBottom() |
| KEndLine | TopOrBottom() |
| KBeginData | TopOrBottom() |
| KEndData | TopOrBottom() |
| KNextField | PrimitiveNextTabGroup() |
| KPrevField | PrimitivePrevTabGroup() |
| KActivate | PrimitiveParentActivate() |
| KCancel | CancelDrag() |
| KHelp | PrimitiveHelp() |

## Action Routines

ScrollBar defines the following action routines:

`CancelDrag()`
: In Motif 1.2, cancels the scrolling operation and returns the slider to its previous location if the event happened during a drag. Otherwise, passes the event to the parent if it is a manager.

`IncrementDownOrRight(`*`flag`*`):`
: Moves the slider by one increment—downward if *`flag`* is 0; to the right if *`flag`* is 1. Depending on the value of the `XmNprocessingDirection` resource, the slider's movement invokes the callbacks listed in either `XmNincrementCallback` or `XmNdecrementCallback` (or `XmNvalueChangedCallback` if the appropriate callback resource is NULL).

`IncrementUpOrLeft(`*`flag`*`):`
: Same as `IncrementDownOrRight` except that the slider moves upward if *`flag`* is 0 and to the left if *`flag`* is 1.

`Moved()`
: This action applies when the mouse button is pressed in the slider. When this is done, moving the pointer moves the slider along with it and also invokes the callbacks specified by `XmNdragCallback`.

`PageDownOrRight(`*`flag`*`):`
: Moves the slider by one page increment—downward if *`flag`* is 0; to the right if *`flag`* is 1. Depending on the value of the `XmNprocessingDirection` resource, the slider's movement invokes the callbacks listed in either `XmNpageIncrementCallback` or `XmNpageDecrementCallback` (or `XmNvalueChangedCallback` if the appropriate callback resource is NULL).

`PageUpOrLeft(`*`flag`*`):`
: Same as `IncrementDownOrRight` except that the slider moves upward if *`flag`* is 0 and to the left if *`flag`* is 1.

`PrimitiveHelp()`
: Invokes the list of callbacks specified by `XmNhelpCallback`. If the ScrollBar doesn't have any help callbacks, the `Help()` routine invokes those associated with the nearest ancestor that has them.

`PrimitiveNextTabGroup()`
`PrimitivePrevTabGroup()`
: Traverses to the first item in the next/previous tab group, wrapping if necessary.

`PrimitiveParentActivate()`
: In Motif 1.2, passes the event to the parent if it is a manager.

`Release()`
: If the `Moved()` action changes the slider's position, then the `Release()` action invokes the callbacks specified by `XmNvalueChangedCallback`.

`Select()`

The results of this action depend on the location in which it's applied: Within an arrow, this action is the same as `IncrementDownOrRight()` or `Increment-UpOrLeft()`—incrementing or decrementing according to the value of the `XmN-processingDirection` resource, and invoking the appropriate increment or decrement callback. Within the scrolling area that lies between an arrow and the slider, this action works like the page increment action routines—moving by one page increment according to the value of the `XmNprocessingDirection` resource, and invoking the appropriate page increment or page decrement callback. Within either of these locations, keeping the button pressed repeats the incremental movement of the slider. This behavior is triggered when the duration of the button press exceeds the value of the `XmNinitialDelay` resource; the slider movement then repeats with a time interval specified by the `XmNrepeatDelay` resource. Within the slider, this action begins slider dragging, which is subsequently affected by the actions `Moved()` and `Release()`.

`TopOrBottom()`

Moves the slider to its minimum value and invokes the callbacks specified by `XmNtoTopCallback`, or moves the slider to its maximum value and invokes the callbacks specified by `XmNtoBottomCallback`. The direction of the slider's movement depends on the value of the `XmNprocessingDirection` resource. This action can be applied using either keyboard or mouse events.

## See Also

*XmCreateObject*(1), *XmScrollBarGetValues*(1), *Core*(2), *XmPrimitive*(2).

# XmScrolledList



## Name

XmScrolledList – a List as a child of a ScrolledWindow.

## Synopsis

**Public Header:** *<Xm/List.h>*

**Instantiation:** `widget = XmCreateScrolledList(...)`

**Functions/Macros:** `XmCreateScrolledList()`, `XmCreateScrolledWindow()`

## Description

A ScrolledList is a compound object created by a call to `XmCreateScrolledList()` that provides scroll bars for a list that is not visible all at once. A ScrolledList consists of a ScrolledWindow widget with a List widget as its child.

A ScrolledList automatically creates the necessary scroll bars. The ScrolledWindow resource `XmNscrollingPolicy` is set to `XmAPPLICATION_DEFINED` and `XmNvisualPolicy` is set to `XmVARIABLE`. The ScrolledWindow resource `XmNscrollBarDisplayPolicy` is set to `XmSTATIC`, but no initial value is set for the List `XmNscrollBarDisplayPolicy` resource.

## Default Resource Values

A ScrolledList sets the following default values for ScrolledWindow resources:

| Name | Default |
|---|---|
| XmNscrollBarDisplayPolicy | XmSTATIC |
| XmNscrollingPolicy | XmAPPLICATION_DEFINED |
| XmNvisualPolicy | XmVARIABLE |

## Widget Hierarchy

When a ScrolledList is created with a specified `name`, the ScrolledWindow is named `nameSW` and the List is called `name`. The horizontal and vertical scroll bars are named `HorScrollBar` and `VertScrollBar`, respectively.

## See Also

*XmCreateObject*(1),
*XmList*(2), *XmScrolledWindow*(2).

## Name

XmScrolledText – a Text widget as a child of a ScrolledWindow.

## Synopsis

**Public Header:** *<Xm/Text.h>*

**Instantiation:** `widget = XmCreateScrolledText(...)`

**Functions/Macros:** `XmCreateScrolledText()`, `XmCreateScrolledWindow()`

## Description

ScrolledText is a compound object created by a call to `XmCreateScrolledText()` that provides scroll bars for text that is not visible all at once. A ScrolledText object consists of a ScrolledWindow widget with a multi-line Text widget as its child.

ScrolledText automatically creates the necessary scroll bars. The ScrolledWindow resource `XmNscrollingPolicy` is set to `XmAPPLICATION_DEFINED`, `XmNvisualPolicy` is set to `XmVARIABLE` and `XmNscrollBarDisplayPolicy` is set to `XmSTATIC`.

## Default Resource Values

ScrolledText sets the following default values for ScrolledWindow resources:

| Name | Default |
|---|---|
| XmNscrollBarDisplayPolicy | XmSTATIC |
| XmNscrollingPolicy | XmAPPLICATION_DEFINED |
| XmNvisualPolicy | XmVARIABLE |

## Widget Hierarchy

When a ScrolledText object is created with a specified `name`, the ScrolledWindow is named `nameSW` and the Text widget is called `name`. The horizontal and vertical scroll bars are named `HorScrollBar` and `VertScrollBar` respectively.

## See Also

*XmCreateObject*(1),
*XmScrolledWindow*(2), *XmText*(2).

# XmScrolledWindow

## Name

XmScrolledWindow widget class – a manager widget that provides scroll bars for the data display.

## Synopsis

**Public Header:** *<Xm/ScrolledW.h>*

**Class Name:** XmScrolledWindow

**Class Hierarchy:** Core → Composite → Constraint → XmManager → XmScrolledWindow

**Class Pointer:** `xmScrolledWindowWidgetClass`

**Instantiation:** `widget = XtCreateWidget(name, xmScrolledWindowWidgetClass, ...)`

**Functions/Macros:** `XmCreateScrolledList()`, `XmCreateScrolledText()`, `XmCreateScrolledWindow()`, `XmIsScrolledWindow()`, `XmScrollVisible()`, `XmScrolledWindowSetAreas()`

## Description

ScrolledWindow provides a scrollable view of data that may not be visible all at once. ScrollBars allow a user to scroll the visible part of the window through the larger display. A ScrolledWindow widget can be created so that it scrolls automatically without application intervention or so that an application provides support for all scrolling operations. When scrolling is handled automatically, ScrolledWindow creates the scroll bars, which are named `HorScrollBar` and `VertScrollBar`.

Each of the ScrolledWindow regions is associated with a ScrolledWindow resource; `XmScrolledWindowSetAreas()` sets the associated resources. If an application does not call `XmScrolledWindowSetAreas()`, the widget may still set some of the standard regions. If ScrollBars are added as children, the `XmNhorizontalScrollBar` and `XmNverticalScrollBar` resources may be set if they have not already been specified. Any child that is not a ScrollBar is used for the `XmNworkWindow`. If you want to be certain about which widgets are used for the different regions, it is wise to call `XmScrolledWindowSetAreas()` explicitly.

## New Resources

ScrolledWindow defines the following resources:

| Name | Class | Type | Default | Access |
|---|---|---|---|---|
| XmNclipWindow | XmCClipWindow | Window | dynamic | G |
| XmNhorizontalScrollBar | XmCHorizontalScrollBar | Widget | dynamic | CSG |
| XmNscrollBarDisplayPolicy | XmCScrollBarDisplayPolicy | unsigned char | dynamic | CSG |

| Name | Class | Type | Default | Access |
|---|---|---|---|---|
| XmNscrollBar-Placement | XmCScrollBar-Placement | unsigned char | XmBOTTOM_RIGHT | CSG |
| XmNscrolledWindow-MarginHeight | XmCScrolledWindow-MarginHeight | Dimension | 0 | CSG |
| XmNscrolledWindow-MarginWidth | XmCScrolledWindow-MarginWidth | Dimension | 0 | CSG |
| XmNscrollingPolicy | XmCScrollingPolicy | unsigned char | XmAPPLICATION_DEFINED | CG |
| XmNspacing | XmCSpacing | Dimension | 4 | CSG |
| XmNverticalScroll-Bar | XmCVerticalScroll-Bar | Widget | dynamic | CSG |
| XmNvisualPolicy | XmCVisualPolicy | unsigned char | dynamic | G |
| XmNworkWindow | XmCWorkWindow | Widget | NULL | CSG |

XmNclipWindow

The widget ID of the clipping area. The clipping window exists only when the XmNvisualPolicy resource is set to XmCONSTANT. The XmNclipWindow resource cannot be set to a new value.

XmNhorizontalScrollBar

The widget ID of the horizontal ScrollBar.

XmNscrollBarDisplayPolicy

Controls the placement of ScrollBars, depending on the value of the XmNscrolling-Policy resource. Possible values:

```
XmSTATIC        /* vertical ScrollBar always displays */
XmAS_NEEDED     /* add ScrollBar when view is clipped */
```

If XmNscrollingPolicy is set to XmAUTOMATIC, then XmNscrollBar-DisplayPolicy defaults to a value of XmAS_NEEDED, and ScrollBars are displayed only when the workspace cannot fit within the clip area. If XmNscrollingPolicy is set to XmAPPLICATION_DEFINED, then XmNscrollBarDisplayPolicy defaults to (and must remain with) a value of XmSTATIC. This means that ScrollBars will always be displayed.

XmNscrollBarPlacement

The positions of the ScrollBars relative to the work window. The default value of this resource depends on the value of the XmNstringDirection resource. Possible values:

```
XmTOP_LEFT        /* vertical ScrollBar on left; horizontal on top */
XmBOTTOM_LEFT     /* vertical ScrollBar on left; horizontal on bottom */
XmTOP_RIGHT       /* vertical ScrollBar on right; horizontal on top */
XmBOTTOM_RIGHT    /* vertical ScrollBar on right; horizontal on bottom */
```

`XmNscrolledWindowMarginHeight`
The spacing at the top and bottom of the ScrolledWindow.

`XmNscrolledWindowMarginWidth`
The spacing at the right and left sides of the ScrolledWindow.

`XmNscrollingPolicy`
Determines how automatic scrolling occurs. Possible values:

```
XmAUTOMATIC               /* ScrolledWindow handles scrolling */
XmAPPLICATION_DEFINED     /* application handles scrolling */
```

`XmNspacing`
The distance between each ScrollBar and the work window.

`XmNverticalScrollBar`
The widget ID of the vertical ScrollBar.

`XmNvisualPolicy`
The visual layout policy of the ScrolledWindow. Possible values:

```
XmCONSTANT          /* viewing area is clipped if needed; */
                    /* default when XmNscrollingPolicy is XmAUTOMATIC */
XmVARIABLE          /* layout grows or shrinks; default otherwise */
```

`XmNworkWindow`
The widget ID of the viewing area.

### Callback Resources

ScrolledWindow defines the following callback resources:

| Callback | Reason Constant |
|---|---|
| XmNtraverseObscuredCallback | XmCR_OBSCURED_TRAVERSAL |

`XmNtraverseObscuredCallback`
List of callbacks that are called when the keyboard focus is moved to a widget or gadget that is obscured from view.

### Callback Structure

Each callback function is passed the following structure:

```
typedef struct
{
        int         reason;         /* the reason that the callback was called */
        XEvent      *event;         /* event structure that triggered callback */
        Widget      traversal_destination;/* widget or gadget to traverse to */
        XmTraversalDirection        direction;/* direction of traversal */
} XmTraverseObscuredCallbackStruct;
```

## Inherited Resources

ScrolledWindow inherits the following resources. The resources are listed alphabetically, along with the superclass that defines them. ScrolledWindow sets the default value of XmNshadowThickness dynamically. The default value of XmNborderWidth is reset to 0 by Manager.

| Resource | Inherited From | Resource | Inherited From |
|---|---|---|---|
| XmNaccelerators | Core | XmNinitialResources-Persistent | Core |
| XmNancestorSensitive | Core | XmNinsertPosition | Composite |
| XmNbackground | Core | XmNmappedWhenManaged | Core |
| XmNbackgroundPixmap | Core | XmNnavigationType | Manager |
| XmNborderColor | Core | XmNnumChildren | Composite |
| XmNborderPixmap | Core | XmNscreen | Core |
| XmNborderWidth | Core | XmNsensitive | Core |
| XmNbottomShadowColor | Manager | XmNshadowThickness | Manager |
| XmNbottomShadowPixmap | Manager | XmNstringDirection | Manager |
| XmNchildren | Composite | XmNtopShadowColor | Manager |
| XmNcolormap | Core | XmNtopShadowPixmap | Manager |
| XmNdepth | Core | XmNtranslations | Core |
| XmNdestroyCallback | Core | XmNtraversalOn | Manager |
| XmNforeground | Manager | XmNunitType | Manager |
| XmNheight | Core | XmNuserData | Manager |
| XmNhelpCallback | Manager | XmNwidth | Core |
| XmNhighlightColor | Manager | XmNx | Core |
| XmNhighlightPixmap | Manager | XmNy | Core |
| XmNinitialFocus | Manager | | |

## Translations

The translations for ScrolledWindow include those from Manager.

## Additional Behavior

ScrolledWindow has the following additional behavior when the XmNscrollingPolicy resource is XmAUTOMATIC:

| Event | Scrolls window... |
|---|---|
| KPageUp | up by the size of the viewing window |
| KPageDown | down by the size of the viewing window |
| KPageLeft | left by the size of the viewing window |
| KPageRight | right by the size of the viewing window |
| KBeginLine | horizontally to ScrollBar's minimum value |
| KEndLine | horizontally to ScrollBar's maximum value |

| Event | Scrolls window . . . |
|---|---|
| `KBeginData` | vertically to ScrollBar's minimum value |
| `KEndData` | vertically to ScrollBar's maximum value |

## See Also

*XmCreateObject*(1), *XmScrollVisible*(1), *XmScrolledWindowSetAreas*(1), *Composite*(2), *Constraint*(2), *Core*(2), *XmManager*(2), *XmScrollBar*(2), *XmScrolledList*(2), *XmScrolledText*(2).

## Name

XmSelectionBox widget class – a widget for selecting one of a list of alternatives.

## Synopsis

**Public Header:** *<Xm/SelectioB.h>*

**Class Name:** XmSelectionBox

**Class Hierarchy:** Core → Composite → Constraint → XmManager → XmBulletinBoard → XmSelectionBox

**Class Pointer:** `XmSelectionBoxWidgetClass`

**Instantiation:** `widget = XtCreateWidget(name, XmSelectionBoxWidgetClass, ...)`

**Functions/Macros:** `XmCreateSelectionBox()`, `XmCreateSelectionDialog()`, `XmCreatePromptDialog()`, `XmXmIsSelectionBox()`, `XmSelectionBoxGetChild()`

## Description

SelectionBox is a composite widget that displays a scrollable list of alternatives from which the user can choose items. A SelectionBox contains a text field in which the user can enter a selection, the scrollable list of selections, labels for the text field and the scrollable list, a separator, and a group of three or four buttons. The names of these components in the SelectionBox are `Items`, `ItemsList`, `Selection`, `Text`, and `Separator`, respectively.

In Motif 1.2, the default button labels can be localized. In the C locale, and in Motif 1.1, the PushButtons are labeled **OK**, **Apply**, **Cancel**, and **Help** by default. The **Apply** button is created but not always managed. If the parent of the SelectionBox is a DialogShell the button is managed, otherwise it is not.

You can customize a SelectionBox by removing existing children or adding new children. Use `XmSelectionBoxGetChild()` to retrieve the widget ID of an existing child and then unmanage the child. With Motif 1.2, multiple widgets can be added as children of a SelectionBox. The first child is considered a work area and is placed based on the value of the `XmNchildPlacement` resource. If a menu bar is added, it is placed at the top of the window. Any buttons are placed after the **OK** button. Any additional children are placed below the message. In Motif 1.1, only a single widget can be added as a child of a SelectionBox. This child is placed below the selection text and acts as a work area.



## New Resources

SelectionBox defines the following resources, which are all `CSG` access, except for `XmNdialogType` (CG access) and `XmNselectionLabelString` (C access):

| Name | Class | Type | Default |
|---|---|---|---|
| `XmNapplyLabelString` | `XmCApplyLabelString` | `XmString` | dynamic |
| `XmNcancelLabelString` | `XmCCancelLabelString` | `XmString` | dynamic |

| Name | Class | Type | Default |
|---|---|---|---|
| XmNchildPlacement | XmCChildPlacement | unsigned char | XmPLACE_ ABOVE_ SELECTION |
| XmNdialogType | XmCDialogType | unsigned char | dynamic |
| XmNhelpLabelString | XmCHelpLabelString | XmString | dynamic |
| XmNlistItemCount | XmCItemCount | int | 0 |
| XmNlistItems | XmCItems | XmStringTable | NULL |
| XmNlistLabelString | XmCListLabelString | XmString | dynamic |
| XmNlistVisibleItemCount | XmCVisibleItemCount | int | dynamic |
| XmNminimizeButtons | XmCMinimizeButtons | Boolean | False |
| XmNmustMatch | XmCMustMatch | Boolean | False |
| XmNokLabelString | XmCOkLabelString | XmString | dynamic |
| XmNselectionLabelString | XmCSelectionLabelString | XmString | dynamic |
| XmNtextAccelerators | XmCTextAccelerators | XtAccelerators | default |
| XmNtextColumns | XmCColumns | short | dynamic |
| XmNtextString | XmCTextString | XmString | dynamic |

`XmNapplyLabelString`

The string that labels the **Apply** button. In Motif 1.2, the default value is locale-dependent. In the C locale, and in Motif 1.1, the default value is `"Apply"`.

`XmNcancelLabelString`

The string that labels the **Cancel** button. In Motif 1.2, the default value is locale-dependent. In the C locale, and in Motif 1.1, the default value is `"Cancel"`.

`XmNchildPlacement`

In Motif 1.2, determines the placement of the work area child. Possible values:

```
XmPLACE_ABOVE_SELECTION     /* above the text area */
XmPLACE_BELOW_SELECTION     /* below the text area */
XmPLACE_TOP                 /* above the list area */
```

`XmNdialogType`

Determines which children of the SelectionBox widget will be initially created and managed. Possible values:

```
XmDIALOG_WORK_AREA        /* default, when parent isn't a DialogShell */
XmDIALOG_PROMPT           /* all children except list and label */
XmDIALOG_SELECTION        /* default, when parent is a DialogShell */
XmDIALOG_COMMAND          /* only list, selection label and text field */
XmDIALOG_FILE_SELECTION   /* all standard children */
```

Note that in Release 1.1, Command and FileSelectionBox are separate widget classes, and they can no longer be created by setting `XmNdialogType`.

`XmNhelpLabelString`
The string that labels the **Help** button. In Motif 1.2, the default value is locale-dependent. In the C locale, and in Motif 1.1, the default value is `"Help"`.

`XmNlistItems`
The items in the SelectionBox list. A call to `XtGetValues()` returns the actual list items (not a copy), so don't have your application free these items.

`XmNlistItemCount`
The number of items in the SelectionBox list.

`XmNlistLabelString`
The string that labels the SelectionBox list. The default string is `NULL` when the `XmNdialogType` resource is set to `XmDIALOG_PROMPT`; otherwise, in Motif 1.2, the default value is locale-dependent. In the C locale, and in Motif 1.1, the default value is `"Items"`.

`XmNlistVisibleItemCount`
The number of items that appear in the SelectionBox list. The default value depends on the height of the list. This resource has a value of 0 when the `XmNdialogType` resource is set to `XmDIALOG_PROMPT`.

`XmNminimizeButtons`
If `False` (default), all buttons are standardized to be as wide as the widest button and as high as the highest button. If `True`, buttons will keep their preferred size.

`XmNmustMatch`
If `True`, the selection that a user types in the text edit field must match an existing entry in the SelectionBox list. If `False` (default), the typed selection doesn't need to match a list entry. (When the user activates the `Ok` button, the widget calls one of two lists of callbacks: if this resource is `True` but the selections don't match, then the SelectionBox widget calls the callbacks specified by the `XmNnoMatchCallback` resource; if this resource is `False` or if the selections do match, then the widget calls the callbacks specified by the `XmNokCallback` resource.)

`XmNokLabelString`
The string that labels the **Ok** button. In Motif 1.2, the default value is locale-dependent. In the C locale, and in Motif 1.1, the default value is `"OK"`.

`XmNselectionLabelString`
The string that labels the text edit field. In Motif 1.2, the default value is locale-dependent. In the C locale, and in Motif 1.1, the default value is `"Selection"`.

`XmNtextAccelerators`
The translations to add to the SelectionBox's Text widget child. The default bindings allow the up and down keys to be used in selecting list items. This resource is meaningful only when the SelectionBox widget is using the default values in the `XmNaccelerators` resource.

XmNtextColumns
: The number of columns in the Text widget.

XmNtextString
: The text string that appears in the text edit selection field.

### Callback Resources

SelectionBox defines the following callback resources:

| Callback | Reason Constant |
|---|---|
| XmNapplyCallback | XmCR_APPLY |
| XmNcancelCallback | XmCR_CANCEL |
| XmNnoMatchCallback | XmCR_NO_MATCH |
| XmNokCallback | XmCR_OK |

XmNapplyCallback
: List of callbacks that are called when the **Apply** button is activated.

XmNcancelCallback
: List of callbacks that are called when the **Cancel** button is activated.

XmNnoMatchCallback
: List of callbacks that are called when the user types a selection in the text area that does not match an item in the list.

XmNokCallback
: List of callbacks that are called when the **OK** button is activated. If XmNmustMatch is True and the selection text does not match an item in the list, the XmNnoMatchCallback callbacks are called instead.

### Callback Structure

Each callback function is passed the following structure:

```
typedef struct
{
   int       reason;      /* the reason that the callback was called */
   XEvent    *event;      /* event structure that triggered callback */
   XmString  value;       /* selection string that was either chosen */
                          /* from the SelectionBox list or typed in */
   int       length;      /* number of bytes of value */
} XmSelectionBoxCallbackStruct;
```

### Inherited Resources

SelectionBox inherits the following resources. The resources are listed alphabetically, along with the superclass that defines them. The default value of XmNborderWidth is reset to 0 by Manager. BulletinBoard sets the values of XmNinitialFocus to the text entry area, XmNdefaultButton to the **Cancel** button, and resets the default XmNshadowThickness from 0 to 1 if the SelectionBox is a child of a DialogShell.

| Resource | Inherited From | Resource | Inherited From |
|---|---|---|---|
| XmNaccelerators | Core | XmNinsertPosition | Composite |
| XmNallowOverlap | BulletinBoard | XmNlabelFontList | BulletinBoard |
| XmNancestorSensitive | Core | XmNmapCallback | BulletinBoard |
| XmNautoUnmanage | BulletinBoard | XmNmappedWhenManaged | Core |
| XmNbackground | Core | XmNmarginHeight | BulletinBoard |
| XmNbackgroundPixmap | Core | XmNmarginWidth | BulletinBoard |
| XmNborderColor | Core | XmNnavigationType | Manager |
| XmNborderPixmap | Core | XmNnoResize | BulletinBoard |
| XmNborderWidth | Core | XmNnumChildren | Composite |
| XmNbottomShadowColor | Manager | XmNresizePolicy | BulletinBoard |
| XmNbottomShadowPixmap | Manager | XmNscreen | Core |
| XmNbuttonFontList | BulletinBoard | XmNsensitive | Core |
| XmNcancelButton | BulletinBoard | XmNshadowThickness | Manager |
| XmNchildren | Composite | XmNshadowType | BulletinBoard |
| XmNcolormap | Core | XmNstringDirection | Manager |
| XmNdefaultButton | BulletinBoard | XmNtextFontList | BulletinBoard |
| XmNdefaultPosition | BulletinBoard | XmNtextTranslations | BulletinBoard |
| XmNdepth | Core | XmNtopShadowColor | Manager |
| XmNdestroyCallback | Core | XmNtopShadowPixmap | Manager |
| XmNdialogStyle | BulletinBoard | XmNtranslations | Core |
| XmNdialogTitle | BulletinBoard | XmNtraversalOn | Manager |
| XmNfocusCallback | BulletinBoard | XmNunitType | Manager |
| XmNforeground | Manager | XmNunmapCallback | BulletinBoard |
| XmNheight | Core | XmNuserData | Manager |
| XmNhelpCallback | Manager | XmNwidth | Core |
| XmNhighlightColor | Manager | XmNx | Core |
| XmNhighlightPixmap | Manager | XmNy | Core |
| XmNinitialFocus | Manager | | |
| XmNinitialResources-Persistent | Core | | |



## Translations

The translations for SelectionBox are inherited from BulletinBoard.

## Action Routines

SelectionBox defines the following action routines:

SelectionBoxUpOrDown(*flag*):

This action applies when the location cursor is within the item list. This action selects a list item from one of four possible positions and uses this item to replace the selection text. A *flag* value of 0, 1, 2, or 3 selects the previous, next, first, or last item, respectively. These four action routines are respectively bound to KUp, KDown, KBeginData, and KEndData, which represent four of the default accelerators in the XmNtextAccelerators resource.

SelectionBoxRestore()
: Like SelectionBoxUpOrDown except that this action replaces the selection text with the current list item. This action clears the selection text if no list item is currently selected. This action routine is bound to KRestore, a default accelerator for XmNtextAccelerators.

## Additional Behavior

SelectionBox has the following additional behavior:

MAny KCancel
: For a sensitive **Cancel** button, invokes the XmNactivateCallback callbacks.

KActivate
: For the button that has keyboard focus (or else the default button), invokes the callbacks in XmNactivateCallback. In a List or Text widget, this event calls the associated List or Text action before the associated SelectionBox action.

<Ok Button Activated>
: Invokes the XmNokCallback callback or the XmNnoMatchCallback if XmN-mustMatch is True and the text does not match an item in the list.

<Apply Button Activated>
: Invokes the XmNapplyCallback callbacks.

<Cancel Button Activated>
: Invokes the XmNcancelCallback callbacks.

<Help Button Activated>
: Invokes the XmNhelpCallback callbacks.

<MapWindow>
: Invokes the callbacks for XmNmapCallback if the parent is a DialogShell.

<UnmapWindow>
: Invokes the callbacks for XmNunmapCallback if the parent is a DialogShell.

## See Also

*XmCreateObject*(1), *XmSelectionBoxGetChild*(1),
*Composite*(2), *Constraint*(2), *Core*(2),
*XmBulletinBoard*(2), *XmManager*(2), *XmPromptDialog*(2), *XmSelectionDialog*(2).

# XmSelectionDialog

## Name

XmSelectionDialog – an unmanaged SelectionBox as a child of a Dialog Shell.

## Synopsis

**Public Header:** *<Xm/SelectioB.h>*

**Instantiation:** `widget = XmCreateSelectionDialog(...)`

**Functions/Macros:** `XmCreateSelectionBox()`, `XmCreateSelectionDialog()`, `XmSelectionBoxGetChild()`

## Description

A SelectionDialog is a compound object created by a call to `XmCreateSelectionDialog()` that an application can use to allow a user to make a selection from a dialog box. A SelectionDialog consists of a DialogShell with an unmanaged SelectionBox widget as its child. The SelectionBox resource `XmNdialogType` is set to `XmDIALOG_SELECTION`.

A SelectionDialog displays a scrollable list of alternatives from which the user can choose items. A SelectionDialog also contains a text field in which the user can edit a selection, labels for the text field and for the scrollable list, and four buttons. In Motif 1.2, the default button labels can be localized. In the C locale, and in Motif 1.1, the PushButtons are labeled **OK**, **Apply**, **Cancel**, and **Help** by default.

## Default Resource Values

A SelectionDialog sets the following default values for SelectionBox resources:

| Name | Default |
|---|---|
| `XmNdialogType` | `XmDIALOG_SELECTION` |

## Widget Hierarchy

When a SelectionDialog is created with a specified `name`, the DialogShell is named `name_popup` and the SelectionBox is called `name`.

## See Also

*XmCreateObject*(1), *XmSelectionBoxGetChild*(1), *XmDialogShell*(2), *XmSelectionBox*(2).

# XmSeparator

## Name

XmSeparator widget class – a widget that draws a line to separate other widgets visually.

## Synopsis

**Public Header:** *<Xm/Separator.h>*

**Class Name:** XmSeparator

**Class Hierarchy:** Core → XmPrimitive → XmSeparator

**Class Pointer:** `xmSeparatorWidgetClass`

**Instantiation:** `widget = XtCreateWidget(name, xmSeparatorWidgetClass, ...)`

**Functions/Macros:** `XmCreateSeparator()`, `XmIsSeparator()`

## Description

A Separator is a widget that draws a horizontal or vertical line between components in an application. Several line styles are available for the Separator. A pixmap separator can also be made by specifying a pixmap for the Core resource `XmNbackgroundPixmap` and then setting `XmNseparatorType` to `XmNO_LINE`.

## New Resources

Separator defines the following resources, all with `CSG` access:

| Name | Class | Type | Default |
|---|---|---|---|
| XmNmargin | XmCMargin | Dimension | 0 |
| XmNorientation | XmCOrientation | unsigned char | XmHORIZONTAL |
| XmNseparatorType | XmCSeparatorType | unsigned char | XmSHADOW_ETCHED_IN |

`XmNmargin`

The spacing on either end of the Separator. This would be the left and right margins for a horizontally drawn Separator and the top and bottom margins for a vertically drawn Separator.

`XmNorientation`

The direction in which to display the Separator. Possible values:

```
XmVERTICAL          /* top-to-bottom creation */
XmHORIZONTAL        /* left-to-right creation */
```

`XmNseparatorType`

The line style in which to draw the Separator. Possible values:

```
XmNO_LINE           XmSINGLE_DASHED_LINE     XmSHADOW_ETCHED_IN
XmSINGLE_LINE       XmDOUBLE_DASHED_LINE     XmSHADOW_ETCHED_OUT
XmDOUBLE_LINE
```

## Inherited Resources

Separator inherits the following resources. The resources are listed alphabetically, along with the superclass that defines them. Separator sets the default values of `XmNhighlight-Thickness` to 0 `XmNtraversalOn` to `False`. The default value of `XmNborderWidth` is reset to 0 by Primitive.

| Resource | Inherited From | Resource | Inherited From |
|---|---|---|---|
| XmNaccelerators | Core | XmNhighlightPixmap | Primitive |
| XmNancestorSensitive | Core | XmNhighlightThickness | Primitive |
| XmNbackground | Core | XmNinitialResourcesPersistent | Core |
| XmNbackgroundPixmap | Core | XmNmappedWhenManaged | Core |
| XmNborderColor | Core | XmNnavigationType | Primitive |
| XmNborderPixmap | Core | XmNscreen | Core |
| XmNborderWidth | Core | XmNsensitive | Core |
| XmNbottomShadowColor | Primitive | XmNshadowThickness | Primitive |
| XmNbottomShadowPixmap | Primitive | XmNtopShadowColor | Primitive |
| XmNcolormap | Core | XmNtopShadowPixmap | Primitive |
| XmNdepth | Core | XmNtranslations | Core |
| XmNdestroyCallback | Core | XmNtraversalOn | Primitive |
| XmNforeground | Primitive | XmNunitType | Primitive |
| XmNheight | Core | XmNuserData | Primitive |
| XmNhelpCallback | Primitive | XmNwidth | Core |
| XmNhighlightColor | Primitive | XmNx | Core |
| XmNhighlightOnEnter | Primitive | XmNy | Core |

## See Also

*XmCreateObject*(1),
*Core*(2), *XmPrimitive*(2).

Motif and Xt Widget Classes

# XmSeparatorGadget



## Name

XmSeparatorGadget widget class – a gadget that draws a line to separate other widgets visually.

## Synopsis

**Public Header:** *<Xm/SeparatoG.h>*

**Class Name:** XmSeparatorGadget

**Class Hierarchy:** Object → RectObj → XmGadget → XmSeparatorGadget

**Class Pointer:** xmSeparatorGadgetClass

**Instantiation:** `widget = XtCreateWidget(name, xmSeparatorGadgetClass, ...)`

**Functions/Macros:** `XmCreateSeparatorGadget()`, `XmIsSeparatorGadget()`

## Description

SeparatorGadget is the gadget variant of Separator.

SeparatorGadget's new resources are the same as those for Separator.

## Inherited Resources

SeparatorGadget inherits the following resources. The resources are listed alphabetically, along with the superclass that defines them. SeparatorGadget sets the default values of `XmNhighlightThickness` to 0 and `XmNtraversalOn` to `False`. The default value of `XmNborderWidth` is reset to 0 by Gadget.

| Resource | Inherited From | Resource | Inherited From |
|---|---|---|---|
| `XmNancestorSensitive` | `RectObj` | `XmNsensitive` | `RectObj` |
| `XmNborderWidth` | `RectObj` | `XmNshadowThickness` | `Gadget` |
| `XmNbottomShadowColor` | `Gadget` | `XmNtopShadowColor` | `Gadget` |
| `XmNdestroyCallback` | `Object` | `XmNtraversalOn` | `Gadget` |
| `XmNheight` | `RectObj` | `XmNunitType` | `Gadget` |
| `XmNhelpCallback` | `Gadget` | `XmNuserData` | `Gadget` |
| `XmNhighlightColor` | `Gadget` | `XmNwidth` | `RectObj` |
| `XmNhighlightOnEnter` | `Gadget` | `XmNx` | `RectObj` |
| `XmNhighlightThickness` | `Gadget` | `XmNy` | `RectObj` |
| `XmNnavigationType` | `Gadget` | | |

## See Also

*XmCreateObject*(1),
*Object*(2), *RectObj*(2), *XmGadget*(2), *XmSeparator*(2).

# XmTemplateDialog

## Name

XmTemplateDialog – an unmanaged MessageBox as a child of DialogShell.

## Synopsis

**Public Header:** *<Xm/MessageB.h>*

**Instantiation:** `widget = XmCreateTemplateDialog(...)`

**Functions/Macros:** `XmCreateTemplateDialog()`, `XmMessageBoxGetChild()`

## Description

A TemplateDialog is a compound object created by a call to `XmCreateTemplateDialog()` that an application can use to present a customized message to the user. A TemplateDialog consists of a DialogShell with an unmanaged MessageBox widget as its child. The MessageBox resource `XmNdialogType` is set to `XmDIALOG_TEMPLATE`. By default, a TemplateDialog includes only a separator. An application can create a customized dialog by adding children to the TemplateDialog. To create the standard MessageBox PushButtons, an application can specify the label string and callback resources for the desired buttons. Setting either the `XmNmessageString` or `XmNsymbolPixmap` resource creates a message or a symbol.

## Default Resource Values

A TemplateDialog sets the following default values for MessageBox resources:

| Name | Default |
|---|---|
| `XmNdialogType` | `XmDIALOG_TEMPLATE` |

## Widget Hierarchy

When a TemplateDialog is created with a specified `name`, the DialogShell is named `name_popup` and the MessageBox is called `name`.

## See Also

*XmCreateObject*(1), *XmMessageBoxGetChild*(1), *XmDialogShell*(2), *XmMessageBox*(2).

## Name

XmText widget class – text-editing widget.

## Synopsis

**Public Header:** *<Xm/Text.h>*

**Class Name:** XmText

**Class Hierarchy:** Core → XmPrimitive → XmText

**Class Pointer:** `xmTextWidgetClass`

**Instantiation:** `widget = XtCreateWidget(name, xmTextWidgetClass, ...)`

**Functions/Macros:** `XmCreateScrolledText()`, `XmCreateText()`, `XmIsText()`, `XmText...` routines

## Description

A Text widget provides a text editor that allows text to be inserted, modified, deleted, and selected. Text provides both single-line and multi-line text editing capabilities.

## New Resources

Text defines the following resources:

| Name | Class | Type | Default | Access |
|---|---|---|---|---|
| XmNautoShowCursorPosition | XmCAutoShowCursorPosition | Boolean | True | CSG |
| XmNcursorPosition | XmCCursorPosition | XmTextPosition | 0 | CSG |
| XmNeditable | XmCEditable | Boolean | True | CSG |
| XmNeditMode | XmCEditMode | int | See below | CSG |
| XmNmarginHeight | XmCMarginHeight | Dimension | 5 | CSG |
| XmNmarginWidth | XmCMarginWidth | Dimension | 5 | CSG |
| XmNmaxLength | XmCMaxLength | int | largest integer | CSG |
| XmNsource | XmCSource | XmTextSource | default source | CSG |
| XmNtopCharacter | XmCTextPosition | XmTextPosition | 0 | CSG |
| XmNvalue | XmCValue | String | "" | CSG |
| XmNvalueWcs | XmCValueWcs | wchar_t * | (wchar_t *)"" | CSG |
| XmNverifyBell | XmCVerifyBell | Boolean | True | CSG |

`XmNautoShowCursorPosition`

If `True` (default), the visible portion of the Text widget will always contain the insert cursor. The Text widget will scroll its contents, if necessary, to ensure that the cursor remains visible.

`XmNcursorPosition`

The location at which to place the current insert cursor. Values for this resource are relative to the beginning of the text; the first character position is defined as 0.

`XmNeditable`

If `True` (default), the user is allowed to edit the text string; if `False`, the user is not allowed to do so.

`XmNeditMode`

Determines which group of keyboard bindings to use. Possible values:

```
XmMULTI_LINE_EDIT     /* key bindings for multi-line edits */
XmSINGLE_LINE_EDIT    /* key bindings for single line edits; the default value */
```

`XmNmarginHeight`
`XmNmarginWidth`

The spacing between the edges of the widget and the text. (Top and bottom edges for height; left and right for width.)

`XmNmaxLength`

The maximum length of the text string that a user can enter from the keyboard. This resource does not affect strings that are entered via the `XmNvalue` resource or the `XmTextSetString()` routine.

`XmNsource`

A source that the Text widget uses for displaying text, thereby allowing Text widgets to share the same text source.

`XmNtopCharacter`

The location of the text to display at the top of the window. Values for this resource are relative to the beginning of the text, with the first character position defined as 0.

`XmNvalue`

The string value to display in the Text widget, expressed as a `char *`. If `XmNvalue` and `XmNvalueWcs` are both defined, `XmNvalueWcs` takes precedence. Use `XtSetValues()` to copy string values to the internal buffer and use `XtGetValues()` to return the value of the internal buffer.

`XmNvalueWcs`

In Motif 1.2, the string value to display in the Text widget, expressed as a `wchar_t *`. If `XmNvalue` and `XmNvalueWcs` are both defined, `XmNvalueWcs` takes precedence. Use `XtSetValues()` to copy string values to the internal buffer and use `XtGetValues()` to return the value of the internal buffer. This resource cannot be set in a resource file.

`XmNverifyBell`

If `True` (default), a bell will sound when a verification produces no action.

## Text Input Resources

| Name | Class | Type | Default | Access |
|---|---|---|---|---|
| XmNpendingDelete | XmCPendingDelete | Boolean | True | CSG |
| XmNselectionArray | XmCSelectionArray | XtPointer | default array | CSG |
| XmNselectionArrayCount | XmCSelectionArrayCount | int | 4 | CSG |
| XmNselectThreshold | XmCSelectThreshold | int | 5 | CSG |

XmNpendingDelete
: If True (default), the Text widget's pending delete mode is on, meaning that selected text will be deleted as soon as the next text insertion occurs.

XmNselectionArray
: The array of possible actions caused by multiple mouse clicks. UIL does not define these values for the Text widget. Possible values:

```
XmSELECT_POSITION     /* single-click; reset position of insert cursor */
XmSELECT_WORD         /* double-click; select a word */
XmSELECT_LINE         /* triple-click; select a line */
XmSELECT_ALL          /* quadruple-click; select all text */
```

XmNselectionArrayCount
: The number of items in the array specified by XmNselectionArray.

XmNselectThreshold
: The number of pixels the insertion cursor must be dragged during selection in order to select the next character.

## Text Output Resources

| Name | Class | Type | Default | Access |
|---|---|---|---|---|
| XmNblinkRate | XmCBlinkRate | int | 500 | CSG |
| XmNcolumns | XmCColumns | short | dynamic | CSG |
| XmNcursorPositionVisible | XmCCursorPositionVisible | Boolean | True | CSG |
| XmNfontList | XmCFontList | XmFontList | dynamic | CSG |
| XmNresizeHeight | XmCResizeHeight | Boolean | False | CSG |
| XmNresizeWidth | XmCResizeWidth | Boolean | False | CSG |
| XmNrows | XmCRows | short | dynamic | CSG |
| XmNwordWrap | XmCWordWrap | Boolean | False | CSG |

XmNblinkRate
: The time in milliseconds that the cursor spends either being visible or invisible. A value of 0 prevents the cursor from blinking.

XmNcolumns
: The number of character spaces that should fit horizontally in the text window. The XmNwidth resource determines the default value of XmNcolumns, but if no width has been set, the default is 20. See also XmNrows.

XmNcursorPositionVisible
: If True (default), the text cursor will be visible.

XmNfontList
: The font list used for the widget's text. If this value is initially NULL, the font list is derived from the font list resource from the nearest parent that is a subclass of BulletinBoard, MenuShell, or VendorShell.

XmNresizeHeight
: If False (default), the Text widget will not expand vertically to fit all of the text (in other words, the widget will need to have scrollbars so that the rest of the text can be scrolled into view). If True, the Text widget always begins its display with the text at the beginning of the source. This resource has no effect in a ScrolledText widget whose XmNscrollVertical resource is set to True.

XmNresizeWidth
: If False (default), the Text widget will not expand horizontally to fit its text. If True, the widget tries to change its width. This resource has no effect when the XmNwordWrap resource is set to True.

XmNrows
: The number of character spaces that should fit vertically in the text window. The XmNheight resource determines the default value of XmNrows, but if no height has been set, the default is 1. This resource is meaningful only when XmNeditMode is XmMULTI_LINE_EDIT. See also XmNcolumns.

XmNwordWrap
: If False (default), does not break lines automatically between words (in which case text can disappear beyond the window's edge). If True, breaks lines at spaces, tabs, or newlines. This resource is meaningful only when XmNeditMode is XmMULTI_LINE_EDIT.

## Scrolled Text Resources

| Name | Class | Type | Default | Access |
|---|---|---|---|---|
| XmNscrollHorizontal | XmCScroll | Boolean | True | CG |
| XmNscrollLeftSide | XmCScrollSide | Boolean | dynamic | CG |
| XmNscrollTopSide | XmCScrollSide | Boolean | False | CG |
| XmNscrollVertical | XmCScroll | Boolean | True | CG |

XmNscrollHorizontal
: If True, the Text widget adds a horizontal ScrollBar. The default is True; however, the value changes to False if the widget is in a ScrolledWindow whose XmNscrollingPolicy resource is set to XmAUTOMATIC. This resource is meaningful only when XmNeditMode is XmMULTI_LINE_EDIT.

XmNscrollLeftSide
: If True, the vertical ScrollBar is placed to the left of the scrolled text window. The default value depends on how the XmNstringDirection resource is set. This resource is meaningful only when XmNeditMode is XmMULTI_LINE_EDIT and when XmNscrollVertical is True.

XmNscrollTopSide
: If True, the horizontal ScrollBar is placed above the scrolled text window, rather than below by default.

XmNscrollVertical
: If True, the Text widget adds a vertical ScrollBar. The default is True; however, the value changes to False if the widget is in a ScrolledWindow whose XmNscrollingPolicy resource is set to XmAUTOMATIC.

## Callback Resources

Text defines the following callback resources:

| Callback | Reason Constant |
|---|---|
| XmNactivateCallback | XmCR_ACTIVATE |
| XmNfocusCallback | XmCR_FOCUS |
| XmNgainPrimaryCallback | XmCR_GAIN_PRIMARY |
| XmNlosePrimaryCallback | XmCR_LOSE_PRIMARY |
| XmNlosingFocusCallback | XmCR_LOSING_FOCUS |
| XmNmodifyVerifyCallback | XmCR_MODIFYING_TEXT_VALUE |
| XmNmodifyVerify CallbackWcs | XmCR_MODIFYING_TEXT_VALUE |
| XmNmotionVerifyCallback | XmCR_MOVING_INSERT_CURSOR |
| XmNvalueChangedCallback | XmCR_VALUE_CHANGED |

XmNactivateCallback
: List of callbacks that are called when the user causes the Text widget to be activated.

XmNfocusCallback
: List of callbacks that are called when the Text widget receives the input focus.

XmNgainPrimaryCallback
: List of callbacks that are called when the Text widget gains ownership of the primary selection.

`XmNlosePrimary`
: List of callbacks that are called when the Text widget loses ownership of the primary selection.

`XmNlosingFocusCallback`
: List of callbacks that are called when the Text widget loses the input focus.

`XmNmodifyVerifyCallback`
: List of callbacks that are called before the value of the Text widget is changed. If there are callbacks for both `XmNmodifyVerifyCallback` and `XmNmodifyVerify-CallbackWcs`, the `XmNmodifyVerifyCallback` callbacks are called first.

`XmNmodifyVerifyCallbackWcs`
: List of callbacks that are called before the value of the Text widget is changed. If there are callbacks for both `XmNmodifyVerifyCallback` and `XmNmodifyVerify-CallbackWcs`, the `XmNmodifyVerifyCallback` callbacks are called first.

`XmNmotionVerifyCallback`
: List of callbacks that are called before the insertion cursor is moved in the Text widget.

`XmNvalueChangedCallback`
: List of callbacks that are called after the value of the Text widget is changed.

## Callback Structure

Each callback function is passed the following structure:

```
typedef struct
{
   int     reason;      /* the reason that the callback was called */
   XEvent  *event;      /* event structure that triggered callback */
} XmAnyCallbackStruct;
```

In addition, the callback resources `XmNlosingFocusCallback`, `XmNmodifyVerify-Callback`, and `XmNmotionVerifyCallback` reference the following structure:

```
typedef struct
{
   int             reason;         /* the reason that the callback was called */
   XEvent          *event;         /* structure that triggered callback */
   Boolean         doit;           /* do the action (True) or undo it (False) */
   XmTextPosition current_insert;/* the insert cursor's current position */
   XmTextPosition new_insert;      /* desired new position of insert cursor */
   XmTextPosition start_pos;       /* start of text to change */
   XmTextPosition end_pos;         /* end of text to change */
   XmTextBlock     text;           /* describes the text to insert */
} XmTextVerifyCallbackStruct, *XmTextVerifyPtr;
```

`start_pos` specifies the location at which to start modifying text. `start_pos` is unused if the callback resource is `XmNmotionVerifyCallback`, and is the same as the `current_-insert` member if the callback resource is `XmNlosingFocusCallback`.

end_pos specifies the location at which to stop modifying text (however, if no text was modified, end_pos has the same value as start_pos). end_pos is unused if the callback resource is XmNmotionVerifyCallback, and is the same as the current_insert member if the callback resource is XmNlosingFocusCallback.

text points to the structure below, which specifies information about the text to be inserted.

```
typedef struct
{
   char           *ptr;          /* pointer to the text to insert */
   int            length;        /* length of this text */
   XmTextFormat   format;        /* text format (e.g., FMT8BIT, FMT16BIT) */
} XmTextBlockRec, *XmTextBlock;
```

The callback resource XmNmodifyVerifyCallbackWcs references the following structure:

```
typedef struct
{
   int             reason;        /* the reason that the callback was called */
   XEvent          *event;        /* structure that triggered callback */
   Boolean         doit;          /* do the action (True) or undo it (False) */
   XmTextPosition current_insert;/* the insert cursor's current position */
   XmTextPosition new_insert;     /* desired new position of insert cursor */
   XmTextPosition start_pos;      /* start of text to change */
   XmTextPosition end_pos;        /* end of text to change */
   XmTextBlockWcs text;           /* describes the text to insert */
} XmTextVerifyCallbackStructWcs, *XmTextVerifyPtrWcs;
```

All of the fields in this structure are the same as the fields in the XmTextVerifyCallback-Struct except text, which points to the structure below and specifies information about the text to be inserted.

```
typedef struct
{
   wchar_t        *wcsptr;       /* pointer to the text to insert */
   int            length;        /* length of this text */
} XmTextBlockRecWcs, *XmTextBlockWcs;
```

## Inherited Resources

Text inherits the following resources. The resources are listed alphabetically, along with the superclass that defines them. Text sets the default value of XmNnavigationType to XmTAB_GROUP. The default value of XmNborderWidth is reset to 0 by Primitive.

| Resource | Inherited From | Resource | Inherited From |
|---|---|---|---|
| XmNaccelerators | Core | XmNhighlightPixmap | Primitive |
| XmNancestorSensitive | Core | XmNhighlightThickness | Primitive |
| XmNbackground | Core | XmNinitialResourcesPersistent | Core |
| XmNbackgroundPixmap | Core | XmNmappedWhenManaged | Core |

| Resource | Inherited From | Resource | Inherited From |
|---|---|---|---|
| XmNborderColor | Core | XmNnavigationType | Primitive |
| XmNborderPixmap | Core | XmNscreen | Core |
| XmNborderWidth | Core | XmNsensitive | Core |
| XmNbottomShadowColor | Primitive | XmNshadowThickness | Primitive |
| XmNbottomShadowPixmap | Primitive | XmNtopShadowColor | Primitive |
| XmNcolormap | Core | XmNtopShadowPixmap | Primitive |
| XmNdepth | Core | XmNtranslations | Core |
| XmNdestroyCallback | Core | XmNtraversalOn | Primitive |
| XmNforeground | Primitive | XmNunitType | Primitive |
| XmNheight | Core | XmNuserData | Primitive |
| XmNhelpCallback | Primitive | XmNwidth | Core |
| XmNhighlightColor | Primitive | XmNx | Core |
| XmNhighlightOnEnter | Primitive | XmNy | Core |

## Translations

The translations for Text include those from Primitive, as well as the following. (Note that some of the associated actions will be reversed for a language environment in which text is not read from left to right.)

| Event | Action |
|---|---|
| BSelect Press | grab-focus() |
| BSelect Motion | extend-adjust() |
| BSelect Release | extend-end() |
| BExtend Press | extend-start() |
| BExtend Motion | extend-adjust() |
| BExtend Release | extend-end() |
| BToggle Press | move-destination() |
| BTransfer Press | process-bdrag() (1.2) |
| | secondary-start() (1.1) |
| BTransfer Motion | secondary-adjust() |
| BTransfer Release | copy-to() |
| MCtrl BTransfer Press | process-bdrag() (1.2) |
| | secondary-start() (1.1) |
| MCtrl BTransfer Motion | secondary-adjust() |
| MCtrl BTransfer Release | copy-to() |
| MAlt BTransfer Press | process-bdrag() (1.2) |
| | secondary-start() (1.1) |
| MAlt BTransfer Motion | secondary-adjust() |
| MAlt BTransfer Release | copy-to() |
| MShift BTransfer Press | process-bdrag() |

| Event | Action |
|---|---|
| MShift BTransfer Motion | secondary-adjust() |
| MShift BTransfer Release | move-to() |
| MAlt MCtrl BTransfer Release | copy-to() |
| MAlt MShift BTransfer Release | move-to() |
| KUp | process-up() |
| MShift KUp | process-shift-up() |
| MCtrl KUp | backward-paragraph() |
| MShift MCtrl KUp | backward-paragraph(extend) |
| KDown | process-down() |
| MShift KDown | process-shift-down() |
| MCtrl KDown | forward-paragraph() |
| MShift MCtrl KDown | forward-paragraph(extend) |
| KLeft | backward-character() |
| MShift KLeft | key-select(left) |
| MCtrl KLeft | backward-word() |
| MShift MCtrl KLeft | backward-word(extend) |
| KRight | forward-character() |
| MShift KRight | key-select(right) |
| MCtrl KRight | forward-word() |
| MShift MCtrl KRight | forward-word(extend) |
| KPageUp | previous-page() |
| MShift KPageUp | previous-page(extend) |
| KPageDown | next-page() |
| MShift KPageDown | next-page(extend) |
| KPageLeft | page-left() |
| KPageRight | page-right() |
| KBeginLine | beginning-of-line() |
| MShift KBeginLine | beginning-of-file(extend) |
| KEndLine | end-of-line() |
| MShift KEndLine | end-of-line(extend) |
| KBeginData | beginning-of-file() |
| MShift KBeginData | beginning-of-file(extend) |
| KEndData | end-of-file() |
| MShift KEndData | end-of-file(extend) |
| KTab | process-tab() |
| KNextField | next-tab-group() |
| KPrevField | prev-tab-group() |
| KEnter | process-return() |

| Event | Action |
|---|---|
| `KActivate` | `activate()` |
| `KDelete` | `delete-next-character()` |
| `KBackSpace` | `delete-previous-character()` |
| `KAddMode` | `toggle-add-mode()` |
| `KSpace` | `self-insert()` |
| `MShift KSpace` | `self-insert()` |
| `KSelect` | `set-anchor()` |
| `KExtend` | `key-select()` |
| `MAny KCancel` | `process-cancel()` |
| `KClear` | `clear-selection()` |
| `KSelectAll` | `select-all()` |
| `KDeselectAll` | `deselect-all()` |
| `KCut` | `cut-clipboard()` |
| `KCopy` | `copy-clipboard()` |
| `KPaste` | `paste-clipboard()` |
| `KPrimaryCut` | `cut-primary()` |
| `KPrimaryCopy` | `copy-primary()` |
| `KPrimaryPaste` | `copy-primary()` |
| `KQuickCut` | `quick-cut-set (1.1)()` |
| `KQuickCopy` | `quick-copy-set() (1.1)` |
| `KQuickPaste` | `quick-copy-set() (1.1)` |
| `KQuickExtend` | `do-quick-action() (1.1)` |
| `KHelp` | `Help()` |
| `KAny` | `self_insert()` |



## Action Routines

Text defines the action routines below. For actions that involve movement such as `next`, `previous`, `start`, `end`, `back`, `forward`, etc., the actual cursor movement depends on whether the language environment is left-to-right or right-to-left. In addition, some actions accept an optional argument, *`extend`*. When applied with no argument, these actions move the cursor; when applied with the *`extend`* argument, these actions move the cursor but also extend the text selection. In all descriptions, the term cursor refers to the insertion cursor.

`activate()`
: Invokes the callbacks specified by `XmNactivateCallback`.

`backward-character()`
: Moves the cursor back one character.

`backward-paragraph(extend)`
: Moves the cursor back to the first non-blank character that follows a blank line (or back to the start of the text if there is no previous blank line). If the cursor is

already located at a non-blank character (i.e., if it's already at the beginning of the paragraph), the cursor moves to the start of the previous paragraph. (Multiline edit mode only.)

`backward-word(`*`extend`*`)`
: Moves the cursor back to the first non-blank character that follows a blank character (or back to the start of the line if there is no previous blank character). If the cursor is already located at a non-blank character (i.e., if it's already at the beginning of a word), the cursor moves to the start of the previous word.

`beep()` Makes the terminal beep.

`beginning-of-file(`*`extend`*`)`
: Moves the cursor to the start of the text.

`beginning-of-line(`*`extend`*`)`
: Moves the cursor to the start of the line.

`clear-selection()`
: Replaces each character (except a newline) with a space, effectively clearing the current selection.

`copy-clipboard()`
: Copies the current text selection into the clipboard.

`copy-primary()`
: Inserts a copy of the primary selection at the cursor location.

`copy-to()`
: Inserts a copy of the secondary selection at the cursor location, or, if there is no secondary selection, inserts a copy of the primary selection at the pointer location.

`cut-clipboard()`
: Deletes the current selection and moves it to the clipboard.

`cut-primary()`
: Deletes the primary selection and inserts it at the cursor.

`delete-next-character()`
`delete-previous-character()`
: If the cursor is inside the selection and `XmNpendingDelete` is `True`, deletes the selection. Otherwise, deletes the character following/preceding the cursor.

`delete-next-word()`
`delete-previous-word()`
: If the cursor is inside the selection and `XmNpendingDelete` is `True`, deletes the selection. Otherwise, deletes from the character following/preceding the cursor to the next/previous space, tab, or end of line.

`delete-selection()`
: Deletes the current selection.

`delete-to-end-of-line()`
: Deletes forward from the character after the cursor up to and including the end of the line.

`delete-to-start-of-line()`
: Deletes back from the character before the cursor up to and including the beginning of the line.

`deselect-all()`
: Deselects the current selection.

`do-quick-action()`
: In Motif 1.1, Ends a secondary selection and does the action that was started by either of the actions `quick-copy-set` or `quick-cut-set`.

`end-of-file(`*`extend`*`)`
: Moves the cursor to the end of the text.

`end-of-line(`*`extend`*`)`
: Moves the cursor to the end of the line.

`extend-adjust()`
: Selects text that is between the anchor and the pointer location, while deselecting text that is outside this area. As a result of this action, when the pointer moves past lines of text, these lines are selected and the current line is selected up to the position of the pointer.

`extend-end()`
: Moves the cursor to the pointer location and ends the selection performed by `extend-adjust`.

`extend-start()`
: Adjusts the anchor in preparation for selecting text via the `extend-adjust` action.

`forward-character()`
: Moves the cursor forward one character.

`forward-paragraph(`*`extend`*`)`
: Moves the cursor forward to the first non-blank character that follows a blank line. If the cursor is already located at a non-blank character (i.e., if it's already at the beginning of the paragraph), the cursor moves to the start of the next paragraph. (Multiline edit mode only.)

`forward-word(`*`extend`*`)`
: Moves the cursor forward to the first blank character that follows a nonblank character (or forward to the end of the line if there is no blank character to move to). If the cursor is already located at a blank character (i.e., if it's already at the end of a word), the cursor moves to the end of the next word.

`grab-focus()`
: Processes multiclicks as defined in the `XmNselectionArray` resource. By default, one click resets the cursor to the pointer location, two clicks select a word, three clicks select a line, and four clicks select all of the text.

`Help()`
: Invokes the list of callbacks specified by `XmNhelpCallback`. If the Text widget doesn't have any help callbacks, this action routine invokes those associated with the nearest ancestor that has them.

`insert-string(`*`text`*`)`
: Inserts `text` at the cursor, or replaces the current selection with `text` (when `XmNpendingDelete` is `True`).

`key-select(`*`direction`*`)`
: Extends the selection and moves the cursor one character to the right (when `direction` is `right`), one character to the left (`direction` is `left`), or not at all (no argument).

`kill-next-character()`
`kill-next-word()`
`kill-previous-character()`
`kill-previous-word()`
: These four actions are similar to their delete action counterparts, but the kill actions have the added feature of storing the deleted text in the cut buffer.

`kill-selection()`
: Deletes the current selection and stores this text in the cut buffer.

`kill-to-end-of-line()`
: Deletes forward from the character after the cursor up to and including the end of the line; stores this text in the cut buffer.

`kill-to-start-of-line()`
: Deletes back from the character before the cursor up to and including the beginning of the line; stores this text in the cut buffer.

`move-destination()`
: Moves the cursor to the pointer location, leaving existing selections unaffected.

`move-to()`
: Deletes the secondary selection and inserts it at the cursor, or, if there is no secondary selection, deletes the primary selection and inserts it at the pointer location.

`newline()`
: If the cursor is inside the selection and `XmNpendingDelete` is `True`, deletes the selection and inserts a newline at the cursor. Otherwise, only inserts a newline at the cursor.

`newline-and-backup()`
: If the cursor is inside the selection and `XmNpendingDelete` is `True`, deletes the selection, inserts a newline at the cursor and moves the cursor to the previous end of line. Otherwise, only inserts a newline and then moves the cursor to the previous end of line.

`newline-and-indent()`
: If the cursor is inside the selection and `XmNpendingDelete` is `True`, deletes the selection, inserts a newline at the cursor, and adds blanks (as needed) so that the cursor aligns with the first nonblank character in the previous line. Otherwise, only inserts a newline and adds blanks (as needed) so that the cursor aligns with the first nonblank character in the previous line.

`next-line()`
: Places the cursor on the next line.

`next-page(`*`extend`*`)`
: Moves the cursor one page forward.

`next-tab-group()`
: Traverses to the next tab group.

`page-left()`
`page-right()`
: Scrolls the visible area one page to the left or right.

`paste-clipboard()`
: Pastes text from the clipboard to the position before the cursor.

`prev-tab-group()`
: Traverses to the previous tab group.

`previous-line()`
: Places the cursor on the previous line.

`previous-page(extend)`
: Moves the cursor one page backward.

`process-bdrag()`
: In Motif 1.2, copies the current selection to the insertion cursor if text is selected, the location cursor is outside of the selection, and no motion is detected. Performs a secondary selection and copies the selection to the position where text was last edited if the cursor is outside of the selection and motion is detected. Otherwise, initiates a drag and drop operation using the current selection.

`process-cancel()`
: Cancels the `extend-adjust()` or `secondary-adjust()` actions that are currently being applied, restoring the selection to its previous state.

`process-down()`
`process-up()`
: If `XmNnavigationType` is `XmNONE`, descends/ascends to the adjacent widget in the tab group (single-line edit mode only). Moves the cursor one line down/up (multi-line edit mode only).

`process-home()`
: Moves the cursor to the start of the line. (Similar to `beginning-of-line`.)

`process-return()`
: Invokes the `XmNactivateCallback` callbacks (in single-line editing) or inserts a newline (in multi-line editing).

`process-shift-down()`
`process-shift-up()`
: Moves the cursor one line down or up (in multi-line editing only).

`process-tab()`
: Traverses to the next tab group (in single-line editing) or inserts a tab (in multi-line editing).

`quick-copy-set()`
: In Motif 1.1, marks this text location as the start of the secondary selection to use in quick copying.

`quick-cut-set()`
: In Motif 1.1, marks this text location as the start of the secondary selection to use in quick cutting.

`redraw-display()`
: Redraws the text in the viewing window.

`scroll-one-line-down()`
`scroll-one-line-up()`
: Scrolls the text region one line down or up.

`secondary-adjust()`
: Extends the secondary selection to the location of the pointer.

`secondary-notify()`
: Inserts a copy of the secondary selection at the destination cursor.

`secondary-start()`
: In Motif 1.1, marks this text location as the start of a secondary selection.

`select-adjust()`
: Extends the selection via the multiple mouse clicks defined by the `XmNselectionArray` resource.

`select-all()`
: Selects all text.

`select-end()`
: Ends the selection made using the `select-adjust()` action.

`select-start()`
: Begins a text selection.

`self-insert()`
: The basic method of inserting text. Typing at the keyboard inserts new text and (if `XmNpendingDelete` is `True`) replaces selected text that the cursor is in.

`set-anchor()`
: Changes the anchor point used when making extended selections; changes the destination cursor used for secondary selections.

`set-insertion-point()`
: Sets the position of the cursor.

`set-selection-hint()`
: Sets the selection's text source and the selection's location.

`toggle-add-mode()`
: Turns Add Mode either on or off.

`traverse-home()`
`traverse-next()`
`traverse-prev()`
: Traverse within the tab group to the first widget, the next widget, and the previous widget, respectively.

`unkill()`
: Restores the most recently deleted text to the cursor's location.

## Additional Behavior

Text has the following additional behavior:

`<FocusIn>`
: Draws a solid insertion cursor and makes it blink.

`<FocusOut>`
: Draws a stippled I-beam insertion cursor, unless it is the destination widget.

## See Also

*XmCreateObject*(1), *XmTextClearSelection*(1), *XmTextCopy*(1), *XmTextCut*(1), *XmTextDisableRedisplay*(1), *XmTextEnableRedisplay*(1), *XmTextFindString*(1), *XmTextFindStringWcs*(1), *XmTextGetBaseline*(1), *XmTextGetCursorPosition*(1), *XmTextGetEditable*(1), *XmTextGetInsertionPosition*(1), *XmTextGetLastPosition*(1), *XmTextGetMaxLength*(1), *XmTextGetSelection*(1), *XmTextGetSelectionPosition*(1), *XmTextGetSelectionWcs*(1), *XmTextGetSource*(1), *XmTextGetString*(1), *XmTextGetStringWcs*(1), *XmTextGetSubstring*(1), *XmTextGetSubstringWcs*(1), *XmTextGetTopCharacter*(1), *XmTextInsert*(1),

*XmTextInsertWcs*(1), *XmTextPaste*(1), *XmTextPosToXY*(1), *XmTextRemove*(1), *XmTextReplace*(1), *XmTextReplaceWcs*(1), *XmTextScroll*(1), *XmTextSetAddMode*(1), *XmTextSetCursorPosition*(1), *XmTextSetEditable*(1), *XmTextSetHighlight*(1), *XmTextSetInsertionPosition*(1), *XmTextSetMaxLength*(1), *XmTextSetSelection*(1), *XmTextSetSource*(1), *XmTextSetString*(1), *XmTextSetStringWcs*(1), *XmTextSetTopCharacter*(1), *XmTextShowPosition*(1), *XmTextXYToPos*(1),
*Core*(2), *XmPrimitive*(2), *XmTextField*(2).

## Name

XmTextField widget class – a single-line text-editing widget.

## Synopsis

**Public Header:** *<Xm/TextF.h>*

**Class Name:** XmTextField

**Class Hierarchy:** Core → XmPrimitive → XmTextField

**Class Pointer:** `xmTextFieldWidgetClass`

**Instantiation:** `widget = XtCreateWidget(name, xmTextWidgetClass, ...)`

**Functions/Macros:** `XmCreateTextField()`, `XmIsTextField()`, `XmTextField...` routines

## Description

A TextField widget provides a single-line text editor that has a subset of the functionality of the Text widget.

## New Resources

TextField defines the following resources, all with access CSG:

| Name | Class | Type | Default |
|---|---|---|---|
| XmNblinkRate | XmCBlinkRate | int | 500 |
| XmNcolumns | XmCColumns | short | dynamic |
| XmNcursorPosition | XmCCursorPosition | XmTextPosition | 0 |
| XmNcursorPositionVisible | XmCCursorPositionVisible | Boolean | True |
| XmNeditable | XmCEditable | Boolean | True |
| XmNfontList | XmCFontList | XmFontList | dynamic |
| XmNmarginHeight | XmCMarginHeight | Dimension | 5 |
| XmNmarginWidth | XmCMarginWidth | Dimension | 5 |
| XmNmaxLength | XmCMaxLength | int | largest integer |
| XmNpendingDelete | XmCPendingDelete | Boolean | True |
| XmNresizeWidth | XmCResizeWidth | Boolean | False |
| XmNselectionArray | XmCSelectionArray | Pointer | default array |
| XmNselectionArrayCount | XmCSelectionArrayCount | int | 3 |
| XmNselectThreshold | XmCSelectThreshold | int | 5 |
| XmNvalue | XmCValue | String | "" |
| XmNvalueWcs | XmCValueWcs | wchar_t * | (wchar_t *)"" |
| XmNverifyBell | XmCVerifyBell | Boolean | dynamic |

`XmNblinkRate`
The time in milliseconds that the cursor spends either being visible or invisible. A value of 0 prevents the cursor from blinking.

`XmNcolumns`
The number of character spaces that should fit horizontally in the text window. The `XmNwidth` resource determines the default value of `XmNcolumns`, but if no width has been set, the default is 20.

`XmNcursorPosition`
The location at which to place the current insert cursor. Values for this resource are relative to the beginning of the text, with the first character position defined as 0.

`XmNcursorPositionVisible`
If `True` (default), the text cursor will be visible.

`XmNeditable`
If `True` (default), the user is allowed to edit the text string; if `False`, the user is not allowed to do so.

`XmNfontList`
The font list used for the widget's text. If this value is initially `NULL`, the font list is derived from the font list resource from the nearest parent that is a subclass of BulletinBoard, MenuShell, or VendorShell.

`XmNmarginHeight`
`XmNmarginWidth`
The spacing between the edges of the widget and the text. (Top and bottom edges for height; left and right for width.)

`XmNmaxLength`
The maximum length of the text string that a user can enter from the keyboard. This resource doesn't affect strings that are entered via the `XmNvalue` resource or the `XmTextFieldSetString()` routine.

`XmNpendingDelete`
If `True` (default), the TextField widget's pending delete mode is on, meaning that selected text will be deleted as soon as the next text insertion occurs.

`XmNresizeWidth`
If `False` (default), the TextField widget will not expand horizontally to fit its text. If `True`, the widget tries to change its width.

`XmNselectionArray`
The array of possible actions caused by multiple mouse clicks. UIL does not define these values for the Text widget. Possible values:

```
XmSELECT_POSITION      /* single-click; reset position of insert cursor */
XmSELECT_WORD          /* double-click; select a word */
XmSELECT_LINE          /* triple-click; select a line */
```

XmNselectionArrayCount
The number of items in the array specified by XmNselectionArray.

XmNselectThreshold
The number of pixels the insertion cursor must be dragged during selection in order to select the next character.

XmNvalue
The string value to display in the TextField widget, expressed as a char *. If XmNvalue and XmNvalueWcs are both defined, XmNvalueWcs takes precedence. Use XtSetValues() to copy string values to the internal buffer and use XtGetValues() to return the value of the internal buffer.

XmNvalueWcs
In Motif 1.2, the string value to display in the TextField widget, expressed as a wchar_t *. If XmNvalue and XmNvalueWcs are both defined, XmNvalueWcs takes precedence. Use XtSetValues() to copy string values to the internal buffer and use XtGetValues() to return the value of the internal buffer. This resource cannot be set in a resource file.

XmNverifyBell
If True, a bell will sound when a verification produces no action.

## Callback Resources

TextField defines the same callback resources and references the same callback structures as the Text widget.

## Inherited Resources

TextField inherits the following resources. The resources are listed alphabetically, along with the superclass that defines them. TextField sets the default value of XmNnavigationType to XmTAB_GROUP. The default value of XmNborderWidth is reset to 0 by Primitive.

| Resource | Inherited From | Resource | Inherited From |
|---|---|---|---|
| XmNaccelerators | Core | XmNhighlightPixmap | Primitive |
| XmNancestorSensitive | Core | XmNhighlightThickness | Primitive |
| XmNbackground | Core | XmNinitialResourcesPersistent | Core |
| XmNbackgroundPixmap | Core | XmNmappedWhenManaged | Core |
| XmNborderColor | Core | XmNnavigationType | Primitive |
| XmNborderPixmap | Core | XmNscreen | Core |
| XmNborderWidth | Core | XmNsensitive | Core |
| XmNbottomShadowColor | Primitive | XmNshadowThickness | Primitive |
| XmNbottomShadowPixmap | Primitive | XmNtopShadowColor | Primitive |
| XmNcolormap | Core | XmNtopShadowPixmap | Primitive |
| XmNdepth | Core | XmNtranslations | Core |
| XmNdestroyCallback | Core | XmNtraversalOn | Primitive |
| XmNforeground | Primitive | XmNunitType | Primitive |

| Resource | Inherited From | Resource | Inherited From |
|---|---|---|---|
| XmNheight | Core | XmNuserData | Primitive |
| XmNhelpCallback | Primitive | XmNwidth | Core |
| XmNhighlightColor | Primitive | XmNx | Core |
| XmNhighlightOnEnter | Primitive | XmNy | Core |

## Translations

TextField has the same translation as a Text widget whose XmNeditMode resource is set to XmSINGLE_LINE_EDIT.

## Actions

TextField defines the same action routines as a Text widget whose XmNeditMode resource is set to XmSINGLE_LINE_EDIT.

## See Also

*XmCreateObject*(1), *XmTextClearSelection*(1), *XmTextCopy*(1), *XmTextCut*(1), *XmTextGetBaseline*(1), *XmTextGetCursorPosition*(1), *XmTextGetEditable*(1), *XmTextGetInsertionPosition*(1), *XmTextGetLastPosition*(1), *XmTextGetMaxLength*(1), *XmTextGetSelection*(1), *XmTextGetSelectionPosition*(1), *XmTextGetSelectionWcs*(1), *XmTextGetString*(1), *XmTextGetStringWcs*(1), *XmTextGetSubstring*(1), *XmTextGetSubstringWcs*(1), *XmTextInsert*(1), *XmTextInsertWcs*(1), *XmTextPaste*(1), *XmTextPosToXY*(1), *XmTextRemove*(1), *XmTextReplace*(1), *XmTextReplaceWcs*(1), *XmTextScroll*(1), *XmTextSetAddMode*(1), *XmTextSetCursorPosition*(1), *XmTextSetEditable*(1), *XmTextSetHighlight*(1), *XmTextSetInsertionPosition*(1), *XmTextSetMaxLength*(1), *XmTextSetSelection*(1), *XmTextSetSource*(1), *XmTextSetString*(1), *XmTextSetStringWcs*(1), *XmTextSetTopCharacter*(1), *XmTextShowPosition*(1), *XmTextXYToPos*(1), *Core*(2), *XmPrimitive*(2), *XmText*(2).

# XmToggleButton

## Name

XmToggleButton widget class – a button widget that maintains a Boolean state.

## Synopsis

**Public Header:** *<Xm/ToggleB.h>*

**Class Name:** XmToggleButton

**Class Hierarchy:** Core → XmPrimitive → XmLabel → XmToggleButton

**Class Pointer:** `xmToggleButtonWidgetClass`

**Instantiation:** `widget = XtCreateWidget(name, xmToggleButtonWidgetClass, ...)`

**Functions/Macros:** `XmCreateToggleButton()`, `XmToggleButtonGetState()`, `XmToggleButtonSetState()`, `XmIsToggleButton()`

## Description

A ToggleButton is a button that is either set or unset. ToggleButtons are typically used in groups, called RadioBoxes and CheckBoxes, depending on the behavior of the buttons. In a RadioBox, a ToggleButton displays *one-of-many* behavior, which means that only one button in the group can be set at a time. When a button is selected, the previously selected button is unset. In a CheckBox, a ToggleButton displays *n-of-many* behavior, which means that any number of ToggleButtons can be set at one time. ToggleButton uses an indicator to show its state; the shape of the indicator specifies the type of behavior. A diamond-shaped indicator is used for one-of-many ToggleButtons and a square-shaped indicator is used for n-of-many ToggleButtons.

## New Resources

ToggleButton defines the following resources, all having access CSG:

| Name | Class | Type | Default |
|---|---|---|---|
| XmNfillOnSelect | XmCFillOnSelect | Boolean | dynamic |
| XmNindicatorOn | XmCIndicatorOn | Boolean | True |
| XmNindicatorSize | XmCIndicatorSize | Dimension | dynamic |
| XmNindicatorType | XmCIndicatorType | unsigned char | dynamic |
| XmNselectColor | XmCSelectColor | Pixel | dynamic |
| WXmNselectInsensitivePixmap | XmCSelectInsensitivePixmap | Pixmap | XmUNSPECIFIED_PIXMAP |
| XmNselectPixmap | XmCSelectPixmap | Pixmap | XmUNSPECIFIED_PIXMAP |
| XmNset | XmCSet | Boolean | False |
| XmNspacing | XmCSpacing | Dimension | 4 |
| XmNvisibleWhenOff | XmCVisibleWhenOff | Boolean | dynamic |

`XmNfillOnSelect`
If `True`, selection of this ToggleButton fills the indicator with the color given by the `XmNselectColor` resource and switches the button's top and bottom shadow colors. If `False`, only the top and bottom shadow colors are switched.

`XmNindicatorOn`
If `True` (default), the indicator is visible and its shadows are switched when the button is toggled. If `False`, the indicator is invisible and no space is set aside for it; in addition, the shadows surrounding the button are switched when it is toggled.

`XmNindicatorSize`
The size of the indicator. This value changes if the size of the button's text string or pixmap changes.

`XmNindicatorType`
Determines whether the indicator is drawn as a diamond (signifying a one-of-many indicator) or as a square (signifying an n-of-many indicator). Possible values:

```
XmN_OF_MANY              /* creates a square button */
XmONE_OF_MANY            /* creates a diamond-shaped button */
```

The default value is `XmONE_OF_MANY` for a ToggleButton in a RadioBox widget, and `XmN_OF_MANY` otherwise. This resource only sets the indicator; it is RowColumn's `XmNradioBehavior` resource that actually enforces radioButton or checkButton behavior.

`XmNselectColor`
The color with which to fill the indicator when the button is selected. On a color display, the default is a value between the background color and the bottom shadow color; on a monochrome display, the default is the foreground color.

`XmNselectInsensitivePixmap`
The pixmap used for an insensitive ToggleButton when it's selected. An unselected, insensitive ToggleButton uses the pixmap specified by the Label resource `XmNlabel-InsensitivePixmap`. However, if this Label resource wasn't specified, it is set to the value of `XmNselectInsensitivePixmap`. This resource is meaningful only when the Label resource `XmNlabelType` is set to `XmPIXMAP`.

`XmNselectPixmap`
The pixmap used for a (sensitive) ToggleButton when it's selected. An unselected ToggleButton uses the pixmap specified by the Label resource `XmNlabelPixmap`. This resource is meaningful only when the Label resource `XmNlabelType` is set to `XmPIXMAP`.

`XmNset`
The selection state of the button.

`XmNspacing`
The distance between the toggle indicator and its label.

`XmNvisibleWhenOff`
: If `True`, the toggle indicator remains visible when the button is unselected. This is the default behavior in a RadioBox. The default is `False` in a menu.

### Callback Resources

ToggleButton defines the following callback resources:

| Callback | Reason Constant |
|---|---|
| XmNarmCallback | XmCR_ARM |
| XmNdisarmCallback | XmCR_DISARM |
| XmNvalueChangedCallback | XmCR_VALUE_CHANGED |

`XmNarmCallback`
: List of callbacks that are called when `BSelect` is pressed while the pointer is inside the widget.

`XmNdisarmCallback`
: List of callbacks that are called when `BSelect` is released after it has been pressed inside the widget.

`XmNvalueChangedCallback`
: List of callbacks that are called when the value of the ToggleButton is changed.

### Callback Structure

Each callback function is passed the following structure:

```
typedef struct
{
    int     reason;      /* the reason that the callback was called */
    XEvent  *event;      /* points to event structure that triggered callback */
    int     set;         /* button is selected (True) or unselected (False) */
} XmToggleButtonCallbackStruct;
```

### Inherited Resources

ToggleButton inherits the following resources. The resources are listed alphabetically, along with the superclass that defines them. ToggleButton sets the default values of `XmNmarginBottom`, `XmNmarginTop`, `XmNmarginWidth`, and `XmNshadowThickness` dynamically. The default value of `XmNborderWidth` is reset to 0 by Primitive.

| Resource | Inherited From | Resource | Inherited From |
|---|---|---|---|
| XmNaccelerator | Label | XmNlabelString | Label |
| XmNaccelerators | Core | XmNlabelType | Label |
| XmNacceleratorText | Label | XmNmappedWhenManaged | Core |
| XmNalignment | Label | XmNmarginBottom | Label |
| XmNancestorSensitive | Core | XmNmarginHeight | Label |

| Resource | Inherited From | Resource | Inherited From |
|---|---|---|---|
| XmNbackground | Core | XmNmarginLeft | Label |
| XmNbackgroundPixmap | Core | XmNmarginRight | Label |
| XmNborderColor | Core | XmNmarginTop | Label |
| XmNborderPixmap | Core | XmNmarginWidth | Label |
| XmNborderWidth | Core | XmNmnemonic | Label |
| XmNbottomShadowColor | Primitive | XmNmnemonicCharSet | Label |
| XmNbottomShadowPixmap | Primitive | XmNnavigationType | Primitive |
| XmNcolormap | Core | XmNrecomputeSize | Label |
| XmNdepth | Core | XmNscreen | Core |
| XmNdestroyCallback | Core | XmNsensitive | Core |
| XmNfontList | Label | XmNshadowThickness | Primitive |
| XmNforeground | Primitive | XmNstringDirection | Label |
| XmNheight | Core | XmNtopShadowColor | Primitive |
| XmNhelpCallback | Primitive | XmNtopShadowPixmap | Primitive |
| XmNhighlightColor | Primitive | XmNtranslations | Core |
| XmNhighlightOnEnter | Primitive | XmNtraversalOn | Primitive |
| XmNhighlightPixmap | Primitive | XmNunitType | Primitive |
| XmNhighlightThickness | Primitive | XmNuserData | Primitive |
| XmNinitialResourcesPersistent | Core | XmNwidth | Core |
| XmNlabelInsensitivePixmap | Label | XmNx | Core |
| XmNlabelPixmap | Label | XmNy | Core |

## Translations

The translations for ToggleButton include those from Primitive. In addition, ToggleButtons that are not in a menu system have the following translations:

| Event | Action |
|---|---|
| BTransfer Press | ProcessDrag() |
| BSelect Press | Arm() |
| BSelect Release | Select() |
| | Disarm() |
| KHelp | Help() |
| KSelect | ArmAndActivate() |

For ToggleButtons that are in a menu system, translations include the menu traversal translations inherited from the Label widget, as well as the following:

| Event | Action |
|---|---|
| `BSelect Press` | `BtnDown()` |
| `BSelect Release` | `BtnUp()` |
| `KHelp` | `Help()` |
| `KActivate` | `ArmAndActivate()` |
| `KSelect` | `ArmAndActivate()` |
| `MAny KCancel` | `MenuShellPopdownOne()` |

## Action Routines

ToggleButton defines the following action routines:

`Arm()` Sets the button if it was previously unset, unsets the button if it was previously set, and invokes the callbacks specified by `XmNarmCallback`. Setting the button means displaying it so that it appears selected. The selected state can be shown by: Highlighting the indicator so it appears pressed in. Filling in the indicator (using the color given by `XmNselectColor`). Highlighting the button so it appears pressed in. (This is done only if the indicator isn't displayed). Drawing the button face using the pixmap given by `XmNselectPixmap`.

The unselected state can be shown by: Highlighting the indicator so it appears raised. Filling in the indicator with the background color. Highlighting the button so it appears raised. (This is done only if the indicator isn't displayed). Drawing the button face using the pixmap given by `XmNlabelPixmap`.

`ArmAndActivate()`
Sets the button if it was previously unset, unsets the button if it was previously set, and invokes the callbacks specified by `XmNarmCallback` (if the button isn't yet armed), `XmNvalueChangedCallback`, and `XmNdisarmCallback`. Inside a menu, this action unposts the menu hierarchy. Outside a menu, this action displays the button as selected or unselected, as described for `Arm()`.

`BtnDown()`
Unposts any menus that were posted by the parent menu of the ToggleButton, changes from keyboard traversal to mouse traversal, draws a shadow to show the ToggleButton as armed, and (assuming the button is not yet armed) invokes the callbacks specified by `XmNarmCallback`.

`BtnUp()` Unposts the menu hierarchy, changes the ToggleButton's state, and invokes first the callbacks specified by `XmNvalueChangedCallback` and then those specified by `XmNdisarmCallback`.

`Disarm()`
Invokes the callbacks specified by `XmNdisarmCallback`.

`Help()` Unposts the menu hierarchy, restores the previous keyboard focus, and invokes the callbacks specified by the `XmNhelpCallback` resource.

`MenuShellPopdownOne()`
Unposts the current menu and (unless the menu is a pulldown submenu) restores keyboard focus to the tab group or widget that previously had it. In a top-level pulldown menu pane attached to a menu bar, this action routine also disarms the cascade button and the menu bar.

`ProcessDrag()`
In Motif 1.2, initiates a drag and drop operation using the label of the ToggleButton.

`Select()`
Switches the state of the ToggleButton and invokes the callbacks specified by `XmNvalueChangedCallback`.

## Additional Behavior

ToggleButton has the following additional behavior:

`<EnterWindow>`
Displays the ToggleButton as armed.

`<LeaveWindow>`
Displays the ToggleButton as unarmed.

## See Also

*XmCreateObject*(1), *XmToggleButtonGetState*(1), *XmToggleButtonSetState*(1), *Core*(2), *XmCheckBox*(2), *XmLabel*(2), *XmPrimitive*(2), *XmRadioBox*(2), *XmRowColumn*(2).

# XmToggleButtonGadget

## Name

XmToggleButtonGadget widget class – a button gadget that maintains a Boolean state.

## Synopsis

**Public Header:** <*Xm/ToggleBG.h*>

**Class Name:** XmToggleButtonGadget

**Class Hierarchy:** Object → RectObj → XmGadget → XmLabelGadget → XmToggleButtonGadget

**Class Pointer:** xmToggleButtonGadgetClass

**Instantiation:** `widget = XtCreateWidget(name, xmToggleButtonGadgetClass, ...)`

**Functions/Macros:** `XmCreateToggleButtonGadget()`, `XmToggleButtonGadgetGetState()`, `XmToggleButtonGadgetSetState()`, `XmIsToggleButtonGadget()`

## Description

ToggleButtonGadget is the gadget variant of ToggleButton.

ToggleButtonGadget's new resources, callback resources, and callback structure are the same as those for ToggleButton.

## Inherited Resources

ToggleButtonGadget inherits the following resources. The resources are listed alphabetically, along with the superclass that defines them. ToggleButtonGadget sets the default values of `XmNmarginBotton`, `XmNmarginTop`, `XmNmarginWidth`, and `XmNshadowThickness` dynamically. The default value of `XmNborderWidth` is reset to 0 by Primitive.

| Resource | Inherited From | Resource | Inherited From |
|---|---|---|---|
| XmNaccelerator | LabelGadget | XmNmarginRight | LabelGadget |
| XmNacceleratorText | LabelGadget | XmNmarginTop | LabelGadget |
| XmNalignment | LabelGadget | XmNmarginWidth | LabelGadget |
| XmNancestorSensitive | RectObj | XmNmnemonic | LabelGadget |
| XmNborderWidth | RectObj | XmNmnemonicCharSet | LabelGadget |
| XmNbottomShadowColor | Gadget | XmNnavigationType | Gadget |
| XmNfontList | LabelGadget | XmNrecomputeSize | LabelGadget |
| XmNheight | RectObj | XmNsensitive | RectObj |
| XmNhelpCallback | Gadget | XmNshadowThickness | Gadget |
| XmNhighlightColor | Gadget | XmNstringDirection | LabelGadget |
| XmNhighlightOnEnter | Gadget | XmNtopShadowColor | Gadget |
| XmNhighlightThickness | Gadget | XmNtraversalOn | Gadget |
| XmNlabelInsensitivePixmap | LabelGadget | XmNunitType | Gadget |
| XmNlabelPixmap | LabelGadget | XmNuserData | Gadget |

| Resource | Inherited From | Resource | Inherited From |
|---|---|---|---|
| XmNlabelString | LabelGadget | XmNwidth | RectObj |
| XmNlabelType | LabelGadget | XmNx | RectObj |
| XmNmarginBottom | LabelGadget | XmNy | RectObj |
| XmNmarginHeight | LabelGadget | | |
| XmNmarginLeft | LabelGadget | | |

## Behavior

As a gadget subclass, ToggleButtonGadget has no translations associated with it. However, ToggleButtonGadget behavior corresponds to the action routines of the ToggleButton widget. See the ToggleButton action routines for more information.

| Behavior | Equivalent ToggleButton Action Routine |
|---|---|
| BTransfer Press | ProcessDrag() |
| BSelect Press | Arm() |
| | BtnDown() (in a menu) |
| BSelect Release | Select(), Disarm() |
| | BtnUp() (in a menu) |
| KActivate or KSelect | ArmAndActivate() |
| KHelp | Help() |
| MAny KCancel | MenuShellPopdownOne() |

ToggleButtonGadget has additional behavior associated with `<Enter>` and `<Leave>`, which draw the shadow in the armed or unarmed state, respectively.

## See Also

*XmCreateObject*(1), *XmToggleButtonGetState*(1), *XmToggleButtonSetState*(1), *Object*(2), *RectObj*(2), *XmCheckBox*(2), *XmGadget*(2), *XmLabelGadget*(2), *XmRadioBox*(2), *XmRowColumn*(2), *XmToggleButton*(2).

## Name

XmWarningDialog – an unmanaged MessageBox as a child of a DialogShell.

## Synopsis

**Public Header:** <*Xm/MessageB.h*>

**Instantiation:** `widget = XmCreateWarningDialog(...)`

**Functions/Macros:** `XmCreateWarningDialog()`, `XmMessageBoxGetChild()`

## Description

A WarningDialog is a compound object created by a call to `XmCreateWarningDialog()` that an application can use to warn the user about a potentially hazardous action. A WarningDialog consists of a DialogShell with an unmanaged MessageBox widget as its child. The MessageBox resource `XmNdialogType` is set to `XmDIALOG_WARNING`.

A WarningDialog includes four components: a symbol, a message, three buttons, and a separator between the message and the buttons. By default, the symbol is an exclamation point. In Motif 1.2, the default button labels can be localized. In the C locale, and in Motif 1.1, the PushButtons are labeled **OK**, **Cancel**, and **Help** by default.

## Default Resource Values

A WarningDialog sets the following default values for MessageBox resources:

| Name | Default |
|---|---|
| XmNdialogType | XmDIALOG_WARNING |
| XmNsymbolPixmap | xm_warning |

## Widget Hierarchy

When a WarningDialog is created with a specified name, the DialogShell is named `name_popup` and the MessageBox is called `name`.

## See Also

*XmCreateObject*(1), *XmMessageBoxGetChild*(1), *XmDialogShell*(2), *XmMessageBox*(2).

# XmWorkingDialog

## Name

XmWorkingDialog – an unmanaged MessageBox as a child of a DialogShell.

## Synopsis

**Public Header:** *<Xm/MessageB.h>*

**Instantiation:** *widget* = XmCreateWorkingDialog( . . . )

**Functions/Macros:** XmCreateWorkingDialog(), XmMessageBoxGetChild()

## Description

A WorkingDialog is a compound object created by a call to XmCreateWorkingDialog() that an application can use to warn the user about a potentially hazardous action. A Working-Dialog consists of a DialogShell with an unmanaged MessageBox widget as its child. The MessageBox resource XmNdialogType is set to XmDIALOG_WORKING.

A WorkingDialog includes four components: a symbol, a message, three buttons, and a separator between the message and the buttons. By default, the symbol is an hourglass. In Motif 1.2, the default button labels can be localized. In the C locale, and in Motif 1.1, the PushButtons are labeled **OK**, **Cancel**, and **Help** by default.

## Default Resource Values

A WorkingDialog sets the following default values for MessageBox resources:

| Name | Default |
|---|---|
| XmNdialogType | XmDIALOG_WORKING |
| XmNsymbolPixmap | xm_working |

## Widget Hierarchy

When a WorkingDialog is created with a specified name, the DialogShell is named name_popup and the MessageBox is called name.

## See Also

*XmCreateObject*(1), *XmMessageBoxGetChild*(1),
*XmDialogShell*(2), *XmMessageBox*(2).

# Section 3

## Mrm Functions

*This section describes the Motif Resource Manager (Mrm) functions that are used in conjunction with the User Interface Language (UIL) to create user interfaces. Functions are presented alphabetically.*

*The first reference page,* Introduction, *explains the format and contents of each of the following pages.*

### In This Section:

# Introduction

This page describes the format and contents of each reference page in Section 3, which covers the Motif Resource Manager (Mrm) functions.

## Name

Function – a brief description of the function.

## Synopsis

This section shows the signature of the function: the names and types of the arguments, and the type of the return value. The header file *<Mrm/MrmPublic.h>* declares all of the public Mrm functions.

### Inputs

This subsection describes each of the function arguments that pass information to the function.

### Outputs

This subsection describes any of the function arguments that are used to return information from the function. These arguments are always of some pointer type, so you should use the C address-of operator (**&**) to pass the address of the variable in which the function will store the return value. The names of these arguments are sometimes suffixed with *_return* to indicate that values are returned in them. Some arguments both supply and return a value; they will be listed in this section and in the "Inputs" section above. Finally, note that because the list of function arguments is broken into "Input" and "Output" sections, they do not always appear in the same order that they are passed to the function. See the function signature for the actual calling order.

### Returns

This subsection explains the return values of the function. Mrm functions typically return one of the following values: `MrmSUCCESS`, `MrmPARTIAL_SUCCESS`, `MrmBAD_HIERARCHY`, `MrmNOT_FOUND`, `MrmWRONG_TYPE`, `MrmNOT_VALID`, `MrmDISPLAY_NOT_OPENED`, or `MrmFAILURE`. To be safe, you should check the return value against `MrmSUCCESS` or `MrmPARTIAL_SUCCESS`, and then check for specific errors on non-success. When an error occurs, the functions call `XtWarning()` with a descriptive error message.

## Availability

This section appears for functions that were added in Motif 1.2, and also for functions that are now superceded by other, preferred, functions.

## Description

This section explains what the function does and describes its arguments and return value. If you've used the function before and are just looking for a refresher, this section and the synopsis above should be all you need.

## Usage

This section appears for most functions and provides less formal information about the function: when and how you might want to use it, things to watch out for, and related functions that you might want to consider.

### Example

This section provides an example of the use of the function. It also shows the corresponding UIL code needed for the example.

### Structures

This section shows the definition of any structures, enumerated types, typedefs, or symbolic constants used by the function.

### Procedures

This section shows the syntax of any prototype procedures used by the function.

### See Also

This section refers you to related functions, UIL file format sections, and UIL data types. The numbers in parentheses following each reference refer to the sections of this book in which they are found.

# MrmCloseHierarchy

## Name

MrmCloseHierarchy – close an Mrm hierarchy.

## Synopsis

```
#include <Mrm/MrmPublic.h>
Cardinal MrmCloseHierarchy (hierarchy)
    MrmHierarchy hierarchy;
```

### Inputs

*hierarchy* Specifies an Mrm hierarchy obtained from a previous call to `MrmOpenHierarchy()` or `MrmOpenHierarchyPerDisplay()`.

### Returns

`MrmSUCCESS` On success.

`MrmBAD_HIERARCHY`
If *hierarchy* is `NULL` or does not point to a valid Mrm hierarchy.

`MrmFAILURE` On failure.

## Description

`MrmCloseHierarchy()` closes an Mrm hierarchy that has been previously opened with a call to `MrmOpenHierarchy()` or `MrmOpenHierarchyPerDisplay()`. The UID files associated with the hierarchy are closed and the memory used by the hierarchy is freed. However, as of Motif 1.2, the memory used by Mrm to register any values or procedures with `MrmRegisterNamesInHierarchy()` is not freed.

## Usage

An application calls `MrmCloseHierarchy()` when it is done accessing an Mrm hierarchy in order to free file descriptions and memory consumed by the hierarchy. As of Motif 1.2, this function cannot fail; it always returns `MrmSUCCESS` or `MrmBAD_HIERARCHY`.

## Example

The following code fragment illustrates the use of `MrmCloseHierarchy()`:

```
...
extern MrmHierarchy hierarchy;  /* Previously opened Mrm hierarchy. */

if (MrmCloseHierarchy (hierarchy) != MrmSUCCESS)
  error_handler();
hierarchy = NULL;               /* Protect from future misuse. */
...
```

## See Also

*MrmOpenHierarchy*(3), *MrmOpenHierarchyPerDisplay*(3).

# MrmFetchBitmapLiteral

## Name

MrmFetchBitmapLiteral – retrieve an exported bitmap from an Mrm hierarchy.

## Synopsis

```
#include <Mrm/MrmPublic.h>
Cardinal MrFetchBitmapLiteral (hierarchy, name, screen, display, pixmap,
        width, height);
    MrmHierarchy hierarchy;
    String name;
    Screen *screen;
    Display *display;
    Pixmap *pixmap;
    Dimension *width, *height;
```

### Inputs

| | |
|---|---|
| *hierarchy* | Specifies an Mrm hierarchy obtained from a previous call to `MrmOpenHierarchy()` or `MrmOpenHierarchyPerDisplay()`. |
| *name* | Specifies the name of an `icon` to retrieve as a bitmap. |
| *screen* | Specifies the screen of the display on which the pixmap is created. |
| *display* | Specifies the display on which the pixmap is created. |

### Outputs

| | |
|---|---|
| *pixmap* | Returns the specified *bitmap* as a pixmap of depth 1 on the specified screen of the specified display. |
| *width* | Returns the width of the pixmap. |
| *height* | Returns the height of the pixmap. |

## Returns

`MrmSUCCESS` On success.

`MrmBAD_HIERARCHY`
If *hierarchy* is `NULL` or does not point to a valid Mrm hierarchy.

`MrmNOT_FOUND`
If the `icon` is not found.

`MrmWRONG_TYPE`
If the named value is not an `icon`.

`MrmNOT_VALID`
If the `icon` uses a color table which contains colors other than `foreground color` and `background color`.

`MrmFAILURE` On failure.

### Availability

Motif 1.2 and later.

### Description

MrmFetchBitmapLiteral() retrieves the named icon and converts it to a pixmap of depth 1 on the specified screen of the specified display. The icon must be defined as an exported value in a UIL source module. Foreground color pixels in the icon are set to 1 in the pixmap and background color pixels in the icon are set to 0 (zero) in the pixmap. The application is responsible for freeing the pixmap using XFreePixmap().

### Usage

An icon retrieved with MrmFetchBitmapLiteral() can only use the special colors foreground color and background color in its color table. If the color table contains any other colors, MrmFetchBitmapLiteral() fails and returns MrmNOT_VALID.

As of Motif 1.2, values of type xbitmapfile cannot be converted to a pixmap using this function. xbitmapfile values can only be retrieved using MrmFetchIconLiteral().

### Example

The following UIL and C code fragments show the retrieval of a bitmap from an Mrm hierarchy:

UIL:

```
...
! Declare a cursor icon using the default color table.
value
  resize_down : exported icon ('********',
                                '   **   ',
                                '   **   ',
                                '** ** **',
                                ' ****** ',
                                '   **   ');
...
```

C:

```
...
extern MrmHierarchy hierarchy;      /* Previously opened hierarchy. */
extern Widget w;                    /* Previously created widget. */
Pixmap cursor_bits;
Dimension width, height;
Cardinal status;
static XColor white = { 0, ~0, ~0, ~0, DoRed | DoGreen | DoBlue };
static XColor black = { 0,  0,  0,  0, DoRed | DoGreen | DoBlue };
```

Motif Resource Manager Functions

```
/* Get the icon as a pixmap of depth 1. */
status = MrmFetchBitmapLiteral (hierarchy, "resize_down", XtScreen(w),
                                XtDisplay(w), &cursor_bits,
                                &width, &height);
if (status != MrmSUCCESS)
  error_handler();
else {
  /* Create a cursor using the pixmap. */
  cursor = XCreatePixmapCursor (XtDisplay(w), cursor_bits, cursor_bits,
                                &black, &white, width/2, height-1);

  /* Set the cursor in the widget. */
  XDefineCursor (XtWindow(w), cursor);
}
...
```

## See Also

*MrmFetchIconLiteral*(3), *MrmFetchLiteral*(3),
*value*(5),
*color_table*(6), *icon*(6), *xbitmapfile*(6).

# MrmFetchColorLiteral

## Name

MrmFetchColorLiteral – retrieve an exported color value from an Mrm hierarchy.

## Synopsis

```
#include <Mrm/MrmPublic.h>
Cardinal MrmFetchColorLiteral (hierarchy, name, display, colormap, pixel)
    MrmHierarchy hierarchy;
    String name;
    Display *display;
    Colormap colormap;
    Pixel *pixel;
```

### Inputs

*hierarchy* — Specifies an Mrm hierarchy obtained from a previous call to `MrmOpenHierarchy()` or `MrmOpenHierarchyPerDisplay()`.

*name* — Specifies the name of the `color` to retrieve.

*display* — Specifies the display.

*colormap* — Specifies the colormap in which the color is allocated.

### Outputs

*pixel* — Returns a pixel value for the named color.

### Returns

`MrmSUCCESS` — On success.

`MrmBAD_HIERARCHY` — If *hierarchy* is `NULL` or does not point to a valid Mrm hierarchy.

`MrmNOT_FOUND` — If the specified `color` is not found or cannot be allocated.

`MrmWRONG_TYPE` — If the named value is not a `color` or `rgb` value.

`MrmFAILURE` — On failure.

## Description

`MrmFetchColorLiteral()` retrieves a named `color` value and attempts to allocate a color cell containing it. The `color` must be defined as an exported value in a UIL source module. The color cell is allocated with `XAllocColor()` if the type of the value is `rgb` or with `XAllocNamedColor` if the type of the value is `color`. The *colormap* argument is used as a parameter to these functions. If *colormap* ise `NULL`, Mrm uses the colormap returned by the `DefaultColormap()` macro.

## Usage

If the `color` cannot be allocated because the specified colormap is full, `MrmFetchColorLiteral()` fails and returns `MrmNOT_FOUND`, not `MrmFAILURE`. The OSF documentation claims that when a color cannot be allocated, black or white is substituted, but as of Motif 1.2.2 this translation does not take place, so you have to handle the error yourself.

## Example

The following UIL and C code fragments show the retrieval of color values from an Mrm hierarchy:

UIL:

```
...
value
  foreground : exported rgb (255, 167, 0);
  background : exported color ('mutant ninja turtle');
...
```

C:

```
Widget       toplevel;                /* Previously created widget. */
MrmHierarchy hierarchy;               /* Previously opened Mrm hierarchy. */
Pixel        foreground, background;
Cardinal     status;
...
status =
  MrmFetchColorLiteral (hierarchy, "foreground", XtDisplay (toplevel),
                        NULL, &foreground);
if (status != MrmSUCCESS)
  error_handler();

status =
  MrmFetchColorLiteral (hierarchy, "background", XtDisplay (toplevel),
                        NULL, &background);
if (status != MrmSUCCESS)
  error_handler();
...
```

## See Also

*MrmFetchBitmapLiteral*(3), *MrmFetchIconLiteral*(3), *MrmFetchLiteral*(3),
*value*(5),
*color*(6), *color_table*(6), *rgb*(6).

# MrmFetchIconLiteral

## Name

MrmFetchIconLiteral – retrieve an exported icon from an Mrm hierarchy.

## Synopsis

```
#include <Mrm/MrmPublic.h>
Cardinal MrmFetchIconLiteral (hierarchy, name, screen, display, foreground,
        background, pixmap)
    MrmHierarchy hierarchy;
    String name;
    Screen *screen;
    Display *display;
    Pixel foreground;
    Pixel background;
    Pixmap *pixmap;
```

### Inputs

*hierarchy* Specifies an Mrm hierarchy obtained from a previous call to MrmOpenHierarchy() or MrmOpenHierarchyPerDisplay().

*name* Specifies the name of an icon or xbitmapfile to retrieve.

*screen* Specifies the screen of the display on which the pixmap is created.

*display* Specifies the display.

*foreground* Specifies the foreground color to use for the pixmap.

*background* Specifies the background color to use for the pixmap.

### Outputs

*pixmap* Returns a pixmap created on the specified screen and display.

### Returns

MrmSUCCESS On success.

MrmBAD_HIERARCHY
If *hierarchy* is NULL or does not point to a valid Mrm hierarchy.

MrmNOT_FOUND
If the specified icon or xbitmapfile is not found or a color in the icon's color table cannot be allocated.

MrmWRONG_TYPE
If the named value is not an icon or xbitmapfile value.

MrmFAILURE On failure.

## Description

MrmFetchIconLiteral() retrieves the named icon or xbitmapfile value and attempts to convert it to a pixmap on the specified screen of the display. The icon or xbitmapfile must be defined as an exported value in a UIL source module. The `foreground` pixel argument is used as the color for foreground pixels in an `icon` and pixels set to 1 in an `xbitmapfile`. The *background* pixel argument is used as the color for background pixels in an `icon` and pixels set to 0 (zero) in an `xbitmapfile`. Additional colors used by an `icon` are allocated in the colormap returned by the `DefaultColormap()` macro. The application is responsible for freeing the pixmap using `XFreePixmap()`.

## Usage

If a `color` cannot be allocated because the specified colormap is full, `MrmFetchIcon-Literal()` fails and returns `MrmNOT_FOUND`, not `MrmFAILURE`. The OSF documentation claims that when a color cannot be allocated, black or while is substituted, but as of Motif 1.2.2 this translation does not take place, so you have to handle the error yourself.

## Example

The following UIL and C code fragments illustrate the retrieval of a pixmap from an Mrm hierarchy:

UIL:

```
...
! Declare an icon using the default color table.
value
  box : exported
        icon ('****',
              '*  *',
              '*  *',
              '****');
...
```

C:

```
extern MrmHierarchy hierarchy;      /* Previously opened hierarchy. */
extern Widget drawing_area;         /* Previously created widget.   */
extern GC     drawing_area_gc;      /* Previously defined graphics context. */
Pixel foreground, background;
Pixmap box_pixmap;
unsigned int box_width, box_height;
unsigned int dont_care;
Cardinal status;

/* Get values to use for pixmap foreground and background. */
XtVaGetValues (drawing_area,
               XmNforeground, &foreground, XmNbackground, &background,
               NULL);

/* Create the pixmap from the box icon in the hierarchy. */
status = MrmFetchIconLiteral (hierarchy, "box", XtScreen (drawing_area),
                              XtDisplay (drawing_area), foreground,
                              background, &box_pixmap);
if (status != MrmSUCCESS)
```

```
    error_handler();
  else {
    /* Get the size of the pixmap. */
    XGetGeometry (XtDisplay(drawing_area), box_pixmap, (Window *) &dont_care,
                  (int *) &dont_care, (int *) &dont_care,
                  &box_width, &box_height, &dont_care, &dont_care);

    /* Draw the box in the drawing area. */
    XCopyArea (XtDisplay(drawing_area), box_pixmap, XtWindow(drawing_area),
               drawing_area_gc, 0, 0, box_width, box_height, 10, 10);
    }
    /* Free the pixmap. */
    XFreePixmap (box_pixmap);
  }
```

## See Also

*MrmFetchBitmapLiteral*(3), *MrmFetchColorLiteral*(3), *MrmFetchLiteral*(3),
*value*(5),
*color*(6), *color_table*(6), *icon*(6), *rgb*(6), *xbitmapfile*(6).

# MrmFetchLiteral

## Name

MrmFetchLiteral – retrieve an exported value from an Mrm hierarchy.

## Synopsis

```
#include <Mrm/MrmPublic.h>
Cardinal MrmFetchLiteral (hierarchy, name, display, value, type)
    MrmHierarchy hierarchy;
    String name;
    Display *display;
    XtPointer *value;
    MrmCode *type;
```

### Inputs

*hierarchy* Specifies an Mrm hierarchy obtained from a previous call to MrmOpen-Hierarchy() or MrmOpenHierarchyPerDisplay().

*name* Specifies the name of the value to retrieve.

*display* Specifies the display.

### Outputs

*value* Returns a pointer to the value with the specified name.

*type* Returns the type of the value retrieved.

### Returns

MrmSUCCESS On success.

MrmBAD_HIERARCHY
If *hierarchy* is NULL or does not point to a valid Mrm hierarchy.

MrmNOT_FOUND
If the specified value is not found.

MrmWRONG_TYPE
If the type of the value specified cannot be converted by this procedure.

## Description

MrmFetchLiteral() retrieves the named value and its type from the specified Mrm *hierarchy*. The value must be defined as an exported value in a UIL source module. The *display* argument is used to convert values of type font, fontset, and font_table. On success, this routine returns a pointer to the named value and the type of the value. The possible type values begin with MrmRtype and are defined in the include file *<Mrm/MrmPublic.h>*. The application is responsible for freeing the returned value, except when it is a font or a fontset. font and fontset values are cached by Mrm and freed when the display is closed.

## Usage

`MrmFetchLiteral()` cannot be used to retrieve values of certain types. You should retrieve `icon` values with `MrmFetchIconLiteral()` or `MrmFetchBitmapLiteral()`, `xbitmapfile` values with `MrmFetchIconLiteral()`, and `color` or `rgb` values with `MrmFetchColorLiteral()`.

The storage allocated by Mrm for a `boolean` value is `sizeof(int)` not `sizeof(Boolean)`. Because `sizeof(Boolean)` is less than `sizeof(int)` on many systems, applications should use an `int` pointer rather than a `Boolean` pointer as the *`value`* argument when retrieving a boolean.

## Example

The following UIL and C code fragments illustrate the use of `MrmFetchLiteral()` to fetch various values from an Mrm hierarchy:

UIL:

```
...
value
  int_val : 10;
  string_val : 'okemo';
...
```

C:

```
...
extern MrmHierarchy hierarchy;  /* Previously opened hierarchy. */
extern Display      *display;   /* Previously opened display.   */
int                 *int_ptr;
String              string;
MrmCode             type;
Cardinal            status;

status = MrmFetchLiteral (hierarchy, "int_val", display,
                          (XtPointer *) &int_ptr, &type);
if (status != MrmSUCCESS || type != MrmRtypeInteger)
  error_handler();
else
  printf ("Fetched integer %d\n", *int_ptr);

status = MrmFetchLiteral (hierarchy, "string_val", display,
                          (XtPoitner *) &string, &type);
if (status != MrmSUCCESS || type != MrmRtypeCString)
  error_handler();
else
  printf ("Fetched string '%s'\n", string);
...
```

## See Also

*MrmFetchBitmapLiteral*(3), *MrmFetchColorLiteral*(3), *MrmFetchIconLiteral*(3), *MrmFetchSetValues*(3), *value*(5),
*asciz_string_table*(6), *boolean*(6), *class_rec_name*(6), *color*(6), *compound_string*(6), *compound_string_table*(6), *float*(6), *font*(6), *font_table*(6), *fontset*(6), *icon*(6), *integer*(6), *integer_table*(6), *keysym*(6), *rgb*(6), *single_float*(6), *string*(6), *translation_table*(6), *wide_character*(6), *widget*(6), *xbitmapfile*(6).

# MrmFetchSetValues

## Name

MrmFetchSetValues – set widget resources to values retrieved from an Mrm hierarchy.

## Synopsis

```
#include <Mrm/MrmPublic.h>
Cardinal MrmFetchSetValues (hierarchy, widget, args, num_args)
    MrmHierarchy hierarchy;
    Widget widget;
    ArgList arg_list;
    Cardinal num_args;
```

### Inputs

*hierarchy* Specifies an Mrm hierarchy obtained from a previous call to `MrmOpenHierarchy()` or `MrmOpenHierarchyPerDisplay()`.

*widget* Specifies the object whose resouces are modified.

*arg_list* Specifies an array of name/UID-value pairs to be set.

*num_args* Specifies the number of elements in *arg_list*.

### Returns

`MrmSUCCESS` On success.

`MrmPARTIAL_SUCCESS`
On partial success.

`MrmBAD_HIERARCHY`
If *hierarchy* is NULL or does not point to a valid Mrm hierarchy.

`MrmFAILURE` On failure.

## Description

`MrmFetchSetValues()` sets the resources for an widget to named values obtained from the specified Mrm *hierarchy*. If a named value is not found or cannot be converted, the resource corresponding to that value is not set. If all the named values in *arg_list* are successfully retrieved, `MrmFetchSetValues()` returns `MrmSUCCESS`. If some values are successfully retrieved and others are not, `MrmPARTIAL_SUCCESS` is returned. If no values are successfully retrieved, `MrmFAILURE` is returned. When at least one value is successfully retrieved, `XtSetValues()` is called to modify the resources of *object*.

## Usage

`MrmFetchSetValues()` sets the resources named in the `name` member of each item in *arg_list* to the value from the Mrm hierarchy named by the `value` member. This use differs from `XtSetValues()`, in that `value` member contains the name of a value to retrieve, not the value itself. Each named value must be defined as an exported value in a UIL source module.

The conversion of certain types may require a display pointer, screen pointer, background color, or foreground color. When these values are needed, Mrm obtains them from *widget*. If foreground and background colors are needed for a conversion and *widget* does not have a background or foreground resource, Mrm uses black or white instead. If foreground and background colors are needed for a conversion and the XmNbackground or XmNforeground resources are specified in *arg_list*, they are used instead of the foreground and background of *widget*. As a result, if both an icon and foreground and/or background values are specified in the same argument list, the icon uses the colors specified in the list, rather than the colors of the widget.

## Example

The following UIL and C code fragments illustrate the use of MrmFetchSetValues() to fetch a resource value from an Mrm hierarchy:

UIL:

```
...
value
  ! English language version of the confirm quit message:
  confirm_quit_msg : 'Do you really want to quit?';
...
```

C:

```
extern MrmHierarchy hierarchy;    /* Previously opened Mrm hierarchy. */
extern Widget yes_no_dialog;      /* Previosly created yes/no dialog. */

void DisplayConfirmQuit()
{
  static Arg args[] = { { XmNmessageString,
                          (XtArgVal) "confirm_quit_msg" } };

  /* Set the message string for confirm quit. */
  MrmFetchSetValues (hierarchy, yes_no_dialog, args, XtNumber (args));

 /* Make the dialog appear. */
 XtManageChild (yes_no_dialog);
}
```

## Structures

ArgList is defined as follows:

```
typedef struct {
    String name;
    XtArgVal value;
} Arg, *ArgList;
```

## See Also

*MrmFetchBitmapLiteral*(3), *MrmFetchColorLiteral*(3), *MrmFetchIconLiteral*(3), *MrmFetchLiteral*(3), *value*(5).

# MrmFetchWidget

## Name

MrmFetchWidget – create the widget tree rooted at a named widget.

## Synopsis

```
#include <Mrm/MrmPublic.h>
Cardinal MrmFetchWidget (hierarchy, name, parent, widget, class)
    MrmHierarchy hierarchy;
    String name;
    Widget parent;
    Widget *widget;
    MrmType *class;
```

### Inputs

*hierarchy* Specifies an Mrm hierarchy obtained from a previous call to `MrmOpenHierarchy()` or `MrmOpenHierarchyPerDisplay()`.

*name* Specifies the name of the root widget of the widget tree to create.

*parent* Specifies the parent of the root widget.

### Outputs

*widget* Returns the widget ID of the root widget.

*class* Returns the UID class code for the widget class of the root widget.

### Returns

`MrmSUCCESS` On success.

`MrmBAD_HIERARCHY`
If *hierarchy* is `NULL` or does not point to a valid Mrm hierarchy.

`MrmNOT_FOUND`
If the specified widget is not found.

`MrmFAILURE` On failure.

## Description

`MrmFetchWidget()` creates the named widget and recursively creates all of its children. Each child is managed by Mrm, unless declared `unmanaged` in the UIL source module. The root widget should be defined as exported in a UIL source module. Mrm supports the `MrmNcreateCallback`, which if defined, is called after a widget is created. The prototype of an `MrmNcreateCallback` is the same as any other Xt callback procedure. The *call_data* passed to the callback is an `XmAnyCallbackStruct`.

## Usage

Each successful call to `MrmFetchWidget()` results in the creation of a new widget tree, even if *name* has been fetched previously. As a result, you can use a widget tree definition from an Mrm hierarchy as a template for creating multiple instances of the same widget tree.

The widget at the root of the tree is not managed by Mrm, so your application must manage this widget to make the tree visible.

In Motif 1.2 and earlier, `MrmFetchWidget()` returns `MrmSUCCESS` if the root widget is retrieved successfully, even if one or more of its children are not. As of Motif 1.2.1, if `MrmFetchWidget()` cannot find a child widget, it returns `MrmNOT_FOUND` and does not create any widgets.

As of Motif 1.2, the possible `MrmType` values returned in *`class`* are not defined in any of the Mrm include files, although the OSF documentation claims that they are defined in *<Mrm/Mrm.h>*. If you need to check the widget class of a widget created with `MrmFetchWidget()`, use `XtClass()` or one of the `XmIs*()` macros.

## Example

The following UIL and C code fragments illustrate the retrieval of a widget hierarchy from an Mrm hierarchy:

UIL:

```
...
! Define a simple widget tree, with form at the root.
object label : XmLabel { };
object button : XmPushButton { };
object form : exported XmForm {
  controls {
    XmLabel label;
    XmPushButton button;
  };
};
...
```

C:

```
extern Widget toplevel;          /* Previously defined widget. */
extern MrmHierarchy hierarchy;   /* Previously opened hierarchy. */
Widget form;
MrmType class;
Cardinal status;

status = MrmFetchWidget (hierarchy, "form", toplevel, &form, &class);

if (status != MrmSUCCESS)
  error_handler();
...
```

## Structures

The `MrmNcreateCallback` function is passed an `XmAnyCallbackStruct`, which is defined as follows:

```
typedef struct {
    int     reason;         /* MrmCR_CREATE */
    XEvent  *event;         /* NULL */
} XmAnyCallbackStruct;
```

## See Also

*MrmFetchWidgetOverride*(3), *MrmOpenHierarchy*(3), *MrmOpenHierarchyPerDisplay*(3), *object*(5), *widget*(6).

# MrmFetchWidgetOverride

## Name

MrmFetchWidgetOverride – create the widget tree rooted at a named widget and override the resources set in the UID file.

## Synopsis

```
#include <Mrm/MrmPublic.h>
Cardinal MrmFetchWidgetOverride (hierarchy, name, parent, override_name,
        arg_list, num_args, widget, class)
    MrmHierarchy hierarchy;
    String name;
    Widget parent;
    String override_name;
    ArgList arg_list;
    Cardinal num_args;
    Widget *widget;
    MrmType *class;
```

### Inputs

*hierarchy* Specifies an Mrm hierarchy obtained from a previous call to MrmOpenHierarchy() or MrmOpenHierarchyPerDisplay().

*name* Specifies the name of the root widget of the widget tree to create.

*parent* Specifies the parent of the root widget.

*override_name*
Specifies the name to use when creating the root widget. If NULL, *name* is used.

*arg_list* Specifies an array of resource/value pairs to set on the root widget when it is created. If NULL, no resources are set.

*num_args* Specifies the number of elements in *arg_list*. Must be 0 (zero) if *arg_list* is NULL.

### Outputs

*widget* Returns the widget ID of the root widget.

*class* Returns the UID class code for the widget class of the root widget.

### Returns

MrmSUCCESS On success.

MrmBAD_HIERARCHY
If *hierarchy* is NULL or does not point to a valid Mrm hierarchy.

MrmNOT_FOUND
If the specified widget is not found.

MrmFAILURE On failure.

### Description

MrmFetchWidgetOverride() creates the named widget and recursively creates all of its children. The root widget should be defined as exported in a UIL source module. *arg_list* is used to specify additional resource/value pairs that override those specified in the widget definition in a UIL source module. Each child is managed by Mrm unless declared unmanaged in the UIL source module. Mrm supports the MrmNcreateCallback, which if defined, is called after a widget is created. The prototype of an MrmNcreateCallback is the same as any other Xt callback procedure. The *call_data* passed to the callback is an XmAnyCallbackStruct.

### Usage

MrmFetchWidgetOverride() allows an application to create a widget defined in an Mrm hierarchy while specifying application-defined resource values that can supplement or override those specified in the UIL defintion. The function sets the resources of the root widget that are named in the name member of each item in *arg_list* to value specified in the value member. The resource of any children of the root widget are not affected.

Each successful call to MrmFetchWidgetOverride() results in the creation of a new widget tree, even if *name* has been fetched previously. As a result, you can use a widget tree definition from an Mrm hierarchy as a template for creating multiple instances of the same widget tree. The widget at the root of the tree is not managed by Mrm, so your application must manage this widget to make the tree visible.

In Motif 1.2 and earlier, MrmFetchWidget() returns MrmSUCCESS if the root widget is retrieved successfully, even if one or more of its children are not. As of Motif 1.2.1, if Mrm-FetchWidget() cannot find a child widget, it returns MrmNOT_FOUND and does not create any widgets.

As of Motif 1.2, the possible MrmType values returned in *class* are not defined in any of the Mrm include files, although the OSF documentation claims that they are defined in *<Mrm/Mrm.h>*. If you need to check the widget class of a widget created with MrmFetch-WidgetOverride(), use XtClass() or one of the XmIs*() macros.

### Example

The following UIL and C code fragments illustrate the retrieval of a widget hierarchy from an Mrm hierarchy using MwmFetchWidgetOverride():

UIL:

```
...
object error_dialog : exported XmErrorDialog {
  arguments {
    XmNmessageString = "If you can read this, file a bug report.";
    XmNdialogStyle = XmDIALOG_FULL_APPLICATION_MODAL;
  };
};
...
```

C:

```
extern Widget toplevel;            /* Previously created widget. */
extern MrmHierarchy hierarchy;     /* Previously opened hierarchy. */

void
display_error (String message)
{
  Arg arg_list[1];
  XmString s;
  Cardinal status;
  Widget error_dialog;
  MrmType class;

  s = XmStringCreateLocalized (message);
  XtSetArg (arg_list[0], XmNmessageString, s);

  status = MrmFetchWidgetOverride (hierarchy, "error_dialog", toplevel,
                                   "error_dialog", arg_list, 1,
                                   &error_dialog, &class);

  XmStringFree (s);

  if (status != MrmSUCCESS)
    handle_error();
  else
    XtManageChild (error_dialog);
}
```

## Structures

`ArgList` is defined as follows:

```
typedef struct {
    String name;
    XtArgVal value;
} Arg, *ArgList;
```

The `MrmNcreateCallback` function is passed an `XmAnyCallbackStruct`, which is defined as follows:

```
typedef struct {
     int     reason;        /* MrmCR_CREATE */
     XEvent  *event;        /* NULL */
} XmAnyCallbackStruct;
```

## See Also

*MrmFetchWidget*(3), *MrmOpenHierarchy*(3), *MrmOpenHierarchyPerDisplay*(3),
*object*(5),
*widget*(6).

# MrmInitialize

## Name

MrmInitialize – prepare the Mrm library for use.

## Synopsis

```
#include <Mrm/MrmPublic.h>
void MrmInitialize ()
```

## Description

`MrmInitialize()` initializes the Mrm library. As part of the initialization, all Motif widget classes are registered in the Mrm widget class database with `MrmRegisterClass()`.

## Usage

Applications should call `MrmInitialize()` before the Xt Toolkit is initialized and before calling any other Mrm functions. If the routine is not called before `MrmOpenHierarchyPerDisplay()`, future calls to `MrmFetchWidget()` and `MrmFetchWidgetOverride()` will fail. Applications should only call `MrmInitialize()` once.

## Example

The following code fragment illustrates the use of `MrmInitialize()`:

```
...
Widget toplevel;
XtAppContext app_context;
MrmHierarchy hierarchy;
Cardinal status;

XtSetLanguageProc (NULL, (XtLanguageProc)NULL, NULL);

MrmInitialize();

toplevel = XtAppInitialize (&app_context, "App", NULL, 0,
                             (Cardinal *) &argv, &argv, NULL, NULL, 0);
...
```

## See Also

*MrmFetchWidget*(3), *MrmFetchWidgetOverride*(3), *MrmOpenHierarchy*(3), *MrmOpenHierarchyPerDisplay*(3), *MrmRegisterClass*(3).

# MrmOpenHierarchy

## Name

MrmOpenHierarchy – open an Mrm hierarchy.

## Synopsis

```
#include <Mrm/MrmPublic.h>
Cardinal MrmOpenHierarchy (num_files, file_name_list, os_params, hierarchy)
    MrmCount num_files;
    String file_name_list[];
    MrmOsOpenParamPtr *os_params;
    MrmHierarchy *hierarchy;
```

### Inputs

*num_files* Specifies the number of files in *file_name_list*.

*file_name_list*
Specifies an array of UID file names to associate with the hierarchy.

*os_params* Specifies operating system dependent settings.

### Outputs

*hierarchy* Returns an open Mrm hierarchy consisting of the specified files.

### Returns

`MrmSUCCESS` On success.

`MrmNOT_FOUND`
If one or more files cannot be opened.

`MrmNOT_VALID`
If the version of Mrm is older than the version of any UID file.

`MrmDISPLAY_NOT_OPENED`
If a display pointer cannot be found.

`MrmFAILURE` On failure.

## Availability

In Motif 1.2, `MrmOpenHierarchy()` is obsolete. It has been superceded by `MrmOpen-HierarchyPerDisplay()`.

## Description

`MrmOpenHierarchy()` opens an Mrm hierarchy consisting of one or more UID files. This routine is similar to `MrmOpenHierarchyPerDisplay()`, except that it does not take a *display* parameter. `MrmOpenHierarchy()` is retained for compatibility with Motif 1.1 and should not be used in newer applications.

Motif Resource Manager Functions

## Usage

`MrmOpenHierarchy()` relies on the Motif widget library to locate a display pointer. To ensure that a display pointer can be found, an application must create an ApplicationShell before calling `MrmOpenHierarchy()`. The display pointer is used as a parameter to `XtResolvePathname()`, which locates the files in *`file_name_list`*. If an application creates multiple ApplicationShells on different displays, the display pointer chosen by this routine is undefined.

See the `MrmOpenHierarchyPerDisplay()` manual page for a full explanation of the process of opening an Mrm hierarchy, including the search path that is used to find the UID files.

## See Also

*MrmCloseHierarchy*(3), *MrmOpenHierarchyPerDisplay*(3).

## Name

MrmOpenHierarchyPerDisplay – open an Mrm hierarchy.

## Synopsis

```
#include <Mrm/MrmPublic.h>
Cardinal MrmOpenHierarchyPerDisplay (display, num_files, file_name_list,
        os_params_list, hierarchy)
    Display *display;
    MrmCount num_files;
    String file_name_list[]
    MrmOsOpenParamPtr os_params_list[];
    MrmHierarchy *hierarchy;
```

### Inputs

*display* Specifies the display.

*num_files* Specifies the number of files in *file_name_list*.

*file_name_list*
Specifies an array of file names to associate with the hierarchy.

*os_params_list*
Specifies an array of operating system dependent settings.

### Outputs

*hierarchy* Returns an open Mrm hierarchy consisting of the specified files.

### Returns

MrmSUCCESS On success.

MrmNOT_FOUND
If one or more files cannot be opened.

MrmNOT_VALID
If the version of Mrm is older than version of the any UID file.

MrmDISPLAY_NOT_OPENED
If a display pointer cannot be found.

MrmFAILURE On failure.

## Availability

Motif 1.2 and later.

## Description

MrmOpenHierarchyPerDisplay() opens an Mrm hierarchy consisting of one or more UID files. An Mrm hierarchy must be opened before any values are retrieved or widgets created with the MrmFetch*() routines. When an Mrm hierarchy is successfully opened, each UID file specified in *file_name_list* is opened and consumes a file descriptor. No files are opened if a value other than MrmSUCCES is returned. The UID files are subsequently closed when the hierarchy is closed with `MrmCloseHierarchy()`. As of Motif 1.2, settings in the *`os_params_list`* parameter are only useful to the UIL compiler. Application programs should always specify `NULL` for this argument.

## Usage

The `MrmFetch*()` routines retrieve a named value or widget by searching the UID files for a hierarchy in the order that they are specified in *`file_name_list`*. If a named value or widget occurs in more than one of the UID files, the value is retrieved from the file that occurs first in the array. Once an Mrm hierarchy has been opened, the UID files associated with the hierarchy must not be modified or deleted until the hierarchy is closed.

Files specified in *`file_name_list`* may be full or partial path names. When a file name starts with a slash (/), it specifies a full path name and `MrmOpenHierarchyPerDisplay()` opens the file. Otherwise, the file name specifies a partial path name which causes `MrmOpenHierarchyPerDisplay()` to look for the file using a search path.

`XtResolvePathname()` is used to locate the file in the search path. The UIDPATH environment variable specified the search path for UID files. Each directory in the search path can contain the substitution character %U; the partial path name specified by *`file_name_list`* is substituted for %U. In addition, the path can also use the substitution characters accepted by `XtResolvePathname`. The path is first searched with %S mapped to *.uid*. If the file is not found the path is searched again with %S mapped to `NULL`.

If UIDPATH is not set, `MrmOpenHierarchyPerDisplay()` uses a default search path. If the XAPPLRESDIR environment variable is set, the routine searches the following path; the class name of the application is substituted for %N, the language string of the *`display`* argument is substituted for %L, and the language component of the language string is substituted for %l.

*%U%S*
*$XAPPLRESDIR/%L/uid/%N/%U%S*
*$XAPPLRESDIR/%l/uid/%N/%U%S*
*$XAPPLRESDIR/uid/%N/%U%S*
*$XAPPLRESDIR/%L/uid/%U%S*
*$XAPPLRESDIR/%l/uid/%U%S*
*$XAPPLRESDIR/uid/%U%S*
*$HOME/uid/%U%S*
*$HOME/%U%S*
*/usr/lib/X11/%L/uid/%N/%U%S*
*/usr/lib/X11/%l/uid/%N/%U%S*
*/usr/lib/X11/uid/%N/%U%S*
*/usr/lib/X11/%L/uid/%U%S*
*/usr/lib/X11/%l/uid/%U%S*
*/usr/lib/X11/uid/%U%S*
*/usr/include/X11/uid/%U%S*

If XAPPLRESDIR is not set, (`MrmOpenHierarchyPerDisplay()` searches the same path, except that XAPPLRESDIR is replaced by HOME. These paths are vendor-dependent and a vendor may use different directories for */usr/lib/X11* and */usr/include/X11*.

## Example

The following code fragment illustrates the use of `MrmOpenHierarchyPerDisplay()`:

```
...
MrmHierarchy hierarchy;
XtAppContext app_context;
Widget toplevel;
String uid_files[ ] = { "/usr/lib/app/app", "strings" };
Cardinal status;

XtSetLanguageProc (NULL, NULL, NULL);

MrmInitialize();

toplevel = XtAppInitialize (&app_context, "App", NULL, 0, &argc, argv,
                            NULL, 0);

status = MrmOpenHierarchyPerDisplay (XtDisplay (toplevel),
                                     XtNumber (uid_files), uid_files, NULL,
                                     &hierarchy);
if (status != MrmSUCCESS)
  error_handler();
...
```

## See Also

*MrmCloseHierarchy*(3), *MrmFetchBitmapLiteral*(3), *MrmFetchColorLiteral*(3), *MrmFetchIconLiteral*(3), *MrmFetchLiteral*(3), *MrmFetchWidget*(3), *MrmFetchWidgetOverride*(3).

Motif Resource Manager Functions

# MrmRegisterClass

## Name

MrmRegisterClass – register a widget creation function for a non-Motif widget.

## Synopsis

```
#include <Mrm/MrmPublic.h>
Cardinal MrmRegisterClass (class_code, class_name, create_proc_name,
        create_proc, widget_class)
    MrmType class_code;
    String class_name;
    String create_proc_name;
    Widget (*create_proc) ();
    WidgetClass widget_class;
```

### Inputs

*class_code* — This argument is obsolete and is ignored.

*class_name* — This argument is obsolete and is ignored.

*create_proc_name* — Specifies the case-sensitive name of the widget creation function.

*create_proc* — Specifies a pointer to the widget creation procedure.

*widget_class* — Specifies a pointer to the widget class record or NULL.

### Returns

MrmSUCCESS — On success.

MrmFAILURE — On failure.

## Description

MrmRegisterClass() supplies Mrm with information it needs to create a user-defined widget, which is any widget that is not built into UIL and Mrm. A user-defined widget cannot be created until its class is registered.

## Usage

A user-defined widget is defined in a UIL source module by specifying the *create_-proc_name* in its declaration. *create_proc_name* must be all uppercase characters when used in a UIL module compiled with case_insensitive names because this setting causes the UIL compiler to store procedure name references in all uppercase characters.

If MrmRegisterClass() is called with a *class_name* that has been registered previously, the new *create_proc* and *widget_class* replace the previous values. There is no way to unregister a previously registered class. As of Motif 1.2, a small amount of memory may be leaked when a class is registered multiple times.

The *widget_class* argument allows Mrm to convert a class name specified in a UIL class_rec_name literal into a widget class pointer. If NULL is specified, the widget class pointer is not accessible with the class_rec_name type.

## Example

The following UIL and C code fragments illustrate the creation of an instance of the Athena panner widget from UIL. Like any other widget defined in a UIL module, it is created with a call to MrmFetchWidget() or MrmFetchWidgetOverride():

UIL:

```
...
procedure XawCreatePannerWidget;

object panner : user_defined procedure XawCreatePannerWidget
  { };
...
```

C:

```
Widget
XawCreatePannerWidget (Widget parent, String name, ArgList args,
                      Cardinal num_args)
{
  return (XtCreateWidget (name, pannerWidgetClass, parent, args, num_args);
}

...
MrmRegisterClass (0, NULL, "XawCreatePannerWidget", XawCreatePannerWidget,
                  &pannerWidgetClass);
...
```

## Procedures

The *create_proc* parameter has the following syntax:

```
Widget create_proc (Widget, String, ArgList, Cardinal)
    Widget parent;
    String name;
    ArgList args;
    Cardinal num_args;
```

The procedure takes four arguments. The first, *parent*, is the parent of the widget that is being created. *name* is the name of the widget. The last two arguments, *args* and *num_args*, specify the initial resource settings for the widget. The procedure returns the widget ID of the newly created widget.

## See Also

*MrmInitialize*(3), *MrmFetchWidget*(3), *MrmFetchWidgetOverride*(3),
*object*(5),
*class_rec_name*(6).

# MrmRegisterNames

## Name

MrmRegisterNames – register application-defined values and procedures.

## Synopsis

```
#include <Mrm/MrmPublic.h>
Cardinal MrmRegisterNames (name_list, count);
    MrmRegisterArgList name_list;
    MrmCount count;
```

### Inputs

| | |
|---|---|
| *name_list* | Specifies an array of name/value pairs to be registered with Mrm. |
| *count* | Specifies the number of elements in *name_list*. |

### Returns

| | |
|---|---|
| MrmSUCCESS | On success. |
| MrmFAILURE | On failure. |

## Description

MrmRegisterNames() registers an array of name/value pairs that are used as identifiers and procedures in a UIL source module. Names registered with this routine are accessible from any open Mrm hierarchy. By contrast, names registered with MrmRegisterNamesInHierarchy() are only accessible from the hierarchy in which they are registered.

If MrmRegisterNames() is called with a name that has been registered previously, the old value associated with the name is replaced by the new value. There is no way to unregister a previously registered name.

## Usage

The MrmRegisterArg structure consists of a name and an associated value. The case of name is significant. name must be in all uppercase characters if name is used in a UIL module compiled with case_insensitive names, because this setting causes the UIL compiler to store procedure and identifier name references in all uppercase characters.

The *name_list* array can contain names that represent both callback procedures and identifier values. A procedure value in *name_list* should be a pointer to a function of type XtCallbackProc. An identifier value is any application-defined value that is exactly sizeof (XtPointer). Mrm makes no distinction between procedures and identifiers, although an application may organize them in two separate arrays for clarity. A distinction is made in a UIL source module, where any name used must be declared as either a procedure or an identifier.

Procedures and identifiers must be registered with MrmRegisterNames() or MrmRegisterNamesInHierarchy() before an application attempts to create a widget that references them. Mrm converts a procedure or identifier reference to a value by first searching hierarchy-local names registered with `MrmRegisterNamesInHierarchy()`. If the value is not found, the search continues with global names registered with `MrmRegisterNames()`.

## Example

The following UIL and C code fragments illustrate the use of `MrmRegisterNames()`:

UIL:

```
...
identifier user_id;
procedure activate();

object button : XmPushButton {
  callbacks {
    XmNactivateCallback = procedure activate;
  };
};
...
```

C:

```
..
extern XtCallbackProc activate;
int user_id;

MrmRegisterArg names[ ] =
{
  { "activate", (XtPointer) activate },
  { "user_id",  (XtPointer) user_id },
};

user_id = getuid();

MrmRegisterNames (names, XtNumber (names));
...
```

## Structures

`MrmRegisterArgList` is defined as follows:

```
typedef struct {
    String name;              /* case-sensitive name */
    XtPointer value;          /* procedure/value to associate with name */
} MrmRegisterArg, *MrmRegisterArglist;
```

## See Also

*MrmRegisterNamesInHierarchy*(3),
*identifier*(5), *procedure*(5).

# MrmRegisterNamesInHierarchy

## Name

MrmRegisterNamesInHierarchy – register application-defined values and procedures for use in a specific UIL hierarchy.

## Synopsis

```
#include <Mrm/MrmPublic.h>
Cardinal MrmRegisterNamesInHierarchy (hierarchy, name_list, count);
    MrmHierarchy hierarchy;
    MrmRegisterArgList name_list;
    MrmCount count;
```

### Inputs

| | |
|---|---|
| *hierarchy* | Specifies an Mrm hierarchy obtained from a previous call to `MrmOpenHierarchy()` or `MrmOpenHierarchyPerDisplay()`. |
| *name_list* | Specifies an array of name/value pairs to be registered with Mrm. |
| *count* | Specifies the number elements in *name_list*. |

### Returns

| | |
|---|---|
| `MrmSUCCESS` | On success. |
| `MrmFAILURE` | On failure. |

## Description

`MrmRegisterNames()` registers an array of name/value pairs that are used as identifiers and procedures in a UIL source module. Names registered with this routine are accessible only within the specified *hierarchy*. By contrast, names registered with `MrmRegisterNames()` are accessible from any open hierarchy.

If `MrmRegisterNamesInHierarchy()` is called with a name that has been registered previously in the same hierarchy, the old value associated with the name is replaced by the new value. There is no way to unregister a previously registered name while the hierarchy is open. However, closing the hierarchy automatically unregisters all names.

## Usage

The `MrmRegisterArg` structure consists of a `name` and an associated `value`. The case of `name` is significant. `name` must be in all uppercase characters if `name` is used in a UIL module compiled with `case_insensitive` names, because this setting causes the UIL compiler to store procedure and identifier name references in all uppercase characters.

The *name_list* array can contain names that represent both callback procedures and identifier values. A procedure value in *name_list* should be a pointer to a function of type `XtCallbackProc`. An identifier value is any application-defined value that is exactly `sizeof (XtPointer)`. Mrm makes no distinction between procedures and identifiers, although an application may orgranize them in two separate arrays for clarity. A distinction is made in a UIL source module, where any name used must be declared as either a procedure or an identifier.

Procedures and identifiers must be registered with `MrmRegisterNames()` or `MrmRegisterNamesInHierarchy()` before an application attempts to create a widget which references them. Mrm converts a procedure or identifier reference to a value by first searching hierarchy-local names registered with `MrmRegisterNamesInHierarchy()`. If the value is not found, the search continues with global names registered with `MrmRegisterNames()`.

## Example

The following code fragment illustrates the use of `MrmRegisterNamesInHierarchy()`:

```
/* Open a hierarchy and register it's file name list. */
Cardinal
register_and_open (Display display, MrmCount count, String *files)
{
  Cardinal status;
  int *count = (int *) malloc (sizeof (int));
  MrmRegisterArg names[ ] =
  {
    { "file_list", files },
    { "file_count", count },
  };

  if (count == NULL)
    return (MrmFAILURE);

  status = MrmOpenHierarchyPerDisplay (display, count, files,
    NULL, &hierarchy);
  if (status != MrmSUCCESS)
    return (status);

  status = MrmRegisterNamesInHierarchy (*hierarchy, names, XtNumber (names));

  return (status);
}
```

## Structures

`MrmRegisterArgList` is defined as follows:

```
typedef struct {
    String name;              /* case-sensitive name */
    XtPointer value;          /* procedure/value to associate with name */
} MrmRegisterArg, *MrmRegisterArglist;
```

## See Also

*MrmRegisterNames*(3),
*identifier*(5), *procedure*(5).

Motif Resource Manager Functions

# Section 4

## Motif Clients

*This section describes the Motif clients: mwm, uil, and xmbind. The first reference page,* Introduction*, explains the format and contents of each of the following pages.*

### In This Section:

# Introduction



This page describes the format and contents of each reference page in Section 4, which covers the Motif clients.

## Name

Client – a brief description of the client.

## Syntax

This section describes the command-line syntax for invoking the client. Anything in **bold** type should be typed exactly as shown. Items in *italics* are parameters that should be replaced by actual values when you enter the command. Anything enclosed in brackets is optional.

## Availability

This section appears for clients that were added in Motif 1.2.

## Description

This section explains the operation of the client. In some cases, additional descriptive sections appear later on in the reference page.

## Options

This section lists available command-line options.

## Environment

If present, this section lists shell environment variables used by the client. This section does not list the DISPLAY and XENVIRONMENT variables, which are used by all clients. These variables are used as follows:

DISPLAY

To get the default display name (specifically, the host, server/display, and screen). The DISPLAY variable typically has the form:

*hostname*:*server*.*screen*

XENVIRONMENT

To get the name of a resource file containing host-specific resources. If this variable is not set, the resource manager will look for a file called *.Xdefaults-**hostname*** (where ***hostname*** is the name of a particular host) in the user's home directory.

## Example

This section provides an example of the use of the client.

## Bugs

If present, this section lists any problems that could arise when using the client.

### See Also

This section refers you to related functions and widget classes. The numbers in parentheses following each reference refer to the sections of this book in which they are found.

## Name

mwm – the Motif Window Manager (*mwm*).

## Syntax

**mwm** [*options*]

## Description

The Motif Window Manager, *mwm*, provides all of the standard window management functions. It allows you to move, resize, iconify/deiconify, maximize, and close windows and icons, focus input to a window or icon, and refresh the display. *mwm* provides much of its functionality via a frame that (by default) is placed around every window on the display. The *mwm* frame has the three-dimensional appearance characteristic of the OSF/Motif graphical user interface.

The rest of this reference page describes how to customize *mwm*. It does not provide information on using *mwm*. For information on using the window manager, see Volume Three, *X Window System User's Guide, Motif Edition*.

## Options

`-display` [*host*]`:`*server*[`.`*screen*]
: Specifies the name of the display on which to run *mwm*. *host* is the hostname of the physical display, *server* specifies the server number, and *screen* specifies the screen number. Either or both of the *host* and *screen* elements can be omitted. If *host* is omitted, the local display is assumed. If *screen* is omitted, screen 0 is assumed (and the period is unnecessary). The colon and (display) *server* are necessary in all cases.

`-multiscreen`
: Specifies that *mwm* should manage all screens on the display. The default is to manage only screen 0. You can specify an alternate screen by setting the DISPLAY environment variable or using the `-display` option. You can also specify that *mwm* manage all screens by assigning a value of `True` to the `multiScreen` resource variable.

`-name` *app_name*
: Specifies the name under which resources for the window manager should be found.

`-screens` *screen_name* [*screen_name* ]...
: Assigns resource names to the screens *mwm* is managing. (By default, the screen number is used as the *screen_name*.) If *mwm* is managing a single screen, only the first name in the list is used. If *mwm* is managing multiple screens, the names are assigned to the screens in order, starting with screen 0. If there are more screens than names, resources for the remaining screens will be retrieved using the first *screen_name*.

`-xrm` *resourcestring*
: Specifies a resource name and value to override any defaults. This option is very useful for setting resources that do not have explicit command-line arguments.

## Window Manager Components

The *mwm* window frame contains various components that perform different functions. The title bar stretches across the top of the window and contains the title area and the minimize, maximize, and window menu buttons. The title area displays the window title and can be used to move the window. The minimize button iconifies the window, while the maximize button enlarges the window to fill the entire screen. The window menu button posts the **Window Menu**. The resize border handles surround the window; they are used to resize the window in a particular direction. A window can also have an optional matte decoration between the client area and the window frame. The matte is not part of the window frame and it has no functionality. At times, *mwm* uses dialog boxes or feedback windows to communicate with the user.

An icon is a small graphic representation of a window. When a window is iconified using the minimize button, it is replaced on the screen by its icon. Iconifying windows reduces clutter on the screen. *mwm* provides a separate window, call the icon box, that can hold icons. Using the icon box keeps icons from cluttering the screen.

By default, *mwm* uses an explicit keyboard selection policy, which means that once a window has the keyboard focus, it keeps it until another window is explicitly given the focus. Windows can overlap, which means that they are arranged in a global stacking order on the screen. A window that is higher in the stacking order obscures windows below it in the stacking order if they overlap. Each application has its own local stacking order; transient windows remain above their parents by default in the local stacking order.

## Customization

Like any X application, *mwm* uses resources to control its appearance and behavior. The window manager builds its resource database just like any other X client. `Mwm` is the resource class name for *mwm*. You can place *mwm* resources in your regular resource file (*.Xdefaults*) in your home directory or you can create a file called *Mwm* (also in your home directory) for *mwm* resources only. If you place conflicting specifications in both files, the resources in *.Xdefaults* take precedence.

The default operation of the mouse, the keyboard, and menus in *mwm* is controlled by a system-wide resource description file, *system.mwmrc*. This file describes the contents of the **Window Menu** and **Root Menu**, as well as the key and button combinations that manage windows. To modify the behavior of *mwm*, you can edit a copy of this file in your home directory. The version of the file in your home directory should be called *.mwmrc*, unless you specify an alternate name using the `configFile` resource.

An *mwm* resource description file is a standard text file. Items are separated by blanks, tabs, and newlines. A line that begins with an exclamation mark (`!`) or a number sign (#) is treated as a comment. If a line ends with a backslash (\), the subsequent line is considered a continuation of that line.

### Component Appearance Resources

*mwm* provides some resources that specify the appearance of particular window manager components, such as the window frame, menus, and icons. Component appearance resources can be specified for particular window manager components or all components. To specify a resource for all components, use the following syntax:

`Mwm*`*resource_name*`:` *resource_value*

The window manager components have the following resource names associated with them:

| Component | Resource name |
|---|---|
| Menu | `menu` |
| Icon | `icon` |
| Client window frame | `client` |
| Feedback/dialog box | `feedback` |
| Title bar | `title` |

These resource names can be used to specify particular window manager components in a resource specification. To specify a resource for a specific component, use the following syntax:

`Mwm*[`*component_name* `]*`*resource_name*`:` *resource_value*

The title bar is a descendant of the client window frame, so you can use `title` to specify the appearance of the title bar separately from the rest of the window frame. You can also specify resources for individual menus by using `menu`, followed by the name of the menu.

The following component appearance resources apply to all window manager components. Unless a default value is specified, the default varies based on system specifics such as the visual type of the screen:

`background` (class `Background`)
: Specifies the background color.

`backgroundPixmap` (class `BackgroundPixmap`)
: Specifies the background pixmap of the *mwm* decoration when the window does not have the input focus.

`bottomShadowColor` (class `Foreground`)
: Specifies the color to be used for the lower and right bevels of the window manager decoration.

`bottomShadowPixmap` (class `BottomShadowPixmap`)
: Specifies the pixmap to be used for the lower and right bevels of the window manager decoration.

`fontList` (class `FontList`)
: Specifies the font to be used in the window manager decoration. The default is `fixed`.

`foreground` (class `Foreground`)
: Specifies the foreground color.

`saveUnder` (class `SaveUnder`)
: Specifies whether save unders are used for *mwm* components. The default value is `False`, which means that save unders are not used on any window manager frames.

`topShadowColor` (class `Background`)
: Specifies the color to be used for the upper and left bevels of the window manager decoration.

`topShadowPixmap` (class `TopShadowPixmap`)
: Specifies the pixmap to be used for the upper and left bevels of the window manager decoration.

The following component appearance resources apply to the window frame and icons. Unless a default value is specified, the default varies based on system specifics such as the visual type of the screen:

`activeBackground` (class `Background`)
: Specifies the background color of the *mwm* decoration when the window has the input focus.

`activeBackgroundPixmap` (class `ActiveBackgroundPixmap`)
: Specifies the background pixmap of the *mwm* decoration when the window has the input focus.

`activeBottomShadowColor` (class `Foreground`)
: Specifies the bottom shadow color of the *mwm* decoration when the window has the input focus.

`activeBottomShadowPixmap` (class `BottomShadowPixmap`)
: Specifies the bottom shadow pixmap of the *mwm* decoration when the window has the input focus.

`activeForeground` (class `Foreground`)
: Specifies the foreground color of the *mwm* decoration when the window has the input focus.

`activeTopShadowColor` (class `Background`)
: Specifies the top shadow color of the *mwm* decoration when the window has the input focus.

`activeTopShadowPixmap` (class `TopShadowPixmap`)
: Specifies the top shadow Pixmap of the *mwm* decoration when the window has the input focus.

### General Appearance and Behavior Resources

*mwm* also provides resources that control the appearance and behavior of the window manager as a whole. These resources specify features such as the focus policy, interactive window placement, and the icon box. To specify a general appearance and behavior resource, use the following syntax:

`Mwm*`*resource_name*`:` *resource_value*

The following general appearance and behavior resources can be specified:

autoKeyFocus (class AutoKeyFocus)
If True (the default), when the focus window is withdrawn from window management or is iconified, the focus bounces back to the window that previously had the focus. This resource is available only when keyboardFocusPolicy is explicit. If False, the input focus is not set automatically. autoKeyFocus and startupKeyFocus should both be True to work properly with tear-off menus.

autoRaiseDelay (class AutoRaiseDelay)
Specifies the amount of time (in milliseconds) that *mwm* will wait before raising a window after it receives the input focus. The default is 500. This resource is available only when focusAutoRaise is True and the keyboardFocusPolicy is pointer.

bitmapDirectory (class BitmapDirectory)
Identifies the directory to be searched for bitmaps referenced by *mwm* resources (if an absolute pathname to the bitmap file is not given). The default is */usr/include/X11/-bitmaps*, which is considered the standard location on many systems. Note, however, that the location of the bitmap directory may vary in different environments. If a bitmap is not found in the specified directory, XBMLANGPATH is searched.

buttonBindings (class ButtonBindings)
Identifies the set of button bindings to be used for window management functions; must correspond to a set of button bindings specified in the *mwm* startup file. Button bindings specified in the startup file are merged with built-in default bindings. The default is DefaultButtonBindings.

cleanText (class CleanText)
Specifies whether text that appears in *mwm* title and feedback windows is displayed over the existing background pattern. If True (the default), text is drawn with a clear (no stipple) background. (Only the stippling in the area immediately around the text is cleared.) This enhances readability, especially on monochrome systems where a backgroundPixmap is specified. If False, text is drawn on top of the existing background.

clientAutoPlace (class ClientAutoPlace)
Specifies the location of a window when the user has not specified a location. If True (the default), windows are positioned with the upper-left corners of the frames offset horizontally and vertically, so that no two windows completely overlap. If False, the currently configured position of the window is used. In either case, *mwm* attempts to place the windows totally on screen.

colormapFocusPolicy (class ColormapFocusPolicy)
Specifies the colormap focus policy. Takes three possible values: keyboard, pointer, and explicit. If keyboard (the default) is specified, the input focus window has the colormap focus. If explicit is specified, a colormap selection

action is done on a client window to set the colormap focus to that window. If `pointer` is specified, the client window containing the pointer has the colormap focus.

`configFile` (class `ConfigFile`)

Specifies the pathname for the *mwm* startup file. The default startup file is *.mwmrc*.

*mwm* searches for the configuration file in the user's home directory. If the `configFile` resource is not specified or the file does not exist, *mwm* defaults to an implementation-specific standard directory (the default is */usr/lib/X11/system.mwmrc*).

If the LANG environment variable is set, *mwm* looks for the configuration file in a *$LANG* subdirectory first. For example, if the LANG environment variable is set to Fr (for French), *mwm* searches for the configuration file in the directory *$HOME/Fr* before it looks in *$HOME*. Similarly, if the `configFile` resource is not specified or the file does not exist, *mwm* defaults to */usr/lib/X11/$LANG/system.mwmrc* before it reads */usr/lib/X11/system.mwmrc*.

If the `configFile` pathname does not begin with ~/, *mwm* considers it to be relative to the current working directory.

`deiconifyKeyFocus` (class `DeiconifyKeyFocus`)

If `True` (the default), a window receives the input focus when it is normalized (deiconified). This resource applies only when the `keyboardFocusPolicy` is `explicit`.

`doubleClickTime` (class `DoubleClickTime`)

Specifies the maximum time (in milliseconds) between the two clicks of a double click. The default is the display's multi-click time.

`enableWarp` (class `EnableWarp`)

If `True` (the default), causes *mwm* to *warp* the pointer to the center of the selected window during resize and move operations invoked using keyboard accelerators. (The cursor symbol disappears from its current location and reappears at the center of the window.) If `False`, *mwm* leaves the pointer at its original place on the screen, unless the user explicitly moves it.

`enforceKeyFocus` (class `EnforceKeyFocus`)

If `True` (the default), the input focus is always explicitly set to selected windows even if there is an indication that they are "globally active" input windows. (An example of a globally active window is a scrollbar that can be operated without setting the focus to that client.) If the resource is `False`, the keyboard input focus is not explicitly set to globally active windows.

`fadeNormalIcon` (class `FadeNormalIcon`)

If `True`, an icon is greyed out when it has been normalized. The default is `False`.

`feedbackGeometry` (class `FeedbackGeometry`)

Specifies the position of the small, rectangular feedback box that displays coordinate and size information during move and resize operations. By default, the feedback window appears in the center of the screen. This resource takes the argument:

[=]±*xoffset*±*yoffset*

With the exception of the optional leading equal sign, this string is identical to the second portion of the standard geometry string. Note that `feedbackGeometry` allows you to specify location only. The size of the feedback window is not configurable using this resource. Available as of *mwm* version 1.2.

`frameBorderWidth` (class `FrameBorderWidth`)

Specifies the width in pixels of a window frame border, without resize handles. (The border width includes the three-dimensional shadows.) The default is determined according to screen specifics.

`iconAutoPlace` (class `IconAutoPlace`)

Specifies whether the window manager arranges icons in a particular area of the screen or places each icon where the window was when it was iconified. If `True` (the default), icons are arranged in a particular area of the screen, determined by the `iconPlacement` resource. If `False`, an icon is placed at the location of the window when it is iconified.

`iconBoxGeometry` (class `IconBoxGeometry`)

Specifies the initial position and size of the icon box. Takes as its argument the standard geometry string:

*width*x*height*±*xoff*±*yoff*

where *width* and *height* are measured in icons. The default geometry string is `6x1+0-0`, which places an icon box six icons wide by one icon high in the lower-left corner of the screen.

You can omit either the dimensions or the x and y offsets from the geometry string and the defaults apply. If the offsets are not provided, the `iconPlacement` resource is used to determine the initial placement.

The actual screen size of the icon box depends on the `iconImageMaximum` and `iconDecoration` resources, which specify icon size and padding. The default value for size is (6 × *icon_width* + padding) wide by (1 × *icon_height* + padding) high.

`iconBoxName` (class `IconBoxName`)

Specifies the name under which icon box resources are to be found. The default is `iconbox`.

`iconBoxSBDisplayPolicy` (class `IconBoxSBDisplayPolicy`)

Specifies what scrollbars are displayed in the icon box. The resource has three possible values: `all`, `vertical`, and `horizontal`. If `all` is specified (the default), both vertical and horizontal scrollbars are displayed at all times. `vertical` specifies that a single vertical scrollbar is displayed and sets the orientation of the icon box to horizontal, regardless of the `iconBoxGeometry` specification. `horizontal` specifies that a single horizontal scrollbar is displayed in the icon box and sets the orientation of the icon box to vertical, regardless of the `iconBoxGeometry` specification.

`iconBoxTitle` (class `IconBoxTitle`)
: Specifies the name to be used in the title area of the icon box. The default is `Icons`.

`iconClick` (class `IconClick`)
: If `True` (the default), the **Window Menu** is displayed when the pointer is clicked on an icon.

`iconDecoration` (class `IconDecoration`)
: Specifies how much icon decoration is used. The resource value takes four possible values (multiple values can also be supplied): `label`, which specifies that only the label is displayed; `image`, which specifies that only the image is displayed; and `activelabel`, which specifies that a label (not truncated to the width of the icon) is used when the icon has the focus.

The default decoration for icons in an icon box is `label image`, which specifies that both the label and image parts are displayed. The default decoration for individual icons on the screen proper is `activelabel label image`.

`iconImageMaximum` (class `IconImageMaximum`)
: Specifies the maximum size of the icon image. Takes a value of *width*x*height* (e.g., `80×80`). The maximum size supported is `128×128`. The default is `50×50`.

`iconImageMinimum` (class `IconImageMinimum`)
: Specifies the minimum size of the icon image. Takes a value of *width*x*height* (e.g., `36×48`). The minimum size supported is `16×16` (which is also the default).

`iconPlacement` (class `IconPlacement`)
: Specifies an icon placement scheme. Note that this resource is only useful when `useIconBox` is `False` (the default). The `iconPlacement` resource takes a value of the syntax:

*primary_layout secondary_layout* `[tight]`

There are four possible layout policies. `top` specifies that icons are placed from the top of the screen to the bottom, `bottom` specifies a bottom-to-top arrangement, `left` specifies that icons are placed from the left to the right, and `right` specifies a right-to-left arrangement. The optional argument `tight` specifies that there is no space between icons.

The *primary_layout* specifies whether icons are placed in a row or a column and the direction of placement. The *secondary_layout* specifies where to place new rows or columns. For example, a value of `top right` specifies that icons should be placed from top to bottom on the screen and that columns should be added from right to left on the screen.

A horizontal (vertical) layout value should not be used for both the *primary_layout* and the *secondary_layout*. For example, do not use `top` for the *primary_layout* and `bottom` for the *secondary_layout*.

The default placement is `left bottom` (i.e., icons are placed left to right on the screen, with the first row on the bottom of the screen, and new rows are added from the bottom of the screen to the top of the screen).

`iconPlacementMargin` (class `IconPlacementMargin`)
: Sets the distance from the edge of the screen at which icons are placed. The value should be greater than or equal to 0. A default value is used if an invalid distance is specified. The default value is equal to the space between icons as they are placed on the screen, which is based on maximizing the number of icons in each row and column.

`interactivePlacement` (class `InteractivePlacement`)
: If `True`, specifies that new windows are to be placed interactively on the screen using the pointer. When a client is run, the pointer shape changes to an upper-left corner cursor; move the pointer to the location you want the window to appear and click the first button; the window is displayed in the selected location. If `False` (the default), windows are placed according to the initial window configuration attributes.

`keyBindings` (class `KeyBindings`)
: Identifies the set of key bindings to be used for window management functions; must correspond to a set of key bindings specified in the *mwm* startup file. Note that key bindings specified in the startup file replace the built-in default bindings. The default is `DefaultKeyBindings`.

`keyboardFocusPolicy` (class `KeyboardFocusPolicy`)
: If `explicit` focus is specified (the default), placing the pointer on a window (including the frame) or icon and pressing the first pointer button focuses keyboard input on the client. If `pointer` is specified, the keyboard input focus is directed to the client window on which the pointer rests (the pointer can also rest on the frame).

`limitResize` (class `LimitResize`)
: If `True` (the default), the user is not allowed to resize a window to greater than the maximum size.

`lowerOnIconify` (class `LowerOnIconify`)
: If `True` (the default), a window's icon is placed on the bottom of the stack when the window is iconified. If `False`, the icon is placed in the stacking order at the same place as its associated window.

`maximumMaximumSize` (class `MaximumMaximumSize`)
Specifies the maximum size of a client window (as set by the user or client). Takes a value of *width*x*height* (e.g., `1024x1024`) where *width* and *height* are in pixels. The default is twice the screen width and height.

`moveThreshold` (class `MoveThreshold`)
Controls the sensitivity of dragging operations, such as those used to move windows and icons on the display. Takes a value of the number of pixels that the pointing device is moved while a button is held down before the move operation is initiated. The default is `4`. This resource helps prevent a window or icon from moving when you click or double click and inadvertently jostle the pointer while a button is down.

`moveOpaque` (class `MoveOpaque`)
If `False` (the default), when you move a window or icon, its outline is moved before it is redrawn in the new location. If `True`, the actual (and thus, opaque) window or icon is moved. Available as of *mwm* version 1.2.

`multiScreen` (class `MultiScreen`)
If `False` (the default), *mwm* manages only a single screen. If `True`, *mwm* manages all screens on the display.

`passButtons` (class `PassButtons`)
Specifies whether button press events are passed to clients after the events are used to invoke a window manager function in the client context. If `False` (the default), button presses are not passed to the client. If `True`, button presses are passed to the client. The window manager function is done in either case.

`passSelectButton` (class `PassSelectButton`)
Specifies whether select button press events are passed to clients after the events are used to invoke a window manager function in the client context. If `True` (the default), button presses are passed to the client window. If `False`, button presses are not passed to the client. The window manager function is done in either case.

`positionIsFrame` (class `PositionIsFrame`)
Specifies how *mwm* should interpret window position information from the WM_NORMAL_HINTS property and from configuration requests. If `True` (the default), the information is interpreted as the position of the *mwm* client window frame. If `False`, it is interpreted as being the position of the client area of the window.

`positionOnScreen` (class `PositionOnScreen`)
If `True` (the default), specifies that windows should initially be placed (if possible) so that they are not clipped by the edge of the screen. If a window is larger than the size of the screen, at least the upper-left corner of the window is placed is on the screen. If `False`, windows are placed in the requested position even if totally off the screen.

`quitTimeout` (class `QuitTimeout`)

Specifies the amount of time (in milliseconds) that *mwm* will wait for a client to update the WM_COMMAND property after *mwm* has sent the WM_SAVE_-YOURSELF message. The default is `1000`. (See the `f.kill` function for additional information.)

`raiseKeyFocus` (class `RaiseKeyFocus`)

If `True`, specifies that a window raised by means of the `f.normalize_-and_raise` function also receives the input focus. This function is available only when the `keyboardFocusPolicy` is `explicit`. The default is `False`.

`resizeBorderWidth` (class `ResizeBorderWidth`)

Specifies the width in pixels of a window frame border, with resize handles. (The border width includes the three-dimensional shadows.) The default is determined according to screen specifics.

`resizeCursors` (class `ResizeCursors`)

If `True` (the default), the resize cursors are always displayed when the pointer is in the window resize border.

`screens` (class `Screens`)

Assigns resource names to the screens *mwm* is managing. If *mwm* is managing a single screen, only the first name in the list is used. If *mwm* is managing multiple screens, the names are assigned to the screens in order, starting with screen 0.

`showFeedback` (class `ShowFeedback`)

Specifies whether *mwm* feedback windows and confirmation dialog boxes are displayed. (Feedback windows are used to display: window coordinates during interactive placement and subsequent moves; and dimensions during resize operations. A typical confirmation dialog is the window displayed to allow the user to allow or cancel a window manager restart operation.)

`showFeedback` accepts a list of options, each of which corresponds to the type of feedback given in a particular circumstance. Depending on the syntax in which the options are entered, you can either enable or disable a feedback option (as explained later).

The possible feedback options are: `all`, which specifies that *mwm* show all types of feedback (this is the default); `behavior`, which specifies that feedback is displayed to confirm a behavior switch; `kill`, which specifies that feedback is displayed on receipt of a KILL signal; `move`, which specifies that a box containing the coordinates of a window or icon is displayed during a move operation; `placement`, which specifies that a box containing the position and size of a window is displayed during initial (interactive) placement; `quit`, which specifies that a dialog box is displayed so that the user can confirm (or cancel) the procedure to quit *mwm*; `resize`, which specifies that a box containing the window size is displayed during a resize operation;

`restart`, which displays a dialog box so that the user can confirm (or cancel) an *mwm* restart procedure; the `none` option specifies that no feedback is shown.

To limit feedback to particular cases, you can use one of two syntaxes: with the first syntax, you disable feedback in specified cases (all other default feedback is still used); with the second syntax, you enable feedback only in specified cases. You supply this resource with a list of options to be enabled or disabled. If the first item is preceded by a minus sign, feedback is disabled for all options in the list. If the first item is preceded by a plus sign (or no sign is used), feedback is enabled only for options in the list.

`startupKeyFocus` (class `StartupKeyFocus`)
If `True` (the default), the input focus is transferred to a window when the window is mapped (i.e., initially managed by the window manager). This function is available only when `keyboardFocusPolicy` is `explicit`. `startupKeyFocus` and `autoKeyFocus` should both be `True` to work properly with tear-off menus.

`transientDecoration` (class `TransientDecoration`)
Specifies the amount of decoration *mwm* puts on transient windows. The decoration specification is exactly the same as for the `clientDecoration` (client-specific) resource. Transient windows are identified by the WM_TRANSIENT_FOR property, which is added by the client to indicate a relatively temporary window. The default is `menu title`, which specifies that transient windows have resize borders and a title bar with a window menu button. If the client application also specifies which decorations the window manager should provide, *mwm* uses only those features that both the client and the `transientDecoration` resource specify.

`transientFunctions` (class `TransientFunctions`)
Specifies which window management functions are applicable (or not applicable) to transient windows. The function specification is exactly the same as for the `clientFunctions` (client-specific) resource. The default is `-minimize maximize`. If the client application also specifies which window management functions should be applicable, *mwm* provides only those functions that both the client and the `transientFunctions` resource specify.

`useIconBox` (class `UseIconBox`)
If `True`, icons are placed in an icon box. By default, the individual icons are placed on the root window.

`wMenuButtonClick` (class `WMenuButtonClick`)
If `True` (the default), a pointer button click on the window menu button displays the **Window Menu** and leaves it displayed.

`wMenuButtonClick2` (class `WMenuButtonClick2`)
If `True`, double clicking on the window menu button removes the client window, which means that `f.kill` is invoked.

### Client-Specific Resources

Some *mwm* resources can be set to apply to certain client applications or classes of applications. To specify a client-specific resource, use the following syntax:

Mwm**client_name***resource_name*: *resource_value*

Client-specific specifications take precendence over specifications for all clients. Client-specific resources can be specified for all clients using the following syntax:

Mwm**resource_name*: *resource_value*

The class name `defaults` can be used to specify resources for clients that have an unknown name and class.

The following client-specific resources can be specified:

`clientDecoration` (class `ClientDecoration`)

Specifies the amount of window frame decoration. The default frame is composed of several component parts: the title bar, resize handles, border, and the minimize, maximize, and window menu buttons. You can limit the frame decoration for a client using the `clientDecoration` resource.

`clientDecoration` accepts a list of options, each of which corresponds to a part of the client frame. The options are: `maximize`, `minimize`, `menu`, `border`, `title`, `resize`, `all`, which encompasses all decorations previously listed, and `none`, which specifies that no decorations are used.

Some decorations require the presence of others; if you specify such a decoration, any decorations required with it are used automatically. Specifically, if any of the command buttons are specified, a title bar is also used; if resize handles or a title bar is specified, a border is also used.

By default, a client window has `all` decoration. To specify only certain parts of the default frame, you can use one of two syntaxes: with the first syntax, you disable certain frame features; with the second syntax, you enable only certain features. You supply `clientDecoration` with a list of options to be enabled or disabled. If the first item is preceded by a minus sign, the features in the list are disabled. If the first item is preceded by a plus sign (or no sign is used), only those features listed are enabled.

`clientFunctions` (class `ClientFunctions` )

Specifies whether certain *mwm* functions can be invoked on a client window. The only functions that can be controlled are those that are executable using the pointer on the default window frame.

`clientFunctions` accepts a list of options, each of which corresponds to an *mwm* function. The options are: `resize`, `move`, `minimize`, `maximize`, `close`, `all`, which encompasses all of the previously listed functions, and `none`, which specifies that no default functions are allowed.

By default, a client recognizes `all` functions. To limit the functions a client recognizes, you can use one of two syntaxes: with the first syntax, you disallow certain functions; with the second syntax, you allow only certain functions. You supply `clientFunctions` with a list of options (corresponding to functions) to be allowed or disallowed. If the first item is preceded by a minus sign, the functions in the list are disallowed. If the first option is preceded by a plus sign (or no sign is used), only those functions listed are allowed.

A less than obvious repercussion of disallowing a particular function is that the client window frame is also altered to prevent your invoking that function. For instance, if you disallow the `f.resize` function for a client, the client's frame does not include resize borders. In addition, the **Size** item on the **Window Menu**, which invokes the `f.resize` function, no longer appears on the menu.

If the client application also specifies which window management functions should be applicable, *mwm* provides only those functions that both the client and the `clientFunctions` resource specify.

`focusAutoRaise` (class `FocusAutoRaise`)
: If `True`, a window is raised when it receives the input focus. Otherwise, directing focus to a window does not affect the stacking order. The default depends on the value assigned to the `keyboardFocusPolicy` resource. If the `keyboardFocusPolicy` is `explicit`, the default for `focusAutoRaise` is `True`. If the `keyboardFocusPolicy` is `pointer`, the default for `focusAutoRaise` is `False`.

`iconImage` (class `IconImage`)
: Specifies the pathname of a bitmap file to be used as an icon image for a client. The default is to display an icon image supplied by the window manager. If the `useClientIcon` resource is set to `True`, an icon image supplied by the client takes precedence over an icon image supplied by the user.

`iconImageBackground` (class `Background`)
: Specifies the background color of the icon image. The default is the color specified by `Mwm*background` or `Mwm*icon*background`.

`iconImageBottomShadowColor` (class `Foreground`)
: Specifies the bottom shadow color of the icon image. The default is the color specified by `Mwm*icon*bottomShadowColor`.

`iconImageBottomShadowPixmap` (class `BottomShadowPixmap`)
: Specifies the bottom shadow pixmap of the icon image. The default is the pixmap specified by `Mwm*icon*bottomShadowPixmap`.

`iconImageForeground` (class `Foreground`)
: Specifies the foreground color of the icon image. The default varies based on the icon background.

iconImageTopShadowColor (class Background)
Specifies the top shadow color of the icon image. The default is the color specified by Mwm*icon*topShadowColor.

iconImageTopShadowPixmap (class TopShadowPixmap)
Specifies the top shadow Pixmap of the icon image. The default is the pixmap specified by Mwm*icon*topShadowPixmap.

matteBackground (class Background)
Specifies the background color of the matte. The default is the color specified by Mwm*background or Mwm*client*background. This resource is only relevant if matteWidth is positive.

matteBottomShadowColor (class Foreground)
Specifies the bottom shadow color of the matte. The default is the color specified by Mwm*bottomShadowColor or Mwm*client*bottomShadowColor. This resource is only relevant if matteWidth is positive.

matteBottomShadowPixmap (class BottomShadowPixmap)
Specifies the bottom shadow pixmap of the matte. The default is the pixmap specified by Mwm*bottomShadowPixmap or Mwm*client*bottomShadowPixmap. This resource is only relevant if matteWidth is positive.

matteForeground (class Foreground)
Specifies the foreground color of the matte. The default is the color specified by Mwm*foreground or Mwm*client*foreground. This resource is only relevant if matteWidth is positive.

matteTopShadowColor (class Background)
Specifies the top shadow color of the matte. The default is the color specified by Mwm*topShadowColor or Mwm*client*topShadowColor. This resource is only relevant if matteWidth is positive.

matteTopShadowPixmap (class TopShadowPixmap)
Specifies the top shadow pixmap of the matte. The default is the pixmap specified by Mwm*topShadowPixmap or Mwm*client*topShadowPixmap. This resource is only relevant if matteWidth is positive.

matteWidth (class MatteWidth)
Specifies the width of the matte. The default is 0, which means no matte is used.

maximumClientSize (class MaximumClientSize)
Specifies how a window is to be maximized, either to a specific size (*width*x*height*), or as much as possible in a certain direction (vertical or horizontal). If the value is of the form *width*x*height*, the width and height are interpreted in the units used by the client. For example, *xterm* measures width and height in font characters and lines.

If `maximumClientSize` is not specified, and the WM_NORMAL_HINTS property is set, the default is obtained from it. If WM_NORMAL_HINTS is not set, the default is the size (including borders) that fills the screen. *mwm* also uses `maximumMaximumSize` to constrain the value in this case.

`useClientIcon` (class `UseClientIcon`)
: If `True`, an icon image supplied by the client takes precedence over an icon image supplied by the user. The default is `False`.

`usePPosition` (class `UsePPosition`)
: Specifies whether *mwm* uses initial coordinates supplied by the client application. If `True`, *mwm* always uses the program specified position. If `False`, *mwm* never uses the program specified position. The default is `nonzero`, which means that *mwm* will use any program specified position except 0,0. Available as of *mwm* version 1.2.

`windowMenu` (class `WindowMenu`)
: Specifies a name for the **Window Menu** (which must be defined in the startup file). The default is `DefaultWindowMenu`.

### Functions

*mwm* supports a number of functions that can be bound to different key and button combinations and assigned to menus in the *mwm* resource description file (*system.mwmrc* or *.mwmrc*). Most window manager functions can be used in key bindings, button bindings, and menus. The function descriptions below note any exceptions to this policy. Most window manager functions can also be specified for three contexts: `root`, `window`, and `icon`. The `root` context means that the function is applied to the root window, `window` means that the function is applied to the selected client window, and `icon` means that the function is applied to the selected icon. The function descriptions below note any functions that cannot be used in all three contexts.

When a function is specified with the context `icon | window` and you invoke the function from the icon box, the function applies to the icon box itself, rather than to any of the icons it contains.

A function is treated as `f.nop` if it is not a valid function name, if it is specified inappropriately, or if it is invoked in an invalid way.

*mwm* recognizes the following functions:

`f.beep`
: Causes a beep from the keyboard.

`f.circle_down [icon | window]`
: Causes the window or icon on the top of the stack to be lowered to the bottom of the stack. If the `icon` argument is specified, the function applies only to icons. If the `window` argument is specified, the function applies only to windows.

`f.circle_up [icon | window]`
Causes the window or icon on the bottom of the stack to be raised to the top. If the `icon` argument is specified, the function applies only to icons. If the `window` argument is specified, the function applies only to windows.

`f.exec` [*command*]
`!` [*command*]
Executes *command* using the shell specified by the MWMSHELL environment variable. If MWMSHELL is not set, the command is executed using the shell specified by the SHELL environment variable; otherwise, the command is executed using */bin/sh*.

`f.focus_color`
Sets the colormap focus to a client window. If this function is invoked in the `root` context, the default colormap (specified by X for the screen where *mwm* is running) is installed and there is no specific client window colormap focus. For the `f.focus_color` function to work, the `colormapFocusPolicy` should be specified as `explicit`; otherwise the function is treated as `f.nop`.

`f.focus_key`
Sets the input focus to a window or icon. For the `f.focus_key` function to work, the `keyboardFocusPolicy` should be specified as `explicit`. If `keyboardFocusPolicy` is not `explicit` or if the function is invoked in the `root` context, it is treated as `f.nop`.

`f.kill`
Terminates a client. It sends the WM_DELETE_WINDOW message to the selected window if the client application has requested it through the WM_PROTOCOLS property. The application is supposed to respond to the message by removing the indicated window. If the WM_SAVE_YOURSELF protocol is set up and the WM_DELETE_WINDOW protocol is not, the client is sent a message that indicates that the client needs to prepare to be terminated. If the client does not have the WM_DELETE_WINDOW or WM_SAVE_YOURSELF protocol set, the `f.kill` function causes a client's X connection to be terminated.

`f.lower` [`-`*client* | `within` | `freeFamily`]
Without arguments, lowers a window or icon to the bottom of the stack. By default, the context in which the function is invoked indicates to the window or icon to lower. If an application window has one or more transient windows (e.g., dialog boxes), the transient windows are lowered with the parent (within the global stack) and remain on top of it.

If the `-`*client* argument is specified, the function is invoked on the named client. *client* must be the instance or class name of a program.

The `within` argument is used to lower a transient window within the application's local window hierarchy; all transients remain above the parent window and that window remains in the same position in the global window stack. In practice, this function is only useful when there are two or more transient windows and you want to shuffle them.

The `freeFamily` argument is used to lower a transient below its parent in the application's local window hierarchy. Again, the parent is not moved in the global window stack. However, if you use this function on the parent, the entire family stack is lowered within the global stack.

`f.maximize`
: Causes a window to be redisplayed at its maximum size. This function cannot be invoked in the context `root` or on a window that is already maximized.

`f.menu` *menu_name*
: Associates a cascading menu with a menu item or associates a menu with a button or key binding. The *menu_name* argument specifies the menu.

`f.minimize`
: Causes a window to be minimized (i.e., iconified). When no icon box is being used, icons are placed on the bottom of the stack, which is generally in the lower-left corner of the screen. If an icon box is being used, icons are placed inside the box. This function cannot be invoked in the context `root` or on an iconified window.

`f.move`
: Allows you to move a window interactively, using the pointer.

`f.next_cmap`
: Installs the next colormap in the list of colormaps for the window with the colormap focus.

`f.next_key [icon | window | transient]`
: Without any arguments, this function advances the input focus to the next window or icon in the stack. You can specify `icon` or `window` to make the function apply only to icons or windows, respectively. Generally, the focus is moved to windows that do not have an associated secondary window that is application modal. If the `transient` argument is specified, transient windows are also traversed. Otherwise, if only `window` is specified, focus is moved to the last window in a transient group to have the focus. For this function to work, `keyboardFocusPolicy` must be `explicit`; otherwise, the function is treated as `f.nop`.

`f.nop` Specifies no operation.

`f.normalize`
: Causes a client window to be displayed at its normal size. This function cannot be invoked in the context `root` or on a window that is already at its normal size.

`f.normalize_and_raise`
: Causes the client window to be displayed at its normal size and raised to the top of the stack. This function cannot be invoked in the context `root` or on a window that is already at its normal size.

`f.pack_icons`
: Rearranges icons in an optimal fashion based on the layout policy being used, either on the root window or in the icon box.

`f.pass_keys`
: Toggles processing of key bindings for window manager functions. When key binding processing is disabled, all keys are passed to the window with the keyboard input focus and no window manager functions are invoked. If the `f.pass_keys` function is set up to be invoked with a key binding, the binding can be used to toggle key binding processing.

`f.post_wmenu`
: Displays the **Window Menu**. If a key is used to display the menu and a window menu button is present, the upper-left corner of the menu is placed at the lower-left corner of the command button. If no window menu button is present, the menu is placed in the upper-left corner of the window.

`f.prev_cmap`
: This function installs the previous colormap in the list of colormaps for the window with the colormap focus.

`f.prev_key [icon | window | transient]`
: Without any arguments, this function moves the input focus to the previous window or icon in the stack. You can specify `icon` or `window` to make the function apply only to icons or windows, respectively. Generally, the focus is moved to windows that do not have an associated secondary window that is application modal. If the `transient` argument is specified, transient windows are also traversed. Otherwise, if only `window` is specified, focus is moved to the last window in a transient group to have the focus. For this function to work, `keyboardFocusPolicy` must be `explicit`; otherwise, the function is treated as `f.nop`.

`f.quit_mwm`
: Stops the *mwm* window manager. Note that this function does not stop the X server. This function cannot be invoked from a non-root menu.

`f.raise` [*-client* | `within` | `freeFamily` ]
: Without arguments, raises a window or icon to the top of the stack. By default, the context in which the function is invoked indicates the window or icon to raise. If an application window has one or more transient windows (e.g., dialog boxes), the transient windows are raised with the parent (within the global stack) and remain on top of it.

  If the *-client* argument is specified, the function is invoked on the named client. *client* must be the instance or class name of a program.

  The `within` argument is used to raise a transient window within the application's local window hierarchy; all transients remain above the parent window and that window remains in the same position in the global window stack. In practice, this function is only useful when there are two or more transient windows and you want to shuffle them.

The `freeFamily` argument raises a transient to the top of the application's local window hierarchy. The parent window is also raised to the top of the global stack.

`f.raise_lower [within | freeFamily ]`

Raises a primary application window to the top of the stack or lowers a window to the bottom of the stack, as appropriate to the context.

The `within` argument is intended to raise a transient window within the application's local window hierarchy. All transients remain above the parent window and the parent window should also remain in the same position in the global window stack. If the transient is not obscured by another window in the local stack, the transient window is lowered within the family.

The preceding paragraph describes how `within` *should* work. However, we have found that the parent window does not always remain in the same position in the global window stack.

The `freeFamily` argument raises a transient to the top of the family stack and also raises the parent window to the top of the global stack. If the transient is not obscured by another window, this function lowers the transient to the bottom of the family stack and lowers the family in the global stack.

`f.refresh`

Redraws all windows.

`f.refresh_win`

Redraws a single window.

`f.resize`

Allows you to resize a window interactively, using the pointer.

`f.restart`

Restarts the *mwm* window manager. The function causes the current *mwm* process to be stopped and a new *mwm* process to be started. It cannot be invoked from a non-root menu.

`f.restore`

Causes the client window to be displayed at its previous size. If invoked on an icon, `f.restore` causes the icon to be converted back to a window at its previous size. Thus, if the window was maximized, it is restored to this state. If the window was previously at its normal size, it is restored to this state. If invoked on a maximized window, the window is restored to its normal size. This function cannot be invoked in the context `root` or on a window that is already at its normal size.

`f.restore_and_raise`
Causes the client window to be displayed at its previous size and raised to the top of the stack. This function cannot be invoked in the context `root` or on a window that is already at its normal size.

`f.screen` [`next` | `prev` | `back` | *screen_number*]
Causes the pointer to be warped to another screen, which is determined by one of four mutually exclusive parameters. The `next` argument means skip to the next managed screen, `prev` means skip back to the previous managed screen, `back` means skip to the last screen visited, and *screen_number* specifies a particular screen. Screens are numbered beginning at 0.

`f.send_msg` *message_number*
Sends a message of the type _MOTIF_WM_MESSAGES to a client; the message type is indicated by the *message_number* argument. The message is sent only if the client's _MOTIF_WM_MESSAGES property includes *message_number*. If a menu item is set up to invoke `f.send_msg` and the *message_number* is not included in the client's _MOTIF_WM_MESSAGES property, the menu item label is greyed out, which indicates that it is not available for selection.

`f.separator`
Creates a divider line in a menu. Any associated label is ignored.

`f.set_behavior`
Restarts *mwm*, toggling between the default behavior for the particular system and the user's custom environment. In any case, a dialog box asks the user to confirm or cancel the action. By default this function is invoked using the following key sequence: `Shift Ctrl Meta !`.

`f.title`
Specifies the title of a menu. The title string is separated from the menu items by a double divider line.

### Event Specification

In order to specify button bindings, key bindings, and menu accelerators, you need to be able to specify events in the *mwm* resource description file. Use the following syntax to specify button events for button bindings:

[*modifier_key* ... ]<*button_event*>

The acceptable values for *modifier_key* are: `Ctrl`, `Shift`, `Alt`, `Meta`, `Lock`, `Mod1`, `Mod2`, `Mod3`, `Mod4`, and `Mod5`. *mwm* considers `Alt` and `Meta` to be equivalent. The acceptable values for *button_event* are:

```
Btn1Down     Btn2Down     Btn3Down     Btn4Down     Btn5Down
Btn1Up       Btn2Up       Btn3Up       Btn4Up       Btn5Up
Btn1Click    Btn2Click    Btn3Click    Btn4Click    Btn5Click
Btn1Click2   Btn2Click2   Btn3Click2   Btn4Click2   Btn5Click2
```

Use the following syntax to specify key events for key bindings and menu accelerators:

```
[modifier_key ... ]<Key>key_name
```

Any X11 keysym name is an acceptable value for *key_name*.

### Button Bindings

The `buttonBindings` resource specifies the name of a set of button bindings that control mouse behavior in *mwm*. You can create your own set of button bindings or use one of the sets defined in *system.mwmrc*: `DefaultButtonBindings`, `ExplicitButtonBindings`, or `PointerButtonBindings`. Use the following syntax to specify a set of button bindings:

```
Buttons button_set_name
{
 button  context  function
 button  context  function
   ...
 button  context  function
}
```

The *context* specifies where the pointer must be located for the button binding to work. The context is also used for window manager functions that are context-sensitive. The valid contexts for button bindings are `root`, `window`, `icon`, `title`, `border`, `frame`, and `app`. The `title` context refers to the title area of the frame. `border` refers to the frame exclusive of the title bar. `frame` refers to the entire frame. The `app` context refers to the application window proper. The `window` context includes the application window and the frame. A context specification can include multiple contexts; use a vertical bar ( | ) to separate multiple context values.

### Key Bindings

The `keyBindings` resource specifies the name of a set of key bindings that control keyboard behavior in *mwm*. You can create your own set of key bindings or use the default key bindings, `DefaultKeyBindings`, defined in *system.mwmrc*. Use the following syntax to specify a set of key bindings:

```
Keys key_set_name
{
 key  context  function
 key  context  function
   ...
 key  context  function
}
```

The *context* specifies where the keyboard focus must be for the key binding to work. The context is also used for window manager functions that are context-sensitive. The valid contexts for key bindings are `root`, `window`, `icon`, `title`, `border`, `frame`, and `app`. The `title`, `border`, `frame`, and `app` contexts are all equivalent to `window`. A context specification can include multiple contexts; use a vertical bar ( | ) to separate multiple context values.

### Menus

The window manager functions `f.post_wmenu` and `f.menu` post menus. These functions both take the name of a menu to post. You can create your own menus or use the default menus defined in *system.mwmrc*: `DefaultRootMenu` and `DefaultWindowMenu`. Use the following syntax to specify a menu:

```
Menu menu_name
{
 label [mnemonic] [accelerator] function
 label [mnemonic] [accelerator] function
  ...
 label [mnemonic] [accelerator] function
}
```

Each line in a menu specification indicates the label for the menu item, optional keyboard mnemonics and accelerators, and the window manager function that is performed. *label* can be a string or a bitmap file. If the string contains multiple words, it must be enclosed in quotation marks. A bitmap file specification is preceded by an at sign (`@`). A *mnemonic* is specified as *_character*. An *accelerator* specification uses the key event specification syntax.

The context of a window manager function that is activated from a menu is based on how the menu is posted. If it is posted from a button binding, the context of the menu is the context of the button binding. If it is posted from a key binding, the context of the menu is based on the location of the keyboard focus.

## Environment

*mwm* uses the following environment variables:

HOME The user's home directory.

LANG The language to be used for the *mwm* message catalog and the *mwm* startup file.

XBMLANGPATH
: Used to search for bitmap files.

XFILESEARCHPATH
: Used to determine the location of system-wide class resource files. If the LANG variable is set, the *$LANG* subdirectory is also searched.

XUSERFILESEARCHPATH, XAPPLRESDIR
: Used to determine the location of user-specific class resource files. If the LANG variable is set, the *$LANG* subdirectory is also searched.

MWMSHELL, SHELL
: MWMSHELL specifies the shell to use when executing a command supplied as an argument to the `f.exec` function. If MWMSHELL is not set, SHELL is used.

## Files

*/usr/lib/X11/$LANG/system.mwmrc*
*/usr/lib/X11/system.mwmrc*
*/usr/lib/X11/app-defaults/Mwm*
*$HOME/Mwm*
*$HOME/$LANG/.mwmrc*
*$HOME/.mwmrc*
*$HOME/.motifbind*

## See Also

*XmIsMotifWMRunning*(1), *XmInstallImage*(1),
*VendorShell*(2),
*xmbind*(4).

## Name

uil – the User Interface Language (UIL) compiler.

## Syntax

`uil` [*options*] *file*

## Description

The *uil* command invokes the User Interface Language (UIL) compiler. If the file does not contain any errors, the compiler generates a User Interface Description (UID) file that contains a compiled form of the input file. UIL is a specification language that can be used to describe the initial state of a user interface that uses the OSF/Motif widget set, as well as other widgets. The user interface for an application is created at run-time using the Motif Resource Manager (Mrm) library; the interface is based on compiled interface descriptions stored in one or more UID files.

## Options

`-I`*pathname*
: Specifies a search path for include files. By default, the current directory and */usr/include* are searched. Path names may be relative or absolute. The paths specified with this option are searched in order after the current directory and before */usr/include*.

`-m`
: When specified with the `-v` option, the UIL compiler includes machine code in the listing file. The machine code provides binary and text descriptions of the data that is stored in the UID file. This option is useful for determining exactly how the compiler interprets a particular statement and how much storage is used for the variables, declarations, and assignments.

`-o` *ofile*
: Specifies the name of the UID file to output. The default filename is *a.uid*. The customary suffix for UID files is *.uid*.

`-s`
: Specifies that the UIL compiler set the locale before compiling any files. Setting the locale determines the behavior of locale-dependent routines like character string operations. Although setting the locale is an implementation-dependent operation, on ANSI-C-based systems, the locale is set with the call:

```
setlocale (LC_ALL, "")
```

See the `setlocale()` man page on your system for more information.

`-v` *lfile*
: Directs the UIL compiler to produce a listing of the compilation. The file indicates the name of the output file. If this option is not specified, the compiler does not generate a listing. On UNIX systems, a filename of */dev/tty* usually causes the listing to be output on the terminal where *uil* was invoked.

`-w`
: Directs the compiler to suppress warning and informational messages and to print only error messages. The default behavior is to print error, warning and informational messages.

-wmd *wfile*

Specifies a compiled Widget Meta-Language (WML) description file that is loaded in place of the default WML description. The default WML description file contains a description of all of the Motif widgets. This option is normally used to debug a WML description file without rebuilding the UIL compiler.

## Environment

The LANG environment variable affects the way that the UIL compiler parses and generates compound strings, fonts, fontsets, and font tables (font lists). The exact effect is described by the UIL reference pages for these types.

## Example

```
% uil -o myfile.uid -v /dev/tty myfile.uil

% uil -I/project/include/uil -o mainui.uid mainui.uil
```

## Bugs

If the LANG environment variable is set to an invalid value and the -s option is specified, the UIL compiler crashes.

## See Also

*Uil*(7).

## Name

xmbind – configure virtual key bindings.

## Syntax

**xmbind** [*options*] [*file*]

## Availability

Motif 1.2 and later.

## Description

The *xmbind* command configures the virtual key bindings for Motif applications. Since this action is performed by *mwm* on startup, *xmbind* is only needed when *mwm* is not being used or when a user wants to change the bindings without restarting *mwm*.

When a file is specified, its contents are used for the virtual bindings. Otherwise, *xmbind* uses the *.motifbind* file in the user's home directory. A sample specification is shown below:

```
osfBackSpace :      <Key>BackSpace
osfInsert :         <Key>InsertChar
osfDelete :         <Key>DeleteChar
```

If *xmbind* cannot find the *.motifbind* file, it loads the default virtual bindings for the server. *xmbind* searches for a vendor-specific set of bindings located using the file *xmbind.alias*. If this file exists in the user's home directory, it is searched for a pathname associated with the vendor string or the vendor string and vendor release. If the search is unsuccessful, Motif continues looking for *xmbind.alias* in the directory specified by XMBINDDIR or in */usr/lib/Xm/bindings* if the variable is not set. If this file exists, it is searched for a pathname as before. If either search locates a pathname and the file exists, the bindings in that file are used. An *xmbind.alias* file contains lines of the following form:

"*vendor_string*[ *vendor_release* ] "*bindings_file*

If *xmbind* still has not located any bindings, it loads fixed fallback default bindings.

The Motif toolkit uses a mechanism called *virtual bindings* to map one set of keysyms to another set. This mapping permits widgets and applications to use one set of keysyms in translation tables; applications and users can then customize the keysyms used in the translations based on the particular keyboard that is being used. Keysyms that can be used in this way are called *osf keysyms*. Motif maintains a mapping between the osf keysyms and the actual keysyms that represent keys on a particular keyboard. See the Introduction to Section 2, *Motif and Xt Widget Classes* for more information about virtual bindings.

## Options

`-display` [*host*]`:`*server*[`.`*screen*]

Specifies the name of the display on which to run *xmbind*. *host* is the hostname of the physical display, *server* specifies the server number, and *screen* specifies the screen number. Either or both of the *host* and *screen* elements can be omitted. If *host* is omitted, the local display is assumed. If *screen* is omitted, screen 0 is assumed (and the period is unnecessary). The colon and (display) *server* are necessary in all cases.

## Environment

The XMBINDDIR environment variable affects the way that *xmbind* searches for vendor-specific default virtual bindings.

## See Also

*XmTranslateKey*(1).

# Section 5

## UIL File Format

*This section describes the file format of a User Interface Language (UIL) module. The module reference page describes the UIL module structure. The rest of the reference pages document the syntax and usage of each of the UIL sections. The section reference pages appear in the order that the UIL sections typically appear in a UIL module.*

*The first reference page,* Introduction*, explains the format and contents of each of the following pages. It also describes the overall structure and syntax of a UIL module.*

## In This Section:

# Introduction

This page describes the format and contents of each reference page in Section 5, which covers the UIL file format.

## Name

Section – a brief description of the file section.

## Syntax

This section describes the syntax for the section of the UIL file. Anything in `constant width` type should be typed exactly as shown. Items in *italics* are expressions that should be replaced by actual names and values when you write a UIL file. Anything enclosed in brackets is optional. An ellipsis (`. . .`) means that the previous expression can be repeated multiple times and a vertical bar ( | ) means to select one of a set of choices.

## Description

This section provides an overview of the particular section in the UIL module and it explains the syntax that is expected for the section. A UIL source file, also known as a UIL module, describes the user interface for an application. It consists of a module name, optional module settings, optional include directives, zero or more sections that describe all or part of a user interface, and an end module statement. The module specifies the widgets used in the interface, as well as the resources and callbacks of these widgets. UIL gives you the ability to use variables, procedures, lists, and objects to describe the interface.

A major portion of a UIL module is the sections that describe the user interface. They are the `value` section, for defining and declaring variables; the `procedure` section, for declaring callback routines; the `identifier` section, for declaring values registered by the application at run-time; the `list` section, for defining lists of procedures, resources, callbacks, and widgets; and the `object` section, for defining the widgets, their resources, and the widget hierarchy.

In this section, we provide reference pages for each section of a UIL source file, as well as for the overall `module` structure and the `include` directive. Figure 5-1 shows an example of a UIL module that contains all of these sections.

### UIL Syntax

Symbols and identifiers in a UIL module must be separated by whitespace or punctuation characters in order to be recognized by the UIL compiler. Like C, no other restrictions are placed on the formatting of a UIL module, although the maximum line length accepted by the compiler is 132 characters.

Comments in UIL can take two different forms: single-line and multi-line. A single-line comment begins with a exclamation point (`!`) and continues to the end of the line. A multi-line comment begins with the characters `/*` and ends with the characters `*/`. Since the UIL compiler suspends normal parsing within comments, they cannot be nested.

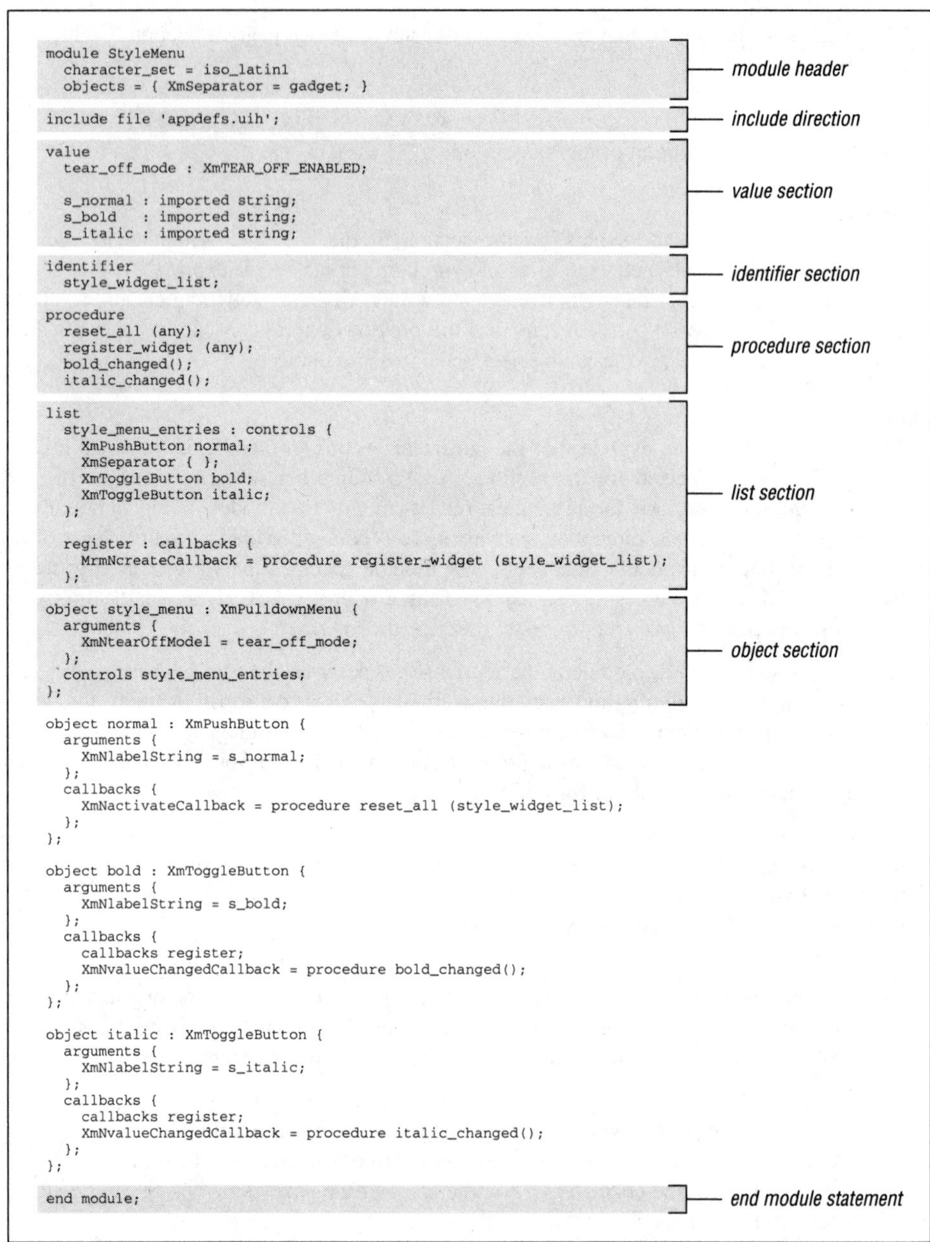

```
module StyleMenu
  character_set = iso_latin1
  objects = { XmSeparator = gadget; }

include file 'appdefs.uih';

value
  tear_off_mode : XmTEAR_OFF_ENABLED;

  s_normal : imported string;
  s_bold   : imported string;
  s_italic : imported string;

identifier
  style_widget_list;

procedure
  reset_all (any);
  register_widget (any);
  bold_changed();
  italic_changed();

list
  style_menu_entries : controls {
    XmPushButton normal;
    XmSeparator { };
    XmToggleButton bold;
    XmToggleButton italic;
  };

  register : callbacks {
    MrmNcreateCallback = procedure register_widget (style_widget_list);
  };

object style_menu : XmPulldownMenu {
  arguments {
    XmNtearOffModel = tear_off_mode;
  };
  controls style_menu_entries;
};

object normal : XmPushButton {
  arguments {
    XmNlabelString = s_normal;
  };
  callbacks {
    XmNactivateCallback = procedure reset_all (style_widget_list);
  };
};

object bold : XmToggleButton {
  arguments {
    XmNlabelString = s_bold;
  };
  callbacks {
    callbacks register;
    XmNvalueChangedCallback = procedure bold_changed();
  };
};

object italic : XmToggleButton {
  arguments {
    XmNlabelString = s_italic;
  };
  callbacks {
    callbacks register;
    XmNvalueChangedCallback = procedure italic_changed();
  };
};

end module;
```



*Figure 5-1. A sample UIL source file*

Values, identifiers, procedures, lists, and objects are declared or defined with programmer-assigned names. Names can be composed of upper and lowercase characters from A to Z, the digits from 0 to 9, and the underscore (_) and dollar sign ($) characters. Names may be up to 31 characters in length; they cannot begin with a digit. The `names` option, which is described on the `module` reference page, affects the case sensitivity of names. The UIL compiler maintains a single name-space for all UIL keywords and programmer-defined names. This means that the name of each value, identifier, procedure, list, and object must be unique.

### UIL Keywords

UIL keywords are categorized into reserved and unreserved keywords. Reserved keywords cannot be redefined by the programmer, while unreserved keywords can be used as programmer-defined names. In general, you should avoid redefining unreserved keywords because it can lead to confusion and programming errors. UIL uses the following reserved and unreserved keywords:

| Type | Reserved Keywords |
|---|---|
| General | `module`, `end`, `widget`, `gadget` |
| Section and list names | `arguments`, `callbacks`, `controls`, `identifier`, `include`, `list`, `object`, `procedure`, `procedures`, `value` |
| Storage classes | `exported`, `private` |
| Boolean constants | `on`, `off`, `true`, `false` |

| Type | Unreserved Keywords |
|---|---|
| Resource names | `XmNaccelerators`, `XmNactivateCallback`, et al. |
| Character set names | `iso_latin1`, `iso_greek`, et al. |
| Enumerated values | `XmATTACH_FORM`, `XmSHADOW_ETCHED_IN`, et al. |
| Widget class names | `XmPushButton`, `XmSeparator`, et al. |
| Option names and values | `background`, `case_insensitive`, `case_sensitive`, `file`, `foreground`, `imported`, `managed`, `names`, `objects`, `right_to_left`, `unmanaged`, `user_defined` |
| Type names | `any`, `argument`, `asciz_table`, `asciz_string_table`, `boolean`, `character_set`, `color`, `color_table`, `compound_string`, `compound_string_table`, `float`, `font`, `font_table`, `fontset`, `icon`, `integer`, `integer_table`, `keysym`, `reason`, `rgb`, `single_float`, `string`, `string_table`, `translation_table`, `wide_character`, `xbitmapfile` |

## Usage

This section provides less formal information about the section: how you might want to use it in a UIL module and things to watch out for.

## Example

This section provides examples of the use of the section in a UIL module.

## See Also

This section refers you to related functions, UIL file format sections, and UIL data types. The numbers in parentheses following each reference refer to the sections of this book in which they are found.

## Name

module – module structure.

## Syntax

```
module module_name
  [ names = [ case_insensitive | case_sensitive ] ]
  [ character_set = character_set ]
  [ objects = { widget_name = gadget | widget; [...] } ]
  [ [ include_directive ] | [ value_section ] | [ procedure_section ] |
    [ identifier_section ] | [ list_section ] | [ object_section ] ]
  [...]
end module;
```

## Description

A UIL module must begin with the keyword `module`, followed by the name of the module. You may name a module anything you like, as long as it is a valid UIL identifier. The name of a module is defined as a symbol in the compiler's symbol table, and therefore may not be a UIL reserved keyword. In addition, the name of the module cannot be used as the name of an object, variable, identifier, widget, or procedure elsewhere in the module. Option settings for the module are specified following the module statement. There are three different options that you can set: the case sensitivity of the module, the default character set, and the default object variant.

The `names` option specifies the case sensitivity of keywords and symbols in the UIL module. The syntax of this option is the keyword `names`, followed by either `case_sensitive` or `case_insensitive`. The default is `case_sensitive`, which means that all keywords must be lowercase and the case of symbols is significant. If `case_insensitive` is specified, keywords may be in upper, lower, or mixed case, and all programmer-defined values, procedures, identifiers, and objects are stored as uppercase in the UID file. For example, the three symbols `JellyBean`, `jellybean`, and `JELLYBEAN` are considered different symbols when names are `case_sensitive`, but are considered the same symbol when names are `case_insensitive`. If this option is specified, it must be the first option after the module name and must be specified in lowercase only.

The `character_set` option specifies the character set used for `compound_string`, `font`, and `fontset` values that are not defined with an explicit character set. The syntax of this option is the keyword `character_set`, followed by the name of a built-in character set. (See the `character_set` reference page for a list of the built-in character sets.) A user-defined character set cannot be used for this option. If this option is not specified, the default character set is determined from the codeset portion of the LANG environment variable if it is set, or `XmFALLBACK_CHARSET` otherwise. Setting this option overrides the LANG environment variable and turns off localized string parsing specified by the `-s` compiler option. When the `character_set` defaults to `XmFALLBACK_CHARSET`, the UIL compiler may use ISO8859-1 as the character set, even if the value has been changed by the vendor. Therefore, you should specify a character set explicitly instead of relying on the value of `XmFALLBACK_CHARSET`.

The `objects` option specifies whether the widget or gadget variant is used by default for CascadeButton, Label, PushButton, Separator, and ToggleButton objects. The syntax of the option is the keyword `objects`, followed by a list of object-specific settings. Like all lists in UIL, each setting is separated by a semicolon and enclosed by curly braces. Each object setting is the name of one of the classes listed above, followed by either `widget` or `gadget`. The default value for all of the classes is `widget`. You can override these settings when you define a specific object by adding `widget` or `gadget` after the object class name.

UIL also supports a version option setting, which consists of the string `version`, followed by a string representing the version of the module. This option is obsolete in Motif 1.2 and is retained for backward compatibility. You may encounter this setting in older UIL source files but you should not use it in new ones. The version string is stored in the UID file, but is not used by Mrm and cannot be accessed by the application. To make a version identifier that is accessible by the application through Mrm, you can store a version value in an exported UIL variable.

The bulk of a UIL module is the sections that describe the user interface, which occur after the module name and optional module settings. Briefly, the sections are the value section, for defining and declaring variables; the procedure section, for declaring callback routines; the identifier section, for declaring values registered by the application at run-time; the list section, for defining lists of procedures, resources, callbacks, or widgets; and the object section, for defining the widgets and their resources, and the widget hierarchy. Each section is described completely in a separate reference page.

Every UIL module must end with the end module statement, which is simply the string `end module` followed by a semicolon (`;`). A final newline is required after the end module statement or the UIL compiler generates an error message stating that the line is too long.

## Example

```
module print_panel
  names = case_insensitive
  character_set = iso_latin1
  objects = { XmPushButton = gadget; }

! sections ...

end module;
```

## See Also

*identifier*(5), *include*(5), *list*(5), *object*(5), *procedure*(5), *value*(5), *character_set*(6), *compound_string*(6), *font*(6), *fontset*(6), *font_table*(6), *string*(6).

# include

## Name

include – include file directive.

## Syntax

```
include file 'file_name';
```

## Description

The `include` directive tells the UIL compiler to suspend parsing of the current file and switch to the specified file. Parsing of the original file resumes after the end of the included file has been reached. `Include` directives may be nested, which means that an included file can contain `include` directives.

If an include file is specified an absolute pathname, which means that it begins with a slash (/), the compiler looks for the file in that specific location. Otherwise, the compiler tries to locate the file by searching in one or more directories. The directory that contains the UIL source file specified on the command line is searched first. (This directory may or may not be the same as the directory the compiler was invoked from.) If the file is not found there, the compiler searches any directories specified on the command line with the `-I` option in the order that they were specified. Next, the compiler searches the */usr/include* directory. Finally, if the specified file cannot be found, the compiler generates an error message and exits.

When an `include` directive is encountered, the UIL compiler ends the current section. Therefore, an include file must specifically use one of the section name keywords to begin a new section.

## Usage

Include files are used to break up modules into more manageable pieces or to provide a common place for definitions and declarations that are shared by several modules. Include files should not be used for defining strings. Strings should be defined in a separate UIL module and loaded at run-time as part of an Mrm hierarchy. The `MrmOpenHierarchyPerDisplay()` reference page explains how different UID files can be loaded based on the LANG environment variable. String declarations, however, are suitable for placement in an include file.

A UIL module can include a maximum of 99 files. This is not a nesting limit, but a limit on the total number of files that can be included. Because the UIL compiler maintains an open file descriptor for each included file, even after it has been included, the limit may be less than 99 due to operating-system imposed limits. If the UIL compiler tries to include a file and the maximum number of open file descriptors have been used, the compiler prints an error and exits. If this situation occurs, you should reduce the number of files included or increase the maximum number of open file descriptors.

If the string containing the include filename is missing a closing quotation mark, or if extraneous characters precede or follow the string, the UIL compiler may generate many strange errors.

### Example

From *callbacks.uih*:

```
procedure
  save();
  save_as (string);
  open (string);
  select (integer_table);
  quit();
```

From *edit_window.uil*:

```
module edit_window

! Include callback definitions.
include file 'callbacks.uih';

...

end module;
```

### See Also

*MrmOpenHierarchyPerDisplay*(3),
*uil*(4),
*module*(5).

## Name

value – variable definition and declaration section.

## Syntax

```
value
  value_name : [ exported | private ] value_expression | imported value_type ;
  [...]
```

## Description

The `value` section contains variable definitions and declarations. A variable is defined by assigning a value to it. A variable declaration is used to inform the UIL compiler of the existence of a variable defined in another module. The value assigned to a variable may be an arithmetic or string expression, a literal value, or another variable or identifier.

A value can be declared with a storage class of `private`, `exported`, or `imported`. Values are private by default. Private and exported values consist of a named variable and the value that is assigned to it. Private values are only accessible within the module in which they are defined. An exported variable definition includes the symbol `exported` before the value assigned. Exported values are accessible in other modules and from the application, in addition to the module in which they are defined.

You can access an exported value in another module by declaring it as an imported value in the module where you want to access it. Imported value declarations consist of a named variable, the symbol `imported`, and the type of the variable. If an imported value is exported from more than one module, the value from the module that occurs first in the array passed to `MrmOpenHierarchyPerDisplay()` is used.

Values of all types can be declared as private; values of most types can be declared as exported and imported. The Introduction to Section 6, *UIL Data Types*, contains a table that summarizes the storage classes that are allowed for each type.

## Usage

Variables used in an expression can be forward referenced. However, the specification of some complex literals cannot contain forward-referenced values. The UIL compiler indicates a value cannot be found in these cases. Refer to the reference page for a type to see if its literal representation can contain forward references.

Typically, the value of a variable used in an expression or in the specification of a complex literal must be accessible in the module in which it is used. As a result, in most cases you cannot use an imported variable in an expression or complex value specification. If an imported value is used in an invalid context, the UIL compiler issues an error message.

## Example

```
...
! See individual type reference pages for additional examples.
value
  version : exported 1002;
```

```
    Soothsayer : 'Beware the ides of March.';
    ides : 15;
    background : imported color;
  ...
```

## See Also

*MrmFetchBitmapLiteral*(3), *MrmFetchColorLiteral*(3), *MrmFetchIconLiteral*(3), *MrmFetchSetValues*(3), *argument*(6), *asciz_string_table*(6), *boolean*(6), *color*(6), *color_table*(6), *compound_string*(6), *compound_string_table*(6), *float*(6), *font*(6), *fontset*(6), *font_table*(6), *icon*(6), *integer*(6), *integer_table*(6), *keysym*(6), *reason*(6), *rgb*(6), *single_float*(6), *string*(6), *translation_table*(6), *wide_character*(6), *xbitmapfile*(6).

# procedure



## Name

procedure – procedure declaration section.

## Syntax

```
procedure
  procedure_name [ ( [ value_type ] ) ];
  [...]
```

## Description

The `procedure` section contains declarations of procedures that can be used as a callback for a widget or as a user-defined widget creation function. Procedures can also be used in a procedure list; procedure lists are used to associate more than one callback procedure with a specific callback. Procedure lists are described on the `list` reference page.

The procedure section begins with the UIL keyword `procedure`, followed by list of procedure declarations. Each declaration consists of the procedure name followed by optional parentheses enclosing an optional parameter type. Valid type names are listed in the Introduction to Section 6, *UIL Data Types*.

## Usage

A procedure declaration can be used to specify whether a procedure expects a parameter, and if so, the type of the parameter. The UIL compiler verifies that a procedure reference conforms to its declaration. If a procedure name is not followed by parentheses, the compiler does not count parameters or perform any type checking when the procedure is used. Zero arguments, or one argument of any type, can be used in the reference.

If the procedure name is followed by an empty pair of parentheses, a reference to the procedure must contain zero arguments. User-defined widget creation functions should be declared as taking no parameters, although the UIL compiler does not enforce this rule.

If the procedure name is followed by a parenthesized type name or widget class, a reference to the procedure must contain exactly one argument of the specified type or class. If the type `any` is specified, the reference can contain an argument of any type. Prior to Motif 1.2.1, the UIL compiler generates an error if a widget class name is specified as the type in a procedure declaration. If the parameter to a callback procedure is an imported value or an identifier that cannot be resolved at run-time, a segmentation fault may occur when the callback is called.

Because identifiers and procedures are registered in the same name space with `MrmRegisterName()` and `MrmRegisterNamesInHierarchy()`, it is possible to declare a value as a procedure in the UIL source, even though the entry that is registered may not be a procedure. An attempt to call a non-procedure value usually causes an application to crash.

## Example

```
...
procedure
  exit();
  print (string);
```

```
    XawCreateForm();
    popup (XmPopupMenu);

  object form : user_defined procedure XawCreateForm { };

  object quit : XmPushButton {
    callbacks {
      MrmNcreateCallback = procedure print ('Hello!');
      XmNactivateCallback = procedure exit();
      XmNdestroyCallback = procedure print ('Goodbye!');
    };
  };
```

## See Also

*MrmFetchWidget*(3), *MrmFetchWidgetOverride*(3), *MrmRegisterNames*(3), *MrmRegisterNamesInHierarchy*(3),
*identifier*(5), *list*(5), *object*(5).

# identifier

## Name

identifier – run-time variable declaration section.

## Syntax

```
identifier
  identifier_name ;
  [...]
```

## Description

The `identifier` section contains variable declarations that are registered at run-time by the application with `MrmRegisterNames()` or `MrmRegisterNamesInHierarchy()`. The section begins with the UIL keyword `identifier`, followed by a list of names separated by semicolons.

## Usage

A value declared as an identifier can be assigned to a named variable in a `value` section, it can be passed as the parameter to a callback procedure, or it can be assigned to a resource in the `arguments` section of an object definition. An identifier value cannot be used in an expression or as part of a complex literal type definition. An identifier value does not have any type associated with it, so it can be passed as a parameter to any callback that can take an argument or it can be assigned to any resource, regardless of the type of parameter or resource expected.

## Example

```
...
identifier
  display_name;
  highlight_color;

value
  alias : display_name;

procedure
  highlight (color);

object label : XmLabel {
  arguments {
    XmNlabelString : display_name;
  }
  callbacks {
    XmNfocusInCallback = procedure highlight (highlight_color);
  };
}
...
```

## See Also

*MrmRegisterNames*(3), *MrmRegisterNamesInHierarchy*(3),
*procedure*(5), *object*(5).

# list

## Name

list - list definition section.

## Syntax

```
list
  list_name : arguments {
    argument_name = value_expression ; |
    arguments arguments_list_name ;
    [...] } ; |
  list_name : callbacks {
    reason_name = procedure procedure_name [ ( [ value_expression ] ) ]; |
    reason_name = procedures {
        procedure_name [ ( [ value_expression ] ) ];
        [...] } ; |
    reason_name = procedures procedure_list_name ; |
    callbacks callbacks_list_name ;
    [...] } ; |
  list_name : controls {
    [managed | unmanaged] object_class object_name ; |
    [managed | unmanaged] object_class [widget | gadget] { [attributes] } ; |
    [managed | unmanaged] user_defined procedure creation_procedure
        { [attributes] } ; |
    auto_created_object_name { [attributes] } ; |
    controls controls_list_name ;
    [...] } ; |
  list_name : procedures {
    procedure_name [ ( [ value_expression ] ) ]; |
    procedures procedures_list_name ;
    [...] } ;
  [...]
```

## Description

The `list` section is used to define lists of resources, callbacks, procedures, or controls that can be used when setting attributes of a widget defined in an `object` section. Each list definition consists of a list name followed by a colon, a list type, and a list of items of that type separated by semicolons. Each item can be a single item (resource, callback, procedure, or widget) or a list of that type of item. When a list contains another list, the result is the same as if the items in the included list were specified directly in the including list. The storage class of lists is limited to private. Unlike variables and objects, lists cannot be exported, imported, or retrieved by an application at run-time.

The type of a list determines the type and the format of the items it contains. UIL allows the following types of lists: `arguments`, `callbacks`, `controls`, and `procedures`. The format of the items in arguments, callbacks, and controls lists is the same as the format for the corresponding subsection in an object definition. The exact syntax is described in the `object` section reference page.

The procedures list type exists to allow the specification of a list of procedures for a single callback. Each routine in a procedures list is invoked by the specified callback. A procedures list is specified by the symbol `procedures`, followed by a list of procedures declared elsewhere in the module. An individual procedure is specified with the name of the procedure and an argument specification consistent with the routine's declaration. The order in which routines in a procedures list are invoked is not specified by the Xt Intrinsics. If you need to have several procedures called in a particular order, you should register a single callback that calls the procedures in that order.

Like many values in UIL, a list can be specified directly in the `arguments`, `callbacks`, or `controls` subsection or as a callback procedures list. An inline list is specified by the type of the list, followed by a list of items of that type.



## Usage

A list can be used to group collections of resources, callbacks, and widget children that are common to several object definitions. To specify more than one procedure for a single callback, you must use a list. A simple style/behavior hierarchy can be specified by using nested list definitions, as the example below illustrates. If a resource or callback setting occurs more than once in an arguments or callbacks list, the last occurrence has precedence over earlier occurrences. This feature allows you to define a list that includes settings from another list but overrides some of the settings. The UIL compiler issues an informational message about multiple occurrences, but the messages can be turned off by using the -w compiler option.

## Example

```
...
! Declare procedures used below.
procedure
  shift();
  floor_it();
  armed();
  ready();

list
  ! Declare some lists to implement widget styles.
  base_style : arguments {
    ! This list contains individual elements only.
    XmNforeground = default_foreground;
    XmNbackground = default_background;
  };
  button_style : arguments {
    ! Include another list in this list.
    arguments base_style;
    XmNfontList = font ('*helvetica-bold-r-normal-*-120-100-100*');
  };
```

```
! Declare a list of procedures to be set on an individual callback.
list
  super_button_activate : procedures {
    shift();
    floor_it();
  };

list
  super_button_callbacks : callbacks {
    XmNactivateCallback = procedures super_button_activate;
    ! Set the arm callback to an inline list of procedures.
    XmNarmCallback = procedures {
                       armed();
                       ready();
                     };
  };

object
  super_button : XmPushButton {
    arguments {
      ! Use arguments in button_style list and add one of our own.
      arguments button_style;
      XmNarmColor = color ('yellow');
    };
    callbacks super_button_callbacks;
  };
...
```

## See Also

*object*(5), *procedure*(5).

# object



## Name

object – widget declaration and definition section.

## Syntax

```
object object_name : imported object_type ; or

object object_name : [ exported | private ]
                         object_type [ widget | gadget ] |
                         user_defined procedure creation_procedure
 { [
   arguments {
     arguments argument_list_name ; |
     argument_name = value_expression ;
     [...] } ; |
   callbacks {
     callbacks callback_list_name ; |
     reason_name = procedure procedure_name [ ( [ value_expression ] ) ]; |
     reason_name = procedures {
         procedure_name [ ( [ value_expression ] ) ];
         [...] } ; |
     reason_name = procedures procedures_list_name ;
     [...] } ; |
   controls {
     controls controls_list_name ; |
     [ managed | unmanaged ] object_class object_name ; |
     [ managed | unmanaged ] object_class [ widget | gadget ] { [ attributes ] } ; |
     [ managed | unmanaged ] user_defined procedure creation_procedure
         { [ attributes ] } ; |
     auto_created_object_name { [ attributes ] } ;
     [...] } ;
   [...]
 ] } ;
```

## Description

The `object` section is used to declare or define the objects that compose the user interface of an application. These objects can be either widgets or gadgets and are created at run-time with the routines `MrmFetchWidget()` and `MrmFetchWidgetOverride()`. Both built-in Motif widgets and user-defined widgets can be defined in an `object` section.

An object declaration informs the UIL compiler about an object that is defined in another UIL module. A declaration consists of the object name followed by a colon, the keyword `imported`, and the type of the imported widget.

An object definition consists of an object name followed by a colon, an optional storage class, a built-in widget class name or used-defined creation procedure, and a list of attributes. An object's attributes may include resource settings, callbacks, and a list of the object's children. The storage class may be either `private` or `exported`. The default storage class is `exported`. Widgets defined as `private` are not prevented from being retrieved directly with Mrm, but you can still declare widgets as `private` to indicate that they should not be retrieved directly.

When defining an instance of a built-in widget, the name of a Motif class (such as XmPushButton or XmMessageDialog) follows the optional storage class. A class that has both widget and gadget variants can be followed by `widget` or `gadget` to indicate which variant is used. The default variant is `widget`, unless `gadget` is specified in the `objects` setting in the UIL module header. For gadget variants, the UIL compiler also allows the name `Gadget` to be appended directly to the widget class name (as in XmPushButtonGadget). This syntax is inconsistent, however, so you should avoid using it.

When defining an instance of a user-defined widget, the optional storage class is followed by the string `user_defined procedure` and the name of a widget creation procedure. The procedure must be declared in a `procedure` section elsewhere in the module. It must also be registered by the application at run-time with `MrmRegisterClass()` before the widget is retrieved. The C prototype of a creation procedure is described in the `MrmRegisterClass()` manual page in Section 3, *Mrm Functions*.

The remainder of an object definition consists of three optional subsections that define the widget's resources, callbacks, and children. The subsections are enclosed by curly braces, which must be present, even when none of the subsections are specified. Each subsection consists of the name of the subsection followed by the name of a list defined in a list section or a list of items enclosed by curly braces. The `arguments` subsection specifies resource settings, the `callbacks` subsection specifies callback procedures, and the `controls` section specifies child widgets.

### Arguments

The `arguments` subsection, if present, specifies one or more resource settings and/or resource lists. A list is specified with the symbol `arguments`, followed by the name of an arguments list defined elsewhere in the module. Resource settings are of the form `resourceName = value`. The resource name may be built-in or user-defined. (See the `argument` reference page in Section 6, *UIL Data Types*, for information about creating user-defined resource names.) If the same resource is set more than once in a widget's `arguments` section, the last occurrence of the setting is used and the UIL compiler issues an informational message.

If the widget instance being defined is from a built-in Motif widget class, the predefined resources set in the `arguments` section must be valid for the widget class, but any user-defined resource can be set. It can be useful to set user-defined constraint resources on a built-in widget when it is the child of a user-defined constraint widget. If the widget instance being defined is a user-defined widget, any predefined or user-defined resources can be set in its `arguments` section. You should take care to set resources that are valid for user-defined widgets, as the UIL compiler is unable to detect invalid resources.

The UIL compiler normally verifies that the type of a value matches the type of the resource to which it is assigned. Type checking is not possible, however, when a value is assigned to a user-defined resource of type `any`, or when a variable declared in an identifier section is assigned to a resource.

The type of a resource and the value assigned to it do not always have to be an exact match. The UIL compiler automatically converts certain values to the appropriate type for a resource. If a type mismatch occurs and a conversion cannot be performed, the compiler generates an error message and a UID file is not generated. The table below summarizes the supported conversions:

| Value Type | Can Be Assigned To |
|---|---|
| `string` | `compound_string` |
| `asciz_string_table` | `compound_string_table` |
| `icon` | `pixmap` |
| `xbitmapfile` | `pixmap` |
| `rgb` | `color` |
| `font` | `font_list` |
| `fontset` | `font_list` |

When a built-in array resource is specified in the `arguments` subsection, the UIL compiler automatically sets the associated count resource. All but one of the built-in arrays with associated counts are `XmStringTable` resources; they are listed in the `compound_string_table` reference page in Section 6, *UIL Data Types*. The other resource is the Text and TextField resource `XmNselectionArray` and its associated count resource, `XmNselectionArrayCount`.

### Callbacks

The `callbacks` subsection, if present, specifies one or more callback settings and/or callback lists. A list is specified with the symbol `callbacks`, followed by the name of a callback list defined elsewhere in the module. A callback setting consists of the callback name, such as `XmNactivateCallback`, followed by an equal sign (=) and either a single procedure name or the name of a list of procedures defined elsewhere in the module. A single procedure is specified by the symbol `procedure` followed by its name, and an argument specification consistent with the procedure's declaration. A list is specified by the symbol `procedures` followed by the name of the list. If the same callback is set more than once in a widget's callbacks section, the last occurrence of the setting is used and the UIL compiler issues an informational message.

A procedure used in the `callbacks` section must be declared in a `procedure` section elsewhere in the module. It must also be registered by the application at run-time with `MrmRegisterNames()` or `MrmRegisterNamesInHierarchy()` before any widgets that reference it are created.

If the widget instance being defined is from a built-in Motif widget class, the predefined callbacks set in the `callbacks` section must be valid for the widget class, but any user-defined callbacks can be set. There should not be any need to set a user-defined callback on a built-in widget, however. If the widget instance being defined is a user-defined widget, any built-in or user-defined callbacks can be set in the `callbacks` section.

In addition to the standard Motif callbacks, Mrm supports the `MrmNcreateCallback`, which is called by Mrm when a widget is created. The prototype of an `MrmNcreate-Callback` is the same as any other Xt callback procedure. The `call_data` passed to the callback is an `XmAnyCallbackStruct`.

### Controls

The `controls` subsection, if present, specifies a list of children. Each entry in the list may be a list of children, an object defined elsewhere, an object defined inline, or an automatically-created child. A list is specified with the symbol `controls` followed by the name of a controls lists defined elsewhere in the module. Specify an object defined elsewhere using an optional initial state of `managed` or `unmanaged`, followed by `user_defined` or a widget class and the name of the child widget. If the same child widget occurs more than once in a widget's `controls` section, an instance of the child is created for each occurrence.

An inline object definition is similar, but the name of the child widget is replaced by a set of widget attributes. The name of the inline widget is automatically generated by the UIL compiler. Inline definitions can be used to define widget instances that have few or no attributes and that do not need to be referenced by name. You may wish to avoid inline definitions, however, since the widget name is not well-defined, which makes customization via X resources difficult. An automatically-created child is specified by the name of the child followed by an attributes list. Appendix D, *Table of UIL Objects*, lists the automatically-created children of the built-in Motif widgets. The ability to specify attributes for automatically-created children is only available in Motif 1.2 and later.

If the widget instance being defined is from a built-in Motif widget class, the children specified in the `controls` section must be valid for the widget class, but any user-defined children can be specified. If the widget instance being defined is a user-defined widget, any built-in or used-defined children can be specified in the `controls` section. The UIL compiler verifies that the children specified in the `controls` section are allowable children for the widget being defined. Appendix D, *Table of UIL Objects*, lists the valid children for each built-in widget class. Any children are allowed for user-defined widgets. If an invalid child is specified in a widget's `controls` section, the UIL compiler generates an error and no UID file is produced.

## Usage

A named widget can be specified as a value for a resource of type `widget`, such as the Form constraint resource `XmNleftWidget`, or as the argument of a callback procedure declared with a parameter of type `any` or `widget`. Prior to Motif 1.2.1, UIL does not allow the type `widget` to be used as an argument type in a procedure declaration. You can specify type `any` to work around this problem. Older versions of UIL may require the widget class name to precede a widget value that is assigned to a resource or used as callback parameter. Since all versions of UIL accept this syntax, you can avoid potential difficulties by always using it.

Mrm places some restrictions on the widgets that can be assigned to a resource or used as a callback parameter. The widget must be a member of the same hierarchy as the widget definition in which it is used. A widget hierarchy includes the widget named in the call to `MrmFetchWidget()` or `MrmFetchWidgetOverride()` and the widgets created in the widget tree below it. If a named widget does not exist when a reference to it is encountered, Mrm waits until all of the widgets in the hierarchy have been created and tries to resolve the name again. If a widget reference still cannot be resolved, Mrm does not set the specified resource or add the specified callback. As of Motif 1.2, Mrm does not generate a warning message when this situation occurs.

The advantage of this functionality is that, unlike in C, you do not have to worry about the creation order of a widget hierarchy when you are specifying a widget as a resource value or callback parameter. UIL also makes the creation of OptionMenus and MenuBars easier by allowing you to specify a PulldownMenu as the child of an OptionMenu or CascadeButton. The `XmNsubMenuId` resource of the object is automatically set to widget ID of the menu. When specified as the child of a CascadeButton, the menu is created as a child of the MenuBar that contains the button. As a convenience, you can also specify a PopupMenu as the child of any widget (but not gadget).

As of Motif 1.2, the UIL compiler does not support user-defined imported widgets. If you need to import a user-defined widget, declare it with the type of a built-in widget that is a valid child for the context where the imported widget is used.



## Example

```
...
object romulus : XmPushButton gadget {
  callbacks {
    XmNactivateCallback = procedure create_Rome();
  };
};
object remus : imported XmPushButton;

object mars : XmForm {
  arguments {
    XmNbackground = color ('orange');
  };
  controls {
    ! Define a couple of children.
    XmPushButton romulus;
    unmanaged XmPushButton remus;
    ! Define an inline separator.
    XmSeparator { };
  };
};

object thing : user_defined procedure create_thing {
  ...
};
```

```
object scale : XmScale {
  controls {
    ! Set the labelString on the automatically created label.
    Xm_Title {
      arguments { XmNlabelString = 'Temperature'; };
    };
  };
};
...
```

## See Also

*MrmFetchWidget*(3), *MrmFetchWidgetOverride*(3), *MrmRegisterNames*(3), *MrmRegisterNamesInHierarchy*(3), *list*(5), *procedure*(5), *value*(5), *any*(6), *argument*(6), *compound_string_table*(6), *reason*(6), *widget*(6).

# Section 6

## UIL Data Types

*This section describes the data types supported by the User Interface Language (UIL). Many UIL data types correspond to types defined by Xlib, the Xt Intrinsics, the Motif toolkit, while some exist exclusively in UIL to aid in the definition of a user interface. Data types are presented alphabetically.*

*The first reference page,* Introduction, *explains the format and contents of each of the following pages. It also describes UIL expression syntax and summarizes the valid uses of each UIL type.*

### In This Section:

# Introduction

This page describes the format and contents of each reference page in Section 6, which covers each of the UIL data types.

## Name

Type – a brief description of the data type.

## Synopsis

**Syntax:** The literal syntax for specifying a value of the data type. Anything in `constant width` type should be typed exactly as shown. Items in *italics* are expressions that should be replaced by actual values when you specify a value. Anything enclosed in brackets is optional. An ellipsis ( . . . ) means that the previous expression can be repeated multiple times and a vertical bar ( | ) means to select one of a set of choices.

**MrmType:** The Mrm value type that corresponds to the data type. These types are returned by `MrmFetchLiteral()`.

## Availability

This section appears for data types that were added in Motif 1.2.

## Description

This section gives an overview of the data type. It explains the literal syntax that is used to specify a value of the type in a UIL module.

The UIL compiler supports `integer`, `float`, `single_float`, `boolean`, `string`, and `compound_string` expressions in most contexts where a value of one of the types is expected. Expressions can include literal or named values, but any named values that are used must be declared `private` or `exported` because the result of an expression cannot be computed if it contains an `imported` value.

The UIL compiler allows both string and arithmetic expressions. String expressions contain `NULL`-terminated strings and compound strings, while arithmetic expressions can contain `integer`, `float`, `single_float`, and `boolean` values.

A string expression, consists of two or more `string` or `compound_string` values concatenated with the string concatenation operator (&). The `string` and `compound_string` reference sections contains more details and examples of string concatenation.

An arithmetic expression consists of one or more `boolean`, `integer`, `single_float`, or `float` values and one or more arithmetic operators. The following operations can be used in arithmetic expressions:

| Operator | Type | Operand Types | Operation | Precedence |
|---|---|---|---|---|
| ~ | unary | boolean | NOT | 1 (highest) |
| | | integer | One's complement | 1 |
| - | unary | integer | Negation | 1 |
| | | float | Negation | 1 |

| Operator | Type | Operand Types | Operation | Precedence |
|---|---|---|---|---|
| + | unary | integer | None | 1 |
| | | float | None | 1 |
| * | binary | integer | Multiplication | 2 |
| | | float | Multiplication | 2 |
| / | binary | integer | Division | 2 |
| | | float | Division | 2 |
| + | binary | integer | Addition | 3 |
| | | float | Addition | 3 |
| – | binary | integer | Subtraction | 3 |
| | | float | Subtraction | 3 |
| >> | binary | integer | Shift right | 4 |
| << | binary | integer | Shift left | 4 |
| & | binary | boolean | AND | 5 |
| | | integer | Bitwise AND | 5 |
| \| | binary | boolean | OR | 6 |
| | | integer | Bitwise OR | 6 |
| ^ | binary | boolean | XOR | 6 |
| | | integer | Bitwise XOR | 6 (lowest) |

When the UIL compiler evaluates an expression, higher precedence operations are performed before those of lower precedence. Binary operations of equal precedence are evaluated from left to right, while unary operations of equal precedence are evaluated from right to left. You can change the default order of evaluation by using parentheses to group subexpressions that should be evaluated first. For example, in the expression `2+4*5`, `4*5` is evaluated first, followed by `20+2`. If the expression is written `(2+4)*5`, then `2+4` is evaluated first, followed by `6*5`.

The type of an expression is the type of its most complex operand. The UIL compiler converts the value of the less complex type in an operation to a value of the most complex type. The order of complexity for operands in a string expression is `string` followed by `compound_string`. For operations in an arithmetic expression, the order is `boolean`, `integer`, `single_float`, and `float`.

For example, if a string expression contains only strings, the type of the concatenated expression is `string`, but if it contains both strings and compound strings, its type is `compound_string`. The result of concatenating two `NULL`-terminated strings is a `NULL`-terminated string, unless the two strings have different character sets or writing directions, in which case the result is a compound string. If an arithmetic expression contains only integers, the type of an expression is `integer`, but if it contains both integers and floats, its type is `float`.

The table below summarizes the valid uses of the types documented in this section. For each type, the table indicates the supported storage classes. It also specifies whether or not values of the type can be specified literally and whether or not the type can be used for a procedure parameter and as an argument type. The final column lists the Motif Resource Manager (Mrm) routine that can be used to fetch values of the type. If certain information is not relevant for a type, the table entry indicates that it is not applicable (NA).

| Type | Supported Storage Classes | | | Literal | Reason/ | Fetch |
|---|---|---|---|---|---|---|
| | Private | Exported | Imported | Value | Parameter | Function |
| `any` | NA | NA | NA | No | Yes | NA |
| `argument` | Yes | No | No | Yes | No | NA |
| `asciz_table` | Yes | Yes | es | Yes | Yes | MrmFetchLiteral |
| `boolean` | Yes | Yes | Yes | Yes | Yes | MrmFetchLiteral |
| `character_set` | NA | NA | NA | Yes | No | NA |
| `class_rec_name` | Yes | Yes | Yes | Yes | Yes | MrmFetchLiteral |
| `color` | Yes | Yes | Yes | Yes | Yes | MrmFetchColor Literal |
| `color_table` | Yes | No | No | Yes | No | NA |
| `compound_string` | Yes | Yes | Yes | Yes | Yes | MrmFetchLiteral |
| `compound_string_table` | Yes | Yes | Yes | Yes | Yes | MrmFetchLiteral |
| `float` | Yes | Yes | Yes | Yes | Yes | MrmFetchLiteral |
| `font` | Yes | Yes | Yes | Yes | Yes | MrmFetchLiteral |
| `fontset` | Yes | Yes | Yes | Yes | Yes | MrmFetchLiteral |
| `font_table` | Yes | Yes | Yes | Yes | Yes | MrmFetchLiteral |
| `icon` | Yes | Yes | Yes | Yes | Yes | MrmFetchIcon Literal, MrmFetchBitmap Literal |
| `integer` | Yes | Yes | Yes | Yes | Yes | MrmFetchLiteral |
| `integer_table` | Yes | Yes | Yes | Yes | Yes | MrmFetchLiteral |
| `keysym` | Yes | Yes | Yes | Yes | Yes | MrmFetchLiteral |
| `pixmap` | No | No | Yes | No | Yes | NA |
| `reason` | Yes | No | No | Yes | No | NA |
| `rgb` | Yes | Yes | Yes | Yes | Yes | MrmFetchColor Literal |
| `single_float` | Yes | Yes | Yes | Yes | Yes | MrmFetchLiteral |
| `string` | Yes | Yes | Yes | Yes | Yes | MrmFetchLiteral |
| `translation_table` | Yes | Yes | Yes | Yes | Yes | MrmFetchLiteral |
| `wide_character` | Yes | Yes | Yes | Yes | Yes | MrmFetchLiteral |
| `widget` | Yes | Yes | Yes | Yes | Yes | MrmFetchWidget, MrmFetchWidget Override |
| `xbitmapfile` | Yes | Yes | Yes | Yes | Yes | MrmFetchIcon Literal |

The UIL compiler may not generate errors when some of the types are used incorrectly. These cases are documented in the individual type reference pages.

As of Motif version 1.2, the UIL compiler does not support the assignment of a `character_set` value to a named variable. A built-in or literal character set must be specifed in all contexts in which a character set is expected. In addition, prior to Motif 1.2.1, UIL may generate an error if the type `widget` is used as an argument or reason type. In this case, the type `any` can be used as a workaround.

### Usage

This section provides less formal information about the data type: when and how you might want to use it and things to watch out for.

### Example

This section provides examples of the use of the type.

### See Also

This section refers you to related functions, UIL file format sections, and UIL data types. The numbers in parentheses following each reference refer to the sections of this book in which they are found.

# any

## Name

any – type checking suppression type.

## Synopsis

**Syntax:** `any`

**MrmType:** `MrmRtypeAny`

## Description

The `any` type is used to suppress type checking for values passed to callback procedures or assigned to user-defined arguments. When a callback parameter or user defined-argument type is specified as `any`, the UIL compiler allows a value of any type to be used. Because the type `any` is only used to specify an expected type in these two cases, it does not have a literal syntax and values of type `any` cannot be defined or declared.

## Usage

The `any` type specifier is used when values of more than one type can be passed as a callback parameter or assigned to an argument. It can also be used when a callback or argument expects a type that is not predefined by the UIL compiler.

Since no type checking is performed on callback parameters or arguments declared as type `any`, it is possible to specify a value that is not expected by the callback or widget. You should use caution when specifying the value for a callback or argument that uses the `any` type.

## Example

```
...
! Define activate procedure that takes different arguments depending upon
! usage context.  Context must be checked in C code before value is used.
procedure
  activate (any);

! Define a resource that can be set to different types.
! Widget checks type field at run-time to determine value type.
value
  XtNlabelValue : argument ('labelValue', any);
  XtNlabelType  : argument ('labelType', integer);
```

## See Also

*procedure*(5),
*argument*(6).

UIL Data Types

# argument



## Name

argument – user-defined resource type.

## Synopsis

**Syntax:** `argument` ( *string_expression* [, *argument_type* ] )

**MrmType:** none

## Description

An `argument` value represents a user-defined resource. An `argument` is represented literally by the symbol `argument`, followed by a string expression that evaluates to the name of the resource and an optional resource type. The name of the resource is assigned to the name member of the `ArgList` structure passed to `XtSetValues()`. The name is typically the name of a resource with the `XmN` or `XtN` prefix removed. The type of the argument, if specified, is used by the UIL compiler to perform type checking of assignments to the resource. If omitted, the type defaults to `any`.

## Usage

A user-defined resource can be used in the `arguments` section of a UIL module, for both built-in Motif widgets and user-defined widgets. While user-defined arguments are typically assigned to a named variable in the `value` section, they can also be specified literally in the `arguments` section of an `object` definition. If you are defining arguments for a widget or widget set that is not predefined, you should define them as named variables in a separate UIL module that can be included by any module that uses the widget(s).

Arguments must be private values; they cannot be imported or exported. The UIL compiler allows imported and exported declarations, but it generates an error when the user-defined `argument` is used. Since `argument` values cannot be exported, they cannot be retrieved by an application.

The `argument` type can only be used to define non-callback resource types. The `reason` type is used to specify user-defined callback resources.

Some versions of the UIL compiler may not allow the definition of arguments of type `widget`. If you encounter this problem, use the type `any` as a workaround. The compiler may allow the definition of arguments of type `argument` or `reason`. If arguments with these types are used, the actual value set as the widget's resource is undefined.

## Example

From *Xaw/Tree.uih*:

```
! Resource and definitions for the Athena Tree widget.
value
  XtNautoReconfigure : argument ('autoReconfigure', boolean);
  XtNgravity : argument ('gravity', integer);
    NorthGravity  : 2;
    WestGravity   : 4;
```

```
      EastGravity  : 6;
      SouthGravity : 8;
    ! Use any type because compiler may not allow widget:
    XtNtreeParent : argument ('treeParent', any);
    ...
```

From *my_module.uil*:

```
include file 'Xaw/Tree.uih';

object parent : XmPushButton { }
object child : XmPushButton {
  arguments {
    XtNtreeParent = parent;
  };
};
object tree : procedure user_defined XawCreateTreeWidget {
  arguments {
    XtNautoReconfigure = false;
    XtNgravity = NorthGravity;
  };
  controls {
    XmPushButton parent;
    XmPushButton child;
  };
};
```

## See Also

*MrmRegisterClass*(3),
*include*(5), *object*(5),
*reason*(6).

# asciz_string_table



## Name

asciz_string_table – array of NULL-terminated strings.

## Synopsis

**Syntax:** `asciz_table` ( *string_expression* [, ... ] ) or

`asciz_string_table` ( *string_expression* [, ... ] )

**MrmType:** `MrmRtypeChar8Vector`

## Description

An `asciz_string_table` value represents an array of NULL-terminated strings. An `asciz_string_table` is represented literally by the symbol `asciz_table` or `asciz_string_table`, followed by a list of string expressions separated by commas. String variables in this list can be forward referenced.

## Usage

There are no built-in Motif resources of type `asciz_string_table`, so values of this type are usually passed as callback parameters or retrieved with `MrmFetchLiteral()`. The type `asciz_string_table` can be used as the type of an imported value, as a parameter type in a procedure declaration, or as the type in an `argument` literal. An `asciz_string_table` obtained by the application as a callback parameter, a widget resource, or with `MrmFetch-Literal()` is NULL-terminated.

## Example

```
...
! Declare a procedure that expects an array of NULL-terminated strings.
procedure
  set_names (asciz_table);

! Define a couple of asciz_tables
value
  dwarfs : asciz_table ('Dopey', 'Doc', 'Sneezy', 'Sleepy',
                        'Happy', 'Grumpy', 'Bashful');
  numbers : asciz_string_table (one, two);
  one   : 'one';
  two   : 'two';
  reindeer : imported asciz_string;

! Define some asciz_table resources.
value
  XtNniceList : argument ('niceList', asciz_table);
  XtNnaughtyList : argument ('naughtyList', asciz_table);
```

```
object doit : XmPushButton {
  callbacks {
    XmNactivateCallback = procedure set_names (dwarfs);
  };
};
...
```

## See Also

*MrmFetchLiteral*(3),
*procedure*(5),
*argument*(6), *compound_string*(6), *compound_string_table*(6), *string*(6).

# boolean

## Name

boolean – true/false type.

## Synopsis

**Syntax:** true | on | false | off

**MrmType:** MrmRtypeBoolean

## Description

Values of type boolean may be either true (on) or false (off). A boolean value is represented literally by true, false, on, or off. A boolean variable can be defined in the value section by setting a named variable to one of these literal values or to another boolean variable.

## Usage

The type name boolean can be used as the type of an imported value, as a parameter type in a procedure declaration, or as the type in an argument literal.

A boolean value can be explicitly converted to an integer, float, or single_float value by specifying the conversion type followed by the boolean value in parentheses. true and on convert to the value 1 or 1.0, while false and off convert to the value 0 or 0.0.

The storage allocated by Mrm for a boolean value is sizeof(int) not sizeof(Boolean). Because sizeof(Boolean) is less than sizeof(int) on many systems, you should use an int pointer rather than a Boolean pointer when retrieving a boolean value with MrmFetchLiteral().

## Example

```
...
procedure
  set_sleepy_state (boolean);

value
  map_flag : true;
  one      : integer (true);
  zero     : integer (false);
  debug    : imported boolean;
  XtNtimed : argument ('timed', boolean);

object sleep : XmPushButton {
  arguments {
    XmNmapWhenManaged = map_flag;
    XmNtraversalOn = off;
  };
```

```
        callbacks {
          XmNactivateCallback = procedure set_sleepy_state (true);
        };
      };
      ...
```

## See Also

*MrmFetchLiteral*(3),
*procedure*(5),
*argument*(6), *float*(6), *integer*(6), *single_float*(6).

# character_set

## Name

character_set – character set type for use with strings and font lists.

## Synopsis

**Syntax:**

```
character_set ( string_expression
                [, right_to_left = boolean_expression ]
                [, sixteen_bit = boolean_expression ] )
```

**MrmType:** none

## Description

The character_set type represents a user-defined character set that can be used when defining strings, compound_strings, fonts, fontsets, and font_tables. A character set specifies the encoding that is used for character values. A character_set is represented literally by the symbol character_set, followed by a string expression that names the character set and two optional properties.

If the right_to_left property of the character set for a string is set to true, the string is parsed and stored from right to left and compound strings created from the string have a direction component of XmSTRING_DIRECTION_R_TO_L. The default value of this property is false. The direction component used by a compound_string can be specified independently of the parsing direction using the compound_string literal syntax.

If the sixteen_bit property of the character set for a string is set to true, the string is interpreted as having double-byte characters. Strings with this property set to true must contain an even number of bytes or the UIL compiler generates an error.

## Usage

A character_set value is used to specify the character set for string, compound_string, font, fontset, and font_table values. The right_to_left and sixteen_bit properties only apply to strings and compound strings and have no effect on character sets specified for fonts and fontsets.

Unlike most of the UIL types, the character_set type cannot be assigned to a named variable in a value section, or used as the type of an imported value, as a parameter type in a procedure declaration, or as the type in an argument literal. A character set value can only be specified with the character_set literal syntax.

If a font, fontset, or font_table that uses a user-defined character set is exported or used as a resource value, the UIL compiler may exit with a severe internal error. As a result, only the predefined character sets can be used with font, fontset, and font_list values. You can work around this problem by specifying values of these types in an X resource file.

The UIL compiler may allow the use of string variables and the string concatenation operator (&) in a character_set name specification. Although no errors are generated, a string using such a character set may be incorrectly converted to a compound_string value. To avoid this problem, you should always specify a quoted string as the name in a `character_set` literal.

UIL defines a number of built-in character sets that you can use to define `string`, `compound_string`, `font`, `fontset`, and `font_table` values. The following table summarizes the built-in character sets:

| UIL Name | Character Set | Parse Direction | Writing Direction | 16 Bit |
|---|---|---|---|---|
| `iso_latin1` | ISO8859-1 | L to R | L to R | No |
| `iso_latin2` | ISO8859-2 | L to R | L to R | No |
| `iso_latin3` | ISO8859-3 | L to R | L to R | No |
| `iso_latin4` | ISO8859-4 | L to R | L to R | No |
| `iso_latin5` | ISO8859-5 | L to R | L to R | No |
| `iso_cyrillic` | ISO8859-5 | L to R | L to R | No |
| `iso_arabic` | ISO8859-6 | L to R | L to R | No |
| `iso_greek` | ISO8859-7 | L to R | L to R | No |
| `iso_latin8` | ISO8859-8 | R to L | R to L | No |
| `iso_latin8_lr` | ISO8859-8 | L to R | R to L | No |
| `iso_hebrew` | ISO8859-8 | R to L | R to L | No |
| `iso_hebrew_lr` | ISO8859-8 | L to R | R to L | No |
| `gb_hanzi` | GB2313.1980-0 | L to R | L to R | Yes |
| `gb_hanzi_gr` | GB2313.1980-1 | L to R | L to R | Yes |
| `jis_kanji` | JISX0208.1983-0 | L to R | L to R | Yes |
| `jis_kanji_gr` | JISX0208.1983-1 | L to R | L to R | Yes |
| `jis_katakana` | JISX0201.1976-0 | L to R | L to R | No |
| `ksc_hangul` | KSC5601.1987-0 | L to R | L to R | Yes |
| `ksc_hangul_gr` | KSC5601.1987-1 | L to R | L to R | Yes |

## Example

```
...
value
  ! Define font with user-defined character set.
  big: font ('*times-medium-r-normal-*-240-75-75-*',
              character_set = character_set ('body'));
  ! Declare some strings with user-defined character sets.
  player : #character_set (big) "Mookie Wilson";


  hello : exported #iso_hebrew "\355\\345\\354\\371\";
...
```

## See Also

*compound_string*(6), *font*(6), *fontset*(6), *font_table*(6), *string*(6).

# class_rec_name

## Name

class_rec_name – widget class pointer type.

## Synopsis

**Syntax:** `class_rec_name` ( *string_expression* )

**MrmType:** `MrmRtypeClassRecName`

## Availability

Motif 1.2 and later.

## Description

The `class_rec_name` type represents a pointer to a widget class record. A `class_rec_name` value is represented literally by the symbol `class_rec_name`, followed by a string that specifies the class name. The string can either be the name of a class from a widget's class definition or the name of a widget creation function registered with `MrmRegisterClass()`. The string is converted to a widget class pointer at run-time by Mrm when a `class_rec_name` value is referenced. Mrm finds the widget class pointer corresponding to the name by searching the list of widgets registered with `MrmRegisterClass()`. This list includes the built-in Motif widgets and any user-defined widgets that have been registered.

## Usage

The type `clas_rec_name` can be used as the type of an imported value, as the parameter type in a procedure declaration, or as the type in an `argument` literal. None of the built-in Motif widgets have a `class_rec_name` resource, however. If a `class_rec_name` value is specified as a resource value for a widget and the conversion of the class name string to a widget class pointer fails at run-time (inside a call to `MrmFetchWidget()`, `MrmFetchWidgetOverride()`, or `MrmFetchSetValues()`), Mrm does not set the resource. If `MrmFetchLiteral()` is used to retrieve the value and the conversion fails, `MrmNOT_FOUND` is returned.

## Example

```
...
value
  pbclass : class_rec_name ('XmPushButton');
...
```

## See Also

*MrmFetchSetValues*(3), *MrmFetchWidget*(3), *MrmFetchWidgetOverride*(3), *MrmInitialize*(3), *MrmRegisterClass*(3),
*procedure*(5),
*argument*(6).

# color

## Name

color – color specified as color name.

## Synopsis

**Syntax:** `color` ( *string_expression* [ `foreground` | `background` ] )

**MrmType:** `MrmRtypeColor`

## Description

A `color` value represents a named color. A `color` is represented literally by the symbol `color`, followed by a string expression that evaluates to the color name and an optional `foreground` or `background` property to indicate how the color is displayed on a monochrome screen. Mrm converts the color name to an X `Color` at run-time with `XAllocNamedColor()` on a color display, or chooses black or white on a monochrome display. The X server maintains a color name database that is used to map color names to RGB values. The text version of this database is typically in the file */usr/lib/x11/rgb.txt*. See Volume One, *Xlib Programming Manual* and Volume Two, *Xlib Reference Manual*, for more information on color allocation.

## Usage

The `color` type can be used as the type of an imported value, as a parameter type in a procedure declaration, or as the type in an `argument` literal. An `rgb` value can also be specified in any context that a `color` value is valid. There are several built-in Motif `color` resources, such as `XmNforeground` and `XmNbackground`.

The optional `foreground` and `background` properties can be used to specify the mapping of colors on a monochrome display or when a color allocation fails because the colormap is full. Mrm dynamically determines the appropriate foreground or background color based on the context in which a `color` value is used.

When a `color` is used as a resource value for a widget (directly or indirectly in an icon's `color_table`), the background and foreground colors are obtained from the widget. When a color is retrieved for the `color_table` of an icon retrieved with `MrmFetchIconLiteral()`, the background and foreground colors are supplied by the application as arguments to the function.

If the `foreground` or `background` property is not specified, Mrm uses the `Color` returned by `XAllocNamedColor()` on a monochrome display. When an allocation fails on a color display and neither property is specified, black is used. In addition, black is always used when an allocation on a color display fails in `MrmFetchColorLiteral()`; the procedure does not take fallback `background` and `foreground` colors arguments.

As of Motif version 1.2.1, the color substitutions described above do not take place. When a color allocation fails for a `color` specified directly or indirectly as a resource value, the resource is not set. If the allocation fails in a call to `MrmFetchColorLiteral()` or `MrmFetchIconLiteral()`, `MrmNOT_FOUND` is returned.

## Example

```
...
value
  background : color ('chocolate mint', background);
  foreground : color ('whipped cream', foreground);

object label: XmLabel {
  arguments {
    XmNbackground = color('red');
  };
};
...
```

## See Also

*MrmFetchColorLiteral*(3), *MrmFetchIconLiteral*(3), *MrmFetchSetValues*(3), *MrmFetchWidget*(3), *MrmFetchWidgetOverride*(3),
*color_table*(6), *icon*(6), *rgb*(6).

# color_table

## Name

color_table – character-to-color mapping type.

## Synopsis

**Syntax:** `color_table` ( *color_expression* = *'character'* [, ...] )

**MrmType:** none

## Description

A `color_table` value is used to define a mapping from color names or RGB values to the single characters that are used to represent pixel values in icons. A `color_table` is represented literally by the symbol `color_table`, followed by a list of mappings. Each mapping associates a previously-defined color value with a single character. A color value can be a variable or a literal of type `color` or `rgb`, the global `background color`, or the symbol `foreground color`.

## Usage

The sole purpose of a `color_table` is to define colors that can be used in an `icon` definition. Because the color mappings are needed at compile-time to construct an icon, a `color_table` value must be `private`. The UIL compiler may allow an imported or exported `color_table` definition, but it generates an error when the value is used. Unlike most other UIL types, a `color_table` cannot be used as a parameter type in a procedure declaration or as the type in an `argument` literal.

The color values `background color` and `foreground color` can be used to map a character to the background or foreground color. These colors are determined at run-time by Mrm, based on the context in which an `icon` is used. When an `icon` is a resource value for a widget, the foreground and background colors are obtained from the widget. When an `icon` is retrieved by the application with `MrmFetchIconLiteral()`, the foreground and background colors are supplied by the application as arguments to the function.

The colors in a `color_table` are allocated at run-time by Mrm when an icon that uses the color table is retrieved as the value for a widget resource or retrieved by the application with `MrmFetchIconLiteral()`. See the `color` reference page for a description of how Mrm allocates colors and what happens when a color allocation fails.

The UIL compiler may not perform type checking on the color values in a `color_table`. If the compiler allows the use of a value that is not a `color`, it will crash when the `color_table` is used.

## Example

```
...
value
  blue : color ('blue');
  yellow : rgb (65535,65535,0);
  pallete :
    color_table (background color = ' ', foreground color = '*',
```

```
                    color ('red') = 'r', rgb (0,65535,0) = 'g',
                    blue = 'b', yellow = 'y');

    plus : icon (color_table = pallete,
                 'brb',
                 'rrr',
                 'brb');
   ...
```

## See Also

*MrmFetchIconLiteral*(3),
*color*(6), *icon*(6), *rgb*(6).

# compound_string

## Name

compound_string – Motif compound string type.

## Synopsis

**Syntax:** `compound_string (` *string_expression*
`[, character_set =` *character_set* `]`
`[, right_to_left =` *boolean_expression* `]`
`[, separate =` *boolean_expression* `] )`

**MrmType:** `MrmRtypeCString`

## Description

A `compound_string` value represents a Motif `XmString`. An `XmString` is the data type for a Motif compound string. The Motif toolkit uses compound strings, rather than character strings, to represent most text values. A compound string is composed of one or more segments, where each segment can contain a font list element tag, a string direction, and a text component. The tag specifies the font, and thus the character set, that is used to display the text component.

UIL-generated `compound_strings` can contain up to four components: a single-byte, multi-byte, or wide-character string, a character set, a writing direction, and a separator. Like NULL-terminated strings, `compound_strings` can be concatenated with the concatenation operator (&). A `compound_string` is represented literally by the symbol `compound_string`, followed by a string expression and an optional list of properties. The valid properties are `character_set`, `right_to_left`, and `separate`. They may be specified in any order, but each may occur only once.

The `character_set` property is used to establish the character set of the `compound_string`. It can be set to one of the UIL built-in character sets or to a user-defined character set. If a character set is specified in the definition of the string using the `#`*`character_set`* notation, it takes precedence over the `character_set` property setting. If the `character_set` property is omitted, the default character set of the module is used.

The `right_to_left` property is used to set the writing direction of the `compound_string`. If the `right_to_left` property is omitted, the writing direction defaults to that of the character set of the compound_string.

When the `separate` property is set to `true`, UIL adds a separator component to the end of the `compound_string`. Separators usually appear as line breaks when a compound string is displayed. If omitted, the `separate` property defaults to `false`. Newline characters present in the string expression of a compound string literal are not converted to separators.

## Usage

When a `compound_string` literal contains a string expression consisting of two or more concatenated strings, they are combined into a single component if the character set and writing direction of each is the same. If any of the character sets differ, each string is placed in a separate string component with its own character set and direction components. If the separate property is set to true, a separator component is added to the end of the entire compound_string.

A compound_string with a character_set that differs from XmFALLBACK_-CHARSET is only displayed correctly in a Motif widget if the XmFontList of the widget includes an XFontStruct or an XFontSet entry for the character_set.

The type compound_string can also be used as the type of an imported value, as a parameter type in a procedure declaration, or as the type in an argument literal.

## Example

```
...
procedure
  set_label_string (compound_string);

value
  ying  : "Ying";
  yang  : #iso_latin1"Yang";

  left  : compound_string (ying, character_set=iso_latin1, separate=true);
  right : compound_string (yang, right_to_left=true);
  day   : compound_string ('moon' & ' ' & 'sun');
  other : imported compound_string;

  lines : exported left & right;

object verse : XmLabel {
  arguments {
    XmNlabelString = lines;
  };
};

value
  XtNgraphicCaption : argument ('graphicCaption', compound_string);
...
```

## See Also

*XmStringCreate*(1), *XmStringCreateLocalized*(1),
*character_set*(6), *compound_string_table*(6), *string*(6).

# compound_string_table

## Name

compound_string_table – array of compound strings.

## Synopsis

**Syntax:** `compound_string_table` ( *string_expression* [, ...] ) or

`string_table` ( *string_expression* [, ...] )

**MrmType:** `MrmRtypeCStringVector`

## Description

A `compound_string_table` value represents an array of Motif `XmStrings`. An `XmString` is the data type for a Motif compound string. The Motif toolkit uses compound strings, rather than character strings, to represent most text values. A compound string is composed of one or more segments, where each segment can contain a font list element tag, a string direction, and a text component. The tag specifies the font, and thus the character set, that is used to display the text component.

A `compound_string_table` is represented literally by the symbol `compound_string_table` or `string_table`, followed by a list of `string` or `compound_string` expressions. The UIL compiler automatically converts a `string` expression to a `compound_string`.

## Usage

A common use of `compound_string_table` values is to set resources of the type `XmStringTable` in a UIL module or in the application with `MrmFetchSetValues()`. When a `compound_string_table` is assigned to a built-in `XmStringTable` resource, UIL automatically sets the corresponding count resource. The table below lists the `XmStringTable` resources and their related count resources.

| Widget | XmStringTable Resource | Related Resource |
|---|---|---|
| XmList | `XmNitems` | `XmNitemCount` |
| XmList | `XmNselectedItems` | `XmNselectedItemCount` |
| XmSelectionBox | `XmNlistItems` | `XmNlistItemCount` |
| XmCommand | `XmNhistoryItems` | `XmNhistoryItemCount` |
| XmFileSelectionBox | `XmNdirListItems` | `XmNdirListItemCount` |
| XmFileSelectionBox | `XmNfileListItems` | `XmNfileListItemCount` |

The associated count is not automatically set for `compound_string_tables` that are assigned using `MrmFetchSetValues()`.

The type `compound_string_table` can also be used as the type of an imported value, as a parameter type in a procedure declaration, or as the type in an `argument` literal. A `compound_string_table` that is obtained by the application as a callback parameter, a widget resource, or with `MrmFetchLiteral()` is `NULL`-terminated.

If a compound_string_table contains a forward reference to a compound_string value, all items in the list before that entry may be lost by the UIL compiler. To avoid this problem, you should be sure to define all compound_strings used in a compound_string_table before they are referenced.

## Example

```
...
procedure
  set_items (string_table);

value
  fruit_list : string_table ('apple', 'banana', 'grape');

object list : XmList {
  arguments {
    XmNitems = fruit_list;
  };
};

value
  XtNnameList : argument ('nameList', compound_string_list);
...
```

## See Also

*character_set*(6), *compound_string*(6), *string*(6).

## Name

float – double-precision floating point type.

## Synopsis

**Syntax:** [ + | - ]*integer* . *integer* [ e [ + | - ]*integer* ]

**MrmType:** `MrmRtypeFloat`

## Description

A `float` value represents a negative or positive double-precision floating point number. A `float` is represented literally by an optional sign, one or more consecutive digits which must include a decimal point, and an optional exponent. The UIL compiler uses `atof()` to convert literal float values to the architecture's internal representation.

A `float` can also be represented literally by the symbol `float` followed by a `boolean`, `integer`, or `single_float` expression. The expression is converted to a `float` and can be used in any context that a `float` value is valid. A `float` is formed from a `boolean` by converting `true` and `on` to 1.0 and `false` and `off` to 0.0.

## Usage

The allowable range of a `float` value is determined by the size of a C `double` on the machine where the UIL module is compiled. Since a `double` on most architectures is typically a minimum of four bytes, `float` values may safely range from 1.4013e-45 to 3.40282e+38 (positive or negative). Although many architectures represent a `double` using eight bytes, you can ensure greater portability by keeping `float` values within the four-byte range. The UIL compiler generates an error if it encounters a `float` outside of the machine's representable range.

The type `float` can be used as the type of an imported value, as a parameter type in a procedure declaration, or as the type in an `argument` literal.

## Example

```
...
! Declare some floating point values.
value
  pi : 3.14159;
  burn_rate : imported float;
  one_point_oh : float (true);
  ten_even: float (10);

! Declare a procedure which takes a float parameter.
procedure
  set_temperature (float);

! Declare an argument of type float.
value
  XtNorbitalVelocity : argument ('orbitalVelocity', float);
...
```

## See Also

*boolean*(6), *integer*(6), *single_float*(6).

# font

## Name

font – XFontStruct type.

## Synopsis

**Syntax:** font ( *string_expression* [, character_set = *character_set* ] )

**MrmType:** MrmRtypeFont

## Description

A font value represents an XFontStruct, which is an Xlib structure that specifies font metric information. A font is represented literally by the symbol font, followed by a string expression that evaluates to the name of the font and an optional character_set. All parts of the string expression that make up the font name must be private to the UIL module. The character_set is associated with the font if it appears in a font_table. If character_set is not specified, it is determined from the codeset portion of the LANG environment variable if it is set, or XmFALLBACK_CHARSET otherwise.

The string expression that specifies the font name is an X Logical Font Description (XLFD) string. This string is stored in the UID file and used as a parameter to XLoadQueryFont() at run-time to load the font. See Volume One, *Xlib Programming Manual*, and Volume Two, *Xlib Reference Manual*, for more information on fonts.

## Usage

You can use a font value to specify a font or font_table resource. When a font is assigned to a font_table resource, at run-time Mrm automatically creates an XmFont-List that contains only the specified font. A font value can also be used as an element in font_table, although in this context it must be private to the UIL module.

The font type can be used as the type of an imported value, as a parameter type in a procedure declaration, or as the type in an argument literal.

In some versions of UIL, the default character_set is always ISO8859-1, instead of being based on the LANG environment variable or XmFALLBACK_CHARSET.

The UIL compiler may exit with a severe interal error if a user-defined character_set is used in a font that is exported or specified as a resource value. If this problem occurs in your version of UIL, only predefined character_set values can be used in font, fontset, and font_table values. The workaround is to specify these problematic values in an X resource file.

## Example

```
...
procedure
  change_font (font);

value
  title_font : font ('-*-helvetica-bold-r-normal-*-160-100-100-*-iso8859-1');
  family : 'courier';
```

```
  style  : 'medium';
  body_font : font ('-*-' & family &'-'& style &
                    '-r-normal-*-120-100-100*-iso8859-1');
  kanjiFont : font ('-*-JISX0208.1983-1', character_set = jis_kanji);

  default_font : imported font;

value
  XtNheadlineFont : argument ('headlineFont', font);

object label: XmLabel {
  arguments {
    XmNfontList = title_font;
  };
};
...
```

## See Also

*character_set*(6), *fontset*(6), *font_table*(6).

# fontset

## Name

fontset – XFontSet type.

## Synopsis

**Syntax:** fontset ( *string_expression* [, ...] [, character_set = *character_set* ] )

**MrmType:** MrmRtypeFontSet

## Availability

Motif 1.2 and later.

## Description

A fontset value represents an XFontSet, which is an Xlib structure that specifies all of the fonts that are needed to display text in a particular locale. A fontset is represented literally by the symbol fontset, followed by a list of string expressions that evaluate to font names and an optional character_set. All parts of the string expressions that make up the list of font names must be private to the UIL module. The character_set is associated with the fontset if it appears in a font_table. If character_set is not specified, it is determined from the codeset portion of the LANG environment variable if it is set, or XmFALLBACK_CHARSET otherwise.

The string expression that specifies the font name is a list or wildcarded set of X Logical Font Description (XLFD) strings. This list is stored in the UID file and used as a parameter to XCreateFontSet() at run-time to load the font set. See Volume One, *Xlib Programming Manual*, and Volume Two, *Xlib Reference Manual*, for more information on fonts.

## Usage

You can use a fontset value to specify a fontset or font_table resource. When a fontset is assigned to a font_table resource, at run-time Mrm automatically creates an XmFontList that contains only the specified fontset. A fontset value can also be used as an element in font_table, although in this context it must be private to the UIL module.

The fontset type can be used as the type of an imported value, as a parameter type in a procedure declaration, or as the type in an argument literal.

In some versions of UIL, the default character set is always ISO8859-1, instead of being based on the LANG environment variable or XmFALLBACK_CHARSET.

The UIL compiler may exit with a severe internal error if a user-defined character_set is used in a fontset that is exported or specified as a resource value. If this problem occurs in your version of UIL, only predefined character_set values can be used in font, fontset, and font_table values. The workaround is to specify these problematic values in an X resource file.

## Example

```
...
procedure
  change_fontset (fontset);

value
  japanese_font : fontset ('-misc-fixed-*-75-75-*');
  default_font : imported font;

value
  XtNbodyFontSet : argument ('bodyFontSet', fontset);

object label: XmLabel {
  arguments {
    XmNfontList = japanese_font;
  };
};
...
```

## See Also

*character_set*(6), *font*(6), *font_table*(6).

# font_table

## Name

font_table – Motif font list type.

## Synopsis

**Syntax:** `font_table ( [ character_set = ] font_expression [, ...] )`

**MrmType:** `MrmRtypeFontList`

## Description

A `font_table` value represents a Motif `XmFontList`. An `XmFontList` is a data type that specifies the fonts that are in use. Each entry in a font list specifies a font or a font set and an associated tag. When a Motif compound string (`XmString`) is displayed, the font list tag for the string is used to match the string with a font or a font set, so that the compound string is displayed appropriately.

In UIL, a `font_table` is represented literally by the symbol `font_table`, followed by a list of one or more `font` or `fontset` values. The elements of a `font_table` must be defined as `private` values. The `character_set` of an entry in the list can be overridden by preceding it with a predefined or user-defined `character_set` and an equal sign (=).



## Usage

The `font_table` type can be used as the type of an imported value, as a parameter type in a procedure declaration, or as the type in an `argument` literal. A `font_table` is converted to an `XmFontList` at run-time by Mrm.

The UIL compiler may exit with a severe interal error if a user-defined `character_set` is used in a `font_table` that is exported or specified as a resource value. This situation can occur if `character_set` is specified directly or indirectly in one of the entries. If this problem occurs in your version of UIL, only predefined `character_set` values can be used in `font`, `fontset`, and `font_table` values. The workaround is to specify these problematic values in an X resource file.

## Example

```
...
procedure
  switch_styles (font_table);

value
  latin1 : font ('*-iso8859-1', character_set = iso_latin1);
  hebrew : font ('*-iso8859-8', character_set = iso_hebrew);
  list : font_table (latin1, hebrew);

value
  XtNdefaultFonts : argument ('defaultFonts', font_table);

object label: XmLabel {
  arguments {
    XmNfontList = list;
```

```
    };
  };
  ...
```

## See Also

*XmFontListAppendEntry*(1), *XmFontListEntryCreate*(1), *XmFontListEntryLoad*(1), *character_set*(6), *font*(6), *fontset*(6).

# icon

## Name

icon – multi-color rectangular pixmap type.

## Synopsis

**Syntax:** `icon ( [ color_table =` *color_table_name* ,] *row* [, ... ] )

**MrmType:** `MrmRtypeIconImage`

## Description

An `icon` value represents a multi-color rectangular pixmap, or array of pixel values. An `icon` is represented literally by the symbol `icon`, followed by an optional `color_table` specification and a list of strings that represent the rows of pixel values in the `icon`.

If a `color_table` is specified, it must be a `private` value and cannot be forward referenced. If a `color_table` is not specified, the following default `color_table` is used:

```
color_table (background_color = ' ', foreground color = '*')
```

Each *row* in the `icon` is a character expression that represents a row of pixel values. Each character in the row represents a single pixel. All of the rows in the `icon` must be the same length and must contain only characters defined in the `color_table` for the icon. The UIL compiler generates an error if these rules are violated.



## Usage

The type `icon` can be used as the type of an imported value, as a parameter type in a procedure declaration, or as the type in an `argument` literal. An `icon` can be retrieved by an application with `MrmFetchIconLiteral()` or `MrmFetchBitmapLiteral()`.

When an `icon` is specified as a resource value for a widget, the depth of the pixmap created by Mrm at run-time is the same as the depth of the widget. When an `icon` is retrieved with `MrmFetchIconLiteral()`, the depth of the resulting pixmap is the value returned from the `DefaultDepthOfScreen()` macro. When an `icon` is retrieved with `MrmFetchBitmapLiteral()`, the depth of the resulting pixmap is always one. The `color_table` of an `icon` retrieved with this function must only contain mappings for `background color` and `foreground color` or the function fails and returns `MrmNOT_FOUND`.

The UIL compiler may not check the type of the value specified as the `color_table` for an `icon`. If the compiler allows the specification of a value that is not a `color_table`, it generates an error message when the icon is referenced. If no reference to the icon occurs in the module, the compiler exits with a severe internal error.

If the row values in an `icon` literal do not consist entirely of string literals, the UIL compiler may generate an error message or crash with a segmentation violation.

If a named value is declared as an imported `icon` in one UIL module file, but defined with a different type in another, an error is generated at run time when Mrm attempts to retrieve the `icon`. If you attempt to define a named variable with the value of an `icon` variable, the UIL compiler may generate a large number of errors that are seemingly unrelated to the assignment.

## Example

```
...
value
  ! Define an icon that uses default color table and can be retrieved
  ! as a resource or with any of the fetch procedures including
  ! MrmFetchBitmapLiteral():

  checker : icon ('* *',
                  ' * ',
                  '* *');

  ! Define an icon that uses a custom color table which contains named
  ! colors.  This icon cannot be retrieved with MrmFetchBitmapLiteral().

  red_blue : color_table (color('red') = 'r', color('blue') = 'b');

  plus : icon (color_table = red_blue,
               'brb',
               'rrr',
               'brb');

  ! Declare an argument of type icon.
  XtNwmIcon : argument ('wmIcon', icon);

! Declare a procedure taking an icon parameter.
procedure
  display_icon (icon);

! Use an icon for a resource value.
object label: XmLabel {
  arguments {
    XmNlabelType = XmPIXMAP;
    XmNlabelPixmap = plus;
  };
};
...
```

## See Also

*MrmFetchBitmapLiteral*(3), *MrmFetchIconLiteral*(3), *MrmFetchSetValues*(3), *MrmFetchWidget*(3), *MrmFetchWidgetOverride*(3),
*color_table*(6), *pixmap*(6), *xbitmapfile*(6).

## Name

integer – whole number type.

## Synopsis

**Syntax:** `[ + | - ]0-9[...]`

**MrmType:** `MrmRtypeInteger`

## Description

An `integer` value represents a negative or positive whole number. An `integer` is represented literally by an optional sign followed by one or more consecutive digits.

An `integer` can also be represented literally by the symbol `integer` followed by a `float`, `single_float`, or `boolean` expression. The expression is converted to an `integer` and can be used in any context that an `integer` value is valid. An `integer` is formed from a `float` or `single_float` by truncating the fractional value. You can add 0.5 to the `float` or `single_float` value if rounding is desired. If a `float` or `single_float` larger (smaller) than `MAXINT` (`-MAXINT`) is converted to an `integer`, the resulting value is `MAXINT` (`MININT`). An `integer` is formed from a `boolean` by converting `true` and `on` to 1 and `false` and `off` to 0.

## Usage

The allowable range of an `integer` value is determined by the size of an integer on the machine where the UIL module is compiled. Since an integer on most architectures is typically a minimum of four bytes, `integer` values may safely range from -2147483647 (`-MAXINT`) to 2147483647 (`MAXINT`). You can ensure greater portability by keeping `integer` values within the four-byte range. The UIL compiler generates an error if it encounters an `integer` outside of the machine's representable range.

The type `integer` can be used as the type of an imported value, as a parameter type in a procedure declaration, or as the type in an `argument` literal.

Widget resources of type `Position` (`short`) and `Dimension` (`unsigned short`) are specified as integers in UIL. As a result, the UIL compiler does not generate an error if an out-of-range value is assigned to such a resource. If the `sizeof(short)` is smaller than `sizeof(int)`, part of the out-of-range value is truncated, which produces an undefined result. The part truncated depends on the C compiler and byte-ordering of the machine on which the UIL module is compiled. For maximum portability, `Position` values should be limited to the range -32768 to 32767 and `Dimension` values should be limited to the range 0 to 65536.

The UIL compiler uses `-MAXINT` to `MAXINT`, not `MININT` to `MAXINT`, as the allowable range for integers, which means that on an architecture with four-byte integers, the minimum `integer` value allowed is -2147483647, not -2147483648. The value `MININT` can be used, however, by converting a `float` smaller than `-MAXINT` to an `integer`.

## Example

```
...
! Declare a procedure taking an integer value.
procedure
  set_speed (integer);

! Define some integer variables.
value
  meaning_of_life: 41;
  the_question : imported integer;
  half_life: meaning_of_life / 2;
  ten : integer (10.75);
  round_factor : 0.5;
  eleven : integer (10.75 + round_factor);
  one : integer (true);
  ! Generate MININT value by converting large negative float:
  minint : integer (-3.0e30);

! Define an argument of type integer.
value
  XtNsize : argument ('size', integer);

object pb : XmPushButton {
  arguments {
    XmNleftOffset = -3;
  };
};
...
```

## See Also

*boolean*(6), *float*(6), *integer_table*(6), *single_float*(6).

# integer_table

## Name

integer_table – array of integers.

## Synopsis

**Syntax:** `integer_table` ( *integer_expression* [, ...] )

**MrmType:** `MrmRtypeIntegerVector`

## Description

An `integer_type` value represents an array of integers. An `integer_table` is represented literally by the symbol `integer_table`, followed by a list of `integer` expressions.

## Usage

The type name `integer_table` can be used as the type of an imported value, as a parameter type in a procedure declaration, or as the type in an `argument` literal. The `XmNselectionArray` resource of the `XmText` and `XmTextField` widgets is the only built-in `integer_table` resource. When the resource is set, UIL automatically sets the `XmNselectionArrayCount` resource to the number of elements in the array.

Unlike `asciz_string_table` and `compound_string_table` values, an `integer_table` is not NULL-terminated. As a result, you must either use `integer_table` values of a set length, include the length explicitly, or use a value to indicate the end of the array. The application code that uses the values must use the same conventions as the UIL module.

## Example

```
...
value
  ! Define table with known number of elements (12).
  days: integer_table (31, 28, 31, 30, 31, 30, 31, 31, 30, 31, 30, 31);

  ! Define table with length as first element.
  grades : integer_table (5, 95, 87, 100, 92, 82);

  ! Define table with last element of MININT.
  end_of_table : integer (3.0e-30);
  ages : integer_table (25, 29, 29, 30, 32, end_of_table);

! Declare a procedure taking an integer_table
procedure
  compute_average (integer_table);

! Declare an argument taking an integer table
value
  XtNdaysPerMonth : argument ('daysPerMonth', integer_table);
...
```

UIL Data Types

## See Also

*integer*(6).

# keysym

## Name

keysym – character type.

## Synopsis

**Syntax:** `keysym` ( *string_literal* )

**MrmType:** `MrmRtypeKeysym`

## Description

A `keysym` value is used to represent a single character. A `keysym` is represented literally by the symbol `keysym`, followed by a string value that contains exactly one character. If the string is a variable, it can be forward referenced and must be private to the UIL module.

## Usage

A `keysym` value is typically used to specify a widget mnemonic resource, such as `XmNmnemonic`. The `keysym` type can be used as the type of an imported value, as a parameter type in a procedure declaration, or as the type in an `argument` literal.

When a `keysym` is retrieved by an application with `MrmFetchLiteral()`, the `value` argument returned is the character value of the `keysym`, not a pointer to the value like many other types.

The UIL compiler may not generate an error if the string expression in a `keysym` literal is more than one character long, but an error will be generated by Mrm at run-time. If an invalid `keysym` is specified as a resource value, the resource is not set. If the application attempts to retrieve an invalid `keysym` with `MrmFetchLiteral()`, `MrmNOT_FOUND` is returned.

## Example

```
...
procedure
  set_keysym (keysym);

value
  d_key : keysym ('d');

  XtNquitKey : argument ('quitKey', keysym);

object the_button : XmPushButton {
  arguments {
    XmNmnemonic = keysym ('b');
  };
};
...
```

## See Also

*MrmFetchLiteral*(3).

# pixmap



## Name

pixmap – generic icon or xbitmapfile type.

## Synopsis

**Syntax:** No literal syntax.

**MrmType:** `MrmRtypeIconImage` or `MrmRtypeXBitmapFile`

## Description

A `pixmap` value can be either an `icon` or `xbitmapfile`. In either case, the type specifies an array of pixel values. A `pixmap` does not have its own literal representation; a `pixmap` value is specified with either the `icon` or `xbitmapfile` literal syntax.

## Usage

The type `pixmap` can be used as the type of an imported value, as a parameter type in a procedure declaration, or as the type in an `argument` literal. The purpose of the `pixmap` type is to allow either an `icon` or an `xbitmapfile` value to be imported, passed as a callback argument, or specified as a resource value.

## Example

```
...
value
  ! Declare an imported pixmap that can be defined as an icon or xbitmapfile.
  stop_pixmap : imported pixmap;

  ! Declare an argument to which an icon or xbitmapfile can be assigned.
  XtNstipplePixmap : argument ('stipplePixmap', pixmap);

! Declare a procedure to which an icon or xbitmapfile can be passed.
procedure
  print_pixmap (pixmap);
...
```

## See Also

*icon*(6), *xbitmapfile*(6).

## Name

reason – user-defined callback type.

## Synopsis

**Syntax:** `reason` ( *string_expression* )

**MrmType:** none

## Description

A `reason` value represents a user-defined callback. A `reason` is represented literally by the symbol `reason`, followed by a string expression that evaluates to the name of a callback. The name of the `reason` is assigned to the name member of the `ArgList` structure passed to `XtSetValues()`. The name is typically the name of a callback with the `XmN` or `XtN` prefix removed.

## Usage

A user-defined callback can be used in the `callbacks` section of a UIL module for both built-in Motif widgets and user-defined widgets. While user-defined callbacks are typically assigned to a named variable in the `value` section, they can also be specified literally in the `arguments` section of an `object` definition. If you are defining arguments for a widget or widget set which is not predefined, you should define them as named variables in a separate UIL module that can be included by any module that uses the widget(s).

Reasons must be private values; they cannot be imported or exported. The UIL compiler allows imported and exported declarations, but it generates an error when the user-defined `reason` is used. Since `reason` values cannot be exported, they cannot be retrieved by an application.

The `reason` type can only be used to define callback resource types. The `argument` type is used to specify other user-defined resources.

## Example

From *Xaw/Panner.uih*:

```
! Resources and definitions for the Athena Panner widget.
...
! Callback definitions
value
  XtNreportCallback = reason ('XtNreportCallback');
...
```

From *my_module.uil*:

```
include file 'Xaw/Panner.uih';

procedure
  panner_report();

object panner : user_defined procedure XawCreatePanner {
```

```
    callbacks {
      XtNreportCallback = procedure panner_report();
    };
  };
  ...
```

## See Also

*MrmRegisterClass*(3),
*include*(5), *object*(5),
*argument*(6).

# rgb

## Name

rgb – color specified with the values of red, green, and blue components.

## Synopsis

**Syntax:** `rgb` ( *red_integer*, *green_integer*, *blue_integer* )

**MrmType:** `MrmRtypeColor`

## Description

The type `rgb` represents a color as a mixture of red, green, and blue values. An `rgb` value is represented literally by the symbol `rgb`, followed by a list of three integers that specify the red, green, and blue components of the color. The amount of each color component can range from 0 (0 percent) to 65,535 (100 percent). Mrm allocates `rgb` values with `XAllocColor()`. See Volume One, *Xlib Programming Manual*, and Volume Two, *Xlib Reference Manual*, for more information on color allocation.

## Usage

An `rgb` value or literal can be used anywhere a `color` value is expected: as a callback argument, as a resource value, or in a `color_table`. Unlike `color` values, it is not possible to specify a foreground or background fallback for `rgb` values. For this reason, and to maximize the number of sharable color cells, you should use named colors defined with the `color` type whenever possible.

If a color cannot be allocated, Mrm substitutes black, unless the color is specified as the `background color` or `foreground color` in a `color_table` and the `foreground color` or `background color` is already black. In this situation, white is substituted.

As of Motif version 1.2.1, the color substitutions described above do not take place. When a color allocation fails for an `rgb` value specified directly or indirectly (in the `color_table` of an `icon`) the resource is not set. If the allocation fails in a call to `MrmFetchColorLiteral()` or `MrmFetchIconLiteral()`, `MrmNOT_FOUND` is returned.

Note that the values that specify that red, green, and blue components cannot be integer expressions. The UIL compiler, however, does not generate an error if an integer expression is encountered; it silently replaces the expression with the value 0. In addition, the UIL compiler does not report an error if an integer specified for a color value is less than 0 or greater than 65,535. If any of the three components is out-of-range, the three values stored in the UID file are undefined.

## Example

```
value
  white  : rgb (65535, 65535, 65535);
  orange : exported rgb (65535, 32767, 0);
  grape  : imported rgb;
  ctable : color_table (white = 'w, orange = 'o', grape = 'g');
...
```

UIL Data Types

```
object label : XmLabel {
  arguments {
    XmNforeground = rgb (0, 0, 32767);
    XmNbackground = orange;
  };
};
...
```

## See Also

*MrmFetchColorLiteral*(3), *MrmFetchIconLiteral*(3), *MrmFetchSetValues*(3), *MrmFetchWidget*(3), *MrmFetchWidgetOverride*(3),
*color*(6), *color_table*(6), *icon*(6).

# single_float

## Name

single_float – single-precision floating point type.

## Synopsis

**Syntax:** `single_float` ( *numeric_expression* )

**MrmType:** `MrmRtypeSingleFloat`

## Description

A `single_float` value represents a negative or positive single-precision floating point number. A `single_float` is represented literally by the symbol `single_float`, followed by a `boolean`, `float` or `integer` expression. The expression is converted to a `single_float` and can be used in any context in which a `single_float` value is valid. A `single_float` is formed from a `boolean` by converting `true` and `on` to 1.0 and `false` and `off` to 0.0. If a `float` expression is greater than (less than) the largest (smallest) representable `float`, the resulting `single_float` is +infinity (-infinity).

## Usage

The type `single_float` can be used as the type of an imported value, as a parameter type in a procedure declaration, or as the type in an `argument` literal. A `single_float` value is used to save space, as the storage used by a `single_float` is usually less than that used by a `float`.

The allowable range of a `single_float` value is determined by the size of a C `float` on the machine where the UIL module is compiled. Since a `float` on most architectures is typically a minimum of four bytes, `single_float` values may safely range from 1.4013e-45 to 3.40282e+38 (positive or negative). You can ensure greater portability by keeping `single_float` values within the four-byte range.

## Example

```
...
! Declare a procedure taking a single_float value.
procedure
  sqrt (single_float);

value
  avogadro   : single_float (6.023e+23);
  prime_rate : imported single_float;

! Define an argument of type single_float.
value
  XtNarea : argument ('area', single_float);
...
```

## See Also

*boolean*(6), *float*(6), *integer*(6).

UIL Data Types

# string



## Name

string – NULL-terminated character string type.

## Synopsis

**Syntax:** [ #*character_set* ] "*character_expression*" or

'*character_expression*'

**MrmType:** MrmRtypeChar8

## Description

A string value represents a NULL-terminated single-byte, multi-byte, or wide-character string. A string literal is represented by either a double or single-quoted sequence of characters, that may be up to 2000 characters long. Newer versions of UIL may allow even longer strings. The type of quotes used to delimit a string literal determines how the string is parsed by the UIL compiler.

Both double and single-quoted strings can directly contain characters with decimal values in the range 32 to 126 and 160 to 255. Characters with values outside of the range can only be entered using the escape sequence *value*\, where *value* represents the character code desired. To allow the easy specification of commonly-used non-printing characters codes, UIL recognizes the following escape sequences:

| Character | Meaning |
|---|---|
| \b | Backspace |
| \f | Formfeed |
| \n | Newline |
| \r | Carriage return |
| \t | Horizontal tab |
| \v | Vertical tab |
| \\ | Backslash |
| \' | Single quote |
| \" | Double quote |

A double-quoted string consists of an optional character_set, followed by a sequence of characters surrounded by a double quotes. Double-quoted strings cannot span multiple lines, but may contain the \n escape sequence. If a character_set is specified, it preceeds the string and is indicated by a pound sign (#). Either a built-in or user-defined character_set can be specified. If a character_set is not specified, the default character set of the module is used. The default character_set can be specified with the character_set option in the module header of a UIL module. If this option is not set, the default is determined from the codeset portion of the LANG environment variable if it is set, or XmFALLBACK_CHARSET otherwise.

If the UIL compiler is invoked with the -s option, double-quoted strings are parsed in the current locale. When UIL parses localized strings, escape sequences may be interpreted literally.

You can avoid unexpected results by restricting the use of escape sequences to single quoted strings.

A single-quoted `string` consists of a sequence of characters surrounded by single quotes. Unlike double-quoted strings, single-quoted strings can span multiple lines by using a backslash (\) to indicate that the string is continued on the next line. The newline character following the backslash is not included in the string. The \n escape sequence should be used if an embedded newline is desired. The `character_set` of a single-quoted string defaults to the codeset portion of the LANG environment variable if it is set, or `XmFALLBACK_CHARSET` otherwise.

The parsing direction of either `string` variant is determined by the `character_set` of the string. A string that is parsed right-to-left is stored in the UID file in the reverse order that it appeared in the UIL source module. The parsing direction and `character_set` writing direction determine the order of individual characters when a string is printed or displayed. The writing direction of a string is generally the same as the parsing direction, unless explicitly overridden in a `compound_string` literal. The order of the characters in escape sequences is always the same, regardless of the parsing direction.

## Usage

A single or double-quoted `string` value can be used anywhere a string or string expression is expected. A string expression can be a single string value or two or more string values concatenated with the string concatentation operator (&). A string or string expression can also be used anywhere a `compound_string` is expected, since the UIL compiler automatically converts the string to a compound string, with the character set determined by the rules described above. (When determining the character set, the UIL compiler may use ISO8859-1 as the fallback character set, even if the value has been changed by the vendor. Therefore, you should specify a character set explicitly instead of relying on `XmFALLBACK_CHARSET`.)

Any newline characters in a NULL-terminated `string` that is converted into a `compound_string` are not converted into separator components to make a multi-line compound string. If you need a multi-line compound string, it must be specified as a concatenated set of values using the `compound_string` literal syntax with the `separate` property set to `true`.

The type `string` can be used as the type of an imported value, as a parameter type in a procedure declaration, or as the type in an `argument` literal. String values used in string expressions or in `compound_string` literals must be private to the module in which they are used.

## Example

```
...
procedure
  tie_knot (string);

value
  display : imported string;
  skit_name : 'Unfrozen Caveman Lawyer';
  hello : #iso_hebrew"\237\\229\\236\\249\";
```

```
    quote : exported 'Quoth the Raven, `Nevermore.\'\n';
    concat : 'The Cat' & ' in the Hat';

    multi : '\
All that we see or seem\n\
Is but a dream within a dream.';

    ! Define a resource of type string.
    XtNfilename : argument ('filename', string);

  object play : XmPushButton {
    arguments {
      ! String automatically converted to XmString
      XmNlabelString = skit_name;
    };
  };
  ...
```

## See Also

*asciz_string_table*(6), *character_set*(6), *compound_string*(6), *compound_string_table*(6).

# translation_table

## Name

translation_table – Xt translation table type.

## Synopsis

**Syntax:** `translation_table ( [ '#override' | '#augment' | '#replace' ] string_expression [, ...] )`

**MrmType:** `MrmRtypeTransTable`

## Description

A `translation_table` value represents an X Toolkit translation table. A translation table is a list of translations, where each translation maps an event or an event sequence to an action name. In UIL, a `translation_table` is represented literally by the symbol `translation_table`, followed by an optional directive and list of string expressions that are interpreted as translations. If specified, the directive must be one of `#override`, `#augment`, or `#replace`. The translations are specified as a list of string expressions, one per translation. The individual translations are concatenated and separated with newline charcters before they are stored in the UID file.

## Usage

The `translation_table` type can be used as the type of an imported value, as a parameter type in a procedure declaration, or as the type in an `argument` literal.

The syntax of a `translation_table` is not verified by the UIL compiler. Instead, Mrm converts a `translation_table` literal to an `XtTranslations` value with `XtParseTranslationTable()` at run-time. Errors that occur when parsing the `translation_table` are passed to `XtWarning()`. Because `XtParseTranslationTable()` always returns a valid `XtTranslations` value, even when parsing errors occur, the run-time conversion of a `translation_table` cannot fail. See Volume Four, *X Toolkit Intrinsics Programming Manual*, and Volume Five, *X Toolkit Intrinsics Reference Manual*, for more information about translation tables.

## Example

```
...
procedure
  set_translations (translation_table);
  exit();

value
  XtNquickKeys : argument ('translations', translation_table);

value
  quit_tt : translation_table ('#override', '<Key>q: ArmAndActivate()');
  other_tt : imported translation_table;

object quit : XmPushButton {
  arguments {
    XmNtranslations = quit_tt;
```

```
    };
    callbacks {
      XmNactivateCallback = procedure exit();
    };
  };
  ...
```

## See Also

*MrmFetchLiteral*(3).

# wide_character

## Name

wide_character – wide-character string type.

## Synopsis

**Syntax:** `wide_character` ( *string_expression* )

**MrmType:** `MrmRtypeWideCharacter`

## Availability

Motif 1.2 and later.

## Description

A `wide_character` value represents a wide-character string. The corresponding C type is `wchar_t *`. A `wide_character` literal is represented by the symbol `wide_-character`, followed by a string expression.

## Usage

A `wide_character` literal is used to make the UIL compiler parse a regular character string as a wide-character string. A `wide_character` string is parsed with the `mbstowcs()` function. The operation of this function depends on the setting of the locale. See the *uil* reference page for more information regarding the locale setting. The `wide_character` literal syntax may not work in early releases of Motif 1.2. However, you can specify a wide-character string using the normal UIL `string` syntax. The difference is that the UIL compiler does not verify that a wide-character string specified in this way is properly formed.

The type `wide_character` can also be used as the type of an imported value, as a parameter type in a procedure declaration, or as the type in an `argument` literal.

## Example

```
...
procedure
  print_wcs (wide_character);

value
  wcs : wide_character ('\204\\176\\224\\189\');
  name : imported wide_character;

  XtNwideCharacterString : argument ('wideCharacterString', wide_character);

object text : XmText {
  arguments {
    XmNvalueWcs = wcs;
  };
};
...
```



UIL Data Types

## See Also

*uil*(4),
*procedure*(5),
*argument*(6), *string*(6).

## Name

widget – widget type.

## Synopsis

**Syntax:** See the `object` section of the UIL file format reference page.

**MrmType:** none

## Description

Objects that are declared or defined in a UIL `object` section are of type `widget`. Values of type `widget` are the only UIL values that are not declared or defined in a `value` section. The literal representation of a `widget` is described in the `object` section of the UIL file format reference page.

## Usage

The type `widget` can be used as a parameter type in a procedure declaration or as the type in an `argument` literal. When a widget is used as a callback parameter or resource value in the declaration of another widget, it must be part of the same hierarchy as that widget. A widget hierarchy is defined by the widget passed to `MrmFetchWidget()` or `MrmFetchWidgetOverride()` and it includes all of the descendants of that widget. If you need to specify a widget in a different hierarchy as a callback parameter, you can use the string name of the widget instead and convert it to a widget pointer in the callback with `XtNameToWidget()`.

Widgets can be forward referenced. If Mrm encounters a reference to a widget that has not been created in the current hierarchy, it creates the remainder of the hierarchy and makes another attempt to resolve the reference. If the reference cannot be resolved at that point, Mrm does not add the callback or set the resource for which the widget is specified. As of Motif 1.2, Mrm does not generate a warning when a widget reference cannot be resolved.

Prior to Motif 1.2.1, the UIL compiler generates an error when `widget` is used as a procedure parameter or type in an `argument` literal. To work around this problem, you can use the type `any`.

## Example

```
...
value
  ! Declare Athena tree widget constraint argument.
  XtNtreeParent : argument ('treeParent', widget);

procedure
  manage (widget);

object
  button1 : XmPushButton {
    callbacks {
      XmNactivateCallback = manage (button3);
    }
    arguments {
```



UIL Data Types

```
            XmNbottomAttachment = XmATTACH_FORM;
            XmNbottomOffset = 40;
            XmNrightAttachment = XmATTACH_WIDGET;
            XmNrightWidget = button1;
    };
    button2 : XmPushButton { };
    button3 : XmPushButton {
      arguments {
        XmNbottomAttachment = XmATTACH_FORM;
      };
    };
    form : XmForm {
      controls {
        XmPushButton button1;
        XmPushButton button2;
        unmanaged XmPushButton button3;
      };
    };
  ...
```

## See Also

*MrmFetchWidget*(3), *MrmFetchWidgetOverride*(3),
*object*(5), *procedure*(5),
*argument*(6).

# xbitmapfile

## Name

xbitmapfile – X bitmap file type.

## Synopsis

**Syntax:** `xbitmapfile` ( *string_expression* )

**MrmType:** `MrmRtypeXBitmapFile`

## Description

An `xbitmapfile` value represents a file that contains a bitmap in the standard X bitmap file format. An `xbitmapfile` literal is represented by the symbol `xbitmapfile`, followed by a string expression that evaluates to the name of the file containing the bitmap. The X bitmap is loaded at run-time by Mrm using `XmGetPixmapByDepth()`. See Volume One, *Xlib Programming Manual*, for more information about the X bitmap file format.

## Usage

The type `xbitmapfile` can be used as the type of an imported value, as a parameter type in a procedure declaration, or as the type in an `argument` literal. An `xbitmapfile` value can be retrieved by an application with `MrmFetchIconLiteral()`. The `MrmFetchBitmap-Literal()` procedure cannot be used to retrieve values of the `xbitmapfile` type.

When an `xbitmapfile` is specified as a resource value for a widget, the depth of the pixmap created by Mrm at run-time is the same as the depth of the widget. When an `xbitmapfile` is retrieved with `MrmFetchIconLiteral()`, the depth of the resulting pixmap is the value returned from the `DefaultDepthOfScreen()` macro.

The UIL compiler stores the specified file name in the UID output file, not the X bitmap to which the name refers. The compiler does not verify that the specified file exists. If an `xbitmapfile` specified as a resource cannot be loaded, the resource is not set. If `Mrm-FetchIconLiteral` fails to load an `xbitmapfile()`, MrmNOT_FOUND is returned.

## Example

```
...
! Declare a bitmap of the most challenging ski slope in the Northeast.
value
  goat : xbitmapfile ('goat.xbm');

object scary : XmLabel {
  arguments {
    XmNlabelType = XmPIXMAP;
    XmNlabelPixmap = goat;
  };
};
...
```

## See Also

*XmGetPixmapByDepth*(2),
*MrmFetchBitmapLiteral*(3), *MrmFetchIconLiteral*(3), *MrmFetchWidget*(3),
*MrmFetchWidgetOverride*(3),
*icon*(6), *pixmap*(6).

# Section 7

## UIL Functions

*This section contains the reference pages for Uil(), the application callable UIL compiler, and UilDumpSymbolTable(), the routine that prints the parse tree that the callable compiler can be directed to generate.*

*The first reference page,* Introduction*, explains the format and contents of the following pages.*

### In This Section:

# Introduction

This page describes the format and contents of each reference page in Section 7, which covers the User Interface Language (UIL) functions.

## Name

Function – a brief description of the function.

## Synopsis

This section shows the signature of the function: the names and types of the arguments, and the type of the return value. The header file *<uil/UilDef.h>* declares both of the public UIL functions.

### Inputs

This subsection describes each of the function arguments that pass information to the function.

### Outputs

This subsection describes any of the function arguments that are used to return information from the function. These arguments are always of some pointer type, so you should use the C address-of operator (**&**) to pass the address of the variable in which the function will store the return value. The names of these arguments are sometimes suffixed with `_return` to indicate that values are returned in them. Some arguments both supply and return a value; they will be listed in this section and in the "Inputs" section above. Finally, note that because the list of function arguments is broken into "Input" and "Output" sections, they do not always appear in the same order that they are passed to the function. See the function signature for the actual calling order.

### Returns

This subsection explains the return value of the function, if any.

## Description

This section explains what the function does and describes its arguments and return value. If you've used the function before and are just looking for a refresher, this section and the synopsis above should be all you need.

## Usage

This section appears for most functions and provides less formal information about the function: when and how you might want to use it, things to watch out for, and related functions that you might want to consider.

## Example

This section provides an example of the use of the function.

## Structures

This section shows the definition of any structures, enumerated types, typedefs, or symbolic constants used by the function.

## Procedures

This section shows the syntax of any prototype procedures used by the function.

## See Also

This section refers you to related functions, clients, and UIL data types. The numbers in parentheses following each reference refer to the sections of this book in which they are found.

# Uil

## Name

Uil – call the UIL compiler from an application.

## Synopsis

```
#include <uil/UilDef.h>
Uil_status_type Uil (command_desc, compile_desc, message_cb, message_data,
        status_cb, status_data)
    Uil_command_type *command_desc;
    Uil_compile_desc_type *compile_desc;
    Uil_continue_type (*message_cb)();
    char *message_data;
    Uil_continue_type (*status_cb)();
    char *status_data;
```

### Inputs

*command_desc*
Specifies a structure containing the compilation options.

*message_cb* Specifies a callback function that is called when error, warning and informational messages are generated by the compiler.

*message_data*
Specifies data that is passed to the message_cb function.

*status_cb* Specifies a callback function that is called periodically during the compilation to indicate progress.

*status_data* Specifies data that is passed to the status_cb function.

### Outputs

*compile_desc*
Returns a structure containing the results of the compilation.

### Returns

Uil_k_success_status on success and if no problems are detected, Uil_k_info_-status on success and if informational messages are generated, Uil_k_warning_-status on success and if warning messages are generated, Uil_k_error_status on failure and if error messages are generated, and Uil_k_severe_status on failure and if the compilation stopped prematurely.

## Description

Uil() invokes the UIL compiler from within an application. Options for the compiler, including the input, output and listing files, are provided in the *command_desc* argument. The calling application can supply a message handling function in *message_cb* that displays compiler messages in an application-defined manner. The application can also supply a status-monitoring function in *status_cb*. This function is called periodically by the compiler to report progress. Upon completion, the Uil() function fills in the *compile_desc* structure with information about the compilation and returns the status of the compilation.

## Usage

An application that calls `Uil()` is responsible for allocating the `command_desc` and `compile_desc` arguments. The application must initialize all members of the `command_desc` structure. Members of the `compile_desc` structure are set by the compiler. If the `parse_tree_flag` in *command_desc* is set, the compiler returns a pointer to the root of the parse tree in the `parse_tree_root` field of the *compile_desc*. This parse table cannot be freed by the calling application. Therefore, you should not set the `parse_tree_flag` unless you plan to use the parse tree. To limit memory consumption, if you set the `parse_tree_flag`, invoke the `Uil()` routine once and exit soon thereafter.

An application can specify a function for handling compiler generated messages in the `message_cb` argument. You can specify `NULL` for this argument if you want to use the default message handling routine. This routine prints all messages to *stderr*. If you specify a function, the value of `message_data` is passed to each invocation of the function.

An application can also specify a function for monitoring the status of the compilation in the `status_cb` argument. You can specify `NULL` to indicate that no status function should be called. If you specify a function, the value of `status_data` is passed to each invocation of the function. In addition to monitoring progress, the function can also be used to process X events in an X application.

The `Uil()` function installs signal handers for `SIGBUS`, `SIGSYS`, and `SIGFPE` with no regard for application installed handlers. These installed handlers remain set after the function returns, so you may wish to change them.

Applications that call the `Uil()` function must be linked with the UIL library, *libUil.a*, in addition to the Mrm, Motif, Xt, and X libraries.

## Structures

The `Uil_command_type` is defined as follows:

```
typedef struct {
    char            *source_file;           /* name of UIL source file */
    char            *resource_file;         /* name of UID output file */
    char            *listing_file;          /* name of listing file */
    unsigned int    include_dir_count;      /* length of include_dir array */
    char            **include_dir;          /* array of include file directories */
    unsigned int    listing_file_flag : 1;  /* write listing file flag */
    unsigned int    resource_file_flag : 1; /* write UID file flag */
    unsigned int    machine_code_flag : 1;  /* write machine code flag */
    unsigned int    report_info_msg_flag : 1;/* report informational messages */
    unsigned int    report_warn_msg_flag : 1;/* report warning messages */
    unsigned int    parse_tree_flag : 1;    /* generate parse tree flag */
    unsigned int    issue_summary : 1;      /* write diagnostic summary flag */
    unsigned int    status_update_delay;    /* delay between status_cb calls */
    char            *database;              /* WML database filename */
```

```
    unsigned int     database_flag : 1;       /* read WML database flag */
    unsigned int     use_setlocale_flag : 1; /* parse strings in locale flag */
} Uil_command_type;
```

`Uil_command_type` describes the compilation options for the `Uil()` routine. `source_file` is the name of the UIL module to compile. `resource_file` is the name of the UID file that is output if `resource_file_flag` is set. `listing_file` is the name of the compilation listing file that is output if `listing_file_flag` is set. Setting `machine_code_flag` causes the compiler to output a binary description of the UID file when a listing is generated.

`include_dir` specifies an array of `include_dir_count` directory names that the compiler searches for UIL include files. If set, `report_info_msg_flag`, `report_warn_msg_flag`, and `issue_summary` cause the compiler to generate informational messages, warning messages, and a summary message, respectively.

If `parse_tree_flag` is set, it instructs the compiler to return a pointer to the parse tree of the module in the *compile_desc* structure. `status_update_delay` specifies how many status check points must be passed before the *status_cb* callback is called. If the field is set to zero, the function is called at every check point.

`use_setlocale_flag` directs the UIL compiler to parse double-quoted strings in the current locale. (See the UIL string type man page for more information.) `database` specifies the name of a Widget Meta-Language (WML) description file that the compiler loads if `database_flag` is set.

The `Uil_compile_desc_type` is defined as follows:

```
typedef struct _Uil_comp_desc
{
    unsigned int     compiler_version;        /* UIL compiler version */
    unsigned int     data_version;            /* UIL structures version */
    char             *parse_tree_root;        /* parse tree for module */
    unsigned int     message_count[ ];        /* status messages counts */
} Uil_compile_desc_type;
```

`Uil_compile_desc_type` describes the return data for the `Uil()` routine. `compiler_version` specifies the version of the UIL compiler, while `data_version` specifies the version of the structures used by the compiler. If `parse_tree_flag` is set in the *command_desc* argument, `parse_tree_root` contains a pointer to a compiler-generated parse tree if the compilation succeeds. `message_count` is an array of integers that contains the number of each type of compiler message generated by the routine. Valid indices to the array are `Uil_k_info_status`, `Uil_k_warning_status`, `Uil_k_error_status`, and `Uil_k_severe_status`.

UIL Functions

### Procedures

A message_cb function has the following syntax:

```
Uil_continue_type *message_cb (message_data, message_number, severity,
                               message_string, source_text,
                               column_string, location_string,
                               message_count);
    char *message_data;
    int  message_number;
    int  severity;
    char *message_string;
    char *source_text;
    char *column_string;
    char *location_string;
    int  message_count[ ];
```

A message_cb function takes eight arguments. The first argument, message_data, is the value of the *message_data* argument passed to the Uil() function. message_number is the internal index of the message, which is used by the UIL compiler. severity specifies the severity of the message, which is one of Uil_k_info_status, Uil_k_warning_-status, Uil_k_error_status, or Uil_k_severe_status.

message_string is a string describing the problem. source_text is a copy of the source line to which the message refers, with a tab character prepended. If the source line is not available, source_text is the empty string. column_string is a string that consists of a leading tab character followed by zero or more spaces and an * (asterick) in the same column as the problem in the source line. This string is suitable for printing beneath message_-string to indicate the location of the problem. If the column that contains the error or the source line is not available, column_string is the empty string.

location_string describes the location where the problem occured. The format of this string is "\t\t line: %d file: %s" if both source and column number are available, or if no column number is available. If the column number, but no source line is available, the format is "\t\t line: %d position: %d file: %s". If the location is unavailable, the value of location_string is the empty string. If an application does not specify a message_cb routine, the compiler prints source_text, column_string, message_string, and location_string in that order.

message_count is an array of integers that contains the number of each type of compiler message generated by the routine so far. Valid indices to the array are Uil_k_info_-status, Uil_k_warning_status, Uil_k_error_status, and Uil_k_severe_-status.

A message_cb function should return Uil_k_continue if the compilation can continue or Uil_k_terminate if the compilation should be terminated.

A `status_cb` function has the following format:

```
Uil_continue_type *status_cb (status_data, percent_complete, lines_processed,
                              current_file, message_count);
    char *status_data;
    int  percent_complete;
    int  lines_processed;
    char *current_file;
    int  message_count[];
```

A `status_cb` function takes five parameters. The first argument, `status_data`, is the value of the *`status_data`* argument passed to the `Uil()` function. `percent_complete` specifies an estimate of the percentage of the compilation that has been completed. The value of this field falls within a fixed range of values for each step of the compilation. The value ranges from 0 to 50 while `source_file` is being parsed, from 60 to 80 while the `resource_file` is written, and from 80 to 100 while the `listing_file` is generated. Some versions of the UIL compiler may only report percent-complete values on the boundaries of these ranges. `lines_processed` indicates the number of lines that have been read from the input file.

When the UIL compiler is invoked, it parses the `source_file`, writes the `resource_file`, and then generates the `listing_file`, based on the settings of the *`command_desc`* argument. The `current_file` field changes to reflect the file that the compiler is accessing.

`message_count` is an array of integers that contains the number of each type of compiler message generated by the routine so far. Valid indices to the array are `Uil_k_info_status`, `Uil_k_warning_status`, `Uil_k_error_status`, and `Uil_k_severe_status`.

A `status_cb` function should return `Uil_k_continue` if the compilation can continue or `Uil_k_terminate` if the compilation should be terminated.

The frequency with which the compiler calls the `status_cb` function at check points is based on the value of `status_update_delay` field in *`command_desc`*. A check point occurs every time a symbol is found during the parsing of `source_file`, every time an element is written to the `resource_file`, and every time a line is written to the `listing_file`.

UIL Functions

## Example

The following routines illustrate the use of the `Uil()` routine in a very basic way:

```
#include <uil/UilDef.h>
#include <stdio.h>

static char *last_current_file;

static char *status_string_list[Uil_k_max_status] = { NULL };

Uil_continue_type
```

```
message_cb (char *message_data, int message_number, int severity,
        char *message_string, char *line_text,
        char *error_col_string, char *line_and_file_string,
        int *message_count)
{
  if (*line_text != ' ')
    puts (line_text);
  if (*error_col_string != ' ')
    puts (error_col_string);
  if (*message_string != ' ')
    printf ("%s: %s\n", status_string_list[severity], message_string);
  if (*line_and_file_string != ' ')
    puts (line_and_file_string);

  return (Uil_k_continue);
}

Uil_continue_type
status_cb (char *status_data, int percent_complete, int lines_processed,
        char *current_file, int *message_count)
{
  if (last_current_file == NULL ||
      strcmp (last_current_file, current_file) != 0)
    {
      fprintf (stderr, "Working on file %s...\n", current_file);
      last_current_file = current_file;
    }

  return (Uil_k_continue);
}

Uil_compile_desc_type *
compile (char *filename)
{
  Uil_command_type command_desc;
  static Uil_compile_desc_type compile_desc;
  Uil_status_type status;

  if (status_string_list[Uil_k_success_status] == NULL)
    {
      status_string_list[Uil_k_success_status] = "Success";
      status_string_list[Uil_k_info_status]    = "Informational";
      status_string_list[Uil_k_warning_status] = "Warning";
      status_string_list[Uil_k_error_status]   = "Error";
      status_string_list[Uil_k_severe_status]  = "Severe Error";
    }

  command_desc.source_file = filename;
  command_desc.resource_file = "a.uid";
```

```
    command_desc.listing_file = "uil.lst";
    command_desc.include_dir_count = 0;
    command_desc.include_dir = NULL;
    command_desc.listing_file_flag = TRUE;
    command_desc.resource_file_flag = TRUE;
    command_desc.machine_code_flag = FALSE;
    command_desc.report_info_msg_flag = TRUE;
    command_desc.report_warn_msg_flag = TRUE;
    command_desc.parse_tree_flag = FALSE;
    command_desc.issue_summary = TRUE;
    command_desc.status_update_delay = 0;
    command_desc.database = NULL;
    command_desc.database_flag = FALSE;
    command_desc.use_setlocale_flag = FALSE;

    last_current_file = NULL;
    status =
      Uil (&command_desc, &compile_desc, message_cb, NULL, status_cb, NULL);

    if (status == Uil_k_error_status ||
        status == Uil_k_severe_status)
      return (NULL);
    else
      return (&compile_desc);
}

int
main (int argc, char **argv)
{
    Uil_compile_desc_type *compile_desc;
    if (argc != 2)
      {
        printf ("usage: Uil filename\n");
        exit (1);
      }

    compile_desc = compile (argv[1]);

    if (compile_desc != NULL)
      fprintf (stderr, "Compilation Successful.\n");
    else
      fprintf (stderr, "Compilation Failed.\n");
}
```

## See Also

*uil*(4),
*string*(6),
*UilDumpSymbolTable*(7).

# UilDumpSymbolTable

## Name

UilDumpSymbolTable – produce a listing of a UIL symbol table.

## Synopsis

```
#include <uil/UilDef.h>
void UilDumpSymbolTable (parse_tree_root)
    sym_entry_type *parse_tree_root;
```

### Inputs

*parse_tree_root*
Specifies a pointer to the root entry of a symbol table.

## Description

`UilDumpSymbolTable()` prints a listing of the symbols parsed in a UIL module to *stdout*. A parse tree is generated by a call to `Uil()`. If the `parse_tree_flag` of the `Uil_command_type` structure passed to the routine is set and the compilation is successful, the `Uil()` routine returns a pointer to the root of the parse tree in the `parse_tree_root` member of the `Uil_compile_desc_type` structure. If the compilation is unsuccessful, the `parse_tree_root` field is set to NULL.

## Usage

`UilDumpSymbolTable()` generates a listing of the internal representation of UIL structures and symbols, which is really only useful for people who are quite familiar with the internals of the UIL compiler. The `-m` option of the **uil** command, or the `machine_code_flag` option of the `Uil()` routine, generates far more useful information for most users of UIL.

Instead of calling `UilDumpSymbolTable()`, an application can examine the parse tree directly. The structures used in the parse tree are defined in the file *<uil/UilSymDef.h>* and definitions of constants used in the structures are in *<uil/UilDBDef.h>*. Both of these files are included by *<uil/UilDef.h>*.

The parse table generated by the `Uil()` routine cannot be freed by the calling application. Therefore, you should not set the `parse_tree_flag` unless you plan to use the parse tree. To limit memory consumption, if you set the `parse_tree_flag`, invoke the `Uil()` routine once and exit soon thereafter.

## See Also

*uil*(4).
*Uil*(7).

# Appendices

*This part of the manual contains handy lists of functions, as well as useful reference information on data types, events, and the like.*

## In The Appendices:

# A
# Function Summaries

This quick reference is intended to help you find and use the right function for a particular task. It organizes the Section 1 and Section 3 reference pages into two lists:

- List of functions and macros by groups.
- Alphabetical list of functions and macros.

The first column indicates which section to find the routines in. If the name is followed by a (3), the routine can be found in Section 3; otherwise, the routine can be found in Section 1.

## A.1 Group Listing with Brief Descriptions

### Atoms

| | |
|---|---|
| `XmGetAtomName()` | Get the string representation of an atom. |
| `XmInternAtom()` | Return an atom for a given property name string. |

### CascadeButton

| | |
|---|---|
| `XmCascadeButtonGadgetHighlight()` | Set the highlight state of a CascadeButton. |
| `XmCascadeButtonHighlight()` | Set the highlight state of a CascadeButton. |

### Clipboard

| | |
|---|---|
| `XmClipboardBeginCopy()` | Set up storage for a clipboard copy operation. |
| `XmClipboardCancelCopy()` | Cancel a copy operation to the clipboard. |
| `XmClipboardCopy()` | Copy a data item to temporary storage for later copying to the clipboard. |
| `XmClipboardCopyByName()` | Copy a data item passed by name. |
| `XmClipboardEndCopy()` | End a copy operation to the clipboard |
| `XmClipboardEndRetrieve()` | End a copy operation from the clipboard. |
| `XmClipboardInquireCount()` | Get the number of data item formats available on the clipboard. |
| `XmClipboardInquireFormat()` | Get the specified clipboard data format name. |
| `XmClipboardInquireLength()` | Get the length of the data item on the clipboard. |
| `XmClipboardInquirePendingItems()` | Get a list of pending data ID/private ID pairs. |
| `XmClipboardLock()` | Lock the clipboard. |
| `XmClipboardRegisterFormat()` | Register a new format for clipboard data items. |

| | |
|---|---|
| `XmClipboardRetrieve()` | Retrieve a data item from the clipboard. |
| `XmClipboardStartCopy()` | Set up storage for a clipboard copy operation. |
| `XmClipboardStartRetrieve()` | Start a clipboard retrieval operation. |
| `XmClipboardUndoCopy()` | Remove the last item copied to the clipboard. |
| `XmClipboardUnlock()` | Unlock the clipboard. |
| `XmClipboardWithdrawFormat()` | Indicate that an application does not want to supply a data item any longer. |

## Colors

| | |
|---|---|
| `XmChangeColor()` | Update the colors for a widget. |
| `XmGetColorCalculation()` | Get the procedure that calculates default colors. |
| `XmGetColors()` | Get the foreground, select, and shadow colors. |
| `XmSetColorCalculation()` | Set the procedure that calculates default colors. |

## Command

| | |
|---|---|
| `XmCommandAppendValue()` | Append a compound string to the command. |
| `XmCommandError()` | Display an error message in a Command widget. |
| `XmCommandGetChild()` | Get the specified child of a Command widget. |
| `XmCommandSetValue()` | Replace the command string. |

## Compound Strings

| | |
|---|---|
| `XmCvtCTToXmString()` | Convert compound text to a compound string |
| `XmCvtXmStringToCT()` | Convert a compound string to compound text. |
| `XmMapSegmentEncoding()` | Get the compound text encoding format for a font list element tag. |
| `XmRegisterSegmentEncoding()` | Register a compound text encoding format for a font list element tag. |
| `XmStringBaseline()` | Get the baseline spacing for a compound string. |
| `XmStringByteCompare()` | Compare two compound strings byte-by-byte. |
| `XmStringCompare()` | Compare two compound strings. |
| `XmStringConcat()` | Concatenate two compound strings. |
| `XmStringCopy()` | Copy a compound string. |
| `XmStringCreate()` | Create a compound string. |
| `XmStringCreateLocalized()` | Create a compound string in the current locale. |
| `XmStringCreateLtoR()` | Create a compound string. |
| `XmStringCreateSimple()` | Create a compound string in the current language environment. |
| `XmStringDirectionCreate()` | Create a compound string containing a direction component. |
| `XmStringDraw()` | Draw a compound string. |
| `XmStringDrawImage()` | Draw a compound string. |
| `XmStringDrawUnderline()` | Draw a compound string with an underlined sub-string. |
| `XmStringEmpty()` | Determine whether there are text segments in a compound string. |
| `XmStringExtent()` | Get the smallest rectangle that contains a compound string. |
| `XmStringFree()` | Free the memory used by a compound string. |
| `XmStringFreeContext()` | Free a string context. |
| `XmStringGetLtoR()` | Get a text segment from a compound string. |

| | |
|---|---|
| `XmStringGetNextComponent()` | Retrieves information about the next compound string component. |
| `XmStringGetNextSegment()` | Retrieves information about the next compound string segment. |
| `XmStringHasSubstring()` | Determine whether a compound string contains a substring. |
| `XmStringHeight()` | Get the line height of a compound string. |
| `XmStringInitContext()` | Create a string context. |
| `XmStringLength()` | Get the length of a compound string. |
| `XmStringLineCount()` | Get the number of lines in a compound string. |
| `XmStringNConcat()` | Concatenate a specified portion of a compound string to another compound string. |
| `XmStringNCopy()` | Copy a specified portion of a compound string. |
| `XmStringPeekNextComponent()` | Returns the type of the next compound string component. |
| `XmStringSegmentCreate()` | Create a compound string segment. |
| `XmStringSeparatorCreate()` | Create a compound string containing a separator component. |
| `XmStringWidth()` | Get the width of the longest line of text in a compound string. |

## Cursors

| | |
|---|---|
| `XmGetMenuCursor()` | Get the current menu cursor. |
| `XmSetMenuCursor()` | Set the current menu cursor. |

## Display

| | |
|---|---|
| `XmGetXmDisplay()` | Get the Display object for a display. |
| `XmUpdateDisplay()` | Update the display. |

## Drag and Drop

| | |
|---|---|
| `XmDragCancel()` | Cancel a drag operation. |
| `XmDragStart()` | Start a drag operation. |
| `XmDropSiteConfigureStackingOrder()` | Change the stacking order of a drop site. |
| `XmDropSiteEndUpdate()` | End an update of multiple drop sites. |
| `XmDropSiteQueryStackingOrder()` | Get the stacking order of a drop site. |
| `XmDropSiteRegister()` | Register a drop site. |
| `XmDropSiteRetrieve()` | Get the resource values for a drop site. |
| `XmDropSiteStartUpdate()` | Start an update of multiple drop sites. |
| `XmDropSiteUnregister()` | Remove a drop site. |
| `XmDropSiteUpdate()` | Change the resource values for a drop site. |
| `XmDropTransferAdd()` | Add drop transfer entries to a drop operation. |
| `XmDropTransferStart()` | Start a drop operation. |
| `XmGetDragContext()` | Get information about a drag and drop operation. |
| `XmTargetsAreCompatible()` | Determine whether or not the target types of a drag source and a drop site match. |

## FileSelectionBox

| | |
|---|---|
| `XmFileSelectionBoxGetChild()` | Get the specified child of a FileSelectionBox widget. |
| `XmFileSelectionDoSearch()` | Start a directory search. |

## Font Lists

| | |
|---|---|
| XmFontListAdd() | Create a new font list. |
| XmFontListAppendEntry() | Append a font entry to a font list. |
| XmFontListCopy() | Copy a font list. |
| XmFontListCreate() | Create a font list. |
| XmFontListEntryCreate() | Create a font list entry. |
| XmFontListEntryFree() | Free the memory used by a font list entry. |
| XmFontListEntryGetFont() | Get the font information from a font list entry. |
| XmFontListEntryGetTag() | Get the tag of a font list entry. |
| XmFontListEntryLoad() | Load a font or create a font set and then create a font list entry. |
| XmFontListFree() | Free the memory used by a font list. |
| XmFontListFreeFontContext() | Free a font context. |
| XmFontListGetNextFont() | Retrieve information about the next font list element. |
| XmFontListInitFontContext() | Create a font context. |
| XmFontListNextEntry() | Retrieve the next font list entry in a font list. |
| XmFontListRemoveEntry() | Remove a font list entry from a font list. |

## Fonts

| | |
|---|---|
| XmSetFontUnit() | Set the font unit values. |
| XmSetFontUnits() | Set the font unit values. |

## Keyboard Handling

| | |
|---|---|
| XmTranslateKey() | Convert a keycode to a keysym using the default translator. |

## Keyboard Traversal

| | |
|---|---|
| XmAddTabGroup() | Add a widget to a list of tab groups. |
| XmGetDestination() | Get the current destination widget. |
| XmGetFocusWidget() | Get the widget that has the keyboard focus. |
| XmGetTabGroup() | Get the tab group for a widget. |
| XmGetVisibility() | Determine whether or not a widget is visible. |
| XmIsTraversable() | Determine whether or not a widget can receive the keyboard focus. |
| XmProcessTraversal() | Set the widget that has the keyboard focus. |
| XmRemoveTabGroup() | Remove a widget from a list of tab groups. |

## List

| | |
|---|---|
| XmListAddItem() | Add an item to a list. |
| XmListAddItems() | Add items to a list. |
| XmListAddItemUnselected() | Add an item to a list. |
| XmListAddItemsUnselected() | Add items to a list. |
| XmListDeleteAllItems() | Delete all of the items from a list. |
| XmListDeleteItem() | Delete an item from a list. |
| XmListDeleteItems() | Delete items from a list. |
| XmListDeleteItemsPos() | Delete items starting at a specified position from a list. |
| XmListDeletePos() | Delete an item at the specified position from a list. |

| | |
|---|---|
| `XmListDeletePositions()` | Delete items at the specified positions from a list. |
| `XmListDeselectAllItems()` | Deselect all items in a list. |
| `XmListDeselectItem()` | Deselect an item from a list. |
| `XmListDeselectPos()` | Deselect an item at the specified position from a list. |
| `XmListGetKbdItemPos()` | Get the position of the item in a list that has the location cursor. |
| `XmListGetMatchPos()` | Get all occurences of an item in a list. |
| `XmListItemExists()` | Determine if a specified item is in a list. |
| `XmListItemPos()` | Return the position of an item in a list. |
| `XmListPosSelected()` | Check if the item at a specified position is selected in a list. |
| `XmListPosToBounds()` | Return the bounding box of an item at the specified position in a list. |
| `XmListReplaceItems()` | Replace specified items in a list. |
| `XmListReplaceItemsPos()` | Replace specified items in a list. |
| `XmListReplaceItemsPosUnselected()` | Replace specified items in a list. |
| `XmListReplaceItemsUnselected()` | Replace specified items in a list. |
| `XmListReplacePositions()` | Replace items at the specified postions in a list. |
| `XmListSelectedPos()` | Get the positions of the selected items in a list. |
| `XmListSelectItem()` | Select an item from a list. |
| `XmListSelectPos()` | Select an item at the specified position from a list. |
| `XmListSetAddMode()` | Set add mode in a list. |
| `XmListSetBottomItem()` | Set the last visible item in a list. |
| `XmListSetBottomPos()` | Set the last visible item in a list. |
| `XmListSetHorizPos()` | Set the horizontal position of a list. |
| `XmListSetItem()` | Set the first visible item in a list. |
| `XmListSetKbdItemPos()` | Set the position of the location cursor in a list. |
| `XmListSetPos()` | Sets the first visible item in a list. |
| `XmListUpdateSelectedList()` | Update the list of selected items in a list. |
| `XmListYToPos()` | Get the position of the item at the specified y-coordinate in a list. |

## MainWindow

| | |
|---|---|
| `XmMainWindowSep1()` | Get the widget ID of a MainWindow Separator. |
| `XmMainWindowSep2()` | Get the widget ID of a MainWindow Separator. |
| `XmMainWindowSep3()` | Get the widget ID of a MainWindow Separator. |
| `XmMainWindowSetAreas()` | Specify the children for a MainWindow. |

## Menus

| | |
|---|---|
| `XmGetPostedFromWidget()` | Get the widget that posted a menu. |
| `XmGetTearOffControl()` | Get the tear-off control for a menu. |
| `XmMenuPosition()` | Position a popup menu. |
| `XmOptionButtonGadget()` | Get the CascadeButtonGadget in an option menu. |
| `XmOptionLabelGadget()` | Get the LabelGadget in an option menu. |

## MessageBox

| | |
|---|---|
| `XmMessageBoxGetChild()` | Get the specified child of a MessageBox widget. |

## Mrm Functions

| | |
|---|---|
| `MrmCloseHierarchy()` | Close an Mrm hierarchy. |
| `MrmFetchBitmapLiteral()` | Retrieve an exported bitmap from an Mrm hierarchy. |
| `MrmFetchColorLiteral()` | Retrieve an exported color value from an Mrm hierarchy. |
| `MrmFetchIconLiteral()` | Retrieve an exported icon from an Mrm hierarchy. |
| `MrmFetchLiteral()` | Retrieve an exported value from an Mrm hierarchy. |
| `MrmFetchSetValues()` | Set widget resources to values retrieved from an Mrm hierarchy. |
| `MrmFetchWidget()` | Create the widget tree rooted at a named widget. |
| `MrmFetchWidgetOverride()` | Create the widget tree rooted at a named widget and override the resources set in the UID file. |
| `MrmInitialize()` | Prepare the Mrm library for use. |
| `MrmOpenHierarchy()` | Open an Mrm hierarchy. |
| `MrmOpenHierarchyPerDisplay()` | Open an Mrm hierarchy. |
| `MrmRegisterClass()` | Register a widget creation function for a non-Motif widget |
| `MrmRegisterNames()` | Register application-defined values and procedures. |
| `MrmRegisterNamesInHierarchy()` | Register application-defined values and procedures for use in a specific UIL hierarchy. |

## Pixmaps

| | |
|---|---|
| `XmDestroyPixmap()` | Remove a pixmap from the pixmap cache. |
| `XmGetPixmap()` | Create and return a pixmap. |
| `XmGetPixmapByDepth()` | Create and return a pixmap of the specified depth. |
| `XmInstallImage()` | Install an image in the image cache. |
| `XmUninstallImage()` | Remove an image from the image cache. |

## Protocols

| | |
|---|---|
| `XmActivateProtocol()` | Activate a protocol. |
| `XmActivateWMProtocol()` | Activate the XA_WM_PROTOCOLS protocol. |
| `XmAddProtocolCallback()` | Add client callbacks to a protocol. |
| `XmAddProtocols()` | Add protocols to the protocol manager. |
| `XmAddWMProtocolCallback()` | Add client callbacks to a XA_WM_PROTOCOLS protocol. |
| `XmAddWMProtocols()` | Add the XA_WM_PROTOCOLS protocols to the protocol manager. |
| `XmDeactivateProtocol()` | Deactivate a protocol. |
| `XmDeactivateWMProtocol()` | Deactivate the XA_WM_PROTOCOLS protocol. |
| `XmRemoveProtocolCallback()` | Remove client callback from a protocol. |
| `XmRemoveProtocols()` | Remove protocols from the protocol manager. |
| `XmRemoveWMProtocolCallback()` | Remove client callbacks from a XA_WM_PROTOCOLS protocol. |
| `XmRemoveWMProtocols()` | Remove the XA_WM_PROTOCOLS protocols from the protocol manager. |
| `XmSetProtocolHooks()` | Set prehooks and posthooks for a protocol. |
| `XmSetWMProtocolHooks()` | Set prehooks and posthooks for the XA_WM_PROTOCOLS protocol. |

## Resolution Independence

| | |
|---|---|
| `XmConvertUnits()` | Convert a value to a specified unit type. |

## Resource Conversion

| | |
|---|---|
| `XmCvtStringToUnitType()` | Convert a string to a unit-type value. |
| `XmRepTypeAddReverse()` | Install the reverse converter for a representation type. |
| `XmRepTypeGetId()` | Get the ID number of a representation type. |
| `XmRepTypeGetNameList()` | Get the list of value names for a representation type. |
| `XmRepTypeGetRecord()` | Get information about a representation type. |
| `XmRepTypeGetRegistered()` | Get the registered representation types. |
| `XmRepTypeInstallTearOffModelConverter()` | Install the resource converter for `XmNtearOffModel`. |
| `XmRepTypeRegister()` | Register a representation type resource. |
| `XmRepTypeValidValue()` | Determine the validity of a numerical value for a representation type. |

## Scale

| | |
|---|---|
| `XmScaleGetValue()` | Get the slider value for a Scale widget. |
| `XmScaleSetValue()` | Set the slider value for a Scale widget. |

## Screen

| | |
|---|---|
| `XmGetXmScreen()` | Get the Screen object for a screen. |

## ScrollBar

| | |
|---|---|
| `XmScrollBarGetValues()` | Get information about the current state of a ScrollBar widget. |
| `XmScrollBarSetValues()` | Set the current state of a ScrollBar widget. |

## ScrolledWindow

| | |
|---|---|
| `XmScrolledWindowsSetAreas()` | Specify the children for a scrolled window. |
| `XmScrollVisible()` | Make an obscured child of a ScrolledWindow visible. |

## SelectionBox

| | |
|---|---|
| `XmSelectionBoxGetChild()` | Get the specified child of a SelectionBox widget. |

## Text

| | |
|---|---|
| `XmTextClearSelection()` | Clear the primary selection. |
| `XmTextCopy()` | Copy the primary selection to the clipboard. |
| `XmTextCut()` | Copy the primary selection to the clipboard and remove the selected text. |
| `XmTextDisableRedisplay()` | Prevent visual update of a Text widget. |
| `XmTextEnableRedisplay()` | Allow visual update of a Text widget. |
| `XmTextFieldClearSelection()` | Clear the primary selection. |
| `XmTextFieldCopy()` | Copy the primary selection to the clipboard. |

| | |
|---|---|
| `XmTextFieldCut()` | Copy the primary selection to the clipboard and remove the selected text. |
| `XmTextFieldGetBaseline()` | Get the position of the baseline. |
| `XmTextFieldGetCursorPosition()` | Get the position of the insertion cursor. |
| `XmTextFieldGetEditable()` | Get the edit permission state. |
| `XmTextFieldGetInsertionPosition()` | Get the position of the insertion cursor. |
| `XmTextFieldGetLastPosition()` | Get the position of the last character of text. |
| `XmTextFieldGetMaxLength()` | Get the maximum possible length of a text string. |
| `XmTextFieldGetSelection()` | Get the value of the primary selection. |
| `XmTextFieldGetSelectionPosition()` | Get the position of the primary selection. |
| `XmTextFieldGetSelectionWcs()` | Get the wide-character value of the primary selection. |
| `XmTextFieldGetString()` | Get the text string. |
| `XmTextFieldGetStringWcs()` | Get the wide-character text string. |
| `XmTextFieldGetSubstring()` | Get a copy of part of the text string. |
| `XmTextFieldGetSubstringWcs()` | Get a copy of part of the wide-character text string. |
| `XmTextFieldInsert()` | Insert a string into the text string. |
| `XmTextFieldInsertWcs()` | Insert a wide-character string into the text string. |
| `XmTextFieldPaste()` | Insert the clipboard selection. |
| `XmTextFieldPosToXY()` | Get the x, y position of a character position. |
| `XmTextFieldRemove()` | Delete the primary selection. |
| `XmTextFieldReplace()` | Replace part of the text string. |
| `XmTextFieldReplaceWcs()` | Replace part of the wide-character text string. |
| `XmTextFieldSetAddMode()` | Set the add mode state. |
| `XmTextFieldSetCursorPosition()` | Set the position of the insertion cursor. |
| `XmTextFieldSetEditable()` | Set the edit permission state. |
| `XmTextFieldSetHighlight()` | Highlight text. |
| `XmTextFieldSetInsertionPosition()` | Set the position of the insertion cursor. |
| `XmTextFieldSetMaxLength()` | Set the maximum possible length of a text string. |
| `XmTextFieldSetSelection()` | Set the value of the primary selection. |
| `XmTextFieldSetString()` | Set the text string. |
| `XmTextFieldSetStringWcs()` | Set the wide-character text string. |
| `XmTextFieldShowPosition()` | Display the text at a specified position. |
| `XmTextFieldXYToPos()` | Get the character position for an x, y position. |
| `XmTextFindString()` | Find the beginning position of a text string. |
| `XmTextFindStringWcs()` | Find the beginning position of a wide-character text string. |
| `XmTextGetBaseline()` | Get the position of the baseline. |
| `XmTextGetCursorPosition()` | Get the position of the insertion cursor. |
| `XmTextGetEditable()` | Get the edit permission state. |
| `XmTextGetInsertionPosition()` | Get the position of the insertion cursor. |
| `XmTextGetLastPosition()` | Get the position of the last character of text. |
| `XmTextGetMaxLength()` | Get the maximum possible length of a text string. |
| `XmTextGetSelection()` | Get the value of the primary selection. |
| `XmTextGetSelectionPosition()` | Get the position of the primary selection. |
| `XmTextGetSelectionWcs()` | Get the wide-character value of the primary selection. |
| `XmTextGetSource()` | Get the text source. |
| `XmTextGetString()` | Get the text string. |
| `XmTextGetStringWcs()` | Get the wide-character text string. |
| `XmTextGetSubstring()` | Get a copy of part of the text string. |
| `XmTextGetSubstringWcs()` | Get a copy of part of the wide-character text string. |

| | |
|---|---|
| `XmTextGetTopCharacter()` | Get the position of the first character of text that is displayed. |
| `XmTextInsert()` | Insert a string into the text string. |
| `XmTextInsertWcs()` | Insert a wide-character string into the text string. |
| `XmTextPaste()` | Insert the clipboard selection. |
| `XmTextPosToXY()` | Get the x, y position of a character position. |
| `XmTextRemove()` | Delete the primary selection. |
| `XmTextReplace()` | Replace part of the text string. |
| `XmTextReplaceWcs()` | Replace part of the wide-character text string. |
| `XmTextScroll()` | Scroll the text. |
| `XmTextSetAddMode()` | Set the add mode state. |
| `XmTextSetCursorPosition()` | Set the position of the insertion cursor. |
| `XmTextSetEditable()` | Set the edit permission state. |
| `XmTextSetHighlight()` | Highlight text. |
| `XmTextSetInsertionPosition()` | Set the position of the insertion cursor. |
| `XmTextSetMaxLength()` | Set the maximum possible length of a text string. |
| `XmTextSetSelection()` | Set the value of the primary selection. |
| `XmTextSetSource()` | Set the text source. |
| `XmTextSetString()` | Set the text string. |
| `XmTextSetStringWcs()` | Set the wide-character text string. |
| `XmTextSetTopCharacter()` | Set the position of the first character of text that is displayed. |
| `XmTextShowPosition()` | Display the text at a specified position. |
| `XmTextXYToPos()` | Get the character position for an x, y position. |

## ToggleButton

| | |
|---|---|
| `XmToggleButtonGadgetGetState()` | Get the state of a ToggleButton. |
| `XmToggleButtonGadgetSetState()` | Set the state of a ToggleButton. |
| `XmToggleButtonGetState()` | Get the state of a ToggleButton. |
| `XmToggleButtonSetState()` | Set the state of a ToggleButton. |

## Widget Class

| | |
|---|---|
| `XmIs`*`Object`*`()` | Determine whether a widget is a subclass of a class. |

## Widget Creation

| | |
|---|---|
| `XmCreate`*`Object`*`()` | Create an instance of a particular widget class or compound object. |
| `XmCreateSimpleOptionMenu()` | Create an OptionMenu compound object. |
| `XmVaCreateSimpleCheckBox()` | Create a CheckBox compound object. |
| `XmVaCreateSimpleMenuBar()` | Create a MenuBar compound object. |
| `XmVaCreateSimplePopupMenu()` | Create a PopupMenu compound object as the child of a MenuShell. |
| `XmVaCreateSimplePulldownMenu()` | Create a PulldownMenu compound object as the child of a MenuShell. |
| `XmVaCreateSimpleRadioBox()` | Create a RadioBox compound object. |

## Widget Internals

| | |
|---|---|
| `XmGetSecondaryResourceData()` | Retrieve secondary widget resource data. |
| `XmResolveAllPartOffset()` | Ensure upward-compatible widgets and applications. |

| | |
|---|---|
| `XmResolvePartOffsets()` | Ensure upward-compatible widgets and applications. |

### Widget Layout

| | |
|---|---|
| `XmWidgetGetBaselines()` | Get the positions of the baselines in a widget. |
| `XmWidgetGetDisplayRect()` | Get the display rectangle for a widget. |

### Widget Selection

| | |
|---|---|
| `XmTrackingEvent()` | Allow for modal selection of a component. |
| `XmTrackingLocate()` | Allow for modal selection of a component. |

### Window Manager

| | |
|---|---|
| `XmIsMotifWMRunning()` | Check whether the Motif Window Manager (*mwm*) is running. |

## A.2 Alphabetical Listing

| | |
|---|---|
| `MrmCloseHierarchy(3)` | Close an Mrm hierarchy. |
| `MrmFetchBitmapLiteral(3)` | Retrieve an exported bitmap from an Mrm hierarchy. |
| `MrmFetchColorLiteral(3)` | Retrieve an exported color value from an Mrm hierarchy. |
| `MrmFetchIconLiteral(3)` | Retrieve an exported icon from an Mrm hierarchy. |
| `MrmFetchLiteral(3)` | Retrieve an exported value from an Mrm hierarchy. |
| `MrmFetchSetValues(3)` | Set widget resources to values retrieved from an Mrm hierarchy. |
| `MrmFetchWidget(3)` | Create the widget tree rooted at a named widget. |
| `MrmFetchWidgetOverride(3)` | Create the widget tree rooted at a named widget and override the resources set in the UID file. |
| `MrmInitialize(3)` | Prepare the Mrm library for use. |
| `MrmOpenHierarchy(3)` | Open an Mrm hierarchy. |
| `MrmOpenHierarchyPerDisplay(3)` | Open an Mrm hierarchy. |
| `MrmRegisterClass(3)` | Register a widget creation function for a non-Motif widget |
| `MrmRegisterNames(3)` | Register application-defined values and procedures. |
| `MrmRegisterNamesInHierarchy(3)` | Register application-defined values and procedures for use in a specific UIL hierarchy. |
| `XmActivateProtocol()` | Activate a protocol. |
| `XmActivateWMProtocol()` | Activate the XA_WM_PROTOCOLS protocol. |
| `XmAddProtocolCallback()` | Add client callbacks to a protocol. |
| `XmAddProtocols()` | Add protocols to the protocol manager. |
| `XmAddTabGroup()` | Add a widget to a list of tab groups. |
| `XmAddWMProtocolCallback()` | Add client callbacks to a XA_WM_PROTOCOLS protocol. |

| | |
|---|---|
| `XmAddWMProtocols()` | Add the XA_WM_PROTOCOLS protocols to the protocol manager. |
| `XmCascadeButtonGadgetHighlight()` | Set the highlight state of a CascadeButton. |
| `XmCascadeButtonHighlight()` | Set the highlight state of a CascadeButton. |
| `XmChangeColor()` | Update the colors for a widget. |
| `XmClipboardBeginCopy()` | Set up storage for a clipboard copy operation. |
| `XmClipboardCancelCopy()` | Cancel a copy operation to the clipboard. |
| `XmClipboardCopy()` | Copy a data item to temporary storage for later copying to the clipboard. |
| `XmClipboardCopyByName()` | Copy a data item passed by name. |
| `XmClipboardEndCopy()` | End a copy operation to the clipboard |
| `XmClipboardEndRetrieve()` | End a copy operation from the clipboard. |
| `XmClipboardInquireCount()` | Get the number of data item formats available on the clipboard. |
| `XmClipboardInquireFormat()` | Get the specified clipboard data format name. |
| `XmClipboardInquireLength()` | Get the length of the data item on the clipboard. |
| `XmClipboardInquirePendingItems()` | Get a list of pending data ID/private ID pairs. |
| `XmClipboardLock()` | Lock the clipboard. |
| `XmClipboardRegisterFormat()` | Register a new format for clipboard data items. |
| `XmClipboardRetrieve()` | Retrieve a data item from the clipboard. |
| `XmClipboardStartCopy()` | Set up storage for a clipboard copy operation. |
| `XmClipboardStartRetrieve()` | Start a clipboard retrieval operation. |
| `XmClipboardUndoCopy()` | Remove the last item copied to the clipboard. |
| `XmClipboardUnlock()` | Unlock the clipboard. |
| `XmClipboardWithdrawFormat()` | Indicate that an application does not want to supply a data item any longer. |
| `XmCommandAppendValue()` | Append a compound string to the command. |
| `XmCommandError()` | Display an error message in a Command widget. |
| `XmCommandGetChild()` | Get the specified child of a Command widget. |
| `XmCommandSetValue()` | Replace the command string. |
| `XmConvertUnits()` | Convert a value to a specified unit type. |
| `XmCreate()`*`Object`* | Create an instance of a particular widget class or compound object. |
| `XmCreateSimpleOptionMenu()` | Create an OptionMenu compound object. |
| `XmCvtCTToXmString()` | Convert compound text to a compound string |
| `XmCvtStringToUnitType()` | Convert a string to a unit-type value. |
| `XmCvtXmStringToCT()` | Convert a compound string to compound text. |
| `XmDeactivateProtocol()` | Deactivate a protocol. |
| `XmDeactivateWMProtocol()` | Deactivate the XA_WM_PROTOCOLS protocol. |
| `XmDestroyPixmap()` | Remove a pixmap from the pixmap cache. |
| `XmDragCancel()` | Cancel a drag operation. |
| `XmDragStart()` | Start a drag operation. |
| `XmDropSiteConfigureStackingOrder()` | Change the stacking order of a drop site. |
| `XmDropSiteEndUpdate()` | End an update of multiple drop sites. |
| `XmDropSiteQueryStackingOrder()` | Get the stacking order of a drop site. |
| `XmDropSiteRegister()` | Register a drop site. |
| `XmDropSiteRetrieve()` | Get the resource values for a drop site. |

| | |
|---|---|
| `XmDropSiteStartUpdate()` | Start an update of multiple drop sites. |
| `XmDropSiteUnregister()` | Remove a drop site. |
| `XmDropSiteUpdate()` | Change the resource values for a drop site. |
| `XmDropTransferAdd()` | Add drop transfer entries to a drop operation. |
| `XmDropTransferStart()` | Start a drop operation. |
| `XmFileSelectionBoxGetChild()` | Get the specified child of a FileSelectionBox widget. |
| `XmFileSelectionDoSearch()` | Start a directory search. |
| `XmFontListAdd()` | Create a new font list. |
| `XmFontListAppendEntry()` | Append a font entry to a font list. |
| `XmFontListCopy()` | Copy a font list. |
| `XmFontListCreate()` | Create a font list. |
| `XmFontListEntryCreate()` | Create a font list entry. |
| `XmFontListEntryFree()` | Free the memory used by a font list entry. |
| `XmFontListEntryGetFont()` | Get the font information from a font list entry. |
| `XmFontListEntryGetTag()` | Get the tag of a font list entry. |
| `XmFontListEntryLoad()` | Load a font or create a font set and then create a font list entry. |
| `XmFontListFree()` | Free the memory used by a font list. |
| `XmFontListFreeFontContext()` | Free a font context. |
| `XmFontListGetNextFont()` | Retrieve information about the next font list element. |
| `XmFontListInitFontContext()` | Create a font context. |
| `XmFontListNextEntry()` | Retrieve the next font list entry in a font list. |
| `XmFontListRemoveEntry()` | Remove a font list entry from a font list. |
| `XmGetAtomName()` | Get the string representation of an atom. |
| `XmGetColorCalculation()` | Get the procedure that calculates default colors. |
| `XmGetColors()` | Get the foreground, select, and shadow colors. |
| `XmGetDestination()` | Get the current destination widget. |
| `XmGetDragContext()` | Get information about a drag and drop operation. |
| `XmGetFocusWidget()` | Get the widget that has the keyboard focus. |
| `XmGetMenuCursor()` | Get the current menu cursor. |
| `XmGetPixmap()` | Create and return a pixmap. |
| `XmGetPixmapByDepth()` | Create and return a pixmap of the specified depth. |
| `XmGetPostedFromWidget()` | Get the widget that posted a menu. |
| `XmGetSecondaryResourceData()` | Retrieve secondary widget resource data. |
| `XmGetTabGroup()` | Get the tab group for a widget. |
| `XmGetTearOffControl()` | Get the tear-off control for a menu. |
| `XmGetVisibility()` | Determine whether or not a widget is visible. |
| `XmGetXmDisplay()` | Get the Display object for a display. |
| `XmGetXmScreen()` | Get the Screen object for a screen. |
| `XmInstallImage()` | Install an image in the image cache. |
| `XmInternAtom()` | Return an atom for a given property name string. |
| `XmIs()`*`Object`* | Determine whether a widget is a subclass of a class. |
| `XmIsMotifWMRunning()` | Check whether the Motif Window Manager (*mwm*) is running. |

| | |
|---|---|
| XmIsTraversable() | Determine whether or not a widget can receive the keyboard focus. |
| XmListAddItem() | Add an item to a list. |
| XmListAddItems() | Add items to a list. |
| XmListAddItemUnselected() | Add an item to a list. |
| XmListAddItemsUnselected() | Add items to a list. |
| XmListDeleteAllItems() | Delete all of the items from a list. |
| XmListDeleteItem() | Delete an item from a list. |
| XmListDeleteItems() | Delete items from a list. |
| XmListDeleteItemsPos() | Delete items starting at a specified position from a list. |
| XmListDeletePos() | Delete an item at the specified position from a list. |
| XmListDeletePositions() | Delete items at the specified positions from a list. |
| XmListDeselectAllItems() | Deselect all items in a list. |
| XmListDeselectItem() | Deselect an item from a list. |
| XmListDeselectPos() | Deselect an item at the specified position from a list. |
| XmListGetKbdItemPos() | Get the position of the item in a list that has the location cursor. |
| XmListGetMatchPos() | Get all occurences of an item in a list. |
| XmListItemExists() | Determine if a specified item is in a list. |
| XmListItemPos() | Return the position of an item in a list. |
| XmListPosSelected() | Check if the item at a specified position is selected in a list. |
| XmListPosToBounds() | Return the bounding box of an item at the specified position in a list. |
| XmListReplaceItems() | Replace specified items in a list. |
| XmListReplaceItemsPos() | Replace specified items in a list. |
| XmListReplaceItemsPosUnselected() | Replace specified items in a list. |
| XmListReplaceItemsUnselected() | Replace specified items in a list. |
| XmListReplacePositions() | Replace items at the specified postions in a list. |
| XmListSelectedPos() | Get the positions of the selected items in a list. |
| XmListSelectItem() | Select an item from a list. |
| XmListSelectPos() | Select an item at the specified position from a list. |
| XmListSetAddMode() | Set add mode in a list. |
| XmListSetBottomItem() | Set the last visible item in a list. |
| XmListSetBottomPos() | Set the last visible item in a list. |
| XmListSetHorizPos() | Set the horizontal position of a list. |
| XmListSetItem() | Set the first visible item in a list. |
| XmListSetKbdItemPos() | Set the position of the location cursor in a list. |
| XmListSetPos() | Sets the first visible item in a list. |
| XmListUpdateSelectedList() | Update the list of selected items in a list. |
| XmListYToPos() | Get the position of the item at the specified y-coordinate in a list. |
| XmMainWindowSep1() | Get the widget ID of a MainWindow Separator. |
| XmMainWindowSep2() | Get the widget ID of a MainWindow Separator. |
| XmMainWindowSep3() | Get the widget ID of a MainWindow Separator. |

| | |
|---|---|
| `XmMainWindowSetAreas()` | Specify the children for a MainWindow. |
| `XmMapSegmentEncoding()` | Get the compound text encoding format for a font list element tag. |
| `XmMenuPosition()` | Position a popup menu. |
| `XmMessageBoxGetChild()` | Get the specified child of a MessageBox widget. |
| `XmOptionButtonGadget()` | Get the CascadeButtonGadget in an option menu. |
| `XmOptionLabelGadget()` | Get the LabelGadget in an option menu. |
| `XmProcessTraversal()` | Set the widget that has the keyboard focus. |
| `XmRegisterSegmentEncoding()` | Register a compound text encoding format for a font list element tag. |
| `XmRemoveProtocolCallback()` | Remove client callback from a protocol. |
| `XmRemoveProtocols()` | Remove protocols from the protocol manager. |
| `XmRemoveTabGroup()` | Remove a widget from a list of tab groups. |
| `XmRemoveWMProtocolCallback()` | Remove client callbacks from a XA_WM_PROTOCOLS protocol. |
| `XmRemoveWMProtocols()` | Remove the XA_WM_PROTOCOLS protocols from the protocol manager. |
| `XmRepTypeAddReverse()` | Install the reverse converter for a representation type. |
| `XmRepTypeGetId()` | Get the ID number of a representation type. |
| `XmRepTypeGetNameList()` | Get the list of value names for a representation type. |
| `XmRepTypeGetRecord()` | Get information about a representation type. |
| `XmRepTypeGetRegistered()` | Get the registered representation types. |
| `XmRepTypeInstallTearOffModelConverter()` | Install the resource converter for `XmNtearOffModel`. |
| `XmRepTypeRegister()` | Register a representation type resource. |
| `XmRepTypeValidValue()` | Determine the validity of a numerical value for a representation type. |
| `XmResolveAllPartOffset()` | Ensure upward-compatible widgets and applications. |
| `XmResolvePartOffsets()` | Ensure upward-compatible widgets and applications. |
| `XmScaleGetValue()` | Get the slider value for a Scale widget. |
| `XmScaleSetValue()` | Set the slider value for a Scale widget. |
| `XmScrollBarGetValues()` | Get information about the current state of a ScrollBar widget. |
| `XmScrollBarSetValues()` | Set the current state of a ScrollBar widget. |
| `XmScrolledWindowsSetAreas()` | Specify the children for a scrolled window. |
| `XmScrollVisible()` | Make an obscured child of a ScrolledWindow visible. |
| `XmSelectionBoxGetChild()` | Get the specified child of a SelectionBox widget. |
| `XmSetColorCalculation()` | Set the procedure that calculates default colors. |
| `XmSetFontUnit()` | Set the font unit values. |
| `XmSetFontUnits()` | Set the font unit values. |
| `XmSetMenuCursor()` | Set the current menu cursor. |
| `XmSetProtocolHooks()` | Set prehooks and posthooks for a protocol. |

| | |
|---|---|
| `XmSetWMProtocolHooks()` | Set prehooks and posthooks for the XA_WM_-PROTOCOLS protocol. |
| `XmStringBaseline()` | Get the baseline spacing for a compound string. |
| `XmStringByteCompare()` | Compare two compound strings byte-by-byte. |
| `XmStringCompare()` | Compare two compound strings. |
| `XmStringConcat()` | Concatenate two compound strings. |
| `XmStringCopy()` | Copy a compound string. |
| `XmStringCreate()` | Create a compound string. |
| `XmStringCreateLocalized()` | Create a compound string in the current locale. |
| `XmStringCreateLtoR()` | Create a compound string. |
| `XmStringCreateSimple()` | Create a compound string in the current language environment. |
| `XmStringDirectionCreate()` | Create a compound string containing a direction component. |
| `XmStringDraw()` | Draw a compound string. |
| `XmStringDrawImage()` | Draw a compound string. |
| `XmStringDrawUnderline()` | Draw a compound string with an underlined sub-string. |
| `XmStringEmpty()` | Determine whether there are text segments in a compound string. |
| `XmStringExtent()` | Get the smallest rectangle that contains a compound string. |
| `XmStringFree()` | Free the memory used by a compound string. |
| `XmStringFreeContext()` | Free a string context. |
| `XmStringGetLtoR()` | Get a text segment from a compound string. |
| `XmStringGetNextComponent()` | Retrieves information about the next compound string component. |
| `XmStringGetNextSegment()` | Retrieves information about the next compound string segment. |
| `XmStringHasSubstring()` | Determine whether a compound string contains a substring. |
| `XmStringHeight()` | Get the line height of a compound string. |
| `XmStringInitContext()` | Create a string context. |
| `XmStringLength()` | Get the length of a compound string. |
| `XmStringLineCount()` | Get the number of lines in a compound string. |
| `XmStringNConcat()` | Concatenate a specified portion of a compound string to another compound string. |
| `XmStringNCopy()` | Copy a specified portion of a compound string. |
| `XmStringPeekNextComponent()` | Returns the type of the next compound string component. |
| `XmStringSegmentCreate()` | Create a compound string segment. |
| `XmStringSeparatorCreate()` | Create a compound string containing a separator component. |
| `XmStringWidth()` | Get the width of the longest line of text in a compound string. |
| `XmTargetsAreCompatible()` | Determine whether or not the target types of a drag source and a drop site match. |
| `XmTextClearSelection()` | Clear the primary selection. |

| | |
|---|---|
| `XmTextCopy()` | Copy the primary selection to the clipboard. |
| `XmTextCut()` | Copy the primary selection to the clipboard and remove the selected text. |
| `XmTextDisableRedisplay()` | Prevent visual update of a Text widget. |
| `XmTextEnableRedisplay()` | Allow visual update of a Text widget. |
| `XmTextFieldClearSelection()` | Clear the primary selection. |
| `XmTextFieldCopy()` | Copy the primary selection to the clipboard. |
| `XmTextFieldCut()` | Copy the primary selection to the clipboard and remove the selected text. |
| `XmTextFieldGetBaseline()` | Get the position of the baseline. |
| `XmTextFieldGetCursorPosition()` | Get the position of the insertion cursor. |
| `XmTextFieldGetEditable()` | Get the edit permission state. |
| `XmTextFieldGetInsertionPosition()` | Get the position of the insertion cursor. |
| `XmTextFieldGetLastPosition()` | Get the position of the last character of text. |
| `XmTextFieldGetMaxLength()` | Get the maximum possible length of a text string. |
| `XmTextFieldGetSelection()` | Get the value of the primary selection. |
| `XmTextFieldGetSelectionPosition()` | Get the position of the primary selection. |
| `XmTextFieldGetSelectionWcs()` | Get the wide-character value of the primary selection. |
| `XmTextFieldGetString()` | Get the text string. |
| `XmTextFieldGetStringWcs()` | Get the wide-character text string. |
| `XmTextFieldGetSubstring()` | Get a copy of part of the text string. |
| `XmTextFieldGetSubstringWcs()` | Get a copy of part of the wide-character text string. |
| `XmTextFieldInsert()` | Insert a string into the text string. |
| `XmTextFieldInsertWcs()` | Insert a wide-character string into the text string. |
| `XmTextFieldPaste()` | Insert the clipboard selection. |
| `XmTextFieldPosToXY()` | Get the x, y position of a character position. |
| `XmTextFieldRemove()` | Delete the primary selection. |
| `XmTextFieldReplace()` | Replace part of the text string. |
| `XmTextFieldReplaceWcs()` | Replace part of the wide-character text string. |
| `XmTextFieldSetAddMode()` | Set the add mode state. |
| `XmTextFieldSetCursorPosition()` | Set the position of the insertion cursor. |
| `XmTextFieldSetEditable()` | Set the edit permission state. |
| `XmTextFieldSetHighlight()` | Highlight text. |
| `XmTextFieldSetInsertionPosition()` | Set the position of the insertion cursor. |
| `XmTextFieldSetMaxLength()` | Set the maximum possible length of a text string. |
| `XmTextFieldSetSelection()` | Set the value of the primary selection. |
| `XmTextFieldSetString()` | Set the text string. |
| `XmTextFieldSetStringWcs()` | Set the wide-character text string. |
| `XmTextFieldShowPosition()` | Display the text at a specified position. |
| `XmTextFieldXYToPos()` | Get the character position for an x, y position. |
| `XmTextFindString()` | Find the beginning position of a text string. |
| `XmTextFindStringWcs()` | Find the beginning position of a wide-character text string. |
| `XmTextGetBaseline()` | Get the position of the baseline. |
| `XmTextGetCursorPosition()` | Get the position of the insertion cursor. |
| `XmTextGetEditable()` | Get the edit permission state. |

| | |
|---|---|
| `XmTextGetInsertionPosition()` | Get the position of the insertion cursor. |
| `XmTextGetLastPosition()` | Get the position of the last character of text. |
| `XmTextGetMaxLength()` | Get the maximum possible length of a text string. |
| `XmTextGetSelection()` | Get the value of the primary selection. |
| `XmTextGetSelectionPosition()` | Get the position of the primary selection. |
| `XmTextGetSelectionWcs()` | Get the wide-character value of the primary selection. |
| `XmTextGetSource()` | Get the text source. |
| `XmTextGetString()` | Get the text string. |
| `XmTextGetStringWcs()` | Get the wide-character text string. |
| `XmTextGetSubstring()` | Get a copy of part of the text string. |
| `XmTextGetSubstringWcs()` | Get a copy of part of the wide-character text string. |
| `XmTextGetTopCharacter()` | Get the position of the first character of text that is displayed. |
| `XmTextInsert()` | Insert a string into the text string. |
| `XmTextInsertWcs()` | Insert a wide-character string into the text string. |
| `XmTextPaste()` | Insert the clipboard selection. |
| `XmTextPosToXY()` | Get the x, y position of a character position. |
| `XmTextRemove()` | Delete the primary selection. |
| `XmTextReplace()` | Replace part of the text string. |
| `XmTextReplaceWcs()` | Replace part of the wide-character text string. |
| `XmTextScroll()` | Scroll the text. |
| `XmTextSetAddMode()` | Set the add mode state. |
| `XmTextSetCursorPosition()` | Set the position of the insertion cursor. |
| `XmTextSetEditable()` | Set the edit permission state. |
| `XmTextSetHighlight()` | Highlight text. |
| `XmTextSetInsertionPosition()` | Set the position of the insertion cursor. |
| `XmTextSetMaxLength()` | Set the maximum possible length of a text string. |
| `XmTextSetSelection()` | Set the value of the primary selection. |
| `XmTextSetSource()` | Set the text source. |
| `XmTextSetString()` | Set the text string. |
| `XmTextSetStringWcs()` | Set the wide-character text string. |
| `XmTextSetTopCharacter()` | Set the position of the first character of text that is displayed. |
| `XmTextShowPosition()` | Display the text at a specified position. |
| `XmTextXYToPos()` | Get the character position for an x, y position. |
| `XmToggleButtonGadgetGetState()` | Get the state of a ToggleButton. |
| `XmToggleButtonGadgetSetState()` | Set the state of a ToggleButton. |
| `XmToggleButtonGetState()` | Get the state of a ToggleButton. |
| `XmToggleButtonSetState()` | Set the state of a ToggleButton. |
| `XmTrackingEvent()` | Allow for modal selection of a component. |
| `XmTrackingLocate()` | Allow for modal selection of a component. |
| `XmTranslateKey()` | Convert a keycode to a keysym using the default translator. |
| `XmUninstallImage()` | Remove an image from the image cache. |
| `XmUpdateDisplay()` | Update the display. |
| `XmVaCreateSimpleCheckBox()` | Create a CheckBox compound object. |

| | |
|---|---|
| `XmVaCreateSimpleMenuBar()` | Create a MenuBar compound object. |
| `XmVaCreateSimplePopupMenu()` | Create a PopupMenu compound object as the child of a MenuShell. |
| `XmVaCreateSimplePulldownMenu()` | Create a PulldownMenu compound object as the child of a MenuShell. |
| `XmVaCreateSimpleRadioBox()` | Create a RadioBox compound object. |
| `XmWidgetGetBaselines()` | Get the positions of the baselines in a widget. |
| `XmWidgetGetDisplayRect()` | Get the display rectangle for a widget. |

Data Types

# B
# Data Types

This appendix summarizes the data types used as arguments or return values in Motif toolkit and Motif Resource Manager functions. Xt and Xlib data types used by the routines are included. For each data type, the description states the header file that defines the type. Data types (which include simple typedefs as well as structures and enums) are listed alphabetically. Defined symbols (for example, constants used to specify the value of a mask or a field in a structure) or other data types used only to set structure members are listed with the data type in which they are used.

**ArgList**

An `ArgList` is used for setting resources in calls to widget creation routines. It is defined as follows in *<X11/Intrinsic.h>*:

```
typedef struct {
    String      name;
    XtArgVal    value;
} Arg, *ArgList;
```

The `name` field is typically a defined constant of the form `XtN`*`resourcename`* from either *<X11/Stringdefs.h>* or a widget public header file. It identifies the name of the argument to be set. The `value` field is an `XtArgVal`, a system-dependent typedef chosen to be large enough to hold a pointer to a function. It is often not large enough to hold a `float` or `double`.

**Atom**

To optimize communication with the server, a property is referenced by string name only once, and subsequently by a unique integer ID called an Atom. Predefined atoms are defined in *<X11/Xatom.h>* using defined symbols beginning with `XA_`; other atoms can be obtained from the server by calling the Xlib function `XInternAtom()`. The Motif toolkit supports an atom-caching mechanism with `XmInternAtom()`. Atoms are used by the Motif protocol routines.

**Boolean**

A typedef from *<X11/Intrinsic.h>* used to indicate `True` (1) or `False` (0). Use either the symbols `TRUE` or `FALSE`, defined in *<X11/Intrinsic.h>* or `True` or `False`, defined in *<X11/Xlib.h>*.

**Cardinal**

A typedef from *<X11/Intrinsic.h>* used to specify any unsigned integer value.

**`Colormap`**

An `XID` (server resource ID) from *<X11/X.h>* that identifies a colormap resource maintained by the server. `XmGetColors()` and `MrmFetchColorLiteral()` use `Colormap` values.

**`Cursor`**

A typedef in *<X11/X.h>* for an `XID` (server resource ID) that identifies a cursor resource maintained by the server. A `Cursor` is used to set the menu cursor in Motif. `XmTrackingEvent()` and `XmTrackingLocate()` also have a `Cursor` parameter.

**`Dimension`**

A typedef from *<X11/Intrinsic.h>* used to specify window sizes.

**`Display`**

A structure defined in *<X11/Xlib.h>* that contains information about the display the program is running on. `Display` structure fields should not be accessed directly; Xlib provides a number of macros to return essential values. In Xt, a pointer to the current `Display` is returned by a call to `XtDisplay()`. The Motif clipboard routines and string drawing routines, among others, use `Display` parameters. This data type should not be confused with the Display object in Motif 1.2.

**`GC`**

A graphics context, which is defined in *<X11/X.h>*. A GC is a pointer to a structure that contains a copy of the settings in a server resource. The server resource, in turn, contains information about how to interpret a graphics primitive. A pointer to a structure of this type is returned by the Xlib call `XCreateGC()` or the Xt call `XtGetGC()`. The Motif string drawing routines use `GC` parameters. The members of this structure should not be accessed directly.

**`KeyCode`**

A server-dependent code that describes a key that has been pressed. A `KeyCode` is defined as an unsigned character in *<X11/X.h>*. `XmTranslateKey()` takes a `KeyCode` argument.

**`KeySym`**

A portable representation of the symbol on the cap of a key. The Motif toolkit use both virtual keysyms (osfkeysyms) and actual keysyms. The toolkit maps osfkeysyms to actual keysyms. Individual `KeySyms` are symbols defined in *<X11/keysymdef.h>*. The keycode-to-keysym lookup tables are maintained by the server, and hence a `KeySym` is actually an `XID`. `XmVaCreateSimpleOptionMenu` and `XmTranslateKey()` take `KeySym` arguments.

**`Modifiers`**

Any bitmask that describes modifier keys. The `Modifiers` type and its values are defined as follows in *<X11/Intrinsic.h>* and *<X11/X.h>*:

```
typedef unsigned int Modifiers;
#define ShiftMask (1<<0)
#define LockMask (1<<1)
#define ControlMask (1<<2)
#define Mod1Mask (1<<3)
#define Mod2Mask (1<<4)
#define Mod3Mask (1<<5)
```

```
#define Mod4Mask (1<<6)
#define Mod5Mask (1<<7)
```

XmTranslateKey() takes an argument of type Modifiers.

**MrmCode**

Indicates the type of a value returned by MrmFetchLiteral(). Codes are prefixed with MrmRtype and are defined in *<Mrm/MrmPublic.h>*.

**MrmCount**

A typedef in *<Mrm/MrmPublic.h>* for specifying a count of items.

**MrmHierarchy**

A pointer to an Mrm hierarchy opened with MrmOpenHierarchy() or MrmOpenHierarchyPerDisplay(). The type is defined in *<Mrm/MrmPublic.h>*. The functions associate one or more UID files with the hierarchy. An MrmHierarchy is a required argument of most of the Mrm functions.

**MrmOsOpenParamPtr**

A structure of operating system-dependent settings used as an argument to MrmOpenHierarchy() and MrmOpenHierarchyPerDisplay() and defined in *<Mrm/MrmPublic.h>*. As of Motif 1.2, the settings are only useful to the UIL compiler.

**MrmRegisterArg**

See MrmRegisterArgList.

**MrmRegisterArgList**

A type used for registering application-defined procedures and identifiers with MrmRegisterNames() and MrmRegisterNamesInHierarchy(). It is defined as follows in *<Mrm/MrmPublic.h>*:

```
typedef struct {
    String name;            /* case-sensitive name */
    XtPointer value;        /* value/procedure to associate with name */
} MrmRegisterArg, *MrmRegisterArglist;
```

**MrmType**

Indicates the class of a widget created with MrmFetchWidget() or MrmFetchWidgetOverride(). As of Motif 1.2, the types are not defined in any of the Mrm include files, although the OSF documentation states that they are defined in *<Mrm/Mrm.h>*.

**Pixel**

An unsigned long integer (defined in *<X11/Intrinsic.h>*) that serves as an index to a colormap. The Motif pixmap and color routines, as well as some Mrm functions, use Pixel values.

**Pixmap**

An XID (server resource ID) that represents a two-dimensional array of pixels—a drawable with a specified width, height, and depth (number of planes), but no screen coordinates. The Motif pixmap routines, as well as some Mrm functions, use Pixmap parameters.

**Position**

A typedef from <*X11/Intrinsic.h*> used to specify x- and y-coordinates. The Motif string drawing routines, among others, use `Position` values.

**Screen**

A structure that describes the characteristics of a screen (one or more of which make up a display). A pointer to a list of these structures is a member of the `Display` structure. A pointer to a structure of this type is returned by `XtScreen()` and `XGetWindowAttributes()`. The Motif pixmap routines, among others, as well as some of the Mrm functions, use `Screen` values. This data type should not be confused with the Screen object in Motif 1.2.

```
typedef struct {
    XExtData *ext_data;         /* hook for extension to hang data */
    struct _XDisplay *display;/* back pointer to display structure */
    Window root;                /* root window ID */
    int width, height;          /* width and height of screen */
    int mwidth, mheight;        /* width and height of  in millimeters */
    int ndepths;                /* number of depths possible */
    Depth *depths;              /* list of allowable depths on the screen */
    int root_depth;             /* bits per pixel */
    Visual *root_visual;        /* root visual */
    GC default_gc;              /* GC for the root root visual */
    Colormap cmap;              /* default colormap */
    unsigned long white_pixel;
    unsigned long black_pixel;/* white and black pixel values */
    int max_maps, min_maps;     /* max and min colormaps */
    int backing_store;          /* Never, WhenMapped, Always */
    Bool save_unders;
    long root_input_mask;       /* initial root input mask */
} Screen;
```

**String**

A typedef for `char *`.

**StringTable**

A pointer to a list of `Strings`.

**Time**

An `unsigned long` value (defined in <*X11/X.h*>) that contains a time value in milliseconds. The constant `CurrentTime` is interpreted as the time in milliseconds since the server was started. The `Time` data type is used in event structures and as an argument to some Motif clipboard, drag and drop, and text selection routines.

**Visual**

A structure that defines a way of using color resources on a particular screen.

**Widget**

A structure returned by calls to create a widget, such as `XtAppInitialize()`, `XtCreateWidget()`, and `XtCreateManagedWidget()`, as well as the Motif widget creation routines. The members of this structure should not be accessed directly from applications; they should regard it as an opaque pointer. Type `Widget` is actually a pointer to a widget instance structure. Widget code accesses instance variables from this structure.

**WidgetClass**

A pointer to the widget class structure, used to identify the widget class in various routines that create widgets or that return information about widgets. Widget class names have the form *nameWidgetClass*, with the exception of the widget-precursor classes, `Object` and `RectObj`, which have the class pointers `objectClass` and `rectObjClass`, respectively.

**WidgetList**

A pointer to a list of `Widgets`.

**Window**

A resource maintained by the server, and known on the client side only by an integer ID. In Xt, a widget's window can be returned by the `XtWindow()` macro. Given the window, the corresponding widget can be returned by `XtWindowToWidget()`. The Motif clipboard and string drawing routines use `Window` values.

**XEvent**

A union of all thirty event structures. The first member is always the type, so it is possible to branch on the type, and do event-specific processing in each branch. Both `XmDragStart()` and `XmTrackingEvent()` take `XEvent` parameters. An `XButtonPressedEvent`, which is one of the event structures in the union, is used by `XmMenuPosition()`.

**XFontSet**

Specifies all of the fonts needed to display text in a particular locale. The Motif font list entry routines can use `XFontSet` values.

**XFontStruct**

Specifies metric information (in pixels) for an entire font. This structure (defined in *<X11/Xlib.h>*) is filled by means of the Xlib routines `XLoadQueryFont()` and `XQueryFont()`. `XListFontsWithInfo()` also fills it, but with metric information for the entire font only, not for each character. Some of the Motif font list routines use `XFontStructs`.

```
typedef struct {
    XExtData      *ext_data;            /* hook for extension to hang data */
    Font          fid;                  /* font ID for this font */
    unsigned      direction;            /* direction the font is painted */
    unsigned      min_char_or_byte2;    /* first character */
    unsigned      max_char_or_byte2;    /* last character */
    unsigned      min_byte1;            /* first row that exists */
    unsigned      max_byte1;            /* last row that exists */
    Bool          all_chars_exist;      /* flag if all characters have nonzero size*/
    unsigned      default_char;         /* char to print for undefined character */
    int           n_properties;         /* how many properties there are */
    XFontProp     *properties;          /* pointer to array of additional properties*/
    XCharStruct   min_bounds;           /* minimum bounds over all existing char*/
    XCharStruct   max_bounds;           /* maximum bounds over all existing char*/
    XCharStruct   *per_char;            /* first_char to last_char information */
    int           ascent;               /* logical extent of largest character */
                                        /* above baseline */
    int           descent;              /* logical descent of largest character */
                                        /* below baseline */
} XFontStruct;
```

The `direction` member is specified by one of the following constants from *<X11/X.h>*:

```
FontLeftToRight            FontRightToLeft            FontChange
```

### XImage

Describes an area of the screen. This structure (defined in *<X11/Xlib.h>*) is used by `XmInstallImage` and `XmUninstallImage`.

```
typedef struct _XImage {
    int              width, height;       /* size of image in pixels */
    int              xoffset;             /* number of pixels offset in X direction */
    int              format;              /* XYBitmap, XYPixmap, ZPixmap */
    char             *data;               /* pointer to image data */
    int              byte_order;          /* data byte order:  LSBFirst, MSBFirst */
    int              bitmap_unit;         /* quant. of scan line 8, 16, 32 */
    int              bitmap_bit_order;    /* LSBFirst, MSBFirst */
    int              bitmap_pad;          /* 8, 16, 32 */
    int              depth;               /* depth of image */
    int              bytes_per_line;      /* accelerator to next line */
    int              bits_per_pixel;      /* bits per pixel (ZPixmap only) */
    unsigned long    red_mask;            /* bits in z arrangement */
    unsigned long    green_mask;
    unsigned long    blue_mask;
    char             *obdata;             /* hook for the object routines to hang on */
    struct funcs {                        /* image manipulation routines */
    struct _XImage *(*create_image)();
        int (*destroy_image)();
        unsigned long (*get_pixel)();
        int (*put_pixel)();
        struct _XImage *(*sub_image)();
        int (*add_pixel)();
    } f;
} XImage;
```

The `format` member is specified by one of the following constants defined in *<X11/X.h>*:

```
XYBitmap        /* depth 1, XYFormat */
XYPixmap        /* pixmap viewed as stack of planes; depth == drawable depth */
ZPixmap         /* pixels in scan-line order; depth == drawable depth */
```

`byte_order` and `bitmap_bit_order` are specified by either `LSBFirst` or `MSBFirst`, which are defined in *<X11/X.h>*.

### XRectangle

Specifies a rectangle. This structure (defined in *<X11/Xlib.h>*) is used by the Motif string drawing routines and `XmGetDisplayRect()`.

```
typedef struct {
    short                    x, y;
    unsigned short           width, height;
} XRectangle;
```

**XmAnyCallbackStruct**

The generic Motif callback structure. It is defined as follows in <*Xm/Xm.h*>:

```
typedef struct {
     int      reason;    /* the reason that the callback was called */
     XEvent   *event;    /* event structure that triggered callback */
} XmAnyCallbackStruct;
```

**XmArrowButtonCallbackStruct**

The callback structure passed to ArrowButton callback routines. It is defined as follows in <*Xm/Xm.h*>:

```
typedef struct {
     int      reason;          /* the reason that the callback was called */
     XEvent   *event;          /* event structure that triggered callback */
     int      click_count;     /* number of clicks in multi-click sequence */
} XmArrowButtonCallbackStruct;
```

**XmButtonType**

An enumerated type that specifies the type of button used in a simple menu creation routine. The valid values for the type are:

```
XmPUSHBUTTON           XmTOGGLEBUTTON
XmRADIOBUTTON          XmCHECKBUTTON
XmCASCADEBUTTON        XmTITLE
XmSEPARATOR            XmDOUBLE_SEPARATOR
```

**XmButtonTypeList**

A pointer to a list of `XmButtonTypes`.

**XmClipboardPendingList**

A structure used in calls to `XmClipboardInquirePendingItems()` to specify a *data_id*/*private_id* pair. It is defined as follows in <*X11/CutPaste.h*>:

```
typedef struct {
    intDataId;
    intPrivateId;
} XmClipboardPendingRec, *XmClipboardPendingList;
```

**XmColorProc**

The prototype for the color calculation procedure used by `XmGetColorCalculation()` and `XmSetColorCalculation()`. It is defined as follows in <*Xm/Xm.h*>:

```
typedef void (*XmColorProc) (XColor, XColor, XColor, XColor, XColor)
    XColor *bg_color;   /* specifies the background color */
    XColor *fg_color;   /* returns the foreground color */
    XColor *sel_color;  /* returns the select color */
    XColor *ts_color;   /* returns the top shadow color */
    XColor *bs_color;   /* returns the bottom shadow color */
```

An `XmColorProc` takes five arguments. The first argument, *bg_color*, is a pointer to an `XColor` structure that specifies the background color. The `red`, `green`, `blue`, and `pixel` fields in the structure contain valid values. The rest of the arguments are pointers to `XColor` structures for the colors that are to be calculated. The procedure fills in the `red`, `green`, and `blue` fields in these structures.

**XmCommandCallbackStruct**

The callback structure passed to Command widget callback routines. It is defined as follows in *<Xm/Xm.h>*:

```
typedef struct {
      int         reason;     /* the reason that the callback was called */
      XEvent      *event;     /* event structure that triggered callback */
      XmString    value;      /* the string contained in the command area */
      int         length;     /* the size of this string */
} XmCommandCallbackStruct;
```

**XmCutPasteProc**

The prototype for the procedure that copies data passed by name to the clipboard. `XmClipboardStartCopy()` specifies a procedure of this type. It is defined as follows in *<Xm/CutPaste.h>*:

```
typedef void (*XmCutPasteProc) (Widget, * int, * int, * int)
    Widget widget;
    int *data_id;
    int *private_id;
    int *reason;
```

An `XmCutPasteProc` takes four arguments. The first argument, *widget*, is the widget passed to the callback routine, which is the same widget as passed to `XmClipboardBeginCopy()`. The *data_id* argument is the ID of the data item that is returned by `XmClipboardCopy()` and *private_id* is the private data passed to `XmClipboardCopy()`. The *reason* argument takes the value `XmCR_CLIPBOARD_DATA_REQUEST`, which indicates that the data must be copied to the clipboard, or `XmCR_CLIPBOARD_DATA_DELETE`, which indicates that the client can delete the data from the clipboard. Although the last three parameters are pointers to integers, the values are read-only and changing them has no effect.

**XmDragDropFininshCallbackStruct**

The callback structure passed to the `XmNdragDropFinishCallback` of a DragContext object. It is defined as follows in *<Xm/DragC.h>*:

```
typedef struct {
      int       reason;     /* the reason the callback was called */
      XEvent    *event;     /* event structure that triggered callback */
      Time      timeStamp; /* time at which operation completed */
} XmDragDropFinishCallbackStruct, *XmDragDropFinishCallback;
```

**XmDragMotionCallbackStruct**

The callback structure passed to the `XmNdragMotionCallback` of a DragContext object. It is defined as follows in *<Xm/DragC.h>*:

```
typedef struct {
      int             reason;         /* the reason the callback was called */
      XEvent          *event;         /* event structure that triggered callback */
      Time            timeStamp;      /* timestamp of logical event */
      unsigned char   operation;      /* current operation */
      unsigned char   operations;     /* supported operations */
      unsigned char   dropSiteStatus; /* valid, invalid, or none */
      Position        x;              /* x-coordinate of pointer */
      Position        y;              /* y-coordinate of pointer */
} XmDragMotionCallbackStruct, *XmDragMotionCallback;
```

### XmDragProcCallbackStruct

The callback structure passed to the XmNdragProc of a drop site. It is defined as follows in *<Xm/DropSMgr.h>*:

```
typedef struct {
    int             reason;         /* the reason the callback was called */
    XEvent          *event;         /* event structure that triggered callback */
    Time            timeStamp;      /* timestamp of logical event */
    Widget          dragContext;    /* DragContext widget assoc. with operation */
    Position        x;              /* x-coordinate of pointer */
    Position        y;              /* y-coordinate of pointer */
    unsigned char   dropSiteStatus; /* valid or invalid */
    unsigned char   operation;      /* current operation */
    unsigned char   operations;     /* supported operations */
    Boolean         animate;        /* toolkit or receiver does animation */
} XmDragProcCallbackStruct, *XmDragProcCallback;
```

### XmDrawingAreaCallbackStruct

The callback structure passed to DrawingArea callback routines. It is defined as follows in *<Xm/Xm.h>*:

```
typedef struct {
    int     reason;         /* the reason that the callback was called */
    XEvent  *event;         /* event structure that triggered callback; */
                            /* for XmNresizeCallback, this is NULL */
    Window  window;         /* the widget's window */
} XmDrawingAreaCallbackStruct;
```

### XmDrawnButtonCallbackStruct

The callback structure pased to DrawnButton callback routines. It is defined as follows in *<Xm/Xm.h>*:

```
typedef struct {
    int     reason;         /* the reason that the callback was called */
    XEvent  *event;         /* event structure that triggered callback */
    Window  window;         /* ID of window in which the event occurred */
    int     click_count;    /* number of multi-clicks */
} XmDrawnButtonCallbackStruct;
```

### XmDropFinishCallbackStruct

The callback structure passed to the XmNdropFinishCallback of a DragContext object. It is defined as follows in *<Xm/DragC.h>*:

```
typedef struct {
    int             reason;           /* the reason the callback was called */
    XEvent          *event;           /* event structure that triggered callback */
    Time            timeStamp;        /* time at which drop completed */
    unsigned char   operation;        /* current operation */
    unsigned char   operations;       /* supported operations */
    unsigned char   dropSiteStatus;   /* valid, invalid, or none */
    unsigned char   dropAction;       /* drop, cancel, help, or interrupt */
    unsigned char   completionStatus; /* success or failure */
} XmDropFinishCallbackStruct, *XmDropFinishCallback;
```

**XmDropProcCallbackStruct**

The callback structure passed to the XmNdropProc of a drop site. It is defined as follows in *<Xm/DropSMgr.h>*:

```
typedef struct {
    int             reason;         /* the reason the callback was called */
    XEvent          *event;         /* event structure that triggered callback */
    Time            timeStamp;      /* timestamp of logical event */
    Widget          dragContext;    /* DragContext widget associated */
                                    /* with operation */
    Position        x;              /* x-coordinate of pointer */
    Position        y;              /* y-coordinate of pointer */
    unsigned char   dropSiteStatus; /* valid or invalid */
    unsigned char   operation;      /* current operation */
    unsigned char   operations;     /* supported operations */
    unsigned char   dropAction;     /* drop or help */
} XmDropProcCallbackStruct, *XmDropProcCallback;
```

**XmDropSiteEnterCallbackStruct**

The callback structure passed to the XmNdropSiteEnterCallback of a DragContext object. It is defined as follows in *<Xm/DragC.h>*:

```
typedef struct {
    int             reason;         /* the reason the callback was called */
    XEvent          *event;         /* event structure that triggered callback */
    Time            timeStamp;      /* time of crossing event */
    unsigned char   operation;      /* current operation */
    unsigned char   operations;     /* supported operations */
    unsigned char   dropSiteStatus; /* valid, invalid, or none */
    Position        x;              /* x-coordinate of pointer */
    Position        y;              /* y-coordinate of pointer */
} XmDropSiteEnterCallbackStruct, *XmDropSiteEnterCallback;
```

**XmDropSiteLeaveCallbackStruct**

The callback structure passed to the XmNdropSiteLeaveCallback of a DragContext object. It is defined as follows in *<Xm/DragC.h>*:

```
typedef struct {
    int     reason;         /* the reason the callback was called */
    XEvent  *event;         /* the event structure that triggered callback */
    Time    timeStamp;      /* time of crossing event */
} XmDropSiteLeaveCallbackStruct, *XmDropSiteLeaveCallback;
```

**XmDropStartCallbackStruct**

The callback structure passed to the XmNdropStartCallback of a DragContext object. It is defined as follows in *<Xm/DragC.h>*:

```
typedef struct {
    int             reason;         /* the reason the callback was called */
    XEvent          *event;         /* event structure that triggered callback */
    Time            timeStamp;      /* time at which drag completed */
    unsigned char   operation;      /* current operation */
    unsigned char   operations;     /* supported operations */
    unsigned char   dropSiteStatus; /* valid, invalid, or none */
    unsigned char   dropAction;     /* drop, cancel, help, or interrupt */
    Position        x;              /* x-coordinate of pointer */
```

```
    Position        y;              /* y-coordinate of pointer */
} XmDropStartCallbackStruct, *XmDropStartCallback;
```



**XmDropTransferEntryRec**

A structure that specifies the targets of a drop operation for a Drop Transfer object. It is defined as follows in *<Xm/DropTrans.h>*:

```
typedef struct {
    XtPointer   client_data;    /* data passed to the transfer proc */
    Atom        target;         /* target format of the transfer */
} XmDropTransferEntryRec, *XmDropTransferEntry;
```

**XmDropTransferEntry**

See XmDropTransferEntryRec.

**XmFileSelectionBoxCallbackStruct**

The callback structure passed to FileSelectionBox callback routines. It is defined as follows in *<Xm/Xm.h>*:

```
typedef struct {
     int        reason;           /* the reason that the callback was called */
     XEvent     *event;           /* event structure that triggered callback */
     XmString   value;            /* current value of XmNdirSpec resource */
     int        length;           /* number of bytes in value member */
     XmString   mask;             /* current value of XmNdirMask resource */
     int        mask_length;      /* number of bytes in mask member */
     XmString   dir;              /* current base directory */
     int        dir_length;       /* number of bytes in dir member */
     XmString   pattern;          /* current search pattern */
     int        pattern_length;   /* number of bytes in pattern member */
} XmFileSelectionBoxCallbackStruct;
```

**XmFontContext**

A typedef for a font list context that lets an application access the font list entries and font list tags in a font list. This data type is an opaque structure returned by a call to XmFontListInitFontContext(), and is used in subsequent calls to XmFontListGetNextEntry(), XmFontListGetNextFont() and XmFontListFreeFontContext().

**XmFontList**

A font list contains entries that describe the fonts that are in use. In Motif 1.1, each entry associates a font and a character set. In Motif 1.2, each entry consists of a XmFontListEntry and an associated tag, where the XmFontListEntry specifies a font or a font set. XmFontList is an opaque data type used in calls to font list routines and string manipulation routines. When a Motif compound string is displayed, the font list tag is used to match the string with a font or font set, so that the compound string is displayed appropriately. The font list tag XmFONTLIST_DEFAULT_TAG causes compound strings to be displayed using the font for the current locale.

To specify a font list in a resource file, use the following syntax:

*resource_spec*: *font_entry* [, *font_entry* ] ...

The value specification consists of at least one font list entry, with multiple entries separated by commas. Each *font_entry* specifies a font or a font set and an optional font list entry tag. Use the following syntax to specify a single font:

*font_name* [ = *font_list_entry_tag* ]

To specify the optional tag for a single font, separate the *font_name* and the *font_list_entry_tag* by an equal sign (=). Use the following syntax to specify a font set:

*font_name* [ ; *font_name* ] ... : [ *font_list_entry_tag* ]

Separate multiple *font_names* with semicolons and end the specification with a colon, followed by the optional tag. A *font_name* is an X Logical Font Description (XLFD) string. If a *font_list_entry_tag* is not specified for an entry, XmFONTLIST_DEFAULT_TAG is used.

**XmFontListEntry**

In Motif 1.2, a font list entry is an element of an XmFontList that specifies a font or a font set. Each XmFontListEntry is associated with a font list entry tag. XmFontListEntry is an opaque type.

**XmFontType**

An enumerated type that specifies the type of entry in a XmFontListEntry. It is defined as follows in *<Xm/Xm.h>*:

```
typedef enum {
    XmFONT_IS_FONT,          /* specifies a font */
    XmFONT_IS_FONTSET        /* specifies a font set */
} XmFontType;
```

**XmHighlightMode**

An enumerated type that defines the kind of text highlighting that results from calls to XmTextSetHighlight() and XmTextFieldSetHighlight(). It is defined as follows in *<Xm/Xm.h>*:

```
typedef enum {
   XmHIGHLIGHT_NORMAL,                        /* no highlighting */
   XmHIGHLIGHT_SELECTED,                      /* highlight in reverse video */
   XmHIGHLIGHT_SECONDARY_SELECTED             /* highlight by underlining */
} XmHighlightMode;
```

**XmKeySymTable**

A pointer to a list of KeySyms.

**XmListCallbackStruct**

The callback structure passed to List widget callback routines. It is defined as follows in *<Xm/Xm.h>*:

```
typedef struct {
   int        reason;              /* the reason that callback was called */
   XEvent     *event;              /* event structure that triggered callback */
   XmString   item;                /* item most recently selected at the */
                                   /* time event occurred */
   int        item_length;         /* number of bytes in item member */
   int        item_position;       /* item's position within XmNitems array */
```

```
    XmString *selected_items;       /* list of items selected at the */
                                    /* time event occurred */
    int      selected_item_count;   /* number of items in selected_items */
    int      *selected_item_positions;/* array of int. marking selected items */
    int      selection_type;        /* type of the most recent selection */
  } XmListCallbackStruct;
```

The structure members event, item, item_length, and item_position are valid for any value of reason. The structure members selected_items, selected_item_count, and selected_item_ positions are valid when the reason field has a value of XmCR_MULTIPLE_SELECT or XmCR_EXTENDED_SELECT. The structure member selection_type is valid only when the reason field is XmCR_EXTENDED_SELECT.

For the strings pointed to by item and selected_items, as well as for the integers pointed to by selected_item_positions, storage is overwritten each time the callback is invoked. Applications that need to save this data should make their own copies of it.

selected_item_positions is an integer array. The elements of the array indicate the positions of each selected item within the List widget's XmNitems array.

selection_type specifies what kind of extended selection was most recently made. One of three values is possible:

```
XmINITIAL           /* selection was the initial selection */
XmMODIFICATION      /* selection changed an existing selection */
XmADDITION          /* selection added non-adjacent items to an existing selection */
```

**XmNavigationType**

An enumerated type that specifies the type of keyboard navigation associated with a widget. The valid values for the type are:

```
XmNONE                      XmTAB_GROUP
XmSTICKY_TAB_GROUP          XmEXCLUSIVE_TAB_GROUP
```

**XmOffset**

A long integer that represents the units used in calculating the offsets into a widget's instance data. The type is used internally to Motif. See also XmOffsetPtr.

**XmOffsetPtr**

A pointer to an XmOffset value, which is returned by a calls to XmResolveAll-PartOffsets() and XmResolvePartOffsets().

**XmOperationChangedCallbackStruct**

The callback structure passed to the XmNoperationChangedCallback of a Drag-Context object. It is defined as follows in *<Xm/DragC.h>*:

```
typedef struct {
    int             reason;          /* the reason the callback was called */
    XEvent          *event;          /* event structure that triggered callback */
    Time            timeStamp;       /* timestamp of logical event */
    unsigned char   operation;       /* current operation */
    unsigned char   operations;      /* supported operations */
    unsigned char   dropSiteStatus;  /* valid, invalid, or none */
} XmOperationChangedCallbackStruct, *XmOperationChangedCallback;
```

**XmPushButtonCallbackStruct**

The callback structure passed to PushButton callback routines. It is defined as follows in *<Xm/Xm.h>*:

```
typedef struct {
     int      reason;         /* the reason that the callback was called */
     XEvent   *event;         /* event structure that triggered callback */
     int      click_count;    /* number of multi-clicks */
} XmPushButtonCallbackStruct;
```

**XmQualifyProc**

The prototype for the qualification procedure that produces a qualified directory mask, base directory, and search pattern for the directory and file search procedures in a FileSelectionBox. The `XmNqualifySearchDataProc` resource specifies a procedure of this type, which is defined as follows in *<Xm/FileSB.h>*:

```
typedef void (*XmQualifyProc)(Widget, XtPointer, XtPointer);
    Widgetwidget;
    XtPointerinput_data;
    XtPointeroutput_data;
```

An `XmQualifyProc` takes three arguments. The first argument, *`widget`*, is the FileSelectionBox widget. The *`input_data`* argument is a pointer to an `XmFileSelectionBoxCallbackStruct` that contains input data to be qualified. The *`output_data`* argument is a pointer to an `XmFileSelectionBoxCallbackStruct` that is to be filled in by the qualification procedure.

**XmRepTypeEntry**

A pointer to a representation type entry structure which contains information about the value names and values for an enumerated type. The Motif representation type manager routines use values of this type, which is defined as follows in *<Xm/RepType.h>*:

```
typedef struct {
    String          rep_type_name;       /* name of representation type */
    String          *value_names;        /* array of value names */
    unsigned char   *values;             /* array of numeric values */
    unsigned char   num_values;          /* number of values */
    Boolean         reverse_installed;   /* reverse converter installed flag */
    XmRepTypeId     rep_type_id;         /* representation type ID /*
} XmRepTypeEntryRec, *XmRepTypeEntry, XmRepTypeListRec, *XmRepTypeList;
```

**XmRepTypeId**

An unsigned short that specifies the identification number of a representation type registered with the representation type manager. The representation type manager routines use values of this type.

**XmRepTypeList**

See `XmRepTypeEntry`.

**XmRowColumnCallbackStruct**

The callback structure passed to RowColumn callback routines. It is defined as follows in *<Xm/Xm.h>*:

```
typedef struct {
     int      reason;         /* the reason that the callback was called */
```

```
        XEvent   *event;          /* event structure that triggered callback */
        Widget   widget;          /* ID of activated RowColumn item */
        char     *data;           /* value of application's client data */
        char     *callbackstruct; /* created when item is activated */
    } XmRowColumnCallbackStruct;
```



**XmScaleCallbackStruct**

The callback structure passed to Scale widget callback routines. It is defined as follows in <*Xm/Xm.h*>:

```
typedef struct {
        int      reason;          /* the reason that the callback was called */
        XEvent   *event;          /* event structure that triggered callback */
        int      value;           /* new value of the slider */
    } XmScaleCallbackStruct;
```

**XmScrollBarCallbackStruct**

The callback structure passed to ScrollBar callback routines. It is defined as follows in <*Xm/Xm.h*>:

```
typedef struct {
        int      reason;          /* the reason that the callback was called */
        XEvent   *event;          /* event structure that triggered callback */
        int      value;           /* value of the slider's new location */
        int      pixel;           /* coordinate where selection occurred */
    } XmScrollBarCallbackStruct;
```

**XmSearchProc**

The prototype for a search procedure that searches the directories or files in a FileSelectionBox. The `XmNdirSearchProc` and `XmNfileSearchProc` resources specify procedures of this type, which is defined as follows in <*Xm/FileSB.h*>:

```
typedef void (*XmQualifyProc)(Widget, XtPointer);
    Widgetwidget;
    XtPointersearch_data;
```

An `XmQualifyProc` takes two arguments. The first argument, *`widget`*, is the FileSelectionBox widget. The *`search_data`* argument is a pointer to an `XmFileSelectionBoxCallbackStruct` that contains the information for performing a search.

**XmSecondaryResourceData**

A structure that specifies information about secondary resources associated with a widget class. `XmGetSecondaryResourceData()` returns an array of these values. The type is defined as follows in <*Xm/Xm.h*>:

```
typedef struct {
    XmResourceBaseProcbase_proc;
    XtPointer          client_data;
    String             name;
    String             res_class;
    XtResourceList     resources;
    Cardinal           num_resources;
} XmSecondaryResourceDataRec, *XmSecondaryResourceData;
```

**XmSelectionBoxCallbackStruct**

The callback structure passed to SelectionBox callback routines. It is defined as follows in *<Xm/Xm.h>*:

```
typedef struct {
    int        reason;        /* the reason that the callback was called */
    XEvent     *event;        /* event structure that triggered callback */
    XmString   value;         /* selection string that was either chosen */
                              /* from the SelectionBox list or typed in */
    int        length;        /* number of bytes of value */
} XmSelectionBoxCallbackStruct;
```

**XmString**

The data type for Motif compound strings. In Motif 1.2, a compound string is composed of one or more segments, where each segment can contain a font list element tag, a string direction, and a text component. The font list element tag `XmFONTLIST_DEFAULT_TAG` specifies a text segment encoded in the current locale. In Motif 1.1, compound strings use character set identifiers rather than font list element tags. The character set identifier for a compound string can have the value `XmSTRING_DEFAULT_CHARSET`, which takes the character set from the current language environment, but this value may be removed from future versions of Motif.

**XmStringCharSet**

A typedef for `char *` that is used to define the character set of a compound string in Motif 1.1. Variables of this type can have the following values, among others:

```
XmSTRING_ISO8859_1
XmSTRING_OS_CHARSET
XmSTRING_DEFAULT_CHARSET
```

`XmSTRING_DEFAULT_CHARSET` specifies the character set from the current language environment, but this value may be removed from future versions of Motif.

**XmStringCharSetTable**

A pointer to a list of `XmStringCharSets`.

**XmStringComponentType**

An `unsigned char` value that specifies the type of component in a compound string segment. Values of this type are returned by calls to `XmStringGetNextComponent()` and `XmStringPeekNextComponent()`. The valid values for the type are:

```
XmSTRING_COMPONENT_FONTLIST_ELEMENT_TAG   /* font list element tag component */
XmSTRING_COMPONENT_CHARSET                /* character set identifier component; */
                                          /* obsolete in Motif 1.2 */
XmSTRING_COMPONENT_TEXT                   /* text component */
XmSTRING_COMPONENT_LOCALE_TEXT            /* locale-encoded text component */
XmSTRING_COMPONENT_DIRECTION              /* direction component */
XmSTRING_COMPONENT_SEPARATOR              /* separator component */
XmSTRING_COMPONENT_END                    /* last component in string */
XmSTRING_COMPONENT_UNKNOWN                /* unknown component */
```

**XmStringContext**

A typedef for a string context that lets an application access the components or segments within a compound string. This data type is an opaque structure returned by a call to `XmStringInitContext()`, and is used in subsequent calls to the four other string context routines: `XmStringFreeContext()`, `XmStringGetNextSegment()`, `XmStringGetNextComponent()`, and `XmStringPeekNextComponent()`.



**XmStringDirection**

An `unsigned char` used for determining the direction in which a compound string is displayed. The type is used in calls to `XmStringDirectionCreate()` and `XmStringSegmentCreate()`. The valid values for the type are:

```
XmSTRING_DIRECTION_L_TO_R            XmSTRING_DIRECTION_R_TO_L
XmSTRING_DIRECTION_DEFAULT
```

**XmStringTable**

An opaque typedef for `XmString *` that is used for arrays of compound strings.

**XmTextBlockRec**

A structure that specifies information about a block of text in a Text or TextField widget. The `text` field in an `XmTextVerifyCallbackStruct` points to a structure of this type, which is defined as follows in *<Xm/Xm.h>*:

```
typedef struct {
   char            *ptr;          /* pointer to the text to insert */
   int             length;        /* length of this text */
   XmTextFormat    format;        /* text format (e.g., FMT8BIT, FMT16BIT) */
} XmTextBlockRec, *XmTextBlock;
```

**XmTextBlockRecWcs**

A structure that specifies information about a block of text in wide-character format in a Text or TextField widget. The `text` field in an `XmTextVerifyCallbackStructWcs` points to a structure of this type, which is defined as follows in *<Xm/Xm.h>*:

```
typedef struct {
   wchar_t         *wcsptr;       /* pointer to the text to insert */
   int             length;        /* length of this text */
} XmTextBlockRecWcs, *XmTextBlockWcs;
```

**XmTextDirection**

An enumerated type that specifies the search direction in calls to `XmTextFindString()` and `XmTextFindStringWcs()`. It is defined as follows in *<Xm/Xm.h>*:

```
typedef enum {
    XmTEXT_FORWARD,       /* search forward */
    XmTEXT_BACKWARD       /* search backward */
} XmTextDirection;
```

**XmTextPosition**

A long integer, used by Text and TextField routines for determining the position of a character inside the text string.

**XmTextSource**

A pointer to an opaque structure that specifies a text source. The type is used in calls to `XmTextGetSource()` and `XmTextSetSource()`.

**XmTextVerifyCallbackStruct**

The callback structure passed to the XmNlosingFocusCallback, XmNmodifyVerifyCallback, and XmNmotionVerifyCallback callback routines of Text and TextField widgets. It is defined as follows in *<Xm/Xm.h>*:

```
typedef struct {
    int             reason;          /* the reason that the callback was called */
    XEvent          *event;          /* event structure that triggered callback */
    Boolean         doit;            /* do the action (True) or undo it (False) */
    XmTextPosition  current_insert;  /* the insert cursor's current position */
    XmTextPosition  new_insert;      /* desired new position of insert cursor */
    XmTextPosition  start_pos;       /* start of text to change */
    XmTextPosition  end_pos;         /* end of text to change */
    XmTextBlock     text;            /* describes the text to insert */
} XmTextVerifyCallbackStruct, *XmTextVerifyPtr;
```

start_pos specifies the location at which to start modifying text. start_pos is unused if the callback resource is XmNmotionVerifyCallback, and is the same as the current_insert member if the callback resource is XmNlosingFocusCallback.

end_pos specifies the location at which to stop modifying text (however, if no text was modified, end_pos has the same value as start_pos). end_pos is unused if the callback resource is XmNmotionVerifyCallback, and is the same as the current_insert member if the callback resource is XmNlosingFocusCallback.

**XmTextVerifyCallbackStructWcs**

The callback structure passed to the XmNmodifyVerifyCallbackWcs of Text and TextField widgets. It is defined as follows in *<Xm/Xm.h>*:

```
typedef struct {
    int             reason;          /* the reason that the callback was called */
    XEvent          *event;          /* event structure that triggered callback */
    Boolean         doit;            /* do the action (True) or undo it (False) */
    XmTextPosition  current_insert;  /* the insert cursor's current position */
    XmTextPosition  new_insert;      /* desired new position of insert cursor */
    XmTextPosition  start_pos;       /* start of text to change */
    XmTextPosition  end_pos;         /* end of text to change */
    XmTextBlockWcs  text;            /* describes the text to insert */
} XmTextVerifyCallbackStructWcs, *XmTextVerifyPtrWcs;
```

All of the fields in this structure are the same as the fields in the XmTextVerifyCallbackStruct except text, which points to a XmTextBlockRecWcs structure.

**XmToggleButtonCallbackStruct**

The callback structure passed to ToggleButton callback routines. It is defined as follows in *<Xm/Xm.h>*:

```
typedef struct {
      int     reason;         /* the reason that the callback was called */
      XEvent  *event;         /* event structure that triggered callback */
      int     set;            /* button is selected (True) or unselected (False) */
} XmToggleButtonCallbackStruct;
```

**XmTopLevelEnterCallbackStruct**

The callback structure passed to the XmNtopLevelEnterCallback of a DragContext object. It is defined as follows in *<Xm/DragC.h>*:

```
typedef struct {
    int           reason;           /* the reason the callback was called */
    XEvent        *event;           /* event structure that triggered callback */
    Time          timestamp;        /* timestamp of logical event */
    Screen        screen;           /* screen of top-level window */
    Window        window;           /* window being entered */
    Position      x;                /* x-coordinate of pointer */
    Position      y;                /* y-coordinate of pointer */
    unsigned char dragProtocolStyle;/* drag protocol of initiator */
} XmTopLevelEnterCallbackStruct, *XmTopLevelEnterCallback;
```

**XmTopLevelLeaveCallbackStruct**

The callback structure passed to the XmNtopLevelLeaveCallback of a DragContext object. It is defined as follows in *<Xm/DragC.h>*:

```
typedef struct {
    int     reason;         /* the reason the callback was called */
    XEvent  *event;         /* event structure that triggered callback */
    Time    timestamp;      /* timestamp of logical event */
    Screen  screen;         /* screen of top-level window */
    Window  window;         /* window being left */
} XmTopLevelLeaveCallbackStruct, *XmTopLevelLeaveCallback;
```

**XmTraversalDirection**

An enumerated type that specifies direction of traversal in a XmTraverseObscuredCallbackStruct. It is defined as follows in *<Xm/Xm.h>*:

```
typedef enum {
    XmTRAVERSE_CURRENT,             XmTRAVERSE_NEXT,
    XmTRAVERSE_PREV,                XmTRAVERSE_HOME,
    XmTRAVERSE_NEXT_TAB_GROUP,      XmTRAVERSE_PREV_TAB_GROUP,
    XmTRAVERSE_UP,                  XmTRAVERSE_DOWN,
    XmTRAVERSE_LEFT,                XmTRAVERSE_RIGHT
} XmTraversalDirection ;
```

**XmTraverseObscureCallbackStruct**

The callback structure passed to the XmNtraverseObscuredCallback of a ScrolledWindow widget. It is defined as follows in *<Xm/Xm.h>*:

```
typedef struct {
        int     reason;  /* reason the callback was called */
        XEvent  *event;  /* event structure that triggered callback */
        Widget  traversal_destination;      /* widget or gadget to traverse to */
        XmTraversalDirection  direction;  /* direction of traversal */
} XmTraverseObscuredCallbackStruct;
```

**XmVisibility**

An enumerated type that specifies the visibility state of a widget. A value of type XmVisibility is returned by XmGetVisibility(). It is defined as follows in <*Xm/Xm.h*>:

```
typedef enum {
    XmVISIBILITY_UNOBSCURED,          /* completely visible */
    XmVISIBILITY_PARTIALLY_OBSCURED, /* partially visible */
    XmVISIBILITY_FULLY_OBSCURED       /* not visible */
} XmVisibility;
```

**XrmValue**

A structure defined in <*X11/Xresource.h*>, used in XtConvert() and other resource conversion routines:

```
typedef struct {
    unsigned intsize;
    XPointeraddr;
} XrmValue, *XrmValuePtr;
```

**XrmValuePtr**

See XrmValue.

**XtAccelerators**

A pointer to an opaque internal type, a compiled accelerator table. A pointer to an XtAccelerators structure is returned by a call to XtParseAcceleratorTable(). Usually, the compiled accelerator table is produced automatically by resource conversion of a string accelerator table stored in a resource file.

**XtCallbackList**

A structure defined as follows in <*X11/Intrinsic.h*>:

```
typedef struct _XtCallbackRec {
    XtCallbackProc        callback;
    XtPointer             closure;
} XtCallbackRec, *XtCallbackList;
```

An XtCallbackList is statically defined just after the callback function itself is declared or defined. Then the callback list is used to set a callback resource with any of the calls that set resources, including XtCreateWidget(). In most documentation, the closure member is referred to as *client_data*. In application code, when XtAddCallback() and XtRemoveCallback() are used, an XtCallbackList is not required.

**XtCallbackProc**

The prototype for callback functions. It is defined as follows in <*X11/Intrinsic.h*>:

```
typedef void (*XtCallbackProc)(Widget, XtPointer, XtPointer);
    Widget       widget;
    XtPointer    client_data;
    XtPointer    call_data;
```

**XtConvertSelectionIncrProc**

The prototype for an incremental selection conversion procedure. The `XmNconvertProc` for a DragContext object is of this type, which is defined as follows in *<X11/Intrinsic.h>*:

```
typedef Boolean (*XtConvertSelectionIncrProc)(Widget, Atom *, Atom *, Atom *,
        XtPointer *, unsigned long *, int *, unsigned long *, XtPointer,
        XtRequestId *);
    Widget             widget;
    Atom               *selection;
    Atom               *target;
    Atom               *type_return;
    XtPointer          *value_return;
    unsigned long      *length_return;
    int                *format_return;
    unsigned long      *max_length;
    XtPointer          client_data;
    XtRequestId        *request_id;
```

**XtCreatePopupChildProc**

The prototype for a procedure that pops up the child of a shell when the shell is popped up. The `XmNcreatePopupChildProc` resource of Shell specifies a procedure of this type, which is defined as follows in *<X11/Intrinsic.h>*:

```
typedef void (*XtCreatePopupChildProc)(Widget);
    Widgetshell;
```

**XtOrderProc**

The prototype for a keycode-to-keysym translation procedure. `XmTranslateKey()` is the default `XtKeyProc` for Motif applications. The prototype is defined as follows in *<X11/Intrinsic.h>*:

```
typedef void (*XtKeyProc)(Display *, KeyCode, Modifiers, Modifiers *,
        KeySym *);
    Display*display;
    KeyCodekeycode;
    Modifiersmodifiers;
    Modifiers*modifiers_return;
    KeySym*keysym_return;
```

**XtKeyProc**

The prototype for a procedure that allows composite widgets to order their children. The `XmNinsertPosition` resource of Composite specifies a procedure of this type, which is defined as follows in *<X11/Composite.h>*:

```
typedef Cardinal (*XtOrderProc)(Widget);
    Widgetchild;
```

**XtPointer**

A datum large enough to contain the largest of a `char*`, `int*`, function pointer, structure pointer, or long value. A pointer to any type or function, or a long, may be converted to an `XtPointer` and back again and the result will compare equally to the original value. In ANSI-C environments, it is expected that `XtPointer` will be defined as `void`.

**XtSelectionCallbackProc**

The prototype for a selection callback procedure. The XmNtransferProc for a DropTransfer object is of this type, which is defined as follows in *<X11/Intrinsic.h>*:

```
typedef void (*XtSelectionCallbackProc)(Widget, XtPointer, Atom *, Atom *,
        XtPointer, unsigned long*, int *);
    Widget              widget;
    XtPointer           client_data;
    Atom                *selection;
    Atom                *type;
    XtPointer           value;
    unsigned long       *length;
    int                 *format;
```

**XtTranslations**

A pointer to an opaque internal type, a compiled translation table. A pointer to an XtTranslations structure is returned by a call to XtParseTranslationTable(). Usually, the compiled translation table is produced automatically by resource conversion of a string translation table stored in a resource file.

# C
# Table of Motif Resources



This appendix lists all of the resources for the widget classes provided by the Motif toolkit and the X Toolkit Intrinsics. The table lists the appropriate data types for specifying each resource with both Motif and UIL. For resources that cannot be specified in UIL, the table entry indicates that the resource is not applicable (NA). The table also specifies the widget classes that define each resource. If a widget class has a corresponding gadget class, the table lists only the widget class as defining resources, even though the resources pertain to both the widget and gadget classes. For more information on each resource, see the appropriate reference pages in Section 2, *Motif and Xt Widget Classes*.

| Resource Name | Motif Type | UIL Type | Defined in Class |
|---|---|---|---|
| XmNaccelerator | String | string | XmLabel |
| XmNacceleratorText | XmString | compound_string | XmLabel |
| XmNaccelerators | XtAccelerators | translation_table | Core |
| XmNactivateCallback | XtCallbackList | procedure | XmArrowButton, XmCascadeButton, XmDrawnButton, XmPushButton, XmText, XmTextField |
| XmNadjustLast | Boolean | boolean | XmRowColumn |
| XmNadjustMargin | Boolean | boolean | XmRowColumn |
| XmNalignment | unsigned char | integer | XmLabel |
| XmNallowOverlap | Boolean | boolean | XmBulletinBoard |
| XmNallowResize | Boolean | boolean | XmPanedWindow |
| XmNallowShellResize | Boolean | boolean | Shell |
| XmNancestorSensitive | Boolean | boolean | Core, XmRectObj |
| XmNanimationMask | Pixmap | NA | XmDropSite |
| XmNanimationPixmap | Pixmap | NA | XmDropSite |
| XmNanimationPixmapDepth | int | NA | XmDropSite |
| XmNanimationStyle | unsigned char | NA | XmDropSite |
| XmNapplyCallback | XtCallbackList | procedure | XmSelectionBox |
| XmNapplyLabelString | XmString | compound_string | XmSelectionBox |

| Resource Name | Motif Type | UIL Type | Defined in Class |
|---|---|---|---|
| XmNargc | int | NA | ApplicationShell |
| XmNargv | String * | NA | ApplicationShell |
| XmNarmCallback | XtCallbackList | procedure | XmArrowButton, XmDrawnButton, XmPushButton, XmToggleButton |
| XmNarmColor | Pixel | color | XmPushButton |
| XmNarmPixmap | Pixmap | pixmap | XmPushButton |
| XmNarrowDirection | unsigned char | integer | XmArrowButton |
| XmNattachment | unsigned char | NA | XmDragIcon |
| XmNaudibleWarning | unsigned char | integer | VendorShell |
| XmNautoShowCursorPosition | Boolean | boolean | XmText |
| XmNautoUnmanage | Boolean | boolean | XmBulletinBoard |
| XmNautomaticSelection | Boolean | boolean | XmList |
| XmNbackground | Pixel | color | Core |
| XmNbackgroundPixmap | Pixmap | pixmap | Core |
| XmNbaseHeight | int | integer | WMShell |
| XmNbaseWidth | int | integer | WMShell |
| XmNblendModel | unsigned char | NA | XmDragContext |
| XmNblinkRate | int | integer | XmText, XmTextField |
| XmNborderColor | Pixel | color | Core |
| XmNborderPixmap | Pixmap | pixmap | Core |
| XmNborderWidth | Dimension | integer | Core, XmRectObj |
| XmNbottomAttachment | unsigned char | integer | XmForm |
| XmNbottomOffset | int | integer | XmForm |
| XmNbottomPosition | int | integer | XmForm |
| XmNbottomShadowColor | Pixel | color | XmGadget, XmManager, XmPrimitive |
| XmNbottomShadowPixmap | Pixmap | pixmap | XmManager, XmPrimitive |
| XmNbottomWidget | Widget | widget_ref | XmForm |
| XmNbrowseSelectionCallback | XtCallbackList | procedure | XmList |
| XmNbuttonAcceleratorText | XmStringTable | NA | XmRowColumn |
| XmNbuttonAccelerators | StringTable | NA | XmRowColumn |
| XmNbuttonCount | int | NA | XmRowColumn |
| XmNbuttonFontList | XmFontList | font_table | XmBulletinBoard, XmMenuShell, XmVendorShell |
| XmNbuttonMnemonicCharSets | XmStringCharSetTable | NA | XmRowColumn |
| XmNbuttonMnemonics | XmKeySymTable | NA | XmRowColumn |
| XmNbuttonSet | int | NA | XmRowColumn |
| XmNbuttonType | XmButtonTypeTable | NA | XmRowColumn |

| Resource Name | Motif Type | UIL Type | Defined in Class |
|---|---|---|---|
| XmNbuttons | XmStringTable | NA | XmRowColumn |
| XmNcancelButton | Window | widget_ref | XmBulletinBoard |
| XmNcancelCallback | XtCallbackList | procedure | XmMessageBox, XmSelectionBox |
| XmNcancelLabelString | XmString | compound_string | XmMessageBox, XmSelectionBox |
| XmNcascadePixmap | Pixmap | pixmap | XmCascadeButton |
| XmNcascadingCallback | XtCallbackList | procedure | XmCascadeButton |
| XmNchildHorizontalAlignment | unsigned char | integer | XmFrame |
| XmNchildHorizontalSpacing | Dimension | integer | XmFrame |
| XmNchildPlacement | unsigned char | integer | XmSelectionBox |
| XmNchildType | unsigned char | integer | XmFrame |
| XmNchildVerticalAlignment | unsigned char | integer | XmFrame |
| XmNchildren | WidgetList | NA | Composite |
| XmNclientData | XtPointer | NA | XmDragContext |
| XmNclipWindow | Window | NA | XmScrolledWindow |
| XmNcolormap | Colormap | identifier | Core |
| XmNcolumns | short | integer | XmText, XmTextField |
| XmNcommand | XmString | compound_string | XmCommand |
| XmNcommandChangedCallback | XtCallbackList | procedure | XmCommand |
| XmNcommandEnteredCallback | XtCallbackList | procedure | XmCommand |
| XmNcommandWindow | Window | widget_ref | XmMainWindow |
| XmNcommandWindowLocation | unsigned char | integer | XmMainWindow |
| XmNconvertProc | XtConvertSelection IncrProc | NA | XmDragContext |
| XmNcreatePopupChildProc | XtCreatePopup ChildProc | any | Shell |
| XmNcursorBackground | Pixel | NA | XmDragContext |
| XmNcursorForeground | Pixel | NA | XmDragContext |
| XmNcursorPosition | XmTextPosition | integer | XmText, XmTextField |
| XmNcursorPositionVisible | Boolean | boolean | XmText, XmTextField |
| XmNdarkThreshold | int | NA | XmScreen |
| XmNdecimalPoints | short | integer | XmScale |
| XmNdecrementCallback | XtCallbackList | procedure | XmScrollBar |
| XmNdefaultActionCallback | XtCallbackList | procedure | XmList |
| XmNdefaultButton | Window | widget_ref | XmBulletinBoard |
| XmNdefaultButtonShadowThickness | Dimension | integer | XmPushButton |
| XmNdefaultButtonType | unsigned char | integer | XmMessageBox |
| XmNdefaultCopyCursorIcon | Widget | NA | XmScreen |
| XmNdefaultFontList | XmFontList | font_table | XmMenuShell, XmVendorShell |
| XmNdefaultInvalidCursorIcon | Widget | NA | XmScreen |
| XmNdefaultLinkCursorIcon | Widget | NA | XmScreen |

Motif Resources

| Resource Name | Motif Type | UIL Type | Defined in Class |
|---|---|---|---|
| XmNdefaultMoveCursorIcon | Widget | NA | XmScreen |
| XmNdefaultNoneCursorIcon | Widget | NA | XmScreen |
| XmNdefaultPosition | Boolean | boolean | XmBulletinBoard |
| XmNdefaultSourceCursorIcon | Widget | NA | XmScreen |
| XmNdefaultValidCursorIcon | Widget | NA | XmScreen |
| XmNdefaultVirtualBindings | String | NA | XmDisplay |
| XmNdeleteResponse | unsigned char | integer | VendorShell |
| XmNdepth | int | identifier | Core, XmDragIcon |
| XmNdestroyCallback | XtCallbackList | procedure | Core, XmObject |
| XmNdialogStyle | unsigned char | integer | XmBulletinBoard |
| XmNdialogTitle | XmString | compound_string | XmBulletinBoard |
| XmNdialogType | unsigned char | integer | XmMessageBox, XmSelectionBox |
| XmNdirListItemCount | int | integer | XmFileSelectionBox |
| XmNdirListItems | XmStringTable | string_table | XmFileSelectionBox |
| XmNdirListLabelString | XmString | compound_string | XmFileSelectionBox |
| XmNdirMask | XmString | compound_string | XmFileSelectionBox |
| XmNdirSearchProc | XmSearchProc | any | XmFileSelectionBox |
| XmNdirSpec | XmString | compound_string | XmFileSelectionBox |
| XmNdirectory | XmString | compound_string | XmFileSelectionBox |
| XmNdirectoryValid | Boolean | NA | XmFileSelectionBox |
| XmNdisarmCallback | XtCallbackList | procedure | XmArrowButton, XmDrawnButton, XmPushButton, XmToggleButton |
| XmNdoubleClickInterval | int | integer | XmList |
| XmNdragCallback | XtCallbackList | procedure | XmScale, XmScrollBar |
| XmNdragDropFinishCallback | XtCallbackList | NA | XmDragContext |
| XmNdragInitiatorProtocolStyle | unsigned char | NA | XmDisplay |
| XmNdragMotionCallback | XtCallbackList | NA | XmDragContext |
| XmNdragOperations | unsigned char | NA | XmDragContext |
| XmNdragProc | XtCallbackProc | NA | XmDropSite |
| XmNdragReceiverProtocolStyle | unsigned char | NA | XmDisplay |
| XmNdropFinishCallback | XtCallbackList | NA | XmDragContext |
| XmNdropProc | XtCallbackProc | NA | XmDropSite |
| XmNdropRectangles | XRectangle * | NA | XmDropSite |
| XmNdropSiteActivity | unsigned char | NA | XmDropSite |
| XmNdropSiteEnterCallback | XtCallbackList | NA | XmDragContext |
| XmNdropSiteLeaveCallback | XtCallbackList | NA | XmDragContext |
| XmNdropSiteOperations | unsigned char | NA | XmDropSite |
| XmNdropSiteType | unsigned char | NA | XmDropSite |
| XmNdropStartCallback | XtCallbackList | NA | XmDragContext |

| Resource Name | Motif Type | UIL Type | Defined in Class |
|---|---|---|---|
| XmNdropTransfers | XmDropTransfer EntryRec * | NA | XmDropTransfer |
| XmNeditMode | int | integer | XmText |
| XmNeditable | Boolean | boolean | XmText, XmTextField |
| XmNentryAlignment | unsigned char | integer | XmRowColumn |
| XmNentryBorder | Dimension | integer | XmRowColumn |
| XmNentryCallback | XtCallbackList | procedure | XmRowColumn |
| XmNentryClass | WidgetClass | class_rec_name | XmRowColumn |
| XmNentryVerticalAlignment | unsigned char | integer | XmRowColumn |
| XmNexportTargets | Atom * | NA | XmDragContext |
| XmNexposeCallback | XtCallbackList | procedure | XmDrawingArea, XmDrawnButton |
| XmNextendedSelectionCallback | XtCallbackList | procedure | XmList |
| XmNfileListItemCount | int | integer | XmFileSelectionBox |
| XmNfileListItems | XmStringTable | string_table | XmFileSelectionBox |
| XmNfileListLabelString | XmString | compound_string | XmFileSelectionBox |
| XmNfileSearchProc | XmSearchProc | any | XmFileSelectionBox |
| XmNfileTypeMask | unsigned char | integer | XmFileSelectionBox |
| XmNfillOnArm | Boolean | boolean | XmPushButton |
| XmNfillOnSelect | Boolean | boolean | XmToggleButton |
| XmNfilterLabelString | XmString | compound_string | XmFileSelectionBox |
| XmNfocusCallback | XtCallbackList | procedure | XmBulletinBoard, XmText, XmTextField |
| XmNfont | XFontStruct * | NA | XmScreen |
| XmNfontList | XmFontList | font_table | XmLabel, XmList, XmScale, XmText, XmTextField |
| XmNforeground | Pixel | color | XmManager, XmPrimitive |
| XmNforegroundThreshold | int | NA | XmScreen |
| XmNfractionBase | int | integer | XmForm |
| XmNgainPrimaryCallback | XtCallbackList | procedure | XmText, XmTextField |
| XmNgeometry | String | string | Shell |
| XmNheight | Dimension | integer | Core, XmDragIcon, XmRectObj |
| XmNheightInc | int | integer | WMShell |
| XmNhelpCalback | XtCallbackList | procedure | XmGadget, XmManager, XmPrimitive |
| XmNhelpLabelString | XmString | compound_string | XmMessageBox, XmSelectionBox |
| XmNhighlightColor | Pixel | color | XmGadget, XmManager, XmPrimitive |

Motif Resources

| Resource Name | Motif Type | UIL Type | Defined in Class |
|---|---|---|---|
| XmNhighlightOnEnter | Boolean | boolean | XmGadget, XmPrimitive, XmScale |
| XmNhighlightPixmap | Pixmap | pixmap | XmManager, XmPrimitive |
| XmNhighlightThickness | Dimension | integer | XmGadget, XmPrimitive, XmScale |
| XmNhistoryItemCount | int | integer | XmCommand |
| XmNhistoryItems | XmStringTable | string_table | XmCommand |
| XmNhistoryMaxItems | int | integer | XmCommand |
| XmNhistoryVisibleItemCount | int | integer | XmCommand |
| XmNhorizontalFontUnit | int | NA | XmScreen |
| XmNhorizontalScrollBar | Widget | widget_ref | XmScrolledWindow |
| XmNhorizontalSpacing | Dimension | integer | XmForm |
| XmNhotX | Position | NA | XmDragIcon |
| XmNhotY | Position | NA | XmDragIcon |
| XmNiconMask | Pixmap | pixmap | WMShell |
| XmNiconName | String | NA | TopLevelShell |
| XmNiconNameEncoding | Atom | NA | TopLevelShell |
| XmNiconPixmap | Pixmap | pixmap | WMShell |
| XmNiconWindow | Window | any | WMShell |
| XmNiconX | int | integer | WMShell |
| XmNiconY | int | integer | WMShell |
| XmNiconic | Boolean | NA | TopLevelShell |
| XmNimportTargets | Atom * | NA | XmDropSite |
| XmNincrement | int | integer | XmScrollBar |
| XmNincrementCallback | XtCallbackList | procedure | XmScrollBar |
| XmNincremental | Boolean | NA | XmDragContext, XmDropTransfer |
| XmNindicatorOn | Boolean | boolean | XmToggleButton |
| XmNindicatorSize | Dimension | integer | XmToggleButton |
| XmNindicatorType | unsigned char | integer | XmToggleButton |
| XmNinitialDelay | int | integer | XmScrollBar |
| XmNinitialFocus | Widget | widget_ref | XmManager |
| XmNinitialResourcesPersistent | Boolean | boolean | Core |
| XmNinitialState | int | integer | WMShell |
| XmNinput | Boolean | boolean | WMShell |
| XmNinputCallback | XtCallbackList | procedure | XmDrawingArea |
| XmNinputMethod | String | string | VendorShell |
| XmNinsertPosition | XtOrderProc | identifier | Composite |
| XmNinvalidCursorForeground | Pixel | NA | XmDragContext |
| XmNisAligned | Boolean | boolean | XmRowColumn |
| XmNisHomogeneous | Boolean | boolean | XmRowColumn |
| XmNitemCount | int | integer | XmList |

| Resource Name | Motif Type | UIL Type | Defined in Class |
|---|---|---|---|
| XmNitems | XmStringTable | string_table | XmList |
| XmNkeyboardFocusPolicy | unsigned char | integer | VendorShell |
| XmNlabelFontList | XmFontList | font_table | XmBulletinBoard, XmMenuShell, XmVendorShell |
| XmNlabelInsensitivePixmap | Pixmap | pixmap | XmLabel |
| XmNlabelPixmap | Pixmap | pixmap | XmLabel |
| XmNlabelString | XmString | compound_string | XmLabel, XmRowColumn |
| XmNlabelType | unsigned char | integer | XmLabel |
| XmNleftAttachment | unsigned char | integer | XmForm |
| XmNleftOffset | int | integer | XmForm |
| XmNleftPosition | int | integer | XmForm |
| XmNleftWidget | Widget | widget_ref | XmForm |
| XmNlightThreshold | int | NA | XmScreen |
| XmNlistItemCount | int | integer | XmSelectionBox |
| XmNlistItems | XmStringTable | string_table | XmSelectionBox |
| XmNlistLabelString | XmString | compound_string | XmSelectionBox |
| XmNlistMarginHeight | Dimension | integer | XmList |
| XmNlistMarginWidth | Dimension | integer | XmList |
| XmNlistSizePolicy | unsigned char | integer | XmList |
| XmNlistSpacing | Dimension | integer | XmList |
| XmNlistUpdated | Boolean | boolean | XmFileSelectionBox |
| XmNlistVisibleItemCount | int | integer | XmSelectionBox |
| XmNlosePrimaryCallback | XtCallbackList | procedure | XmText, XmTextField |
| XmNlosingFocusCallback | XtCallbackList | procedure | XmText, XmTextField |
| XmNmainWindowMarginHeight | Dimension | integer | XmMainWindow |
| XmNmainWindowMarginWidth | Dimension | integer | XmMainWindow |
| XmNmapCallback | XtCallbackList | procedure | XmBulletinBoard, XmRowColumn |
| XmNmappedWhenManaged | Boolean | boolean | Core |
| XmNmappingDelay | int | integer | XmCascadeButton |
| XmNmargin | Dimension | integer | XmSeparator |
| XmNmarginBottom | Dimension | integer | XmLabel |
| XmNmarginHeight | Dimension | integer | XmBulletinBoard, XmDrawingArea, XmFrame, XmLabel, XmPanedWindow, XmRowColumn, XmText, XmTextField |
| XmNmarginLeft | Dimension | integer | XmLabel |
| XmNmarginRight | Dimension | integer | XmLabel |
| XmNmarginTop | Dimension | integer | XmLabel |

| Resource Name | Motif Type | UIL Type | Defined in Class |
|---|---|---|---|
| XmNmarginWidth | Dimension | integer | XmBulletinBoard, XmDrawingArea, XmFrame, XmLabel, XmPanedWindow, XmRowColumn, XmText, XmTextField |
| XmNmask | Pixmap | NA | XmDragIcon |
| XmNmaxAspectX | int | integer | WMShell |
| XmNmaxAspectY | int | integer | WMShell |
| XmNmaxHeight | int | integer | WMShell |
| XmNmaxLength | int | integer | XmText, XmTextField |
| XmNmaxWidth | int | integer | WMShell |
| XmNmaximum | int | integer | XmScale, XmScrollBar |
| XmNmenuAccelerator | String | string | XmRowColumn |
| XmNmenuBar | Window | widget_ref | XmMainWindow |
| XmNmenuCursor | String | NA | XmScreen |
| XmNmenuHelpWidget | Widget | widget_ref | XmRowColumn |
| XmNmenuHistory | Widget | widget_ref | XmRowColumn |
| XmNmenuPost | String | string | XmRowColumn |
| XmNmessageAlignment | unsigned char | integer | XmMessageBox |
| XmNmessageString | XmString | compound_string | XmMessageBox |
| XmNmessageWindow | Window | widget_ref | XmMainWindow |
| XmNminAspectX | int | integer | WMShell |
| XmNminAspectY | int | integer | WMShell |
| XmNminHeight | int | integer | WMShell |
| XmNminWidth | int | integer | WMShell |
| XmNminimizeButtons | Boolean | boolean | XmMessageBox, XmSelectionBox |
| XmNminimum | int | integer | XmScale, XmScrollBar |
| XmNmnemonic | KeySym | keysym | XmLabel, XmRowColumn |
| XmNmnemonicCharSet | String | string | XmLabel, XmRowColumn |
| XmNmodifyVerifyCallback | XtCallbackList | procedure | XmText, XmTextField |
| XmNmodifyVerifyCallbackWcs | XtCallbackList | procedure | XmText, XmTextField |
| XmNmotionVerifyCallback | XtCallbackList | procedure | XmText, XmTextField |
| XmNmoveOpaque | Boolean | NA | XmScreen |
| XmNmultiClick | unsigned char | integer | XmArrowButton, XmDrawnButton, XmPushButton |
| XmNmultipleSelectionCallback | XtCallbackList | procedure | XmList |
| XmNmustMatch | Boolean | boolean | XmSelectionBox |

| Resource Name | Motif Type | UIL Type | Defined in Class |
|---|---|---|---|
| XmNmwmDecorations | int | integer | VendorShell |
| XmNmwmFunctions | int | integer | VendorShell |
| XmNmwmInputMode | int | integer | VendorShell |
| XmNmwmMenu | String | string | VendorShell |
| XmNnavigationType | XmNavigationType | integer | XmGadget, XmManager, XmPrimitive |
| XmNnoMatchCallback | XtCallbackList | procedure | XmSelectionBox |
| XmNnoMatchString | XmString | compound_string | XmFileSelectionBox |
| XmNnoResize | Boolean | boolean | XmBulletinBoard |
| XmNnoneCursorForeground | Pixel | NA | XmDragContext |
| XmNnumChildren | Cardinal | NA | Composite |
| XmNnumColumns | short | integer | XmRowColumn |
| XmNnumDropRectangles | Cardinal | NA | XmDropSite |
| XmNnumDropTransfers | Cardinal | NA | XmDropTransfer |
| XmNnumExportTargets | Cardinal | NA | XmDragContext |
| XmNnumImportTargets | Cardinal | NA | XmDropSite |
| XmNoffsetX | Position | NA | XmDragIcon |
| XmNoffsetY | Position | NA | XmDragIcon |
| XmNokCallback | XtCallbackList | procedure | XmMessageBox, XmSelectionBox |
| XmNokLabelString | XmString | compound_string | XmMessageBox, XmSelectionBox |
| XmNoperationChangedCallback | XtCallbackList | NA | XmDragContext |
| XmNoperationCursorIcon | Widget | NA | XmDragContext |
| XmNoptionLabel | XmString | NA | XmRowColumn |
| XmNoptionMnemonic | KeySym | NA | XmRowColumn |
| XmNorientation | unsigned char | integer | XmRowColumn, XmScale, XmScrollBar, XmSeparator |
| XmNoverrideRedirect | Boolean | boolean | Shell |
| XmNpacking | unsigned char | integer | XmRowColumn |
| XmNpageDecrementCallback | XtCallbackList | procedure | XmScrollBar |
| XmNpageIncrement | int | integer | XmScrollBar |
| XmNpageIncrementCallback | XtCallbackList | procedure | XmScrollBar |
| XmNpaneMaximum | Dimension | integer | XmPanedWindow |
| XmNpaneMinimum | Dimension | integer | XmPanedWindow |
| XmNpattern | XmString | compound_string | XmFileSelectionBox |
| XmNpendingDelete | Boolean | boolean | XmTextField |
| XmNpixmap | Pixmap | NA | XmDragIcon |
| XmNpopdownCallback | XtCallbackList | procedure | Shell |
| XmNpopupCallback | XtCallbackList | procedure | Shell |

| Resource Name | Motif Type | UIL Type | Defined in Class |
|---|---|---|---|
| XmNpopupEnabled | Boolean | boolean | XmRowColumn |
| XmNpositionIndex | short | integer | XmPanedWindow, XmRowColumn |
| XmNpostFromButton | int | NA | XmRowColumn |
| XmNpreeditType | String | string | VendorShell |
| XmNprocessingDirection | unsigned char | integer | XmScale, XmScrollBar |
| XmNpromptString | XmString | compound_string | XmCommand |
| XmNpushButtonEnabled | Boolean | boolean | XmDrawnButton |
| XmNqualifySearchDataProc | XmQualifyProc | any | XmFileSelectionBox |
| XmNradioAlwaysOne | Boolean | boolean | XmRowColumn |
| XmNradioBehavior | Boolean | boolean | XmRowColumn |
| XmNrecomputeSize | Boolean | boolean | XmLabel |
| XmNrefigureMode | Boolean | boolean | XmPanedWindow |
| XmNrepeatDelay | int | integer | XmScrollBar |
| XmNresizable | Boolean | boolean | XmForm |
| XmNresizeCallback | XtCallbackList | procedure | XmDrawingArea, XmDrawnButton |
| XmNresizeHeight | Boolean | boolean | XmRowColumn, XmText |
| XmNresizePolicy | unsigned char | integer | XmBulletinBoard, XmDrawingArea |
| XmNresizeWidth | Boolean | boolean | XmRowColumn, XmText, XmTextField |
| XmNrightAttachment | unsigned char | integer | XmForm |
| XmNrightOffset | int | integer | XmForm |
| XmNrightPosition | int | integer | XmForm |
| XmNrightWidget | Widget | widget_ref | XmForm |
| XmNrowColumnType | unsigned char | integer | XmRowColumn |
| XmNrows | short | integer | XmText |
| XmNrubberPositioning | Boolean | boolean | XmForm |
| XmNsashHeight | Dimension | integer | XmPanedWindow |
| XmNsashIndent | Position | integer | XmPanedWindow |
| XmNsashShadowThickness | Dimension | integer | XmPanedWindow |
| XmNsashWidth | Dimension | integer | XmPanedWindow |
| XmNsaveUnder | Boolean | boolean | Shell |
| XmNscaleHeight | Dimension | integer | XmScale |
| XmNscaleMultiple | int | integer | XmScale |
| XmNscaleWidth | Dimension | integer | XmScale |
| XmNscreen | Screen * | identifier | Core |
| XmNscrollBarDisplayPolicy | unsigned char | integer | XmList, XmScrolledWindow |
| XmNscrollBarPlacement | unsigned char | integer | XmScrolledWindow |

| Resource Name | Motif Type | UIL Type | Defined in Class |
|---|---|---|---|
| XmNscrollHorizontal | Boolean | boolean | XmText |
| XmNscrollLeftSide | Boolean | boolean | XmText |
| XmNscrollTopSide | Boolean | boolean | XmText |
| XmNscrollVertical | Boolean | boolean | XmText |
| XmNscrolledWindowMarginHeight | Dimension | integer | XmScrolledWindow |
| XmNscrolledWindowMarginWidth | Dimension | integer | XmScrolledWindow |
| XmNscrollingPolicy | unsigned char | integer | XmScrolledWindow |
| XmNselectColor | Pixel | color | XmToggleButton |
| XmNselectInsensitivePixmap | Pixmap | pixmap | XmToggleButton |
| XmNselectPixmap | Pixmap | pixmap | XmToggleButton |
| XmNselectThreshold | int | integer | XmTextField |
| XmNselectedItemCount | int | integer | XmList |
| XmNselectedItems | XmStringTable | string_table | XmList |
| XmNselectionArray | Pointer | any | XmTextField |
| XmNselectionArrayCount | int | integer | XmTextField |
| XmNselectionLabelString | XmString | compound_string | XmSelectionBox |
| XmNselectionPolicy | unsigned char | integer | XmList |
| XmNsensitive | Boolean | boolean | Core, XmRectObj |
| XmNseparatorOn | Boolean | boolean | XmPanedWindow |
| XmNseparatorType | unsigned char | integer | XmSeparator |
| XmNset | Boolean | boolean | XmToggleButton |
| XmNshadowThickness | Dimension | integer | XmGadget, XmManager, XmPrimitive |
| XmNshadowType | unsigned char | integer | XmBulletinBoard, XmDrawnButton, XmFrame |
| XmNshellUnitType | unsigned char | integer | VendorShell |
| XmNshowArrows | Boolean | boolean | XmScrollBar |
| XmNshowAsDefault | Dimension | integer | XmPushButton |
| XmNshowSeparator | Boolean | boolean | XmMainWindow |
| XmNshowValue | Boolean | boolean | XmScale |
| XmNsimpleCallback | XtCallbackProc | procedure | XmRowColumn |
| XmNsingleSelectionCallback | XtCallbackList | procedure | XmList |
| XmNskipAdjust | Boolean | boolean | XmPanedWindow |
| XmNsliderSize | int | integer | XmScrollBar |
| XmNsource | XmTextSource | any | XmText |
| XmNsourceCursorIcon | Widget | NA | XmDragContext |
| XmNsourcePixmapIcon | Widget | NA | XmDragContext |
| XmNspacing | Dimension | integer | XmPanedWindow, XmRowColumn, XmScrolledWindow, XmToggleButton |

| Resource Name | Motif Type | UIL Type | Defined in Class |
|---|---|---|---|
| XmNstateCursorIcon | Widget | NA | XmDragContext |
| XmNstringDirection | XmStringDirection | integer | XmLabel, XmList, XmManager |
| XmNsubMenuId | Widget | widget_ref | XmCascadeButton, XmRowColumn |
| XmNsymbolPixmap | Pixmap | pixmap | XmMessageBox |
| XmNtearOffMenuActivateCallback | XtCallbackList | procedure | XmRowColumn |
| XmNtearOffMenuDeactivateCallback | XtCallbackList | procedure | XmRowColumn |
| XmNtearOffModel | unsigned char | integer | XmRowColumn |
| XmNtextAccelerators | XtAccelerators | translation_table | XmSelectionBox |
| XmNtextColumns | short | integer | XmSelectionBox |
| XmNtextFontList | XmFontList | font_table | XmBulletinBoard, XmVendorShell |
| XmNtextString | XmString | compound_string | XmSelectionBox |
| XmNtextTranslations | XtTranslations | translation_table | XmBulletinBoard |
| XmNtitle | String | string | WMShell |
| XmNtitleEncoding | Atom | any | WMShell |
| XmNtitleString | XmString | compound_string | XmScale |
| XmNtoBottomCallback | XtCallbackList | procedure | XmScrollBar |
| XmNtoTopCallback | XtCallbackList | procedure | XmScrollBar |
| XmNtopAttachment | unsigned char | integer | XmForm |
| XmNtopCharacter | XmTextPosition | integer | XmText |
| XmNtopItemPosition | int | integer | XmList |
| XmNtopLevelEnterCallback | XtCallbackList | NA | XmDragContext |
| XmNtopLevelLeaveCallback | XtCallbackList | NA | XmDragContext |
| XmNtopOffset | int | integer | XmForm |
| XmNtopPosition | int | integer | XmForm |
| XmNtopShadowColor | Pixel | color | XmGadget, XmManager, XmPrimitive |
| XmNtopShadowPixmap | Pixmap | pixmap | XmManager, XmPrimitive |
| XmNtopWidget | Widget | widget_ref | XmForm |
| XmNtransferProc | XtSelectionCallbackProc | NA | XmDropTransfer |
| XmNtransferStatus | unsigned char | NA | XmDropTransfer |
| XmNtransient | Boolean | boolean | WMShell |
| XmNtransientFor | Widget | widget_ref | TransientShell |
| XmNtranslations | XtTranslations | translation_table | Core |
| XmNtraversalOn | Boolean | boolean | XmGadget, XmManager, XmPrimitive |
| XmNtraverseObscuredCallback | XtCallbackList | procedure | XmScrolledWindow |
| XmNtroughColor | Pixel | color | XmScrollBar |

| Resource Name | Motif Type | UIL Type | Defined in Class |
|---|---|---|---|
| XmNunitType | unsigned char | integer | XmGadget, XmManager, XmPrimitive |
| XmNunmapCallback | XtCallbackList | procedure | XmBulletinBoard, XmRowColumn |
| XmNunpostBehavior | unsigned char | integer | XmScreen |
| XmNuseAsyncGeometry | Boolean | boolean | VendorShell |
| XmNuserData | XtPointer | any | XmGadget, XmManager, XmPrimitive |
| XmNvalidCursorForeground | Pixel | NA | XmDragContext |
| XmNvalue | String | | XmText, XmTextField |
| XmNvalue | int | string | XmScale, XmScrollBar |
| XmNvalueChangedCallback | XtCallbackList | procedure | XmScale, XmScrollBar, XmText, XmTextField, XmToggleButton |
| XmNvalueWcs | wchar_t * | wide_character | XmText, XmTextField |
| XmNverifyBell | Boolean | boolean | XmText, XmTextField |
| XmNverticalFontUnit | int | NA | XmScreen |
| XmNverticalScrollBar | Widget | widget_ref | XmScrolledWindow |
| XmNverticalSpacing | Dimension | integer | XmForm |
| XmNvisibleItemCount | int | integer | XmList |
| XmNvisibleWhenOff | Boolean | boolean | XmToggleButton |
| XmNvisual | Visual * | any | Shell |
| XmNvisualPolicy | unsigned char | integer | XmScrolledWindow |
| XmNwaitForWm | Boolean | boolean | WMShell |
| XmNwhichButton | unsigned int | integer | XmRowColumn |
| XmNwidth | Dimension | integer | Core, XmDragIcon, XmRectObj |
| XmNwidthInc | int | integer | WMShell |
| XmNwinGravity | int | integer | WMShell |
| XmNwindowGroup | Window | any | WMShell |
| XmNwmTimeout | int | integer | WMShell |
| XmNwordWrap | Boolean | boolean | XmText |
| XmNworkWindow | Widget | widget_ref | XmScrolledWindow |
| XmNx | Position | integer | Core, XmRectObj |
| XmNy | Position | integer | Core, XmRectObj |

# D
# Table of UIL Objects

This appendix lists all of the objects supported by the User Interface Language (UIL). For each object, the table lists the corresponding widget or widgets in the Motif toolkit. The resources and callbacks for each object are the same as the resources and callbacks for the corresponding widget(s). UIL provides one additional callback, `MrmNcreateCallback`, for each object. This callback is invoked when the object is instantiated by the Motif Resource Manager (Mrm). The table also specifies the types of objects that can be children of a particular object, as well as the names and classes of any automatically-created children. For more information on each object, see the appropriate reference pages in Section 2, *Motif and Xt Widget Classes*.

| UIL Object | Corresponding Motif Widget(s) | Allowable Children | Automatically Created Children | |
|---|---|---|---|---|
| | | | Name | Class |
| XmArrowButton | XmArrowButton | XmPopupMenu | | |
| XmArrowButton Gadget | XmArrowButton Gadget | none | | |
| XmBulletinBoard | XmBulletinBoard | all UIL objects | | |
| XmBulletinBoard Dialog | XmDialogShell with XmBulletinBoard child | all UIL objects | | |
| XmCascadeButton | XmCascadeButton | XmPopupMenu, XmPulldownMenu | | |
| XmCascadeButton Gadget | XmCascadeButton Gadget | XmPulldownMenu | | |
| XmCommand | XmCommand | XmPopupMenu | | |
| XmDialogShell | XmDialogShell | XmBulletinBoard, XmDrawingArea, XmFileSelection Box, XmForm, XmFrame, XmMessageBox, XmPanedWindow, XmRadioBox, | | |

UIL Objects

| UIL Object | Corresponding Motif Widget(s) | Allowable Children | Automatically Created Children Name | Class |
|---|---|---|---|---|
| | | XmRowColumn, XmScale, XmScrolledWindow, XmSelectionBox, XmWorkArea | | |
| XmDrawingArea | XmDrawingArea | all UIL objects | | |
| XmDrawnButton | XmDrawnButton | XmPopupMenu | | |
| XmErrorDialog | XmDialogShell with XmMessageBox child | all UIL objects | Xm_Symbol<br>Xm_Separator<br>Xm_Message<br>Xm_OK<br>Xm_Cancel<br>Xm_Help | XmLabel<br>XmSeparator<br>XmLabel<br>XmPushButton<br>XmPushButton<br>XmPushButton |
| XmFileSelection Box | XmFileSelection Box | all UIL objects | Xm_Items<br>Xm_ItemsList<br>Xm_Separator<br>Xm_OK<br>Xm_Cancel<br>Xm_Help<br>Xm_FilterLabel<br>Xm_FilterText<br>Xm_DirList<br>Xm_Dir<br>Xm_Filter | XmLabel<br>XmScrolledList<br>XmSeparator<br>XmPushButton<br>XmPushButton<br>XmPushButton<br>XmLabel<br>XmText<br>XmScrolledList<br>XmLabel<br>XmPushButton |
| XmFileSelection Dialog | XmDialogShell with XmFileSelection Box child | all UIL objects | Xm_Items<br>Xm_ItemsList<br>Xm_Separator<br>Xm_OK<br>Xm_Cancel<br>Xm_Help<br>Xm_FilterLabel<br>Xm_FilterText<br>Xm_DirList<br>Xm_Dir<br>Xm_Filter | XmLabel<br>XmScrolledList<br>XmSeparator<br>XmPushButton<br>XmPushButton<br>XmPushButton<br>XmLabel<br>XmText<br>XmScrolledList<br>XmLabel<br>XmPushButton |
| XmForm | XmForm | all UIL objects | | |
| XmFormDialog | XmDialogShell with XmForm child | all UIL objects | | |
| XmFrame | XmFrame | all UIL objects | | |
| XmInformation Dialog | XmDialogShell with XmMessageBox child | all UIL objects | Xm_Symbol<br>Xm_Separator<br>Xm_Message<br>Xm_OK<br>Xm_Cancel<br>Xm_Help | XmLabel<br>XmSeparator<br>XmLabel<br>XmPushButton<br>XmPushButton<br>XmPushButton |

| UIL Object | Corresponding Motif Widget(s) | Allowable Children | Automatically Created Children | |
|---|---|---|---|---|
| | | | Name | Class |
| XmLabel | XmLabel | XmPopupMenu | | |
| XmLabelGadget | XmLabelGadget | none | | |
| XmList | XmList | XmPopupMenu | | |
| XmMainWindow | XmMainWindow | all UIL objects | Xm_Separator1<br>Xm_Separator2<br>Xm_Separator3 | XmSeparator<br>XmSeparator<br>XmSeparator |
| XmMenuBar | XmRowColumn | XmCascadeButton<br>XmCascadeButton Gadget<br>XmDrawnButton<br>XmLabel<br>XmLabelGadget<br>XmPopupMenu<br>XmPushButton<br>XmPushButton Gadget<br>XmSeparator<br>XmSeparator Gadget<br>XmToggleButton<br>XmToggleButton Gadget<br>user_defined object | | |
| XmMenuShell | XmMenuShell | XmRowColumn | | |
| XmMessageBox | XmMessageBox | all UIL objects | Xm_Symbol<br>Xm_Separator<br>Xm_Message<br>Xm_OK<br>Xm_Cancel<br>Xm_Help | XmLabel<br>XmSeparator<br>XmLabel<br>XmPushButton<br>XmPushButton<br>XmPushButton |
| XmMessageDialog | XmDialogShell with XmMessageBox child | all UIL objects | Xm_Symbol<br>Xm_Separator<br>Xm_Message<br>Xm_OK<br>Xm_Cancel<br>Xm_Help | XmLabel<br>XmSeparator<br>XmLabel<br>XmPushButton<br>XmPushButton<br>XmPushButton |
| XmOptionMenu | XmRowColumn | XmPulldownMenu | Xm_OptionLabel<br>Xm_OptionButton | XmLabelGadget<br>XmCascadeButton Gadget |
| XmPanedWindow | XmPanedWindow | all UIL objects | | |
| XmPopupMenu | XmDialogShell with XmRowColumn child | XmCascadeButton<br>XmCascadeButton Gadget<br>XmDrawnButton<br>XmLabel<br>XmLabelGadget | | |

UIL Objects

| UIL Object | Corresponding Motif Widget(s) | Allowable Children | Automatically Created Children Name | Class |
|---|---|---|---|---|
| | | XmPushButton<br>XmPushButton Gadget | | |
| XmSeparator<br>XmSeparator Gadget<br>XmToggleButton<br>XmToggleButton Gadget<br>user_defined object | Xm_TearOffControl | XmTearOffButton | | |
| XmPromptDialog | XmDialogShell with XmSelectionBox child | all UIL objects | Xm_Items<br>Xm_ItemsList<br>Xm_Selection<br>Xm_Text<br>Xm_Separator<br>Xm_OK<br>Xm_Cancel<br>Xm_Help<br>Xm_Apply | XmLabel<br>XmScrolledList<br>XmLabel<br>XmText<br>XmSeparator<br>XmPushButton<br>XmPushButton<br>XmPushButton<br>XmPushButton |
| XmPulldownMenu | XmDialogShell with XmRowColumn child | XmCascadeButton<br>XmCascadeButton Gadget<br>XmDrawnButton<br>XmLabel<br>XmLabelGadget<br>XmPushButton<br>XmPushButton Gadget<br>XmSeparator<br>XmSeparator Gadget<br>XmToggleButton<br>XmToggleButton Gadget<br>user_defined object | Xm_TearOffControl | XmTearOffButton |
| XmPushButton | XmPushButton | XmPopupMenu | | |
| XmPushButton Gadget | XmPushButton Gadget | none | | |
| XmQuestionDialog | XmDialogShell with XmMessageBox child | all UIL objects | Xm_Symbol<br>Xm_Separator<br>Xm_Message<br>Xm_OK<br>Xm_Cancel<br>Xm_Help | XmLabel<br>XmSeparator<br>XmLabel<br>XmPushButton<br>XmPushButton<br>XmPushButton |
| XmRadioBox | XmRowColumn | all UIL objects | | |

| UIL Object | Corresponding Motif Widget(s) | Allowable Children | Automatically Created Children | |
|---|---|---|---|---|
| | | | Name | Class |
| XmRowColumn | XmRowColumn | all UIL objects | | |
| XmScale | XmScale | all UIL objects | Xm_Title | XmLabel |
| XmScrollBar | XmScrollBar | XmPopupMenu | | |
| XmScrolledList | XmScrolledWindow with XmList child | XmPopupMenu | Xm_VertScrollBar<br>Xm_HorScrollBar | XmScrollBar<br>XmScrollBar |
| XmScrolledText | XmScrolledWindow with XmText child | XmPopupMenu | Xm_VertScrollBar<br>Xm_HorScrollBar | XmScrollBar<br>XmScrollBar |
| XmScrolledWindow | XmScrolledWindow | all UIL objects | Xm_VertScrollBar<br>Xm_HorScrollBar | XmScrollBar<br>XmScrollBar |
| XmSelectionBox | XmSelectionBox | all UIL objects | Xm_Items<br>Xm_ItemsList<br>Xm_Selection<br>Xm_Text<br>Xm_Separator<br>Xm_OK<br>Xm_Cancel<br>Xm_Help<br>Xm_Apply | XmLabel<br>XmScrolledList<br>XmLabel<br>XmText<br>XmSeparator<br>XmPushButton<br>XmPushButton<br>XmPushButton<br>XmPushButton |
| XmSelection Dialog | XmDialogShell with XmSelectionBox child | all UIL objects | Xm_Items<br>Xm_ItemsList<br>Xm_Selection<br>Xm_Text<br>Xm_Separator<br>Xm_OK<br>Xm_Cancel<br>Xm_Help<br>Xm_Apply | XmLabel<br>XmScrolledList<br>XmLabel<br>XmText<br>XmSeparator<br>XmPushButton<br>XmPushButton<br>XmPushButton<br>XmPushButton |
| XmSeparator | XmSeparator | XmPopupMenu | | |
| XmSeparator Gadget | XmSeparator Gadget | none | | |
| XmTearOffButton | none | XmPopupMenu | | |
| XmTemplateDialog | XmDialogShell with XmMessageBox child | all UIL objects | Xm_Symbol<br>Xm_Separator<br>Xm_Message<br>Xm_OK<br>Xm_Cancel<br>Xm_Help | XmLabel<br>XmSeparator<br>XmLabel<br>XmPushButton<br>XmPushButton<br>XmPushButton |
| XmText | XmText | XmPopupMenu | | |
| XmTextField | XmTextField | XmPopupMenu | | |
| XmToggleButton | XmToggleButton | XmPopupMenu | | |
| XmToggleButton Gadget | XmToggleButton Gadget | none | | |
| XmWarningDialog | XmDialogShell with | all UIL objects | Xm_Symbol<br>Xm_Separator | XmLabel<br>XmSeparator |

UIL Objects

| UIL Object | Corresponding Motif Widget(s) | Allowable Children | Automatically Created Children | |
|---|---|---|---|---|
| | | | Name | Class |
| | XmMessageBox child | | Xm_Message<br>Xm_OK<br>Xm_Cancel<br>Xm_Help | XmLabel<br>XmPushButton<br>XmPushButton<br>XmPushButton |
| XmWorkArea | XmRowColumn | all UIL objects | | |
| XmWorkingDialog | XmDialogShell with XmMessageBox child | all UIL objects | Xm_Symbol<br>Xm_Separator<br>Xm_Message<br>Xm_OK<br>Xm_Cancel<br>Xm_Help | XmLabel<br>XmSeparator<br>XmLabel<br>XmPushButton<br>XmPushButton<br>XmPushButton |

# E
# New Features in Motif 1.2

This appendix provides a summary of the new features in Motif 1.2. It lists the new toolkit functions and widget classes in Motif 1.2, as well as any new resources added to existing widget classes. For more information on the functions and widgets, see the appropriate reference pages in Section 1, *Motif Functions and Macros* and Section 2, *Motif and Xt Widget Classes*.

The appendix also lists the new Motif Resource Manager (Mrm) functions and User Interface Language (UIL) data types in Motif 1.2. For more information on these functions and data types, see the reference pages in Section 3, *Mrm Functions* and Section 6, *UIL Data Types*.

The *xmbind* client is new in Motif 1.2; see the reference page in Section 4, *Motif Clients* for more information.

## New Toolkit Functions

| | |
|---|---|
| `XmChangeColor()` | Update the colors for a widget. |
| `XmCreateDragIcon()` | Create a drag icon. |
| `XmCreateTemplateDialog()` | Create a template dialog. |
| `XmDragCancel()` | Cancel a drag operation. |
| `XmDragStart()` | Start a drag operation. |
| `XmDropSiteConfigureStackingOrder()` | Change the stacking order of a drop site. |
| `XmDropSiteEndUpdate()` | End an update of multiple drop sites. |
| `XmDropSiteQueryStackingOrder()` | Get the stacking order of a drop site. |
| `XmDropSiteRegister()` | Register a drop site. |
| `XmDropSiteRetrieve()` | Get the resource values for a drop site. |
| `XmDropSiteStartUpdate()` | Start an update of multiple drop sites. |
| `XmDropSiteUnregister()` | Remove a drop site. |
| `XmDropSiteUpdate()` | Change the resource values for a drop site. |
| `XmDropTransferAdd()` | Add drop transfer entries to a drop operation. |
| `XmDropTransferStart()` | Start a drop operation. |
| `XmFontListAppendEntry()` | Append a font entry to a font list. |
| `XmFontListEntryCreate()` | Create a font list entry. |
| `XmFontListEntryFree()` | Free the memory used by a font list entry. |
| `XmFontListEntryGetFont()` | Get the font information from a font list entry. |
| `XmFontListEntryGetTag()` | Get the tag of a font list entry. |

| | |
|---|---|
| `XmFontListEntryLoad()` | Load a font or create a font set and then create a font list entry. |
| `XmFontListNextEntry()` | Retrieve the next font list entry in a font list. |
| `XmFontListRemoveEntry()` | Remove a font list entry from a font list. |
| `XmGetDragContext()` | Get information about a drag and drop operation. |
| `XmGetFocusWidget()` | Get the widget that has the keyboard focus. |
| `XmGetPixmapByDepth()` | Create and return a pixmap of the specified depth. |
| `XmGetSecondaryResourceData()` | Retrieve secondary widget resource data. |
| `XmGetTabGroup()` | Get the tab group for a widget. |
| `XmGetTearOffControl()` | Get the tear-off control for a menu. |
| `XmGetVisibility()` | Determine whether or not a widget is visible. |
| `XmGetXmDisplay()` | Get the Display object for a display. |
| `XmGetXmScreen()` | Get the Screen object for a screen. |
| `XmIsTraversable()` | Determine whether or not a widget can receive the keyboard focus. |
| `XmListAddItemUnselected()` | Add an item to a list. |
| `XmListAddItemsUnselected()` | Add items to a list. |
| `XmListDeletePositions()` | Delete items at the specified positions from a list. |
| `XmListGetKbdItemPos()` | Get the position of the item in a list that has the location cursor. |
| `XmListPosSelected()` | Check if the item at a specified position is selected in a list. |
| `XmListPosToBounds()` | Return the bounding box of an item at the specified position in a list. |
| `XmListReplaceItemsPosUnselected()` | Replace specified items in a list. |
| `XmListReplaceItemsUnselected()` | Replace specified items in a list. |
| `XmListReplacePositions()` | Replace items at the specified postions in a list. |
| `XmListSetKbdItemPos()` | Set the position of the location cursor in a list. |
| `XmListUpdateSelectedList()` | Update the list of selected items in a list. |
| `XmListYToPos()` | Get the position of the item at the specified y-coordinate in a list. |
| `XmMapSegmentEncoding()` | Get the compound text encoding format for a font list element tag. |
| `XmRegisterSegmentEncoding()` | Register a compound text encoding format for a font list element tag. |
| `XmRepTypeAddReverse()` | Install the reverse converter for a representation type. |
| `XmRepTypeGetId()` | Get the ID number of a representation type. |
| `XmRepTypeGetNameList()` | Get the list of value names for a representation type. |
| `XmRepTypeGetRecord()` | |
| `XmRepTypeGetRegistered()` | Get the registered representation types. |
| `XmRepTypeInstallTearOffModelConverter()` | Install the resource converter for `XmNtearOffModel`. |
| `XmRepTypeRegister()` | Register a representation type resource. |
| `XmRepTypeValidValue()` | Determine the validity of a numerical value for a representation type. |

| | |
|---|---|
| `XmScrollVisible()` | Make an obscured child of a ScrolledWindow visible. |
| `XmStringCreateLocalized()` | Create a compound string in the current locale. |
| `XmTargetsAreCompatible()` | Determine whether or not the target types of a drag source and a drop site match. |
| `XmTextDisableRedisplay()` | Prevent visual update of a Text widget. |
| `XmTextEnableRedisplay()` | Allow visual update of a Text widget. |
| `XmTextFieldGetSelectionWcs()` | Get the wide-character value of the primary selection. |
| `XmTextFieldGetStringWcs()` | Get the wide-character text string. |
| `XmTextFieldGetSubstring()` | Get a copy of part of the text string. |
| `XmTextFieldGetSubstringWcs()` | Get a copy of part of the wide-character text string. |
| `XmTextFieldInsertWcs()` | Insert a wide-character string into the text string. |
| `XmTextFieldReplaceWcs()` | Replace part of the wide-character text string. |
| `XmTextFieldSetStringWcs()` | Set the wide-character text string. |
| `XmTextFindString()` | Find the beginning position of a text string. |
| `XmTextFindStringWcs()` | Find the beginning position of a wide-character text string. |
| `XmTextGetSelectionWcs()` | Get the wide-character value of the primary selection. |
| `XmTextGetStringWcs()` | Get the wide-character text string. |
| `XmTextGetSubstring()` | Get a copy of part of the text string. |
| `XmTextGetSubstringWcs()` | Get a copy of part of the wide-character text string. |
| `XmTextInsertWcs()` | Insert a wide-character string into the text string. |
| `XmTextReplaceWcs()` | Replace part of the wide-character text string. |
| `XmTextSetStringWcs()` | Set the wide-character text string. |
| `XmTrackingEvent()` | Allow for modal selection of a component. |
| `XmTranslateKey()` | Convert a keycode to a keysym using the default translator. |
| `XmWidgetGetBaselines()` | Get the positions of the baselines in a widget. |
| `XmWidgetGetDisplayRect()` | Get the display rectangle for a widget. |

## Obsolete Toolkit Functions

| | |
|---|---|
| `XmAddTabGroup()` | Superseded by setting `XmNnavigationType` to `XmEXCLUSIVE_TAB_GROUP`. |
| `XmCvtStringToUnitType()` | Superseded by a representation type manager converter. |
| `XmFontListAdd()` | Superseded by `XmFontListAppendEntry()`. |
| `XmFontListCreate()` | Superseded by `XmFontListAppendEntry()`. |
| `XmFontListGetNextFont()` | Superseded by `XmFontListGetNextEntry()`. |
| `XmGetMenuCursor()` | Superseded by getting the Screen resource `XmNmenuCursor`. |
| `XmRemoveTabGroup()` | Superseded by setting `XmNnavigationType` to `XmNONE`. |
| `XmSetFontUnit()` | Superseded by setting the Screen resources `XmNhorizontalFontUnit` and `XmNverticalFontUnit`. |
| `XmSetFontUnits()` | Superseded by setting the Screen resources `XmNhorizontalFontUnit` and `XmNverticalFontUnit`. |

| | |
|---|---|
| `XmSetMenuCursor()` | Superseded by setting the Screen resource `XmNmenuCursor`. |
| `XmStringCreateSimple()` | Superseded by `XmStringCreateLocalized()`. |
| `XmTrackingLocate()` | Superseded by `XmTrackingEvent()`. |

## New Widget Classes

| | |
|---|---|
| XmDisplay | An object to store display-specific information. |
| XmDragContext | An object used to store information about a drag transaction. |
| XmDragIcon | An object used to represent the data in a drag and drop operation. |
| XmDropSite | An object that defines the characteristics of a drop site. |
| XmDropTransfer | An object used to store information about a drop transaction. |
| XmScreen | An object used to store screen-specific information. |

## New Resources in Existing Widget Classes

| | | |
|---|---|---|
| VendorShell | `XmNbuttonFontList` | Font used for button children. |
| | `XmNinputMethod` | Sets the locale modifier for the input method. |
| | `XmNlabelFontList` | Font used for label children. |
| | `XmNpreeditType` | Specifies the available input method styles. |
| | `XmNtextFontList` | Font used for text children. |
| XmFrame | `XmNchildHorizontalAlignment` | Constraint resource for horizontal alignment. |
| | `XmNchildHorizontalSpacing` | Constraint resource for horizontal spacing. |
| | `XmNchildType` | Constraint resource for type of child. |
| | `XmNchildVerticalAlignment` | Constraint resource for vertical spacing. |
| XmGadget | `XmNbottomShadowColor` | Color used for bottomw shadow. |
| | `XmNhighlightColor` | Color used for highlighting rectangle. |
| | `XmNtopShadowColor` | Color used for top shadow. |
| XmManager | `XmNinitialFocus` | Widget that receives initial keyboard focus. |
| XmMenuShell | `XmNbuttonFontList` | Font used for button children. |
| | `XmNlabelFontList` | Font used for label children. |
| XmPanedWindow | `XmNpositionIndex` | Constraint resource for position of child. |
| XmRowColumn | `XmNentryVerticalAlignment` | Specifies vertical alignment of children. |
| | `XmNtearOffModel` | Specifies whether tear-off behavior is enabled or disabled. |
| | `XmNpositionIndex` | Constraint resource for position of child. |
| XmText | `XmNvalueWcs` | Specifies wide-character value string. |
| XmTextField | `XmNvalueWcs` | Specifies wide-character value string. |

## New Mrm Functions

| | |
|---|---|
| `MrmFetchBitmapLiteral()` | Retrieve an exported bitmap from an Mrm hierarchy. |
| `MrmOpenHierarchyPerDisplay()` | Open an Mrm hierarchy. |

## Obsolete Mrm Functions

| | |
|---|---|
| `MrmOpenHierarchy()` | Superseded by `MrmOpenHierarchyPerDisplay()`. |

## New UIL Data Types

| | |
|---|---|
| `class_rec_name` | Widget class pointer type. |
| `fontset` | `XFontSet` type. |
| `wide_character` | Wide-character string type. |

# Index

# Index

Index

Index

Index

## *About the Authors*

**Paula Ferguson** is a writer for O'Reilly & Associates. In addition to co-authoring this book, she has written articles for The X Resource and helped update other volumes in the X series. Paula has also developed and taught courses on Motif for the Open Software Foundation and worked on interface-design and software development projects.

Paula graduated from the Massachusetts Institute of Technology in 1990 with a B.S. in Computer Science and Engineering. She lives in Somerville, Massachusetts with her two cats, but spends as much time outside of the city as possible. When she can escape, Paula likes to go rock climbing, cycling, hiking, backpacking, and mountaineering.

**Dave Brennan** is a senior software engineer at HaL Computer Systems, where he is a member of the On-Line Information Access System (OLIAS) group. He is responsible for the user interface of the on-line documentation browser, as well as a number of other insidious hacks to which he'll never admit. In addition, Dave maintains the Emacs lisp archive at Ohio State University. Dave graduated from Rensselaer Polytechnic Institute in 1989 with a B.S. in Computer Science. After a brief stint in Raleigh, North Carolina, where he worked at Data General, Dave moved to Austin, Texas, where he now lives. In his non-existent spare time, Dave likes to play hockey, rock climb, kayak, and sail.

X BOOKS FROM O'REILLY & ASSOCIATES, INC.

### *Volume 0: X Protocol Reference Manual for X11 Release 4 and Release 5*

*Edited by Adrian Nye*
*3rd Edition, February 1992*

*Volume 0, X Protocol Reference Manual*, describes the X Network Protocol which underlies all software for Version 11 of the X Window System. The manual is updated for R5. Contents are divided into three parts:

Part One provides a conceptual introduction to the X Protocol. It describes the role of the server and client and demonstrates the network transactions that take place during a minimal client session.

Part Two contains an extensive set of reference pages for each protocol request and event. It is a reformatted and reorganized version of the Consortium's Protocol specification. All material from the original document is present in this manual, and the material in the reference pages is reorganized to provide easier access. Each protocol request or event is treated as a separate, alphabetized reference page. Reference pages include the encoding requests and replies.

Part Three consists of several appendixes describing particular parts of the X Protocol, along with several reference aids. It includes the most recent version of the ICCCM and the Logical Font Conventions Manual.

The Third Edition of Volume 0 can be used with any release of X.

*516 pages, ISBN: 1-56592-008-2*

### *Volume 1: Xlib Programming Manual for X11 Release 4 and Release 5*

*By Adrian Nye*
*3rd Edition, July 1992*

Newly updated to cover X11 Release 5, *Volume 1, Xlib Programming Manual* is a complete guide to programming to the X library (Xlib), the lowest level of programming interface to X. New features include introductions to internationalization, device-independent color, font service, and scalable fonts.

Includes chapters on:

- X Window System concepts
- Simple client application
- Window attributes
- The graphics context
- Graphics in practice
- Color and Events
- Interclient communication
- The Resource Manager
- A complete client application
- Window management

*824 pages, ISBN: 1-56592-002-3*

### *Volume 2: Xlib Reference Manual for X11 Release 4 and Release 5*

*By Adrian Nye*
*3rd Edition, June 1992*

*Volume 2, Xlib Reference Manual*, is a complete programmer's reference for Xlib, updated for X11 Release 4 and Release 5.

Includes:

- Reference pages for Xlib functions
- Reference pages for event types
- Permuted links to Xlib functions
- Description of macros and reference pages for their function versions
- Listing of the server-side color database
- Alphabetical index and description of structures
- Alphabetical index and description of defined symbols
- KeySyms and their meaning
- Illustration of the standard cursor font
- Function group index to the right routine for a particular task
- Reference pages for Xlib-related Xmu functions (miscellaneous utilities)
- 4 single-page reference aids for the GC and window attributes

New features in the 3rd Edition include:

- Over 100 new manpages covering Xcms, internationalization, and the function versions of macros
- Updating to the R5 spec
- New "Returns" sections on all the functions which return values, making this information easier to find

*1138 pages, ISBN: 1-56592-006-6*

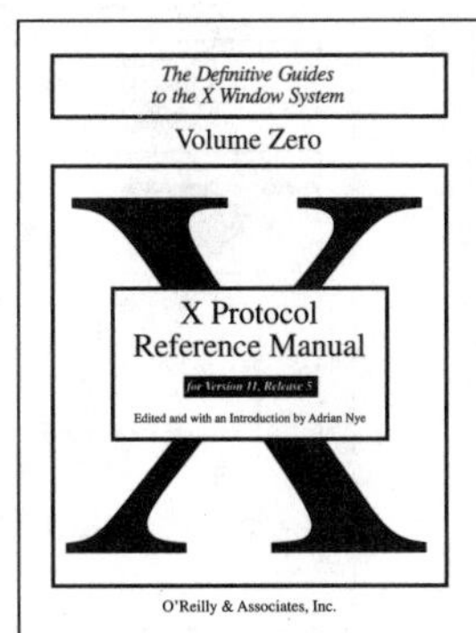

The Definitive Guides to the X Window System
Volume Zero
X Protocol Reference Manual
Edited and with an Introduction by Adrian Nye
O'Reilly & Associates, Inc.


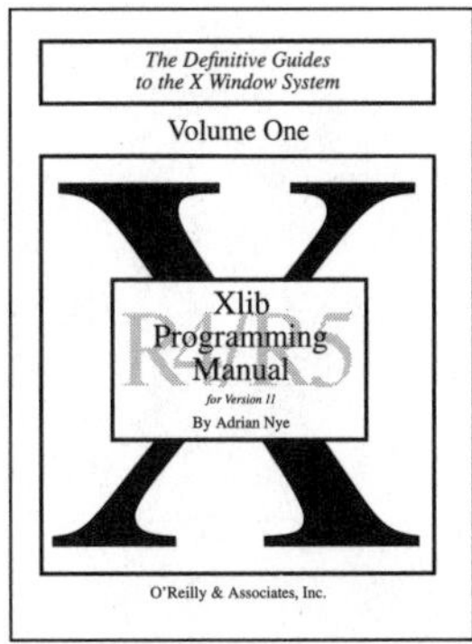

The Definitive Guides to the X Window System
Volume One
Xlib Programming Manual
R4/R5
for Version 11
By Adrian Nye
O'Reilly & Associates, Inc.

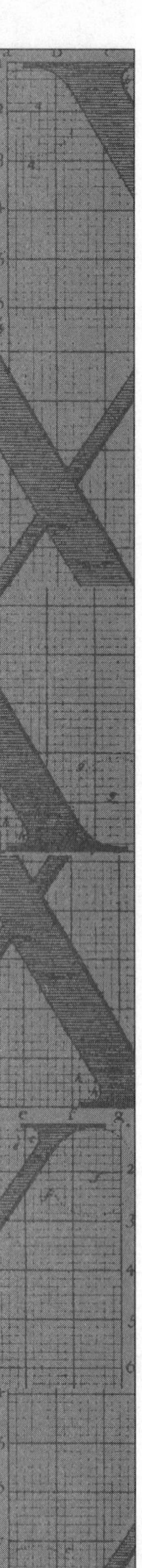

## *Volume 3: X Window System User's Guide for X11 Release 4*

*By Valerie Quercia and Tim O'Reilly*
*3rd Edition, May 1990*

*Volume 3, X Window System User's Guide*, orients the new user to window system concepts and provides detailed tutorials for many client programs, including the xterm terminal emulator and window managers.

Building on this basic knowledge, later chapters explain how to customize the X environment and provide sample configurations.

This popular manual is available in two editions, one for users of the MIT software, one for users of Motif. The Standard Edition uses the twm manager in most examples and illustrations, and has been updated for X11 Release 4.

Topics include:

- Starting the system and opening windows
- Using the xterm terminal emulator and window managers
- Most standard release clients, including programs for graphics, printing, font manipulation, window/display information, removing windows, as well as several desktop utilities
- Customizing the window manager, keyboard, display, and certain basicfeatures of any client program
- Using and customizing the mwm window manager, for those using the OSF/Motif graphical user interface
- System administration tasks, including managing fonts, starting X automatically, and using the display manager, xdm, to run X on a single or multiple display

*Standard Edition: 752 pages, ISBN: 0-937175-14-5*

## *Volume 3M: X Window System User's Guide OSF/Motif Edition*

*By Valerie Quercia and Tim O'Reilly*
*2nd Edition, January 1993*

Newly revised for Motif 1.2 and X11 Release 5, this alternative edition of the User's Guide highlights the Motif window manager and graphical interface. It will be the first choice for the many users with the Motif graphical user interface.

Topics include:

- Overview of the X Color Management System (Xcms)
- Using the X font server
- Bitmap and xmag
- Tear-off menus and drag-and-drop
- Starting the system and opening client windows
- Using the xterm terminal emulator
- Using standard release clients
- Using Motif's mwm window manager
- Customizing the keyboard, display and basic features of any client program
- Performing system administration tasks, such as managing fonts, starting X automatically, and using the display manager to run X on single or multiple displays

*Motif Edition: 956 pages, ISBN: 1-56592-015-5*

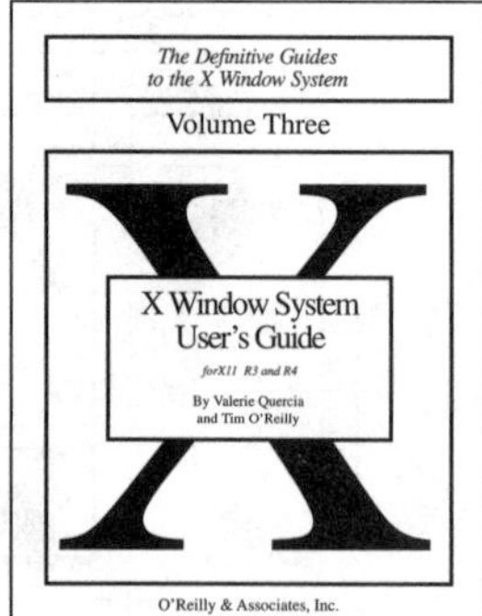


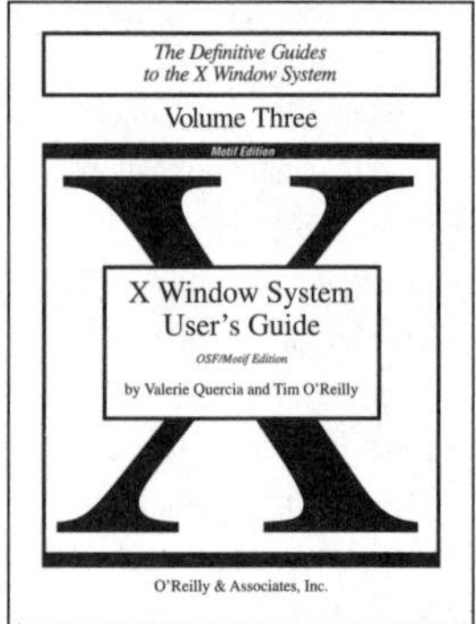

## Volume 4: X Toolkit Intrinsics Programming Manual for X11 Release 4

*By Adrian Nye and Tim O'Reilly*
*Standard: 2nd Edition, September 1990*
*Motif: 2nd Edition, August 1992*

Volume 4 is a complete guide to programming with the X Toolkit Intrinsics, the library of C language routines that facilitate the design of user interfaces, with reusable components called widgets. It provides concepts and examples that show how to use the various X Toolkit routines. The first few chapters are devoted to using widgets; the remainder of the book covers the more complex task of writing new widgets.

Volume 4 is available in two editions. The Standard Edition uses Athena widgets in examples for X11 Release 4 to demonstrate how to use existing widgets but provides a good introduction to programming with any widget set based on Xt. The Motif Edition uses the Motif 1.2 widget set in examples, and has been updated for X11 Release 5. Both books include:

- Introduction to the X Window System
- Building applications with widgets
- Constructing a bitmap editor with widgets
- Basic widget methods
- Events, translations, and accelerators
- Event handlers, timeouts, and work procedures
- Resource management and type conversion
- Selections and window manager interaction
- Geometry management
- Menus, gadgets, and cascaded pop-ups
- Miscellaneous techniques
- Comparison of Athena, OSF/Motif, and AT&T OPEN LOOK widgets
- Master index to volumes 4 and 5

This book is designed to be used with *Volume 5, X Toolkit Intrinsics Reference Manual*, which provides reference pages for each of the Xt functions and the widget classes defined by Xt.Volume 5.

*Standard Edition: 624 pages, ISBN: 0-937175-56-0*

*Motif Edition: 714 pages, ISBN 1-56592-013-9*

## Volume 5: X Toolkit Intrinsics Reference Manual for X11 Release 4 and Release 5

*Edited by David Flanagan*
*3rd Edition, April 1992*

*Volume 5, X Toolkit Intrinsics Reference Manual*, is a complete programmer's reference for the X Toolkit. It provides reference pages for each of the Xt functions as well as the widget classes defined by Xt and the Athena widgets.

This volume is based on Xt documentation from MIT and has been re-edited, reorganized, and expanded. Contents include:

- Reference pages for each of the Xt Intrinsics and macros, organized alphabetically for ease of use
- Reference pages for the interface definitions of functions registered with other Xt functions
- Reference pages for the Core, Composite, and Constraint widget methods
- Reference pages for the Object, RectObj, Core, Composite, Constraint, and Shell widget classes defined by Xt
- Reference pages for Athena widget classes
- Reference pages for Xt-related Xmu functions
- Permuted index
- Many appendixes and quick reference aids
- Index

The 3rd Edition of Volume 5 has been completely revised. In addition to covering Release 4 and Release 5 of X, all the man pages have been completely rewritten for clarity and ease of use, and new examples and descriptions have been added throughout the book.

*916 pages, ISBN: 1-56592-007-4*

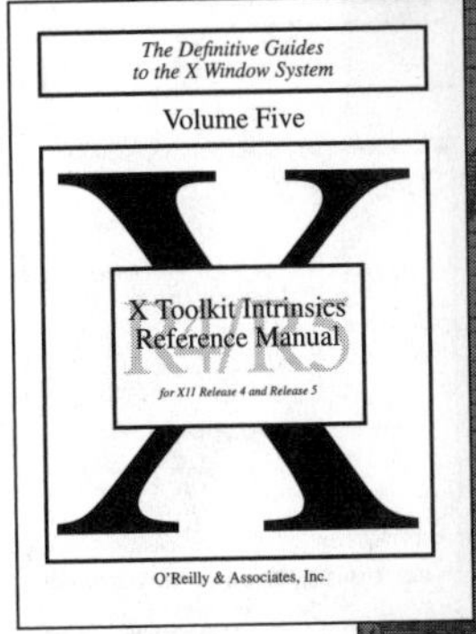

## Volume 6: Motif Programming Manual for OSF/Motif Version 1.1

*By Dan Heller*
*1st Edition, September 1991*

*The Motif Programming Manual* is a source for complete, accurate, and insightful guidance on Motif application programming. There is no other book that covers the ground as thoroughly or as well as this one.

The *Motif Programming Manual* describes how to write applications using the Motif toolkit from the Open Software Foundation (OSF). The book goes into detail on every Motif widget class, with useful examples that will help programmers to develop their own code. Anyone doing Motif programming who doesn't want to have to figure it out on their own needs this book.

In addition to information on Motif, the book is full of tips about programming in general, and about user interface design.

Contents include:

- An introduction to the Motif programming model, how it is based on the X Toolkit Intrinsics, and how it differs from them
- Chapters on each of the Motif widget classes, explaining them in depth, with useful examples that will help you to improve your own code. For example, the chapter on menus shows how to develop utility functions that generalize and simplify menu creation. All of the code shown in the book is available free of charge over the Internet or via UUCP
- Complete quick reference appendices on Motif functions, widgets, and gadgets

This one book can serve both your tutorial and reference needs. The book assumes competence with the C programming language, as well as familiarity with fundamental X Window System concepts. The *Motif Programming Manual* is not only the most comprehensive guide to writing applications with Motif, it is an integral part of the most widely used series of books on X as a whole. It complements and builds upon the earlier books in the X Window System Series from O'Reilly & Associates, as well as on OSF's own Motif Style Guide. Does not cover UIL.

*1032 pages, ISBN: 0-937175-70-6*

The Definitive Guides to the X Window System
Volume Six
Motif Edition
Motif Programming Manual
For OSF/Motif Version 1.1
By Dan Heller
O'Reilly & Associates, Inc.

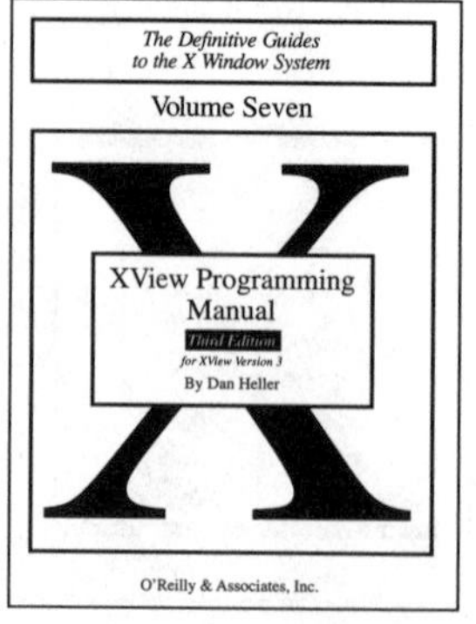


## Volume 7: XView Programming Manual and XView Reference Manual

*Edited by Dan Heller*
*Programming Manual: 3rd Edition, September 1991*
*Reference Manual: 1st Edition, September 1991*

*Volume 7, XView Programming Manual*, has been revised and expanded for XView Version 3. XView was developed by Sun Microsystems and is derived from Sun's proprietary programming toolkit, SunView. It is an easy-to-use object-oriented toolkit that provides an OPEN LOOK user interface for X applications.

For XView Version 3, the major additions are:

- Internationalization support for XView programs
- A new Drag and Drop package that lets the user transfer data between applications by dragging an interface object to a region
- A mouseless input model that means XView applications can be controlled from the keyboard without a mouse. Soft function keys are also supported
- The Notices package has been completely rewritten to incorporate Notice objects
- The Selection package has been rewritten, replacing the SunView-style selection service
- New panel items such as multiline text items and drop target items have been included. The Panels chapter has been reworked to clarify and simplify panel usage
- Panel item extensions are now covered in XView Internals to allow programmers to build custom panel items

The Attribute Summary from the previous edition of the *XView Programming Manual* has been expanded and is now published as a companion volume, the *XView Reference Manual*. It contains complete alphabetical listings of all XView attributes, functions, and macros, as well as other reference information essential for XView programmers.

*XView Programming Manual:*
*798 pages, ISBN: 0-937175-87-0*

*XView Reference Manual:*
*266 pages, ISBN: 0-937175-88-9*

*XView Programming and Reference Manual Set:*
*1064 pages, ISBN: 0-937175-89-7*

## Volume 8: X Window System Administrator's Guide for X11 Release 4 and Release 5

*By Linda Mui and Eric Pearce*
*1st Edition, October 1992*

As X moves out of the hacker's domain and into the "real world," users can't be expected to master all the ins and outs of setting up and administering their own X software. That will increasingly become the domain of system administrators. Even for experienced system administrators X raises many issues, both because of subtle changes in the standard UNIX way of doing things and because X blurs the boundaries between different platforms. Under X, users can run applications across the network, on systems with different resources (including fonts, colors, and screen size) than the applications were designed for originally. Many of these issues are poorly understood, and the technology for dealing with them is in rapid flux. This book is the first and only book devoted to the issues of system administration for X and X-based networks, written not just for UNIX system administrators but for anyone faced with the job of administering X (including those running X on stand-alone workstations).

The book includes:

- An overview of X that focuses on issues that affect the system administrator's job
- Information on obtaining, compiling, and installing the X software, including a discussion of the trade-offs between vendor-supplied and the free MIT versions of X
- How to set up xdm, the X display manager, which takes the place of the login program under X and can be used to create a customized turnkey X session for each user
- How to set up user accounts under X (includes a comparison of the familiar shell setup files and programs to the new mechanisms provided by X)
- Issues involved in making X more secure. X's security features are not strong, but an understanding of what features are available can be very important, since X makes it possible for users to intrude on each other in new and sometimes unexpected ways.
- How fonts are used by X, including a description of the font server
- A discussion of the issues raised by running X on heterogenous networks
- How colors are managed under X and how to get the same colors across multiple devices with different hardware characteristics
- The administration issues involved in setting up and managing X terminal
- How to use PC and Mac X servers to maximize reuse of existing hardware and convert outdated hardware into X terminals
- How to obtain and install additional public domain software and patches for X
- Covers features new in R5, including the font server and Xcms

The *X Window System Administrator's Guide* is available either alone or packaged with the X CD. The CD will provide X source code to complement the instructions for installing the software.

*Without CD-ROM, 372 pages, ISBN: 0-937175-83-8*
*With CD-ROM, ISBN: 1-56592-052-X*

## X Window System Administrator's Guide CD-ROM

The CD-ROM contains the source code for MIT's public domain X Window System, and will be offered with the X Window System's Administrator's Guide. It contains pre-compiled binaries for popular platforms, and comes complete with an installation system that allows custom installation of the CD-ROM.

The CD includes:

- Rock Ridge CD-ROM drivers from Young Minds, so you can install the CD as a UNIX filesystem on several popular UNIX platforms.
- Complete "core" source for MIT X11 Release 4 and 5. This includes the new R5 features, such as the fontserver and XCMS.
- Complete "contrib" source for MIT X11 Release 5. This includes some programs not available in the MIT distribution, such as 'xtici', the Tektronics Color Editor.
- Complete examples and source code for all the books in the X Window System Series.
- Programs and files that are discussed in Volume 8. These were previously available only to administrators with Internet access.
- Pre-compiled X11 Release 5 binaries for Sun3, Sun4, and IBM RS6000 platforms. (The RS6000 server supports the Skyway adaptor, not the new GT3 adaptor.)

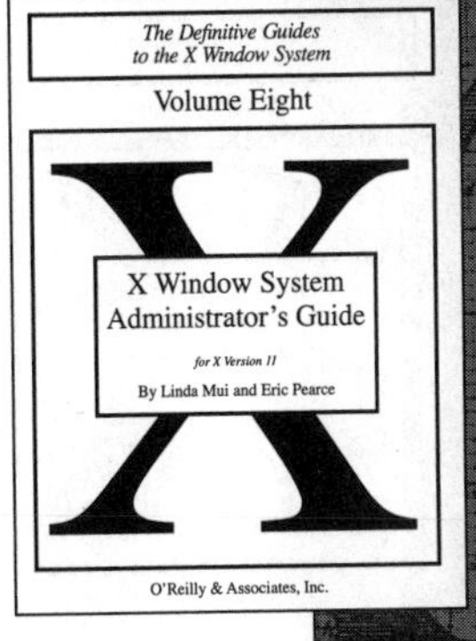

## *Programmer's Supplement for R5 of the X Window System, Version 11*

*By David Flanagan*
*1st Edition, November 1991*

This book is for programmers who are familiar with Release 4 of the X Window System and want to know how to use the new features of Release 5. It is intended as an update for owners of Volumes 1, 2, 4, and 5 of the O'Reilly and Associates' X Window System series, and provides complete tutorial and reference information to all new Xlib and Xt toolkit functions.

It includes:

- Overview of the R5 changes as they affect application programming
- How to write an internationalized application---one that anticipates the needs of a language and culture other than English
- How to use scalable fonts and the fonts provided by the new font server
- How to get consistent color on any display by using the X Color Management System
- Overview of PEX, the new three-dimensional graphics extension for X
- Reference pages for all new and modified Xlib and Xt functions and Athena widgets

Together with Volume 2 and Volume 5, owners of the *Programmer's Supplement for Release 5* have a complete set of reference pages for the current MIT X Consortium standards for Xlib and Xt.

*390 pages, ISBN: 0-937175-86-2*

## *The X Window System in a Nutshell*

*Edited by Ellie Cutler, Daniel Gilly, and Tim O'Reilly*
*2nd Edition, April 1992*

Once programmers have mastered the concepts behind X and learned how to program in Xlib and Xt there is still a mass of details to remember. *The X Window System in a Nutshell* fills this gap. Experienced X programmers can use this single-volume desktop companion for most common questions, keeping the full X Window System series of manuals for detailed reference. X in a Nutshell contains essential information in a boiled-down quick-reference format that makes it easy to find the answers needed most often:

- Command line options and resources for the standard MIT X clients
- Calling sequence for all Xlib and Xt functions and macros
- Detailed description of structures, enums, and other X data types used as arguments or return values in Xlib or Xt functions
- Description of the code inside a basic widget quick reference to the event structures
- Font name syntax, color names, resource file and translations table syntax, and cursors
- Xlib and Xt error messages

This book has been newly updated to cover R5 but is still useful for R4. The descriptions of the functions have been expanded and clarified, with improved cross-referencing to important related functions. Includes material on Xcms and the internationalization features of R5.

*424 pages, ISBN: 1-56592-017-1*

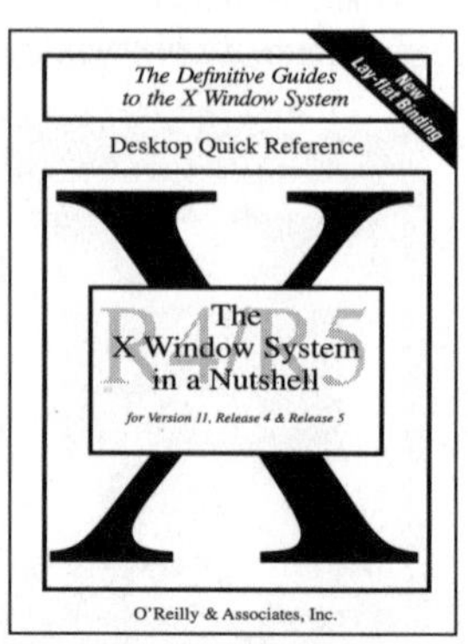

## ***PHIGS Programming Manual: 3D Programming in X***

*By Tom Gaskins*
*1st Edition, February 1992*

A complete and authoritative guide to PHIGS and PHIGS PLUS programming, this book documents the PHIGS and PHIGS PLUS graphics standards and provides full guidance regarding the use of PHIGS within the X environment. The discussions of PHIGS and PHIGS PLUS are fully integrated in this text, which takes as its starting point the PEX Sample Implementation (or PEX-SI)—the publicly available and most widely established base for commercial PHIGS products. In addition, the *PHIGS Programming Manual* explains, at both elementary and advanced levels, how to integrate your PHIGS applications with standard X (Xlib) functions. Window management, event handling, input-output, even lower-level drawing functions---all of these can be made part of your PHIGS programs. Besides Xlib itself, there are detailed examples and explanations based on the Motif, OLIT, and XView toolkits.

The *PHIGS Programming Manual*:

- Offers a clear and comprehensive introduction to PHIGS: output primitives, attributes, color, structure, and all you need to know to begin writing PHIGS programs
- Offers technical know-how. Author Tom Gaskins has for many years been an implementor of PHIGS and is also a key contributor to the international PHIGS standardization efforts.
- Shows how to use PHIGS in your X Window System applications
- Illustrates the concepts of PHIGS and PHIGS PLUS with over 200 figures
- Clearly explains the subtleties of viewing, lighting, and shading, complete with practical code examples, each of them modular and simple to understand, but virtually none of them merely a "toy" program
- Includes the DIS ISO C binding, the closest in existence to the coming ISO standard
- Demonstrates the use of PHIGS and PHIGS PLUS in interactive programs, so that you can do more than merely display pictures
- Fully describes all the PHIGS and PHIGS PLUS functions
- Has a companion reference manual. Taken together, these books are the only documentation you'll need for a product that is changing the way the X world thinks about graphics.

Whether you are starting out in 3D graphics programming or are a seasoned veteran looking for an authoritative work on a fast-rising 3D graphics standard, this book will serve your purposes well.

*Softcover: 968 pages, ISBN: 0-937175-85-4*
*Hardcover: 968 pages, ISBN: 0-937175-92-7*

## ***PHIGS Reference Manual: 3D Programming in X***

*Edited by Linda Kosko*
*1st Edition, October 1992*

The definitive and exhaustive reference documentation for the PHIGS/PEX Sample Implementation ("PEX-SI"). Contains all the reference pages from the MIT X Consortium release, but in upgraded form, with additional reference materials. Together with the *PHIGS Programming Manual*, this book is the most complete and accessible documentation currently available for both the PEX-SI and the PHIGS and PHIGS PLUS standards.

The *PHIGS Reference Manual* is the definitive and exhaustive reference documentation for the PHIGS/PEX Sample Implementation ("PEX-SI"). It contains all the reference pages from the MIT X Consortium release, but in upgraded form. It also contains additional reference materials.

*1116 pages, ISBN: 0-937175-91-9*

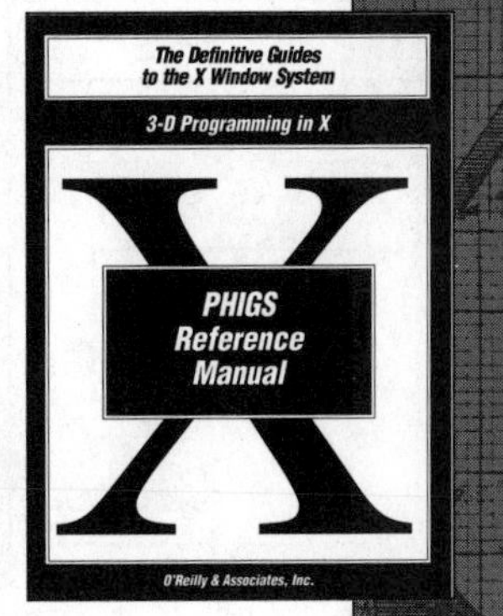

## PEXlib Programming Manual

*By Tom Gaskins*
*1st Edition, December 1992*

The world of workstations changed dramatically with the release of the X Window System. Users can finally count on a consistent interface across almost all makes and models of computers. At the same time, graphics applications become easily portable.

Until recently, X supported only 2D graphics. Now, however, by means of the PEX extensions to X together with the PEXlib applications programming interface, native, 3D graphics have come to the X Window System. PEXlib allows the programmer to create graphics programs of any complexity, and also provides the basis for higher-level graphics systems and toolkits.

The *PEXlib Programming Manual* is the definitive programmer's guide to PEXlib, covering both PEX versions 5.0 and 5.1. Containing over 200 illustrations and 19 color plates, it combines a thorough and gentle tutorial approach with valuable reference features. Along the way, it presents the reader with numerous programming examples, as well as a library of helpful utility routines—all of which are available online. You do not need to have prior graphics programming experience in order to read this manual.

Written by Tom Gaskins—the widely recognized authority who also authored the O'Reilly and Associates' *PHIGS Programming Manual*—this book is the only programming guide to PEXlib you will ever need.

*1154 pages, ISBN: 1-56592-028-7*

## PEXlib Reference Manual

*By O'Reilly & Associates*
*1st Edition, December 1992*

The *PEXlib Reference Manual* is the definitive programmer's reference resource for PEXlib, and contains complete and succinct reference pages for all the callable routines in PEXlib version 5.1. The content of the *PEXlib Reference Manual* stands, with relatively few changes, as it was created by the MIT X Consortium.

The *PEXlib Reference Manual* is a companion volume to the O'Reilly and Associates' *PEXlib Programming Manual*, written by Tom Gaskins. The *Programming Manual* is a thorough tutorial guide to PEXlib, and includes valuable reference features. Together, these books offer the most complete and accessible documentation available for PEXlib version 5.1.

*577 pages, ISBN: 1-56592-029-5*

# About The X Resource

*The X Resource* is a quarterly working journal for X programmers that provides practical, timely information about the programming, administration, and use of the X Window System. *The X Resource* is the Official Publisher of the MIT X Consortium Technical Conference Proceedings, which form the January issue. Issues can be purchased separately or by subscription.

## The X Resource: Issue 2, April 1992

*Edited by Adrian Nye*

Table of Contents, Issue 2 (April 1992):

DEPARTMENTS:

- From the X Consortium: Current Projects, by Bob Scheifler
- Best of Netnews, edited by Marc Albert
- The X User: Designing for Usability, by Scott McGregor
- The X Administrator: Font Formats and Utilities, by Dinah McNutt and Miles O'Neal

PAPERS:

- NASA's TAE PLUS: a GUI Development Tool and Application Environment, by Marti Szczur
- Understanding Grabs and Keyboard Focus, by Wayne Dyksen
- Designing Reusable Widget Classes with C++ and OSF/Motif, by Andreas Baecker
- Visualizing X, by David Lemke and David Rosenthal
- imake Demystified, by Paul Davey

DOCUMENTATION:

- Wcl 2.0: The Widget Creation Library

*190 pages, ISBN: 0-937175-97-8*

## The X Resource: Issue 3, July 1992

*Edited by Adrian Nye*

Table of Contents, Issue 3 (July 1992):

DEPARTMENTS

- Xt Performance Improvements in Release 5, by Gabe Beged-Dov
- The X User: Making Better Use of Resources, by Paul Davey
- The X Administrator: Managing Font Servers, by Eric Pearce
- Best of Network News, edited by Marc Albert

PAPERS

- Multi-user Application Software Using Xt, by Oliver Jones
- An Extension for Server Instrumentation and Tracing, by Mark J. Kilgard
- Using the New Font Capabilities of HP-donated Font Server Enhancements, by Axel Deininger and Nathan Meyers
- Improving X Application Performance, by Chris D. Peterson and Sharon E. Chang
- A Ruler Model for the Motif Form Widget, by Thomas Berlage
- A New Paradigm for Cross-platform Automated GUI Testing, by Lawrence R. Kepple

DOCUMENTATION

- The Nonrectangular Window Shape Extension, by Paula M. Ferguson
- Public-domain XcRichText Widget, by Dan Connolly

*220 pages, ISBN: 0-937175-98-6*

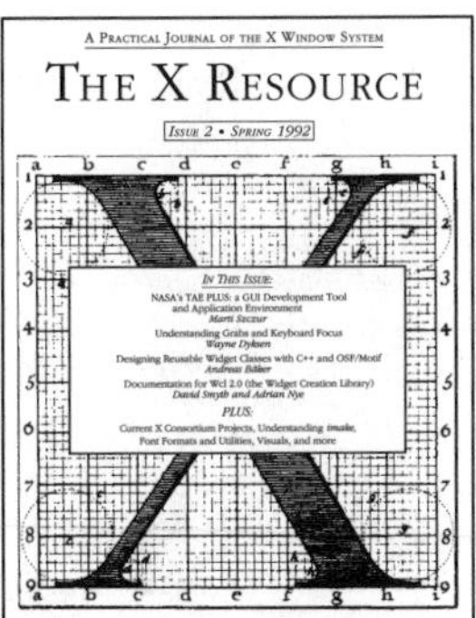


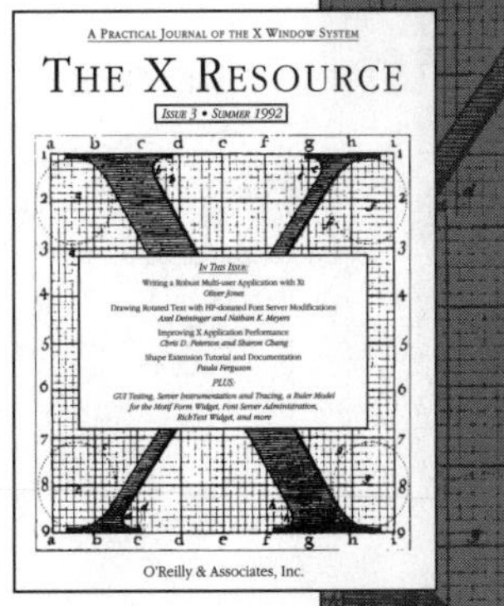

## The X Resource: Issue 4, October 1992

*Edited by Adrian Nye*

Table of Contents, Issue 4 (October 1992):

FROM THE EDITOR

- 7th Annual X Technical Conference
- Xhibition 93 Conference: Call for Participation
- The X Resource Code Archive

DEPARTMENTS

- From The X Consortium: The MIT X Software Distribution After Release 5, by Stephen Gildea, MIT X Consortium
- The X Administrator: Taming the X Display Manager, by Miles O'Neal
- X User Groups
- The PEX Interoperability Center, by Kathy Harris

PAPERS

- Finding Auxiliary Files for an X Toolkit Application, by David Flanagan
- RPC Programming in X Applications, by John Bloomer
- A Bibliography of Windowing Systems and Security, by Jeremy Epstein
- The XGEN Application Generator: Constructing Motif GUIs For TTY Programs, by Kurt Buehler
- Workstation Audio in the X Environment, by Richard Billman, Robert Hammond, Pat McElhatton, Ellen Nordahl Brandt, Francis Sung, and Nancy Yost

DOCUMENTATION

- A Directory of Freely and Commercially Available Widgets
- The Cmap Widget
- The Hdial Widget
- The X11 Input Extension: A Tutorial, by Paula Ferguson
- The X11 Input Extension: Reference Pages

*276 pages, ISBN: 0-937175-99-4*

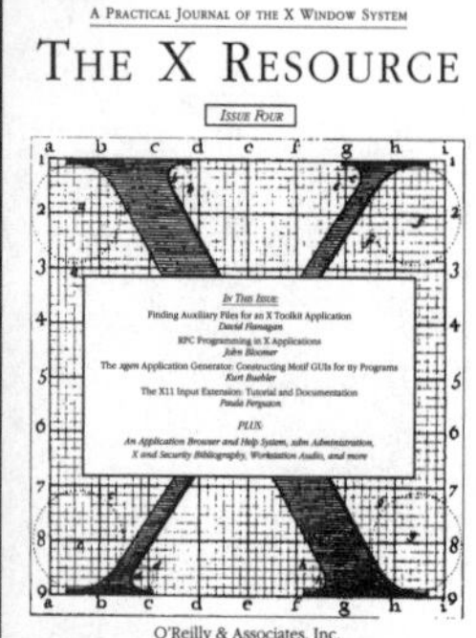


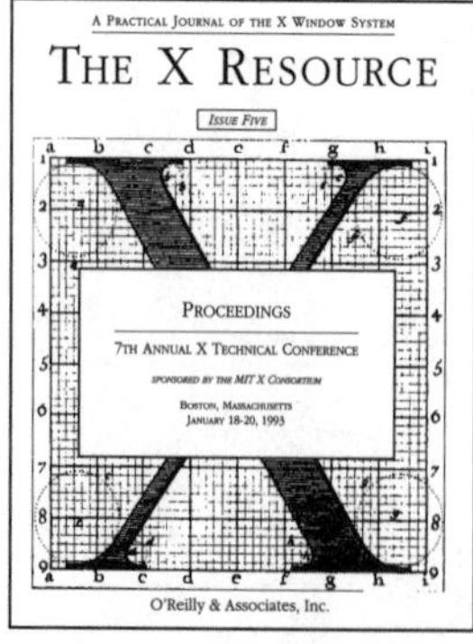


## The X Resource: Issue 5, January 1993

*Edited by Adrian Nye*

Table of Contents, Issue 5 (January 1993):

FROM THE EDITOR

- Proposal for an X-based Online Help Protocol, by Kent J. Summers and Jeffrey L. Vogel
- Describing Formats for X-based Data Interchange, by Ellis S. Cohen
- A Widget Class Extension for Improved Geometry Management, by Steve Humphrey
- The Layout Widget: A TeX-Style Constraint Widget Class, by Keith Packard
- Building Distributed User Interfaces with Fresco, by Mark Linton and Chuck Price
- Melding OSF/Motif, C++ and the Intrinsics, by Douglas S. Rand and Gilles Benati
- The Trestle Toolkit, by Mark S. Manasse
- Hypergraphics and Hypertext in Tk, by John K. Ousterhout
- The X Engine Library: A C++ Library for Constructing X Pseudo-servers, by John Menges
- The X File System, by Jeff Nisewanger
- Trace Analysis of the X Window System Protocol, by Laurence P. G. Cable and Stuart W. Marks
- Multi-threaded Xlib, by Stephen Gildea
- Distributed Memory Multi-computers as X Clients, by Steve R. Ball and Chris W. Johnson
- GUI for Near-Real-Time Applications in X — Programming Tips, by Ilan Aisic
- TaX: A Tool for Building Time Dependent Applications, by Nuno M. Correia and Nuno M. Guimaraes
- Supporting Mobile, Pen-based Computing with X, by James Kempf and Alan Wilson
- Making the X Window System Accessible to People with Disabilities, by Will D. Walker and Mark E. Novak
- Runtime Translation of X Interfaces to Support Visually-Impaired Users, by Keith Edwards and Thomas Rodriguez
- A Fully Functional Implementation of Layered Windows, by Peter Daifuku
- An Update on Low-Bandwidth X (LBX), by Jim Fulton

*272 pages, ISBN: 1-56592-020-1*

YES, send me a subscription to *The X Resource*. I understand that I will receive timely, in-depth, practical articles and documentation. (If I'm not completely satisfied, I can cancel my subscription at any time.)

❑ $65 Quarterly issues. *(Extra shipping for foreign orders: Canada/Mexico—$5; Europe/Africa—$25; Asia/Australia—$30. All foreign shipping by air.)*

❑ $90 Quarterly issues PLUS supplements: Public Review Specifications for proposed X Consortium standards and introductory explanations of the issues involved. *(Extra shipping for foreign orders: Canada/Mexico—$10; Europe/Africa—$50; Asia/Australia—$60. All foreign shipping by air.)*

*Note: Foreign orders must be by credit card or in U.S. dollars drawn on a U.S. bank.*

To subscribe, call (800) 338-6887 (US/Canada) or mail in this card.

NAME

ADDRESS

CITY/STATE/ZIP

COUNTRY

BILL TO MY CREDIT CARD:

❑ MASTERCARD ❑ VISA ❑ AMERICAN EXPRESS

ACCT. # EXP. DATE

NAME AS IT APPEARS ON CARD

SIGNATURE

J21R

# Books That Help People Get More Out of Computers

***If you want more information about our books, or want to know where to buy them, we're happy to send it.***

❑ Send me a free catalog of titles.

❑ What bookstores in my area carry your books (U.S. and Canada only)?

❑ Where can I buy your books outside the U.S. and Canada?

❑ Send me information about consulting services for documentation or programming.

❑ Send me information about bundling books with my product.

Name__________

Address__________

City__________

State, ZIP__________

Country__________

Phone__________

Email Address__________

NAME ______________________________
COMPANY ___________________________
ADDRESS ___________________________
CITY ____________ STATE _____ ZIP __________

NO POSTAGE NECESSARY IF MAILED IN THE UNITED STATES

**BUSINESS REPLY MAIL**

FIRST CLASS MAIL PERMIT NO. 80 SEBASTOPOL, CA

POSTAGE WILL BE PAID BY ADDRESSEE

O'Reilly & Associates, Inc.

103 Morris Street Suite A
Sebastopol CA 95472-9902

NAME ______________________________
COMPANY ___________________________
ADDRESS ___________________________
CITY ____________ STATE _____ ZIP __________

NO POSTAGE NECESSARY IF MAILED IN THE UNITED STATES

**BUSINESS REPLY MAIL**

FIRST CLASS MAIL PERMIT NO. 80 SEBASTOPOL, CA

POSTAGE WILL BE PAID BY ADDRESSEE

O'Reilly & Associates, Inc.

103 Morris Street Suite A
Sebastopol CA 95472-9902